Data Structures
and Algorithms
with Object-Oriented Design Patterns in Java

WORLDWIDE
SERIES IN
COMPUTER
SCIENCE

WORLD WIDE
SERIES IN
COMPUTER
SCIENCE

SERIES EDITORS **Professor David Barron,** *Southampton University, UK*

Professor Peter Wegner, *Brown University, USA*

The Worldwide Series in Computer Science has been created to publish textbooks which both address and anticipate the needs of an ever-evolving curriculum, thereby shaping its future. It is designed for undergraduates majoring in Computer Science and practitioners who need to reskill. Its philosophy derives from the conviction that the discipline of computing needs to produce technically skilled engineers who will inevitably face, and possibly invent, radically new technologies throughout their future careers. New media will be used innovatively to support high-quality texts written by leaders in the field.

Books in Series Ammeraal, *Computer Graphics for Java Programmers*

Ben-Ari, *Ada for Software Engineers*

Gollmann, *Computer Security*

Goodrich & Tamassia, *Data Structures and Algorithms
in Java*

Kotonya & Sommerville, *Requirements Engineering:
Processes and Techniques*

Lowe & Hall, *Hypermedia & the Web:
An Engineering Approach*

Magee & Kramer, *Concurrency: State Models
and Java Programs*

Peters, *Software Engineering: An Engineering Approach*

Preiss, *Data Structures and Algorithms with Object-Oriented
Design Patterns in C++*

Preiss, *Data Structures and Algorithms with Object-Oriented
Design Patterns in Java*

Reiss, *A Practical Introduction to Software Design with C++*

Winder & Roberts, *Developing Java Software*

Data Structures and Algorithms
with Object-Oriented Design Patterns in Java

Bruno R. Preiss

Department of Electrical and Computer Engineering
University of Waterloo

John Wiley & Sons, Inc.

New York   Chichester   Weinheim   Brisbane   Singapore   Toronto

METAFONT is a trademark of Addison Wesley Publishing Company.
SPARCstation, Solaris, and Java are registered trademarks of Sun Microsystems.
TEX is a trademark of the American Mathematical Society.
UNIX is a registered trademark of AT&T Bell Laboratories.

EDITOR   *Bill Zobrist*
MARKETING MANAGER   *Katherine Hepburn*
SENIOR PRODUCTION MANAGER   *Lucille Buonocore*
SENIOR PRODUCTION EDITOR   *Monique Calello*
SENIOR DESIGNER   *Kevin Murphy*
COVER PHOTO   *David Parker/Science Photo Library/Photo Researchers*
ILLUSTRATION COORDINATOR   *Sigmund Malinowski*

This book was set in 10/12 Times Roman by Publication Services and printed and bound by Quebecor
Printing, Fairfield. The cover was printed by Lehigh Press.

This book is printed on acid-free paper. ∞

The paper in this book was manufactured by a mill whose forest management programs include sustained
yield harvesting of its timberlands. Sustained yield harvesting principles ensure that the number of trees cut
each year does not exceed the amount of new growth.

To order books or for customer service call 1 (800) CALL-WILEY (225-5945).

Library of Congress Cataloging in Publication Data:
Preiss, Bruno R.
     Data structures and algorithms with object-oriented
     design patterns in Java/ Bruno R. Preiss.

          p.   cm.
        ISBN 0-471-34613-6 (cloth : alk. paper)
        1. Object-oriented programming (Computer science)   2. Data
     structures (Computer science)   3. Computer algorithms.   I. Title.

     QA76.64.P744   1999
     005.7'3—dc21   99-21792
                                                              CIP

Printed in the United States of America

10 9 8 7 6 5 4 3 2 1

To my parents,
Melanija and Indulis

Preface

This book was motivated by my experience in teaching the course *E&CE 250: Algorithms and Data Structures* in the Computer Engineering program at the University of Waterloo. I have observed that the advent of *object-oriented methods* and the emergence of object-oriented *design patterns* has led to a profound change in the pedagogy of data structures and algorithms. The successful application of these techniques gives rise to a kind of cognitive unification: Ideas that are disparate and apparently unrelated seem to come together when the appropriate design patterns and abstractions are used.

This paradigm shift is both evolutionary and revolutionary. On the one hand, the knowledge base grows incrementally as programmers and researchers invent new algorithms and data structures. On the other hand, the proper use of object-oriented techniques requires a fundamental change in the way the programs are designed and implemented. Programmers who are well schooled in the procedural ways often find the leap to objects to be a difficult one.

Goals

The primary goal of this book is to promote object-oriented design using Java and to illustrate the use of the emerging *object-oriented design patterns*. Experienced object-oriented programmers find that certain ways of doing things work best and that these ways occur over and over again. The book shows how these patterns are used to create good software designs. In particular, the following design patterns are used throughout the text: *singleton*, *container*, *enumeration*, *adapter*, and *visitor*.

Virtually all of the data structures are presented in the context of a *single, unified, polymorphic class hierarchy*. This framework clearly shows the *relationships* between data structures and illustrates how polymorphism and inheritance can be used effectively. In addition, *algorithmic abstraction* is used extensively when presenting classes of algorithms. By using algorithmic abstraction, it is possible to describe a generic algorithm without having to worry about the details of a particular concrete realization of that algorithm.

A secondary goal of the book is to present mathematical tools *just in time*. Analysis techniques and proofs are presented as needed and in the proper context. In the past when the topics in this book were taught at the graduate level, an author could rely on students having the needed background in mathematics. However, because the book is targeted for second- and third-year students, it is necessary to fill in the background as needed. To the extent possible without compromising correctness, the presentation fosters intuitive understanding of the concepts rather than mathematical rigor.

Approach

One cannot learn to program just by reading a book. It is a skill that must be developed by practice. Nevertheless, the best practitioners study the works of others and incorporate their observations into their own practice. I firmly believe that after learning the rudiments of program writing, students should be exposed to examples of complex, yet well-designed program artifacts so that they can learn about designing good software.

Consequently, this book presents the various data structures and algorithms as complete Java program fragments. All of the program fragments presented in this book have been extracted automatically from the source code files of working and tested programs. It has been my experience that by developing the proper abstractions, it is possible to present the concepts as fully functional programs without resorting to *pseudo-code* or hand-waving.

Outline

This book presents material identified in the *Computing Curricula 1991* report of the ACM/IEEE-CS Joint Curriculum Task Force [43]. The book specifically addresses the following *knowledge units*: AL1: Basic Data structures, AL2: Abstract Data Types, AL3: Recursive Algorithms, AL4: Complexity Analysis, AL6: Sorting and Searching, and AL8: Problem-Solving Strategies. The breadth and depth of coverage is typical of what should appear in the second or third year of an undergraduate program in computer science/computer engineering.

In order to analyze a program, it is necessary to develop a model of the computer. Chapter 2 develops several models and illustrates with examples how these models predict performance. Both average-case and worst-case analyses of running time are considered. Recursive algorithms are discussed and it is shown how to solve a recurrence using repeated substitution. This chapter also reviews arithmetic and geometric series summations, Horner's rule, and the properties of harmonic numbers.

Chapter 3 introduces asymptotic (big oh) notation and shows by comparing with Chapter 2 that the results of asymptotic analysis are consistent with models of higher fidelity. In addition to $O(\cdot)$, this chapter also covers other asymptotic notations ($\Omega(\cdot)$, $\Theta(\cdot)$, and $o(\cdot)$) and develops the asymptotic properties of polynomials and logarithms.

Chapter 4 introduces the *foundational data structures*—the array and the linked list. Virtually all of the data structures in the rest of the book can be implemented using either one of these foundational structures. This chapter also covers multi-dimensional arrays and matrices.

Chapter 5 deals with abstraction and data types. It presents the recurring design patterns used throughout the text as well as a unifying framework for the data structures presented in the subsequent chapters. In particular, all of the data structures are viewed as *abstract containers*.

Chapter 6 discusses stacks, queues, and deques. This chapter presents implementations based on both foundational data structures (arrays and linked lists). Applications for stacks and queues are presented.

Chapter 7 covers ordered lists, both sorted and unsorted. In this chapter, a list is viewed as a *searchable container*. Again, several applications of lists are presented.

Chapter 8 introduces hashing and the notion of a hash table. This chapter addresses the design of hashing functions for the various basic data types as well as for the abstract data types described in Chapter 5. Both scatter tables and hash tables are covered in depth and analytical performance results are derived.

Chapter 9 introduces trees and describes their many forms. Both depth-first and breadth-first tree traversals are presented. Completely generic traversal algorithms based on the use of the *visitor* design pattern are presented, thereby illustrating the power of *algorithmic abstraction*. This chapter also shows how trees are used to represent mathematical expressions and illustrates the relationships between traversals and the various expression notations (prefix, infix, and postfix).

Chapter 10 addresses trees as *searchable containers*. Again, the power of *algorithmic abstraction* is demonstrated by showing the relationships between simple algorithms and balancing algorithms. This chapter also presents average case performance analyses and illustrates the solution of recurrences by telescoping.

Chapter 11 presents several priority queue implementations, including binary heaps, leftist heaps, and binomial queues. In particular this chapter illustrates how a more complicated data structure (leftist heap) extends an existing one (tree). Discrete-event simulation is presented as an application of priority queues.

Chapter 12 covers sets and multisets. Also covered are partitions and disjoint set algorithms. The latter topic illustrates again the use of algorithmic abstraction.

Garbage collection is discussed in Chapter 13. This is a topic that is not found often in texts of this sort. However, because the Java language relies on garbage collection, it is important to understand how it works and how it affects the running times of programs.

Chapter 14 surveys a number of algorithm design techniques. Included are brute-force and greedy algorithms, backtracking algorithms (including branch-and-bound), divide-and-conquer algorithms, and dynamic programming. An object-oriented approach based on the notion of an *abstract solution space* and an *abstract solver* unifies much of the discussion. This chapter also covers briefly random number generators, Monte Carlo methods, and simulated annealing.

Chapter 15 covers the major sorting algorithms in an object-oriented style based on the notion of an *abstract sorter*. Using the abstract sorter illustrates the relationships between the various classes of sorting algorithm and demonstrates the use of algorithmic abstractions.

Finally, Chapter 16 presents an overview of graphs and graph algorithms. Both depth-first and breadth-first graph traversals are presented. Topological sort is viewed as yet another special kind of traversal. Generic traversal algorithms based on the *visitor* design pattern are presented, once more illustrating *algorithmic abstraction*. This chapter also covers various shortest-path algorithms and minimum-spanning-tree algorithms.

At the end of each chapter is a set of exercises and a set of programming projects. The exercises are designed to consolidate the concepts presented in the text. The programming projects generally require the student to extend the implementation given in the text.

Suggested Course Outline

This text may be used in either a one-semester or a two-semester course. The course that I teach at Waterloo is a one-semester course consisting of 36 lecture hours on the following topics:

1. Review of the fundamentals of programming in Java and an overview of object-oriented programming with Java (Appendix A). [4 lecture hours]
2. Models of the computer, algorithm analysis, and asymptotic notation (Chapters 2 and 3). [4 lecture hours]
3. Foundational data structures, abstraction, and abstract data types (Chapters 4 and 5). [4 lecture hours]
4. Stacks, queues, ordered lists, and sorted lists (Chapters 6 and 7). [3 lecture hours]
5. Hashing, hash tables, and scatter tables (Chapter 8). [3 lecture hours]
6. Trees and search trees (Chapters 9 and 10). [6 lecture hours]
7. Heaps and priority queues (Chapter 11). [3 lecture hours]
8. Algorithm design techniques (Chapter 14). [3 lecture hours]
9. Sorting algorithms and sorters (Chapter 15). [3 lecture hours]
10. Graphs and graph algorithms (Chapter 16). [3 lecture hours]

Depending on the background of students, a course instructor may find it necessary to review features of the Java language. For example, an understanding of *inner classes* is required for the implementation of *enumerations*. Similarly, students need to understand the workings of *classes*, *interfaces*, and *inheritance* in order to understand the unifying class hierarchy discussed in Chapter 5.

Online Course Materials

Additional material supporting this book can be found on the World Wide Web at the URL:

```
http://www.pads.uwaterloo.ca/Bruno.Preiss/books/opus5
```

In particular, you will find there the source code for all of the program fragments in this book as well as an errata list.

Acknowledgments

I happily acknowledge the many people at UW, Wiley, and elsewhere who supported me in the writing of this book. I thank Regina Brooks for believing in me and my vision for this book. I thank Bill Zobrist for picking up the torch and seeing the work through.

For their careful reviews I thank Mike Clancy, University of California at Berkeley, Eileen Head, Binghamton University, Roberto Ordonez, Andrews University, John Slimick, University of Pittsburgh, and Yabo Wang, North Carolina A&T State University.

For painstakingly guiding the book through the production process I thank Monique Calello. For carefully correcting my grammatical gaffes I thank Helen Walden. For her astute sales and marketing advice I thank Katherine Hepburn.

Thank you to all the students of E&CE 250 who were the guinea pigs on whom various parts of this book were tested. And finally, I apologize to my family and friends who suffered neglect while I single-mindedly pursued my goal.

Bruno Preiss
Waterloo, Canada
December 9, 1998

Contents

1 | Introduction

1.1 What This Book Is About

This book is about the fundamentals of *data structures and algorithms*—the basic elements from which large and complex software artifacts are built. To develop a solid understanding of a data structure requires three things: First, you must learn how the information is arranged in the memory of the computer. Second, you must become familiar with the algorithms for manipulating the information contained in the data structure. And third, you must understand the performance characteristics of the data structure so that when called on to select a suitable data structure for a particular application, you are able to make an appropriate decision.

This book also illustrates object-oriented design and promotes the use of common, object-oriented design patterns. The algorithms and data structures in the book are presented in the Java programming language. Virtually all of the data structures are given in the context of a single class hierarchy. This commitment to a single design allows the programs presented in the later chapters to build on those presented in the earlier chapters.

1.2 Object-Oriented Design

Traditional approaches to the design of software have been either *data oriented* or *process oriented*. Data-oriented methodologies emphasize the representation of information and the relationships between the parts of the whole. The actions that operate on the data are of less significance. On the other hand, process-oriented design methodologies emphasize the actions performed by a software artifact; the data are of lesser importance.

It is now commonly held that *object-oriented* methodologies are more effective for managing the complexity that arises in the design of large and complex software artifacts than either data-oriented or process-oriented methodologies. This is because data and processes are given equal importance. *Objects* are used to combine data with the

1

procedures that operate on those data. The main advantage of using objects is that they provide both *abstraction* and *encapsulation*.

Abstraction

Abstraction can be thought of as a mechanism for suppressing irrelevant details while at the same time emphasizing relevant ones. An important benefit of abstraction is that it makes it easier for the programmer to think about the problem to be solved.

For example, *procedural abstraction* lets the software designer think about the actions to be performed without worrying about how those actions are implemented. Similarly, *data abstraction* lets the software designer think about the objects in a program and the interactions between those objects without having to worry about how those objects are implemented.

There are also many different *levels of abstraction*. The lower levels of abstraction expose more of the details of an implementation whereas the higher levels hide more of the details.

Encapsulation

Encapsulation aids the software designer by enforcing *information hiding*. Objects *encapsulate* data and the procedures for manipulating those data. In a sense, the object *hides* the details of the implementation from the user of that object.

There are two very real benefits from encapsulation—*conceptual* and *physical* independence. Conceptual independence results from hiding the implementation of an object from the user of that object. Consequently, the user is prevented from doing anything with an object that depends on the implementation of that object. This is desirable because it allows the implementation to be changed without requiring the modification of the user's code.

Physical independence arises from the fact that the behavior of an object is determined by the object itself. The behavior of an object is not determined by some external entity. As a result, when we perform an operation on an object, there are no unwanted side-effects.

1.3 Object Hierarchies and Design Patterns

There is more to object-oriented programming than simply encapsulating in an object some data and the procedures for manipulating those data. Object-oriented methods also deal with the *classification* of objects and they address the *relationships* between different classes of objects.

The primary facility for expressing relationships between classes of objects is *derivation*—new classes can be derived from existing classes. What makes derivation so useful is the notion of *inheritance*. Derived classes *inherit* the characteristics of the classes from which they are derived. In addition, inherited functionality can be overridden and additional functionality can be defined in a derived class.

A feature of this book is that virtually all of the data structures are presented in the context of a single class hierarchy. In effect, the class hierarchy is a taxonomy of data structures. Different implementations of a given abstract data structure are all derived from the same abstract base class. Related base classes are in turn derived from classes that abstract and encapsulate the common features of those classes.

In addition to dealing with hierarchically related classes, experienced object-oriented designers also consider very carefully the interactions between unrelated classes. With experience, a good designer discovers the recurring patterns of interactions between objects. By learning to use these patterns, you can make your object-oriented designs more flexible and reusable.

Recently, programmers have started to name the common design patterns. In addition, catalogs of the common patterns are now being compiled and published [14].

The following *object-oriented design patterns* are used throughout this text.

Containers
A container is an object that holds within it other objects. A container has a capacity, it can be full or empty, and objects can be inserted and withdrawn from a container. In addition, a *searchable container* is a container that supports efficient search operations.

Enumerations
An *enumeration* provides a means by which the objects within a container can be accessed one-at-a-time. All enumerations share a common interface, and hide the underlying implementation of the container from the user of that container.

Visitors
A visitor represents an operation to be performed on all the objects within a container. All visitors share a common interface, and thereby hide the operation to be performed from the container. At the same time, visitors are defined separately from containers. Thus, a particular visitor can be used with any container.

Cursors
A *cursor* represents the position of an object in an ordered container. It provides the user with a way to specify where an operation is to be performed without having to know how that position is represented.

Adapters
An *adapter* converts the interface of one class into the interface expected by the user of that class. This allows a given class with an incompatible interface to be used in a situation where a different interface is expected.

Singletons
A singleton is a class of which there is only one instance. The class ensures that there is only one instance created and it provides a way to access that instance.

1.4 The Features of Java You Need to Know

This book does not teach the basics of programming. It is assumed that you have taken an introductory course in programming and that you have learned how to write a program in Java. That is, you have learned the rules of Java syntax and you have learned how to put together Java statements in order to solve rudimentary programming problems. The following paragraphs describe more fully aspects of programming in Java with which you should be familiar.

Variables

You must be very comfortable with the notion of a variable as an abstraction for a region of a memory. A variable has attributes such as *name*, *type*, *value*, *address*, *size*, *lifetime*, and *scope*.

Primitive Types and Reference Types

You must understand the differences between the primitive types and reference types. In particular, you should understand the subtle differences that arise when assigning and comparing reference types.

Parameter Passing

There is one parameter-passing mechanism in Java: *pass-by-value*. It is essential that you understand how pass-by-value works for primitive types and for reference types.

Classes and Objects

A Java class encapsulates a set of values and a set of operations. The values are represented by the fields of the class and the operations by the methods of the class. In Java a class definition introduces a new *type*. The instances of a class type are called objects.

Inheritance

In Java one class may be derived from another. The derived class *inherits* all the fields and the methods of the base class or classes. In addition, inherited methods can be overridden in the derived class and new fields and methods can be defined. You should understand how the compiler determines the code to execute when a particular method is called.

Interfaces and Polymorphism

A Java interface comprises a set of method prototypes. Different classes can *implement* the same interface. In this way, Java facilitates *polymorphism*—the idea that a given abstraction can have many different forms. You should understand how interfaces are used together with abstract classes and inheritance to support polymorphism.

Other Features

This book makes use of other Java features such as exceptions and run-time type information. You can learn about these topics as you work your way through the book.

1.5   How This Book Is Organized

Models and Asymptotic Analysis

To analyze the performance of an algorithm, we need to have a model of the computer. Chapter 2 presents a series of three models, each one less precise but easier to use than its predecessor. These models are similar, in that they require a careful accounting of the operations performed by an algorithm.

Next, Chapter 3 presents *asymptotic analysis*. This is an extremely useful mathematical technique because it simplifies greatly the analysis of algorithms. Asymptotic analysis obviates the need for a detailed accounting of the operations performed by an algorithm, yet at the same time gives a very general result.

Foundational Data Structures

When implementing a data structure, we must decide first whether to use an *array* or a *linked list* as the underlying organizational technique. For this reason, the array and the linked list are called *foundational data structures*. Chapter 4 also covers multi-dimensional arrays and matrices.

Abstract Data Types and the Class Hierarchy

Chapter 5 introduces the notion of an *abstract data type*. All of the data structures discussed in this book are presented as instances of various abstract data types. Chapter 5 also introduces the class hierarchy as well as the various related concepts such as *enumerations* and *visitors*.

Data Structures

Chapter 6 covers *stacks*, *queues*, and *deques*. *Ordered lists* and *sorted lists* are presented in Chapter 7. The concept of hashing is introduced in Chapter 8. This chapter also covers the design of hash functions for a number of different object types. Finally, *hash tables* and *scatter tables* are presented.

Trees and search trees are presented in Chapters 9 and 10. Trees are one of the most important nonlinear data structures. Chapter 9 also covers the various tree traversals, including depth-first traversal and breadth-first traversal. Chapter 11 presents *priority queues* and Chapter 12 covers *sets, multisets, and partitions*

An essential element of the Java run-time system is the pool of dynamically allocated storage. Chapter 13 presents a number of different approaches for implementing garbage collection, in the process illustrating the actual costs associated with dynamic storage allocation.

Algorithms

The last three chapters of the book focus on algorithms, rather than data structures. Chapter 14 is an overview of various algorithmic patterns. By introducing the notion of an abstract problem solver, we show how many of the patterns are related. Chapter 15 uses a similar approach to present various sorting algorithms. That is, we introduce the notion of an abstract sorter and show how the various sorting algorithms are related.

Finally, Chapter 16 gives a brief overview of the subject of graphs and graph algorithms. This chapter brings together various algorithmic techniques from Chapter 14 with the class hierarchy discussed in the earlier chapters.

2 | Algorithm Analysis

What is an algorithm and why do we want to analyze one? An algorithm is "a . . . step-by-step procedure for accomplishing some end" [9]. An algorithm can be given in many ways. For example, it can be written down in English (or French, or any other "natural" language). However, we are interested in algorithms that have been precisely specified using an appropriate mathematical formalism—such as a programming language.

Given such an expression of an algorithm, what can we do with it? Well, obviously we can run the program and observe its behavior. This is not likely to be very useful or informative in the general case. If we run a particular program on a particular computer with a particular set of inputs, then all we know is the behavior of the program in a single instance. Such knowledge is anecdotal and we must be careful when drawing conclusions based on anecdotal evidence.

In order to learn more about an algorithm, we can "analyze" it. By this we mean to study the specification of the algorithm and to draw conclusions about how the implementation of that algorithm—the program—will perform in general. But what can we analyze? We can determine

- the running time of a program as a function of its inputs;
- the total or maximum memory space needed for program data;
- the total size of the program code;
- whether the program correctly computes the desired result;
- the complexity of the program—for example, how easy it is to read, understand, and modify; and,
- the robustness of the program—for example, how well does it deal with unexpected or erroneous inputs?

In this text we are concerned primarily with the running time. We also consider the memory space needed to execute the program. There are many factors that affect the running time of a program. Among these are the algorithm itself, the input data, and the computer system used to run the program. The performance of a computer is determined by

- the hardware:
    - processor used (type and speed),
    - memory available (cache and RAM), and
    - disk available;
- the programming language in which the algorithm is specified;
- the language compiler/interpreter used; and
- the computer operating system software.

A detailed analysis of the performance of a program that takes all of these factors into account is a very difficult and time-consuming undertaking. Furthermore, such an analysis is not likely to have lasting significance. The rapid pace of change in the underlying technologies means that results of such analyses are not likely to be applicable to the next generation of hardware and software.

In order to overcome this shortcoming, we devise a "model" of the behavior of a computer with the goals of simplifying the analysis while still producing meaningful results. The next section introduces the first in a series of such models.

2.1 A Detailed Model of the Computer

In this section we develop a detailed model of the running time performance of Java programs. The model developed is independent of the underlying hardware and system software. Rather than analyze the performance of a particular, arbitrarily chosen physical machine, we model the execution of a Java program on the "Java Virtual Machine" (see Figure 2.1).

A direct consequence of this approach is that we lose some fidelity—the resulting model cannot predict accurately the performance of all possible hardware/software systems. On the other hand, the resulting model is still rather complex and rich in detail.

2.1.1 The Basic Axioms

The running time performance of the Java Virtual Machine is given by a set of axioms that we will now postulate. The first axiom addresses the running time of simple variable references:

Axiom 2.1
The time required to fetch an operand from memory is a constant, τ_{fetch}, and the time required to store a result in memory is a constant, τ_{store}.

FIGURE 2.1
Java system overview.

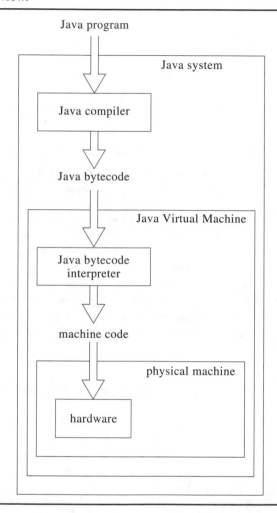

According to Axiom 2.1, the assignment statement

```
y = x;
```

has running time $\tau_{\text{fetch}} + \tau_{\text{store}}$. That is, the time taken to fetch the value of variable **x** is τ_{fetch} and the time taken to store the value in variable **y** is τ_{store}.

We will apply Axiom 2.1 to manifest constants too: the assignment

```
y = 1;
```

also has running time $\tau_{\text{fetch}} + \tau_{\text{store}}$. To see why this should be the case, consider that the constant typically needs to be stored in the memory of the computer, and we can expect the cost of fetching it to be the same as that of fetching any other operand.

The next axiom addresses the running time of simple arithmetic operations:

Axiom 2.2

The times required to perform elementary arithmetic operations, such as addition, subtraction, multiplication, division, and comparison, are all constants. These times are denoted by τ_+, τ_-, $\tau_\times$, $\tau_\div$, and $\tau_<$, respectively.

According to Axiom 2.2, all of the simple operations can be accomplished in a fixed amount of time. In order for this to be feasible, the number of bits used to represent a value must be fixed. In Java, the number of bits needed to represent a number range from 8 (for **byte**s) to 64 (for **long**s and **double**s). It is precisely because the number of bits used is fixed that we can say that the running times are also fixed. If arbitrarily large numbers are allowed, then the basic arithmetic operations can take an arbitrarily long amount of time.

By applying Axiom 2.1 and 2.2, we can determine that the running time of a statement like

```
y = y + 1;
```

is $2\tau_{\text{fetch}} + \tau_+ + \tau_{\text{store}}$. This is because we need to fetch two operands, **y** and **1**; add them; and, store the result back in **y**.

Java syntax provides several alternative ways to express the same computation:

```
y += 1;

++y;

y++;
```

We will assume that these alternatives require exactly the same running time as the original statement.

The third basic axiom addresses the method call/return overhead:

Axiom 2.3

The time required to call a method is a constant, τ_{call}, and the time required to return from a method is a constant, τ_{return}.

When a method is called, certain housekeeping operations need to be performed. Typically this includes saving the return address so that program execution can resume at the correct place after the call, saving the state of any partially completed computations so that they may be resumed after the call, and allocating a new execution context (stack frame or activation record) in which the called method can be evaluated. Conversely, on the return from a method, all of this work is undone. Although the method call/return overhead may be rather large, nevertheless it entails a constant amount of work.

In addition to the method call/return overhead, additional overhead is incurred when parameters are passed to the method:

Axiom 2.4

The time required to pass an argument to a method is the same as the time required to store a value in memory, τ_{store}.

The rationale for making the overhead associated with parameter passing the same as the time to store a value in memory is that the passing of an argument is conceptually the same as assignment of the actual parameter value to the formal parameter of the method.

According to Axiom 2.5, the running time of the statement

```
y = f (x);
```

would be $\tau_{\text{fetch}} + 2\tau_{\text{store}} + \tau_{\text{call}} + T_{\text{f(x)}}$, where $T_{\text{f(x)}}$ is the running time of method **f** for input **x**. The first of the two stores is due to the passing of the parameter **x** to the method **f**; the second arises from the assignment to the variable **y**.

2.1.2   A Simple Example—Arithmetic Series Summation

In this section we apply Axioms 2.1, 2.2, and 2.3 to the analysis of the running time of a program to compute the following simple arithmetic series summation:

$$\sum_{i=1}^{n} i.$$

The algorithm to compute this summation is given in Program 2.1.

The executable statements in Program 2.1 comprise lines 5–8. Table 2.1 gives the running times of each of these statements.

Note that the **for** statement on line 6 of Program 2.1 has been split across three lines in Table 2.1. This is because we analyze the running time of each of the elements of a **for** statement separately. The first element, the *initialization code*, is executed once

---

PROGRAM 2.1
Program to compute $\sum_{i=1}^{n} i$

```
1   public class Example
2   {
3       public static int sum (int n)
4       {
5           int result = 0;
6           for (int i = 1; i <= n; ++i)
7               result += i;
8           return result;
9       }
10  }
```

TABLE 2.1
Computing the Running Time of Program 2.1

Statement	Time	Code
5	$\tau_{\text{fetch}} + \tau_{\text{store}}$	`result = 0`
6a	$\tau_{\text{fetch}} + \tau_{\text{store}}$	`i = 1`
6b	$(2\tau_{\text{fetch}} + \tau_{<}) \times (n + 1)$	`i <= n`
6c	$(2\tau_{\text{fetch}} + \tau_{+} + \tau_{\text{store}}) \times n$	`++i`
7	$(2\tau_{\text{fetch}} + \tau_{+} + \tau_{\text{store}}) \times n$	`result += i`
8	$\tau_{\text{fetch}} + \tau_{\text{return}}$	`return result`
TOTAL	$(6\tau_{\text{fetch}} + 2\tau_{\text{store}} + \tau_{<} + 2\tau_{+}) \times n$ $+ (5\tau_{\text{fetch}} + 2\tau_{\text{store}} + \tau_{<} + \tau_{\text{return}})$	

before the first iteration of the loop. The second element, the *loop termination test*, is executed before each iteration of the loop begins. Altogether, the number of times the termination test is executed is one more than the number of times the loop body is executed. Finally, the third element, the *loop counter increment step*, is executed once per loop iteration.

Summing the entries in Table 2.1, we get that the running time, $T(n)$, of Program 2.1 is

$$T(n) = t_1 + t_2 n, \qquad (2.1)$$

where $t_1 = 5\tau_{\text{fetch}} + 2\tau_{\text{store}} + \tau_{<} + \tau_{\text{return}}$ and $t_2 = 6\tau_{\text{fetch}} + 2\tau_{\text{store}} + \tau_{<} + 2\tau_{+}$.

2.1.3   Array Subscripting Operations

We now address the question of accessing the elements of an array of data. In general, the elements of a one-dimensional array are stored in consecutive memory locations. Therefore, given the address of the first element of the array, a simple addition suffices to determine the address of an arbitrary element of the array:

Axiom 2.5
The time required for the address calculation *implied by an array subscripting operation, for example,* `a[i]`, *is a constant,* $\tau_{[\cdot]}$. *This time does not include the time to compute the subscript expression, nor does it include the time to access (i.e., fetch or store) the array element.*

By applying Axiom 2.5, we can determine that the running time for the statement

```
y = a [i];
```

is $3\tau_{\text{fetch}} + \tau_{[\cdot]} + \tau_{\text{store}}$. Three operand fetches are required: the first to fetch `a`, the base address of the array; the second to fetch `i`, the index into the array; and the third to fetch array element `a[i]`.

2.1.4 Another Example—Horner's Rule

In this section we apply Axioms 2.1, 2.2, 2.3, and 2.4 to the analysis of the running time of a program that evaluates the value of a polynomial. That is, given the $n + 1$ coefficients $a_0, a_1, \ldots, a_n$, and a value x, we wish to compute the following summation:

$$\sum_{i=0}^{n} a_i x^i.$$

The usual way to evaluate such polynomials is to use Horner's rule, which is an algorithm to compute the summation without requiring the computation of arbitrary powers of x. The algorithm to compute this summation is given in Program 2.2. Table 2.2 gives the running times of each of the executable statements in Program 2.2.

PROGRAM 2.2
Program to compute $\sum_{i=0}^{n} a_i x^i$ using Horner's rule

```
1   public class Example
2   {
3       public static int horner (int[] a, int n, int x)
4       {
5           int result = a [n];
6           for (int i = n - 1; i >= 0; --i)
7               result = result * x + a [i];
8           return result;
9       }
10  }
```

TABLE 2.2
Computing the Running Time of Program 2.2

Statement	Time
5	$3\tau_{\text{fetch}} + \tau_{[\cdot]} + \tau_{\text{store}}$
6a	$2\tau_{\text{fetch}} + \tau_- + \tau_{\text{store}}$
6b	$(2\tau_{\text{fetch}} + \tau_<) \times (n + 1)$
6c	$(2\tau_{\text{fetch}} + \tau_- + \tau_{\text{store}}) \times n$
7	$(5\tau_{\text{fetch}} + \tau_{[\cdot]} + \tau_+ + \tau_\times + \tau_{\text{store}}) \times n$
8	$\tau_{\text{fetch}} + \tau_{\text{return}}$
TOTAL	$(9\tau_{\text{fetch}} + 2\tau_{\text{store}} + \tau_< + \tau_{[\cdot]} + \tau_+ + \tau_\times + \tau_-) \times n$ $+ (8\tau_{\text{fetch}} + 2\tau_{\text{store}} + \tau_{[\cdot]} + \tau_- + \tau_< + \tau_{\text{return}})$

Summing the entries in Table 2.2, we get that the running time, $T(n)$, of Program 2.2 is

$$T(n) = t_1 + t_2 n, \tag{2.2}$$

where $t_1 = 8\tau_{\text{fetch}} + 2\tau_{\text{store}} + \tau_{[\cdot]} + \tau_- + \tau_< + \tau_{\text{return}}$ and $t_2 = 9\tau_{\text{fetch}} + 2\tau_{\text{store}} + \tau_< + \tau_{[\cdot]} + \tau_+ + \tau_\times + \tau_-$.

2.1.5 Analyzing Recursive Methods

In this section we analyze the performance of a recursive algorithm that computes the factorial of a number. Recall that the factorial of a non-negative integer n, written $n!$, is defined as

$$n! = \begin{cases} 1 & n = 0, \\ \prod_{i=1}^{n} i & n > 0. \end{cases} \tag{2.3}$$

However, we can also define factorial *recursively* as follows:

$$n! = \begin{cases} 1 & n = 0, \\ n \times (n-1)! & n > 0. \end{cases}$$

It is this latter definition that leads to the algorithm given in Program 2.3 to compute the factorial of n. Table 2.3 gives the running times of each of the executable statements in Program 2.3.

Notice that we had to analyze the running time of the two possible outcomes of the conditional test on line 5 separately. Clearly, the running time of the program depends on the result of this test.

Furthermore, the method **factorial** calls itself recursively on line 8. Therefore, in order to write down the running time of line 8, we need to know the running time, $T(\cdot)$,

---

PROGRAM 2.3
Recursive program to compute $n!$

```
1   public class Example
2   {
3       public static int factorial (int n)
4       {
5           if (n == 0)
6               return 1;
7           else
8               return n * factorial (n - 1);
9       }
10  }
```

TABLE 2.3
Computing the Running Time of Program 2.3

Statement	Time	
	$n = 0$	$n > 0$
5	$2\tau_{\text{fetch}} + \tau_<$	$2\tau_{\text{fetch}} + \tau_<$
6	$\tau_{\text{fetch}} + \tau_{\text{return}}$	—
8	—	$3\tau_{\text{fetch}} + \tau_- + \tau_{\text{store}} + \tau_\times$
		$+ \tau_{\text{call}} + \tau_{\text{return}} + T(n-1)$

of `factorial`. But this is precisely what we are trying to determine in the first place! We escape from this catch-22 by assuming that we already know what is the function $T(\cdot)$, and that we can make use of that function to determine the running time of line 8.

By summing the columns in Table 2.3 we get that the running time of Program 2.3 is

$$T(n) = \begin{cases} t_1 & n = 0, \\ T(n-1) + t_2 & n > 0, \end{cases} \tag{2.4}$$

where $t_1 = 3\tau_{\text{fetch}} + \tau_< + \tau_{\text{return}}$ and $t_2 = 5\tau_{\text{fetch}} + \tau_< + \tau_- + \tau_{\text{store}} + \tau_\times + \tau_{\text{call}} + \tau_{\text{return}}$. This kind of equation is called a *recurrence relation* because the function is defined in terms of itself recursively.

Solving Recurrence Relations—Repeated Substitution

In this section we present a technique for solving a recurrence relation such as Equation 2.4 called *repeated substitution*. The basic idea is this: Given that $T(n) = T(n-1) + t_2$, then we may also write $T(n-1) = T(n-2) + t_2$, provided $n > 1$. Since $T(n-1)$ appears in the right-hand side of the former equation, we can substitute for it the entire right-hand side of the latter. By repeating this process we get

$$\begin{aligned} T(n) &= T(n-1) + t_2 \\ &= (T(n-2) + t_2) + t_2 \\ &= T(n-2) + 2t_2 \\ &= (T(n-3) + t_2) + 2t_2 \\ &= T(n-3) + 3t_2 \\ &\quad\vdots \end{aligned}$$

The next step takes a little intuition: We must try to discern the pattern that is emerging. In this case it is obvious:

$$T(n) = T(n-k) + kt_2,$$

where $1 \leq k \leq n$. Of course, if we have doubts about our intuition, we can always check our result by induction:

Proof (By induction).

Base Case Clearly the formula is correct for $k = 1$, since $T(n) = T(n-k) + kt_2 = T(n-1) + t_2$.

Inductive Hypothesis Assume that $T(n) = T(n-k) + kt_2$ for $k = 1, 2, \ldots, 1$. By this assumption

$$T(n) = T(n-l) + lt_2. \tag{2.5}$$

Note also that using the original recurrence relation we can write

$$T(n-l) = T(n-l-1) + t_2 \tag{2.6}$$

for $l \leq n$. Substituting Equation 2.5 in the right-hand side of Equation 2.6 gives

$$\begin{aligned} T(n) &= T(n-l-1) + t_2 + lt_2 \\ &= T(n-(l+1)) + (l+1)t_2. \end{aligned}$$

Therefore, by induction on l, our formula is correct for all $0 \leq k \leq n$.

So, we have shown that $T(n) = T(n-k) + kt_2$, for $1 \leq k \leq n$. Now, if n was known, we would repeat the process of substitution until we got $T(0)$ on the right-hand side. The fact that n is unknown should not deter us—we get $T(0)$ on the right-hand side when $n - k = 0$. That is, $k = n$. Letting $k = n$, we get

$$\begin{aligned} T(n) &= T(n-k) + kt_2 \\ &= T(0) + nt_2 \\ &= t_1 + nt_2, \end{aligned} \tag{2.7}$$

where $t_1 = 3\tau_{\text{fetch}} + \tau_< + \tau_{\text{return}}$ and $t_2 = 5\tau_{\text{fetch}} + \tau_< + \tau_- + \tau_{\text{store}} + \tau_\times + \tau_{\text{call}} + \tau_{\text{return}}$.

2.1.6 Yet Another Example—Finding the Largest Element of an Array

In this section we consider the problem of finding the largest element of an array. That is, given an array of n non-negative integers, $a_0, a_1, \ldots, a_{n-1}$, we wish to find

$$\max_{0 \leq i < n} a_i.$$

The straightforward way of solving this problem is to perform a *linear search* of the array. The linear search algorithm is given in Program 2.4 and the running times for the various statements are given in Table 2.4.

With the exception of line 8, the running times follow simply from Axioms 2.1, 2.2, and 2.5. In particular, note that the body of the loop is executed $n - 1$ times. This means that the conditional test on line 7 is executed $n - 1$ times. However, the number of times line 8 is executed depends on the data in the array and not on just n.

If we consider that in each iteration of the loop body, the variable **result** contains the largest array element seen so far, then line 8 will be executed in the ith iteration of the loop only if a_i satisfies the following:

$$a_i > \left(\max_{0 \le j < i} a_j \right).$$

Thus, the running time of Program 2.4, $T(\cdot)$, is a function not only of the number of elements in the array, n, but also of the actual array values, $a_0, a_1, \ldots, a_{n-1}$. Summing

---

PROGRAM 2.4
Linear search to find $\max_{0 \le i < n} a_i$

```
1   public class Example
2   {
3       public static int findMaximum (int[] a)
4       {
5           int result = a [0];
6           for (int i = 1; i < a.length; ++i)
7               if (a [i] > result)
8                   result = a [i];
9           return result;
10      }
11  }
```

TABLE 2.4
Computing the Running Time of Program 2.4

Statement	Time
5	$3\tau_{fetch} + \tau_{[\cdot]} + \tau_{store}$
6a	$\tau_{fetch} + \tau_{store}$
6b	$(2\tau_{fetch} + \tau_<) \times n$
6c	$(2\tau_{fetch} + \tau_+ + \tau_{store}) \times (n - 1)$
7	$(4\tau_{fetch} + \tau_{[\cdot]} + \tau_<) \times (n - 1)$
8	$(3\tau_{fetch} + \tau_{[\cdot]} + \tau_{store}) \times ?$
9	$\tau_{fetch} + \tau_{store}$

the entries in Table 2.4, we get

$$T(n, a_0, a_1, \ldots, a_{n-1}) = t_1 + t_2 n + \sum_{\substack{i=1 \\ a_i > \left(\max_{0 \le j < i} a_j\right)}}^{n-1} t_3,$$

where

$$t_1 = 2\tau_{\text{store}} - \tau_{\text{fetch}} - \tau_+ - \tau_<$$

$$t_2 = 8\tau_{\text{fetch}} + 2\tau_< + \tau_{[\cdot]} + \tau_+ + \tau_{\text{store}}$$

$$t_3 = 3\tau_{\text{fetch}} + \tau_{[\cdot]} + \tau_{\text{store}}.$$

Although this result may be correct, it is not terribly useful. In order to determine the running time of the program we need to know the number of elements in the array, n, and we need to know the values of the elements in the array, $a_0, a_1, \ldots,$ a_{n-1}. Even if we know these data, it turns out that in order to compute the running time of the algorithm, $T(n, a_0, a_1, \ldots, a_{n-1})$, we actually have to solve the original problem!

2.1.7 Average Running Times

In the previous section we found the function, $T(n, a_0, a_1, \ldots, a_{n-1})$, which gives the running time of Program 2.4 as a function both of number of inputs, n, and of the actual input values. Suppose instead we are interested in a function $T_{\text{average}}(n)$, which gives the running time *on average* for n inputs, regardless of the values of those inputs. In other words, if we run Program 2.4 a large number of times on a selection of random inputs of length n, what will the average running time be?

We can write the sum of the running times given in Table 2.4 in the following form:

$$T_{\text{average}}(n) = t_1 + t_2 n + \sum_{i=1}^{n-1} p_i t_3, \tag{2.8}$$

where p_i is the probability that line 8 of the program is executed. The probability p_i is given by

$$p_i = P\left[a_i > (\max_{0 \le j < i} a_j)\right].$$

That is, p_i is the probability that the ith array entry, a_i, is larger than the maximum of all the preceding array entries, $a_0, a_1, \ldots, a_{i-1}$.

In order to determine p_i, we need to know (or to assume) something about the distribution of input values. For example, if we know a priori that the array passed to the method **findMaximum** is ordered from smallest to largest, then we know that $p_i = 1$.

Conversely, if we know that the array is ordered from largest to smallest, then we know that $p_i = 0$.

In the general case, we have no a priori knowledge of the distribution of the values in the input array. In this case, consider the ith iteration of the loop. In this iteration a_i is compared with the maximum of the i values, $a_0, a_1, \ldots, a_{i-1}$, preceding it in the array. Line 6 of Program 2.4 is only executed if a_i is the largest of the $i + 1$ values $a_0, a_1, \ldots, a_i$. All things being equal, we can say that this will happen with probability $1/(i + 1)$. Thus

$$p_i = P\left[a_i > (\max_{0 \le j < i} a_j)\right] \qquad (2.9)$$

$$= \frac{1}{i + 1}.$$

Substituting this expression for p_i in Equation 2.8 and simplifying the result, we get

$$T_{\text{average}}(n) = t_1 + t_2 n + \sum_{i=1}^{n-1} p_i t_3$$

$$= t_1 + t_2 n + t_3 \sum_{i=1}^{n-1} \frac{1}{i + 1}$$

$$= t_1 + t_2 n + t_3 \left(\sum_{i=1}^{n} \frac{1}{i} - 1\right)$$

$$= t_1 + t_2 n + t_3 (H_n - 1), \qquad (2.10)$$

where $H_n = \sum_{i=1}^{n} \frac{1}{i}$, is the nth *harmonic number*.

2.1.8   About Harmonic Numbers

The series $1, \frac{1}{2}, \frac{1}{3}, \frac{1}{4}, \ldots$ is called the *harmonic series*, and the summation

$$H_n = \sum_{i=1}^{n} \frac{1}{i}$$

gives rise to the series of *harmonic numbers*, $H_1, H_2, \ldots$. As it turns out, harmonic numbers often creep into the analysis of algorithms. Therefore, we should understand a little bit about how they behave.

A remarkable characteristic of harmonic numbers is that, even though as n gets larger and the difference between consecutive harmonic numbers gets arbitrarily smaller ($H_n - H_{n-1} = 1/n$), *the series does not converge!* That is, $\lim_{n \to \infty} H_n$ does not exist. In other words, the summation $\sum_{i=1}^{\infty} 1/i$ goes off to infinity, but just barely.

FIGURE 2.2
Computing harmonic numbers.

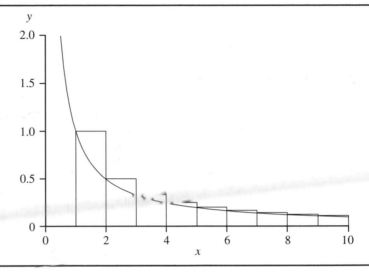

Figure 2.2 helps us to understand the behavior of harmonic numbers. The smooth curve in this figure is the function $y = 1/x$. The descending staircase represents the function $y = 1/\lfloor x \rfloor$.[1]

Notice that the area under the staircase between 1 and n for any integer $n > 1$ is given by

$$\int_1^n \frac{1}{\lfloor x \rfloor} dx = \sum_{i=1}^{n-1} \frac{1}{i}$$
$$= H_{n-1}.$$

Thus, if we can determine the area under the descending staircase in Figure 2.2, we can determine the values of the harmonic numbers.

As an approximation, consider the area under the smooth curve $y = 1/x$:

$$\int_1^n \frac{1}{x} dx = \ln x \Big|_1^n$$
$$= \ln(n).$$

Thus, H_{n-1} is approximately $\ln n$ for $n > 1$.

If we approximate H_{n-1} by $\ln n$, the error in this approximation is equal to the area between the two curves. In fact, the area between these two curves is such an important

---

[1] The notation $\lfloor \cdot \rfloor$ denotes the *floor function*, which is defined as follows: For any real number x, $\lfloor x \rfloor$ is the greatest integer less than or equal to x. While we are on the subject, there is a related function, the *ceiling function*, written $\lceil \cdot \rceil$. For any real number x, $\lceil x \rceil$ is the smallest integer greater than or equal to x.

PROGRAM 2.5
Program to compute γ

```
1   public class Example
2   {
3       public static double gamma ()
4       {
5           double result = 0;
6           for (int i = 1; i <= 500000; ++i)
7               result += 1./i - Math.log ((i + 1.)/i);
8           return result;
9       }
10  }
```

---

quantity that it has its own symbol, γ, which is called *Euler's constant*. The following derivation indicates a way in which to compute Euler's constant:

$$
\begin{aligned}
\gamma &= \lim_{n \to \infty} (H_{n-1} - \ln n) \\
&= \sum_{i=1}^{\infty} \left(\int_{i}^{i+1} \left(\frac{1}{i} - \frac{1}{x} \right) dx \right) \\
&= \sum_{i=1}^{\infty} \left(\frac{1}{i} \int_{i}^{i+1} 1 \, dx - \int_{i}^{i+1} \frac{1}{x} dx \right) \\
&= \sum_{i=1}^{\infty} \left(\frac{1}{i} - \ln \left(\frac{i+1}{i} \right) \right) \\
&\approx 0.577\,215
\end{aligned}
$$

A program to compute Euler's constant on the basis of this derivation is given in Program 2.5. Although this is not necessarily the most accurate or most speedy way to compute Euler's constant, it does give the correct result to six significant digits.

So, with Euler's constant in hand, we can write down an expression for the $(n-1)$th harmonic number

$$H_{n-1} = \ln n + \gamma - \epsilon_n, \tag{2.11}$$

where ϵ_n is the error introduced by the fact that γ is defined as the difference between the curves on the interval $[1, +\infty)$, but we only need the difference on the interval $[1, n]$. As it turns out, it can be shown (but not here), that there exists a constant K such that for large enough values of n, $|\epsilon_n| < K/n$.[2]

---

[2]In fact, we would normally write $\epsilon_n = O(\frac{1}{n})$, but we have not yet seen the $O(\cdot)$ notation, which is introduced in Chapter 3.

Since the error term is less than $1/n$, we can add $1/n$ to both sides of Equation 2.11 and still have an error that goes to zero as n gets large. Thus, the usual approximation for the harmonic number is

$$H_n \approx \ln n + \gamma.$$

We now return to the question of finding the average running time of Program 2.4, which finds the largest element of an array. We can now rewrite Equation 2.10 to give

$$
\begin{aligned}
T_{\text{average}}(n) &= t_1 + t_2 n + t_3(H_n - 1) \\
&\approx t_1 + t_2 n + t_3(\ln n + \gamma - 1) \\
&\approx (t_1 + t_3(\gamma - 1)) + t_2 n + t_3 \ln n.
\end{aligned}
$$

2.1.9   Best-Case and Worst-Case Running Times

In Section 2.1.7 we derived the average running time of Program 2.4 that finds the largest element of an array. In order to do this we had to determine the probability that a certain program statement is executed. To do this, we made an assumption about the *average* input to the program.

The analysis can be significantly simplified if we simply wish to determine the *worst-case* running time. For Program 2.4, the worst-case scenario occurs when line 8 is executed in every iteration of the loop. We saw that this corresponds to the case in which the input array is ordered from smallest to largest. In terms of Equation 2.8, this occurs when $p_i = 1$. Thus, the worst-case running time is given by

$$
\begin{aligned}
T_{\text{worst case}}(n) &= t_1 + t_2 n + \left. \sum_{i=1}^{n-1} p_i t_3 \right|_{p_i = 1} \\
&= t_1 + t_2 n + t_3 \sum_{i=1}^{n-1} 1 \\
&= t_1 + t_2 n + t_3(n - 1) \\
&= (t_1 - t_3) + (t_2 + t_3) \times n.
\end{aligned}
$$

Similarly, the *best-case* running time occurs when line 8 is never executed. This corresponds to the case in which the input array is ordered from largest to smallest. This occurs when $p_i = 0$ and best-case running time is

$$
\begin{aligned}
T_{\text{best case}}(n) &= t_1 + t_2 n + \left. \sum_{i=1}^{n-1} p_i t_3 \right|_{p_i = 0} \\
&= t_1 + t_2 n.
\end{aligned}
$$

In summary, we have the following results for the running time of Program 2.4:

$$T(n, a_0, a_1, \ldots, a_{n-1}) = t_1 + t_2 n + \sum_{\substack{i=1 \\ a_i > \left(\max_{0 \le j < i} a_j\right)}}^{n-1} t_3$$

$$T_{\text{average}}(n) \approx (t_1 + t_3(\gamma - 1)) + t_2 n + t_3 \ln n$$
$$T_{\text{worst case}}(n) = (t_1 - t_3) + (t_2 + t_3) \times n$$
$$T_{\text{best case}}(n) = t_1 + t_2 n.$$

2.1.10   The Last Axiom

In this section we state the last axiom needed for the detailed model of the Java Virtual Machine. This axiom addresses the time required to create a new object instance:

Axiom 2.6
The time required to create a new object instance using the **new** *operator is a constant,* τ_{new}. *This time does not include any time taken to initialize the object.*

By applying Axioms 2.1, 2.3, 2.4, and 2.6, we can determine that the running time of the statement

```
Integer ref = new Integer (0);
```

is $\tau_{\text{new}} + \tau_{\text{fetch}} + 2\tau_{\text{store}} + \tau_{\text{call}} + \mathcal{T}_{\langle \text{Integer}()\rangle}$, where $\mathcal{T}_{\langle \text{Integer}()\rangle}$ is the running time of the **Integer** constructor.

2.2   A Simplified Model of the Computer

The detailed model of the computer given in the previous section is based on a number of different timing parameters—τ_{fetch}, τ_{store}, τ_+, τ_-, $\tau_\times$, $\tau_\div$, $\tau_<$, τ_{call}, τ_{return}, τ_{new}, and $\tau_{[\cdot]}$. Although it is true that a model with a large number of parameters is quite flexible and therefore likely to be a good predictor of performance, keeping track of all of the parameters during the analysis is rather burdensome.

In this section we present a simplified model that makes the performance analysis easier to do. The cost of using the simplified model is that it is likely to be a less accurate predictor of performance than the detailed model.

Consider the various timing parameters in the detailed model. In a real machine, each of these parameters is a multiple of the basic clock period of the machine. The clock frequency of a modern computer is typically between 100 and 500 MHz. Therefore, the clock period is typically between 2 and 10 ns. Let the clock period of the machine be T. Then each of the timing parameters can be expressed as an integer multiple of the clock period. For example, $\tau_{\text{fetch}} = k_{\text{fetch}} T$, where $k_{\text{fetch}} \in \mathbb{Z}$, $k_{\text{fetch}} > 0$.

Note that the term in the first summation in Equation 2.12 is independent of j. Also, the second summation is identical to the left-hand side. Rearranging Equation 2.12, and simplifying gives

$$2\sum_{i=1}^{n} i = n\sum_{j=0}^{n-1} 1 + n$$

$$= n^2 + n$$

$$= n(n + 1)$$

$$\sum_{i=1}^{n} i = \frac{n(n+1)}{2}.$$

There is, of course, a simpler way to arrive at this answer. Consider the series, $1, 2, 3, 4, \ldots, n$, and suppose n is even. The sum of the first and last element is $n + 1$. So too is the sum of the second and second-last element, and the third and third-last element, and so on, and there are $n/2$ such pairs. Therefore, $S_n = \frac{n}{2}(n + 1)$.

And if n is odd, then $S_n = S_{n-1} + n$, where $n - 1$ is even. So we can use the previous result for S_{n-1} to get $S_n = \frac{n-1}{2}n + n = n(n + 1)/2$.

2.2.3 Example—Geometric Series Summation Again

In this example we revisit the problem of computing a *geometric series summation*. We have already seen an algorithm to compute this summation in Section 2.2.1 (Program 2.6). This algorithm was shown to take $\frac{11}{2}n^2 + \frac{47}{2}n + 24$ cycles.

The problem of computing the geometric series summation is identical to that of computing the value of a polynomial in which all of the coefficients are one. This suggests that we could make use of *Horner's rule* as discussed in Section 2.1.4. An algorithm to compute a geometric series summation using Horner's rule is given in Program 2.7.

PROGRAM 2.7
Program to compute $\sum_{i=0}^{n} x^i$ using Horner's rule

```
1   public class Example
2   {
3       public static int geometricSeriesSum (int x, int n)
4       {
5           int sum = 0;
6           for (int i = 0; i <= n; ++i)
7               sum = sum * x + 1;
8           return sum;
9       }
10  }
```

TABLE 2.6
Computing the Running Time
of Program 2.7

Statement	Time
5	2
6a	2
6b	$3(n + 2)$
6c	$4(n + 1)$
7	$6(n + 1)$
8	2
TOTAL	$13n + 22$

The executable statements in Program 2.7 comprise lines 5–8. Table 2.6 gives the running times, as given by the simplified model, for each of these statements.

In Programs 2.6 and 2.7 we have seen two different algorithms to compute the same geometric series summation. We determined the running time of the former to be $\frac{11}{2}n^2 + \frac{47}{2}n + 24$ cycles and of the latter to be $13n + 22$ cycles. In particular, note that for all nonnegative values of n, $(\frac{11}{2}n^2 + \frac{47}{2}n + 24) > 13n + 22$. Hence, according to our simplified model of the computer, Program 2.7, which uses Horner's rule, *always* runs faster than Program 2.6!

2.2.4 About Geometric Series Summation

The series, $1, a, a^2, a^3, \ldots,$ is a *geometric series* and the summation

$$S_n = \sum_{i=0}^{n} a^i$$

is called the *geometric series summation*.

The summation can be solved as follows: First, we make the simple variable substitution $i = j - 1$:

$$\sum_{i=0}^{n} a^i = \sum_{j-1=0}^{n} a^{j-1}$$

$$= \frac{1}{a} \sum_{j=1}^{n+1} a^j$$

$$= \frac{1}{a} \left(\sum_{j=0}^{n} a^j + a^{n+1} - 1 \right). \tag{2.13}$$

Note that the summation that appears on the right is identical to the left-hand side. Rearranging Equation 2.13, and simplifying gives

$$\sum_{i=0}^{n} a_i = \frac{a^{n+1} - 1}{a - 1}.$$ (2.14)

2.2.5 Example—Computing Powers

In this section we consider the running time to raise a number to a given integer power. That is, given a value x and non-negative integer n, we wish to compute the x^n. A naïve way to calculate x^n would be to use a loop such as

```
int result = 1;
for (int i = 0; i <= n; ++i)
    result *= x;
```

Although this may be fine for small values of n, for large values of n the running time may become prohibitive. As an alternative, consider the following recursive definition:

$$x^n = \begin{cases} 1 & n = 0, \\ (x^2)^{\lfloor n/2 \rfloor} & n > 0, n \text{ is even}, \\ x(x^2)^{\lfloor n/2 \rfloor} & n > 0, n \text{ is odd}. \end{cases}$$ (2.15)

For example, using Equation 2.15, we would determine x^{32} as follows:

$$x^{32} = \left(\left(\left(\left(x^2\right)^2\right)^2\right)^2\right)^2,$$

PROGRAM 2.8
Program to compute x^n

```
1  public class Example
2  {
3      public static int power (int x, int n)
4      {
5          if (n == 0)
6              return 1;
7          else if (n % 2 == 0) // n is even
8              return power (x * x, n / 2);
9          else // n is odd
10             return x * power (x * x, n / 2);
11     }
12 }
```

which requires a total of five multiplication operations. Similarly, we would compute x^{31} as follows:

$$x^{31} = \left(\left(\left(\left(x^2\right)x\right)^2 x\right)^2 x\right)^2 x,$$

which requires a total of eight multiplication operations.

A recursive algorithm to compute x^n based on the direct implementation of Equation 2.15 is given in Program 2.8. Table 2.7 gives the running time, as predicted by the simplified model, for each of the executable statements in Program 2.8.

By summing the columns in Table 2.7, we get the following recurrence for the running time of Program 2.8:

$$T(n) = \begin{cases} 5 & n = 0, \\ 18 + T(\lfloor n/2 \rfloor) & n > 0, n \text{ is even,} \\ 20 + T(\lfloor n/2 \rfloor) & n > 0, n \text{ is odd.} \end{cases} \tag{2.16}$$

As the first attempt at solving this recurrence, let us suppose that $n = 2^k$ for some $k > 0$. Clearly, since n is a power of two, it is even. Therefore, $\lfloor n/2 \rfloor = n/2 = 2^{k-1}$.

For $n = 2^k$, Equation 2.16 gives

$$T(2^k) = 18 + T(2^{k-1}), \quad k > 0.$$

This can be solved by repeated substitution:

$$\begin{aligned} T(2^k) &= 18 + T(2^{k-1}) \\ &= 18 + 18 + T(2^{k-2}) \\ &= 18 + 18 + 18 + T(2^{k-3}) \\ &\vdots \\ &= 18j + T(2^{k-j}). \end{aligned}$$

TABLE 2.7
Computing the Running Time of Program 2.8

Statement	$n = 0$	$n > 0$ n is even	$n > 0$ n is odd
5	3	3	3
6	2	—	—
7	—	5	5
8	—	$10 + T(\lfloor n/2 \rfloor)$	—
10	—	—	$12 + T(\lfloor n/2 \rfloor)$
TOTAL	5	$18 + T(\lfloor n/2 \rfloor)$	$20 + T(\lfloor n/2 \rfloor)$

The substitution stops when $k = j$. Thus,

$$T(2^k) = 18k + T(1)$$
$$= 18k + 20 + T(0)$$
$$= 18k + 20 + 5$$
$$= 18k + 25.$$

Note that if $n = 2^k$, then $k = \log_2 n$. In this case, the running time of Program 2.8 is $T(n) = 18 \log_2 n + 25$.

The preceding result is, in fact, the best case—in all but the last two recursive calls of the method, n was even. Interestingly enough, there is a corresponding worst-case scenario. Suppose $n = 2^k - 1$ for some value of $k > 0$. Clearly n is odd, since it is one less than 2^k, which is a power of two and even. Now consider $\lfloor n/2 \rfloor$.

$$\lfloor n/2 \rfloor = \lfloor (2^k - 1)/2 \rfloor$$
$$= (2^k - 2)/2$$
$$= 2^{k-1} - 1.$$

Hence, $\lfloor n/2 \rfloor$ is also odd!

For example, suppose n is 31 ($2^5 - 1$). To compute x^{31}, Program 2.8 calls itself recursively to compute x^{15}, x^7, x^3, x^1, and finally, x^0—all but the last of which are odd powers of x.

For $n = 2^k - 1$, Equation 2.16 gives

$$T(2^k - 1) = 20 + T(2^{k-1} - 1), \quad k > 1.$$

Solving this recurrence by repeated substitution, we get

$$T(2^k - 1) = 20 + T(2^{k-1} - 1)$$
$$= 20 + 20 + T(2^{k-2} - 1)$$
$$= 20 + 20 + 20 + T(2^{k-3} - 1)$$
$$\vdots$$
$$= 20j + T(2^{k-j} - 1).$$

The substitution stops when $k = j$. Thus,

$$T(2^k - 1) = 20k + T(2^0 - 1)$$
$$= 20k + 5.$$

Note that if $n = 2^k - 1$, then $k = \log_2(n + 1)$. In this case, the running time of Program 2.8 is $T(n) = 20 \log_2(n + 1) + 5$.

Consider now what happens for an arbitrary value of n. Table 2.8 shows the recursive calls made by Program 2.8 in computing x^n for various values of n.

TABLE 2.8
Recursive Calls Made in Program 2.8

n	$\lfloor \log_2 n \rfloor + 1$	Powers Computed Recursively
1	1	1,0
2	2	2,1,0
3	2	3,1,0
4	3	4,2,1,0
5	3	5,2,1,0
6	3	6,3,1,0
7	3	7,3,1,0
8	4	8,4,2,1,0

By inspection we determine that the number of recursive calls made in which the second argument is non-zero is $\lfloor \log_2 n \rfloor + 1$. Furthermore, depending on whether the argument is odd or even, each of these calls contributes either 18 or 20 cycles. The pattern emerging in Table 2.7 suggests that, on average, just as many of the recursive calls result in an even number as result in an odd one. The final call (zero argument) adds another 5 cycles. So, on average, we can expect the running time of Program 2.8 to be

$$T(n) = 19(\lfloor \log_2 n \rfloor + 1) + 5. \tag{2.17}$$

2.2.6 Example—Geometric Series Summation Yet Again

In this example we consider the problem of computing a *geometric series summation* for the last time. We have already seen two algorithms to compute this summation in Sections 2.2.1 and 2.2.3 (Programs 2.6 and 2.7).

An algorithm to compute a geometric series summation using the closed-form expression (Equation 2.14) is given in Program 2.9. This algorithm makes use of Program 2.8 to compute x^{n+1}.

PROGRAM 2.9
Program to compute $\sum_{i=0}^{n} x^i$ using the closed-form expression

---

```
1   public class Example
2   {
3       public static int geometricSeriesSum (int x, int n)
4       {
5           return (power (x, n + 1) - 1) / (x - 1);
6       }
7   }
```

To determine the average running time of Program 2.9 we will make use of Equation 2.17, which gives the average running time for the **power** method, which is called on line 5. In this case, the arguments are x and $n + 1$, so the running time of the call to **power** is $19(\lfloor \log_2(n + 1) \rfloor + 1) + 5$. Adding to this the additional work done on line 5 gives the average running time for Program 2.9:

$$T(n) = 19(\lfloor \log_2(n + 1) \rfloor + 1) + 18.$$

The running times of the three programs that compute the geometric series summation presented in this chapter are tabulated in Table 2.9 and are plotted for $1 \le n \le 100$ in Figure 2.3. The plot shows that, according to our simplified model of the computer, Program 2.7 has the best running time for $n < 4$. However, as n increases, Program 2.9 is clearly the fastest of the three and Program 2.6 is the slowest for all values of n.

TABLE 2.9
Running Times of Programs 2.6, 2.7, and 2.9

Program	$T(n)$
Program 2.6	$(\frac{11}{2}n^2 + \frac{47}{2}n + 24)$
Program 2.7	$13n + 22$
Program 2.9	$19(\lfloor \log_2(n + 1) \rfloor + 1) + 18$

FIGURE 2.3
Plot of running time vs. n for Programs 2.6, 2.7, and 2.9.

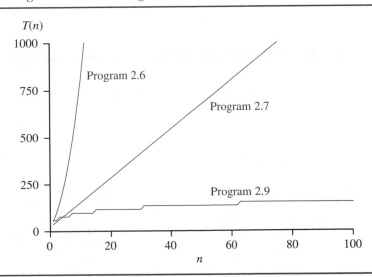

Exercises

2.1   Determine the running times predicted by the detailed model of the computer given in Section 2.1 for each of the following program fragments:

a.
```
for (int i = 0; i < n; ++i)
    ++k;
```

b.
```
for (int i = 1; i < n; i *= 2)
    ++k;
```

c.
```
for (int i = n - 1; i != 0; i /= 2)
    ++k;
```

d.
```
for (int i = 0; i < n; ++i)
    if (i % 2 == 0)
        ++k;
```

e.
```
for (int i = 0; i < n; ++i)
    for (int j = 0; j < n; ++j)
        ++k;
```

f.
```
for (int i = 0; i < n; ++i)
    for (int j = i; j < n; ++j)
        ++k;
```

g.
```
for (int i = 0; i < n; ++i)
    for (int j = 0; j < i * i; ++j)
        ++k;
```

2.2   Repeat Exercise 2.1 this time using the simplified model of the computer given in Section 2.2.

2.3   Prove by induction the following summation formulas:

a. $$\sum_{i=0}^{n} i = \frac{n(n + 1)}{2}$$

b. $$\sum_{i=0}^{n} i^2 = \frac{n(n + 1)(2n + 1)}{6}$$

c. $$\sum_{i=0}^{n} i^3 = \frac{n^2(n + 1)^2}{4}$$

2.4   Evaluate each of the following series summations:

a. $\sum_{i=0}^{n} 2^i$

b. $\sum_{i=0}^{n} \left(\frac{1}{2}\right)^i$

c. $\sum_{i=0}^{\infty} \left(\frac{1}{2}\right)^i$

d. $\sum_{i=-\infty}^{n} 2^i$

2.5   Show that $\sum_{i=0}^{\infty} a^i = \frac{1}{1-a}$, for $0 \le a < 1$. **Hint:** Let $S_n = \sum_{i=0}^{n} a^i$ and show that $\lim_{n \to \infty}(S_n - aS_n) = 1$.

2.6   Show that $\sum_{i=0}^{\infty} i/2^i = 2$. **Hint:** Let $S_n = \sum_{i=0}^{n} i/2^i$ and show that the difference $2S_n - S_n$ is (approximately) a geometric series summation.

2.7   Solve each of the following recurrences by repeated substitution:

a. $T(n) = \begin{cases} 1 & n = 0, \\ T(n-1) + 1 & n > 0. \end{cases}$

b. $T(n) = \begin{cases} 1 & n \le a, a > 0, \\ T(n-a) + 1 & n > a. \end{cases}$

c. $T(n) = \begin{cases} 1 & n = 0, \\ 2T(n-1) + 1 & n > 0. \end{cases}$

d. $T(n) = \begin{cases} 1 & n = 0, \\ 2T(n-1) + n & n > 0. \end{cases}$

e. $T(n) = \begin{cases} 1 & n = 1, \\ T(n/2) + 1 & n > 1. \end{cases}$

f. $T(n) = \begin{cases} 1 & n = 1, \\ 2T(n/2) + 1 & n > 1. \end{cases}$

g. $T(n) = \begin{cases} 1 & n = 1, \\ 2T(n/2) + n & n > 1. \end{cases}$

Programming Projects

2.1   Write a non-recursive method to compute the factorial of n according to Equation 2.3. Calculate the running time predicted by the detailed model given in Section 2.1 and the simplified model given in Section 2.2.

2.2 Write a non-recursive method to compute x^n according to Equation 2.15. Calculate the running time predicted by the detailed model given in Section 2.1 and the simplified model given in Section 2.2.

2.3 Write a program that determines the values of the timing parameters of the detailed model (τ_{fetch}, τ_{store}, τ_+, τ_-, $\tau_\times$, $\tau_\div$, $\tau_<$, τ_{call}, τ_{return}, τ_{new}, and $\tau_{[\cdot]}$) for the machine on which it is run.

2.4 Using the program written for Project 2.3, determine the timing parameters of the detailed model for your computer. Then, measure the actual running times of Programs 2.1, 2.2, and 2.3 and compare the measured results with those predicted by Equations 2.1, 2.2, and 2.7 (respectively).

2.5 Given a sequence of n integers, $\{a_0, a_1, \ldots, a_{n-1}\}$, and a small positive integer k, write an algorithm to compute

$$\sum_{i=0}^{n-1} 2^{ki} a_i,$$

without multiplication. **Hint**: Use Horner's rule and bitwise shifts.

2.6 Verify Equation 2.9 experimentally as follows: Generate a large number of random sequences of length n, $\{a_0, a_1, a_2, \ldots, a_{n-1}\}$. For each sequence, test the hypothesis that the probability that a_i is larger than all its predecessors in the sequence is $p_i = 1/(i + 1)$. (For a good source of random numbers, see Section 14.5.1).

3 | Asymptotic Notation

Suppose we are considering two algorithms, A and B, for solving a given problem. Furthermore, let us say that we have done a careful analysis of the running times of each of the algorithms and determined them to be $T_A(n)$ and $T_B(n)$, respectively, where n is a measure of the problem size. Then it should be a fairly simple matter to compare the two functions $T_A(n)$ and $T_B(n)$ to determine which algorithm is *the best*!

But is it really that simple? What exactly does it mean for one function, say $T_A(n)$, to be *better than* another function, $T_B(n)$? One possibility arises if we know the problem size a priori. For example, suppose the problem size is n_0 and $T_A(n_0) < T_B(n_0)$. Then clearly algorithm A is better than algorithm B for problem size n_0.

In the general case, we have no a priori knowledge of the problem size. However, if it can be shown, say, that $T_A(n) \leq T_B(n)$ for all $n \geq 0$, then algorithm A is better than algorithm B regardless of the problem size.

Unfortunately, we usually don't know the problem size beforehand, nor is it true that one of the functions is less than or equal to the other over the entire range of problem sizes. In this case, we consider the *asymptotic* behavior of the two functions for very large problem sizes.

3.1 An Asymptotic Upper Bound—Big Oh

In 1892, P. Bachmann invented a notation for characterizing the asymptotic behavior of functions. His invention has come to be known as *big oh notation*:

Definition 3.1 (Big Oh)
Consider a function $f(n)$ that is non-negative for all integers $n \geq 0$. We say that "$f(n)$ is big oh $g(n)$," which we write $f(n) = O(g(n))$, if there exists an integer n_0 and a constant $c > 0$ such that for all integers $n \geq n_0$, $f(n) \leq cg(n)$.

3.1.1   A Simple Example

Consider the function $f(n) = 8n + 128$ shown in Figure 3.1. Clearly, $f(n)$ is non-negative for all integers $n \geq 0$. We wish to show that $f(n) = O(n^2)$. According to Definition 3.1, in order to show this we need to find an integer n_0 and a constant $c > 0$ such that for all integers $n \geq n_0$, $f(n) \leq cn^2$.

It does not matter what the particular constants are—as long as they exist! For example, suppose we choose $c = 1$. Then

$$f(n) \leq cn^2 \Rightarrow \quad 8n + 128 \leq n^2$$
$$\Rightarrow \quad 0 \leq n^2 - 8n - 128$$
$$\Rightarrow \quad 0 \leq (n - 16)(n + 8).$$

Since $(n + 8) > 0$ for all values of $n \geq 0$, we conclude that $(n_0 - 16) \geq 0$. That is, $n_0 = 16$.

So, we have that for $c = 1$ and $n_0 = 16$, $f(n) \leq cn^2$ for all integers $n \geq n_0$. Hence, $f(n) = O(n^2)$. Figure 3.1 clearly shows that the function $f(n) = n^2$ is greater than the function $f(n) = 8n + 128$ to the right of $n = 16$.

FIGURE 3.1
Showing that $f(n) = 8n + 128 = O(n^2)$.

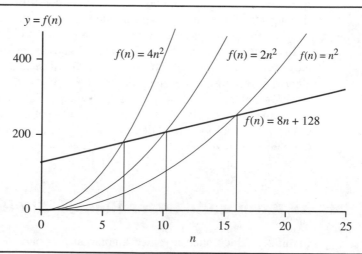

Of course, there are many other values of c and n_0 that will do. For example, $c = 2$ and $n_0 = 2 + 2\sqrt{17} \approx 10.2$ will do, as will $c = 4$ and $n_0 = 1 + \sqrt{33} \approx 6.7$. (See Figure 3.1).

3.1.2 Big Oh Fallacies and Pitfalls

Unfortunately, the way we write big oh notation can be misleading to the naïve reader. This section presents two fallacies that arise because of a misinterpretation of the notation.

Fallacy 3.1
Given that $f_1(n) = O(g(n))$ and $f_2(n) = O(g(n))$, then $f_1(n) = f_2(n)$.

Consider the equations

$$f_1(n) = h(n^2)$$
$$f_2(n) = h(n^2).$$

Clearly, it is reasonable to conclude that $f_1(n) = f_2(n)$.
    However, consider these equations:

$$f_1(n) = O(n^2)$$
$$f_2(n) = O(n^2).$$

It *does not* follow that $f_1(n) = f_2(n)$. For example, $f_1(n) - n$ and $f_2(n) - n^2$ are both $O(n^2)$, but they are not equal.

Fallacy 3.2
If $f(n) = O(g(n))$, then $g(n) = O^{-1}(f(n))$.

Consider functions f, g, and h, such that $f(n) = h(g(n))$. It is reasonable to conclude that $g(n) = h^{-1}(f(n))$ provided that $h(\cdot)$ is an invertible function. However, although we may write $f(n) = O(h(n))$, the equation $g(n) = O^{-1}(f(n))$ is nonsensical and meaningless. Big oh is not a mathematical function, so it has no inverse!
    The reason for these difficulties is that we should read the notation $f(n) = O(n^2)$ as "$f(n)$ is big oh n squared" not "$f(n)$ equals big oh of n squared." The equal sign in the expression does not really denote mathematical equality! And the use of the functional form, $O(\cdot)$, does not really mean that O is a mathematical function!

3.1.3 Properties of Big Oh

In this section we examine some of the mathematical properties of big oh. In particular, suppose we know that $f_1(n) = O(g_1(n))$ and $f_2(n) = O(g_2(n))$.

- What can we say about the asymptotic behavior of the *sum* of $f_1(n)$ and $f_2(n)$? (Theorems 3.1 and 3.2)
- What can we say about the asymptotic behavior of the *product* of $f_1(n)$ and $f_2(n)$? (Theorems 3.3 and 3.4)
- How are $f_1(n)$ and $g_2(n)$ related when $g_1(n) = f_2(n)$? (Theorem 3.5)

The first theorem addresses the asymptotic behavior of the sum of two functions whose asymptotic behaviors are known:

Theorem 3.1
If $f_1(n) = O(g_1(n))$ and $f_2(n) = O(g_2(n))$, then

$$f_1(n) + f_2(n) = O(\max(g_1(n), g_2(n))).$$

Proof   By Definition 3.1, there are two integers, n_1 and n_2 and two constants c_1 and c_2 such that $f_1(n) \leq c_1 g_1(n)$ for $n \geq n_1$ and $f_2(n) \leq c_2 g_2(n)$ for $n \geq n_2$.

Let $n_0 = \max(n_1, n_2)$ and $c_0 = 2\max(c_1, c_2)$. Consider the sum $f_1(n) + f_2(n)$ for $n \geq n_0$:

$$
\begin{aligned}
f_1(n) + f_2(n) &\leq c_1 g_1(n) + c_2 g_2(n), \quad n \geq n_0 \\
&\leq c_0(g_1(n) + g_2(n))/2 \\
&\leq c_0 \max(g_1(n), g_2(n)).
\end{aligned}
$$

Thus, $f_1(n) + f_2(n) = O(\max(g_1(n), g_2(n)))$.

According to Theorem 3.1, if we know that functions $f_1(n)$ and $f_2(n)$ are $O(g_1(n))$ and $O(g_2(n))$, respectively, the *sum* $f_1(n) + f_2(n)$ is $O(\max(g_1(n), g_2(n)))$. The meaning of $\max(g_1(n), g_2(n))$ in this context is the *function $h(n)$*, where $h(n) = \max(g_1(n), g_2(n))$ for integers all $n \geq 0$.

For example, consider the functions $g_1(n) = 1$ and $g_2(n) = 2\cos^2(n\pi/2)$. Then

$$
\begin{aligned}
h(n) &= \max(g_1(n), g_2(n)) \\
&= \max(1, 2\cos^2(n\pi/2)) \\
&= \begin{cases} 1 & n \text{ is even,} \\ 2 & n \text{ is odd.} \end{cases}
\end{aligned}
$$

Theorem 3.2 helps us simplify the asymptotic analysis of the sum of functions by allowing us to drop the max required by Theorem 3.1 in certain circumstances:

Theorem 3.2
If $f(n) = f_1(n) + f_2(n)$ in which $f_1(n)$ and $f_2(n)$ are both non-negative for all integers $n \geq 0$ such that $\lim_{n \to \infty} f_2(n)/f_1(n) = L$ for some limit $L \geq 0$, then $f(n) = O(f_1(n))$.

Proof   According to the definition of limits, the notation

$$\lim_{n \to \infty} \frac{f_2(n)}{f_1(n)} = L$$

means that, given any arbitrary positive value ϵ, it is possible to find a value n_0 such that for all $n \geq n_0$

$$\left| \frac{f_2(n)}{f_1(n)} - L \right| \leq \epsilon.$$

Thus, if we chose a particular value, say ϵ_0, then there exists a corresponding n_0 such that

$$\left| \frac{f_2(n)}{f_1(n)} - L \right| \leq \epsilon_0, \quad n \geq n_0$$

$$\frac{f_2(n)}{f_1(n)} - L \leq \epsilon_0$$

$$f_2(n) \leq (\epsilon_0 + L) f_1(n).$$

Consider the sum $f(n) = f_1(n) + f_2(n)$:

$$\begin{aligned}
f(n) &= f_1(n) + f_2(n) \\
&\leq c_1 f_1(n) + c_2 f_2(n) \\
&\leq c_1 f_1(n) + c_2(\epsilon_0 + L) f_1(n), \quad n \geq n_0 \\
&\leq c_0 f_1(n),
\end{aligned}$$

where $c_0 = c_1 + c_2(\epsilon_0 + L)$. Thus, $f(n) = O(f_1(n))$.

Consider a pair of functions $f_1(n)$ and $f_2(n)$, which are known to be $O(g_1(n))$ and $O(g_2(n))$, respectively. According to Theorem 3.1, the sum $f(n) = f_1(n) + f_2(n)$ is $O(\max(g_1(n), g_2(n)))$. However, Theorem 3.2 says that if $\lim_{n \to \infty} f_2(n)/f_1(n)$ exists, then the sum $f(n)$ is simply $O(f_1(n))$, which, by the transitive property (see Theorem 3.5), is $O(g_1(n))$.

In other words, if the ratio $f_1(n)/f_2(n)$ asymptotically approaches a constant as n gets large, we can say that $f_1(n) + f_2(n)$ is $O(g_1(n))$, which is often a lot simpler than $O(\max(g_1(n), g_2(n)))$.

Theorem 3.2 is a particularly useful result. Consider $f_1(n) = n^3$ and $f_2(n) = n^2$:

$$\begin{aligned}
\lim_{n \to \infty} \frac{f_2(n)}{f_1(n)} &= \lim_{n \to \infty} \frac{n^2}{n^3} \\
&= \lim_{n \to \infty} \frac{1}{n} \\
&= 0.
\end{aligned}$$

From this we can conclude that $f_1(n) + f_2(n) = n^3 + n^2 = O(n^3)$. Thus, Theorem 3.2 suggests that the sum of a series of powers of n is $O(n^m)$, where m is the largest power of n in the summation. We will confirm this result in Section 3.1.4.

The next theorem addresses the asymptotic behavior of the product of two functions whose asymptotic behaviors are known:

Theorem 3.3
If $f_1(n) = O(g_1(n))$ and $f_2(n) = O(g_2(n))$, then

$$f_1(n) \times f_2(n) = O(g_1(n) \times g_2(n)).$$

Proof   By Definition 3.1, there are two integers n_1 and n_2 and two constants c_1 and c_2 such that $f_1(n) \leq c_1 g_1(n)$ for $n \geq n_1$ and $f_2(n) \leq c_2 g_2(n)$ for $n \geq n_2$. Furthermore, by Definition 3.1, $f_1(n)$ and $f_2(n)$ are both non-negative for all integers $n \geq 0$.

Let $n_0 = \max(n_1, n_2)$ and $c_0 = c_1 c_2$. Consider the product $f_1(n) \times f_2(n)$ for $n \geq n_0$:

$$f_1(n) \times f_2(n) \leq c_1 g_1(n) \times c_2 g_2(n), \quad n \geq n_0$$
$$\leq c_0(g_1(n) \times g_2(n)).$$

Thus, $f_1(n) \times f_2(n) = O(g_1(n) \times g_2(n))$.

Theorem 3.3 describes a simple but extremely useful property of big oh. Consider the functions $f_1(n) = n^3 + n^2 + n + 1 = O(n^3)$ and $f_2(n) = n^2 + n + 1 = O(n^2)$. By Theorem 3.3, the asymptotic behavior of the product $f_1(n) \times f_2(n)$ is $O(n^3 \times n^2) = O(n^5)$. That is, we are able to determine the asymptotic behavior of the product without having to go through the gory details of calculating that $f_1(n) \times f_2(n) = n^5 + 2n^4 + 3n^3 + 3n^2 + 2n + 1$.

The next theorem is closely related to the preceding one, in that it also shows how big oh behaves with respect to multiplication.

Theorem 3.4
If $f_1(n) = O(g_1(n))$ and $g_2(n)$ is a function whose value is non-negative for integers $n \geq 0$, then

$$f_1(n) \times g_2(n) = O(g_1(n) \times g_2(n)).$$

Proof   By Definition 3.1, there are integers n_0 and constant c_0 such that $f_1(n) \leq c_0 g_1(n)$ for $n \geq n_0$. Since $g_2(n)$ is never negative,

$$f_1(n) \times g_2(n) \leq c_0 g(n) \times g_2(n), \quad n \geq n_0.$$

Thus, $f_1(n) \times g_2(n) = O(g_1(n) \times g_2(n))$.

Theorem 3.4 applies when we multiply a function, $f_1(n)$, whose asymptotic behavior is known to be $O(g_1(n))$, by another function $g_2(n)$. The asymptotic behavior of the result is simply $O(g_1(n) \times g_2(n))$.

One way to interpret Theorem 3.4 is that it allows us to do the following mathematical manipulation:

$$f_1(n) = O(g_1(n)) \Rightarrow f_1(n) \times g_2(n) = O(g_1(n)) \times g_2(n)$$

$$\Rightarrow f_1(n) \times g_2(n) = O(g_1(n) \times g_2(n)).$$

That is, Fallacy 3.1 notwithstanding, we can multiply both sides of the "equation" by $g_2(n)$ and the "equality" still holds. Furthermore, when we multiply $O(g_1(n))$ by $g_2(n)$, we simply bring the $g_2(n)$ inside the $O(\cdot)$.

The last theorem in this section introduces the *transitive property* of big oh:

Theorem 3.5 (Transitive Property)
If $f(n) = O(g(n))$ and $g(n) = O(h(n))$ then $f(n) = O(h(n))$.

Proof By Definition 3.1, there are two integers n_1 and n_2 and two constants c_1 and c_2 such that $f(n) \leq c_1 g(n)$ for $n \geq n_1$ and $g(n) \leq c_2 h(n)$ for $n \geq n_2$.

Let $n_0 = \max(n_1, n_2)$ and $c_0 = c_1 c_2$. Then

$$f(n) \leq c_1 g(n), \quad n \geq n_1$$

$$\leq c_1 c_2 h(n), \quad n \geq n_0$$

$$\leq c_0 h(n).$$

Thus, $f(n) = O(h(n))$.

The transitive property of big oh is useful in conjunction with Theorem 3.2. Consider $f_1(n) = 5n^3$, which is clearly $O(n^3)$. If we add to $f_1(n)$ the function $f_2(n) = 3n^2$, then by Theorem 3.2, the sum $f_1(n) + f_2(n)$ is $O(f_1(n))$ because $\lim_{n \to \infty} f_2(n)/f_1(n) = 0$. That is, $f_1(n) + f_2(n) = O(f_1(n))$. The combination of the fact that $f_1(n) = O(n^3)$ *and* the transitive property of big oh allows us to conclude that the sum is $O(n^3)$.

3.1.4 About Polynomials

In this section we examine the asymptotic behavior of polynomials in n. In particular, we will see that as n gets larger, the term involving the highest power of n will dominate all the others. Therefore, the asymptotic behavior is determined by that term.

Theorem 3.6
Consider a polynomial in n of the form

$$f(n) = \sum_{i=0}^{m} a_i n^i$$

$$= a_m n^m + a_{m-1} n^{m-1} + \cdots + a_2 n^2 + a_1 n + a_0$$

where $a_m > 0$. Then $f(n) = O(n^m)$.

Proof   Each of the terms in the summation is of the form $a_i n^i$. Since n is non-negative, a particular term will be negative only if $a_i < 0$. Hence, for each term in the summation, $a_i n^i \leq |a_i| n^i$. Recall too that we have stipulated that the coefficient of the largest power of n is positive, that is, $a_m > 0$.

$$f(n) \leq \sum_{i=0}^{m} |a_i| n^i$$

$$\leq n^m \sum_{i=0}^{m} |a_i| n^{i-m}, \quad n \geq 1$$

$$\leq n^m \sum_{i=0}^{m} |a_i| \frac{1}{n^{m-i}}.$$

Note that for integers $n \geq 1$, $1/(n^{m-i}) \leq 1$ for $0 \leq i \leq m$. Thus

$$f(n) \leq \underbrace{n^m}_{g(n)} \underbrace{\sum_{i=0}^{m} |a_i|}_{c}, \quad n \geq \underbrace{1}_{n_0}. \tag{3.1}$$

From Equation 3.1 we see that we have found the constants $n_0 = 1$ and $c = \sum_{i=0}^{m} |a_i|$, such that for all $n \geq n_0$, $f(n) = \sum_{i=0}^{n} a_i n^m \leq c n^m$. Thus, $f(n) = O(n^m)$.

This property of the asymptotic behavior of polynomials is used extensively. In fact, whenever we have a function, which is a polynomial in n, $f(n) = a_m n^m + a_{m-1} n^{m-1} + \cdots + a_2 n^2 + a_1 n + a_0$, we will immediately "drop" the less significant terms (i.e., terms involving powers of n that are less than m), as well as the leading coefficient, a_m, to write $f(n) = O(n^m)$.

3.1.5   About Logarithms

In this section we determine the asymptotic behavior of logarithms. Interestingly, despite the fact that $\log n$ diverges as n gets large, $\log n < n$ for all integers $n \geq 0$. Hence, $\log n = O(n)$. Furthermore, as the following theorem will show, $\log n$ raised to any integer power $k \geq 1$ is still $O(n)$.

Theorem 3.7
For every integer $k \geq 1$, $\log^k n = O(n)$.

Proof   This result follows immediately from Theorem 3.5 and the observation that for all integers $k \geq 1$,

$$\lim_{n \to \infty} \frac{\log^k n}{n} = 0. \tag{3.2}$$

This observation can be proved by induction as follows:

Base Case   Consider the limit

$$\lim_{n \to \infty} \frac{\log^k n}{n}$$

for the case $k = 1$. Using L'Hôpital's rule[1] we see that

$$\lim_{n \to \infty} \frac{\log n}{n} = \lim_{n \to \infty} \frac{1}{n} \cdot \frac{1}{\ln 10}$$
$$= 0.$$

Inductive Hypothesis   Assume that Equation 3.2 holds for $k = 1, 2, \ldots, m$. Consider the case $k = m + 1$. Using L'Hôpital's rule we see that

$$\lim_{n \to \infty} \frac{\log^{m+1} n}{n} = \lim_{n \to \infty} \frac{(m + 1) \log^m n \times \frac{1}{n \ln 10}}{1}$$
$$= \frac{(m + 1)}{\ln 10} \lim_{n \to \infty} \frac{\log^m n}{n}$$
$$= 0.$$

Therefore, by induction on m, Equation 3.2 holds for all integers $k \geq 1$.

For example, using this property of logarithms together with the rule for determining the asymptotic behavior of the product of two functions (Theorem 3.3), we can determine that since $\log n = O(n)$, then $n \log n = O(n^2)$.

---

[1] Guillaume François Antoine de L'Hôpital, marquis de Sainte-Mesme, is known for his rule for computing limits, which states that if $\lim_{n \to \infty} g(n) = \infty$ and $\lim_{n \to \infty} h(n) = \infty$, then

$$\lim_{n \to \infty} \frac{g(n)}{h(n)} = \lim_{n \to \infty} \frac{g'(n)}{h'(n)},$$

where $f'(n)$ and $g'(n)$ are the first derivatives with respect to n of $f(n)$ and $g(n)$, respectively. The rule is also effective if $\lim_{n \to \infty} g(n) = 0$ and $\lim_{n \to \infty} h(n) = 0$.

3.1.6 Tight, Big Oh Bounds

Big oh notation characterizes the asymptotic behavior of a function by providing an upper bound on the rate at which the function grows as n gets large. Unfortunately, the notation does not tell us how close the actual behavior of the function is to the bound. That is, the bound might be very close (tight) or it might be overly conservative (loose).

The following definition tells us what makes a bound tight, and how we can test to see whether a given asymptotic bound is the best one available.

Definition 3.2 (Tightness)
Consider a function $f(n) = O(g(n))$. If for every function $h(n)$ such that $f(n) = O(h(n))$ it is also true that $g(n) = O(h(n))$, then we say that $g(n)$ is a tight asymptotic bound on $f(n)$.

For example, consider the function $f(n) = 8n + 128$. In Section 3.1.1, it was shown that $f(n) = O(n^2)$. However, since $f(n)$ is a polynomial in n, Theorem 3.6 tells us that $f(n) = O(n)$. Clearly $O(n)$ is a tighter bound on the asymptotic behavior of $f(n)$ than is $O(n^2)$.

By Definition 3.2, in order to show that $g(n) = n$ is a tight bound on $f(n)$, we need to show that for every function $h(n)$ such that $f(n) = O(h(n))$, it is also true that $g(n) = O(h(n))$.

We will show this result using proof by contradiction: Assume that $g(n)$ is *not* a tight bound for $f(n) = 8n + 128$. Then there is a function $h(n)$ such that $f(n) = 8n + 128 = O(h(n))$, but for which $g(n) \neq O(h(n))$. Since $8n + 128 = O(h(n))$, by the definition of big oh there are positive constants c and n_0 such that $8n + 128 \leq ch(n)$ for all $n \geq n_0$.

Clearly, for all $n \geq 0$, $n \leq 8n + 128$. Therefore, $g(n) \leq ch(n)$. But then, according to the definition of big oh, we have that $g(n) = O(h(n))$—a contradiction! Therefore, the bound $f(n) = O(n)$ is a tight bound.

3.1.7 More Big Oh Fallacies and Pitfalls

The purpose of this section is to dispel some common misconceptions about big oh. The next fallacy is related to the selection of the constants c and n_0 used to show a big oh relation.

Fallacy 3.3
Consider non-negative functions $f(n)$, $g_1(n)$, and $g_2(n)$, such that $f(n) = g_1(n) \times g_2(n)$. Since $f(n) \leq cg_1(n)$ for all integers $n \geq 0$ if $c = g_2(n)$, then by Definition 3.1 $f(n) = O(g_1(n))$.

This fallacy often results from the following line of reasoning: Consider the function $f(n) = n \log n$. Let $c = \log n$ and $n_0 = 1$. Then $f(n)$ must be $O(n)$, since $f(n) \leq cn$ for all $n \geq n_0$. However, this line of reasoning is false because according to Definition 3.1, c must be a *positive constant*, not a function of n.

The next fallacy involves a misunderstanding of the notion of the *asymptotic upper bound*.

Fallacy 3.4

Given non-negative functions $f_1(n)$, $f_2(n)$, $g_1(n)$, and $g_2(n)$, such that $f_1(n) = O(g_1(n))$, $f_2(n) = O(g_2(n))$, and for all integers $n \geq 0$, $g_1(n) < g_2(n)$, then $f_1(n) < f_2(n)$.

This fallacy arises from the following line of reasoning: Consider the function $f_1(n) = O(n^2)$ and $f_2(n) = O(n^3)$. Since $n^2 \leq n^3$ for all values of $n \geq 1$, we might be tempted to conclude that $f_1(n) \leq f_2(n)$. In fact, such a conclusion is erroneous. For example, consider $f_1(n) = n^2 + 1$ and $f_2(n) = n$. Clearly, the former is $O(n^2)$ and the latter is $O(n^3)$. Clearly too, $f_1(n) \geq f_2(n)$ for all values of $n \geq 0$!

The previous fallacy essentially demonstrates that although we may know how the asymptotic upper bounds on two functions are related, we don't necessarily know, in general, the relative behavior of the two bounded functions.

This fallacy often arises in the comparison of the performance of algorithms. Suppose we are comparing two algorithms, A and B, to solve a given problem and we have determined that the running times of these algorithms are $T_A(n) = O(g_1(n))$ and $T_B(n) = O(g_2(n))$, respectively. Fallacy 3.4 demonstrates that it is an error to conclude from the fact that $g_1(n) \leq g_2(n)$ for all $n \geq 0$ that algorithm A will solve the problem faster than algorithm B for all problem sizes.

But what about any one specific problem size? Can we conclude that for a given problem size, say n_0, that algorithm A is faster than algorithm B? The next fallacy addresses this issue.

Fallacy 3.5

Given non-negative functions $f_1(n)$, $f_2(n)$, $g_1(n)$, and $g_2(n)$, such that $f_1(n) = O(g_1(n))$, $f_2(n) = O(g_2(n))$, and for all integers $n \geq 0$, $g_1(n) < g_2(n)$, there is an integer n_0 for which $f_1(n_0) < f_2(n_0)$.

This fallacy arises from a similar line of reasoning as the preceding one. Consider the function $f_1(n) = O(n^2)$ and $f_2(n) = O(n^3)$. Since $n^2 \leq n^3$ for all values of $n \geq 1$, we might be tempted to conclude that there is a value n_0 for which $f_1(n_0) \leq f_2(n_0)$. Such a conclusion is erroneous. For example, consider $f_1(n) = n^2 + 1$ and $f_2(n) = n$. Clearly, the former is $O(n^2)$ and the latter is $O(n^3)$. Clearly too, since $f_1(n) \geq f_2(n)$ for all values of $n \geq 0$, there is not any value $n_0 \geq 0$ for which $f_1(n_0) \leq f_2(n_0)$.

The final fallacy shows that not all functions are *commensurate*:

Fallacy 3.6

Given two non-negative functions $f(n)$ and $g(n)$, then either $f(n) = O(g(n))$ or $g(n) = O(f(n))$.

This fallacy arises from thinking that the relation $O(\cdot)$ is like $\leq$ and can be used to compare any two functions. However, not all functions are commensurate.[2] Consider

---

[2]Functions that are commensurate are functions that can be compared one with the other.

the following functions:

$$f(n) = \begin{cases} n & n \text{ is even,} \\ 0 & n \text{ is odd.} \end{cases}$$

$$g(n) = \begin{cases} 0 & n \text{ is even,} \\ n & n \text{ is odd.} \end{cases}$$

Clearly, there does not exist a constant c for which $f(n) \leq cg(n)$ for any even integer n, since the $g(n)$ is zero and $f(n)$ is not. Conversely, there does not exist a constant c for which $g(n) \leq cf(n)$ for any odd integer n, since the $f(n)$ is zero and $g(n)$ is not. Hence, neither $f(n) = O(g(n))$ nor $g(n) = O(f(n))$ is true.

3.1.8 Conventions for Writing Big Oh Expressions

Certain conventions have evolved that concern how big oh expressions are normally written:

- First, it is common practice when writing big oh expressions to drop all but the most significant terms. Thus, instead of $O(n^2 + n \log n + n)$, we simply write $O(n^2)$.
- Second, it is common practice to drop constant coefficients. Thus, instead of $O(3n^2)$, we simply write $O(n^2)$. As a special case of this rule, if the function is a constant, instead of, say $O(1024)$, we simply write $O(1)$.

Of course, in order for a particular big oh expression to be the most useful, we prefer to find a *tight* asymptotic bound (see Definition 3.2). For example, although it is not wrong to write $f(n) = n = O(n^3)$, we prefer to write $f(n) = O(n)$, which is a tight bound.

Certain big oh expressions occur so frequently that they are given names. Table 3.1 lists some of the commonly occurring big oh expressions and the usual name given to each of them.

TABLE 3.1
The Names of Common Big
Oh Expressions

Expression	Name
$O(1)$	constant
$O(\log n)$	logarithmic
$O(\log^2 n)$	log squared
$O(n)$	linear
$O(n \log n)$	$n \log n$
$O(n^2)$	quadratic
$O(n^3)$	cubic
$O(2^n)$	exponential

3.2 An Asymptotic Lower Bound—Omega

The big oh notation introduced in the preceding section is an asymptotic *upper bound*. In this section, we introduce a similar notation for characterizing the asymptotic behavior of a function, but in this case it is a *lower bound*.

Definition 3.3 (Omega)
Consider a function $f(n)$ that is non-negative for all integers $n \geq 0$. We say that "$f(n)$ is omega $g(n)$," which we write $f(n) = \Omega(g(n))$, if there is an integer n_0 and a constant $c > 0$ such that for all integers $n \geq n_0$, $f(n) \geq cg(n)$.

The definition of omega is almost identical to that of big oh. The only difference is in the comparison—for big oh it is $f(n) \leq cg(n)$; for omega, it is $f(n) \geq cg(n)$. All of the same conventions and caveats apply to omega as they do to big oh.

3.2.1 A Simple Example

Consider the function $f(x) = 5n^2 - 64n + 256$, which is shown in Figure 3.2. Clearly, $f(n)$ is non-negative for all integers $n \geq 0$. We wish to show that $f(n) = \Omega(n^2)$. According to Definition 3.3, in order to show this we need to find an integer n_0 and a constant $c > 0$ such that for all integers $n \geq n_0$, $f(n) \geq cn^2$.

As with big oh, it does not matter what the particular constants are—as long as they exist! For example, suppose we choose $c = 1$. Then

$$f(n) > cn^2 \Rightarrow 5n^2 - 64n + 256 \geq n^2$$
$$\Rightarrow 4n^2 - 64n + 256 \geq 0$$
$$\Rightarrow 4(n - 8)^2 \geq 0.$$

Since $(n - 8)^2 > 0$ for all values of $n \geq 0$, we conclude that $n_0 = 0$.

So, we have that for $c = 1$ and $n_0 = 0$, $f(n) \geq cn^2$ for all integers $n \geq n_0$. Hence, $f(n) = \Omega(n^2)$. Figure 3.2 clearly shows that the function $f(n) = n^2$ is less than the function $f(n) = 5n - 64n + 256$ for all values of $n \geq 0$. Of course, there are many other values of c and n_0 that will do. For example, $c = 2$ and $n_0 = 16$.

3.2.2 About Polynomials Again

In this section we reexamine the asymptotic behavior of polynomials in n. In Section 3.1.4 we showed that $f(n) = O(n^m)$. That is, $f(n)$ grows asymptotically no more quickly than n^m. This time we are interested in the asymptotic lower bound rather than the asymptotic upper bound. We will see that as n gets large, the term involving n^m also dominates the lower bound in the sense that $f(n)$ grows asymptotically *as quickly* as n^m. That is, that $f(n) = \Omega(n^m)$.

FIGURE 3.2
Showing that $f(n) = 4n^2 - 64n + 288 = \Omega(n^2)$.

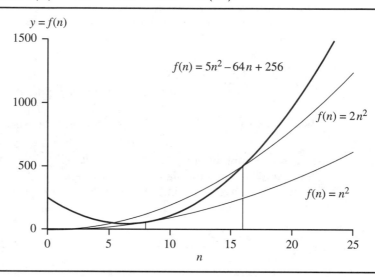

Theorem 3.8
Consider a polynomial in n of the form

$$f(n) = \sum_{i=0}^{m} a_i n^i$$

$$= a_m n^m + a_{m-1} n^{m-1} + \cdots + a_2 n^2 + a_1 n + a_0,$$

where $a_m > 0$. Then $f(n) = \Omega(n^m)$.

Proof   We begin by taking the term $a_m n^m$ out of the summation:

$$f(n) = \sum_{i=0}^{m} a_i n^i$$

$$= a_m n^m + \sum_{i=0}^{m-1} a_i n^i.$$

Since n is a non-negative integer and $a_m > 0$, the term $a_m n^m$ is positive. For each of the remaining terms in the summation, $a_i n^i \geq -|a_i| n^i$. Hence

$$f(n) \geq a_m n^m - \sum_{i=0}^{m-1} |a_i| n^i$$

$$\geq a_m n^m - n^{m-1} \sum_{i=0}^{m-1} |a_i| n^{i-(m-1)}, \quad n \geq 1$$

$$\geq a_m n^m - n^{m-1} \sum_{i=0}^{m-1} |a_i| \frac{1}{n^{(m-1)-i}}.$$

Note that for integers $n \geq 1$, $1/(n^{(m-1)-i}) \leq 1$ for $0 \leq i \leq (m-1)$. Thus

$$f(n) \geq a_m n^m - n^{m-1} \sum_{i=0}^{m-1} |a_i|, \quad n \geq 1$$

$$\geq n^m \left(a_m - \frac{1}{n} \sum_{i=0}^{m-1} |a_i| \right).$$

Consider the term in parentheses on the right. What we need to do is to find a positive constant c and an integer n_0 so that for all integers $n \geq n_0$ this term is greater than or equal to c:

$$\frac{1}{n} \sum_{i=0}^{m-1} |a_i| \succ a_m - \frac{1}{n_0} \sum_{i=0}^{m-1} |a_i|.$$

We choose the value n_0 for which the term is greater than zero:

$$a_m - \frac{1}{n_0} \sum_{i=0}^{m-1} |a_i| > 0$$

$$n_0 > \frac{1}{a_m} \sum_{i=0}^{m-1} |a_i|.$$

The value $n_0 = \left\lceil \frac{1}{a_m} \sum_{i=0}^{m-1} |a_i| \right\rceil + 1$ will suffice! Thus

$$f(n) \geq \underbrace{n^m}_{g(n)} \underbrace{\left(a_m - \frac{1}{n_0} \sum_{i=0}^{m-1} |a_i| \right)}_{c}, \quad n \geq n_0 \tag{3.3}$$

$$n_0 = \left\lceil \frac{1}{a_m} \sum_{i=0}^{m-1} |a_i| \right\rceil + 1.$$

From Equation 3.3 we see that we have found the constants n_0 and c, such that for all $n \geq n_0$, $f(n) = \sum_{i=0}^{n} a_i n^m \geq c n^m$. Thus, $f(n) = \Omega(n^m)$.

This property of the asymptotic behavior of polynomials is used extensively. In fact, whenever we have a function, that is a polynomial in n, $f(n) = a_m n^m + a_{m-1} n^{m-1} + \cdots + a_2 n^2 + a_1 n + a_0$, we will immediately "drop" the less significant terms (i.e., terms involving powers of n that are less than m), as well as the leading coefficient, a_m, to write $f(n) = \Omega(n^m)$.

3.3 More Notation—Theta and Little Oh

This section presents two less commonly used forms of asymptotic notations. They are as follows:

- A notation, $\Theta(\cdot)$, to describe a function that is both $O(g(n))$ and $\Omega(g(n))$, for the same $g(n)$. (Definition 3.4)

- A notation, $o(\cdot)$, to describe a function that is $O(g(n))$ but not $\Theta(g(n))$, for the same $g(n)$. (Definition 3.5)

Definition 3.4 (Theta)
Consider a function $f(n)$ that is non-negative for all integers $n \geq 0$. We say that "$f(n)$ is theta $g(n)$," which we write as $f(n) = \Theta(g(n))$, if and only if $f(n)$ is $O(g(n))$ and $f(n)$ is $\Omega(g(n))$.

Remember that we showed in Section 3.1.4 that a polynomial in n, say $f(n) = a_m n^m + a_{m-1} n^{m-1} + \cdots + a_2 n^2 + a_1 n + a_0$, is $O(n^m)$. We also showed in Section 3.2.2 that such a polynomial is $\Omega(n^m)$. Therefore, according to Definition 3.4, we will write $f(n) = \Theta(n^m)$.

Definition 3.5 (Little Oh)
Consider a function $f(n)$ that is non-negative for all integers $n \geq 0$. We say that "$f(n)$ is little oh $g(n)$," which we write as $f(n) = o(g(n))$, if and only if $f(n)$ is $O(g(n))$, but $f(n)$ is not $\Theta(g(n))$.

Little oh notation represents a kind of *loose asymptotic bound* in the sense that if we are given that $f(n) = o(g(n))$, then we know that $g(n)$ is an asymptotic upper bound since $f(n) = O(g(n))$, but $g(n)$ is *not* an asymptotic lower bound since $f(n) = O(g(n))$ and $f(n) \neq \Theta(g(n))$ implies that $f(n) \neq \Omega(g(n))$.[3]

For example, consider the function $f(n) = n + 1$. Clearly, $f(n) = O(n^2)$. Clearly too, $f(n) \neq \Omega(n^2)$, since no matter what c we choose, for large enough n, $cn^2 \geq n + 1$. Thus, we may write $f(n) = n + 1 = o(n^2)$.

3.4 Asymptotic Analysis of Algorithms

The previous chapter presents a detailed model of the computer that involves a number of different timing parameters: τ_{fetch}, τ_{store}, τ_+, τ_-, $\tau_\times$, $\tau_\div$, $\tau_<$, τ_{call}, τ_{return}, τ_{new}, and $\tau_{[\cdot]}$. We show that keeping track of the details is messy and tiresome. So we simplify the model by measuring time in clock cycles, and by assuming that each of the parameters is equal to one cycle. Nevertheless, keeping track of and carefully counting all of the cycles is still a tedious task.

---

[3]This notion of the looseness (tightness) of an asymptotic bound is related to but not exactly the same as that given in Definition 3.2.

PROGRAM 3.1
Program 2.2 again

```
1   public class Example
2   {
3       public static int horner (int[] a, int n, int x)
4       {
5           int result = a [n];
6           for (int i = n - 1; i >= 0; --i)
7           result = result * x + a [i];
8           return result;
9       }
10  }
```

TABLE 3.2
Computing the Running Time of Program 3.1

Statement	Detailed Model	Simple Model	Big Oh
5	$3\tau_{fetch} + \tau_{[\cdot]} + \tau_{store}$	5	$O(1)$
6a	$2\tau_{fetch} + \tau_- + \tau_{store}$	4	$O(1)$
6b	$(2\tau_{fetch} + \tau_<)\tau_\times(n + 1)$	$3n + 3$	$O(n)$
6c	$(2\tau_{fetch} + \tau_- + \tau_{store})\tau_\times n$	$4n$	$O(n)$
7	$(5\tau_{fetch} + \tau_{[\cdot]} + \tau_+ + \tau_\times + \tau_{store})n$	$9n$	$O(n)$
8	$\tau_{fetch} + \tau_{return}$	2	$O(1)$
TOTAL	$(9\tau_{fetch} + 2\tau_{store} + \tau_< + \tau_{[\cdot]}$ $\mid \tau_\mid + \tau_{\mid\mid} + \tau)n$ $+ (8\tau_{fetch} + 2\tau_{store} + \tau_{[\cdot]} + \tau_- + \tau_< + \tau_{return})$	$16n + 14$	$O(n)$

In this chapter we introduce the notion of asymptotic bounds, principally big oh, and examine the properties of such bounds. As it turns out, the rules for computing and manipulating big oh expressions greatly simplify the analysis of the running time of a program when all we are interested in is its asymptotic behavior.

For example, consider the analysis of the running time of Program 3.1, which is just Program 2.2 again, an algorithm to evaluate a polynomial using Horner's rule.

Table 3.2 shows the running time analysis of Program 3.1 done in three ways: a detailed analysis, a simplified analysis, and an asymptotic analysis. In particular, note that all three methods of analysis are in agreement: Lines 5, 6a, and 8 execute in a constant amount of time; 6b, 6c, and 7 execute in an amount of time that is proportional to n, plus a constant.

The most important observation to make is that, regardless of what the actual constants are, the asymptotic analysis always produces the same answer! Since the result does not depend on the values of the constants, the asymptotic bound tells us something fundamental about the running time of the algorithm. And this fundamental result *does not depend on the characteristics of the computer and compiler actually used to execute the program!*

Of course, you don't get something for nothing. Although the asymptotic analysis may be significantly easier to do, all that we get is an upper bound on the running time of the algorithm. In particular, we know nothing about the *actual* running time of a particular program. (Recall Fallacies 3.3 and 3.4.)

3.4.1   Rules for Big Oh Analysis of Running Time

In this section we present some simple rules for determining a big oh upper bound on the running time of the basic compound statements in a Java program.

Rule 3.1 (Sequential Composition)
The worst-case running time of a sequence of Java statements such as

$$S_1;$$
$$S_2;$$
$$\vdots$$
$$S_m;$$

is $O(\max(T_1(n), T_2(n), \ldots, T_m(n)))$, where the running time of S_i, the ith statement in the sequence, is $O(T_i(n))$.

Rule 3.1 follows directly from Theorem 3.1. The total running time of a sequence of statements is equal to the sum of the running times of the individual statements. By Theorem 3.1, when computing the sum of a series of functions it is the largest one (the max) that determines the bound.

Rule 3.2 (Iteration)
The worst-case running time of a Java **for** *loop such as*

```
for  (S₁ ;  S₂ ;  S₃ )
     S₄ ;
```

is $O(\max(T_1(n), T_2(n) \times (I(n)+1), T_3(n) \times I(n), T_4(n) \times I(n)))$, where the running time of statement S_i is $O(T_i(n))$, for $i = 1, 2, 3,$ and 4, and $I(n)$ is the number of iterations executed in the worst case.

Rule 3.2 appears somewhat complicated due to the semantics of the Java **for** statement. However, it follows directly from Theorem 3.4. Consider the following simple *counted do loop.*

```
for (int i = 0; i < n; ++i)
     S₄ ;
```

Here S_1 is `int i = 0`, so its running time is constant ($T_1(n) = 1$); S_2 is `i < n`, so its running time is constant ($T_2(n) = 1$); and S_3 is `++i`, so its running time is constant ($T_3(n) = 1$). Also, the number of iterations is $I(n) = n$. According to Rule 3.2, the running time of this is $O(\max(1, 1 \times (n + 1), 1 \times n, T_4(n) \times n))$, which simplifies to $O(\max(n, T_4(n) \times n))$. Furthermore, if the loop body *does anything at all*, its running time must be $T_4(n) = \Omega(1)$. Hence, the loop body will dominate the calculation of the maximum, and the running time of the loop is simply $O(n \times T_4(n))$.

If we don't know the exact number of iterations executed, $I(n)$, we can still use Rule 3.2 provided we have an upper bound, $I(n) = O(f(n))$, on the number of iterations executed. In this case, the running time is $O(\max(T_1(n), T_2(n) \times (f(n) + 1), T_3(n) \times f(n), T_4(n) \times f(n)))$.

Rule 3.3 (Conditional Execution)

The worst-case running time of a Java if-then-else statement of the form

```
if (S₁ )
    S₂ ;
else
    S₃ ;
```

is $O(\max(T_1(n), T_2(n), T_3(n)))$, where the running time of statement S_i is $O(T_i(n))$, for

$i = 1, 2, 3.$

Rule 3.3 follows directly from the observation that the total running time for an if-then-else statement will never exceed the sum of the running time of the conditional test, S_1, plus the larger of the running times of the *then part*, S_2, and the *else part*, S_3.

3.4.2 Example—Prefix Sums

In this section, we will determine a tight big oh bound on the running time of a program to compute the series of sums $S_0, S_1, \ldots, S_{n-1}$, where

$$S_j = \sum_{i=0}^{j} a_i.$$

An algorithm to compute this series of summations is given in Program 3.2. Table 3.3 summarizes the running time calculation.

Usually the easiest way to analyze a program that contains nested loops is to start with the body of the innermost loop. In Program 3.2, the innermost loop comprises lines 8 and 9. In all, a constant amount of work is done—this includes the loop body (line 9), the conditional test (line 8b), and the incrementing of the loop index (line 8c).

For a given value of j, the innermost loop is done a total $j + 1$ times. And since the outer loop is done for $j = n - 1, n - 2, \ldots, 0$, in the worst case, the innermost loop is

---

PROGRAM 3.2
Program to compute $\sum_{i=0}^{j} a_i$ for $0 \leq j < n$

```
1   public class Example
2   {
3       public static void prefixSums (int[] a, int n)
4       {
5           for (int j = n - 1; j >= 0; --j)
6           {
7               int sum = 0;
8               for (int i = 0; i <= j; ++i)
9                   sum += a[i];
10              a [j] = sum;
11          }
12      }
13  }
```

TABLE 3.3
Computing the Running Time of
Program 3.2

Statement	Time
5a	$O(1)$
5b	$O(1) \times O(n)$ iterations
5c	$O(1) \times O(n)$ iterations
7	$O(1) \times O(n)$ iterations
8a	$O(1) \times O(n)$ iterations
8b	$O(1) \times O(n^2)$ iterations
8c	$O(1) \times O(n^2)$ iterations
9	$O(1) \times O(n^2)$ iterations
10	$O(1) \times O(n)$ iterations
TOTAL	$O(n^2)$

done n times. Therefore, the contribution of the inner loop to the running time of one iteration of the outer loop is $O(n)$.

The rest of the outer loop (lines 5, 7, and 10) does a constant amount of work in each iteration. This constant work is dominated by the $O(n)$ of the inner loop. The outer loop does exactly n iterations. Therefore, the total running time of the program is $O(n^2)$.

But is this a tight big oh bound? We might suspect that it is not, because of the worst-case assumption we made in the analysis concerning the number of times the inner loop is executed. The innermost loop is done exactly $j + 1$ times for $j = n - 1, n - 2, \ldots, 0$. However, we did the calculation assuming the inner loop is done $O(n)$ times, in each iteration of the outer loop. Unfortunately, in order to determine whether our answer is a tight bound, we must determine more precisely the actual running time of the program.

However, there is one approximate calculation that we can easily make. If we observe that the running time will be dominated by the work done in the innermost loop, and that the work done in one iteration of the innermost loop is constant, then all we need to do is to determine exactly the number of times the inner loop is actually executed. This is given by

$$
\sum_{j=0}^{n-1} j + 1 = \sum_{j=1}^{n} j
$$
$$
= \frac{n(n+1)}{2}
$$
$$
= \Theta(n^2).
$$

Therefore, the result $T(n) = O(n^2)$ is a tight, big oh bound on the running time of Program 3.2.

3.4.3 Example—Fibonacci Numbers

In this section we will compare the asymptotic running times of two different programs that both compute Fibonacci numbers.[4] The *Fibonacci numbers* are the series of numbers $F_0, F_1, \ldots,$ given by

$$
F_n = \begin{cases} 0 & n = 0, \\ 1 & n = 1, \\ F_{n-1} + F_{n-2} & n \geq 2. \end{cases} \tag{3.4}
$$

Fibonacci numbers are interesting because they seem to crop up in the most unexpected situations. However, in this section we are merely concerned with writing an algorithm to compute F_n given n.

Fibonacci numbers are easy enough to compute. Consider the sequence of Fibonacci numbers

$$
0, 1, 1, 2, 3, 5, 8, 13, 21, 34, \ldots .
$$

The next number in the sequence is computed simply by adding together the last two numbers—in this case it is $55 = 21 + 34$. Program 3.3 is a direct implementation of this idea. The running time of this algorithm is clearly $O(n)$ as shown by the analysis in Table 3.4.

Recall that the Fibonacci numbers are defined recursively: $F_n = F_{n-1} + F_{n-2}$. However, the algorithm used in Program 3.3 is non-recursive—it is *iterative*. What happens if instead of using the iterative algorithm, we use the definition of Fibonacci numbers to implement directly a recursive algorithm? Such an algorithm is given in Program 3.4 and its running time is summarized in Table 3.5.

---

[4]Fibonacci numbers are named in honor of Leonardo Pisano (Leonardo of Pisa), the son of Bonaccio (in Latin, *Filius Bonaccii*), who discovered the series in 1202.

PROGRAM 3.3
Non-recursive program to compute Fibonacci numbers

```
1   public class Example
2   {
3       public static int fibonacci (int n)
4       {
5           int previous = -1;
6           int result = 1;
7           for (int i = 0; i <= n; ++i)
8           {
9               int sum = result + previous;
10              previous = result;
11              result = sum;
12          }
13          return result;
14      }
15  }
```

TABLE 3.4
Computing the Running Time of
Program 3.3

Statement	Time
5	$O(1)$
6	$O(1)$
7a	$O(1)$
7b	$O(1) \times (n + 2)$ iterations
7c	$O(1) \times (n + 1)$ iterations
9	$O(1) \times (n + 1)$ iterations
10	$O(1) \times (n + 1)$ iterations
11	$O(1) \times (n + 1)$ iterations
13	$O(1)$
TOTAL	$O(n)$

From Table 3.5 we find that the running time of the recursive Fibonacci algorithm is given by the recurrence

$$T(n) = \begin{cases} O(1) & n < 2, \\ T(n - 1) + T(n - 2) + O(1) & n \geq 2. \end{cases}$$

But how do you solve a recurrence containing big oh expressions?

It turns out that there is a simple trick we can use to solve a recurrence containing big oh expressions *as long as we are only interested in an asymptotic bound on the result.* Simply drop the $O(\cdot)$s from the recurrence, solve the recurrence, and put the $O(\cdot)$ back!

PROGRAM 3.4
Recursive program to compute Fibonacci numbers

```
1   public class Example
2   {
3       public static int fibonacci (int n)
4       {
5           if (n == 0 || n == 1)
6               return n;
7           else
8               return fibonacci (n - 1) + fibonacci (n - 2);
9       }
10  }
```

TABLE 3.5
Computing the Running Time of Program
3.4

	Time	
Statement	$n < 2$	$n \geq 2$
5	$O(1)$	$O(1)$
6	$O(1)$	—
8	—	$T(n-1) + T(n-2) + O(1)$
TOTAL	$O(1)$	$T(n-1) + T(n-2) + O(1)$

In this case, we need to solve the recurrence

$$T(n) = \begin{cases} 1 & n < 2, \\ T(n-1) + T(n-2) + 1 & n \geq 2. \end{cases}$$

In the previous chapter, we used successfully repeated substitution to solve recurrences. However, in the previous chapter, all of the recurrences only had one instance of $T(\cdot)$ on the right-hand side—in this case there are two. As a result, repeated substitution won't work.

There is something interesting about this recurrence: It looks very much like the definition of the Fibonacci numbers. In fact, we can show by induction on n that $T(n) \geq F_{n+1}$ for all $n \geq 0$.

Proof (By induction).

Base Case There are two base cases:

$$T(0) = 1, \quad F_1 = 1 \implies T(0) \geq F_1, \quad \text{and}$$
$$T(1) = 1, \quad F_2 = 1 \implies T(1) \geq F_2.$$

Inductive Hypothesis Suppose that $T(n) \geq F_{n+1}$ for $n = 0, 1, 2, \ldots, k$ for some $k \geq 1$. Then

$$
\begin{aligned}
T(k + 1) &= T(k) + T(k - 1) + 1 \\
&\geq F_{k+1} + F_k + 1 \\
&\geq F_{k+2} + 1 \\
&\geq F_{k+2}.
\end{aligned}
$$

Hence, by induction on k, $T(n) \geq F_{n+1}$ for all $n \geq 0$.

So, we can now say with certainty that the running time of the recursive Fibonacci algorithm, Program 3.4, is $T(n) = \Omega(F_{n+1})$. But is this good or bad? The following theorem shows us how bad this really is!

Theorem 3.9 (Fibonacci numbers)
The Fibonacci numbers are given by the closed form expression

$$
F_n = \frac{1}{\sqrt{5}}(\phi^n - \hat{\phi}^n), \tag{3.5}
$$

where $\phi = (1 + \sqrt{5})/2$ and $\hat{\phi} = (1 - \sqrt{5})/2$.

Proof (By induction).

Base Case There are two base cases:

$$
\begin{aligned}
F_0 &= \frac{1}{\sqrt{5}}(\phi^0 - \hat{\phi}^0) \\
&= 0 \\
F_1 &= \frac{1}{\sqrt{5}}(\phi^1 - \hat{\phi}^1) \\
&= \frac{1}{\sqrt{5}}((1 + \sqrt{5})/2) - (1 - \sqrt{5})/2) \\
&= 1.
\end{aligned}
$$

Inductive Hypothesis Suppose that Equation 3.5 holds for $n = 0, 1, 2, \ldots, k$ for some $k \geq 1$. First, we make the following observation:

$$
\begin{aligned}
\phi^2 &= ((1 + \sqrt{5})/2)^2 \\
&= 1 + (1 + \sqrt{5})/2 \\
&= 1 + \phi.
\end{aligned}
$$

Similarly,

$$\hat{\phi}^2 = ((1 - \sqrt{5})/2)^2$$
$$= 1 + (1 - \sqrt{5})/2$$
$$= 1 + \hat{\phi}.$$

Now, we can show the main result:

$$F_{n+1} = F_n + F_{n-1}$$
$$= \frac{1}{\sqrt{5}}(\phi^n - \hat{\phi}^n) + \frac{1}{\sqrt{5}}(\phi^{n-1} - \hat{\phi}^{n-1})$$
$$= \frac{1}{\sqrt{5}}(\phi^{n-1}(1 + \phi) - \hat{\phi}^{n-1}(1 + \hat{\phi}))$$
$$= \frac{1}{\sqrt{5}}(\phi^{n-1}\phi^2 - \hat{\phi}^{n-1}\hat{\phi}^2)$$
$$= \frac{1}{\sqrt{5}}(\phi^{n+1} - \hat{\phi}^{n+1}).$$

Hence, by induction, Equation 3.5 correctly gives F_n for all $n \geq 0$.

Theorem 3.9 gives us that $F_n = \frac{1}{\sqrt{5}}(\phi^n - \hat{\phi}^n)$ where $\phi = (1 + \sqrt{5})/2$ and $\hat{\phi} = (1 - \sqrt{5})/2$. Consider $\hat{\phi}$. A couple of seconds with a calculator should suffice to convince you that $|\hat{\phi}| < 1$. Consequently, as n gets larger, $|\hat{\phi}^n|$ is vanishingly small. Therefore, $F_n \geq \phi^n - 1$. In asymptotic terms, we write $F_n = \Omega(\phi^n)$. Now, since $\phi \approx 1.62 > (3/2)$, we can write that $F_n = \Omega((3/2)^n)$.

Returning to Program 3.4, recall that we have already shown that its running time is $T(n) = \Omega(F_{n+1})$. And since $F_n = \Omega((3/2)^n)$, we can write that $T(n) = \Omega((3/2)^{n+1}) = \Omega((3/2)^n)$. That is, the running time of the recursive Fibonacci program grows *exponentially* with increasing n. And that is really bad in comparison with the linear running time of Program 3.3!

Figure 3.3 shows the actual running times of both the non-recursive and recursive algorithms for computing Fibonacci numbers.[5] Because the largest Java `int` is 2,147,483,647, it is only possible to compute Fibonacci numbers up to $F_{46} = 1,836,311,903$ before overflowing.

The graph shows that up to about $n = 35$, the running times of the two algorithms are comparable. However, as n increases past 40, the exponential growth rate of Program 3.4 is clearly evident. In fact, the actual time taken by Program 3.4 to compute F_{46} was in excess of four hours!

---

[5]These running times were measured on a Sun SPARCstation 5, Model 85, which has an 85 MHz clock and 32 MB of RAM under the Solaris 2.5 operating system. The programs were compiled using the Solaris Java Platform 1.1 compiler (`javac`) and run under the Java interpreter (`java`).

FIGURE 3.3

Actual running times of Program 3.3 and 3.4.

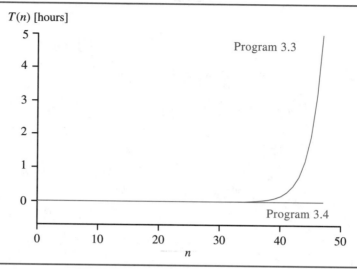

3.4.4   Example—Bucket Sort

So far all of the asymptotic running time analyses presented in this chapter have resulted in tight, big oh bounds. In this section we consider an example which illustrates that a cursory big oh analysis does not always result in a tight bound on the running time of the algorithm.

In this section we consider an algorithm to solve the following problem: Sort an array of n integers $a_0, a_1, \ldots, a_{n-1}$, each of which is known to be between 0 and $m-1$ for some fixed m. An algorithm for solving this problem, called a *bucket sort*, is given in Program 3.5.

A bucket sort works as follows: An array of m counters, or *buckets*, is used. Each of the counters is set initially to zero. Then, a pass is made through the input array, during which the buckets are used to keep a count of the number of occurrences of each value between 0 and $m-1$. Finally, the sorted result is produced by first placing the required number of zeros in the array, then the required number of ones, followed by the twos, and so on, up to $m-1$.

The analysis of the running time of Program 3.5 is summarized in Table 3.6. Clearly, the worst-case running time of the first loop (lines 7–8) is $O(m)$ and that of the second loop (lines 9–10) is $O(n)$.

Consider nested loops on lines 11–13. Exactly m iterations of the outer loop are done—the number of iterations of the outer loop is fixed. But the number of iterations of the inner loop depends on **bucket [j]**—the value of the counter. Since there are n numbers in the input array, in the worst case a counter may have the value n. Therefore, the running time of lines 11–13 is $O(mn)$ and this running time dominates all others, so the running time of Program 3.5 is $O(mn)$. (This is the *cursory analysis* column of Table 3.6).

PROGRAM 3.5
Bucket sort

```
1   public class Example
2   {
3       public static void bucketSort (int[] a, int m)
4       {
5           int[] buckets = new int[m];
6
7           for (int j = 0; j < m; ++j)
8               buckets [j] = 0;
9           for (int i = 0; i < a.length; ++i)
10              ++buckets [a [i]];
11          for (int i = 0, j = 0; j < m; ++j)
12              for (int k = buckets [j]; k > 0; --k)
13                  a [i++] = j;
14      }
15  }
```

TABLE 3.6
Computing the Running Time of Program 3.5

Statement	Time	
	Cursory analysis	Careful analysis
7–8	$O(m)$	$O(m)$
9–10	$O(n)$	$O(n)$
11–13	$O(mn)$	$O(m + n)$
TOTAL	$O(mn)$	$O(m + n)$

Unfortunately, the cursory analysis has not produced a tight bound. To see why this is the case, we must consider the operation of Program 3.5 more carefully. In particular, since we are sorting n items, the final answer will only contain n items. Therefore, line 13 will be executed exactly n times—not mn times as the cursory result suggests.

Consider the inner loop at line 12. During the jth iteration of the outer loop, the inner loop does **bucket**$[j]$ iterations. Therefore, the conditional test at line 12b is done **bucket**$[j] + 1$ times. Therefore, the total number of times the conditional test is done is

$$\sum_{j=0}^{m-1}(\textbf{bucket}[j] + 1) = \sum_{j=0}^{m-1}\textbf{bucket}[j] + \sum_{j=0}^{m-1}1$$
$$= n + m.$$

So, the running time of lines 11–13 is $O(m + n)$ and therefore the running time of Program 3.5 is $O(m + n)$. (This is the *careful analysis* column of Table 3.6.)

TABLE 3.7
Actual Lower Bounds Assuming a 100-MHz Clock, $c = 1$ Cycle, and $n_0 = 0$

	$n = 1$	$n = 8$	$n = 1K$	$n = 1024K$
$\Omega(1)$	10 ns	10 ns	10 ns	10 ns
$\Omega(\log n)$	10 ns	30 ns	100 ns	200 ns
$\Omega(n)$	10 ns	80 ns	$1.02\,\mu s$	10.5 ms
$\Omega(n \log n)$	10 ns	240 ns	$10.2\,\mu s$	210 ms
$\Omega(n^2)$	10 ns	640 ns	$102\,\mu s$	3.05 hours
$\Omega(n^3)$	10 ns	$5.12\,\mu s$	10.7 s	365 years
$\Omega(2^n)$	10 ns	$2.56\,\mu s$	10^{293} years	10^{10^5} years

3.4.5 Reality Check

"Asymptotic analysis is nice in theory," you say, "but of what practical value is it when I don't know what c and n_0 are?" Fallacies 3.3 and 3.4 showed us that if we have two programs, A and B, that solve a given problem, whose running times are $T_A = O(n^2)$ and $T_B = O(n^3)$, say we cannot conclude in general that we should use algorithm A rather than algorithm B to solve a particular instance of the problem. Even if the bounds are both known to be tight, we still don't have enough information. What we do know for sure is that *eventually*, for large enough n, program A is the better choice.

In practice we need not be so conservative. It is almost always the right choice to select program A. To see why this is the case, consider the times shown in Table 3.7. This table shows the running times computed for a very conservative scenario. We assume that the constant of proportionality, c, is one cycle of a 100-MHz clock. This table shows the running times we can expect even if only one instruction is done for each element of the input.

3.4.6 Checking Your Analysis

Having made an asymptotic analysis of the running time of an algorithm, how can you verify that the implementation of the algorithm performs as predicted by the analysis? The only practical way to do this is to conduct an experiment: write out the algorithm in the form of a computer program, compile and execute the program, and measure its actual running time for various values of the parameter, n say, used to characterize the size of the problem.

However, several difficulties immediately arise:

- How do you compare the results of the analysis that, by definition, only applies asymptotically—that is, as n gets arbitrarily larger, with the actual running time of a program that, of necessity, must be measured for fixed and finite values of n?

- How do you explain it when the results of your analysis do not agree with the observed behavior of the program?

Suppose you have conducted an experiment in which you measured the actual running time of a program, $T(n)$, for a number of different values of n. Furthermore, suppose that on the basis of an analysis of the algorithm you have concluded that the worst-case running time of the program is $O(f(n))$. How do you tell from the measurements made that the program behaves as predicted?

One way to do this follows directly from the definition of big oh: there is $c > 0$ such that $T(n) \leq cf(n)$ for all $n \geq n_0$. This suggests that we should compute the ratio $T(n)/f(n)$ for each value of n in the experiment and observe how the ratio behaves as n increases. If this ratio diverges, then $f(n)$ is probably too small; if this ratio converges to zero, then $f(n)$ is probably too big; and if the ratio converges to a constant, then the analysis is probably correct.

What if $f(n)$ turns out too large? There are several possibilities:

- The function $f(n)$ is not a *tight* bound. That is, the analysis is still correct, but the bound is not the tightest bound possible.

- The analysis was for the *worst case* but the worst case did not arise in the set of experiments conducted.

- A mistake was made and the analysis is wrong.

Exercises

3.1 Consider the function $f(n) = 3n^2 - n + 4$. Using Definition 3.1, show that $f(n) = O(n^2)$.

3.2 Consider the function $f(n) = 3n^2 - n + 4$. Using Definition 3.3, show that $f(n) = \Omega(n^2)$.

3.3 Consider the functions $f(n) = 3n^2 - n + 4$ and $g(n) = n \log n + 5$. Using Theorem 3.2, show that $f(n) + g(n) = O(n^2)$.

3.4 Consider the functions $f(n) = \sqrt{n}$ and $g(n) = \log n$. Using Theorem 3.2, show that $f(n) + g(n) = O(\sqrt{n})$.

3.5 For each pair of functions, $f(n)$ and $g(n)$, in the following table, indicate whether $f(n) = O(g(n))$ and whether $g(n) = O(f(n))$.

$f(n)$	$g(n)$
$10n$	$n^2 - 10n$
n^3	$n^2 \log n$
$n \log n$	$n + \log n$
$\log n$	$\sqrt[k]{n}$
$\ln n$	$\log n$
$\log(n + 1)$	$\log n$
$\log \log n$	$\log n$
2^n	10^n
n^m	m^n
$\cos(n\pi/2)$	$\sin(n\pi/2)$
n^2	$(n \cos n)^2$

3.6   Show that the Fibonacci numbers (see Equation 3.4) satisfy the identities

$$F_{2n-1} = (F_n)^2 + (F_{n-1})^2$$
$$F_{2n} = (F_n)^2 + 2F_nF_{n-1}$$

for $n \geq 1$.

3.7   Prove each of the following formulas:

a. $\displaystyle\sum_{i=0}^{n} i = O(n^2)$

b. $\displaystyle\sum_{i=0}^{n} i^2 = O(n^3)$

c. $\displaystyle\sum_{i=0}^{n} i^3 = O(n^4)$

3.8   Show that $\sum_{i=0}^{n} a^i = O(1)$, where $0 \leq a < 1$ and $n \geq 0$.

3.9   Show that $\sum_{i=1}^{n} \frac{1}{i} = O(\log n)$.

3.10   Solve each of the following recurrences:

a. $T(n) = \begin{cases} O(1) & n = 0, \\ aT(n-1) + O(1) & n > 0, \quad a > 1. \end{cases}$

b. $T(n) = \begin{cases} O(1) & n = 0, \\ aT(n-1) + O(n) & n > 0, \quad a > 1. \end{cases}$

c. $T(n) = \begin{cases} O(1) & n = 1, \\ aT(\lfloor n/a \rfloor) + O(1) & n > 1, \quad a \geq 2. \end{cases}$

d. $T(n) = \begin{cases} O(1) & n = 1, \\ aT(\lfloor n/a \rfloor) + O(n) & n > 1, \quad a \geq 2. \end{cases}$

3.11   Derive tight, big oh expressions for the running times of Program 1.2, 2.2, 2.3, 2.4, 2.6, 2.7, 2.8, and 2.9.

3.12   Consider the Java program fragments given in **a–e**. Assume that **n**, **m**, and **k** are non-negative **int**s and that the methods **e**, **f**, **g**, and **h** have the following characteristics:

- The worst-case running time for **e(n,m,k)** is $O(1)$ and it returns a value between 1 and $(n + m + k)$.
- The worst-case running time for **f(n,m,k)** is $O(n + m)$.
- The worst-case running time for **g(n,m,k)** is $O(m + k)$.
- The worst-case running time for **h(n,m,k)** is $O(n + k)$.

Determine a tight, big oh expression for the worst-case running time of each of the following program fragments:

a. ```
   f (n, 10, 0);
   g (n, m, k);
   h (n, m, 1000000);
   ```

b. ```
   for (int i = 0; i < n; ++i)
        f (n, m, k);
   ```

c. ```
   for (int i = 0; i < e (n, 10, 100); ++i)
        f (n, 10, 0);
   ```

d. ```
   for (int i = 0; i < e (n, m, k); ++i)
        f (n, 10, 0);
   ```

e. ```
   for (int i = 0; i < n; ++i)
        for (int j = i; j < n; ++j)
             f (n, m, k);
   ```

**3.13** Consider the following Java program fragment. What value does f compute? (Express your answer as a function of $n$.) Give a tight, big oh expression for the worst-case running time of the method f.

```
class Example
{
    static int f (int n)
    {
        int sum = 0;
        for (int i = 1; i <= n; ++i)
            sum = sum + i;
        return sum;
    }
    // ...
}
```

3.14 Consider the following Java program fragment. (The method f is given in Exercise 3.13.) What value does g compute? (Express your answer as a function of n.) Give a tight, big oh expression for the worst-case running time of the method g.

```
class Example
{
    // ...
    static int g (int n)
    {
        int sum = 0;
        for (int i = 1; i <= n; ++i)
            sum = sum + i + f (i);
        return sum;
    }
}
```
```

3.15   Consider the following Java program fragment. (The method f is given in Exercise 3.13 and the method g is given in Exercise 3.14.) What value does h compute? (Express your answer as a function of n.) Give a tight, big oh expression for the worst-case running time of the method h.

```
class Example
{
    // ...
    int h (int n)
        { return f (n) + g (n); }
}
```

Programming Projects

3.1   Write a Java method that takes a single integer argument n and has a worst-case running time of $O(n)$.

3.2   Write a Java method that takes a single integer argument n and has a worst-case running time of $O(n^2)$.

3.3   Write a Java method that takes two integer arguments n and k and has a worst-case running time of $O(n^k)$.

3.4   Write a Java method that takes a single integer argument n and has a worst-case running time of $O(\log n)$.

3.5   Write a Java method that takes a single integer argument n and has a worst-case running time of $O(n \log n)$.

3.6   Write a Java method that takes a single integer argument n and has a worst-case running time of $O(2^n)$.

3.7   The generalized Fibonacci numbers of order $k \geq 2$ are given by

$$F_n^{(k)} = \begin{cases} 0 & 0 \leq n < k - 1, \\ 1 & n = k - 1, \\ \sum_{i=1}^{k} F_{n-i}^{(k)} & n \geq k. \end{cases} \tag{3.6}$$

Write both *recursive* and *non-recursive* methods that compute $F_n^{(k)}$. Measure the running times of your algorithms for various values of k and n.

4 | Foundational Data Structures

In this book we consider a variety of *abstract data types* (ADTs), including stacks, queues, deques, ordered lists, sorted lists, hash and scatter tables, trees, priority queues, sets, and graphs. In just about every case, we have the option of implementing the ADT using an array or using some kind of linked data structure.

Because they are the base on which almost all of the ADTs are built, we call the *array* and the *linked list* the *foundational data structures*. It is important to understand that we do not view the array or the linked list as ADTs, but rather as alternatives for the implementation of ADTs.

In this chapter we consider arrays first. We review the support for arrays in Java and then show how to provide arrays with arbitrary subscript ranges, resizeable arrays, multi-dimensional arrays, and matrices. Next, we consider a number of linked list implementation alternatives and we discuss in detail the implementation of a singly-linked list class, `LinkedList`. It is important to become familiar with this class, as it is used extensively throughout the remainder of the book.

4.1 Arrays

Probably the most common way to aggregate data is to use an array. In Java an array is an object that contains a collection of objects, all of the same type. For example,

```
int[] a = new int[5];
```

allocates an array of five integers and assigns it to the variable **a**.

The elements of an array are accessed using integer-valued indices. In Java the first element of an array always has index zero. Thus, the five elements of array `a` are `a[0]`, `a[1]`,..., `a[4]`. All array objects in Java have an `int` field called `length`, the value of which is equal to the number of array elements. In this case, `a.length` has the value **5**.

Java checks at run time that the index used in every array access is valid. Valid indices fall between zero and `length` - 1. If an invalid index expression is used, an `IndexOutOfBoundsException` exception is thrown.

It is important to understand that in Java, the variable `a` refers to an array object of type `int[]`. In particular, the sequence of statements

```
int[] b;
b = a;
```

causes the variable `b` to refer to the same array object as variable `a`.

Once allocated, the size of a Java array object is fixed. That is, it is not possible to increase or decrease the size of a given array. Of course, it is always possible to allocate a new array of the desired size, but it is up to the programmer to copy the values from the old array to the new one.

How are Java arrays represented in the memory of the computer? The specification of the Java language leaves this up to the system implementers [16]. However, Figure 4.1 illustrates a typical implementation scenario.

The elements of an array typically occupy consecutive memory locations. That way, given i it is possible to find the position of $a[i]$ in constant time. In addition to the array elements, the array object must have a `length` field.

On the basis of Figure 4.1 we can now estimate the total storage required to represent an array. Let $S(n)$ be the total storage (memory) needed to represent an array of n `int`s. $S(n)$ is given by

$$S(n) \geq \texttt{sizeof}(\texttt{int}[n])$$
$$\geq (n + 1)\texttt{sizeof}(\texttt{int}),$$

FIGURE 4.1

Memory representation of Java arrays.

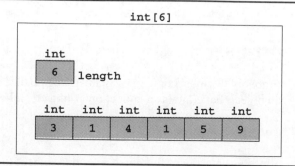

where the function `sizeof(X)` is the number of bytes used for the memory representation of an instance of an object of type **X**.

In Java, the sizes of the primitive data types are fixed constants. Hence, `sizeof(int)` $= O(1)$. In practice, an array object may contain additional fields. For example, it is reasonable to expect that there is a field that records the position in memory of the first array element. In any event, the overhead associated with a fixed number of fields is $O(1)$. Therefore, $S(n) = O(n)$.

4.1.1 Extending Java Arrays

Although the Java programming language does indeed provide built-in support for arrays, that support is not without its shortcomings: Array indices range from zero to $n-1$, where n is the array length. There is no array assignment operator. The size of an array is fixed once it is allocated.

One way to address these deficiencies is to define a new class with the desired functionality. We do this by defining an **Array** class with two fields as shown in Program 4.1. The first is an array of Java **Object**s and the second is an **int**, which records the lower bound for array indices.

4.1.2 Constructors

Program 4.2 gives the code for three **Array** class constructors. The main constructor (lines 6–10) takes two arguments, n and m, which represent the desired array length and the lower bound for array indices, respectively. This constructor allocates an array of **Object**s of length n and sets the **base** field to m. The remaining two constructors (lines 12–16) simply call the main constructor by invoking the `this` method. These constructors simply provide default values for m and n.

In Java, when an array is allocated, two things happen. First, memory is allocated for the array object and its elements. Second, each element of the array is initialized with the appropriate default value (in this case **null**).

For now, we will assume that the first step takes a constant amount of time. Since there are n elements to be initialized, the second step takes $O(n)$ time. Therefore, the running time of the main constructor is $O(n)$.

PROGRAM 4.1
Array fields

```
1   public class Array
2   {
3       protected Object[] data;
4       protected int base;
5
6       // ...
7   }
```

PROGRAM 4.2
Array constructors

```
1   public class Array
2   {
3       protected Object[] data;
4       protected int base;
5
6       public Array (int n, int m)
7       {
8           data = new Object[n];
9           base = m;
10      }
11
12      public Array ()
13          { this (0, 0); }
14
15      public Array (int n)
16          { this (n, 0); }
17      // ...
18  }
```

PROGRAM 4.3
Array class assign method

```
1   public class Array
2   {
3       protected Object[] data;
4       protected int base;
5
6       public void assign (Array array)
7       {
8           if (array != this)
9           {
10              if (data.length != array.data.length)
11                  data = new Object [array.data.length];
12              for (int i = 0; i < data.length; ++i)
13                  data [i] = array.data [i];
14              base = array.base;
15          }
16      }
17      // ...
18  }
```

4.1.3 `assign` Method

Program 4.3 defines the `assign` method of the `Array` class. This method provides a way to assign the elements of one array to another. The `assign` method is intended to be used like this:

```
Array a = new Array (5);
Array b = new Array (5);
// ...
b.assign (a);
```

The effect of doing this is to assign the elements of array **a** to the elements of array **b**. Note that after the assignment, **a** and **b** still refer to distinct `Array` instances.

Program 4.3 shows a simple implementation of the `assign` method. To determine its running time, we need to consider carefully the execution of this method.

First, we observe that the `assign` method detects and avoids self-assignment. That is, the special case

```
a.assign (a);
```

is handled properly by doing nothing.

If the array sizes differ, a new array of `Object`s is allocated. As discussed above, this operation takes $O(n)$ in the worst case, where n is the new array length.

Next, there is a loop that copies one-by-one the elements of the input array to the newly allocated array. Clearly this operation takes $O(n)$ time to perform. Finally, the `base` field is copied in $O(1)$ time. Altogether, the running time of the `assign` method is $T(n) = O(n)$, where n is the size of the array being copied.

4.1.4 Accessor Methods

Program 4.4 defines three `Array` class accessor methods. The methods `getData`, `getBase`, and `getLength` provide a means for the user to *inspect* the contents of the `Array` object. Such methods are known as *accessors*. Clearly, the running times of each of these accessors is a constant.

4.1.5 Array Indexing Methods—`get` and `put`

The elements of a Java array are accessed by enclosing the index expression between brackets `[` and `]` like this:

```
a[2] = b[3];
```

When using the `Array` class, we can access its elements like this:

```
a.getData()[2] = b.getData()[3];
```

PROGRAM 4.4
Array class accessor methods

```
1   public class Array
2   {
3       protected Object[] data;
4       protected int base;
5
6       public Object[] getData ()
7           { return data; }
8
9       public int getBase ()
10          { return base; }
11
12      public int getLength ()
13          { return data.length; }
14      // ...
15  }
```

Unfortunately, the syntax in this case is *ugly*. Unlike C++, in Java there is no way to *overload* the array subscripting operators. We can, however, define methods for indexing an array like this:

```
a.put (2, b.get (3));
```

Program 4.5 defines two methods, **get** and **put**, which provide the means to access and modify the array elements. The **get** method takes an index and returns the element

---

PROGRAM 4.5
Array class **get** and **put** methods

```
1   public class Array
2   {
3       protected Object[] data;
4       protected int base;
5
6       public Object get (int position)
7           { return data [position - base]; }
8
9       public void put (int position, Object object)
10          { data [position - base] = object; }
11      // ...
12  }
```

---

found in the array at the given position. The `put` method takes an index and an `Object` and stores the object in the array at the given position.

Both methods translate the given index by subtracting from it the value of the `base` field. It is in this way that arbitrary subscript ranges are supported. Since the overhead of this subtraction is constant, the running times of `get` and `put` are $O(1)$.

4.1.6   Resizing an Array—`setBase` and `setLength`

The `setBase` and `setLength` methods of the `Array` class are given in Program 4.6. The `setBase` method simply modifies the `base` field as required. The `setLength` method provides a means to change the size of an array at run time. This method can be used both to increase and to decrease the size of an array.

The running time of this algorithm depends only on the new array length. Let n be the original size of the array and let m be the new size of the array. Consider the case where $m \neq n$. The `setLength` method first allocates and initializes a new array of size m. Next, it copies at most $\min(m, n)$ elements from the old array to the new array. Therefore, $T(m, n) = O(m) + O(\min(m, n)) = O(m)$.

PROGRAM 4.6
`Array` class `setBase` and `setLength` methods

```
1  public class Array
2  {
3      protected Object[] data;
4      protected int base;
5
6      public void setBase (int base)
7          { this.base = base; }
8
9      public void setLength (int newLength)
10     {
11         if (data.length != newLength)
12         {
13             Object[] newData = new Object[newLength];
14             int min = data.length < newLength ?
15                 data.length : newLength;
16             for (int i = 0; i < min; ++i)
17                 newData [i] = data [i];
18             data = newData;
19         }
20     }
21     // ...
22 }
```

4.2   Multi-Dimensional Arrays

A *multi-dimensional array* of dimension n (i.e., an n-dimensional array or simply nD array) is a collection of items which is accessed via n subscript expressions. For example, in a language that supports it, the (i, j)th element of the two-dimensional array **x** is accessed by writing **x[i,j]**.

The Java programming language does not really support multi-dimensional arrays. It does, however, support *arrays of arrays*. In Java, a two-dimensional array **x** is really an array of one-dimensional arrays:

```
int[][] x = new int[3][5];
```

The expression **x[i]** selects the ith one-dimensional array; the expression **x[i][j]** selects the jth element from that array.

The built-in multi-dimensional arrays suffer the same indignities that simple one-dimensional arrays do: Array indices in each dimension range from zero to **length**-1, where **length** is the array length in the given dimension. There is no array assignment operator. The number of dimensions and the size of each dimension are fixed once the array has been allocated.

In order to illustrate how these deficiencies of the Java built-in multi-dimensional arrays can be overcome, we will examine the implementation of a multi-dimensional array class, **MultiDimensionalArray**, that is based on the one-dimensional array class discussed in Section 4.1.

4.2.1   Array Subscript Calculations

The memory of a computer is essentially a one-dimensional array—the memory address is the array subscript. Therefore, a natural way to implement a multi-dimensional array is to store its elements in a one-dimensional array. In order to do this, we need a mapping from the n subscript expressions used to access an element of the multi-dimensional array to the one subscript expression used to access the one-dimensional array. For example, suppose we wish to represent a 2×3 array of of **int**s, **a**, using a one-dimensional array like this:

```
int[] b = new int[6];
```

Then we need to determine which element of **b**, say **b[k]**, will be accessed given a reference of the form **a[i][j]**. That is, we need the mapping f such that **k** $= f(\mathbf{i},\mathbf{j})$.

The mapping function determines the way in which the elements of the array are stored in memory. The most common way to represent an array is in *row-major order*, also known as *lexicographic order*. For example, consider the 2×3 two-dimensional array. The row-major layout of this array is shown in Figure 4.2.

In row-major layout, it is the rightmost subscript expression (the column index) that increases the fastest. As a result, the elements of the rows of the matrix end up stored

FIGURE 4.2
Row-major order layout of a 2D array.

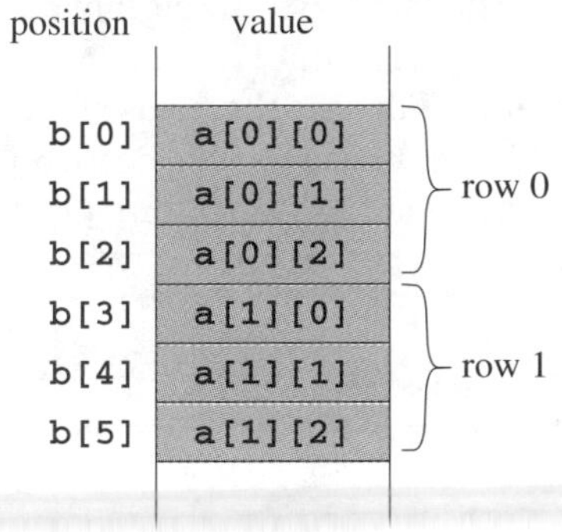

position	value	
b[0]	a[0][0]	⎫
b[1]	a[0][1]	⎬ row 0
b[2]	a[0][2]	⎭
b[3]	a[1][0]	⎫
b[4]	a[1][1]	⎬ row 1
b[5]	a[1][2]	⎭

in contiguous memory locations. In Figure 4.2, the first element of the first row is at position `b[0]`. The first element of the *second* row is at position `b[3]`, since there are three elements in each row.

We can now generalize this to an arbitrary n-dimensional array. Suppose we have an nD array `a` with dimensions

$$\delta_1 \times \delta_2 \times \cdots \times \delta_n.$$

Then, the position of the element `a[`i_1`][`i_2`][`$\cdots$`][`i_n`]` is given by

$$\sum_{j=1}^{n} f_j i_j, \tag{4.1}$$

where

$$f_j = \begin{cases} 1 & j = n, \\ \prod_{k=j+1}^{n} \delta_k & 1 \le j < n. \end{cases} \tag{4.2}$$

The running time required to calculate the position appears to be $O(n^2)$ since the position is the sum of n terms and for each term we need to compute f_j, which requires $O(n)$ multiplications in the worst case. However, the factors f_j are determined solely from the dimensions of the array. Therefore, we need only compute the factors once. Assuming that the factors have been precomputed, the position calculation can be done in $O(n)$ time using the following algorithm:

```
int offset = 0;
for (int j = 1; j <= n; ++j)
    offset +=  f_j * i_j;
```

4.2.2   An Implementation

In this section we illustrate the implementation of a multi-dimensional array using a one-dimensional array. We do this by defining a class called **MultiDimensional-Array** that is very similar to the **Array** class defined in Section 4.1.1.

Program 4.7 defines the fields of the **MultiDimensionalArray** class. Altogether three fields are used. The first, **dimensions**, is an array of length n, where n is number of dimensions and **dimension**$[i]$ is the size of the ith dimension (δ_i).

PROGRAM 4.7
MultiDimensionalArray fields

```
1   public class MultiDimensionalArray
2   {
3       int[] dimensions;
4       int[] factors;
5       Object[] data;
6
7       // ...
8   }
```

PROGRAM 4.8
MultiDimensionalArray constructor

```
1   public class MultiDimensionalArray
2   {
3       int[] dimensions;
4       int[] factors;
5       Object[] data;
6
7       public MultiDimensionalArray (int[] arg)
8       {
9           dimensions = new int[arg.length];
10          factors = new int[arg.length];
11          int product = 1;
12          for (int i = arg.length - 1; i >= 0; --i)
13          {
14              dimensions [i] = arg [i];
15              factors [i] = product;
16              product *= dimensions [i];
17          }
18          data = new Object[product];
19      }
20      // ...
21  }
```

The second field, **factors**, is also an array of length n. The jth element of the **factors** array corresponds to the factor f_j given by Equation 4.2.

The third field, **data**, is a one-dimensional array used to hold the elements of the multi-dimensional array in row-major order.

4.2.3 Constructor

The constructor for the **MultiDimensionalArray** class is defined in Program 4.8. It takes as its lone argument an array of **int**s that represents the dimensions of the array. For example, to create a $3 \times 5 \times 7$ three-dimensional array, we invoke the constructor like this:

```
MultiDimensionalArray a =
    new MultiDimensionalArray (new int[] {3, 5, 7});
```

The constructor copies the dimensions of the array into the **dimensions** array, and then it computes the **factors** array. These operations take $O(n)$, where n is the number of dimensions. The constructor then allocates a one-dimensional array of length m given by

$$m = \prod_{i=0}^{n-1} \delta_i.$$

The worst-case running time of the constructor is $O(m + n)$.

4.2.4 Array Indexing Methods—get and put

The elements of a multi-dimensional array are indexed using the **get** and **put** methods. For example, you can access the (i, j, k)th element of a three-dimensional array **a** like this:

```
a.get (new int[] {i, j, k});
```

and you can modify the (i, j, k)th element like this:

```
a.put (new int[] {i, j, k}, value);
```

Program 4.9 defines the methods **get** and **put** as well as the method **getOffset**. The **getOffset** method takes a set of n indices and computes the position of the corresponding element in the one-dimensional array according to Equation 4.1. This computation takes $O(n)$ time in the worst case, where n is the number of dimensions. Consequently, the running times of **get** and **put** are also $O(n)$.

PROGRAM 4.9
`MultiDimensionalArray` methods

```
1   public class MultiDimensionalArray
2   {
3       int[] dimensions;
4       int[] factors;
5       Object[] data;
6
7       protected int getOffset (int[] indices)
8       {
9           if (indices.length != dimensions.length)
10              throw new IllegalArgumentException (
11                  "wrong number of indices");
12          int offset = 0;
13          for (int i = 0; i < dimensions.length; ++i)
14          {
15              if (indices [i] < 0 || indices [i] >= dimensions [i])
16                  throw new IndexOutOfBoundsException ();
17              offset += factors [i] * indices [i];
18          }
19          return offset;
20      }
21
22      public Object get (int[] indices)
23          { return data [getOffset (indices)]; }
24
25      public void put (int[] indices, Object object)
26          { data [getOffset (indices)] = object; }
27      // ...
28  }
```

4.2.5 Matrices

Multi-dimensional arrays of floating-point numbers arise in many different scientific computations. Such arrays are usually called *matrices*. Mathematicians have studied the properties of matrices for many years and have developed an extensive repertoire of operations on matrices. In this section we consider two-dimensional matrices of **double**s and examine the implementation of simple, matrix multiplication.

The preceding sections show that there are many possible ways to implement matrices. In order to separate *interface* from *implementation*, we define the **Matrix** interface shown in Program 4.10.

This interface defines methods for accessing the elements of a matrix, (**get** and **put**) and methods for some of the elementary operations on matrices such as computing the

PROGRAM 4.10
`Matrix` interface

```
1   public interface Matrix
2   {
3       double get (int i, int j);
4       void put (int i, int j, double d);
5       Matrix transpose ();
6       Matrix times (Matrix matrix);
7       Matrix plus (Matrix matrix);
8   }
```

transpose of a matrix (`transpose`), *adding* matrices (`plus`), and *multiplying* matrices (`times`).

4.26 Dense Matrices

The simplest way to implement a matrix is to use an array of arrays as shown in Program 4.11. In this case, we use three fields. The first two fields, `numberOfRows` and `numberOfColumns`, record the dimensions of the matrix. The third field, `array`, is a Java array of arrays of `double`s.

The constructor takes two arguments, m and n, and constructs the corresponding $m \times n$ matrix. Clearly, the running time of the constructor is $O(mn)$. (Remember, Java initializes all the array elements to zero.)

PROGRAM 4.11
`DenseMatrix` fields and constructor

```
1   public class DenseMatrix
2       implements Matrix
3   {
4       protected int numberOfRows;
5       protected int numberOfColumns;
6       protected double[][] array;
7
8       public DenseMatrix (int numberOfRows, int numberOfColumns)
9       {
10          this.numberOfRows = numberOfRows;
11          this.numberOfColumns = numberOfColumns;
12          array = new double[numberOfRows][numberOfColumns];
13      }
14      // ...
15  }
```

4.2.7 Canonical Matrix Multiplication

Given an $m \times n$ matrix A and an $n \times p$ matrix B, the product $C = AB$ is an $m \times p$ matrix. The elements of the result matrix are given by

$$c_{i,j} = \sum_{k=0}^{n-1} a_{i,k} b_{k,j}. \tag{4.3}$$

Accordingly, in order to compute the product matrix, C, we need to compute mp summations each of which is the sum of n product terms. An algorithm to compute the matrix product is given in Program 4.12. The algorithm given is a direct implementation of Equation 4.3.

PROGRAM 4.12
DenseMatrix class times method

```
1   public class DenseMatrix
2       implements Matrix
3   {
4       protected int numberOfRows;
5       protected int numberOfColumns;
6       protected double[][] array;
7
8       public Matrix times (Matrix mat)
9       {
10          DenseMatrix arg = (DenseMatrix) mat;
11          if (numberOfColumns != arg.numberOfRows)
12              throw new IllegalArgumentException (
13                  "incompatible matrices");
14          DenseMatrix result =
15              new DenseMatrix (numberOfRows, arg.numberOfColumns);
16          for (int i = 0; i < numberOfRows; ++i)
17          {
18              for (int j = 0; j < arg.numberOfColumns; ++j)
19              {
20                  double sum = 0;
21                  for (int k = 0; k < numberOfColumns; ++k)
22                      sum += array [i][k] + arg.array [k][j];
23                  result.array [i][j] = sum;
24              }
25          }
26          return result;
27      }
28      // ...
29  }
```

The algorithm begins by checking to see that the matrices to be multiplied have compatible dimensions. That is, the number of columns of the first matrix must be equal to the number of rows of the second one. This check takes $O(1)$ time in the worst case.

Next, a matrix in which the result will be formed is constructed (lines 14–15). The running time for this is $O(mp)$. For each value of i and j, the innermost loop (lines 21–22) does n iterations. Each iteration takes a constant amount of time.

The body of the middle loop (lines 18–24) takes time $O(n)$ for each value of i and j. The middle loop is done for p iterations, giving the running time of $O(np)$ for each value of i. Since the outer loop does m iterations, its overall running time is $O(mnp)$. Finally, the resulting matrix is returned on line 26. This takes a constant amount of time.

In summary, we have shown that lines 10–13 are $O(1)$; lines 14–15 are $O(mp)$; lines 16–25 are $O(mnp)$; and line 26 is $O(1)$. Therefore, the running time of the canonical matrix multiplication algorithm is $O(mnp)$.

4.3 Singly-Linked Lists

The singly-linked list is the most basic of all the linked data structures. A singly-linked list is simply a sequence of dynamically allocated objects, each of which refers to its successor in the list. Despite this obvious simplicity, there are myriad implementation variations. Figure 4.3 shows several of the most common singly-linked list variants.

FIGURE 4.3
Singly-linked list variations.

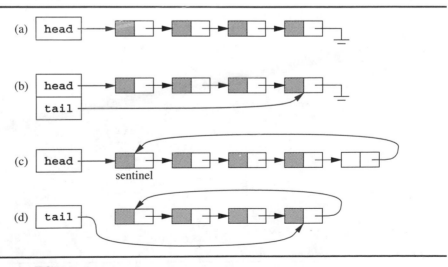

The basic singly-linked list is shown in Figure 4.3 (a). Each element of the list refers to its successor and the last element contains the `null` reference. One variable, labeled `head` in Figure 4.3 (a), is used to keep track of the list.

The basic singly-linked list is inefficient in those cases when we wish to add elements to both ends of the list. Although it is easy to add elements at the head of the list, to add elements at the other end (the *tail*) we need to locate the last element. If the basic singly-linked list is used, the entire list needs to be traversed in order to find its tail.

Figure 4.3 (b) shows a way in which to make adding elements to the tail of a list more efficient. The solution uses a second variable, `tail`, which refers to the last element of the list. Of course, this time efficiency comes at the cost of the additional space used to store the variable `tail`.

The singly-linked list labeled (c) in Figure 4.3 illustrates two common programming tricks. There is an extra element at the head of the list called a *sentinel*. This element is never used to hold data and it is always present. The principal advantage of using a sentinel is that it simplifies the programming of certain operations. For example, since there is always a sentinel standing guard, we never need to modify the `head` variable. Of course, the disadvantage of a sentinel such as that shown in (c) is that extra space is required, and the sentinel needs to be created when the list is initialized.

The list (c) is also a *circular list*. Instead of using a `null` reference to demarcate the end of the list, the last element of the list refers to the sentinel. The advantage of this programming trick is that insertion at the head of the list, insertion at the tail of the list, and insertion at an arbitrary position of the list are all identical operations.

Of course, it is also possible to make a circular, singly-linked list that does not use a sentinel. Figure 4.3 (d) shows a variation in which a single variable is used to keep

---

FIGURE 4.4
Empty singly-linked lists.

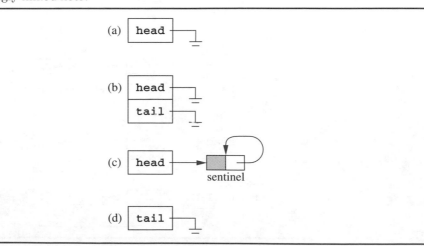

track of the list, but this time the variable, `tail`, refers to the last element of the list. Since the list is circular in this case, the first element follows the last element of the list. Therefore, it is relatively simple to insert both at the head and at the tail of this list. This variation minimizes the storage required, at the expense of a little extra time for certain operations.

Figure 4.4 illustrates how the empty list (i.e., the list containing no list elements) is represented for each of the variations given in Figure 4.3. Notice that the sentinel is always present in list variant (c). On the other hand, in the list variants that do not use a sentinel, the `null` reference is used to indicate the empty list.

In the following sections, we will present the implementation details of a generic singly-linked list. We have chosen to present variation (b)—the one that uses a head and a tail—since it supports append and prepend operations efficiently.

4.3.1 An Implementation

Figure 4.5 illustrates the the singly-linked list scheme we have chosen to implement. Two related structures are used. The elements of the list are represented using instances of the `LinkedList.Element` class, which comprises two fields, `datum` and `next`. The former is used to refer to the objects in the list; the latter is a pointer to the next list element. The main structure is an instance of the `LinkedList` class, which also comprises two fields, `head` and `tail`, which refer to the first and last list elements, respectively.

FIGURE 4.5
Memory representation of a linked list.

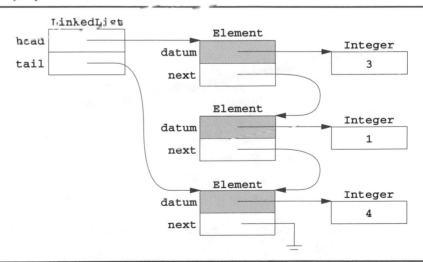

PROGRAM 4.13
LinkedList fields and LinkedList.Element class

```
1   public class LinkedList
2   {
3       protected Element head;
4       protected Element tail;
5
6       public final class Element
7       {
8           Object datum;
9           Element next;
10
11          Element (Object datum, Element next)
12          {
13              this.datum = datum;
14              this.next = next;
15          }
16
17          public Object getDatum ()
18              { return datum; }
19
20          public Element getNext ()
21              { return next; }
22          // ...
23      }
24      // ...
25  }
```

Program 4.13 defines the LinkedList.Element class. It is used to represent the elements of a linked list. It has two fields, datum and next, a constructor and two public accessor methods. Program 4.13 also defines the fields of the LinkedList class, head and tail.

We can calculate the total storage required, $S(n)$, to hold a linked list of n items from the class definitions given in Program 4.13 as follows:

$$S(n) = \texttt{sizeof(LinkedList)} + n\,\texttt{sizeof(LinkedList.Element)}$$
$$= 2\,\texttt{sizeof(LinkedList.Element ref)}$$
$$+ n\,(\texttt{sizeof(Object ref)} + \texttt{sizeof(LinkedList.Element ref)})$$
$$= (n + 2)\,\texttt{sizeof(LinkedList.Element ref)} + n\,\texttt{sizeof(Object ref)}$$

In Java, all object references occupy a constant amount of space. Therefore, $S(n) = O(n)$.

PROGRAM 4.14
LinkedList no-arg constructor

```
1   public class LinkedList
2   {
3       protected Element head;
4       protected Element tail;
5
6       public LinkedList ()
7           {}
8       // ...
9   }
```

4.3.2 List Elements

The definitions of the methods of the **LinkedList.Element** class are given in Program 4.13. Altogether, there are three methods—a constructor and two accessors.

The constructor simply initializes the field to the passed values. Assigning a value to the **datum** and **next** fields takes a constant amount of time. Therefore, the running time of the constructor is $O(1)$.

The two accessor methods, **getDatum** and **getNext**, simply return the values of the corresponding fields. Clearly, the running times of each of these methods is $O(1)$.

4.3.3 **LinkedList** Constructor

The code for the no-arg **LinkedList** constructor is given in Program 4.14. Since the fields **head** and **tail** are initially null, the list is empty by default. As a result, the constructor does nothing. The running time of the no-arg constructor is clearly constant. That is, $T(n) = O(1)$.

4.3.4 **purge** Method

Program 4.15 gives the code for the **purge** method of the **LinkedList** class. The purpose of this method is to discard the current list contents and to make the list empty again. Clearly, the running time of **purge** is $O(1)$.

4.3.5 Accessor Methods

Three **LinkedList** accessors are defined in Program 4.16. The methods **getHead** and **getTail** provide read-only access to the corresponding fields of **LinkedList**. The method **isEmpty** returns a **boolean** result, which indicates whether the list is empty. Clearly, the running time of each accessor is $O(1)$.

PROGRAM 4.15
LinkedList class purge method

```
1   public class LinkedList
2   {
3       protected Element head;
4       protected Element tail;
5
6       public void purge ()
7       {
8           head = null;
9           tail = null;
10      }
11      // ...
12  }
```

PROGRAM 4.16
LinkedList class accessor methods

```
1   public class LinkedList
2   {
3       protected Element head;
4       protected Element tail;
5
6       public Element getHead ()
7           { return head; }
8
9       public Element getTail ()
10          { return tail; }
11
12      public boolean isEmpty ()
13          { return head == null; }
14      // ...
15  }
```

4.3.6 getFirst and getLast Methods

Two more **LinkedList** accessors are defined in Program 4.17. The **getFirst** method returns the first list element. Similarly, the **getLast** method returns the last list element. The code for both methods is almost identical. In the event that the list is empty, a **ContainerEmptyException** exception is thrown.

PROGRAM 4.17
LinkedList class getFirst and getLast methods

```
1   public class LinkedList
2   {
3       protected Element head;
4       protected Element tail;
5
6       public Object getFirst ()
7       {
8           if (head == null)
9               throw new ContainerEmptyException ();
10          return head.datum;
11      }
12
13      public Object getLast ()
14      {
15          if (tail == null)
16              throw new ContainerEmptyException ();
17          return tail.datum;
18      }
19      // ...
20  }
```

We will assume that in a bug-free program, neither the **getFirst** nor the **get-Last** methods will be called for an empty list. In that case, the running time of each of these methods is constant. That is, $T(n) = O(1)$.

4.3.7 prepend Method

To *prepend* an element to a linked list is to insert that element in front of the first element of the list. The prepended list element becomes the new head of the list. Program 4.18 gives the algorithm for the **prepend** method of the **LinkedList** class.

The **prepend** method first creates a new **LinkedList.Element**. Its **datum** field is initialized with the value to be prepended to the list, **item**, and the **next** field refers to the first element of the existing list by initializing it with the current value of **head**. If the list is initially empty, both **head** and **tail** refer to the new element. Otherwise, just **head** needs to be updated.

Note that the **new** operator initializes the new **LinkedList.Element** instance by calling its constructor. In Section 4.3.2 the running time of the constructor was determined to be $O(1)$. And since the body of the **prepend** method adds only a constant amount of work, the running time of the **prepend** method is also $O(1)$.

PROGRAM 4.18
LinkedList class prepend method

```
1   public class LinkedList
2   {
3       protected Element head;
4       protected Element tail;
5
6       public void prepend (Object item)
7       {
8           Element tmp = new Element (item, head);
9           if (head == null)
10              tail = tmp;
11          head = tmp;
12      }
13      // ...
14  }
```

4.3.8 append Method

The append method, the definition of which is given in Program 4.19, adds a new
LinkedList.Element at the tail end of the list. The appended element becomes the
new tail of the list.

PROGRAM 4.19
LinkedList class append method

```
1   public class LinkedList
2   {
3       protected Element head;
4       protected Element tail;
5
6       public void append (Object item)
7       {
8           Element tmp = new Element (item, null);
9           if (head == null)
10              head = tmp;
11          else
12              tail.next = tmp;
13          tail = tmp;
14      }
15      // ...
16  }
```

The **append** method first allocates a new **LinkedList.Element**. Its **datum** field is initialized with the value to be appended, and the **next** field is set to **null**. If the list is initially empty, both **head** and **tail** refer to the new element. Otherwise, the new element is appended to the existing list, and just the **tail** pointer is updated.

The running time analysis of the **append** method is essentially the same as for **prepend**. That is, the running time is $O(1)$.

4.3.9   assign Method

The code for the **assign** method of the **LinkedList** class is given in Program 4.20. The **assign** method is used to assign the elements of one list to another. It does this by discarding the current list elements and then building a copy of the given linked list.

The **assign** method begins by calling **purge** to make sure that the list to which new contents are being assigned is empty. Then, it traverses the list passed to it one-by-one, calling the **append** method to append the items to the list being constructed.

In Section 4.3.8 the running time for the **append** method was determined to be $O(1)$. If the resulting list has n elements, the **append** method will be called n times. Therefore, the running time of the **assign** method is $O(n)$.

PROGRAM 4.20
LinkedList class constructor and **assign** methods

```
1   public class LinkedList
2   {
3       protected Element head;
4       protected Element tail;
5
6       public void assign (LinkedList list)
7       {
8           if (list != this)
9           {
10              purge ();
11              for (Element ptr = list.head;
12                  ptr != null; ptr = ptr.next)
13              {
14                  append (ptr.datum);
15              }
16          }
17      }
18      // ...
19  }
```

4.3.10 extract Method

In this section we consider the **extract** method of the **LinkedList** class. The purpose of this method is to delete the specified element from the linked list.

The **extract** method searches sequentially for the item to be deleted. In the absence of any a priori knowledge, we do not know in which list element the item to be deleted will be found. In fact, the specified item may not even appear in the list!

If we assume that the item to be deleted *is* in the list, and if we assume that there is an equal probability of finding it in each of the possible positions, then on average we will need to search half way through the list before the item to be deleted is found. In the worst case, the item will be found at the tail—assuming it is in the list.

If the item to be deleted does not appear in the list, the algorithm shown in Program 4.21 throws an **IllegalArgumentException** exception. A simpler alternative might be to do nothing—after all, if the item to be deleted is not in the list, then we are already done! However, attempting to delete an item that is not there is more likely

---

PROGRAM 4.21
LinkedList class **extract** method

```
1   public class LinkedList
2   {
3       protected Element head;
4       protected Element tail;
5
6       public void extract (Object item)
7       {
8           Element ptr = head;
9           Element prevPtr = null;
10          while (ptr != null && ptr.datum != item)
11          {
12              prevPtr = ptr;
13              ptr = ptr.next;
14          }
15          if (ptr == null)
16              throw new IllegalArgumentException (
17                  "item not found");
18          if (ptr == head)
19              head = ptr.next;
20          else
21              prevPtr.next = ptr.next;
22          if (ptr == tail)
23              tail = prevPtr;
24      }
25      // ...
26  }
```

---

to indicate a logic error in the programming. It is for this reason that an exception is thrown.

In order to determine the running time of the **extract** method, we first need to determine the time to find the element to be deleted. If the item to be deleted *is not* in the list, then the running time of Program 4.21 up to the point where it throws the exception (line 14) is $T(n) = O(n)$.

PROGRAM 4.22
LinkedList.Element class **insertAfter** and **insertBefore** methods

```
1    public class LinkedList
2    {
3        protected Element head;
4        protected Element tail;
5
6        public final class Element
7        {
8            Object datum;
9            Element next;
10
11           public void insertAfter (Object item)
12           {
13               next = new Element (item, next);
14               if (tail == this)
15                   tail = next;
16           }
17
18           public void insertBefore (Object item)
19           {
20               Element tmp = new Element (item, this);
21               if (this == head)
22                   head = tmp;
23               else
24               {
25                   Element prevPtr = head;
26                   while (prevPtr != null && prevPtr.next != this)
27                       prevPtr = prevPtr.next;
28                   prevPtr.next = tmp;
29               }
30           }
31           // ...
32       }
33       // ...
34   }
```

Now consider what happens if the item to be deleted *is* found in the list. In the worst case the item to be deleted is at the tail. Thus, the running time to find the element is $O(n)$. Actually deleting the element from the list once it has been found is a short sequence of relatively straightforward manipulations. These manipulations can be done in constant time. Therefore, the total running time is $T(n) = O(n)$.

4.3.11 insertAfter and insertBefore Methods

Consider the methods `insertAfter` and `insertBefore` of the `LinkedList.Element` class shown in Program 4.22. Both methods take a single argument that specifies an item to be inserted into the list. The given item is inserted either in front of or immediately following this list element.

The `insertAfter` method is almost identical to `append`. Whereas `append` inserts an item after the tail, `insertAfter` inserts an item after an arbitrary list element. Nevertheless, the running time of `insertAfter` is identical to that of `append`—that is, it is $O(1)$.

To insert a new item *before* a given list element, it is necessary to traverse the linked list starting from the head to locate the list element that precedes the given list element. In the worst case, the given element is at the tail of the list and the entire list needs to be traversed. Therefore, the running time of the `insertBefore` method is $O(n)$.

Exercises

4.1
a. How much space does the `Array` class declared in Program 4.1 use to store an array of `Integers` of length N?
b. How much space does the `LinkedList` class declared in Program 4.14 use to store a list of n `Integers`?
c. For what value of N/n do the two classes use the same amount of space?

4.2 Consider the `assign` method of the `Array` class given in Program 4.3. What is the purpose of the test `array != this` on line 8?

4.3 The `assign` method of the `Array` class defined in Program 4.3 has the effect of making the target of the assignment exactly the same as the source. An alternative version could assign the elements based on their apparent locations in the source and target arrays. That is, assign `a[i]` to `b[i]` for all values of `i` that are valid subscripts in both `a` and `b`. Write an `assign` method with the modified semantics.

4.4 The array subscripting methods defined in Program 4.5 don't test explicitly the index expression to see if it is in the proper range. Explain why the test is not required in this implementation.

4.5 The **setBase** method of the **Array** class defined in Program 4.6 simply changes the value of the **base** field. As a result, after the base is changed, all the array elements appear to have moved. How might the method be modified so that the elements of the array don't change their apparent locations when the base is changed?

4.6 Equation 4.1 is only correct if the subscript ranges in each dimension start at zero. How does the formula change when each dimension is allowed to have an arbitrary subscript range?

4.7 The alternative to *row-major* layout of multi-dimensional arrays is called *column-major order*. In column-major layout the leftmost subscript expression increases fastest. For example, the elements of the columns of a two-dimensional matrix end up stored in contiguous memory locations. Modify Equation 4.1 to compute the correct position for column-major layout.

4.8 Consider the **times** and **plus** methods of the **Matrix** interface defined in Program 4.10. Implement these methods for the **DenseMatrix** class defined in Program 4.11.

4.9 Which methods are affected if we drop the **tail** member variable from the **LinkedList** class declared in Program 4.14? Determine new running times for the affected methods.

4.10 How does the implementation of the **prepend** method of the **LinkedList** class defined in Program 4.18 change when a circular list with a sentinel is used as shown in Figure 4.3 (c)?

4.11 How does the implementation of the **append** method of the **LinkedList** class defined in Program 4.19 change when a circular list with a sentinel is used as shown in Figure 4.3 (c)?

4.12 Consider the assignment operator for the **LinkedList** class given in Program 4.20. What is the purpose of the test **linkedlist != this** on line 8?

Programming Projects

4.1 Complete the implementation of the **Array** class given in Program 4.1 to Program 4.6. Write a test suite to verify all of the functionality. Try to exercise every line of code in the implementation.

4.2 Complete the implementation of the **LinkedList** class given in Program 4.13 to Program 4.22. Write a test suite to verify all of the functionality. Try to exercise every line of code in the implementation.

4.3 Change the implementation of the **LinkedList** class given in Program 4.13 to Program 4.22 by removing the **tail** field. That is, implement the singly-linked list variant shown in Figure 4.3 (a). Write a test suite to verify all of the functionality. Try to exercise every line of code in the implementation.

4.4 Change the implementation of the **LinkedList** class given in Program 4.13 to Program 4.22 so that it uses a circular, singly-linked list with a sentinel as shown in Figure 4.3 (c). Write a test suite to verify all of the functionality. Try to exercise every line of code in the implementation.

4.5 The **MultiDimensionalArray** class given in Program 4.7 to Program 4.9 only supports subscript ranges starting at zero. Modify the implementation to allow an arbitrary subscript base in each dimension.

4.6 Design and implement a three-dimensional matrix class **Matrix3D** based on the two-dimensional class **DenseMatrix** given in Program 4.11 to Program 4.12.

4.7 A row vector is a $1 \times n$ matrix and a column vector is an $n \times 1$ matrix. Define and implement classes **RowVector** and **ColumnVector** as classes derived from the base class **Array** given in Program 4.1 to Program 4.6. Show how these classes can be combined to implement the **Matrix** interface declared in Program 4.10.

5 | Data Types and Abstraction

It is said that "computer science is [the] science of *abstraction*."[2] But what exactly is abstraction? Abstraction is "the idea of a quality thought of apart from any particular object or real thing having that quality"[9]. For example, we can think about the size of an object without knowing what that object is. Similarly, we can think about the way a car is driven without knowing its model or make.

Abstraction is used to suppress irrelevant details, while at the same time emphasizing relevant ones. The benefit of abstraction is that it makes it easier for the programmer to think about the problem to be solved.

5.1 Abstract Data Types

A variable in a procedural programming language such as Fortran, Pascal, C++, and Java is an abstraction. The abstraction comprises a number of *attributes*: name, address, value, lifetime, scope, type, and size. Each attribute has an associated value. For example, if we declare an integer variable in Java, `int x`, we say that the name attribute has value "`x`" and that the type attribute has value "`int`".

Unfortunately, the terminology can be somewhat confusing: The word "value" has two different meanings—in one instance it denotes one of the attributes and in the other it denotes the quantity assigned to an attribute. For example, after the assignment statement `x = 5`, the *value attribute* has the *value* five.

The *name* of a variable is the textual label used to refer to that variable in the text of the source program. The *address* of a variable denotes its location in memory. The *value* attribute is the quantity which that variable represents.[1] The *lifetime* of a variable is the interval of time during the execution of the program in which the variable is said to exist. The *scope* of a variable is the set of statements in the text of the source program in which the variable is said to be *visible*. The *type* of a variable denotes the set of values that can be assigned to the *value* attribute and the set of operations that can be performed on the variable. Finally, the *size* attribute denotes the amount of storage required to represent the variable.

The process of assigning a value to an attribute is called *binding*. When a value is assigned to an attribute, that attribute is said to be *bound* to the value. Depending on the semantics of the programming language and on the attribute in question, the binding may be done statically by the compiler or dynamically at run time. For example, in Java the *type* of a variable is determined at compile time—*static binding*. On the other hand, the *value* of a variable is usually not determined until run time—*dynamic binding*.

In this chapter we are concerned primarily with the *type* attribute of a variable. The type of a variable specifies two sets:

- a set of values, and
- a set of operations.

For example, when we declare a variable, say `x`, of type `int`, we know that `x` can represent an integer in the range $[-2^{31}, 2^{31} - 1]$ and that we can perform operations on `x` such as addition, subtraction, multiplication, and division.

The type `int` is an *abstract data type* in the sense that we can think about the qualities of an `int` apart from any real thing having that quality. In other words, we don't need to know *how* `int`s are represented or how the operations are implemented to be able to use them or reason about them.

In designing *object-oriented* programs, one of the primary concerns of the programmer is to develop an appropriate collection of abstractions for the application at hand, and then to define suitable abstract data types to represent those abstractions. In so doing, the programmer must be conscious of the fact that defining an abstract data type requires the specification of *both* a set of values and a set of operations on those values.

Indeed, it has been only since the advent of the so-called *object-oriented programming languages* that we see programming languages that provide the necessary constructs to properly declare abstract data types. For example, in Java, the `class` construct is the means by which both a set of values and an associated set of operations is declared. Compare this with the `struct` construct of C or Pascal's `record`, which only allow the specification of a set of values!

---

[1] The *address* attribute is sometimes called its *l-value* and the *value* attribute is sometimes called its *r-value*. This terminology arises from considering the semantics of an assignment statement such a `y = x`. The meaning of such a statement is "take the *value* of variable `x` and store it in memory at the *address* of variable `y`." So, when a variable appears on the right-hand side of an assignment, we use its r-value; and when it appears on the left-hand side, we use its l-value.

5.2 Design Patterns

An experienced programmer is in a sense like a concert musician, who has mastered a certain *repertoire* of pieces and is prepared to play them at any time. For the programmer, the repertoire comprises a set of abstract data types with which he or she is familiar and is able to use in programs as the need arises.

The chapters following this present a basic repertoire of abstract data types. In addition to defining the abstractions, we show how to implement them in Java and we analyze the performance of the algorithms.

The repertoire of basic abstract data types has been designed as a hierarchy of Java classes. This section presents an overview of the class hierarchy and lays the groundwork for the following chapters.

5.2.1 Class Hierarchy

The Java class hierarchy that is used to represent the basic repertoire of abstract data types is shown in Figure 5.1. Two kinds of classes are shown in Figure 5.1; *abstract Java classes*, which look like this Abstract Class , and *concrete Java classes*, which look like this Concrete Class . In addition, *Java interfaces* are shown like this (Interface). Solid lines in the figure indicate the "extends" relation between classes and between interfaces; base classes and interfaces always appear to the left of derived classes and interfaces. Dashed lines indicate the "implements" relation between a class and the interface(s) it implements.

A Java *interface* comprises a set of method *declarations*. An interface does not supply *implementations* for the methods it declares. In effect, an interface identifies the set of operations provided by every class that *implements* the interface.

An *abstract class* in Java is a class that defines only part of an implementation. Consequently, it is not possible to create object instances of abstract classes. In Java an abstract class typically contains one or more *abstract methods*. An *abstract* method is one for which no implementation is given.

An abstract class is intended to be used as the *base class* from which other classes are *derived*. By declaring abstract methods in the base class, it is possible to access the implementations provided by the derived classes through the base-class methods. Consequently, we don't need to know how a particular object instance is implemented, nor do we need to know of which derived class it is an instance.

This design pattern uses the idea of *polymorphism*. Polymorphism literally means "having many forms." The essential idea is that a Java interface is used to define the set of values and the set of operations—the abstract data type. Then, various different implementations (*many forms*) of the interface can be made. We do this by defining *abstract classes* that contain shared implementation features and then by deriving concrete classes from the abstract base classes.

The remainder of this section presents the top levels of the class hierarchy, which are shown in Figure 5.2. The top levels define those attributes of objects that are common to all of the classes in the hierarchy. The lower levels of the hierarchy are presented in

FIGURE 5.1
Object class hierarchy.

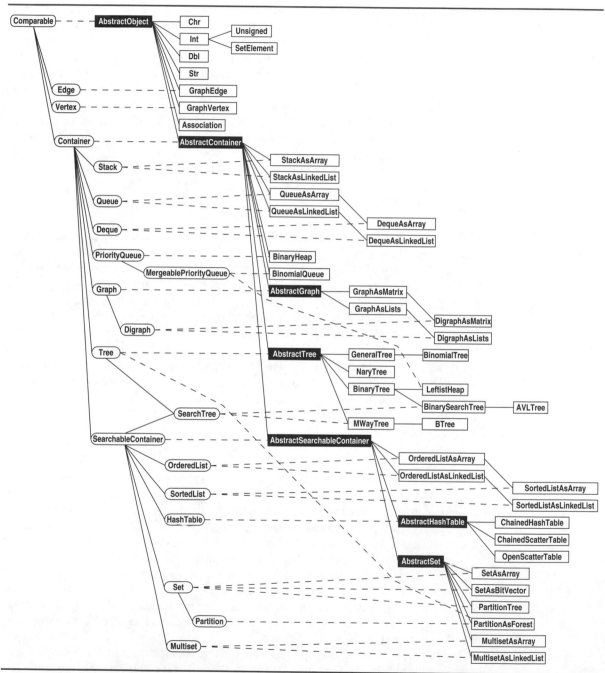

FIGURE 5.2
Object class hierarchy.

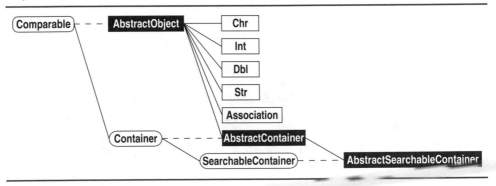

subsequent chapters where the abstractions are defined and various implementations of those abstractions are elaborated.

5.2.2 Java Objects and the `Comparable` Interface

All Java classes, including arrays, are ultimately derived from the base class called `Object`. The following code fragment identifies some of the methods defined in the `Object` class[2]:

```
public class Object
{
    public final Class getClass ();
    public String toString ();
    public boolean equals (Object obj);
    public int hashCode ();
    // ...
}
```

Notice that the Java `Object` class contains a method called `equals`, the purpose of which is to indicate whether some other object is "equal to" this one. By default, `obj1.equals(obj2)` returns `true` only if `obj1` and `obj2` refer to the same object.

Of course, any derived class can override the `equals` method to do the comparison in a way that is appropriate to that class. For example, the `equals` method is overridden in the `Integer` class as follows: If `obj1` and `obj2` are `Integer`s, then `obj1.equals(obj2)` is `true` when `obj1.intValue()` is equal to `obj2.intValue()`.

---

[2]For a complete list of the methods defined in the `Object` class, you should consult *The Java Language Specification* [16].

PROGRAM 5.1
Comparable interface

```
1   public interface Comparable
2   {
3       boolean isLT (Comparable object);
4       boolean isLE (Comparable object);
5       boolean isGT (Comparable object);
6       boolean isGE (Comparable object);
7       boolean isEQ (Comparable object);
8       boolean isNE (Comparable object);
9       int compare (Comparable object);
10  }
```

So, Java objects provide a means to test for equality. Unfortunately, they do not provide a means to test whether one object is "less than" or "greater than" another. To overcome this difficulty, we introduce the `Comparable` interface defined in Program 5.1.

The `Comparable` interface declares seven methods. The first six are used to test whether an object is "less than" (`isLT`), "less than or equal" (`isLE`), "greater than" (`isGT`), "greater than or equal," (`isGE`), "equal" (`isEQ`), or "not equal" (`isNE`) to another given object. For example, given objects `obj1` and `obj2` that implement the `Comparable` interface, the expression `obj1.isLT(obj2)` returns `true` if `obj1` is "less than" `obj2`.

The `compare` method can also be used to compare two object instances. Given two objects `obj1` and `obj2`, calling `obj1.compare (obj2)` *compares* the value of `obj1` with the value of `obj2`. The result is equal to zero if `obj1 = obj2`; less than zero if `obj1 < obj2`; and, greater than zero if `obj1 > obj2`.

Abstract Comparable Objects

The abstract class at the top of the class hierarchy is called `AbstractObject`. All of the other classes in the hierarchy are ultimately derived from this class. As shown in Figure 5.2, the `AbstractObject` class implements the `Comparable` interface discussed in Section 5.2.2.

Program 5.2 shows how the methods `isLT`, `isLE`, `isGT`, `isGE`, `isEQ`, `isNE`, and `equals` are implemented. Notice that all of these methods are declared `final`. This means that they cannot be overridden by derived classes. With the exception of `equals`, all of these methods simply invoke the `compare` method and then interpret the result as needed.

The `equals` method is slightly different because we cannot be sure that the argument passed to `equals` is an instance of a class that implements the `Comparable` interface.

The `compare` method is defined in Program 5.3. Program 5.3 also defines the *abstract method* `compareTo`. To understand the operation of the `compare` method, consider an expression of the form `obj1.compare(obj2)`. First, the `compare` method determines whether `obj1` and `obj2` are instances of the same class (line 8). If they are,

PROGRAM 5.2
`AbstractObject` methods

```
1   public abstract class AbstractObject
2       implements Comparable
3   {
4       public final boolean isLT (Comparable object)
5           { return compare (object) <  0; }
6
7       public final boolean isLE (Comparable object)
8           { return compare (object) <= 0; }
9
10      public final boolean isGT (Comparable object)
11          { return compare (object) >  0; }
12
13      public final boolean isGE (Comparable object)
14          { return compare (object) >= 0; }
15
16      public final boolean isEQ (Comparable object)
17          { return compare (object) == 0; }
18
19      public final boolean isNE (Comparable object)
20          { return compare (object) != 0; }
21
22      public final boolean equals (Object object)
23      {
24          if (object instanceof Comparable)
25              return isEQ ((Comparable) object);
26          else
27              return false;
28      }
29      // ...
30  }
```

the `compareTo` method is called to do the comparison. Thus, the `compareTo` method is only invoked for instances of the same class.

If `obj1` and `obj2` are instances of different classes, then the comparison is based on the *names* of the classes (lines 11–12). Suppose `obj1` is an instance of the class named `Opus5.StackAsArray` and `obj2` is an instance of the class named `Opus5.QueueAsLinkedList`. Then `obj1` is "less than" `obj2` because `StackAsArray` precedes alphabetically `QueueAsLinkedList`.

The use of polymorphism in the way shown gives the programmer enormous leverage. The fact that all objects are derived from the **AbstractObject** base class, together with the fact that every concrete class must implement an appropriate `compareTo` method, ensures that the comparisons always work as expected.

PROGRAM 5.3
AbstractObject class compare and compareTo methods

```
1   public abstract class AbstractObject
2       implements Comparable
3   {
4       protected abstract int compareTo (Comparable arg);
5
6       public final int compare (Comparable arg)
7       {
8           if (getClass () == arg.getClass ())
9               return compareTo (arg);
10          else
11              return getClass ().getName ().compareTo (
12                  arg.getClass ().getName ());
13      }
14      // ...
15  }
```

5.2.3 Wrappers for the Primitive Types

The *primitive types* in Java are boolean, char, short, int, long, float, and double. There is also the "type" void, which is used in the place of the return type to declare a method that returns nothing. For each primitive type, the Java language defines a class that *wraps* the primitive. The wrapper classes are called Boolean, Character, Short, Integer, Long, Float, and Double. There is also a wrapper class for void called Void.

Like all Java classes, the wrapper classes are ultimately derived from the Object class. Therefore, they all provide an equals method to test for equality. However, because the wrapper classes do not implement the Comparable interface given in Program 5.1, the comparison methods isLT, isLE, isGT, isGE, isEQ, and isNE are not supported.

To circumvent this shortcoming, we might be tempted to extend the wrapper classes like this:

```
class ComparableInteger
    extends Integer // Wrong.  Integer is a final class!
    implements Comparable
{
    // ...
}
```

Unfortunately, according to the Java language specification, the Integer class is a final class—it cannot be extended [16].

PROGRAM 5.4
Chr class

```
1   public class Chr
2       extends AbstractObject
3   {
4       protected char value;
5
6       public Chr (char value)
7           { this.value = value; }
8
9       public char charValue ()
10          { return value; }
11
12      protected int compareTo (Comparable object)
13      {
14          Chr arg = (Chr) object;
15          return (int) value - (int) arg.value;
16      }
17      // ...
18  }
```

Consequently, we are forced to implement our own wrapper classes if we want them to implement the **Comparable** interface. Programs 5.4, 5.5, and 5.6 define three such wrapper classes **Chr**, **Int**, and **Dbl**, which are wrappers for Java primitive types **char**, **int**, and **double**.

Java also provides a **String** class for dealing with character sequences. The **String** class is special in that it is closely tied to the definition of the language itself. The Java compiler automatically creates a **String** object for every *string literal*, such as **"Hello world.\n"**, in a Java program.

Because the **String** class does not implement the **Comparable** interface and because the **String** class cannot be extend, we are forced to implement a wrapper class. Program 5.7 defines the class **Str**, which wraps a **String** instance and implements the **Comparable** interface.

5.2.4   Containers

A container is an object that contains within it other objects. Many of the data structures presented in this book can be viewed as containers. For this reason, we develop a common interface that is implemented by the various data structure classes.

The **Container** interface is declared in Program 5.8. It comprises the six methods, **getCount**, **isEmpty**, **isFull**, **purge**, **accept**, and **getEnumeration**.

A container may be empty or it may contain one or more other objects. Typically, a container has finite capacity. The **isEmpty** method returns **true** when the container

---

PROGRAM 5.5
Int class

```
1   public class Int
2       extends AbstractObject
3   {
4       protected int value;
5
6       public Int (int value)
7           { this.value = value; }
8
9       public int intValue ()
10          { return value; }
11
12      protected int compareTo (Comparable object)
13      {
14          Int arg = (Int) object;
15          long diff = (long) value - (long) arg.value;
16          if (diff < 0)
17              return -1;
18          else if (diff > 0)
19              return +1;
20          else
21              return 0;
22      }
23      // ...
24  }
```

---

is empty and the **isFull** method returns **true** when the container is full. The **getCount** method returns the number of objects in the container.

The purpose of the **purge** method is to discard all of the contents of a container. After a container is purged, the **isEmpty** method returns **true** and the **getCount** method returns zero.

Conspicuous by their absence from Program 5.8 are methods for putting objects into a container and for taking them out again. These methods have been omitted from the **Container** interface, because the precise nature of these methods depends on the type of container implemented.

In order to describe the remaining two methods, **accept** and **getEnumeration**, we need to introduce first the concepts of a *visitor* and an *enumeration*, as well as the **Visitor** and **Enumeration** interfaces that represent these concepts. Visitors are discussed in Section 5.2.5 and enumerations are discussed in Section 5.2.6.

Abstract Containers

Program 5.9 introduces an *abstract class* called **AbstractContainer**. It is intended to be used as the base class from which concrete container realizations are

PROGRAM 5.6
Dbl class

```
1   public class Dbl
2       extends AbstractObject
3   {
4       protected double value;
5
6       public Dbl (double value)
7           { this.value = value; }
8
9       public double doubleValue ()
10          { return value; }
11
12      protected int compareTo (Comparable object)
13      {
14          Dbl arg = (Dbl) object;
15          if (value < arg.value)
16              return -1;
17          else if (value > arg.value)
18              return +1;
19          else
20              return 0;
21      }
22      // ...
23  }
```

derived. As illustrated in Figure 5.2, the **AbstractContainer** class extends the **AbstractObject** class (defined in Program 5.2) and it implements the **Container** interface (defined in Program 5.8).

A single field, **count**, is used. This field is used to keep track of the number of objects held in the container. The **count** field is initially zero by default. It is the responsibility of the derived class to update this field as required.

The **getCount** method is an accessor that returns the number of items contained in the container. The **getCount** method simply returns the value of the **count** field.

The **isEmpty** and **isFull** methods are **boolean**-valued accessors that indicate whether a given container is empty or full, respectively. Notice that the **isEmpty** method does not directly access the **count** field. Instead it calls **getCount**. As long as the **getCount** method has the correct semantics, the **isEmpty** method will too.

In some cases, a container is implemented in a way that makes its capacity finite. When this is the case, it is necessary to be able to determine when the container is full. The **isFull** method is a **boolean**-valued accessor that returns the value **true** if the container is full. The default version always returns **false**.

PROGRAM 5.7
`Str` class

```
1   public class Str
2       extends AbstractObject
3   {
4       protected String value;
5
6       public Str (String value)
7           { this.value = value; }
8
9       public String stringValue ()
10          { return value; }
11
12      protected int compareTo (Comparable object)
13      {
14          Str arg = (Str) object;
15          return value.compareTo (arg.value);
16      }
17      // ...
18  }
```

PROGRAM 5.8
`Container` interface

```
1   public interface Container
2       extends Comparable
3   {
4       int getCount ();
5       boolean isEmpty ();
6       boolean isFull ();
7       void purge ();
8       void accept (Visitor visitor);
9       Enumeration getEnumeration ();
10  }
```

5.2.5 Visitors

The `Container` interface described in the preceding section interacts closely with the `Visitor` interface shown in Program 5.10. In particular, the `accept` method of the `Container` interface takes as its argument a reference to any class that implements the `Visitor` interface.

PROGRAM 5.9
`AbstractContainer` fields and methods

```
1   public abstract class AbstractContainer
2        extends AbstractObject
3        implements Container
4   {
5        protected int count;
6
7        public int getCount ()
8            { return count; }
9
10       public boolean isEmpty ()
11           { return getCount () == 0; }
12
13       public boolean isFull ()
14           { return false; }
15       // ...
16  }
```

But what is a visitor? As shown in Program 5.10, a visitor is an object that has the two methods `visit` and `isDone`. Of these, the `visit` method is the most interesting. The `visit` method takes as its argument a reference to an `Object` instance.

The interaction between a container and a visitor goes like this: The container is passed a reference to a visitor by calling the container's `accept` method. That is, the container "accepts" the visitor. What does a container do with a visitor? It calls the `visit` method of that visitor one-by-one for each object contained in the container.

The interaction between a `Container` and its `Visitor` is best understood by considering an example. The following code fragment gives the design framework for the implementation of the `accept` method in some concrete class, say `SomeContainer`,

PROGRAM 5.10
`Visitor` interface

```
1   public interface Visitor
2   {
3        void visit (Object object);
4        boolean isDone ();
5   }
```

that implements the `Container` interface:

```
public class SomeContainer
    implements Container
{
    public void accept (Visitor visitor)
    {
        for each Object i   in this container
        {
            visitor.visit (i);
        }
    }
    // ...
}
```

The `accept` method calls `visit` for each object `i` in the container. Since `Visitor` is an interface, it does not provide an implementation for the `visit` operation. What a visitor actually does with an object depends on the actual class of visitor used.

Suppose that we want to print all of the objects in the container. One way to do this is to create a `PrintingVisitor`, which prints every object it visits, and then to pass the visitor to the container by calling the `accept` method. The following code shows how we can declare the `PrintingVisitor` class, which prints an object on the standard output stream, `System.out`.

```
public class PrintingVisitor
    implements Visitor
{
    public void visit (Object object)
        { System.out.println (object); }
    // ...
}
```

Finally, given an object `c` that is an instance of a concrete class `SomeContainer` that implements the `Container` interface, we can call the `accept` method as follows:

```
Container c = new SomeContainer ();
// ...
c.accept (new PrintingVisitor ());
```

The effect of this is to call the `visit` method of the visitor for each object in the container.

The `isDone` Method

As shown in Program 5.10, the `Visitor` interface also includes the method `isDone`. The `isDone` method is an accessor that is used to determine whether a visitor has finished its work. That is, the `isDone` method returns the `boolean` value `true` if the visitor "is done."

The idea is this: Sometimes a visitor does not need to visit all of the objects in a container. That is, in some cases, the visitor may finish its task after having visited only some of the objects. The `isDone` method can be used by the container to terminate the `accept` method early like this:

```
public class SomeContainer
    implements Container
{
    public void accept (Visitor visitor)
    {
        for each Object i   in this container
        {
            if (visitor.isDone ())
                return;
            visitor.visit (i);
        }
    }
    // ...
}
```

To illustrate the usefulness of `isDone`, consider a visitor that visits the objects in a container with the purpose of finding the first object that matches a given target object. Having found the first matching object in the container, the visitor is done and does not need to visit any more contained objects.

The following code fragment defines a visitor that finds the first object in the container that matches a given object.

```
public class MatchingVisitor
    implements Visitor
{
    private Object target;
    private Object found;

    public MatchingVisitor (Object target)
        { this.target = target; }

    public void visit (Object object)
    {
        if (!isDone () && object.equals (target))
            found = object;
    }

    public boolean isDone ()
        { return found != null; }
}
```

The constructor of the **MatchingVisitor** visitor takes a reference to an **Object** instance that is the target of the search. That is, we wish to find an object in a container that matches the target. For each object the **MatchingVisitor** visitor visits, it compares that object with the target and makes **found** refer to that object if it matches. Clearly, the **MatchingVisitor** visitor is done when the **found** variable is not **null**.

Suppose we have a container **c** that is an instance of a concrete container class, **SomeContainer**, that implements the **Container** interface and an object **x** that is an instance of a concrete object class, **SomeObject**. Then, we can use the **Matching-Visitor** visitor as follows:

```
Container c = new SomeContainer ();
Object x = new SomeObject ();
// ...
c.accept (new MatchingVisitor (x));
```

Abstract Visitors

Program 5.11 defines an abstract class called **AbstractVisitor** that implements the **Visitor** interface. This class is provided simply as a convenience. It provides a default implementation for the **visit** method which does nothing and a default implementation for the **isDone** method which always returns **false**.

The **AbstractContainer** Class **toString** Method

One of the methods defined in the Java **Object** class is the **toString** method. Consequently, every Java object supports the **toString** method. The **toString** method is required to return a string that represents the object "textually." It is typically invoked in situations where it is necessary to print out the representation of an object.

Program 5.12 defines the **toString** method of the **AbstractContainer** class. This method is provided to simplify the implementation of classes derived from the **AbstractContainer** class. The default behavior is to print out the name of the class and then to print each of the elements in the container, by using the **accept** method together with a visitor.

The **toString** method makes use of a **StringBuffer** to accumulate the textual representations of the objects in the container. A Java string buffer is like a Java

---

PROGRAM 5.11
AbstractVisitor class

```
1  public abstract class AbstractVisitor
2      implements Visitor
3  {
4      public void visit (Object object)
5          {}
6      public boolean isDone ()
7          { return false; }
8  }
```

PROGRAM 5.12
AbstractContainer class toString method

```
1   public abstract class AbstractContainer
2       extends AbstractObject
3       implements Container
4   {
5       protected int count;
6
7       public String toString ()
8       {
9           final StringBuffer buffer = new StringBuffer ();
10          Visitor visitor = new AbstractVisitor ()
11          {
12              private boolean comma;
13
14              public void visit (Object object)
15              {
16                  if (comma)
17                      buffer.append (", ");
18                  buffer.append (object);
19                  comma = true;
20              }
21          };
22          accept (visitor);
23          return getClass ().getName () + " {" + buffer + "}";
24      }
25      // ...
26  }
```

String, except it can be modified. In particular, the **StringBuffer** class defines various **append** methods that can be used to append text to the buffer.

In this case, we use a visitor to do the appending. That is, the **visit** method appends to the string buffer the textual representation of every object that it visits. (It also makes sure to put in commas as required.)

The final result returned by the **toString** method consists of the name of the container class, followed by a comma-separated list of the contents of that container enclosed in braces { and }.

5.2.6 Enumerations

In this section we introduce an abstraction called an *enumeration*. An enumeration provides the means to access one-by-one all of the objects in a container. Enumerations are an alternative to using the visitors described in Section 5.2.5.

PROGRAM 5.13
Enumeration interface

```
1  public interface Enumeration
2  {
3      boolean hasMoreElements ();
4      Object nextElement ()
5          throws NoSuchElementException;
6  }
```

The **Container** interface given in Program 5.8 has a method called **getEnumera-tion**, which returns an **Enumeration**. The basic idea is that for every concrete container class we will also implement a related class that implements the **Enumeration** interface.

Program 5.13 defines the **Enumeration** interface.[3] The interface comprises two methods—**hasMoreElements** and **nextElement**.

In order to understand the desired semantics, it is best to consider first an example that illustrates the use of an enumeration. Consider a concrete container class, say **SomeContainer**, that implements the **Container** interface. The following code fragment illustrates the use of the enumeration to access one-by-one the objects contained in the container:

```
Container c = new SomeContainer ();
// ...
Enumeration e = c.getEnumeration ();
while (e.hasMoreElements ())
{
    Object object = e.nextElement ();
    System.out.println (object);
}
```

In order to have the desired effect, the methods **hasMoreElements** and **next-Element** must have the following behaviors:

hasMoreElements   The **hasMoreElements** method is called in the loop-termination test part of the **while** statement. The **hasMoreElements** method returns **true** when there are still more objects in the container to be visited and it returns **false** when all of the contained objects have been visited.

nextElement   The **nextElement** method returns the next object in the container to be visited. When all of the object in a container have been visited, the **nextElement** method throws a **NoSuchElementException** exception.

---

[3]This definition of the **Enumeration** interface is identical to the one given in *The Java Language Specification,* which is called **java.util.Enumeration** [16].

Given these semantics for the enumeration methods, the program fragment shown above systematically visits all of the objects in the container and prints each one on its own line of the standard output stream.

One of the advantages of using an enumeration object that is separate from the container is that it is possible then to have more than one enumeration associated with a given container. This provides greater flexibility than possible using a visitor, since only one visitor can be accepted by a container at any given time. For example, consider the following code fragment:

```
Container c = new SomeContainer ();
// ...
Enumeration e1 = c.getEnumeration ();
while (e1.hasMoreElements ())
{
    Object obj1 = e1.nextElement ();
    Enumeration e2 = c.getEnumeration ();
    while (e2.hasMoreElements ())
    {
        Object obj2 = e2.nextElement ();
        if (obj1.equals (obj2))
        System.out.println (obj1 + "=" + obj2);
    }
}
```

This code compares all pairs of objects in the container **c** and prints out those that are equal.

A certain amount of care is required when defining and using enumerations. In order to simplify the implementation of enumerations, we will assume that while an enumeration is in use, the associated container will not be modified.

5.2.7 Searchable Containers

A *searchable container* is an extension of the container abstraction. It adds to the interface provided for containers methods for putting objects in and taking objects out, for testing whether a given object is in the container, and a method to search the container for a given object.

The definition of the **SearchableContainer** interface is shown in Program 5.14. The **SearchableContainer** interface extends the **Container** interface given in Program 5.8. It adds four methods to the inherited interface.

The **isMember** method is a **boolean**-valued method, which takes as its argument any object that implements the **Comparable** interface. The purpose of this method is to test whether the given object instance is in the container.

The purpose of the **insert** method is to put an object into the container. The **insert** method takes a **Comparable** object and inserts it into the container. Similarly, the **withdraw** method is used to remove an object from a container. The argument refers to the object to be removed.

PROGRAM 5.14
`SearchableContainer` interface

```
1  public interface SearchableContainer
2      extends Container
3  {
4      boolean isMember (Comparable object);
5      void insert (Comparable object);
6      void withdraw (Comparable obj);
7      Comparable find (Comparable object);
8  }
```

The final method, **find**, is used to locate an object in a container and to return a reference to that object. In this case, it is understood that the search is to be done using the comparison methods defined in the **Comparable** interface. That is, the **find** method is *not* to be implemented as a search of the container for the given object but rather as a search of the container for an object that compares equal to the given object.

This is an important subtlety in the semantics of **find**: The search is not for the given object, but rather for an object that compares equal to the given object. These semantics are particularly useful when using *associations*, which are defined in Section 5.2.8.

In the event that the **find** method fails to find an object equal to the specified object, then it will return **null**. Therefore, the user of the **find** method should test explicitly the returned value to determine whether the search was successful. Also, the **find** method does *not* remove the object it finds from the container. An explicit call of the **withdraw** method is needed to actually remove the object from the container.

Abstract Searchable Containers

Program 5.15 introduces an *abstract class* called **AbstractSearchableContainer**. It is intended to be used as the base class from which concrete searchable container realizations are derived. As illustrated in Figure 5.2, the **AbstractSearch-**

PROGRAM 5.15
`AbstractSearchableContainer` class

```
1  public abstract class AbstractSearchableContainer
2      extends AbstractContainer
3      implements SearchableContainer
4  {
5  }
```

ableContainer class extends the AbstractContainer class (defined in Program 5.9) and it implements the SearchableContainer interface (defined in Program 5.14).

5.2.8 Associations

An association is an ordered pair of objects. The first element of the pair is called the *key*; the second element is the *value* associated with the given key.

Associations are useful for storing information in a database for later retrieval. For example, a database can be viewed as a container that holds key-and-value pairs. The information associated with a given key is retrieved from the database by searching the database for an ordered pair in which the key matches the given key.

Program 5.16 introduces the Association class. The Association class is a concrete extension of the AbstractObject class given in Program 5.2.

An association has two fields, key and value. The key field is any object that implements the Comparable interface defined in Program 5.16. The value field is any arbitrary object.

Two constructors and two accessors are defined in Program 5.17. The first constructor takes two arguments and initializes the key and value fields accordingly. The second constructor takes only one argument, which is used to initialize the key field—the value field is set to null.

The getKey and getValue methods are accessors. The former returns the value of the key field; the latter returns the value of the value field.

The remaining methods of the Association class are defined in Program 5.18. The compareTo method is used to compare associations. Its argument is an object that is assumed to be an instance of the Association class. The compareTo method is one place where an association distinguishes between the key and the value. In this case, the result of the comparison is based solely on the keys of the two associations—the values have no role in the comparison.

Program 5.18 also defines a toString method. The purpose of the toString method is to return a textual representation of the association. In this case, the implementation is trivial and needs no further explanation.

PROGRAM 5.16
Association fields

```
1   public class Association
2       extends AbstractObject
3   {
4       protected Comparable key;
5       protected Object value;
6
7       // ...
8   }
```

PROGRAM 5.17
Association constructors

```
1   public class Association
2       extends AbstractObject
3   {
4       protected Comparable key;
5       protected Object value;
6
7       public Association (Comparable key, Object value)
8       {
9           this.key = key;
10          this.value = value;
11      }
12
13      public Association (Comparable key)
14          { this (key, null); }
15
16      public Comparable getKey ()
17          { return key; }
18
19      public Object getValue ()
20          { return value; }
21      // ...
22  }
```

Exercises

5.1 Specify the set of values and the set of operations provided by each of the following Java primitive data types:

  a. `char`

  b. `int`

  c. `double`

  d. `String`

5.2 What are the features of Java that facilitate the creation of *user-defined* data types?

5.3 Explain how each of the following Java features supports *polymorphism*:

  a. interfaces

  b. abstract classes

  c. inheritance

5.4 Suppose we define two concrete classes, **A** and **B**, both of which are derived from the **AbstractObject** class declared in Program 5.2. Furthermore, let **a** and **b**

PROGRAM 5.18
Association methods

```
1   public class Association
2        extends AbstractObject
3   {
4        protected Comparable key;
5        protected Object value;
6
7        protected int compareTo (Comparable object)
8        {
9            Association association = (Association) object;
10           return key.compare (association.getKey ());
11       }
12
13       public String toString ()
14       {
15           String result = "Association {" + key;
16           if (value != null)
17               result += ", " + value;
18           return result + "}";
19       }
20       // ...
21   }
```

---

be instances of classes **A** and **B** (respectively) declared as follows:

```
public class A extends AbstractObject { ... };
public class B extends AbstractObject { ... };
Comparable a = new A();
Comparable b = new B();
```

Give the sequence of methods called in order to evaluate a comparison such as "a.isLT(b)". Is the result of the comparison **true** or **false**? Explain.

5.5 Consider the **Int** wrapper class defined in Program 5.5. Explain the operation of the following program fragment:

```
Comparable i = new Int (5);
Comparable j = new Int (7);
boolean result = i.isLT (j);
```

5.6 Let **c** be an instance of some concrete class derived from the **AbstractContainer** class given in Program 5.9. Explain how the statement

```
System.out.println (c);
```

prints the contents of the container on the standard output stream.

5.7 Suppose we have a container **c** (i.e., an instance of some concrete class derived from the **AbstractContainer** class defined in Program 5.9) that among other things happens to contain itself. What happens when we invoke the **toString** method on **c**?

5.8 Enumerations and visitors provide two ways to do the same thing— to visit one-by-one all the objects in a container. Give an implementation for the **accept** method of the **AbstractContainer** class that uses an enumeration.

5.9 Is it possible to implement an enumeration using a visitor? Explain.

5.10 Suppose we have a container that we know contains only instances of the **Int** class defined in Program 5.5. Design a **Visitor** that computes the sum of all of the integers in the container.

5.11 Consider the following pair of **Association**s:

```
Comparable a = new Association (new Int (3),
                                 new Integer (4));
Comparable b = new Association (new Int (3));
```

Give the sequence of methods called in order to evaluate a comparison such as "**a.isEQ(b)**". Is the result of the comparison **true** or **false**? Explain.

Programming Projects

5.1 Design and implement suitable wrapper classes that implement the **Comparable** interface for the Java primitive types **boolean**, **byte**, **short**, **long**, **float**, and **void**.

5.2 Using *visitors*, devise implementations for the **isMember** and **find** methods of the **AbstractSearchableContainer** class declared in Program 5.15.

5.3 Using *enumerations*, devise implementations for the **isMember** and **find** methods of the **AbstractSearchableContainer** class declared in Program 5.15.

5.4 Devise a scheme using visitors whereby all of the objects contained in one searchable container can be removed from it and transferred to another container.

5.5 A *bag* is a simple container that can hold a collection of objects. Design and implement a concrete class called **Bag** that extends the **AbstractSearchableContainer** class defined in Program 5.15. Use the **Array** class given in Chapter 4 to keep track of the contents of the bag.

5.6 Repeat Project 5.5, this time using the **LinkedList** class given in Chapter 4.

5.7 In C++ it is common to use an *iterator* as the means to iterate through the objects in a container. In Java we can define an iterator like this:

```
public interface Iterator
{
    void init ();
    boolean test ();
    void inc ();
    Object current ();
}
```

Given an iterator **i** from some container **c**, the contents of **c** can be printed like this:

```
for (i.init(); i.test(); i.inc())
    System.out.println (i.current());
```

Devise a wrapper class to encapsulate an enumeration and provide the functionality of an iterator.

6 | Stacks, Queues, and Deques

In this chapter we consider several related abstract data types—stacks, queues, and deques. Each of these can be viewed as a pile of items. What distinguishes each of them is the way in which items are added to or removed from the pile.

In the case of a *stack*, items are added to and removed from the top of the pile. Consider the pile of papers on your desk. Suppose you add papers only to the top of the pile or remove them only from the top of the pile. At any point in time, the only paper that is visible is the one on top. What you have is a *stack*.

Now suppose your boss comes along and asks you to complete a form immediately. You stop doing whatever it is you are doing, and place the form on top of your pile of papers. When you have filled-out the form, you remove it from the top of the stack and return to the task you were working on before your boss interrupted you. This example illustrates that a *stack* can be used to keep track of partially completed tasks.

A *queue* is a pile in which items are added at one end and removed from the other. In this respect, a queue is like the line of customers waiting to be served by a bank teller. As customers arrive, they join the end of the queue while the teller serves the customer at the head of the queue. As a result, a *queue* is used when a sequence of activities must be done on a *first-come, first-served* basis.

Finally, a *deque* extends the notion of a queue. In a deque, items can be added to or removed from either end of the queue. In a sense, a deque is the more general abstraction of which the stack and the queue are just special cases.

As shown in Figure 6.1, we view stacks, queues, and deques as containers. This chapter presents a number of different implementation alternatives for stacks, queues, and deques. All of the concrete classes presented extend the `AbstractContainer` class defined in Chapter 5.

6.1 Stacks

The simplest of all the containers is a *stack*. A stack is a container that provides exactly one method, `push`, for putting objects into the container; and one method, `pop`, for taking objects out of the container. Figure 6.2 illustrates the basic idea.

FIGURE 6.1
Object class hierarchy.

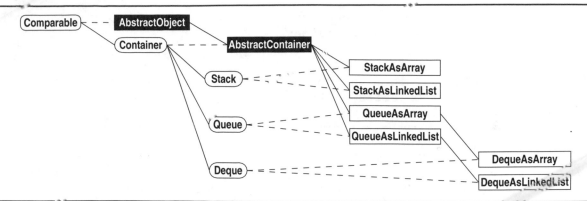

FIGURE 6.2
Basic stack operations.

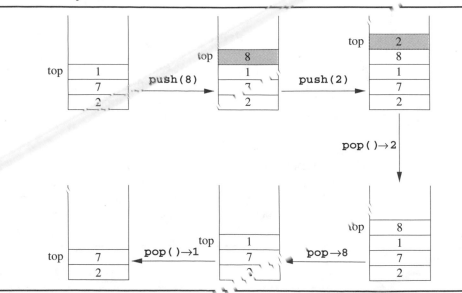

Objects that are stored in a stack are kept in a pile. The last item put into the stack is at the top. When an item is pushed into a stack, it is placed at the top of the pile. When an item is popped it is always the top item that is removed. Since it is always the last item to be put into the stack that is the first item to be removed, a stack is a *last-in, first-out* or *LIFO* data structure.

In addition to the **push** and **pop** operations, the typical stack implementation also provides an accessor called **getTop**, which returns the item at the top of the stack without removing it from the stack.

PROGRAM 6.1
`Stack` interface

```
1   public interface Stack
2       extends Container
3   {
4       Object getTop ();
5       void push (Object object);
6       Object pop ();
7   }
```

Program 6.1 defines the `Stack` interface. The `Stack` interface extends the `Container` interface defined in Program 5.8. Hence, it comprises all of the methods inherited from `Container` plus the three methods `getTop`, `push`, and `pop`.

When implementing a data structure, the first issue to be addressed is which foundational data structure(s) to use. Often, the choice is between an array-based implementation and a linked-list implementation. The next two sections present an array-based implementation of stacks followed by a linked-list implementation.

6.1.1 Array Implementation

This section describes an array-based implementation of stacks. Program 6.2 introduces the `StackAsArray` class. The `StackAsArray` class is a concrete class that extends the `AbstractContainer` class introduced in Program 5.9 and implements the `Stack` interface defined in Program 6.1.

Fields
The `StackAsArray` class contains one field—an array of `Object`s called `array`. In addition, the `StackAsArray` class inherits the `count` field from the `AbstractContainer` class. In the array implementation of the stack, the elements contained in the stack occupy positions 0, 1, . . . , `count` − 1 of the array.

PROGRAM 6.2
`StackAsArray` fields

```
1   public class StackAsArray
2       extends AbstractContainer
3       implements Stack
4   {
5       protected Object[] array;
6
7       // ...
8   }
```

Constructor and `purge` Methods

The definitions of the **StackAsArray** constructor and **purge** methods are given in Program 6.3. The constructor takes a single parameter, **size**, which specifies the maximum number of items that can be stored in the stack. The variable **array** is initialized to be an array of length **size**. The constructor requires $O(n)$ time to construct the array, where $n =$ **size**.

The purpose of the **purge** method is to remove all of the contents of a container. In this case, the objects in the stack occupy the first **count** positions of the array. To empty the stack, the **purge** method simply assigns the value **null** to the first **count** positions of the array. Clearly, the running time for the **purge** method is $O(n)$, where $n =$ **count**.

push, pop, and getTop Methods

Program 6.4 defines the **push**, **pop**, and **getTop**, methods of the **StackAsArray** class. The first of these, **push**, adds an element to the stack. It takes as its argument the **Object** to be pushed onto the stack.

The **push** method first checks to see if there is room left in the stack. If no room is left, it throws a **ContainerFullException** exception. Otherwise, it simply puts the object into the array, and then increases the **count** variable by one. In a correctly functioning program, stack overflow should not occur. If we assume that overflow does not occur, the running time of the **push** method is clearly $O(1)$.

The **pop** method removes an item from the stack and returns that item. The **pop** method first checks whether the stack is empty. If the stack is empty, it throws a **ContainerEmptyException** exception. Otherwise, it simply decreases **count**

PROGRAM 6.3
StackAsArray class constructor and **purge** methods

```
1   public class StackAsArray
2       extends AbstractContainer
3       implements Stack
4   {
5       protected Object[] array;
6
7       public StackAsArray (int size)
8           { array = new Object [size]; }
9
10      public void purge ()
11      {
12          while (count > 0)
13              array [--count] = null;
14      }
15      // ...
16  }
```

PROGRAM 6.4
StackAsArray class push, pop, and getTop methods

```
1  public class StackAsArray
2      extends AbstractContainer
3      implements Stack
4  {
5      protected Object[] array;
6
7      public void push (Object object)
8      {
9          if (count == array.length)
10             throw new ContainerFullException ();
11         array [count++] = object;
12     }
13
14     public Object pop ()
15     {
16         if (count == 0)
17             throw new ContainerEmptyException ();
18         Object result = array [--count];
19         array [count] = null;
20         return result;
21     }
22
23     public Object getTop ()
24     {
25         if (count == 0)
26             throw new ContainerEmptyException ();
27         return array [count - 1];
28     }
29     // ...
30 }
```

---

by one and returns the item found at the top of the stack. In a correctly functioning program, stack underflow will not occur normally. The running time of the **pop** method is $O(1)$.

Finally, the **getTop** method is a stack accessor that returns the top item in the stack. The **getTop** method does not modify the stack. In particular, it does *not* remove the top item from the stack. The **getTop** method first checks whether the stack is empty. If the stack is empty, it throws a **ContainerEmptyException** exception. Otherwise, it returns the top item, which is found at position **count** − 1 in the array. Assuming that stack underflow does not occur normally, the running time of the **getTop** method is $O(1)$.

accept Method

Program 6.5 defines the **accept** method for the **StackAsArray** class. As discussed in Chapter 5, the purpose of the **accept** method of a container is to accept a visitor and to cause it to visit one-by-one all of the contained objects.

The body of the **accept** method is simply a loop that calls the **visit** method for each object in the stack. The running time of the **accept** method depends on the running time of the **visit** method. Let $\mathcal{T}\langle\texttt{visit}\rangle$ be the running time of the **visit** method. In addition to the time for the method call, each iteration of the loop incurs a constant overhead. Consequently, the total running time for **accept** is $n\mathcal{T}\langle\texttt{visit}\rangle + O(n)$, where n is the number of objects in the container. And if $\mathcal{T}\langle\texttt{visit}\rangle = O(1)$, the total running time is $O(n)$.

getEnumeration Method

As discussed in Section 5.2.6, the **getEnumeration** method of a Container returns an **Enumeration**. An enumeration is meant to be used like this:

```
Stack stack = new StackAsArray (57);
stack.push (new Integer (3));
stack.push (new Integer (1));
stack.push (new Integer (4));
Enumeration e = stack.getEnumeration ();
while (e.hasMoreElements ())
{
    Object obj = e.nextElement ();
    System.out.println (obj);
}
```

PROGRAM 6.5
StackAsArray class accept method

```
1   public class StackAsArray
2       extends AbstractContainer
3       implements Stack
4   {
5       protected Object[] array;
6
7       public void accept (Visitor visitor)
8       {
9           for (int i = 0; i < count; ++i)
10          {
11              visitor.visit (array [i]);
12              if (visitor.isDone ())
13                  return;
14          }
15      }
16      // ...
17  }
```

PROGRAM 6.6
`StackAsArray` class `getEnumeration` method

```
1   public class StackAsArray
2       extends AbstractContainer
3       implements Stack
4   {
5       protected Object[] array;
6
7       public Enumeration getEnumeration ()
8       {
9           return new Enumeration ()
10          {
11              protected int position = 0;
12
13              public boolean hasMoreElements ()
14                  { return position < getCount (); }
15
16              public Object nextElement ()
17              {
18                  if (position >= getCount ())
19                      throw new NoSuchElementException ();
20                  return array [position++];
21              }
22          };
23      }
24      // ...
25  }
```

This code creates an instance of the **StackAsArray** class and assigns it to the variable **stack**. Next, several **Integer** objects are pushed onto the stack. Finally, an enumeration is used to systematically print out all of the objects in the stack.

Program 6.6 defines the **getEnumeration** method of the **StackAsArray** class. The **getEnumeration** method returns a new instance of an anonymous, inner class that implements the **Enumeration** interface (lines 9–22).

An *inner class* is a class that is defined inside another. Unless the inner class is declared to be **static**, each instance of an inner class can be thought of as existing inside an instance of the outer class. (Inner classes are non-**static** by default.) Because the inner class instance exists inside an outer class instance, it can directly invoke the methods of outer class instance and it can also access the fields of the outer class instance. In general, there can be more than one inner class instance inside a given outer class instance.

An *anonymous class* is a class that has no name. Anonymous classes are created by extending an existing class or implementing an interface right at the point in the code where the class is being instantiated.

In this case, the `Enumeration` interface is implemented by defining the field `position` (line 11) and the methods `hasMoreElements` (lines 13–14) and `nextElement` (lines 16–21). The `position` field is used in the enumeration to keep track of the position in the array of the next object to be enumerated.

The `hasMoreElements` method is called in the loop termination test of the `while` loop given above. The purpose of the `hasMoreElements` method is to determine whether there are still more objects in the stack to be enumerated. In Program 6.6 this is true as long as the field `position` is less than `count`. Clearly, the running time of `hasMoreElements` is $O(1)$.

The `nextElement` method returns the next object to be enumerated. It returns the appropriate object in the stack, provided that the value of the `position` variable is in the range between 0 and `count` − 1. Otherwise, it throws a `NoSuchElement-Exception` exception. Clearly, the running time of `nextElement` is also $O(1)$.

6.1.2 Linked-List Implementation

In this section we will examine a linked-list implementation of stacks that makes use of the `LinkedList` data structure developed in Chapter 4. Program 6.7 introduces the `StackAsLinkedList` class. The `StackAsLinkedList` class is a concrete class that extends the `AbstractContainer` class introduced in Program 5.9 and implements the `Stack` interface defined in Program 6.1.

Fields
The implementation of the `StackAsLinkedList` class makes use of one field—an instance of the `LinkedList` class called `list`. In addition, the `StackAsLinkedList` class inherits the `count` field from the `AbstractContainer` class. The list is used to keep track of the objects in the stack. As a result, there are as many elements in the linked list as there are objects in the stack.

Constructor and `purge` Methods
The definitions of the constructor and the `purge` methods of the `StackAsLinkedList` class are shown in Program 6.8. With a linked-list implementation, it is not necessary

---

PROGRAM 6.7
`StackAsLinkedList` fields

```
1   public class StackAsLinkedList
2       extends AbstractContainer
3       implements Stack
4   {
5       protected LinkedList list;
6
7       // ...
8   }
```

PROGRAM 6.8
StackAsLinkedList class constructor and purge methods

```
1   public class StackAsLinkedList
2       extends AbstractContainer
3       implements Stack
4   {
5       protected LinkedList list;
6
7       public StackAsLinkedList ()
8           { list = new LinkedList (); }
9
10      public void purge ()
11      {
12          list.purge ();
13          count = 0;
14      }
15      // ...
16  }
```

---

to preallocate storage space for the objects in the stack. Space is allocated dynamically and incrementally on the basis of demand.

The constructor simply creates an empty **LinkedList** and assigns it to the **list** field. Since an empty list can be created in constant time, the running time of the **StackAsLinkedList** constructor is $O(1)$.

The **purge** method of the **StackAsLinkedList** class simply calls the **purge** method of the **LinkedList** class. The **purge** method of the **LinkedList** class discards all the elements of the list in constant time. Consequently, the running time of the **purge** method is also $O(1)$.

push, pop, and getTop Methods

The **push**, **pop**, and **getTop** methods of the **StackAsLinkedList** class are defined in Program 6.9.

The implementation of **push** is trivial. It takes as its argument the **Object** to be pushed onto the stack and simply prepends that object to the linked list **list**. Then, one is added to the **count** variable. The running time of the **push** method is constant, since the **prepend** method has a constant running time, and updating the **count** only takes $O(1)$ time.

The **pop** method is implemented using two of the **LinkedList** methods——**get-First** and **extract**. The **getFirst** method is used to obtain the first item in the linked list. The method **getFirst** runs in constant time. The **extract** method is then called to extract the first item from the linked list. In the worst case, **extract** requires $O(n)$ time to extract an item from a linked list of length n. But the worst-case time arises only when it is the *last* element of the list that is to be extracted. In the case of the **pop** method, it is the *first* element that is extracted. This can be done in constant

PROGRAM 6.9
StackAsLinkedList class push, pop, and getTop methods

```
1   public class StackAsLinkedList
2       extends AbstractContainer
3       implements Stack
4   {
5       protected LinkedList list;
6
7       public void push (Object object)
8       {
9           list.prepend (object);
10          ++count;
11      }
12
13      public Object pop ()
14      {
15          if (count == 0)
16              throw new ContainerEmptyException ();
17          Object result = list.getFirst ();
18          list.extract (result);
19          --count;
20          return result;
21      }
22
23      public Object getTop ()
24      {
25          if (count == 0)
26              throw new ContainerEmptyException ();
27          return list.getFirst ();
28      }
29      // ...
30  }
```

time. Assuming that the exception that is raised when pop is called on an empty list does not occur, the running time for pop is O(1).

The definition of the getTop method is quite simple. It returns the first object in the linked list. Provided the linked list is not empty, the running time of getTop is $O(1)$. If the linked list is empty, the getTop method throws a ContainerEmptyException exception.

accept Method

The accept method of the StackAsLinkedList class is defined in Program 6.10. The accept method takes a visitor and calls its visit method one-by-one for all of the objects on the stack.

PROGRAM 6.10
StackAsLinkedList class accept method

```
1   public class StackAsLinkedList
2       extends AbstractContainer
3       implements Stack
4   {
5       protected LinkedList list;
6
7       public void accept (Visitor visitor)
8       {
9           for (LinkedList.Element ptr = list.getHead ();
10              ptr != null; ptr = ptr.getNext ())
11          {
12              visitor.visit (ptr.getDatum ());
13              if (visitor.isDone ())
14                  return;
15          }
16      }
17      // ...
18  }
```

The implementation of the **accept** method for the **StackAsLinkedList** class mirrors that of the **StackAsArray** class shown in Program 6.5. In this case, the linked list is traversed from front to back—that is, from the top of the stack to the bottom. As each element of the linked list is encountered, the **visit** method is called. If $\mathcal{T}\langle \text{visit} \rangle$ is the running time of the **visit** method, the total running time for **accept** is $n\mathcal{T}\langle \text{visit} \rangle + O(n)$, where $n = $ **count** is the number of objects in the container. If we assume that $\mathcal{T}\langle \text{visit} \rangle = O(1)$, the total running time is $O(n)$.

getEnumeration Method

Program 6.11 defines the **getEnumeration** method of the **StackAsLinkedList** class. The **getEnumeration** method returns a new instance of an anonymous, inner class that implements the **Enumeration** interface (lines 9–25).

In this case, the **Enumeration** interface is implemented by defining the field **position** (lines 11–12) and the methods **hasMoreElements** (lines 14–15) and **nextElement** (lines 17–24). The **position** field is used in the enumeration to keep track of the position in the linked list of the next object to be enumerated.

The purpose of the **hasMoreElements** method is to determine whether there are still more objects in the stack to be enumerated. In Program 6.11 this is true as long as the **position** is not **null**. Clearly, the running time of **hasMoreElements** is $O(1)$.

The **nextElement** method returns the next object to be enumerated. It returns the appropriate object in the linked list, provided that the value of the **position** variable is not **null**. Otherwise, it throws a **NoSuchElementException** exception. Clearly, the running time of **nextElement** is also $O(1)$.

PROGRAM 6.11
`StackAsLinkedList` class `getEnumeration` method

```
1  public class StackAsLinkedList
2      extends AbstractContainer
3      implements Stack
4  {
5      protected LinkedList list;
6
7      public Enumeration getEnumeration ()
8      {
9          return new Enumeration ()
10         {
11             protected LinkedList.Element position =
12                 list.getHead ();
13
14             public boolean hasMoreElements ()
15                 { return position != null; }
16
17             public Object nextElement ()
18             {
19                 if (position == null)
20                     throw new NoSuchElementException ();
21                 Object result = position.getDatum ();
22                 position = position.getNext ();
23                 return result;
24             }
25         };
26     }
27     // ...
28 }
```

6.1.3 Applications

Consider the following expression:

$$(5 + 9) \times 2 + 6 \times 5. \tag{6.1}$$

In order to determine the value of this expression, we first compute the sum $5 + 9$ and then multiply that by 2. Then we compute the product 6×5 and add it to the previous result to get the final answer. Notice that the order in which the operations are to be done is crucial. Clearly if the operations are not done in the correct order, the wrong result is computed.

The expression in (6.1) is written using the usual mathematical notation. This notation is called *infix* notation. What distinguishes this notation is the way that expressions involving binary operators are written. A *binary operator* is an operator that has exactly two operands, such as $+$ and $\times$. In infix notation, binary operators appear *in between* their operands.

Another characteristic of *infix* notation is that the order of operations is determined by *operator precedence*. For example, the $\times$ (multiplication) operator has higher precedence than does the $+$ (addition) operator. When an evaluation order is desired that is different from that provided by the precedence, *parentheses*, "(" and ")", are used to override precedence rules. An expression in parentheses is evaluated first.

As an alternative to infix, the Polish logician *Jan Lukasiewicz* introduced notations that require neither parentheses nor operator precedence rules. The first of these, the so-called *Polish notation*, places the binary operators before their operands. For the expression (6.1) we would write:

$$+ \times + 5\,9\,2 \times 6\,5.$$

This is also called *prefix* notation, because the operators are written in front of their operands.

Although prefix notation is completely unambiguous in the absence of parentheses, it is not very easy to read. A minor syntactic variation on prefix notation is to write the operands as a comma-separated list enclosed in parentheses as follows:

$$+(\times(+(5, 9), 2), \times(6, 5)).$$

Although this notation seems somewhat foreign, in fact it is precisely the notation that is used for static method calls in Java:

```
plus (times (plus (5,9) ,2), times (6,5));
```

The second form of Lukasiewicz notation is the so-called *Reverse-Polish notation* (RPN). Expression (6.1) is written as follows in RPN:

$$5\,9 + 2 \times 6\,5 \times +. \qquad (6.2)$$

This notation is also called *postfix* notation for the obvious reason— the operators are written *after* their operands.

Postfix notation, like prefix notation, does not make use of operator precedence nor does it require the use of parentheses. A postfix expression can always be written without parentheses to express the desired evaluation order. For example, the expression $1 + 2 \times 3$, in which the multiplication is done first, is written $1\,2\,3 \times +$; whereas the expression $(1 + 2) \times 3$ is written $1\,2 + 3 \times$.

Evaluating Postfix Expressions

One of the most useful characteristics of a postfix expression is that the value of such an expression can be computed easily with the aid of a stack of values. The components of a postfix expression are processed from left to right as follows:

1. If the next component of the expression is an operand, the value of the component is pushed onto the stack.

2. If the next component of the expression is an operator, then its operands are in the stack. The required number of operands are popped from the stack, the specified operation is performed, and the result is pushed back onto the stack.

After all the components of the expression have been processed in this fashion, the stack will contain a single result, which is the final value of the expression. Figure 6.3 illustrates the use of a stack to evaluate the RPN expression given in (6.2).

Implementation

Program 6.12 gives the implementation of a simple RPN calculator. The purpose of this example is to illustrate the use of the **Stack** class. The program shown accepts very simplified RPN expressions: The expression may contain only single-digit integers, the addition operator, **+**, and the multiplication operator, *****. In addition, the operator **=** pops the top value off the stack and prints it on the standard output stream. Furthermore, the calculator does its computation entirely with integers.

Notice that the **stack** variable of the **calculator** method may be any object that implements the **Stack** interface. Consequently, the calculator does not depend on the stack implementation used! For example, if we wish to use a stack implemented using an array, we can simply replace line 6 with the following:

```
Stack stack = new StackAsArray (10);
```

The running time of the **run** method depends on the number of symbols, operators, and operands in the expression being evaluated. If there are *n* symbols, the body of

---

FIGURE 6.3
Evaluating the RPN expression in (6.2) using a stack.

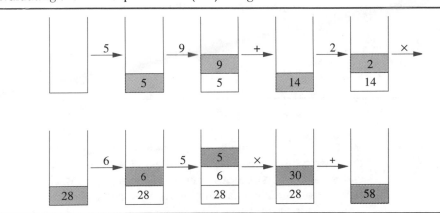

PROGRAM 6.12
Stack application—a single-digit, RPN calculator

```
1   public class Algorithms
2   {
3       public static void calculator (Reader in, PrintWriter out)
4           throws IOException
5       {
6           Stack stack = new StackAsLinkedList ();
7           int i;
8           while ((i = in.read ()) > 0)
9           {
10              char c = (char) i;
11              if (Character.isDigit (c))
12                  stack.push (new Int (
13                      Character.digit (c, 10)));
14              else if (c == '+')
15              {
16                  Int arg2 = (Int) stack.pop ();
17                  Int arg1 = (Int) stack.pop ();
18                  stack.push (new Int (
19                      arg1.intValue () + arg2.intValue ()));
20              }
21              else if (c == '*')
22              {
23                  Int arg2 = (Int) stack.pop ();
24                  Int arg1 = (Int) stack.pop ();
25                  stack.push (new Int (
26                      arg1.intValue () * arg2.intValue ()));
27              }
28              else if (c == '=')
29              {
30                  Int arg = (Int) stack.pop ();
31                  out.println (arg);
32              }
33          }
34      }
35  }
```

---

the **for** loop is executed n times. It should be fairly obvious that the amount of work done per symbol is constant, regardless of the type of symbol encountered. This is the case for both the **StackAsArray** and the **StackAsLinkedList** stack implementations. Therefore, the total running time needed to evaluate an expression comprised of n symbols is $O(n)$.

6.2 Queues

In the preceding section we saw that a stack comprises a pile of objects that can be accessed only at one end—the top. In this section we examine a similar data structure called a *single-ended queue*. Whereas in a stack we add and remove elements at the same end of the pile, in a single-ended queue we add elements at one end and remove them from the other. Since it is always the first item to be put into the queue that is the first item to be removed, a queue is a *first-in, first-out* or *FIFO* data structure. Figure 6.4 illustrates the basic queue operations.

Program 6.13 defines the **Queue** interface. The **Queue** interface extends the **Container** interface defined in Program 5.8. Hence, it comprises all the methods inherited from **Container** plus the three methods, **getHead**, **enqueue**, and **dequeue**. As we did with stacks, we examine two queue implementations—an array based one and a linked-list one.

6.2.1 Array Implementation

Program 6.14 introduces the **QueueAsArray** class. The **QueueAsArray** class is a concrete class that extends the **AbstractContainer** class introduced in Program 5.9 and implements the **Queue** interface defined in Program 6.13.

FIGURE 6.4
Basic queue operations.

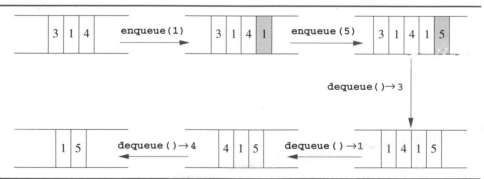

PROGRAM 6.13
Queue interface

```
1  public interface Queue
2      extends Container
3  {
4      Object getHead ();
5      void enqueue (Object object);
6      Object dequeue ();
7  }
```

PROGRAM 6.14
`QueueAsArray` fields

```
public class QueueAsArray
    extends AbstractContainer
    implements Queue
{
    protected Object[] array;
    protected int head;
    protected int tail;

    // ...
}
```

Fields

`QueueAsArray` objects comprise three fields—`array`, `head`, and `tail`. The first, `array`, is an array of `Object`s that is used to hold the contents of the queue. The objects contained in the queue will be held in a contiguous range of array elements as shown in Figure 6.5 (a). The fields `head` and `tail` denote the left and right ends, respectively, of this range.

FIGURE 6.5
Array implementation of a queue.

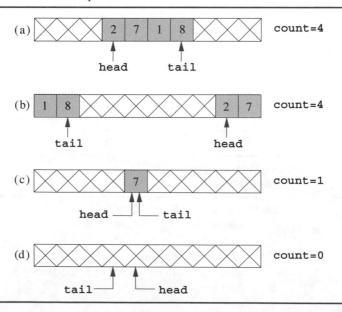

In general, the region of contiguous elements will not necessarily occupy the leftmost array positions. As elements are deleted at the head, the position of the left end will change. Similarly, as elements are added at the tail, the position of the right end will change. In some circumstances, the contiguous region of elements will wrap around the ends of the array as shown in Figure 6.5 (b).

As shown in Figure 6.5, the leftmost element is **array[head]** and the rightmost element is **array[tail]**. When the queue contains only one element, **head = tail** as shown in Figure 6.5 (c).

Finally, Figure 6.5(b) shows if the queue is empty, the **head** position will actually be to the right of the **tail** position. However, this is also the situation that arises when the queue is completely full! The problem is essentially this: Given an array of length n, then $0 \leq \mathbf{head} < n$ and $0 \leq \mathbf{tail} < n$. Therefore, the difference between the **head** and **tail** satisfies $0 \leq \mathbf{head} - \mathbf{tail} \leq n - 1$. Since there are only n distinct differences, there can be only n distinct queue lengths, $0, 1, \ldots, n - 1$. It is not possible to distinguish the queue that is empty from the queue that has n elements solely on the basis of the **head** and **tail** fields.

There are two options for dealing with this problem: The first is to limit the number of elements in the queue to be at most $n - 1$. The second is to use another field, **count**, to keep track explicitly of the actual number of elements in the queue rather than to infer the number from the **head** and **tail** variables. The second approach has been adopted in the implementation given next.

Constructor and purge Methods

The definitions of the **QueueAsArray** class constructor and **purge** methods are given in Program 6.15. The constructor takes a single parameter, **size**, which specifies the maximum number of items that can be stored in the queue. The constructor initializes the fields as follows: The **array** field is initialized to an array of length **size**, and the **head** and **tail** fields are initialized to represent the empty queue. The total running time for the **QueueAsArray** constructor is $O(n)$, where $n = \mathbf{size}$.

The purpose of the **purge** method is to remove all the contents of a container. In this case, the objects in the queue occupy contiguous array positions between **head** and **tail**. To empty the queue, the **purge** method walks through the occupied array positions, assigning to each one the value **null** as it goes. Clearly, the running time for the **purge** method is $O(n)$, where $n = \mathbf{count}$.

getHead, enqueue, and dequeue Methods

Program 6.16 defines the **getHead**, **enqueue**, and **dequeue** methods of the **Queue-AsArray** class.

The **getHead** method simply returns the object found at the head of the queue, having first checked to see that the queue is not empty. If the queue is empty, it throws a **ContainerEmptyException** exception. Under normal circumstances, we expect that the queue will not be empty. Therefore, the normal running time of this method is $O(1)$.

The **enqueue** method takes a single argument, which is the object to be added to the tail of the queue. The **enqueue** method first checks that the queue is not full—a

---

PROGRAM 6.15
QueueAsArray constructor and purge methods

```
1   public class QueueAsArray
2       extends AbstractContainer
3       implements Queue
4   {
5       protected Object[] array;
6       protected int head;
7       protected int tail;
8
9       public QueueAsArray (int size)
10      {
11          array = new Object [size];
12          head = 0;
13          tail = size - 1;
14      }
15
16      public void purge ()
17      {
18          while (count > 0)
19          {
20              array [head] = null;
21              if (++head == array.length)
22                  head = 0;
23              --count;
24          }
25      }
26      // ...
27  }
```

ContainerFullException exception is thrown when the queue is full. Next, the position at which to insert the new element is determined by increasing the tail field by one modulo the length of the array. Finally, the object to be enqueued is put into the array at the correct position and the count is adjusted accordingly. Under normal circumstances (i.e., when the exception is not thrown), the running time of enqueue is $O(1)$.

The dequeue method removes an object from the head of the queue and returns that object. First, it checks that the queue is not empty and throws an exception when it is. If the queue is not empty, the method first sets aside the object at the head in the local variable result, it increases the head field by one modulo the length of the array, adjusts the count accordingly, and returns result. All this can be done in a constant amount of time so the running time of dequeue is $O(1)$.

PROGRAM 6.16
QueueAsArray class getHead, enqueue, and dequeue methods

```
 1  public class QueueAsArray
 2      extends AbstractContainer
 3      implements Queue
 4  {
 5      protected Object[] array;
 6      protected int head;
 7      protected int tail;
 8
 9      public Object getHead ()
10      {
11          if (count == 0)
12              throw new ContainerEmptyException ();
13          return array [head];
14      }
15
16      public void enqueue (Object object)
17      {
18          if (count == array.length)
19              throw new ContainerFullException ();
20          if (++tail == array.length)
21              tail = 0;
22          array [tail] = object;
23          ++count;
24      }
25
26      public Object dequeue ()
27      {
28          if (count == 0)
29              throw new ContainerEmptyException ();
30          Object result = array [head];
31          array [head] = null;
32          if (++head == array.length)
33              head = 0;
34          --count;
35          return result;
36      }
37      // ...
38  }
```

6.2.2 Linked-List Implementation

This section presents a queue implementation that makes use of the singly-linked list data structure, `LinkedList`, that is defined in Chapter 4. Program 6.17 introduces the `QueueAsLinkedList` class. The `QueueAsLinkedList` extends the `AbstractContainer` class and implements the `Queue` interface.

Fields

Just like the `StackAsLinkedList` class, the implementation of the `QueueAsLinkedList` class requires only one field—`list`. The `list` field is an instance of the `LinkedList` class. It is used to keep track of the elements in the queue.

PROGRAM 6.17
`QueueAsLinkedList` fields

```
1   public class QueueAsLinkedList
2       extends AbstractContainer
3       implements Queue
4   {
5       protected LinkedList list;
6
7       // ...
8   }
```

PROGRAM 6.18
`QueueAsLinkedList` class constructor and `purge` methods

```
1   public class QueueAsLinkedList
2       extends AbstractContainer
3       implements Queue
4   {
5       protected LinkedList list;
6
7       public QueueAsLinkedList ()
8           { list = new LinkedList (); }
9
10      public void purge ()
11      {
12          list.purge ();
13          count = 0;
14      }
15      // ...
16  }
```

Constructor and purge Methods

Program 6.18 defines the QueueAsLinkedList constructor and purge methods. In the case of the linked-list implementation, it is not necessary to preallocate storage. The constructor simply initializes the list object as an empty list. The running time of the constructor is $O(1)$.

The purge method empties the queue by invoking the purge method provided by the LinkedList class and then sets the count field to zero. Since a linked list can be purged in constant time, the total running time for the purge method is $O(1)$.

getHead, enqueue, and dequeue Methods

The getHead, enqueue, and dequeue methods of the QueueAsLinkedList class are given in Program 6.19.

PROGRAM 6 19
QueueAsLinkedList class enqueue, getHead and dequeue methods

```
1   public class QueueAsLinkedList
2       extends AbstractContainer
3       implements Queue
4   {
5       protected LinkedList list;
6
7       public Object getHead ()
8       {
9           if (count == 0)
10              throw new ContainerEmptyException ();
11          return list.getFirst ();
12      }
13
14      public void enqueue (Object object)
15      {
16          list.append (object);
17          ++count;
18      }
19
20      public Object dequeue ()
21      {
22          if (count == 0)
23              throw new ContainerEmptyException ();
24          Object result = list.getFirst ();
25          list.extract (result);
26          --count;
27          return result;
28      }
29      // ...
30  }
```

The **getHead** method returns the object at the head of the queue. The head of the queue is in the first element of the linked list. In Chapter 4 we saw that the running time of **LinkedList.getFirst** is a constant. Therefore, the normal running time for the **getHead** method is $O(1)$.

The **enqueue** method takes a single argument—the object to be added to the tail of the queue. The method simply calls the **LinkedList.append** method. Since the running time for **append** is $O(1)$, the running time of **enqueue** is also $O(1)$.

The **dequeue** method removes an object from the head of the queue and returns that object. First, it verifies that the queue is not empty and throws an exception when it is. If the queue is not empty, **dequeue** saves the first item in the linked list in the local variable **result**. Then that item is extracted from the list. Using the **LinkedList** class from Chapter 4, the time required to extract the first item from a list is $O(1)$ regardless of the number of items in the list. As a result, the running time of **dequeue** is also $O(1)$.

6.2.3 Applications

The FIFO nature of queues makes them useful in certain algorithms. For example, we will see in Chapter 16 that a queue is an essential data structure for many different graph algorithms. In this section we illustrate the use of a queue in the *breadth-first traversal* of a tree.

Figure 6.6 shows an example of a tree. A tree is comprised of *nodes* (indicated by the circles) and *edges* (shown as arrows between nodes). We say that the edges point from the *parent* node to a *child* node. The *degree* of a node is equal to the number of children of that node. For example, node A in Figure 6.6 has degree three and its children are nodes B, C, and D. A child and all of its descendents is called a *subtree*.

One way to represent such a tree is to use a collection of linked structures. Consider the following interface definition, which is an abridged version of the **Tree** interface

FIGURE 6.6
A tree.

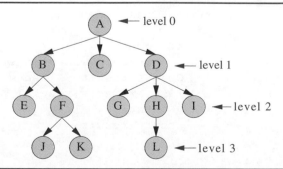

described in Chapter 9:

```
public interface Tree
{
    Object getKey ();
    int getDegree ();
    Tree getSubtree (int i);
}
```

Each node in a tree is represented by an object that implements the `Tree` interface. The `getKey()` method returns an object that represents the contents of the node. For example, in Figure 6.6, each node carries a one-character label, so the `getKey()` method would return a `Character` class instance that represents that label. The `getDegree` method returns the degree of the node, and the `getSubtree` method takes an `int` argument `i` and returns the corresponding child of that node.

One of the essential operations on a tree is a *tree traversal*. A traversal *visits* one-by-one all the nodes in a given tree. To *visit a node* means to perform some computation using the information contained in that node—for example, print the key. The standard tree traversals are discussed in Chapter 9. In this section we consider a traversal that is based on the levels of the nodes in the tree.

Each node in a tree has an associated level that arises from the position of that node in the tree. For example, node A in Figure 6.6 is at level 0, nodes B, C, and D are at level 1; and so on. A *breadth-first traversal* visits the nodes of a tree in the order of their levels. At each level, the nodes are visited from left to right. For this reason, it is sometimes also called a *level-order traversal*. The breadth-first traversal of the tree in Figure 6.6 visits the nodes from A to L in alphabetical order.

One way to implement a breadth-first traversal of a tree is to make use of a queue as follows: To begin the traversal, the root node of the tree is enqueued. Then, we repeat the following steps until the queue is empty:

1. Dequeue and visit the first node in the queue.
2. Enqueue its children in order from left to right.

Figure 6.7 illustrates the breadth-first traversal algorithm by showing the contents of the queue immediately prior to each iteration.

Implementation

Program 6.20 defines the method `breadthFirstTraversal`. This method has as its argument any object that implements the `Tree` interface. The idea is that the method passes a reference to the root of the tree that is to be traversed. The algorithm makes use of the `QueueAsLinkedList` data structure, which was defined in the preceding section, to hold the appropriate tree nodes.

The running time of the `breadthFirstTraversal` algorithm depends on the number of nodes in the tree that is being traversed. Each node of the tree is enqueued exactly once—this requires a constant amount of work. Furthermore, in each iteration

FIGURE 6.7
Queue contents during the breadth-first traversal of the tree in Figure 6.6.

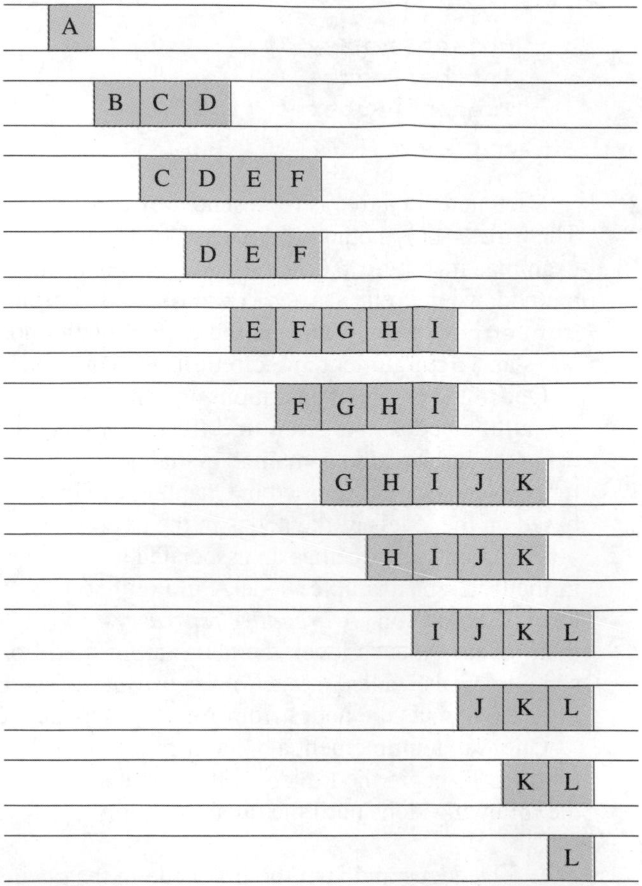

| A |

| B | C | D |

| C | D | E | F |

| D | E | F |

| E | F | G | H | I |

| F | G | H | I |

| G | H | I | J | K |

| H | I | J | K |

| I | J | K | L |

| J | K | L |

| K | L |

| L |

of the loop, each node is dequeued exactly once—again a constant amount of work. As a result, the running time of the `breadthFirstTraversal` algorithm is $O(n)$, where n is the number of nodes in the traversed tree.

6.3 Deques

In the preceding section we saw that a queue comprises a pile of objects into which we insert items at one end and from which we remove items at the other end. In this section we examine an extension of the queue, which provides a means to insert and

PROGRAM 6.20
Queue application—breadth-first tree traversal

```java
public class Algorithms
{
    public static void breadthFirstTraversal (Tree tree)
    {
        Queue queue = new QueueAsLinkedList ();
        if (!tree.isEmpty ())
            queue.enqueue (tree);
        while (!queue.isEmpty ())
        {
            Tree t = (Tree) queue.dequeue ();
            System.out.println (t.getKey ());
            for (int i = 0; i < t.getDegree (); ++i)
            {
                Tree subTree = t.getSubtree (i);
                if (!subTree.isEmpty ())
                    queue.enqueue (subTree);
            }
        }
    }
}
```

remove items at both ends of the pile. This data structure is a *deque*. The word *deque* is an acronym derived from *double-ended queue*.[1]

Figure 6.8 illustrates the basic deque operations. A deque provides three operations that access the head of the queue, `getHead`, `enqueueHead`, and `dequeueHead`,

FIGURE 6.8
Basic deque operations.

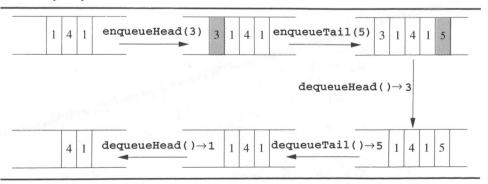

[1] The word *deque* is usually pronounced "deck" and sometimes "deek."

PROGRAM 6.21
Deque interface

```
1  public interface Deque
2      extends Container
3  {
4      Object getHead ();
5      Object getTail ();
6      void enqueueHead (Object object);
7      void enqueueTail (Object object);
8      Object dequeueHead ();
9      Object dequeueTail ();
10 }
```

---

and three operations to access the tail of the queue, `getTail`, `enqueueTail`, and `dequeueTail`.

Program 6.21 defines the `Deque` interface. The `Deque` interface extends the `Container` interface defined in Program 5.8. Hence, it comprises all of the methods inherited from `Container` plus the six methods, `getHead`, `enqueueHead`, `dequeueHead`, `getTail`, `enqueueTail`, and `dequeueTail`.

6.3.1 Array Implementation

Program 6.22 introduces an array implementation of a deque. The `DequeAsArray` class extends the `QueueAsArray` class introduced in Program 6.14 and implements the `Deque` interface defined in Program 6.21. The `QueueAsArray` class provides almost all the required functionality. Only five of the six methods introduced in the `Deque` interface need to be implemented.

The "Head" Methods

Program 6.22 defines the methods `enqueueHead` and `dequeueHead`. The latter is trivial to implement—it simply calls the `dequeue` method inherited from the `QueueAsArray` class.

The `enqueueHead` method takes a single argument, which is the object to be added to the head of the deque. The `enqueueHead` method first checks that the deque is not full—a `ContainerFullException` exception is thrown when the deque is full. Next, the position at which to insert the new element is determined by decreasing the `head` field by one modulo the length of the array. Finally, the object to be enqueued is put into the array at the correct position and the `count` is adjusted accordingly. Under normal circumstances (i.e., when the exception is not thrown), the running time of `enqueueHead` is $O(1)$.

The "Tail" Methods

Program 6.23 defines the `getTail`, `enqueueTail`, and `dequeueTail` methods of the `DequeAsArray` class.

PROGRAM 6.22
DequeAsArray class "Head" methods

```
1   public class DequeAsArray
2       extends QueueAsArray
3       implements Deque
4   {
5       public void enqueueHead (Object object)
6       {
7           if (count == array.length)
8               throw new ContainerFullException ();
9           if (head-- == 0)
10              head = array.length - 1;
11          array [head] = object;
12          ++count;
13      }
14
15      public Object dequeueHead ()
16          { return dequeue (); }
17      // ...
18  }
```

The getTail method simply returns the object found at the tail of the deque, having first checked to see that the deque is not empty. If the deque is empty, it throws a ContainerEmptyException exception. Under normal circumstances, we expect that the deque will not be empty. Therefore, the normal running time of this method is $O(1)$.

The enqueueTail method simply calls the enqueue method inherited from the QueueAsArray class. Its running time was shown to be $O(1)$.

The dequeueTail method removes an object from the tail of the deque and returns that object. First, it checks that the deque is not empty and throws an exception when it is. If the deque is not empty, the method sets aside the object at the tail in the local variable result, it decreases the tail field by one modulo the length of the array, adjusts the count accordingly and returns result. All this can be done in a constant amount of time, so the running time of dequeueTail is a constant.

6.3.2 Linked-List Implementation

Program 6.24 defines a linked-list implementation of a deque. The DequeAsLinked-List class extends the QueueAsLinkedList class introduced in Program 6.17 and implements the Deque interface defined in Program 6.21. The QueueAsLinkedList implementation provides almost all of the required functionality. Only five of the six methods defined in the Deque interface need to be implemented.

PROGRAM 6.23
DequeAsArray class "Tail" methods

```
1   public class DequeAsArray
2       extends QueueAsArray
3       implements Deque
4   {
5       public Object getTail ()
6       {
7           if (count == 0)
8               throw new ContainerEmptyException ();
9           return array [tail];
10      }
11
12      public void enqueueTail (Object object)
13          { enqueue (object); }
14
15      public Object dequeueTail ()
16      {
17          if (count == 0)
18              throw new ContainerEmptyException ();
19          Object result = array [tail];
20          array [tail] = null;
21          if (tail-- == 0)
22              tail = array.length - 1;
23          --count;
24          return result;
25      }
26      // ...
27  }
```

The "Head" Methods
Program 6.24 defines the methods enqueueHead and dequeueHead. The latter is trivial to implement—it simply calls the dequeue method inherited from the QueueAsLinkedList class.

The enqueueHead method takes a single argument—the object to be added to the head of the deque. The method simply calls the LinkedList.prepend method. Since the running time for prepend is $O(1)$, the running time of enqueueHead is also $O(1)$.

The "Tail" Methods
Program 6.25 defines the getTail, enqueueTail, and dequeueTail methods of the DequeAsArray class.

The getTail method returns the object at the tail of the deque. The tail of the deque is in the last element of the linked list. In Chapter 4 we saw that the running time

PROGRAM 6.24
DequeAsLinkedList class "Head" methods

```
1   public class DequeAsLinkedList
2       extends QueueAsLinkedList
3       implements Deque
4   {
5       public void enqueueHead (Object object)
6       {
7           list.prepend (object);
8           ++count;
9       }
10
11      public Object dequeueHead ()
12          { return dequeue (); }
13      // ...
14  }
```

PROGRAM 6.25
DequeAsLinkedList class "Tail" methods

```
1   public class DequeAsLinkedList
2       extends QueueAsLinkedList
3       implements Deque
4   {
5       public Object getTail ()
6       {
7           if (count == 0)
8               throw new ContainerEmptyException ();
9           return list.getLast ();
10      }
11
12      public void enqueueTail (Object object)
13          { enqueue (object); }
14
15      public Object dequeueTail ()
16      {
17          if (count == 0)
18              throw new ContainerEmptyException ();
19          Object result = list.getLast ();
20          list.extract (result);
21          --count;
22          return result;
23      }
24      // ...
25  }
```

of `LinkedList.getLast` is a constant. Therefore, the normal running time for the `getTail` method is $O(1)$.

The `enqueueTail` method simply calls the `enqueue` method inherited from the `QueueAsLinkedList` class. Its running time was shown to be $O(1)$.

The `dequeueTail` method removes an object from the tail of the deque and returns that object. First, it verifies that the deque is not empty and throws an exception when it is. If the deque is not empty, `dequeueTail` saves the last item in the linked list in the local variable `result`. Then that item is extracted from the linked list. When using the `LinkedList` class from Chapter 4, the time required to extract the last item from a list is $O(n)$, where $n =$ `count` is the number of items in the list. As a result, the running time of `dequeueTail` is $O(n)$.

6.3.3 Doubly-Linked and Circular Lists

In the preceding section we saw that the running time of `dequeueHead` is $O(1)$, but that the running time of `dequeueTail` is $O(n)$, for the linked-list implementation of a deque. This is because the linked-list data structure used, `LinkedList`, is a *singly-linked list*. Each element in a singly-linked list contains a single reference—a reference to the successor (next) element of the list. As a result, deleting the head of the linked list is easy: The new head is the successor of the old head.

However, deleting the tail of a linked list is not so easy: The new tail is the predecessor of the original tail. Since there is no reference from the original tail to its predecessor, the predecessor must be found by traversing the linked list from the head. This traversal gives rise to the $O(n)$ running time.

In a *doubly-linked list*, each list element contains two references—one to its successor and one to its predecessor. There are many different variations of doubly-linked lists: Figure 6.9 illustrates three of them.

Figure 6.9 (a) shows the simplest case: Two variables, say *head* and *tail*, are used to keep track of the list elements. One of them refers to the first element of the list, the other refers to the last. The first element of the list has no predecessor, therefore that reference is null. Similarly, the last element has no successor and the corresponding reference is also null. In effect, we have two overlapping, singly-linked lists that go in opposite directions. Figure 6.9 also shows the representation of an empty list. In this case the head and tail variables are both null.

A *circular, doubly-linked list* is shown in Figure 6.9 (b). A circular list is formed by making use of variables that would otherwise be null: The last element of the list is made the predecessor of the first element; the first element, the successor of the last. The upshot is that we no longer need both a head and a tail variable to keep track of the list. Even if only a single variable is used, both the first and the last list elements can be found in constant time.

Finally, Figure 6.9 (c) shows a circular, doubly-linked list that has a single sentinel. This variation is similar to the preceding one in that both the first and the last list elements can be found in constant time. This variation has the advantage that no special cases are required when dealing with an empty list. Figure 6.9 shows that the empty list is represented by a list with exactly one element—the sentinel. In the case of the empty list, the sentinel is both is own successor and predecessor. Since the sentinel is always

FIGURE 6.9
Doubly-linked and circular list variations.

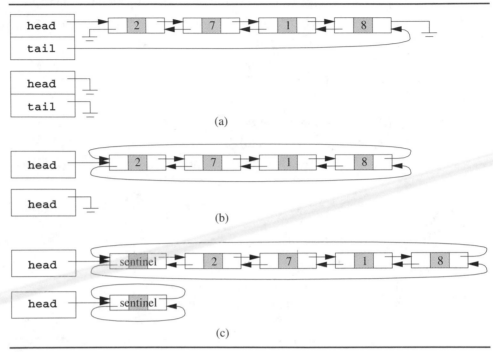

(a)

(b)

(c)

present, and since it always has both a successor and a predecessor, the code for adding elements to the empty list is identical to that for adding elements to a non-empty list.

Exercises

6.1 The array-based stack implementation introduced in Program 6.2 uses a fixed-length array. As a result, it is possible for the stack to become full.

  a. Rewrite the **push** method so that it doubles the length of the array when the array is full.

  b. Rewrite the **pop** method so that it halves the length of the array when the array is less than half full.

  c. Show that the *average* time for both push and pop operations is $O(1)$. **Hint**: Consider the running time required to push $n = 2^k$ items onto an empty stack, where $k \geq 0$.

6.2 Consider a sequence S of push and pop operations performed on a stack that is initially empty. The sequence S is a valid sequence of operations if at no point is a pop operation attempted on an empty stack and if the stack is empty at the end of the sequence. Design a set of rules for generating a valid sequence.

6.3 Devise an implementation of the *queue* abstract data type *using two stacks*. Give algorithms for the **enqueue** and **dequeue** operations, and derive tight big oh expressions for the running times of your implementation.

6.4 Write each of the following *infix* expressions in *postfix* notation:

a. $a + b \times c \div d$

b. $a + b \times (c \div d)$

c. $(a + b) \times c \div d$

d. $(a + b) \times (c \div d)$

e. $(a + b \times c) \div d$

f. $(c \div d) \times (a + b)$

6.5 Write each of the following *postfix* expressions in *infix* notation:

a. $w\, x\, y \div z \times -$

b. $w\, x\, y\, z \times \div -$

c. $w\, x - y \div z \times$

d. $w\, x - y\, z \times \div$

e. $w\, x\, y \div - z \times$

f. $y\, z \times w\, x - \div$

6.6 Devise an algorithm that translates a *postfix* expression to a *prefix* expression. **Hint**: Use a stack of strings.

6.7 The array-based queue implementation introduced in Program 6.14 uses a fixed-length array. As a result, it is possible for the queue to become full.

a. Rewrite the **enqueue** method so that it doubles the length of the array when the array is full.

b. Rewrite the **dequeue** method so that it halves the length of the array when the array is less than half full.

c. Show that the *average* time for both enqueue and dequeue operations is $O(1)$.

6.8 Stacks and queues can be viewed as special cases of deques. Show how all the operations on stacks and queues can be mapped to operations on a deque. Discuss the merits of using a deque to implement a stack or a queue.

6.9 Suppose we add a new operation to the stack ADT called **findMinimum** that returns a reference to the smallest element in the stack. Show that it is possible to provide an implementation for **findMinimum** that has a worst case running time of $O(1)$.

6.10 The *breadth-first traversal* method shown in Program 6.20 visits the nodes of a tree in the order of their levels in the tree. Modify the algorithm so that the nodes are visited in reverse. **Hint**: Use a stack.

Programming Projects

6.1 Enhance the functionality of the RPN calculator given in Program 6.12 in the following ways:

a. Use double-precision, floating-point arithmetic. That is, use the **Dbl** class defined in Program 5.6.

b. Provide the complete repertoire of basic operators: $+$, $-$, $\times$, and $\div$.

c. Add an exponentiation operator and a unary negation operator.

d. Add a *clear* method that empties the operand stack and a *print* method that prints out the contents of the operand stack.

6.2 Modify Program 6.12 so that it accepts expressions written in *prefix* (Polish) notation. **Hint**: See Exercise 6.6.

6.3 Write a program to convert a *postfix* expression to an *infix* expression using a stack. One way to do this is to modify the RPN calculator program given in Program 6.12 to use a stack of infix expressions. The expressions can be represented as instances of the **Str** class defined in Program 5.7. A binary operator should pop two strings from the stack and then push a string that is formed by concatenating the operator and its operands in the correct order. For example, suppose the operator is "*****" and the two strings popped from the stack are "**(b+c)**" and "**a**". Then the result that gets pushed onto the stack is the string "**a*(b+c)**".

6.4 Devise a scheme using a stack to convert an *infix* expression to a *postfix* expression. **Hint**: In a postfix expression operators appear *after* their operands, whereas in an infix expression they appear *between* their operands. Process the symbols in the prefix expression one-by-one. Output operands immediately, but save the operators in a stack until they are needed. Pay special attention to the precedence of the operators.

6.5 Modify your solution to Project 6.4 so that it immediately evaluates the infix expression. That is, create an **infixCalculator** method in the style of Program 6.12.

6.6 Consider a string of characters, S, comprised only of the characters (,), [,], {, and }. We say that S is balanced if it has one of the following forms:

- $S = " "$—that is S is the string of length zero,
- $S = "(T)"$,
- $S = "[T]"$,
- $S = "\{T\}"$,
- $S = "TU"$,

where both T and U are balanced strings. In other words, for every left parenthesis, bracket, or brace, there is a corresponding right parenthesis, bracket, or brace. For example, "**{()[()]}**" is balanced, but "**([)]**" is not. Write a program that uses a stack of characters to test whether a given string is balanced. (Use the **Chr** class defined in Program 5.4.)

6.7 Design and implement a **MultipleStack** class that provides $m \geq 1$ stacks in a single container. The declaration of the class should look something like this:

```
public class MultipleStack
    implements Container
{

    public MultipleStack (int numberOfStacks);
    public void push (Object object, int whichStack);
    public Object pop (int whichStack);
    // ...
}
```

- The constructor takes a single integer argument that specifies the number of stacks in the container.
- The **push** method takes two arguments. The first gives the object to be pushed and the second specifies the stack on which to push it.
- The **pop** method takes a single integer argument which specifies the stack to pop.

Choose one of the following implementation approaches:

a. Keep all of the stack elements in a single array.

b. Use an array of **Stack** objects.

c. Use a linked list of **Stack** objects.

6.8 Design and implement a class called **DequeAsDoublyLinkedList** that implements the **Deque** interface using a doubly-linked list. Select one of the approaches shown in Figure 6.9.

6.9 In Section 6.3, the **DequeAsArray** class extends the **QueueAsArray** class. This is the design paradigm known as *generalization*. The alternative paradigm is *specialization*, in which the **QueueAsArray** extends the **DequeAsArray** class. Redesign the **DequeAsArray** and **QueueAsArray** components of the class hierarchy using specialization.

6.10 Devise an approach for evaluating an arithmetic expression using a *queue* (rather than a stack). **Hint**: Transform the expression into a tree as shown in Figure 6.10 and then do a *breadth-first traversal* of the tree *in reverse* (see Exercise 6.10). For example, the expression $(a + b) \times (c - d)$ becomes $d\,c\,b\,a - + \times$. Evaluate the resulting sequence from left to right using a queue in the same way that a postfix expression is evaluated using a stack.

FIGURE 6.10
Expression tree for $(a + b) \times (c - d)$.

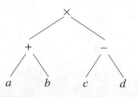

7 | Ordered Lists and Sorted Lists

The most simple, yet one of the most versatile containers is the *list*. In this chapter we consider lists as *abstract data types*. A list is a series of items. In general, we can insert and remove items from a list and we can visit all of the items in a list in the order in which they appear.

In this chapter we consider two kinds of lists—ordered lists and sorted lists. In an *ordered list* the order of the items is significant. Consider a list of the titles of the chapters in this book. The order of the items in the list corresponds to the order in which they appear in the book. However, since the chapter titles are not sorted alphabetically, we cannot consider the list to be sorted. Since it is possible to change the order of chapters in the book, we must be able to do the same with the items of the list. As a result, we may insert an item into an ordered list at any position.

On the other hand, a *sorted list* is one in which the order of the items is defined by some collating sequence. For example, the index of this book is a sorted list. The items in the index are sorted alphabetically. When an item is inserted into a sorted list, it must be inserted at the correct position.

As shown in Figure 7.1, two interfaces are used to represent the different list abstractions—**OrderedList** and **SortedList**. The various list abstractions can be implemented in many ways. In this chapter we examine implementations based on the *array* and the *linked list* foundational data structures presented in Chapter 4.

7.1 Ordered Lists

An *ordered list* is a list in which the order of the items is significant. However, the items in an ordered list are not necessarily *sorted*. Consequently, it is possible to *change* the order of items and still have a valid ordered list.

FIGURE 7.1
Object class hierarchy.

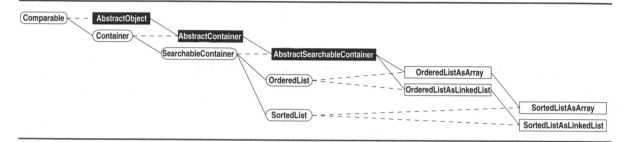

PROGRAM 7.1
`OrderedList` interface

```
1  public interface OrderedList
2      extends SearchableContainer
3  {
4      Comparable get (int i);
5      Cursor findPosition (Comparable object);
6  }
```

Program 7.1 defines the `OrderedList` interface. The `OrderedList` interface extends the `SearchableContainer` interface defined in Program 5.14. Recall that a searchable container is a container that supports the following additional operations:

   insert, used to put objects into the container;

   withdraw, used to remove objects from the container;

   find, used to locate objects in the container;

   isMember, used to test whether a given object instance is in the container.

The `OrderedList` interface adds the following methods:

   get used to access the object at a given position in the ordered list, and

   findPosition used to find the position of an object in the ordered list.

The `findPosition` method of the `List` interface takes a `Comparable` object and searches the list for an object that matches the given one. The return value is a `Cursor`. Program 7.2 defines the `Cursor` interface.

A cursor "remembers" the position of an item in a list. The Program 7.2 interface given in Program 7.2 defines the following methods:

PROGRAM 7.2
Cursor interface

```
1  public interface Cursor
2  {
3      Comparable getDatum ();
4      void insertAfter (Comparable object);
5      void insertBefore (Comparable object);
6      void withdraw ();
7  }
```

---

getDatum, used to access the object in the ordered list at the current cursor position;

insertAfter, used to insert an object into the ordered list after the current cursor position;

insertBefore, used to insert an object into the ordered list before the current cursor position; and

withdraw, used to remove from the ordered list the object at the current cursor position.

As we did in the previous chapter with stacks, queues, and deques, we will examine two ordered list implementations—an array-based one and a linked-list one. Section 7.1.1 presents an array version of ordered lists, and Section 7.1.2 gives an implementation using the **LinkedList** class.

7.1.1 Array Implementation

This section presents an array-based implementation of ordered lists. Program 7.3 introduces the **OrderedListAsArray** class. The **OrderedListAsArray** class extends the **AbstractSearchableContainer** class introduced in Program 5.15 and it implements the **OrderedList** interface defined in Program 7.1.

PROGRAM 7.3
OrderedListAsArray fields

```
1  public class OrderedListAsArray
2      extends AbstractSearchableContainer
3      implements OrderedList
4  {
5      protected Comparable[] array;
6
7      // ...
8  }
```

Fields

The `OrderedListAsArray` class comprises one field, `array`, which is an array of `Comparable` objects. In addition, the `OrderedListAsArray` class inherits the field `count` from `AbstractContainer`. The `array` variable is used to hold the items in the ordered list. Specifically, the items in the list are stored in array positions $0, 1, \ldots,$ `count` $- 1$. In an ordered list the position of an item is significant. The item at position 0 is the first item in the list; the item at position `count` $- 1$, is the last.

An item at position $i + 1$ is the *successor* of the one at position i. That is, the one at $i + 1$ *follows* or comes *after* the one at i. Similarly, an item at position i is the *predecessor* of the one at position $i + 1$; the one at position i is said to *precede* or to come *before* the one at $i + 1$.

Creating a List and Inserting Items

Program 7.4 gives the definitions of the constructor and the `insert` methods of the `OrderedListAsArray` class. The constructor takes a single argument, which specifies the length of array to use in the representation of the ordered list. Thus if we use an array-based implementation, we need to know when a list is declared what will be the maximum number of items in that list. The constructor initializes the `array` variable as an array with the specified length. The running time of the constructor is clearly $O(n)$, where $n =$ `size`.

The `insert` method is part of the interface of all searchable containers. Its purpose is to put an object into the container. The obvious question that arises is: Where should the inserted item be placed in the ordered list? The simple answer is: at the end.

PROGRAM 7.4
`OrderedListAsArray` class constructor and `insert` methods

```
1   public class OrderedListAsArray
2       extends AbstractSearchableContainer
3       implements OrderedList
4   {
5       protected Comparable[] array;
6
7       public OrderedListAsArray (int size)
8           { array = new Comparable [size]; }
9
10      public void insert (Comparable object)
11      {
12          if (count == array.length)
13              throw new ContainerFullException ();
14          array [count] = object;
15          ++count;
16      }
17      // ...
18  }
```

In Program 7.4 we see that the **insert** method simply adds the new item to the end of the list, provided there is still room in the array. Normally, the array will not be full, so the running time of this method is $O(1)$.

Finding Items in a List

Program 7.5 defines two **OrderedListAsArray** class methods, which search for an object in the ordered list. The **isMember** method tests whether a particular object instance is in the ordered list. The **find** method locates in the list an object that *matches* its argument.

The **isMember** method is a **boolean**-valued method that takes as its argument a **Comparable** object. This method compares the argument one-by-one with the contents of the **array**. Note that this method tests whether *a particular object instance* is contained in the ordered list. In the worst case, the object sought is not in the list. In this case, the running time of the method is $O(n)$, where $n = $ count is the number of items in the ordered list.

The **find** method also does a search of the ordered list. However, it uses the **isEQ** method to compare the items. Thus, the **find** method searches the list for an object that matches its argument. The **find** method returns the object found. If no match is

---

PROGRAM 7.5
OrderedListAsArray class isMember and find methods

```
1   public class OrderedListAsArray
2       extends AbstractSearchableContainer
3       implements OrderedList
4   {
5       protected Comparable[] array;
6
7       public boolean isMember (Comparable object)
8       {
9           for (int i = 0; i < count; ++i)
10              if (array [i] == object)
11                  return true;
12          return false;
13      }
14
15      public Comparable find (Comparable arg)
16      {
17          for (int i = 0; i < count; ++i)
18              if (array [i].isEQ (arg))
19                  return array [i];
20          return null;
21      }
22      // ...
23  }
```

found, it returns `null`. The running time of this method depends on the time required for the comparison operator, $\mathcal{T}\langle isEQ \rangle$. In the worst case, the object sought is not in the list. In this case the running time is $n \times \mathcal{T}\langle isEQ \rangle + O(n)$. For simplicity, we will assume that the comparison takes a constant amount of time. Hence, the running time of the method is also $O(n)$, where $n = $ `count` is the number of items in the list.

It is important to understand the subtle distinction between the search done by the `isMember` method and that done by `find`. The `isMember` method searches for a specific object instance, whereas `find` simply looks for a matching object. Consider the following:

```
Comparable object1 = new Int (57);
Comparable object2 = new Int (57);
List list = new OrderedListAsArray (1);
list.insert (object1);
```

This code fragment creates two `Int` class object instances, both of which have the value 57. Only the first object, `object1`, is inserted into the ordered list `list`. Consequently, the method call

```
list.isMember (object1)
```

returns `true`; whereas the method call

```
list.isMember (object2)
```

returns `false`.

On the other hand, if a search is done using the `find` method like this:

```
Comparable object3 = list.find (object2);
```

the search will be successful! After the call, `object3` and `object1` refer to the same object.

Removing Items from a List

Objects are removed from a searchable container using the `withdraw` method. Program 7.6 defines the `withdraw` method for the `OrderedListAsArray` class. This method takes a single argument which is the object to be removed from the container. It is the specific object instance that is removed from the container, not simply one that matches (i.e., compares equal to) the argument.

The withdraw method first needs to find the position of the item to be removed from the list. This part is identical to the main loop of the `isMember` method. An exception is thrown if the list is empty or if the object to be removed is not in the list. The number of iterations needed to find an object depends on its position. If the object to be removed is found at position i, then the search phase takes $O(i)$ time.

Removing an object from position i of an ordered list that is stored in an array requires that all of the objects at positions $i + 1, i + 2, \ldots,$ `count` $- 1$, be moved one position to

PROGRAM 7.6
OrderedListAsArray class withdraw method

```
1  public class OrderedListAsArray
2      extends AbstractSearchableContainer
3      implements OrderedList
4  {
5      protected Comparable[] array;
6
7      public void withdraw (Comparable object)
8      {
9          if (count == 0)
10             throw new ContainerEmptyException ();
11         int i = 0;
12         while (i < count && array [i] != object)
13             ++i;
14         if (i == count)
15             throw new IllegalArgumentException (
16                 "object not found");
17         for ( ; i < count - 1; ++i)
18             array [i] = array [i + 1];
19         array [i] = null;
20         --count;
21     }
22     // ...
23 }
```

the left. Altogether, count $- 1 - i$ objects need to be moved. Hence, this phase takes $O(\text{count} - i)$ time.

The running time of the withdraw method is the sum of the running times of the two phases, $O(i)+O(\text{count} - i)$. Hence, the total running time is $O(n)$, where $n = \text{count}$ is the number of items in the ordered list.

Care must be taken when using the withdraw method. Consider the following:

```
Comparable object1 = new Int (57);
Comparable object2 = new Int (57);
List list = new OrderedListAsArray (1);
list.insert (object1);
```

To remove object1 from the ordered list, we may write

```
list.withdraw (object1);
```

However, the call

```
list.withdraw (object2);
```

PROGRAM 7.7
`OrderedListAsArray.MyCursor` class

```
1   public class OrderedListAsArray
2       extends AbstractSearchableContainer
3       implements OrderedList
4   {
5       protected Comparable[] array;
6
7       protected class MyCursor
8           implements Cursor
9       {
10          int offset;
11
12          MyCursor (int offset)
13              { this.offset = offset; }
14
15          public Comparable getDatum ()
16          {
17              if (offset < 0 || offset >= count)
18                  throw new IndexOutOfBoundsException ();
19              return array [offset];
20          }
21          // ...
22      }
23      // ...
24  }
```

---

will fail because `object2` is not actually in the list. If for some reason we have lost track of `object1`, we can always write:

```
list.withdraw (list.find (object2));
```

which first locates the object in the ordered list (`object1`) that matches `object2` and then deletes that object.

Positions of Items in a List

As shown in Program 7.2, objects that implement the `Cursor` interface can be used to access, insert, and delete objects in an ordered list. Program 7.7 defines an *inner class* called `OrderedListAsArray.MyCursor` that implements the `Cursor` interface. The idea is that instances of this inner class are used by the `OrderedListAsArray` class to represent the abstraction of a *position* in an ordered list.

The `MyCursor` class has a single field, `offset`, that is used to record an offset in the array of objects. A single constructor is provided that simply assigns a given value to the `offset` field. Program 7.7 also defines the `getDatum` method of the `MyCursor` class.

PROGRAM 7.8
`OrderedListAsArray` class `findPosition` and `get` methods

```
1   public class OrderedListAsArray
2       extends AbstractSearchableContainer
3       implements OrderedList
4   {
5       protected Comparable[] array;
6
7       public Cursor findPosition (Comparable object)
8       {
9           int i = 0;
10          while (i < count && array [i].isNE (object))
11              ++i;
12          return new MyCursor (i);
13      }
14
15      public Comparable get (int offset)
16      {
17          if (offset < 0 || offset >= count)
18              throw new IndexOutOfBoundsException ();
19          return array [offset];
20      }
21      // ...
22  }
```

This method simply returns the item in the array at the position record in the offset field, provided that position is valid. The running time of the `getDatum` method is simply $O(1)$.

Finding the Position of an Item and Accessing by Position

Program 7.8 defines two more methods of the `OrderedListAsArray` class, `find-Position` and `get`. The `findPosition` method takes as its argument a `Comparable` object. The purpose of this method is to search the ordered list for an item that matches the object, and to return its position in the form of an object that implements the `Cursor` interface. In this case, the result is an instance of the `MyCursor` inner class.

The search algorithm used in `findPosition` is identical to that used in the `find` method (Program 7.5). The `findPosition` uses the `isEQ` method to locate a contained object that is equal to the search target. Note that if no match is found, the `offset` is set to the value `count`, which is one position to the right of the last item in the ordered list. The running time of `findPosition` is identical to that of `find`: $n \times \mathcal{T}\langle\text{isEQ}\rangle + O(n)$, where $n = $ `count`.

The `get` method defined in Program 7.8 takes an `int` argument and returns the object in the ordered list at the specified position. In this case, the position is specified using an integer-valued subscript expression. The implementation of this method is

FIGURE 7.2
Inserting an item in an ordered list implemented as an array.

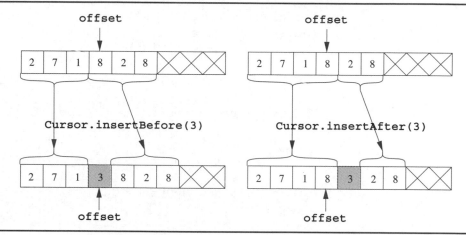

trivial—it simply indexes into the array. Assuming the specified offset is valid, the running time of this method is $O(1)$.

Inserting an Item at an Arbitrary Position

Two methods for inserting an item at an arbitrary position in an ordered list are declared in Program 7.2—**insertBefore** and **insertAfter**. Both of these take one argument—a **Comparable** object. The effects of these two methods are illustrated in Figure 7.2.

Figure 7.2 shows that in both cases a number of items to the right of the insertion point need to be moved over to make room for the item that is being inserted into the ordered list. In the case of **insertBefore**, items to the right *including the item at the point of insertion* are moved; for **insertAfter**, only items to the right of the point of insertion are moved, and the new item is inserted in the array location following the insertion point.

Program 7.9 gives the implementation of the **insertAfter** method for the **OrderedListAsArray.MyCursor** class. The code for the **insertBefore** method is identical except for one line as explained next.

The **insertAfter** method takes one argument—a **Comparable** object. The method begins by performing some simple tests to ensure that the position is valid and that there is room left in the array to do the insertion.

On line 19 the array index where the new item will ultimately be stored is computed. For **insertAfter** the index is **offset** + 1, as shown in Program 7.9. In the case of **insertBefore**, the value required is simply **offset**. The loop on lines 21–22 moves items over and then the object being inserted is put in the array on line 23.

If we assume that no exceptions are thrown, the running time of **insertAfter** is dominated by the loop that moves list items. In the worst case, all items in the array need to be moved. Thus, the running time of both the **insertAfter** and **insertBefore** method is $O(n)$, where n = **count**.

PROGRAM 7.9
OrderedListAsArray.MyCursor class insertAfter method

```
1   public class OrderedListAsArray
2       extends AbstractSearchableContainer
3       implements OrderedList
4   {
5       protected Comparable[] array;
6
7       protected class MyCursor
8           implements Cursor
9       {
10          int offset;
11
12          public void insertAfter (Comparable object)
13          {
14              if (offset < 0 || offset >= count)
15                  throw new IndexOutOfBoundsException ();
16              if (count == array.length)
17                  throw new ContainerFullException ();
18
19              int insertPosition = offset + 1;
20
21              for (int i = count; i > insertPosition; --i)
22                  array [i] = array [i - 1];
23              array [insertPosition] = object;
24              ++count;
25          }
26          // ...
27      }
28      // ...
29  }
```

Removing Arbitrary Items by Position

The final method of the OrderedListAsArray.MyCursor class that we will consider is the withdraw method. The desired effect of this method is to remove from the ordered list the item at the position specified by the cursor.

Figure 7.3 shows the way to delete an item from an ordered list that is implemented with an array. All of the items remaining in the list to the right of the deleted item need to be shifted to the left in the array by one position.

Program 7.10 gives the implementation of the withdraw method. After checking the validity of the position, all of the items following the item to be withdrawn are moved one position to the left in the array.

The running time of the withdraw method depends on the position in the array of the item being deleted and on the number of items in the ordered lists. In the worst case,

---

FIGURE 7.3
Withdrawing an item from an ordered list implemented as an array.

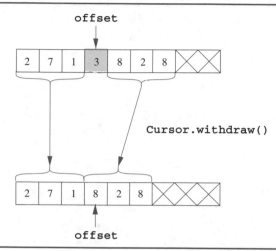

---

the item to be deleted is in the first position. In this case, the work required to move the remaining items left is $O(n)$, where $n = $ count.

7.1.2 Linked-List Implementation

This section presents a linked-list implementation of ordered lists. Program 7.11 introduces the **OrderedListAsLinkedList** class. The **OrderedListAsLinkedList** class extends the **AbstractSearchableContainer** class introduced in Program 5.15 and it implements the **OrderedList** interface defined in Program 7.1.

Fields
Objects of the **OrderedListAsLinkedList** class contain one field, **linkedList**, which is a linked list of **Comparable** objects. The **linkedList** is used to hold the items in the ordered list. Since a linked list is used, there is no notion of an inherent limit on the number of items that can be placed in the ordered list. Items can be inserted until the available memory is exhausted.

Inserting and Accessing Items in a List
Program 7.12 gives the code for the constructor, **insert**, and **get** methods of the **OrderedListAsLinkedList** class. The constructor simply creates an empty linked list. Clearly, the running time of the constructor is $O(1)$.

The **insert** method takes a **Comparable** object and adds it to the ordered list. As in the case of the **ArrayAsLinkedList** class, the object is added at the end of the ordered list. This is done simply by calling the **append** method from the **LinkedList** class.

PROGRAM 7.10
`OrderedListAsArray.MyCursor` class `withdraw` method

```
1   public class OrderedListAsArray
2       extends AbstractSearchableContainer
3       implements OrderedList
4   {
5       protected Comparable[] array;
6
7       protected class MyCursor
8           implements Cursor
9       {
10          int offset;
11
12          public void withdraw ()
13          {
14              if (offset < 0 || offset >= count)
15                  throw new IndexOutOfBoundsException ();
16              if (count == 0)
17                  throw new ContainerEmptyException ();
18
19              int i = offset;
20              while (i < count - 1)
21              {
22                  array [i] = array [i + 1];
23                  ++i;
24              }
25              array [i] = null;
26              --count;
27          }
28          // ...
29      }
30      // ...
31  }
```

PROGRAM 7.11
`OrderedListAsLinkedList` fields

```
1   public class OrderedListAsLinkedList
2       extends AbstractSearchableContainer
3       implements OrderedList
4   {
5       protected LinkedList linkedList;
6
7       // ...
8   }
```

PROGRAM 7.12
OrderedListAsLinkedList class constructor, insert, and get methods

```
1   public class OrderedListAsLinkedList
2       extends AbstractSearchableContainer
3       implements OrderedList
4   {
5       protected LinkedList linkedList;
6
7       public OrderedListAsLinkedList ()
8           { linkedList = new LinkedList (); }
9
10      public void insert (Comparable object)
11      {
12          linkedList.append (object);
13          ++count;
14      }
15
16      public Comparable get (int offset)
17      {
18          if (offset < 0 || offset >= count)
19              throw new IndexOutOfBoundsException ();
20
21          LinkedList.Element ptr = linkedList.getHead ();
22          for (int i = 0; i < offset && ptr != null; ++i)
23              ptr = ptr.getNext ();
24          return (Comparable) ptr.getDatum ();
25      }
26      // ...
27  }
```

The running time of the **insert** method is determined by that of **append**. In Chapter 4 this was shown to be $O(1)$. The only other work done by the **insert** method is to add one to the **count** variable. Consequently, the total running time for **insert** is $O(1)$.

Program 7.12 also defines the **get** method, which takes an argument of type **int**. This method is used to access elements of the ordered list by their position in the list. In this case, the position is specified by a non-negative, integer-valued index. Since there is no way to access directly the ith element of linked list, the implementation of this method comprises a loop, which traverses the list to find the ith item. The method returns a reference to the ith item, provided $0 \leq i < $ **count**. Otherwise, i is not a valid subscript value and the method throws an exception.

The running time of the **get** method depends on the number of items in the list and on the value of the subscript expression. In the worst case, the item sought is at the end of the ordered list. Therefore, the worst-case running time of this algorithm, assuming the subscript expression is valid, is $O(n)$, where $n = $ **count**.

PROGRAM 7.13
OrderedListAsLinkedList class isMember and find methods

```
1   public class OrderedListAsLinkedList
2       extends AbstractSearchableContainer
3       implements OrderedList
4   {
5       protected LinkedList linkedList;
6
7       public boolean isMember (Comparable object)
8       {
9           for (LinkedList.Element ptr = linkedList.getHead ();
10                  ptr != null; ptr = ptr.getNext ())
11          {
12              if ((Comparable) ptr.getDatum () == object)
13                  return true;
14          }
15          return false;
16      }
17
18      public Comparable find (Comparable arg)
19      {
20          for (LinkedList.Element ptr = linkedList.getHead ();
21              ptr != null; ptr = ptr.getNext ())
22          {
23              Comparable object = (Comparable) ptr.getDatum ();
24              if (object.isEQ (arg))
25                  return object;
26          }
27          return null;
28      }
29      // ...
30  }
```

Finding Items in a List

Program 7.13 defines the **isMember** and **find** methods of the **ListAsLinkedList** class. The implementations of these methods are almost identical. However, they differ in two key aspects—the comparison used and the return value.

The **isMember** method tests whether a particular object instance is contained in the ordered list. It returns a **boolean** value indicating whether the object is present. The running time of this method is clearly $O(n)$, where $n =$ **count**, the number of items in the ordered list.

The **find** method locates an object that matches a given object. The match is determined by using the **isEQ** method. **find** returns a reference to the matching object if one is found. Otherwise, it returns the **null** value. The running time for this method

---

PROGRAM 7.14
OrderedListAsLinkedList class withdraw method

```
1   public class OrderedListAsLinkedList
2       extends AbstractSearchableContainer
3       implements OrderedList
4   {
5       protected LinkedList linkedList;
6
7       public void withdraw (Comparable object)
8       {
9           if (count == 0)
10              throw new ContainerEmptyException ();
11          linkedList.extract (object);
12          --count;
13      }
14      // ...
15  }
```

---

is $n \times \mathcal{T}\langle \texttt{isEQ} \rangle + O(n)$, where $\mathcal{T}\langle \texttt{isEQ} \rangle$ is the time required to do the comparison, and $n = \texttt{count}$ is the number of items in the ordered list. This simplifies to $O(n)$ when the comparison can be done in constant time.

Removing Items from a List

The withdraw method is used to remove a specific object instance from an ordered list. The implementation of the withdraw method for the OrderedListAsLinkedList class is given in Program 7.14.

The implementation of withdraw is straightforward: It simply calls the extract method provided by the LinkedList class to remove the specified object from linkedList. The running time of the withdraw method is dominated by that of extract, which was shown in Chapter 4 to be $O(n)$, where n is the number of items in the linked list.

Positions of Items in a List

Program 7.15 gives the definition of the OrderedListAsLinkedList.MyCursor inner class. The MyCursor class implements the Cursor interface defined in Program 7.2. The purpose of this class is to record the position of an item in an ordered list implemented as a linked list.

The MyCursor class has one field, element, which refers to the linked-list element in which a given item appears. Notice that this version of MyCursor is fundamentally different from the array version. In the array version, the position was specified by an offset, that is, by an *ordinal number* that shows the position of the item in the ordered sequence. In the linked-list version, the position is specified by a reference to the element of the linked list in which the item is stored. Regardless of the implementation, both kinds of position provide exactly the same functionality because they both implement the Cursor interface.

PROGRAM 7.15
OrderedListAsLinkedList.MyCursor class

```
1  public class OrderedListAsLinkedList
2      extends AbstractSearchableContainer
3      implements OrderedList
4  {
5      protected LinkedList linkedList;
6
7      protected class MyCursor
8          implements Cursor
9      {
10         LinkedList.Element element;
11
12         MyCursor (LinkedList.Element element)
13             { this.element = element; }
14
15         public Comparable getDatum ()
16             { return (Comparable) element.getDatum (); }
17         // ...
18     }
19     // ...
20 }
```

The getDatum method of the OrderedListAsLinkedList.MyCursor class is also defined in Program 7.15. This method simply dereferences the element field to obtain the required item in the ordered list. The running time is clearly $O(1)$.

Finding the Position of an Item and Accessing by Position

The findPosition method of the OrderedListAsLinkedList class is used to determine the position of an item in an ordered list implemented as a linked list. Its result is an instance of the inner class MyCursor. The findPosition method is defined in Program 7.16.

The findPosition method takes as its argument a Comparable object that is the target of the search. The search algorithm used by findPosition is identical to that of find, which is given in Program 7.13. Consequently, the running time is the same: $n \times \mathcal{T}\langle\text{isEQ}\rangle + O(n)$, where $\mathcal{T}\langle\text{isEQ}\rangle$ is the time required to match two Comparable objects, and $n = \text{count}$ is the number of items in the ordered list.

Inserting an Item at an Arbitrary Position

Once having determined the position of an item in an ordered list, we can make use of that position to insert items into the middle of the list. Two methods are specifically provided for this purpose—insertAfter and insertBefore. Both of these take a single argument—the Comparable object to be inserted into the list.

Program 7.17 gives the implementation for the insertAfter method of the OrderedListAsLinkedList.MyCursor class. This method simply calls the

---

PROGRAM 7.16
`OrderedListAsLinkedList` class `findPosition` method

```
 1   public class OrderedListAsLinkedList
 2       extends AbstractSearchableContainer
 3       implements OrderedList
 4   {
 5       protected LinkedList linkedList;
 6
 7       public Cursor findPosition (Comparable arg)
 8       {
 9           LinkedList.Element ptr;
10           for (ptr = linkedList.getHead ();
11               ptr != null; ptr = ptr.getNext ())
12           {
13               Comparable object = (Comparable) ptr.getDatum ();
14               if (object.isEQ (arg))
15                   break;
16           }
17           return new MyCursor (ptr);
18       }
19       // ...
20   }
```

`insertAfter` method provided by the `LinkedList` class. Assuming no exceptions are thrown, the running time for this method is $O(1)$.

The implementation of `insertBefore` is not shown—its similarity with `insert-After` should be obvious. Since it must call the `insertBefore` method provided by the `LinkedList` class, we expect the worst-case running time to be $O(n)$, where $n =$ count.

Removing Arbitrary Items by Position

The final method to be considered is the `withdraw` method of the `OrderedListAs-LinkedList.MyCursor` class. This method removes an arbitrary item from an ordered list, where the position of that item is specified by a cursor instance. The code for the `withdraw` method is given in Program 7.18.

The item in the linked list at the position specified by the cursor is removed by calling the `extract` method provided by the `LinkedList` class. The running time of the `withdraw` method depends on the running time of the `extract` of the `LinkedList` class. The latter was shown to be $O(n)$, where n is the number of items in the linked list. Consequently, the total running time is $O(n)$.

7.1.3 Performance Comparison: `OrderedListAsArray` vs. `OrderedListAsLinkedList`

The running times calculated for the various methods of the two ordered list implementations, `OrderedListAsArray` and `OrderedListAsLinkedList`, are

---

PROGRAM 7.17
`OrderedListAsLinkedList.MyCursor` class `insertAfter` method.

```
1   public class OrderedListAsLinkedList
2       extends AbstractSearchableContainer
3       implements OrderedList
4   {
5       protected LinkedList linkedList;
6
7       protected class MyCursor
8           implements Cursor
9       {
10          LinkedList.Element element;
11
12          public void insertAfter (Comparable object)
13          {
14              element.insertAfter (object);
15              ++count;
16          }
17          // ...
18      }
19      // ...
20  }
```

---

summarized in Table 7.1. With the exception of two methods, the running times of the two implementations are asymptotically identical.

The two differences are the `get` method and the `insertAfter` method. The subscripting operation can be done in constant time when using an array, but it requires $O(n)$ in a linked list. Conversely, `insertAfter` requires $O(n)$ time when using an array, but can be done in constant time in the singly-linked list.

Table 7.1 does not tell the whole story. The other important difference between the two implementations is the amount of space required. Consider first the array implementation, `OrderedListAsArray`. The storage required for an array was discussed in Chapter 4. Using that result, the storage needed for an `OrderedListAsArray` that can hold *at most M* `Comparable` objects is given by

$$\text{sizeof(count)} + \text{sizeof(array)} + \text{sizeof(Comparable}[M]) =$$
$$2\text{sizeof(int)} + \text{sizeof(array ref)} + M\text{sizeof(Comparable ref)}.$$

Notice that we do not include in this calculation that space required for the objects themselves. Since we cannot know the types of the contained objects, we cannot calculate the space required by those objects.

A similar calculation can also be done for the `OrderedListAsLinkedList` class. In this case, we assume that the actual number of contained objects is n. The total storage

---

PROGRAM 7.18
OrderedListAsLinkedList.MyCursor class withdraw method

```
 1   public class OrderedListAsLinkedList
 2       extends AbstractSearchableContainer
 3       implements OrderedList
 4   {
 5       protected LinkedList linkedList;
 6
 7       protected class MyCursor
 8           implements Cursor
 9       {
10           LinkedList.Element element;
11
12           public void withdraw ()
13           {
14               linkedList.extract (element.getDatum ());
15               --count;
16           }
17           // ...
18       }
19       // ...
20   }
```

TABLE 7.1
Running Times of Operations on Ordered Lists

	Ordered List Implementation		
Method	OrderedListAsArray		OrderedListAsLinkedList
insert	$O(1)$		$O(1)$
isMember	$O(n)$		$O(n)$
find	$O(n)$		$O(n)$
withdraw	$O(n)$		$O(n)$
get	$O(1)$	$\neq$	$O(n)$
findPosition	$O(n)$		$O(n)$
Cursor.getDatum	$O(1)$		$O(1)$
Cursor.insertAfter	$O(n)$	$\neq$	$O(1)$
Cursor.insertBefore	$O(n)$		$O(n)$
Cursor.withdraw	$O(n)$		$O(n)$

$1x + 59x^2$ can be represented by the

$+ 1$. Clearly, there are only two non-
tage of using the sequence of ordered
omit from the sequence those pairs
lynomial $x^{100} + 1$ by the sequence

als, we can consider various opera-
al

ems) =

.Element ref).

bytes each, the storage
$12 + 4M$ bytes; and for
s, the storage needed for
length of the ordered list;
on is $O(n)$, where n is the
o expressions, we get that
$n < (M - 1)/2$, the array
the linked-list version uses

ifferentiating each of the terms to

d be considered when choos-
er the implications of the ex-
res a priori knowledge of the
. The total amount of storage
On the other hand, the linked-
is only constrained by the total
ore, the amount of memory used
ecution. We do not have to com-
rogram.

sequences, if $p(x)$ is represented

.., $(a_n, n)\}$,

ad. In this section we will consider
polynomial. In general, an nth-order
e form

$$x^2 + \cdots + a_n x^n,$$

.., $(na_n, n - 1)\}$.

erentiate a polynomial that is

the ith power of x. We will assume that

ynomial consists of a sequence of ordered

nt by the exponent, and then

nost $n + 1$ ordered pairs, and
ed pair, this is inherently an

$, 2), \ldots, (a_n, n)\}$.

differentiation will depend
d. We will now consider an
nkedList class. To begin
al. Program 7.19 gives the

he term $a_i x^i$ of the polynomial. That is, the
of the ith term together with the subscript of

exponent, which cor-
ssed. The former is a

that term, i. For example, the polynomial $31 + 4$
sequence $\{(31, 0), (41, 1), (59, 2)\}$.

Consider now the 100th-order polynomial x^{100}
zero coefficients: $a_{100} = 1$ and $a_0 = 1$. The advan
pairs to represent such a polynomial is that we ca
that have a zero coefficient. We represent the p
$\{(1, 100), (1, 0)\}$.

Now that we have a way to represent polynom
tions on them. For example, consider the polynom

$$p(x) = \sum_{i=0}^{n} a_i x^i$$

We can compute its *derivative* with respect to x by
get

$$p'(x) = \sum_{i=0}^{n-1} a_i' x^i,$$

where $a_i' = (i + 1)a_{i+1}$. In terms of the corresponding
by the sequence

$$\{(a_0, 0), (a_1, 1), (a_2, 2), \ldots, (a_i, i),$$

then its derivative is the sequence

$$\{(a_1, 0), (2a_2, 1), (3a_3, 2), \ldots, (a_i, i - 1),$$

This result suggests a very simple algorithm to diff
represented by a sequence of ordered pairs:

1. Drop the ordered pair that has a zero exponent.
2. For every other ordered pair, multiply the coefficie
   subtract one from the exponent.

Since the representation of an nth-order polynomial has at
since a constant amount of work is necessary for each orde
$\Omega(n)$ algorithm.

Of course, the worst-case running time of the polynomia
on the way that the sequence of ordered pairs is implemente
implementation that makes use of the **OrderedListAsLi**
with, we need a class to represent the terms of the polynom
definition of the **Term** class and several of its methods.

Each **Term** instance has two fields, **coefficient** an
respond to the elements of the ordered pair as previousl
double and the latter is an **int**.

PROGRAM 7.19
Term class

```
1   public class Term
2       extends AbstractObject
3   {
4       protected double coefficient;
5       protected int exponent;
6
7       public Term (double coefficient, int exponent)
8       {
9           this.coefficient = coefficient;
10          this.exponent = exponent;
11      }
12
13      protected int compareTo (Comparable object)
14      {
15          Term term = (Term) object;
16          if (exponent == term.exponent)
17          {
18              if (coefficient < term.coefficient)
19                  return -1;
20              else if (coefficient > term.coefficient)
21                  return +1;
22              else
23                  return 0;
24          }
25          else
26              return exponent - term.exponent;
27      }
28
29      public void differentiate ()
30      {
31          if (exponent > 0)
32          {
33              coefficient *= exponent;
34              exponent -= 1;
35          }
36          else
37              coefficient = 0;
38      }
39  }
40      // ...
```

The **Term** class extends the **AbstractObject** class introduced in Program 5.2. Therefore, instances of the **Term** class may be put into a container. Program 7.19 defines three methods: a constructor, **compareTo**, and **differentiate**. The constructor simply takes a pair of arguments and initializes the corresponding fields accordingly.

The **compareTo** method is used to compare two **Term** instances. Consider two terms, ax^i and bx^j. We define the relation $<$ on terms of a polynomial as follows:

$$ax^i < bx^j \iff (i < j) \lor (i = j \land a < b).$$

Note that the relation $<$ does not depend on the value of the variable x. The **compareTo** method implements the $<$ relation.

Finally, the **differentiate** method does what its name says: It differentiates a term with respect to x. Given a term such as $(a_0, 0)$, it computes the result $(0, 0)$; and given a term such as (a_i, i), where $i > 0$, it computes the result $(ia_i, i - 1)$.

We now consider the representation of a polynomial. Program 7.20 defines the **Polynomial** interface. The interface comprises three methods—**add**, **differentiate**, and **plus**. The **add** method is used to add terms to a polynomial. The **differentiate** method differentiates the polynomial. Finally, the **plus** method is used to compute the sum of two polynomials.

Program 7.21 introduces the **PolynomialAsOrderedList** class. This concrete class implements the **Polynomial** interface. It has a single field of type **OrderedList**. In this case, an instance of the **OrderedListAsLinkedList** class is used to contain the terms of the polynomial.

Program 7.21 defines the method **differentiate**, which has the effect of changing the polynomial to its derivative with respect to x. To compute this derivative, it is necessary to call the **differentiate** method of the **Term** class for each term in the polynomial. Since the polynomial is implemented as a container, there is an **accept** method that can be used to perform a given operation on all of the objects in that container. In this case, we define a visitor that assumes its argument is an instance of the **Term** class and differentiates it.

After the terms in the polynomial have been differentiated, it is necessary to check for the term $(0, 0)$, which arises from differentiating $(a_0, 0)$. The **find** method is used to locate the term, and if one is found the **withdraw** method is used to remove it.

PROGRAM 7.20
Polynomial interface

```
1   public interface Polynomial
2   {
3       void add (Term term);
4       void differentiate ();
5       Polynomial plus (Polynomial polynomial);
6   }
```

PROGRAM 7.21
PolynomialAsOrderedList class

```
1   public class PolynomialAsOrderedList
2       implements Polynomial
3   {
4       OrderedList list;
5
6       public PolynomialAsOrderedList ()
7           { list = new OrderedListAsLinkedList (); }
8
9       public void add (Term term)
10          { list.insert (term); }
11
12      public void differentiate ()
13      {
14          Visitor visitor = new AbstractVisitor ()
15          {
16              public void visit (Object object)
17                  { ((Term) object).differentiate (); }
18          };
19          list.accept (visitor);
20          Comparable zeroTerm = list.find (new Term (0, 0));
21          if (zeroTerm != null)
22              list.withdraw (zeroTerm);
23      }
24      // ...
25  }
```

The analysis of the running time of the polynomial **differentiate** method is straightforward. The running time required to differentiate a term is clearly $O(1)$. So too is the running time of the **visit** method of the visitor. The latter method is called once for each contained object. In the worst case, given an nth-order polynomial, there are $n + 1$ terms. Therefore, the time required to differentiate the terms is $O(n)$. Locating the zero term is $O(n)$ in the worst case, and so too is deleting it. Therefore, the total running time required to differentiate a nth-order polynomial is $O(n)$.

7.2 Sorted Lists

The next type of searchable container that we consider is a *sorted list*. A sorted list is like an ordered list: It is a searchable container that holds a sequence of objects. However, the position of an item in a sorted list is not arbitrary. The items in the sequence appear

---

PROGRAM 7.22
SortedList interface

```
1   public interface SortedList
2       extends SearchableContainer
3   {
4       Comparable get (int i);
5       Cursor findPosition (Comparable object);
6   }
```

---

in order, say, from the smallest to the largest. Of course, for such an ordering to exist, the relation used to sort the items must be a *total order*.[1]

Program 7.22 defines the SortedList interface. Like its unsorted counterpart, the SortedList interface extends the SearchableContainer interface defined in Program 5.14.

In addition to the basic repertoire of operations supported by all searchable containers, sorted lists provide the following operations:

get, used to access the object at a given position in the sorted list; and

findPosition, used to find the position of an object in the sorted list.

Sorted lists are very similar to ordered lists. As a result, we can make use of the code for ordered lists when implementing sorted lists. Specifically, we will consider an array-based implementation of sorted lists that is derived from the OrderedListAsArray class defined in Section 7.1.1, and a linked-list implementation of sorted lists that is derived from the OrderedListAsLinkedList class given in Section 7.1.2.

7.2.1 Array Implementation

The SortedListAsArray class is introduced in Program 7.23. The SortedList-AsArray class extends the OrderedListAsArray class introduced in Program 7.3 and it implements the SortedList interface defined in Program 7.22.

There are no addition fields required to implement the SortedListAsArray class. That is, the fields provided by the base class OrderedListAsArray are sufficient.

Inserting Items in a Sorted List

When inserting an item into a sorted list we have as a *precondition* that the list is already sorted. Furthermore, once the item is inserted, we have the *postcondition* that the list

---

[1]A *total order* is a relation, say $<$, defined on a set of elements, say $\mathbb{Z}$, with the following properties:

1. For all pairs of elements $(i, j) \in \mathbb{Z} \times \mathbb{Z}$, such that $i \neq j$, exactly one of either $i < j$ or $j < i$ holds. (All elements are commensurate.)

2. For all triples $(i, j, k) \in \mathbb{Z} \times \mathbb{Z} \times \mathbb{Z}, i < j \wedge j < k \iff i < k$. (The relation $\leq$ is transitive.) (See also Definition 15.1.)

PROGRAM 7.23
`SortedListAsArray` class

```
1   public class SortedListAsArray
2       extends OrderedListAsArray
3       implements SortedList
4   {
5       // ...
6   }
```

FIGURE 7.4
Inserting an item into a sorted list implemented as an array.

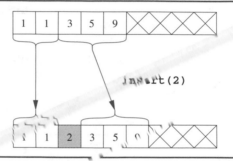

must still be sorted. Therefore, all of the items initially in the list that are larger than the item to be inserted need to be moved to the right by one position as shown in Figure 7.4.

Program 7.24 defines the **insert** method for the **SortedListAsArray** class. This method takes as its argument the object to be inserted in the list. Recall that the **insert** method provided by the **ListAsLinkedList** class simply adds items at the end of the array. Although this is both efficient and easy to implement, it is not suitable for the **SortedListAsArray** class since the items in the array must end up in order.

The **insert** method given in Program 7.24 first checks that there is still room in the array for one more item. Then, to insert the item into the list, all items in the list that are larger than the one to be inserted are moved to the right. This is accomplished by the loop on lines 9–14. Finally the item to be inserted is recorded in the appropriate array position on line 15.

In the worst case, the item to be inserted is smaller than all of the items already in the sorted list. In this case, all $n =$ **count** items must be moved one position to the right. Therefore, the running time of the **insert** method is $O(n)$.

Locating Items in an Array—Binary Search

Given a sorted array of items, an efficient way to locate a given item is to use a *binary search*. The **findOffset** method of the **SortedListAsArray** class defined in Program 7.25 uses a binary search to locate an item in the array that matches a given item.

PROGRAM 7.24
SortedListAsArray class insert method

```
public class SortedListAsArray
    extends OrderedListAsArray
    implements SortedList
{
    public void insert (Comparable object)
    {
        if (count == array.length)
            throw new ContainerFullException ();
        int i = count;
        while (i > 0 && array [i - 1].isGT (object))
        {
            array [i] = array [i - 1];
            --i;
        }
        array [i] = object;
        ++count;
    }
    // ...
}
```

The binary search algorithm makes use of a *search interval* to determine the position of an item in the sorted list. The search interval is a range of array indices in which the item being sought is expected to be found. The initial search interval is $0 \ldots$ count -1. The interval is iteratively narrowed by comparing the item sought with the item found in the array at the middle of the search interval. If the middle item matches the item sought, then we are done. Otherwise, if the item sought is less than the middle item, then we can discard the middle item and the right half of the interval; if the item sought is greater than the middle item, we can discard the middle item and the left half of the interval. At each step, the size of the search interval is approximately halved. The algorithm terminates either when the item sought is found, or if the size of the search interval becomes zero.

In the worst case, the item sought is not in the sorted list. Specifically, the worst case occurs when the item sought is smaller than any item in the list because this case requires two comparisons in each iteration of the binary search loop. In the worst case, $\lceil \log n \rceil + 2$ iterations are required. Therefore, the running time of the findOffset method is $(\lceil \log n \rceil + 2) \times (\mathcal{T}\langle \text{LT} \rangle + \mathcal{T}\langle \text{GT} \rangle) + O(\log n)$, where $\mathcal{T}\langle \text{LT} \rangle$ and $\mathcal{T}\langle \text{GT} \rangle$ represent the running times required to compare two Comparable object instances. If we assume that $\mathcal{T}\langle \text{LT} \rangle = O(1)$ and $\mathcal{T}\langle \text{GT} \rangle = O(1)$, then the total running time is simply $O(\log n)$, where $n =$ count.

Finding Items in a Sorted List
Program 7.26 defines the two methods used to locate items in a sorted list. Both of these methods make use of the findOffset method previously described.

PROGRAM 7.25
`SortedListAsArray` class `findOffset` method

```
1   public class SortedListAsArray
2       extends OrderedListAsArray
3       implements SortedList
4   {
5       protected int findOffset (Comparable object)
6       {
7           int left = 0;
8           int right = count - 1;
9
10          while (left <= right)
11          {
12              int middle = (left + right) / 2;
13
14              if (object.isGT (array [middle]))
15                  left = middle + 1;
16              else if (object.isLT (array [middle]))
17                  right = middle - 1;
18              else
19                  return middle;
20          }
21          return -1;
22      }
23      // ...
24  }
```

The `find` method takes a given object and finds the object contained in the sorted list that matches (i.e., compares equal to) the given one. It calls `findOffset` to determine by doing a binary search the array index at which the matching object is found. `find` returns a reference to the matching object, if one is found; otherwise, it returns `null`. The total running time of `find` is dominated by `findOffset`. Therefore, the running time is $O(\log n)$.

The `findPosition` method also takes an object, but it returns a `Cursor` instead. `findPosition` determines the position in the array of an object that matches its second argument.

The implementation of `findPosition` is trivial: It calls `findOffset` to determine the position at which the matching object is found and returns an instance of an anonymous class derived from the `MyCursor` class. (The `MyCursor` class is defined in Program 7.7.) The anonymous class derived from `MyCursor` overrides the inherited `insertAfter` and `insertBefore` methods with methods that throw an `InvalidOperationException`. These insert operations are not provided for sorted lists because they allow arbitrary insertion, but arbitrary insertions do not necessarily result in sorted lists.

PROGRAM 7.26
`SortedListAsArray` class `find` and `findPosition` methods

```
1   public class SortedListAsArray
2       extends OrderedListAsArray
3       implements SortedList
4   {
5       public Comparable find (Comparable object)
6       {
7           int offset = findOffset (object);
8
9           if (offset >= 0)
10              return array [offset];
11          else
12              return null;
13      }
14
15      public Cursor findPosition (Comparable object)
16      {
17          return new MyCursor (findOffset (object))
18          {
19              public void insertAfter (Comparable object)
20                  { throw new InvalidOperationException (); }
21              public void insertBefore (Comparable object)
22                  { throw new InvalidOperationException (); }
23          };
24      }
25      // ...
26  }
```

The total running time of the `findPosition` method is dominated by `findOffset`. Therefore, like `find`, the running time of `findPosition` is $O(\log n)$.

Removing Items from a List

The purpose of the `withdraw` method is to remove an item from the sorted list. Program 7.27 defines the `withdraw` method, which takes an object and removes it from the sorted list.

The `withdraw` method makes use of `findOffset` to determine the array index of the item to be removed. Removing an object from position i of an ordered list that is stored in an array requires that all of the objects at positions $i + 1, i + 2, \ldots, \text{count} - 1$, be moved one position to the left. The worst case is when $i = 0$. In this case, $\text{count} - 1$ items need to be moved to the left.

Although the `withdraw` method is able to make use of `findOffset` to locate the position of the item to be removed in $O(\log n)$ time, the total running time is dominated by the left shift, which is $O(n)$ in the worst case. Therefore, the running time of `withdraw` is $O(n)$.

variables—**prevPtr** and **ptr**. During the traversal, the latter keeps track of the current element and the former keeps track of the previous element.

By keeping track of the previous element, it is possible to efficiently insert the new item into the sorted list by calling the **insertAfter** method of the **LinkedList** class. In Chapter 4, the **insertAfter** method was shown to be $O(1)$.

In the event that the item to be inserted is smaller than the first item in the sorted list, then rather than using the **insertAfter** method, the **prepend** method is used. The **prepend** method was also shown to be $O(1)$.

In the worst case, the object to be inserted into the linked list is larger than all of the objects already present in the list. In this case, the entire list needs to be traversed before doing the insertion. Consequently, the total running time for the **insert** operation of the **SortedListAsLinkedList** class is $O(n)$, where n = **count**.

Other Operations on Sorted Lists

Unfortunately, it is not possible to do a binary search in a linked list. As a result, it is not possible to exploit the sortedness of the list in the implementation of any of the other required operations on sorted lists. The methods inherited from the **OrderedListAsLinkedList** provide all of the needed functionality.

7.2.3 Performance Comparison: SortedListAsArray vs. SortedListAsLinkedList

The running times calculated for the various methods of the two sorted list implementations, **SortedListAsArray** and **SortedListAsLinkedList**, are summarized in Table 7.2. With the exception of two methods, the running times of the two implementations are asymptotically identical.

Neither the **SortedListAsArray** nor **SortedListAsLinkedList** implementations required any additional fields beyond those of their respective base classes, **OrderedListAsArray** and **OrderedListAsLinkedList**. Consequently, the space requirement analysis of the sorted list implementations is identical to that of the ordered list implementations given in Section 3.1.

TABLE 7.2
Running Times of Operations on Sorted Lists

Method	SortedListAsArray	Sorted List Imp
insert	$O(n)$	
isMember	$O(n)$	
find	$O(\log n)$	$\neq$
withdraw	$O(n)$	
get	$O(1)$	$\neq$
findPosition	$O(\log n)$	$\neq$
Cursor.getDatum	$O(1)$	$O(1)$
Cursor.withdraw	$O(n)$	$O(n)$

7.2.4   Applications

In Section 7.1.4, we saw that an nth-order polynomial,

$$\sum_{i=0}^{n} a_i x^i = a_0 + a_1 x + a_2 x^2 + \cdots + a_n x^n,$$

where $a_n \neq 0$, can be represented by a sequence of ordered pairs thus:

$$\{(a_0, 0), (a_1, 1), (a_2, 2), \ldots, (a_n, n), \}.$$

We also saw that it is possible to make use of an *ordered list* to represent such a sequence and that given such a representation, we can write an algorithm to perform differentiation.

As it turns out, the order of the terms in the sequence does not affect the differentiation algorithm. The correct result is always obtained and the running time is unaffected regardless of the order of the terms in the sequence.

Unfortunately, there are operations on polynomials whose running time depends on the order of the terms. For example, consider the addition of two polynomials:

$$(a_0 + a_1 x + a_2 x^2) + (b_3 x^3 + b_2 x^2 + b_1 x)$$
$$= (a_0) + (a_1 + b_1)x + (a_2 + b_2)x^2 + (b_3)x^3.$$

To perform the addition, all terms involving x raised to the same power need to be grouped together.

If the terms of the polynomials are in an arbitrary order, then the grouping together of the corresponding terms is time consuming. On the other hand, if the terms are ordered, say, from smallest exponent to largest, then the summation can be done rather more efficiently. A single pass through the polynomials will suffice. It makes sense to represent each of the polynomials as a *sorted list* of terms using, say, the `SortedListAsLinkedList` class.

Implementation

To begin with, we need to represent the terms of the polynomial. Program 7.30 extends the definition of the `Term` class introduced in Program 7.19—some additions are needed to support the implementation of polynomial addition.

Four additional methods are declared in Program 7.30. The first is a constructor, which creates a copy of a given term. The next two, `getCoefficient` and `getExponent`, are simple accessor methods that provide read-only access to the corresponding fields of a `Term` instance. Clearly, the running time of each of these methods is $O(1)$.

The final method, `plus`, provides the means to add two `Terms` together. The result of the addition is another `Term`. The working assumption is that the terms to be added have identical exponents. If the exponents are allowed to differ, the result of the addition is a polynomial that cannot be represented using a single term! To add terms with like

---

PROGRAM 7.30
Term methods

```
1   public class Term
2        extends AbstractObject
3   {
4        protected double coefficient;
5        protected int exponent;
6
7        public Term (Term term)
8            { this (term.coefficient, term.exponent); }
9
10       public double getCoefficient ()
11           { return coefficient; }
12
13       public int getExponent ()
14           { return exponent; }
15
16       Term plus (Term arg)
17       {
18           if (exponent != arg.exponent)
19               throw new IllegalArgumentException (
20                   "unequal exponents");
21           return new Term (
22               coefficient + arg.coefficient, exponent);
23       }
24   }
25       // ...
```

---

exponents, we simply need to add their respective coefficients. Therefore, the running time of the **Term** addition operator is $O(1)$.

We now turn to the polynomial itself. Program 7.31 introduces the **PolynomialAsSortedList** class. This class implements the **Polynomial** interface defined in Program 7.20. It has a single field of type **SortedList**. We have chosen in this implementation to use the linked-list sorted list implementation to represent the sequence of terms.

Program 7.31 defines the **plus** method. This method adds two **Polynomials** to obtain a third. It is intended to be used like this:

```
Polynomial p1 = new PolynomialAsSortedList ();
Polynomial p2 = new PolynomialAsSortedList ();
// ...
Polynomial p3 = p1.plus (p2);
```

PROGRAM 7.31
PolynomialAsSortedList class plus method

```
1   public class PolynomialAsSortedList
2       implements Polynomial
3   {
4       SortedList list;
5
6       public Polynomial plus (Polynomial poly)
7       {
8           PolynomialAsSortedList arg =
9               (PolynomialAsSortedList) poly;
10          Polynomial result = new PolynomialAsSortedList ();
11          Enumeration p1 = list.getEnumeration ();
12          Enumeration p2 = arg.list.getEnumeration ();
13          Term term1 = null;
14          Term term2 = null;
15          while (p1.hasMoreElements () && p2.hasMoreElements ()) {
16              if (term1 == null) term1 = (Term) p1.nextElement ();
17              if (term2 == null) term2 = (Term) p2.nextElement ();
18              if (term1.getExponent () < term2.getExponent ()) {
19                  result.add (new Term (term1));
20                  term1 = null;
21              }
22              else if (term1.getExponent() > term2.getExponent()) {
23                  result.add (new Term (term2));
24                  term2 = null;
25              }
26              else {
27                  Term sum = term1.plus (term2);
28                  if (sum.getCoefficient () != 0)
29                      result.add (sum);
30                  term1 = null;
31                  term2 = null;
32              }
33          }
34          while (term1 != null || p1.hasMoreElements ()) {
35              if (term1 == null) term1 = (Term) p1.nextElement ();
36              result.add (new Term (term1));
37              term1 = null;
38          }
39          while (term2 != null || p2.hasMoreElements ()) {
40              if (term2 == null) term2 = (Term) p2.nextElement ();
41              result.add (new Term (term2));
42              term2 = null;
43          }
44          return result;
45      }
46      // ...
47  }
```

Analysis

The proof of the correctness of Program 7.31 is left as an exercise for the reader (Exercise 7.12). We discuss here the running time analysis of the algorithm, as there are some subtle points to remember, which lead to a result that may be surprising.

Consider the addition of a polynomial $p(x)$ with its arithmetic complement $-p(x)$. Suppose $p(x)$ has n terms. Clearly $-p(x)$ also has n terms. The sum of the polynomials is the zero polynomial. An important characteristic of the zero polynomial is that it *has no terms*! In this case, exactly n iterations of the main loop are done (lines 15–33). Furthermore, zero iterations of the second and third loops are required (lines 34–38 and 39–43). Since the result has no terms, there will be no calls to the **add** method. Therefore, the amount of work done in each iteration is a constant. Consequently, the best-case running time is $O(n)$.

Consider now the addition of two polynomials, $p(x)$ and $q(x)$, having l and m terms, respectively. Furthermore, suppose that the largest exponent in $p(x)$ is less than the smallest exponent in $q(x)$. Consequently, there is no power of x that the two polynomials have in common. In this case, since $p(x)$ has the lower-order terms, exactly l iterations of the main loop (lines 15–33) are done. In each of these iterations, exactly one new term is inserted into the result by calling the **add** method. Since all of the terms of $p(x)$ will be exhausted when the main loop is finished, there will be no iterations of the second loop (lines 34–38). However, there will be exactly m iterations of the third loop (lines 39–43), in each of which one new term is inserted into the result by calling the **add** method.

Altogether, $l + m$ calls to the **add** will be made. It was shown earlier that the running time for the insert method is $O(k)$, where k is the number of items in the sorted list. Consequently, the total running time for the $l + m$ insertions is

$$\sum_{k=0}^{l+m-1} O(k) = O((l + m)^2).$$

Consequently, the worst-case running time for the polynomial addition given in Program 7.31 is $O(n^2)$, where $n = l + m$. This is somewhat disappointing. The implementation is not optimal because it fails to take account of the order in which the terms of the result are computed. That is, the **add** method repeatedly searches the sorted list for the correct position at which to insert the next term. But we know that the correct position is at the end! By replacing in Program 7.31 all of the calls to the **add** method by

```
((SortedListAsLinkedList)((PolynomialAsSortedList)result)
.list).linkedList.append (...);
```

the total running time can be reduced to $O(n)$ from $O(n^2)$!

Exercises

7.1 Devise an algorithm to reverse the contents of an ordered list. Determine the running time of your algorithm.

7.2   Devise an algorithm to append the contents of one ordered list to the end of another. Assume that both lists are represented using arrays. What is the running time of your algorithm?

7.3   Repeat Exercise 7.2, but this time assume that both lists are represented using linked lists. What is the running time of your algorithm?

7.4   Devise an algorithm to merge the contents of two sorted lists. Assume that both lists are represented using arrays. What is the running time of your algorithm?

7.5   Repeat Exercise 7.4, but this time assume that both lists are represented using linked lists. What is the running time of your algorithm?

7.6   The `withdraw` method can be used to remove items from a list one at a time. Suppose we want to provide an additional method, `withdrawAll`, that takes one argument and withdraws all items in a list that *match* the given argument. We can provide an implementation of the `withdrawAll` method in the `AbstractSearchableContainer` class like this:

```
public class AbstractSearchableContainer
    extends AbstractContainer
    implements SearchableContainer
{
    void withdrawAll (Comparable arg)
    {
        Comparable object;
        while ((object = Find (arg)) != null)
            withdraw (object);
    }
    // ...
}
```

Determine the worst-case running time of this method for each of the following cases:

a.   an array-based implementation of an ordered list

b.   a linked-list implementation of an ordered list

c.   an array-based implementation of a sorted list

d.   a linked-list implementation of a sorted list

7.7   Devise an $O(n)$ algorithm, to remove from an ordered list all items that match a given item. Assume the list is represented using an array.

7.8   Repeat Exercise 7.7, but this time assume the ordered list is represented using a linked list.

7.9   Consider an implementation of the `OrderedList` interface that uses a doubly-linked list such as the one shown in Figure 6.9(a). Compare the running times of the operations for this implementation with those given in Table 7.1.

7.10   Derive an expression for the amount of space used to represent an ordered list of n elements using a doubly-linked list such as the one shown in Figure 6.9(a). Compare this with the space used by the array-based implementation. Assume that integers and references each occupy four bytes.

7.11 Consider an implementation of the **SortedList** interface that uses a doubly-linked list such as the one shown in Figure 6.9(a). Compare the running times of the operations for this implementation with those given in Table 7.2.

7.12 Verify that Program 7.31 correctly computes the sum of two polynomials.

7.13 Write an algorithm to multiply a polynomial by a scalar. **Hint**: Use a visitor.

Programming Projects

7.1 Write a visitor to solve each of the following problems:

   a. Find the smallest element of a list.

   b. Find the largest element of a list.

   c. Compute the sum of all elements of a list.

   d. Compute the product of all elements of a list.

7.2 Design and implement a class called **OrderedListAsDoublyLinkedList**, which represents an ordered list using a doubly-linked list. Select one of the approaches shown in Figure 6.9.

7.3 Consider the **Polynomial** class given in Program 7.21. Implement a method that computes the value of a polynomial, say $p(x)$, for a given value of x. **Hint**: Use a visitor that visits all of the terms in the polynomial and accumulates the result.

7.4 Devise and implement an algorithm to multiply two polynomials. **Hint**: Consider the identity

$$\left(\sum_{i=0}^{n} a_i x^i \right) \times \left(\sum_{j=0}^{m} b_j x^j \right) = \sum_{i=0}^{n} a_i x^i \left(\sum_{j=0}^{m} b_j x^j \right).$$

Write a method to multiply a **Polynomial** by a **Term** and use the polynomial addition operator defined in Program 7.31.

7.5 Devise and implement an algorithm to compute the kth power of a polynomial, where k is a positive integer. What is the running time of your algorithm?

7.6 For some calculations it is necessary to have very large integers, that is, integers with an arbitrarily large number of digits. We can represent such integers using lists. Design and implement a class for representing arbitrarily large integers. Your implementation should include operations to add, subtract, and multiply such integers, and to compute the kth power of such an integer, where k is a *small* positive integer. **Hint**: Base your design on the **Polynomial** class given in Program 7.21.

8 | Hashing, Hash Tables, and Scatter Tables

A very common paradigm in data processing involves storing information in a table and then later retrieving the information stored there. For example, consider a database of driver's license records. The database contains one record for each driver's license issued. Given a driver's license number, we can look up the information associated with that number.

Similar operations are done by the Java compiler. The compiler uses a *symbol table* to keep track of the user-defined symbols in a Java program. As it compiles a program, the compiler inserts an entry in the symbol table every time a new symbol is declared. In addition, every time a symbol is used, the compiler looks up the attributes associated with that symbol to see that it is being used correctly and to guide the generation of the *bytecodes*.

Typically, the database comprises a collection of key-and-value pairs. Information is retrieved from the database by searching for a given key. In the case of the driver's license database, the key is the driver's license number and in the case of the symbol table, the key is the name of the symbol.

In general, an application may perform a large number of insertion and/or look-up operations. Occasionally it is also necessary to remove items from the database. Because a large number of operations will be done, we want to do them as quickly as possible.

8.1 Hashing—The Basic Idea

In this chapter we examine data structures that are designed specifically with the objective of providing efficient insertion and find operations. In order to meet the design objective, certain concessions are made. Specifically, we do not require that there be any specific ordering of the items in the container. In addition, although we still require the ability to remove items from the container, it is not our primary objective to make removal as efficient as the insertion and find operations.

Ideally we would build a data structure for which both the insertion and find operations are $O(1)$ in the worst case. However, this kind of performance can only be achieved with complete a priori knowledge. We need to know beforehand specifically which items are to be inserted into the container. Unfortunately, we do not have this

194

information in the general case. So, if we cannot guarantee $O(1)$ performance in the *worst case*, then we make it our design objective to achieve $O(1)$ performance in the *average case*.

The constant time performance objective immediately leads us to the following conclusion: Our implementation must be based in some way on an array rather than on a linked list. This is because we can access the kth element of an array in constant time, whereas the same operation in a linked list takes $O(k)$ time.

In the previous chapter we considered two searchable containers—the *ordered list* and the *sorted list*. In the case of an ordered list, the cost of an insertion is $O(1)$ and the cost of the find operation is $O(n)$. For a sorted list the cost of insertion is $O(n)$ and the cost of the find operation is $O(\log n)$ for the array implementation.

Clearly, neither the ordered list nor the sorted list meets our performance objectives. The essential problem is that a search, either linear or binary, is always necessary. In the ordered list, the find operation uses a linear search to locate the item. In the sorted list, a binary search can be used to locate the item because the data are sorted. However, in order to keep the data sorted, insertion becomes $O(n)$.

In order to meet the performance objective of constant time insert and find operations, we need a way to do them *without performing a search*. That is, given an item x, we need to be able to determine directly from x the array position where it is to be stored.

Example *We wish to implement a searchable container that will be used to contain character strings from the set of strings K,*

$$K = \{\texttt{"ett"}, \texttt{"två"}^1, \texttt{"tre"}, \texttt{"fyra"}, \texttt{"fem"}, \texttt{"sex"}^2,$$
$$\texttt{"sju"}, \texttt{"åtta"}, \texttt{"nio"}, \texttt{"tio"}, \texttt{"elva"}, \texttt{"tolv"}\}.$$

Suppose we define a function $h . K \mapsto \mathbb{Z}$ as given by the following table:

x	$h(x)$
`"ett"`	1
`"två"`[1]	2
`"tre"`	3
`"fyra"`	4
`"fem"`	5
`"sex"`[2]	6
`"sju"`	7
`"åtta"`	8
`"nio"`	9
`"tio"`	10
`"elva"`	11
`"tolv"`	12

---

[1]This is the Swedish word for the number two. The symbol å in the *Unicode character set* can be represented in a Java program using the *Unicode escape* "\u00E5".

[2]I have been advised that a book without sex will never be a best-seller. "Sex" is the Swedish word for the number six.

Then, we can implement a searchable container using an array of length $n = 12$. To insert item x, we simply store it at position $h(x) - 1$ of the array. Similarly, to locate item x, we simply check to see if it is found at position $h(x) - 1$. If the function $h(\cdot)$ can be evaluated in constant time, then both insert and find operations are $O(1)$.

We expect that any reasonable implementation of the function $h(\cdot)$ will run in constant time, since the size of the set of strings, K, is a constant! This example illustrates how we can achieve $O(1)$ performance in the worst case when we have complete, a priori knowledge.

8.1.1 Keys and Hash Functions

We are designing a container that will be used to hold some number of items of a given set K. In this context, we call the elements of the set K *keys*. The general approach is to store the keys in an array. The position of a key in the array is given by a function $h(\cdot)$, called a *hash function*, which determines the position of a given key directly from that key.

In the general case, we expect the size of the set of keys, $|K|$, to be relatively large or even unbounded. For example, if the keys are 32-bit integers, then $|K| = 2^{32}$. Similarly, if the keys are arbitrary character strings of arbitrary length, then $|K|$ is unbounded.

On the other hand, we also expect the actual number of items stored in the container to be significantly less than $|K|$. That is, if n is the number of items actually stored in the container, then $n \ll |K|$. Therefore, it seems prudent to use an array of size M, where M is at least as great as the maximum number of items to be stored in the container.

Consequently, what we need is a function $h : K \mapsto \{0, 1, \ldots, M - 1\}$. This function maps the set of values to be stored in the container to subscripts in an array of length M. This function is called a *hash function*.

In general, since $|K| \geq M$, the mapping defined by a hash function will be a *many-to-one mapping*. That is, there will exist many pairs of distinct keys x and y, such that $x \neq y$, for which $h(x) = h(y)$. This situation is called a *collision*. Several approaches for dealing with collisions are explored in the following sections.

What are the characteristics of a good hash function?

- A good hash function avoids collisions.
- A good hash function tends to spread keys evenly in the array.
- A good hash function is easy to compute.

Avoiding Collisions

Ideally, given a set of $n \leq M$ distinct keys, $\{k_1, k_2, \ldots, k_n\}$, the set of hash values $\{h(k_1), h(k_2), \ldots, h(k_n)\}$ contains no duplicates. In practice, unless we know something about the keys chosen, we cannot guarantee that there will not be collisions. However, in certain applications we have some specific knowledge about the keys that we can exploit to reduce the likelihood of a collision. For example, if the keys in our application are telephone numbers, and we know that the telephone numbers are all likely to be from the same geographic area, then it makes little sense to consider the area codes in the hash function—the area codes are all likely to be the same.

Spreading Keys Evenly

Let p_i be the probability that the hash function $h(\cdot) = i$. A hash function that spreads keys evenly has the property that for $0 \le i < M$, $p_i = 1/M$. In other words, the hash values computed by the function $h(\cdot)$ are *uniformly distributed*. Unfortunately, in order to say something about the distribution of the hash values, we need to know something about the distribution of the keys.

In the absence of any information to the contrary, we assume that the keys are equiprobable. Let K_i be the set of keys that map to the value i. That is, $K_i = \{k \in K : h(k) = i\}$. If this is the case, the requirement to spread the keys uniformly implies that $|K_i| = |K|/M$. An equal number of keys should map into each array position.

Ease of Computation

This does not mean necessarily that it is easy for someone to compute the hash function, nor does it mean that it is easy to write the algorithm to compute the function. It means that the running time of the hash function should be $O(1)$.

8.2 Hashing Methods

In this section we discuss several hashing methods. In the following discussion we assume that we are dealing with integer-valued keys, that is, $K = \mathbb{Z}$. Furthermore, we assume that the value of the hash function falls between 0 and $M - 1$.

8.2.1 Division Method

Perhaps the simplest of all the methods of hashing an integer x is to divide x by M and then to use the remainder modulo M. This is called the *division method of hashing*. In this case, the hash function is

$$h(x) = |x| \bmod M.$$

Generally, this approach is quite good for just about any value of M. However, in certain situations some extra care is needed in the selection of a suitable value for M. For example, it is often convenient to make M an even number. But this means that $h(x)$ is even if x is even and $h(x)$ is odd if x is odd. If all possible keys are equiprobable, then this is not a problem. However if, say, even keys are more likely than odd keys, the function $h(x) = x \bmod M$ will not spread the hashed values of those keys evenly.

Similarly, it is often tempting to let M be a power of two. For example, $M = 2^k$ for some integer $k > 1$. In this case, the hash function $h(x) = x \bmod 2^k$ simply extracts the bottom k bits of the binary representation of x. Although this hash function is quite easy to compute, it is not a desirable function because it does not depend on all of the bits in the binary representation of x.

For these reasons M is often chosen to be a prime number. For example, suppose there is a bias in the way the keys are created that makes it more likely for a key to be a multiple of some small constant, say two or three. Then making M a prime increases the likelihood that those keys are spread out evenly. Also, if M is a prime number, the division of x by that prime number depends on all bits of x, not just the bottom k bits, for some small constant k.

The division method is extremely simple to implement. The following Java code illustrates how to do it:

```
public class DivisionMethod
{
    static final int M = 1031; // a prime

    public static int h (int x)
        { return Math.abs (x) % M; }
}
```

In this case, `M` is a constant. However, an advantage of the division method is that `M` need not be a compile-time constant—its value can be determined at run time. In any event, the running time of this implementation is clearly a constant.

A potential disadvantage of the division method is due to the property that consecutive keys map to consecutive hash values:

$$h(i) = i$$
$$h(i + 1) = i + 1 \quad (\text{mod } M)$$
$$h(i + 2) = i + 2 \quad (\text{mod } M)$$
$$\vdots$$

Although this ensures that consecutive keys do not collide, it does mean that consecutive array locations will be occupied. We will see that in certain implementations this can lead to degradation in performance. In the following sections we consider hashing methods that tend to scatter consecutive keys.

8.2.2 Middle-Square Method

In this section we consider a hashing method that avoids the use of division. Since integer division is usually slower than integer multiplication, by avoiding division we can potentially improve the running time of the hashing algorithm. We can avoid division by making use of the fact that a computer does finite-precision integer arithmetic. For example, all arithmetic is done modulo W, where $W = 2^w$ is a power of two such that w is the *word size* of the computer.

The *middle-square hashing method* works as follows: First, we assume that M is a power of two, say $M = 2^k$ for some $k \geq 1$. Then, to hash an integer x, we use the following hash function:

$$h(x) = \left\lfloor \frac{M}{W}(x^2 \text{ mod } W) \right\rfloor.$$

Notice that since M and W are both powers of two, the ratio $W/M = 2^{w-k}$ is also a power two. Therefore, in order to multiply the term $(x^2 \bmod W)$ by M/W we simply shift it to the right by $w - k$ bits! In effect, we are extracting k bits from the middle of the square of the key—hence the name of the method.

The following code fragment illustrates the middle-square method of hashing:

```java
public class MiddleSquareMethod
{
    static final int k = 10; // M==1024
    static final int w = 32;

    public static int h (int x)
        { return (x * x) >>> (w - k); }
}
```

Since `x` is an `int`, the product `x * x` is also an an `int`. In Java, an `int` represents a 32 bit quantity and the product of two `int`s is also a 32-bit quantity. The final result is obtained by shifting the product $w - k$ bits to the right, where w is the number of bits in an integer. Note that we use the Java arithmetic right-shift operator, `>>>`, which inserts zeroes on the left. Therefore, the result always falls between 0 and $M - 1$.

The middle-square method does a pretty good job when the integer-valued keys are equiprobable. The middle-square method also has the characteristic that it scatters consecutive keys nicely. However, since the middle-square method only considers a subset of the bits in the middle of x^2, keys that have a large number of leading zeroes will collide. For example, consider the following set of keys:

$$\{x \in \mathbb{Z} : |x| < \sqrt{W/M}\}.$$

This set contains all keys x such that $|x| < 2^{(w-k)/2}$. For all of these keys, $h(x) = 0$.

A similar line of reasoning applies for keys that have a large number of trailing zeroes. Let W be an even power of two. Consider the set of keys

$$\{x \in \mathbb{Z} : x = \pm n \sqrt{W}, \; n \in \mathbb{Z}\}.$$

The least-significant $w/2$ bits of the keys in this set are all zero. Therefore, the least-significant w bits of of x^2 are also zero and as a result $h(x) = 0$ for all such keys!

8.2.3 Multiplication Method

A very simple variation on the middle-square method that alleviates its deficiencies is the so-called *multiplication hashing method*. Instead of multiplying the key x by itself, we multiply the key by a carefully chosen constant a, and then extract the middle k bits from the result. In this case, the hashing function is

$$h(x) = \left\lfloor \frac{M}{W}(ax \bmod W) \right\rfloor.$$

What is a suitable choice for the constant a? If we want to avoid the problems that the middle-square method encounters with keys having a large number of leading or trailing zeroes, then we should choose an a that has neither leading nor trailing zeroes.

Furthermore, if we choose an a that is *relatively prime*[3] to W, then there exists another number a' such that $aa' = 1 \pmod{W}$. In other words, a' is the *inverse* of a modulo W, since the product of a and its inverse is one. Such a number has the nice property that if we take a key x and multiply it by a to get ax, we can recover the original key by multiplying the product again by a', since $axa' = aa'x = 1x$.

There are many possible constants that have the desired properties. One possibility that is suited for 32-bit arithmetic (i.e., $W = 2^{32}$) is $a = 2\,654\,435\,769$. The binary representation of a is

$$10\,011\,110\,001\,101\,110\,111\,100\,110\,111\,001.$$

This number has neither many leading nor trailing zeroes. Also, this value of a and $W = 2^{32}$ are relatively prime and the inverse of a modulo W is $a' = 340\,573\,321$.

The following code fragment illustrates the multiplication method of hashing:

```
public class MultiplicationMethod
{
    static final int k = 10; // M==1024
    static final int w = 32;
    static final int a = (int) 2654435769L;

    public static int h (int x)
        { return (x * a) >>> (w - k); }
}
```

The code is a simple modification of the middle-square version. Nevertheless, the running time remains $O(1)$.

8.2.4 Fibonacci Hashing

The final variation of hashing to be considered here is called the *Fibonacci hashing method*. In fact, Fibonacci hashing is exactly the multiplication hashing method discussed in the preceding section using a very special value for a. The value we choose is closely related to the number called the golden ratio.

The *golden ratio* is defined as follows: Given two positive numbers x and y, the ratio $\phi = x/y$ is the golden ratio if the ratio of x to y is the same as that of $x + y$ to x. The

---

[3]Two numbers x and y are *relatively prime* if there is no number other than one that divides both x and y evenly.

value of the golden ratio can be determined as follows:

$$\frac{x}{y} = \frac{x+y}{x} \Rightarrow 0 = x^2 - xy - y^2$$
$$\Rightarrow 0 = \phi^2 - \phi - 1$$
$$\Rightarrow \phi = \frac{1 + \sqrt{5}}{2}.$$

There is an intimate relationship between the golden ratio and the Fibonacci numbers. In Section 3.4.3 it was shown that the nth Fibonacci number is given by

$$F_n = \frac{1}{\sqrt{5}}(\phi^n - \hat{\phi}^n),$$

where $\phi = (1 + \sqrt{5})/2$ and $\hat{\phi} = (1 - \sqrt{5})/2$!

The Fibonacci hashing method is essentially the multiplication hashing method in which the constant a is chosen as the integer relatively prime to W that is closest to W/ϕ. The following table gives suitable values of a for various word sizes.

W	$a \approx W/\phi$
2^{16}	40 503
2^{32}	2 654 435 769
2^{64}	11 400 714 819 323 198 485

Why is W/ϕ special? It has to do with what happens to consecutive keys when they are hashed using the multiplicative method. As shown in Figure 8.1, consecutive keys are spread out quite nicely. In fact, when we use $a \approx W/\phi$ to hash consecutive keys, the hash value for each subsequent key falls in between the two widest-spaced hash values already computed. Furthermore, it is a property of the golden ratio, ϕ, that each subsequent hash value divides the interval into which it falls according to the golden ratio!

8.3 Hash Function Implementation

The preceding section presents methods of hashing integer-valued keys. In reality, we cannot expect that the keys will always be integers. Depending on the application, the keys might be letters, character strings, or even more complex data structures such as **Associations** or **Containers**.

FIGURE 8.1
Fibonacci hashing.

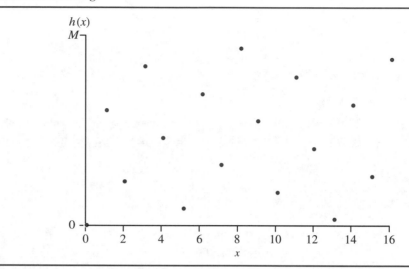

In general, given a set of keys, K, and a positive constant, M, a hash function is a function of the form

$$h : K \mapsto \{0, 1, \ldots, M - 1\}.$$

In practice it is convenient to implement the hash function h as the composition of two functions f and g. The function f maps keys into integers:

$$f : K \mapsto \mathbb{Z},$$

where $\mathbb{Z}$ is the set of integers. The function g maps non-negative integers into $\{0, 1, \ldots, M - 1\}$:

$$g : \mathbb{Z} \mapsto \{0, 1, \ldots, M - 1\}.$$

Given appropriate functions f and g, the hash function h is simply defined as the composition of those functions:

$$h = g \circ f.$$

That is, the hash value of a key x is given by $g(f(x))$.

By decomposing the function h in this way, we can separate the problem into two parts: The first involves finding a suitable mapping from the set of keys K to the non-negative integers. The second involves mapping non-negative integers into the interval $[0, M - 1]$. Ideally, the two problems would be unrelated. That is, the choice of the function f would not depend on the choice of g and vice versa. Unfortunately, this is not always the case. However, if we are careful, we can design the functions in such a way that $h = g \circ f$ is a good hash function.

The hashing methods discussed in the preceding section deal with integer-valued keys. But this is precisely the domain of the function g. Consequently, we have already examined several different alternatives for the function g. On the other hand, the choice of a suitable function for f depends on the characteristics of its domain.

In the following sections, we consider various different domains (sets of keys) and develop suitable hash functions for each of them. Each domain considered corresponds to a Java class. Recall that every Java class is ultimately derived from the **Object** class and that the **Object** class declares a method called **hashCode**:

```
public class Object
{
    public int hashCode ();
    // ...
}
```

The **hashCode** method corresponds to the function f that maps keys into integers.

8.3.1 Integral Keys

Out of all the Java primitive types, the so-called *integral types* are the simplest to hash into integers. The integral data types are **byte**, **short**, **int**, **long**, and **char**. Since the underlying representation of such data types can be viewed as an integer, the hash function is trivial. A suitable function f for an integral data type is the identity function:

$$f(x) = x.$$

Program 8.1 completes the definition of the **Int** wrapper class introduced in Program 5.5. In this case, the **hashCode** method simply returns the contents of the **value** field. Clearly, the running time of the **hashCode** method is $O(1)$.

8.3.2 Floating-Point Keys

Dealing with floating-point numbers involves only a little more work. In Java the floating-point data types are **float** and **double**. The size of a **float** is 32 bits and the size of a **double** is 64 bits.

We seek a function f that maps a floating-point value into a non-negative integer. One possibility is to simply reinterpret the bit pattern used to represent the floating point

---

PROGRAM 8.1
Int class `hashCode` method

```
1   public class Int
2        extends AbstractObject
3   {
4        protected int value;
5
6        public int hashCode ()
7            { return value; }
8        // ...
9   }
```

---

number as an integer. However, this is only possible when the size of the floating-point type does not exceed the size of **int**. This condition is satisfied only by the **float** type.

Another characteristic of floating-point numbers that must be dealt with is the extremely wide range of values that can be represented. For example, when using IEEE floating-point, the smallest double-precision quantity that can be represented is 5×10^{-324} and the largest is $\approx 1.80 \times 10^{308}$. Somehow we need to map values in this large domain into the range of an **int**.

Every non-zero, floating-point quantity x can be written uniquely as

$$x = (-1)^s \times m \times 2^e,$$

where $s \in \{0, 1\}$, $0.5 \leq m < 1$, and $-1023 \leq e \leq 1024$. The quantity s is called the *sign*, m is called the *mantissa* or *significant*, and e is called the *exponent*. This suggests the following definition for the function f:

$$f(x) = \begin{cases} 0 & x = 0, \\ \lfloor 2(m - \frac{1}{2})W \rfloor & x \neq 0, \end{cases} \tag{8.1}$$

where $W = 2^w$ such that w is the word size of the machine.

This hashing method is best understood by considering the conditions under which a collision occurs between two distinct floating-point numbers x and y. Let m_x and m_y be the mantissas of x and y, respectively. The collision occurs when $f(x) = f(y)$.

$$\begin{aligned}
f(x) = f(y) &\Rightarrow f(x) - f(y) = 0 \\
&\Rightarrow \lfloor 2(m_x - \tfrac{1}{2})W \rfloor - \lfloor 2(m_y - \tfrac{1}{2})W \rfloor = 0 \\
&\Rightarrow \left| 2(m_x - \tfrac{1}{2})W - 2(m_y - \tfrac{1}{2})W \right| \leq 1 \\
&\Rightarrow \left| m_x - m_y \right| \leq \frac{1}{2W}
\end{aligned}$$

Thus, x and y collide if their mantissas differ by less than $1/2W$. Notice that the sign of the number is not considered. Thus, x and $-x$ collide. Also, the exponent is not

---

PROGRAM 8.2
Dbl class hashCode method

```
1   public class Dbl
2       extends AbstractObject
3   {
4       protected double value;
5
6       public int hashCode ()
7       {
8           long bits = Double.doubleToLongBits (value);
9           return (int)(bits >>> 20);
10      }
11      // ...
12  }
```

---

considered. Therefore, if x and y collide, then so too do x and $y \times 2^k$ for all permissible values of k.

Program 8.2 completes the definition of the **Dbl** wrapper class introduced in Program 5.6. The **hashCode** function shown computes the hash function defined in Equation (8.1).

This implementation makes use of the fact that in the IEEE standard floating-point format the least-significant 52 bits of a 64-bit floating-point number represent the quantity $m' = (m - \frac{1}{2}) \times 2^{53}$. Since an **int** is a 32-bit quantity, $W = 2^{32}$, and we can rewrite Equation (8.1) as follows:

$$f(n) = 2(m - \tfrac{1}{2})W$$
$$= m' 2^{33} / 2^{53}$$
$$= m' / 2^{20}.$$

Thus, we can compute the hash function simply by shifting the binary representation of the floating-point number 20 bits to the right as shown in Program 8.2. Clearly the running time of the **hashCode** method is $O(1)$.

8.3.3 Character String Keys

Strings of characters are represented in Java as instances of the **String** class. A character string is simply a sequence of characters. Since such a sequence may be arbitrarily long, to devise a suitable hash function we must find a mapping from an unbounded domain into the finite range of **int**.

We can view a character string, s, as a sequence of n characters,

$$\{s_0, s_1, \ldots, s_{n-1}\},$$

where n is the length of the string. (The length of a string can be determined by calling the **String** method **length**.) One very simple way to hash such a string would be to simply sum the numeric values associated with each character:

$$f(s) = \sum_{i=0}^{n-1} s_i. \tag{8.2}$$

As it turns out, this is not a particularly good way to hash character strings. Given that a Java **char** is a 16-bit quantity, $0 \le s_i \le 2^{16} - 1$, for all $0 \le i < n$. As a result, $0 \le f(s) < n(2^{16} - 1)$. For example, given a string of length $n = 5$, the value of $f(s)$ falls between zero and 327 675. In fact, the situation is even worse—in North America we typically use only the *ASCII* subset of the *Unicode* character set. The ASCII character set uses only the least-significant 7 bits of a **char**. If the string is composed of only ASCII characters, the result falls in the range between zero and 640.

Essentially the problem with a function f that produces a result in a relatively small interval is the situation that arises when that function is composed with the function $g(x) = x \bmod M$. If the size of the range of the function f is less than M, then $h = g \circ f$ does not spread its values uniformly on the interval $[0, M - 1]$. For example, if $M = 1031$ only the first 640 values (62% of the range) are used!

Alternatively, suppose we have a priori knowledge that character strings are limited to length $n = 4$. Then we can construct an integer by concatenating the binary representations of each of the characters. For example, given $s = \{s_0, s_1, s_2, s_3\}$, we can construct an integer with the function

$$f(s) = s_0 B^3 + s_1 B^2 + s_2 B + s_3, \tag{8.3}$$

where $B = 2^7$. Since B is a power of two, this function is easy to write in Java:

```
static int f (String s)
{
    return s.charAt(0) << 21 | s.charAt (1) << 14
        | s.charAt (2) << 7 | s.charAt (3);
}
```

Although this function certainly has a larger range, it still has problems—it cannot deal with strings of arbitrary length.

Equation (8.3) can be generalized to deal with strings of arbitrary length as follows:

$$f(s) = \sum_{i=0}^{n-1} B^{n-i-1} s_i.$$

This function produces a unique integer for every possible string. Unfortunately, the range of $f(s)$ is unbounded. A simple modification of this algorithm suffices to bound

TABLE 8.1
Sample Character String Keys and
the Hash Values Obtained Using
Program 8.3.

x	$\mathtt{Hash}(x)$ (octal)
`"ett"`	01446564
`"två "`	01656545
`"tre"`	01656345
`"fyra"`	0147706341
`"fem"`	01474455
`"sex"`	01624470
`"sju"`	01625365
`"åtta"`	0344656541
`"nio"`	01575057
`"tio"`	01655057
`"elva"`	044556741
`"tolv"`	065565566

8.3.4 Hashing Containers

As explained in Section 5.2.4, a container is an object that contains other objects. The **AbstractContainer** class introduced in Program 5.9 implements the **Container** interface defined in Program 5.8. In this section we show how to define a **hashCode** method in the **AbstractContainer** class that computes a suitable hash function on any container.

Given a container c that contains n objects, $o_1, o_2, \ldots, o_n$, we can define the hash function $f(c)$ as follows:

$$f(c) = \left(\sum_{i=1}^{n} h(o_i) \right) \bmod W. \tag{8.5}$$

That is, to hash a container, simply compute the sum of the hash values of the contained objects.

Program 8.4 gives the code for the **hashCode** method of the **AbstractContainer** class. This method makes use of the **accept** method to cause a visitor to visit all of the objects contained in the container. When the visitor visits an object, it calls that object's **hashCode** method and accumulates the result.

Since the **accept** method is an abstract method, every concrete class derived from the **AbstractContainer** class must provide an appropriate implementation. However, it is *not* necessary for any derived class to redefine the behavior of the **hashCode** method—the behavior inherited from the **AbstractContainer** class is completely generic and should suffice for all concrete container classes.

PROGRAM 8.4
`AbstractContainer` class `hashCode` method

```
1   public abstract class AbstractContainer
2       extends AbstractObject
3       implements Container
4   {
5       protected int count;
6
7       public int hashCode ()
8       {
9           Visitor visitor = new AbstractVisitor ()
10          {
11              private int value;
12
13              public void visit (Object object)
14                  { value += object.hashCode (); }
15
16              public int hashCode ()
17                  { return value; }
18          };
19          accept (visitor);
20          return getClass ().hashCode () + visitor.hashCode ();
21      }
22      // ...
23  }
```

There is a slight problem with Equation (8.5). Different container types that happen to contain identical objects produce exactly the same hash value. For example, an empty stack and an empty list both produce the same hash value. We have avoided this situation in Program 8.4 by adding to the sum the value obtained from hashing the class of the container itself.

8.3.5   Using Associations

Hashing provides a way to determine the position of a given object directly from that object itself. Given an object x we determine its position by evaluating the appropriate hash function, $h(x)$. We find the location of object x in exactly the same way. But of what use is this ability to find an object if, in order to compute the hash function $h(x)$, we must be able to access the object x in the first place?

In practice, when using hashing we are dealing with *keyed data*. Mathematically, keyed data consists of ordered pairs

$$A = \{(k, v) : k \in K, v \in V\},$$

PROGRAM 8.5
`Association` class `hashCode` method

```
1   public class Association
2       extends AbstractObject
3   {
4       protected Comparable key;
5       protected Object value;
6
7       public int hashCode ()
8           { return key.hashCode (); }
9       // ...
10  }
```

---

where K is a set of keys, and V is a set of values. The idea is that we will access elements of the set A using the key. That is, the hash function for elements of the set A is given by

$$f_A((k, v)) = f_K(k),$$

where f_K is the hash function associated with the set K.

For example, suppose we wish to use hashing to implement a database that contains driver's license records. Each record contains information about a driver, such as name, address, and perhaps a summary of traffic violations. Furthermore, each record has a unique driver's license number. The driver's license number is the key and the other information is the value associated with that key.

In Section 5.2.8 the `Association` class was declared that comprises two fields, a key, and a value. Given this declaration, the definition of the hash method for `Association`s is trivial. As shown in Program 8.5, it simply calls the `hashCode` method on the `key` field.

8.4 Hash Tables

A *hash table* is a searchable container. As such, its interface provides methods for putting an object into the container, finding an object in the container, and removing an object from the container. Program 8.6 defines the `HashTable` interface. The `HashTable` interface extends the `SearchableContainerInterface` defined in Program 5.14. One additional method, called `getLoadFactor`, is declared. The purpose of this method is explained in Section 8.4.2.

Abstract Hash Tables
As shown in Figure 8.2, we define an `AbstractHashTable` class from which several concrete realizations are derived.

PROGRAM 8.6
`HashTable` interface

```
1   public interface HashTable
2       extends SearchableContainer
3   {
4       double getLoadFactor ();
5   }
```

FIGURE 8.2
Object class hierarchy.

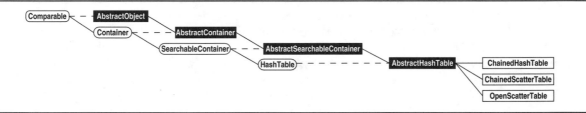

PROGRAM 8.7
`AbstractHashTable` methods

```
1   public abstract class AbstractHashTable
2       extends AbstractSearchableContainer
3       implements HashTable
4   {
5       public abstract int getLength ();
6
7       protected final int f (Object object)
8           { return object.hashCode (); }
9
10      protected final int g (int x)
11          { return Math.abs (x) % getLength (); }
12
13      protected final int h (Object object)
14          { return g(f(object)); }
15      // ...
16  }
```

Program 8.7 introduces the `AbstractHashTable` class. The `AbstractHashTable` class extends the `AbstractSearchableContainer` class introduced in Program 5.15 and it implements the `HashTable` interface defined in Program 8.6.

PROGRAM 8.10
ChainedHashTable class insert and withdraw methods

```
1   public class ChainedHashTable
2       extends AbstractHashTable
3   {
4       protected LinkedList[] array;
5
6       public void insert (Comparable object)
7       {
8           array [h (object)].append (object);
9           ++count;
10      }
11
12      public void withdraw (Comparable object)
13      {
14          array [h (object)].extract (object);
15          --count;
16      }
17      // ...
18  }
```

PROGRAM 8.11
ChainedHashTable class find method

```
1   public class ChainedHashTable
2       extends AbstractHashTable
3   {
4       protected LinkedList[] array;
5
6       public Comparable find (Comparable object)
7       {
8           for (LinkedList.Element ptr = array[h(object)].getHead();
9               ptr != null; ptr = ptr.getNext())
10          {
11              Comparable datum = (Comparable) ptr.getDatum ();
12              if (object.isEQ (datum))
13                  return datum;
14          }
15          return null;
16      }
17      // ...
18  }
```

Program 8.7 introduces four methods—getLength, f, g, and h. The getLength method is an abstract method. This function returns the *length* of a hash table.

The methods f, g, and h correspond to the composition $h = g \circ f$ discussed in Section 8.3. The f method takes an object and calls the hashCode method on that object to compute an integer. The g method uses the *division method* of hashing defined in Section 8.2.1 to map an integer into the interval $[0, M - 1]$, where M is the length of the hash table. Finally, the h method computes the composition of f and g.

In the following we will consider various ways of implementing hash tables. In all cases, the underlying implementation makes use of an array. The position of an object in the array is determined by hashing the object. The main problem to be resolved is how to deal with collisions—two different objects cannot occupy the same array position at the same time. In the following section, we consider an approach that solves the problem of collisions by keeping objects that collide in a linked list.

8.4.1 Separate Chaining

Figure 8.3 shows a hash table that uses *separate chaining* to resolve collisions. The hash table is implemented as an array of linked lists. To insert an item into the table, it is

FIGURE 8.3
Hash table using separate chaining.

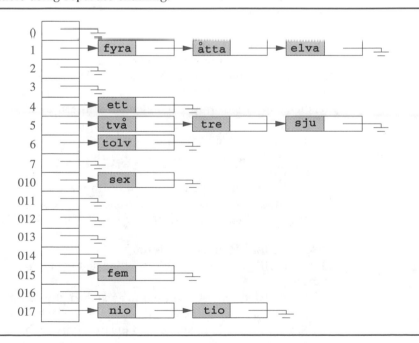

PROGRAM 8.8
ChainedHashTable fields

```
1  public class ChainedHashTable
2      extends AbstractHashTable
3  {
4      protected LinkedList[] array;
5
6      // ...
7  }
```

appended to one of the linked lists. The linked list to which it is appended is determined by hashing that item.

Figure 8.3 illustrates an example in which there are $M = 16$ linked lists. The twelve character strings "ett"–"tolv" have been inserted into the table using the hashed values and in the order given in Table 8.1. Notice that in this example since $M = 16$, the linked list is selected by the least-significant 4 bits of the hashed value given in Table 8.1. In effect, it is only the last letter of a string that determines the linked list in which that string appears.

Implementation

Program 8.8 introduces the **ChainedHashTable** class. The **ChainedHashTable** class extends the **AbstractHashTable** class introduced in Program 8.7. The **ChainedHashTable** class contains a single field called **array**. It is declared as an array of **LinkedList**s. (The **LinkedList** class is described in Chapter 4.)

Constructor, getLength, and purge Methods

The constructor, **getLength**, and **purge** methods of the **ChainedHashTable** class are defined in Program 8.9. The constructor takes a single argument that specifies the size of hash table desired. It creates an array of the specified length and then initializes the elements of the array. Each element of the array is assigned an empty linked list. The running time for the **ChainedHashTable** constructor is $O(M)$, where M is the size of the hash table.

The **getLength** method simply returns the length of the **array** field. Clearly its running time is $O(1)$.

The purpose of the **purge** method is to make the container empty. It does this by invoking the **purge** method one-by-one on each of the linked lists in the array. The running time of the **purge** method is $O(M)$, where M is the size of the hash table.

Inserting and Removing Items

Program 8.10 gives the code for inserting and removing items from a **ChainedHash-Table**.

The implementations of the **insert** and **withdraw** methods are remarkably simple. For example, the **insert** method first calls the hash method **h** to compute an array index, which is used to select one of the linked lists. The **append** method provided by the **LinkedList** class is used to add the object to the selected linked list. The total

PROGRAM 8.9
ChainedHashTable class constructor, getLength, and purge methods

```
1   public class ChainedHashTable
2       extends AbstractHashTable
3   {
4       protected LinkedList[] array;
5
6       public ChainedHashTable (int length)
7       {
8           array = new LinkedList [length];
9           for (int i = 0; i < length; ++i)
10              array [i] = new LinkedList ();
11      }
12
13      public int getLength ()
14          { return array.length; }
15
16      public void purge ()
17      {
18          for (int i = 0; i < getLength (); ++i)
19              array [i].purge ();
20          count = 0;
21      }
22      // ...
23  }
```

running time for the **insert** operation is $\mathcal{T}\langle\text{hashCode}\rangle + O(1)$, where $\mathcal{T}\langle\text{hashCode}\rangle$ i running time of the **hashCode** method. Notice that if the hash method runs in con time, then so too does the hash table insertion operation!

The **withdraw** method is almost identical to the **insert** method. Instead of ing the **append**, it calls the linked-list **extract** method to remove the specifie ject from the appropriate linked list. The running time of **withdraw** is determine the time of the **extract** operation. In Chapter 4 this was shown to be $O(n)$, w n is the number of items in the linked list. In the worst case, all of the items i **ChainedHashTable** have collided with each other and ended up in the same That is, in the worst case if there are n items in the container, all n of them are in a s linked list. In this case, the running time of the **withdraw** operation is $\mathcal{T}\langle\text{hashCo}$ $O(n)$.

Finding an Item

The definition of the **find** method of the **ChainedHashTable** class is given i gram 8.11. The **find** method takes as its argument any **Comparable** object purpose of the **find** operation is to return the object in the container that is equal given object.

The **find** method simply hashes its argument to select the linked list in which it should be found. Then, it traverses the linked list to locate the target object. As for the **withdraw** operation, the worst-case running time of the **find** method occurs when all of the objects in the container have collided, and the item that is being sought does not appear in the linked list. In this case, the running time of the find operation is $n\mathcal{T}\langle\text{isEQ}\rangle + \mathcal{T}\langle\text{hashCode}\rangle + O(n)$.

8.4.2 Average-Case Analysis

The previous section has shown that in the worst case, the running time to insert an object into a separately chained hash table is $O(1)$, and the time to find or delete an object is $O(n)$. But these bounds are no better than the same operations on plain lists! Why have we gone to all the trouble of inventing hash tables?

The answer lies not in the worst-case performance, but in the average expected performance. Suppose we have a hash table of size M. Let there be exactly n items in the hash table. We call the quantity $\lambda = n/M$ the *load factor*. The load factor is simply the ratio of the number of items in the hash table to the array length.

Program 8.12 gives the implementation for the **getLoadFactor** method of the **AbstractHashTable** class. This method computes $\lambda = n/M$ by calling the **getCount** method to determine n and the **getLength** method to determine M.

Consider a chained hash table. Let n_i be the number of items in the ith linked list, for $i = 0, 1, \ldots, M - 1$. The average length of a linked list is

$$\frac{1}{M}\sum_{i=0}^{M-1} n_i = \frac{n}{M}$$
$$= \lambda.$$

The average length of a linked list is exactly the load factor!

If we are given the load factor λ, we can determine the *average* running times for the various operations. The average running time of **insert** is the same as its worst-case

---

PROGRAM 8.12
AbstractHashTable class **getLoadFactor** method

```
1   public abstract class AbstractHashTable
2       extends AbstractSearchableContainer
3       implements HashTable
4   {
5       public abstract int getLength ();
6
7       public final double getLoadFactor ()
8           { return (double) getCount () / getLength (); }
9       // ...
10  }
```

time, $O(1)$—this result does not depend on λ. On the other hand, the average running time for **withdraw** does depend on λ. It is $\mathcal{T}\langle\texttt{hashCode}\rangle + O(1) + O(\lambda)$, since the time required to delete an item from a linked list of length λ is $O(\lambda)$.

To determine the average running time for the **find** operation, we need to make an assumption about whether the item that is being sought is in the table. If the item is not found in the table, the search is said to be *unsuccessful*. The average running time for an unsuccessful search is

$$\mathcal{T}\langle\texttt{hashCode}\rangle + \lambda\mathcal{T}\langle\texttt{isEQ}\rangle + O(1) + O(\lambda).$$

On the other hand, if the search target is in the table, the search is said to be *successful*. The average number of comparisons needed to find an arbitrary item in a linked list of length λ is

$$\frac{1}{\lambda}\sum_{i=1}^{\lambda} i = \frac{\lambda + 1}{2}.$$

Thus, the average running time for a successful search is

$$\mathcal{T}\langle\texttt{hashCode}\rangle + ((\lambda + 1)/2)\mathcal{T}\langle\texttt{isEQ}\rangle + O(1) + O(\lambda).$$

So, although any one search operation can be as bad as $O(n)$, if we do a large number of random searches, we expect that the average running time will be $O(\lambda)$. In fact, if we have a sufficiently good hash function and a reasonable set of objects in the container, we can expect that those objects are distributed throughout the table. Therefore, any one search operation will not be very much worse than the average case.

Finally, if we know how many objects will be inserted into the hash table a priori, then we can choose a table size M that is larger than the maximum number of items expected. By doing this, we can ensure that $\lambda = n/M \leq 1$. That is, a linked list contains no more than one item on average. In this case, the average time for **withdraw** is $\mathcal{T}\langle\texttt{hashCode}\rangle + O(1)$, and for **find** it is $\mathcal{T}\langle\texttt{hashCode}\rangle + \mathcal{T}\langle\texttt{isEQ}\rangle + O(1)$.

8.5   Scatter Tables

The separately chained hash table described in the preceding section is essentially a linked-list implementation. We have seen both linked-list and array-based implementations for all of the data structures considered so far and hash tables are no exception. Array-based hash tables are called *scatter tables*.

The essential idea behind a scatter table is that all of the information is stored within a fixed-size array. Hashing is used to identify the position where an item should be stored. When a collision occurs, the colliding item is stored somewhere else in the array.

One of the motivations for using scatter tables can be seen by considering again the linked-list hash table shown in Figure 8.3. Since most of the linked lists are empty, much of the array is unused. At the same time, for each item that is added to the table, dynamic memory is consumed. Why not simply store the data in the unused array positions?

8.5.1 Chained Scatter Table

Figure 8.4 illustrates a *chained scatter table*. The elements of a chained scatter table are ordered pairs. Each array element contains a key and a "pointer." All keys are stored in the table itself. Consequently, there is a fixed limit on the number of items that can be stored in a scatter table.

Since the pointers point to other elements in the array, they are implemented as integer-valued array subscripts. Since valid array subscripts start from the value zero, the *null* pointer must be represented not as zero, but by an integer value that is outside the array bounds (say, -1).

To find an item in a chained scatter table, we begin by hashing that item to determine the location from which to begin the search. For example, to find the string `"elva"`, which hashes to the value 044556741_8, we begin the search in array location $|044556741_8| \bmod 16 = 1_8$. The item at that location is `"fyra"`, which does not match. So we follow the pointer in location 1_8 to location 2_8. The item there, `"fyra"`, does not match either. We follow the pointer again, this time to location 3_8, where we ultimately find the string we are looking for.

Comparing Figures 8.3 and 8.4, we see that the chained scatter table has embedded within it the linked lists, which appear to be the same as those in the separately chained hash table. However, the lists are not exactly identical. When using the chained scatter table, it is possible for lists to *coalesce*.

FIGURE 8.4
Chained scatter table.

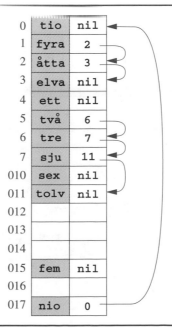

For example, when using separate chaining, the keys **"tre"** and **"sju"** appear in a separate list from the key **"tolv"**. This is because both **"tre"** and **"sju"** hash to position 5_8, whereas **"tolv"** hashes to position 6_8. The same keys appear together in a single list starting at position 5_8 in the chained scatter table. The two lists have *coalesced*.

Implementation

The **ChainedScatterTable** class is introduced in Program 8.13. This class extends the **AbstractHashTableClass** introduced in Program 8.7. The scatter table is implemented as an array of **Entry** objects. The **Entry** class is a *static inner class* defined within the **ChainedScatterTable** class.

Each **Entry** instance has two fields—**object** and **next**. The former refers to a **Comparable** object. The latter indicates the position in the array of the next element of a chain. The value of the enumerated constant **nil** will be used instead of zero to mark the end of a chain. The value zero is not used to mark the end of a chain because zero is a valid array subscript. Notice that the default value for the **next** field is **nil**.

Constructor, getLength, and purge Methods

Program 8.14 defines the constructor, **getLength**, and **purge** methods of the **ChainedScatterTable** class. The constructor takes a single argument, which specifies the size of scatter table desired. It creates an array of the desired length and

---

PROGRAM 8.13
ChainedScatterTable fields and **ChainedScatterTable.Entry** class

---

```
1   public class ChainedScatterTable
2       extends AbstractHashTable
3   {
4       protected Entry[] array;
5
6       static final int nil = -1;
7
8       protected static final class Entry
9       {
10          Comparable object;
11          int next = nil;
12
13          void purge ()
14          {
15              object = null;
16              next = nil;
17          }
18      }
19      // ...
20  }
```

PROGRAM 8.14
ChainedScatterTable class constructor, getLength, and purge methods

```
1  public class ChainedScatterTable
2      extends AbstractHashTable
3  {
4      protected Entry[] array;
5
6      public ChainedScatterTable (int length)
7      {
8          array = new Entry [length];
9          for (int i = 0; i < length; ++i)
10             array [i] = new Entry ();
11     }
12
13     public int getLength ()
14         { return array.length; }
15
16     public void purge ()
17     {
18         for (int i = 0; i < getLength (); ++i)
19             array [i].purge ();
20         count = 0;
21     }
22     // ...
23 }
```

initializes each element of the array by assigning to it a new **Entry** instance. Consequently, the running time for the **ChainedScatterTable** constructor is $O(M)$, where M is the size of the scatter table.

The **getLength** method simply returns the length of the **array** field. Clearly, its running time is $O(1)$.

The **purge** method empties the scatter table by invoking the **purge** method on each **Entry** object in the array. The **purge** method for the **Entry** class is given in Program 8.13. Notice that an entry can be purged in constant time. Therefore, the time required to purge the scatter table is $O(M)$, where M is the length of the table.

Inserting and Finding an Item

Program 8.15 gives the code for the **insert** and **find** methods of the **Chained-ScatterTable** class. To insert an item into a chained scatter table, we need to find an unused array location in which to put the item. We first hash the item to determine the "natural" location for that item. If the natural location is unused, we store the item there and we are done.

However, if the natural position for an item is occupied, then a collision has occurred and an alternate location in which to store that item must be found. When a collision occurs it must be the case that there is a chain emanating from the natural position for

PROGRAM 8.15
ChainedScatterTable class insert and find methods

```
1   public class ChainedScatterTable
2       extends AbstractHashTable
3   {
4       protected Entry[] array;
5
6       public void insert (Comparable object)
7       {
8           if (count == getLength ())
9               throw new ContainerFullException ();
10          int probe = h (object);
11          if (array [probe].object != null)
12          {
13              while (array [probe].next != nil)
14                  probe = array [probe].next;
15              int tail = probe;
16              probe = (probe + 1) % getLength ();
17              while (array [probe].object != null)
18                  probe = (probe + 1) % getLength ();
19              array [tail].next = probe;
20          }
21          array [probe].object = object;
22          array [probe].next = nil;
23          ++count;
24      }
25
26      public Comparable find (Comparable object)
27      {
28          for (int probe = h (object);
29              probe != nil; probe = array [probe].next)
30          {
31              if (object.isEQ (array [probe].object))
32                  return array [probe].object;
33          }
34          return null;
35      }
36      // ...
37  }
```

the item. The insertion algorithm given always adds items at the end of the chain. Therefore, after a collision has been detected, the end of the chain is found (lines 13–15).

After the end of the chain is found, an unused array position in which to store the item must be found. This is done by a simple, linear search starting from the array position immediately following the end of the chain (lines 16–18). Once an unused position is found, it is linked to the end of the chain (line 19), and the item is stored in the unused position (lines 21–22).

The worst-case running time for insertion occurs when the scatter table has only one unused entry—that is, when the number of items in the table is $n = M - 1$, where M is the table size. In the worst case, all of the used array elements are linked into a single chain of length $M - 1$ and the item to be inserted hashes to the head of the chain. In this case, it takes $O(M)$ to find the end of the chain. In the worst case, the end of the chain immediately follows the unused array position. Consequently, the linear search for the unused position is also $O(M)$. Once an unused position has been found, the actual insertion can be done in constant time. Therefore, the running time of the insertion operation is $\mathcal{T}\langle \texttt{hashCode} \rangle + O(M)$ in the worst case.

Program 8.15 also gives the code for the **find** method, which is used to locate a given object in the scatter table. The algorithm is straightforward. The item is hashed to find its natural location in the table. If the item is not found in the natural location but a chain emanates from that location, the chain is followed to determine if that item appears anywhere in the chain.

The worst-case running time occurs when the item for which we are looking is not in the table, the table is completely full, and all of the entries are linked together into a single linked list. In this case, the running time of the **find** algorithm is $\mathcal{T}\langle \texttt{hashCode} \rangle + M\mathcal{T}\langle \texttt{isEQ} \rangle + O(M)$.

Removing Items

Removing items from a chained scatter table is more complicated than putting them into the table. The goal when removing an item is to have the scatter table end up exactly as it would have appeared had that item never been inserted in the first place. Therefore, when an item is removed from the middle of a chain, items that follow it in the chain have to be moved up to fill in the hole. However, the moving-up operation is complicated by the fact that several chains may have coalesced.

Program 8.16 gives an implementation of the **withdraw** method of the **Chained-ScatterTable** class. The algorithm begins by checking that the table is not empty (lines 8–9). To remove an item, we first have to find it. This is what the loop on lines 10–12 does. If the item to be deleted is not in the table, when this loop terminates the variable **i** has the value **nil** and an exception is thrown (lines 13–14). Otherwise, the item in position **i** in the table is to be removed.

The purpose of the loop on lines 15–32 is to fill in the hole in the chain that results when the item at position **i** is removed by moving up items that follow it in the chain. What we need to do is to find the next item that follows the item at **i** that is safe to move into position **i**. The loop on lines 16–28 searches the rest of the chain following the item at **i** to find an item that can be safely moved.

Figure 8.5 illustrates the basic idea. The figure shows a chained scatter table of length ten that contains integer-valued keys. There is a single chain as shown in the figure.

```
1   public class ChainedScatterTable
2       extends AbstractHashTable
3   {
4       protected Entry[] array;
5
6       public void withdraw (Comparable object)
7       {
8           if (count == 0)
9               throw new ContainerEmptyException ();
10          int i = h (object);
11          while (i != nil && object != array [i].object)
12              i = array [i].next;
13          if (i == nil)
14              throw new IllegalArgumentException ("obj not found");
15          for (;;)
16          {   int j = array [i].next;
17              while (j != nil)
18              {   int h = h (array [j].object);
19                  boolean contained = false;
20                  for (int k = array [i].next;
21                      k != array [j].next && !contained;
22                      k = array [k].next)
23                  {
24                      if (k == h) contained = true;
25                  }
26                  if (!contained) break;
27                  j = array [j].next;
28              }
29              if (j == nil) break;
30              array [i].object = array [j].object;
31              i = j;
32          }
33          array [i].object = null;
34          array [i].next = nil;
35          for (int j = (i + getLength () - 1) % getLength ();
36              j != i; j = (j + getLength () - 1) % getLength ())
37          {   if (array [j].next == i)
38              {
39                  array [j].next = nil;
40                  break;
41              }
42          }
43          --count;
44      }
45      // ...
46  }
```

FIGURE 8.5
Removing items from a chained scatter table.

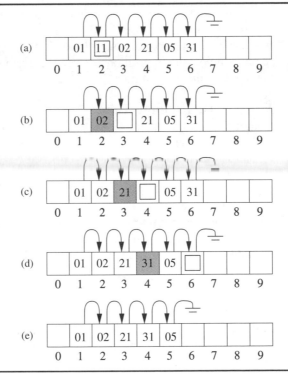

However, notice that the values in the chain are not all equal modulo 10. In fact, this chain must have resulted from the coalescing of three chains—one that begins in position 1, one that begins in position 2, and one that begins in position 5.

Suppose we wish to remove item 11, which is in position 2, as indicated by the box in Figure 8.5(a). To delete it, we must follow the chain to find the next item that can be moved safely up to position 2. Item 02 follows 11 and can be moved safely up to position 2 because that is the location to which it hashes. Moving item 02 up moves the hole down the list to position 3 (Figure 8.5 (b)). Again, we follow the chain to find that item 21 can be moved up safely, giving rise to the situation in Figure 8.5 (c).

Now we have a case where an item cannot be moved. Item 05 is the next candidate to be moved. However, it is in position 5, which is the position to which it hashes. If we were to move it up, then it would no longer be in the chain that emanates from position 5. In effect, the item would no longer be accessible! Therefore, it cannot be moved safely. Instead, we must move item 31 ahead of item 5, as shown in Figure 8.5 (d). Eventually, the hole propagates to the end of the chain, where it can be deleted easily (Figure 8.5 (e)).

The loop on lines 16–28 of Program 8.16 finds the position j of an item that can be safely moved to position i. The algorithm makes use of the following fact: An item can be safely moved up *only if it does not hash to a position that appears in the linked list between i and j*. This is what the code on lines 18–25 tests.

When execution reaches line 29, either we have found an item that can be safely moved, or there does not exist such an item. If an item is found, it is moved up (line 30) and we repeat the whole process again. On the other hand, if there are no more items to be moved up, then the process is finished and the main loop (lines 15–32) terminates.

The statements on lines 33–34 do the actual deed of removing the data from the position **i**, which by now is at the end of the chain. The final task to be done is to remove the pointer to position **i**, since there is no longer a datum at that position. That is the job of the loop on lines 35–42.

Worst-Case Running Time

Computing a tight bound on the worst-case running time of Program 8.16 is tricky. Assuming the item to be removed is actually in the table, then the time required to find the item (lines 10–12) is

$$\mathcal{T}\langle\texttt{hashCode}\rangle + M\mathcal{T}\langle\texttt{isEQ}\rangle + O(M)$$

in the worst case.

The worst-case running time of the main loop occurs when the table is full, there is only one chain, and no items can be safely moved up in the chain. In this case, the running time of the main loop (lines 15–32) is

$$\left(\frac{(M-1)M}{2}\right)\mathcal{T}\langle\texttt{hashCode}\rangle + O(M^2).$$

Finally, the worst-case running time of the last loop (lines 35–42) is $O(M)$.

Therefore, the worst-case running time of the **withdraw** method for chained scatter tables is

$$\left(1 + \frac{(M-1)M}{2}\right)\mathcal{T}\langle\texttt{hashCode}\rangle + M\mathcal{T}\langle\texttt{isEQ}\rangle + O(M^2).$$

Clearly we don't want to be removing items from a chained scatter table very often!

8.5.2   Average-Case Analysis

The previous section has shown that the worst-case running time to insert or to find an object into a chained scatter table is $O(M)$. The average-case analysis of chained scatter tables is complicated by the fact that lists coalesce. However, if we assume that chains never coalesce, then the chains that appear in a chained scatter table for a given set of items are identical to those that appear in a separately chained hash table for the same set of items.

Unfortunately we cannot assume that lists do not coalesce—they do! We therefore expect that the average list will be longer than λ and that the running times are correspondingly slower. Knuth has shown that the average number of probes in an unsuccessful search is

$$U(\lambda) \approx 1 + \frac{1}{4}(e^{2\lambda} - 1 - 2\lambda),$$

and the average number of probes in a successful search is approximately

$$S(\lambda) \approx 1 + \frac{1}{8\lambda}(e^{2\lambda} - 1 - 2\lambda) + \frac{\lambda}{4},$$

where λ is the load factor [27]. The precise functional form of $U(\lambda)$ and $S(\lambda)$ is not so important here. What is important is that when $\lambda = 1$—that is, when the table is full—$U(1) \approx 2.1$ and $S(1) \approx 1.8$. Regardless of the size of the table, an unsuccessful search requires just over two probes on average, and a successful search requires just under two probes on average!

Consequently, the average running time for insertion is

$$\mathcal{T}\langle \mathtt{hashCode} \rangle + O(U(\lambda)) = \mathcal{T}\langle \mathtt{hashCode} \rangle + O(1),$$

since the insertion is always done in the first empty position found. Similarly, the running time for an unsuccessful search is

$$\mathcal{T}\langle \mathtt{hashCode} \rangle + U(\lambda)\mathcal{T}\langle \mathtt{isEQ} \rangle + O(U(\lambda)),$$

and for a successful search it is

$$\mathcal{T}\langle \mathtt{hashCode} \rangle + S(\lambda)\mathcal{T}\langle \mathtt{isEQ} \rangle + O(S(\lambda)).$$

8.6 Scatter Table Using Open Addressing

An alternative method of dealing with collisions that entirely does away with the need for links and chaining is called *open addressing*. The basic idea is to define a *probe sequence* for every key that, when followed, always leads to the key in question.

The probe sequence is essentially a sequence of functions

$$\{h_0, h_1, \ldots, h_{M-1}\},$$

where h_i is a hash function, $h_i : K \mapsto \{0, 1, \ldots, M - 1\}$. To insert item x into the scatter table, we examine array locations $h_0(x), h_1(x), \ldots$, until we find an empty cell. Similarly, to find item x in the scatter table, we examine the same sequence of locations in the same order.

The most common probe sequences are of the form

$$h_i(x) = (h(x) + c(i)) \bmod M,$$

where $i = 0, 1, \ldots, M - 1$. The function $h(x)$ is the same hash function that we have seen before. That is, the function h maps keys into integers in the range from zero to $M - 1$.

The function $c(i)$ represents the collision resolution strategy. It is required to have the following two properties:

Property 1 $c(0) = 0$. This ensures that the first probe in the sequence is

$$h_0(x) = (h(x) + 0) \bmod M = h(x).$$

Property 2 The set of values

$$\{c(0) \bmod M, c(1) \bmod M, c(2) \bmod M, \ldots, c(M-1) \bmod M\}$$

must contain every integer between 0 and $M - 1$. This second property ensures that the probe sequence eventually probes *every possible array position.*

8.6.1 Linear Probing

The simplest collision resolution strategy in open addressing is called *linear probing*. In linear probing, the function $c(i)$ is a linear function in i. That is, it is of the form

$$c(i) = \alpha i + \beta.$$

Property 1 requires that $c(0) = 0$. Therefore, β must be zero.

In order for $c(i) = \alpha i$ to satisfy Property 2, α and M must be relatively prime. If we know that M will always be a prime number, then any α will do. On the other hand, if we cannot be certain that M is prime, then α must be one. Therefore, the linear probing sequence that is usually used is

$$h_i = (h(x) + i) \bmod M,$$

for $i = 0, 1, 2, \ldots, M - 1$.

Figure 8.6 illustrates an example of a scatter table using open addressing together with linear probing. For example, consider the string `"åtta"`. This string hashes to array position 1_8. The corresponding linear probing sequence begins at position 1_8 and goes on to positions $2_8, 3_8, \ldots$. In this case, the search for the string `"åtta"` succeeds after three probes.

To insert an item x into the scatter table, an empty cell is found by following the same probe sequence that would be used in a search for item x. Thus, linear probing finds an empty cell by doing a linear search beginning from array position $h(x)$.

An unfortunate characteristic of linear probing arises from the fact that as the table fills, clusters of consecutive cells form and the time required for a search increases with the size of the cluster. Furthermore, when we attempt to insert an item in the table at a position that is already occupied, that item is ultimately inserted at the end of the cluster— thereby increasing its length. This by itself is not inherently a bad thing. After

FIGURE 8.6
Scatter table using open addressing and linear probing.

0	tio	occupied
1	frya	occupied
2	åtta	occupied
3	elva	occupied
4	ett	occupied
5	två	occupied
6	tre	occupied
7	sju	occupied
010	sex	occupied
011	tolv	occupied
012		empty
013		empty
014		empty
015	fem	occupied
016		empty
017	nio	occupied

all, when using the chained approach, every insertion increases the length of some chain by one. However, whenever an insertion is made between two clusters that are separated by one unoccupied position, the two clusters become one, thereby potentially increasing the cluster length by an amount much greater than one—a bad thing! This phenomenon is called *primary clustering*.

8.6.2 Quadratic Probing

An alternative to linear probing that addresses the primary clustering problem is called *quadratic probing*. In quadratic probing, the function $c(i)$ is a quadratic function in i.[4] The general quadratic has the form

$$c(i) = \alpha i^2 + \beta i + \gamma.$$

However, quadratic probing is usually done using $c(i) = i^2$.

Clearly, $c(i) = i^2$ satisfies Property 1. What is not so clear is whether it satisfies Property 2. In fact, in general it does not. The following theorem gives the conditions

---

[4]What else would it be?

under which quadratic probing works:

Theorem 8.1

When quadratic probing is used in a table of size M, where M is a prime number, the first $\lfloor M/2 \rfloor$ probes are distinct.

Proof (By contradiction). Let us assume that the theorem is false. Then there exist two distinct values i and j, such that $0 \leq i < j < \lfloor M/2 \rfloor$, that probe exactly the same position. Thus,

$$
\begin{aligned}
h_i(x) = h_j(x) &\Rightarrow h(x) + c(i) = h(x) + c(j) \quad (\text{mod } M) \\
&\Rightarrow h(x) + i^2 = h(x) + j^2 \quad (\text{mod } M) \\
&\Rightarrow i^2 = j^2 \quad (\text{mod } M) \\
&\Rightarrow i^2 - j^2 = 0 \quad (\text{mod } M) \\
&\Rightarrow (i - j)(i + j) = 0 \quad (\text{mod } M).
\end{aligned}
$$

Since M is a prime number, the only way that the product $(i - j)(i + j)$ can be zero modulo M is for either $i - j$ to be zero or $i + j$ to be zero modulo M. Since i and j are distinct, $i - j \neq 0$. Furthermore, since both i and j are less than $\lfloor M/2 \rfloor$, the sum $i + j$ is less than M. Consequently, the sum cannot be zero. We have successfully argued an absurdity— if the theorem is false one of two quantities must be zero, neither of which can possibly be zero. Therefore, the original assumption is not correct and the theorem is true.

Applying Theorem 8.1, we get that quadratic probing works as long as the table size is prime and there are fewer than $n = M/2$ items in the table. In terms of the load factor $\lambda = n/M$, this occurs when $\lambda < \frac{1}{2}$.

Quadratic probing eliminates the primary clustering phenomenon of linear probing because instead of doing a linear search, it does a quadratic search:

$$
\begin{aligned}
h_0(x) &= (h(x) + 0 \bmod M) \\
h_1(x) &= (h(x) + 1 \bmod M) \\
h_2(x) &= (h(x) + 4 \bmod M) \\
h_3(x) &= (h(x) + 9 \bmod M)
\end{aligned}
$$

$$\vdots$$

8.6.3 Double Hashing

Although quadratic probing does indeed eliminate the primary clustering problem, it places a restriction on the number of items that can be put in the table— the table must be less than half full. *Double hashing* is yet another method of generating a probing sequence. It requires two distinct hash functions,

$$h : K \mapsto \{0, 1, \ldots, M - 1\},$$
$$h' : K \mapsto \{1, 2, \ldots, M - 1\}.$$

The probing sequence is then computed as follows:

$$h_i(x) = (h(x) + ih'(x)) \bmod M.$$

That is, the scatter table is searched as follows:

$$h_0 = (h(x) + 0 \times h'(x)) \bmod M$$
$$h_1 = (h(x) + 1 \times h'(x)) \bmod M$$
$$h_2 = (h(x) + 2 \times h'(x)) \bmod M$$
$$h_3 = (h(x) + 3 \times h'(x)) \bmod M$$
$$\vdots$$

Since the collision resolution function is $c(i) = ih'(x)$, the probe sequence depends on the key as follows: If $h'(x) = 1$, then the probing sequence for the key x is the same as linear probing. If $h'(x) = 2$, the probing sequence examines every other array position. This works as long as M is not even.

Clearly since $c(0) = 0$, the double-hashing method satisfies Property 1. Furthermore, Property 2 is satisfied as long as $h'(x)$ and M are relatively prime. Since $h'(x)$ can take on any value between 1 and $M - 1$, M must be a prime number.

But what is a suitable choice for the function h'? Recall that h is defined as the composition of two functions, $h = g \circ f$, where $g(x) = x \bmod M$. We can define h' as the composition $g' \circ f$, where

$$g'(x) = 1 + (x \bmod (M - 1)). \tag{8.6}$$

Double hashing reduces the occurrence of primary clustering since it only does a linear search if $h'(x)$ hashes to the value 1. For a good hash function, this should only happen with probability $1/(M - 1)$. However, for double hashing to work at all, the size of the scatter table, M, must be a prime number. Table 8.2 summarizes the characteristics of the various open-addressing probing sequences.

TABLE 8.2
Characteristics of the Open-Addressing Probing Sequences

Probing Sequence	Primary Clustering	Capacity Limit	Size Restriction
linear probing	yes	none	none
quadratic probing	no	$\lambda < \frac{1}{2}$	M must be prime
double hashing	no	none	M must be prime

8.6.4 Implementation

This section describes an implementation of a scatter table using open addressing with linear probing. Program 8.17 introduces the **OpenScatterTable** class. The **OpenScatterTable** class extends the **AbstractHashTable** class introduced in Program 8.7. The scatter table is implemented as an array of elements of the static inner class **Entry**. Each **Entry** instance has two fields—**object** and **state**. The former refers to a **Comparable** object. The latter is an **int**, the value of which is either **empty**, **occupied**, or **deleted**.

Initially, all entries are empty. When an object is recorded in an entry, the state of that entry is changed to **occupied**. The purpose of the third state, **deleted**, will be discussed next in conjunction with the **withdraw** method.

Constructor, getLength, and purge Methods

Program 8.18 defines the constructor, **getLength**, and **purge** methods of the **OpenScatterTable** class. The **OpenScatterTable** constructor takes a single argument, which specifies the size of scatter table desired. It creates an array of the desired length and initializes each element of the array by assigning to it a new **Entry**

PROGRAM 8.17
OpenScatterTable fields and **OpenScatterTable.Entry** class

```
1   public class OpenScatterTable
2       extends AbstractHashTable
3   {
4       protected Entry[] array;
5
6       static final int empty = 0;
7       static final int occupied = 1;
8       static final int deleted = 2;
9
10      protected static final class Entry
11      {
12          int state = empty;
13          Comparable object;
14
15          void purge ()
16          {
17              state = empty;
18              object = null;
19          }
20      }
21      // ...
22  }
```

PROGRAM 8.18
OpenScatterTable class constructor, getLength, and purge methods

```
1    public class OpenScatterTable
2        extends AbstractHashTable
3    {
4        protected Entry[] array;
5
6        public OpenScatterTable (int length)
7        {
8            array = new Entry [length];
9            for (int i = 0; i < length; ++i)
10               array [i] = new Entry ();
11       }
12
13       public int getLength ()
14           { return array.length; }
15
16       public void purge ()
17       {
18           for (int i = 0; i < getLength (); ++i)
19               array [i].purge ();
20           count = 0;
21       }
22       // ...
23   }
```

instance. Consequently, the running time for the **OpenScatterTable** constructor is $O(M)$, where M is the size of the scatter table.

The **getLength** method simply returns the length of the array field. Clearly, its running time is $O(1)$.

The **purge** method empties the scatter table by invoking the **purge** method on each **Entry** object in the array. The **purge** method for the **Entry** class is given in Program 8.17. Notice that an entry can be purged in constant time. Therefore, the time required to purge the scatter table is $O(M)$, where M is the length of the table.

Inserting Items
The method for inserting an item into a scatter table using open addressing is actually quite simple—find an unoccupied array location and then put the item in that location. To find an unoccupied array element, the array is probed according to a probing sequence. In this case, the probing sequence is linear probing. Program 8.19 defines the methods needed to insert an item into the scatter table.

The method c defines the probing sequence. As it turns out, the implementation required for a linear probing sequence is trivial. The method c is the identity function.

PROGRAM 8.19
OpenScatterTable class c, findUnoccupied, and insert methods

```
1   public class OpenScatterTable
2       extends AbstractHashTable
3   {
4       protected Entry[] array;
5
6       protected static int c (int i)
7           { return i; }
8
9       protected int findUnoccupied (Object object)
10      {
11          int hash = h (object);
12          for (int i = 0; i < count + 1; ++i)
13          {
14              int probe = (hash + c (i)) % getLength ();
15              if (array [probe].state != occupied)
16                  return probe;
17          }
18          throw new ContainerFullException ();
19      }
20
21      public void insert (Comparable object)
22      {
23          if (count == getLength ())
24              throw new ContainerFullException ();
25          int offset = findUnoccupied (object);
26          array [offset].state = occupied;
27          array [offset].object = object;
28          ++count;
29      }
30      // ...
31  }
```

The purpose of the private method **findUnoccupied** is to locate an unoccupied array position. The **findUnoccupied** method probes the array according to the probing sequence determined by the **c** method. At most $n + 1$ probes are made, where $n =$ **count** is the number of items in the scatter table. When using linear probing, it is always possible to find an unoccupied cell in this many probes as long as the table is not full. Notice also that we do not search for an **empty** cell. Instead, the search terminates when a cell is found, the state of which is not **occupied**—that is, **empty** or **deleted**. The reason for this subtlety has to do with the way items may be removed from the table. The **findUnoccupied** method returns a value between 0 and $M - 1$, where M is the length of the scatter table, if an unoccupied location is found. Otherwise, it throws an exception that indicates that the table is full.

The **insert** method takes a **Comparable** object and puts that object into the scatter table. It does so by calling **findUnoccupied** to determine the location of an unoccupied entry in which to put the object. The state of the unoccupied entry is set to **occupied** and the object is saved in the entry.

The running time of the **insert** method is dominated by the **findUnoccupied** method. The worst-case running time of **findUnoccupied** is $O(n)$, where n is the number of items in the scatter table. Therefore, the running time of **insert** is $\mathcal{T}\langle \text{hashCode} \rangle + O(n)$.

Finding Items

The **find** and **findMatch** methods of the **OpenScatterTable** class are defined in Program 8.20. The **findMatch** method takes a **Comparable** object and searches the scatter table for an object that matches the given one.

findMatch follows the same probing sequence used by the **insert** method. Therefore, if there is a matching object in the scatter table, **findMatch** will make exactly the same number of probes to locate the object as were made to put the object into the table in the first place. The **findMatch** method makes at most M probes, where M is the size of the scatter table. However, note that the loop immediately terminates should it encounter an **empty** location. This is because if the target has not been found by the time an empty cell is encountered, then the target is not in the table. Notice also that the comparison is only attempted for entries that are marked **occupied**. Any locations marked **deleted** are not examined during the search but they do not terminate the search either.

The running time of the **find** method is determined by that of **findMatch**. In the worst case **findMatch** makes n comparisons, where n is the number of items in the table. Therefore, the running time of **find** is $\mathcal{T}\langle \text{hashCode} \rangle + n\mathcal{T}\langle \text{isEQ} \rangle + O(M)$.

Removing Items

Removing items from a scatter table using open addressing has to be done with some care. The naïve approach would be to locate the item to be removed and then to change the state of its location to **empty**. However, that approach does not work! Recall that the **findMatch** method that is used to locate an item stops its search when it encounters an **empty** cell. Therefore, if we change the state of a cell in the middle of a cluster to **empty**, all subsequent searches in that cluster will stop at the empty cell. As a result, subsequent searches for an object may fail even when the target is still in the table!

One way to deal with this is to make use of the third state, **deleted**. Instead of marking a location **empty**, we mark it **deleted** when an item is deleted. Recall that the **findMatch** method was written in such a way that it continues past deleted cells in its search. Also, the **findUnoccupied** method was written to stop its search when it encounters either an **empty** or a **deleted** location. Consequently, the positions marked **deleted** are available for reuse when insertion is done.

Program 8.21 gives the implementation of the **withdraw** method. The **withdraw** method takes a **Comparable** object and removes that object from the scatter table. It does so by first locating the specific object instance using **findInstance** and then marking the location **deleted**. The implementation of **findInstance** has been elided. It is simply a trivial variation of the **findMatch** method.

PROGRAM 8.20
OpenScatterTable Class findMatch and find methods

```
1   public class OpenScatterTable
2       extends AbstractHashTable
3   {
4       protected Entry[] array;
5
6       protected int findMatch (Comparable object)
7       {
8           int hash = h (object);
9           for (int i = 0; i < getLength (); ++i)
10          {
11              int probe = (hash + c (i)) % getLength ();
12              if (array [probe].state == empty)
13                  break;
14              if (array [probe].state == occupied
15                  && object.isEQ (array [probe].object))
16              {
17                  return probe;
18              }
19          }
20          return -1;
21      }
22
23      public Comparable find (Comparable object)
24      {
25          int offset = findMatch (object);
26          if (offset >= 0)
27              return array [offset].object;
28          else
29              return null;
30      }
31      // ...
32  }
```

The running time of the **withdraw** method is determined by the **findInstance** method. In the worst case **findInstance** has to examine every array position. Therefore, the running time of **withdraw** is $\mathcal{T}\langle\text{hashCode}\rangle + O(M)$.

There is a very serious problem with the technique of marking locations as **deleted**. After a large number of insertions and deletions have been done, it is very likely that there are no cells left that are marked **empty**. This is because nowhere in any of the

---

PROGRAM 8.21
OpenScatterTable class withdraw method

```
1   public class OpenScatterTable
2       extends AbstractHashTable
3   {
4       protected Entry[] array;
5
6       public void withdraw (Comparable object)
7       {
8           if (count == 0)
9               throw new ContainerEmptyException ();
10          int offset = findInstance (object);
11          if (offset < 0)
12              throw new IllegalArgumentException (
13                  "object not found");
14          array [offset].state = deleted;
15          array [offset].object = null;
16          --count;
17      }
18      // ...
19  }
```

---

methods (except **purge**) is a cell ever marked **empty**! This has the very unfortunate consequence that an unsuccessful search—that is, a search for an object that is not in the scatter table—is $\Omega(M)$. Recall that **findMatch** examines at most M array locations and only stops its search early when an **empty** location is encountered. Since there are no more empty locations, the search must examine all M locations.

If we are using the scatter table in an application in which we know a priori that no items will be removed, or perhaps only a very small number of items will be removed, then the **withdraw** method given in Program 8.20 will suffice. However, if the application is such that a significant number of withdrawals will be made, a better implementation is required.

Ideally, when removing an item the scatter table ends up exactly as it would have appeared had that item never been inserted in the first place. Note that exactly the same constraint is met by the **withdraw** method for the **ChainedScatterTable** class given in Program 8.16. It turns out that a variation of that algorithm can be used to implement the **withdraw** method for the **OpenScatterTable** class, as shown in Program 8.22.

The algorithm begins by checking that the scatter table is not empty. Then it calls **findInstance** to determine the position **i** of the item to be removed. If the item to be removed is not in the scatter table, **findInstance** returns -1 and an exception is thrown. Otherwise, **findInstance** falls between 0 and $M - 1$, which indicates that the item was found.

PROGRAM 8.22
OpenScatterTableV2 withdraw method

```
1   public class OpenScatterTableV2
2       extends OpenScatterTable
3   {
4       public void withdraw (Comparable object)
5       {
6           if (count == 0)
7               throw new ContainerEmptyException ();
8           int i = findInstance (object);
9           if (i < 0)
10              throw new IllegalArgumentException (
11                  ''object not found'');
12          for (;;)
13          {
14              int j = (i + 1) % getLength ();
15              while (array [j].state == occupied)
16              {
17                  int h = h (array [j].object);
18                  if ((h <= i && i < j) || (i < j && j < h) ||
19                      (j < h && h <= i))
20                      break;
21                  j = (j + 1) % getLength ();
22              }
23              if (array [j].state == empty)
24                  break;
25              array [i].state = array [j].state;
26              array [i].object = array [j].object;
27              i = j;
28          }
29          array [i].state = empty;
30          array [i].object = null;
31          --count;
32      }
33      // ...
34  }
```

In the general case, the item to be deleted falls in the middle of a cluster. Deleting it would create a hole in the middle of the cluster. What we need to do is to find another item further down in the cluster that can be moved up to fill in the hole that would be created when the item at position i is deleted. The purpose of the loop on lines 14–22 is to find the position j of an item that can be moved safely into position i. Note the implementation here implicitly assumes that a linear probing sequence is used—the c method is not called explicitly. An item at position j can be moved safely to position i

only if the hash value of the item at position j is not cyclically contained in the interval between i and j.

If an item is found at some position j that can be moved safely, then that item is moved to position i on lines 25–26. The effect of moving the item at position j to position i is to move the hole from position i to position j (line 27). Therefore, another iteration of the main loop (lines 12–28) is needed to fill in the relocated hole in the cluster.

If no item can be found to fill in the hole, then it is safe to split the cluster in two. Eventually, either because no item can be found to fill in the hole or because the hole has moved to the end of the cluster, there is nothing more to do other than to delete the hole. Thus, on lines 29–30 the entry at position i is set to **empty** and the associated **object** is set to **null**. Notice that the third state **deleted** is not required by the implementation of **withdraw**.

If we use the **withdraw** implementation of Program 8.22, the scatter table will only ever be in one of two states—**occupied** or **empty**. Consequently, we improve the bound on the worst case for the search from $\mathcal{T}\langle\text{hashCode}\rangle + n\mathcal{T}\langle\text{isEq}\rangle$ to $\mathcal{T}\langle\text{hashCode}\rangle + n\mathcal{T}\langle\text{isEQ}\rangle + O(n)$, where n is the number of items in the scatter table.

Determining the running time of Program 8.22 is a little tricky. Assuming the item to be deleted is actually in the table, the running time to find the position of the item (line 8) is $\mathcal{T}\langle\text{hashCode}\rangle + O(n)$, where $n =$ **count** is the number of items in the scatter table. In the worst case, the scatter table is composed of a single cluster of n items, and we are deleting the first item of the cluster. In this case, the loop on lines 12–28 makes a pass through the entire cluster, in the worst case moving the hole to the end of the cluster one position at a time. Thus, the running time of the loop is $(n-1)\mathcal{T}\langle\text{hashCode}\rangle + O(n)$. The remaining lines require a constant amount of time. Altogether, the running time for the **withdraw** method is $n\mathcal{T}\langle\text{hashCode}\rangle$ in the worst case.

8.6.5 Average-Case Analysis

The average-case analysis of open addressing is easy if we ignore the clustering phenomenon. Given a scatter table of size M that contains n items, each of the $\binom{M}{n}$ combinations of n occupied and $(m-n)$ empty scatter table entries is equally likely. This is the so-called *uniform hashing model*.

In this model we assume that the entries will either be occupied or empty—the **deleted** state is not used. Suppose a search for an empty cell requires i probes. Then the first $i-1$ positions probed must have been occupied and the ith position probed was empty. Consider the i cells that were probed. There are $\binom{M-i}{n-i+1}$ ways in which $i-1$ of the probed cells are occupied and one is empty. Therefore, the probability that exactly i probes are required is

$$P_i = \frac{\dbinom{M-i}{n-i+1}}{\dbinom{M}{n}}.$$

The average number of probes required to find an empty cell in a table that has n occupied cells is $U(n)$, where

$$U(n) = \sum_{i=1}^{M} iP_i.$$

(8.8)

Using Equation (8.7) in Equation (8.8) and simplifying the result gives

$$U(n) = \frac{M+1}{M-n+1}$$

(8.9)

$$= \frac{1 + \dfrac{1}{M}}{1 - \lambda + \dfrac{1}{M}}, \text{ where } \lambda = n/M$$

$$\approx \frac{1}{1 - \lambda}.$$

(8.10)

This result is actually quite intuitive. The load factor, λ, is the fraction of occupied entries. Therefore, $1 - \lambda$ entries are empty so we would expect to have to probe $1/(1-\lambda)$ entries before finding an empty one! For example, if the load factor is 0.75, a quarter of the entries are empty. Therefore, we expect to have to probe four entries before finding an empty one.

To calculate the average number of probes for a successful search, we make the observation that when an item is initially inserted, we need to find an empty cell in which to place it. For example, the number of probes to find the empty position into which the ith item is to be placed is $U(i)$. And this is exactly the number of probes it takes to find the ith item again! Therefore, the average number of probes required for a successful search in a table that has n occupied cells is $S(n)$, where

$$S(n) = \frac{1}{n} \sum_{i=0}^{n-1} U(i).$$

(8.11)

Substituting Equation (8.9) in Equation (8.11) and simplifying gives

$$S(n) = \frac{1}{n} \sum_{i=0}^{n} \frac{M+1}{M-i+1}$$

$$= \frac{M+1}{N}(H_{M+1} - H_{M-n+1})$$

$$\approx \frac{1}{\lambda} \ln \frac{1}{1-\lambda},$$

(8.12)

where H_k is the kth *harmonic number* (see Section 2.1.8). Again, there is an easy intuitive derivation for this result. We can use a simple integral to calculate the mean

number of probes for a successful search using the approximation $U(n) = 1/(1 - \lambda)$ as follows:

$$S(n) = \frac{1}{n} \sum_{i=0}^{n} U(i)$$

$$\approx \frac{1}{\lambda} \int_0^\lambda \frac{1}{1 - x} \, dx$$

$$\approx \frac{1}{\lambda} \ln \frac{1}{1 - \lambda}.$$

Empirical evidence has shown that the formulas derived for the *uniform hashing model* characterize the performance of scatter tables using open addressing with quadratic probing and double hashing quite well. However, they do not capture the effect of primary clustering that occurs when linear probing is used. Knuth has shown that when primary clustering is taken into account, the number of probes required to locate an empty cell is

$$U(n) = \frac{1}{2} \left(1 + \left(\frac{1}{1 - \lambda} \right)^2 \right), \tag{8.13}$$

and the number of probes required for a successful search is

$$S(n) = \frac{1}{2} \left(1 + \frac{1}{1 - \lambda} \right). \tag{8.14}$$

The graph in Figure 8.7 compares the predictions of the uniform hashing model (Equations 8.10 and 8.12)) with the formulas derived by Knuth (Equations 8.13 and 8.14). Clearly, whereas the results are qualitatively similar, the formulas are in agreement for small load factors and they diverge as the load factor increases.

8.7 Applications

Hash and scatter tables have many applications. The principal characteristic of such applications is that keyed information needs to be frequently accessed and the access pattern is either unknown or known to be random. For example, hash tables are often used to implement the *symbol table* of a programming language compiler. A symbol table is used to keep track of information associated with the symbols (variable and method names) used by a programmer. In this case, the keys are character strings and each key hash associated with it some information about the symbol (e.g., type, address, value, lifetime, scope).

FIGURE 8.7
Number of probes vs. load factor for uniform hashing and linear probing.

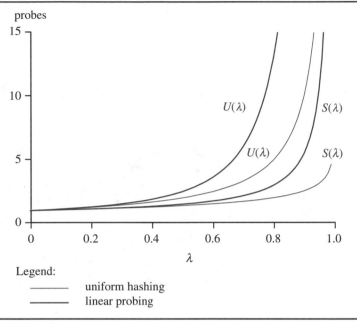

Legend:

———————   uniform hashing
———————   linear probing

This section presents a simple application of hash and scatter tables. Suppose we are required to count the number of occurrences of each distinct word contained in a text file. We can do this easily using a hash or scatter table. Program 8.23 gives an implementation.

The static inner class **Counter** extends the class **Int** defined in Section 5.2.3. In addition to the functionality inherited from the base class, the **Counter** class adds the method **increment**, which increments the value by one.

The **wordCounter** method does the actual work of counting the words in the input file. The local variable **table** refers to a **ChainedHashTable** that is used to keep track of the words and counts. The objects that are put into the hash table are all instances of the class **Association**. Each association has as its key a **String** class instance, and as its value a **Counter** class instance.

The **wordCounter** method reads words from the input stream one at a time. As each word is read, a **find** operation is done on the hash table to determine if there is already an association for the given key. If none is found, a new association is created and inserted into the hash table. The given word is used as the key of the new association and the value is a counter that is initialized to one. On the other hand, if there is already an association for the given word in the hash table, the corresponding counter is incremented. When the **wordCounter** method reaches the end of the input stream, it simply prints the hash table on the given output stream.

PROGRAM 8.23
Hash/scatter table application—counting words

```
1   public class Algorithms
2   {
3       private static final class Counter
4           extends Int
5       {
6           Counter (int value)
7               { super (value); }
8           void increment()
9               { ++value; }
10      }
11
12      public static void wordCounter (Reader in, PrintWriter out)
13          throws IOException
14      {
15          HashTable table = new ChainedHashTable (1031);
16          StreamTokenizer tin = new StreamTokenizer (in);
17          while (tin.nextToken () != StreamTokenizer.TT_EOF)
18          {
19              String word = tin.sval;
20
21              Object obj = table.find (
22                  new Association (new Str (word)));
23
24              if (obj == null)
25                  table.insert (new Association (
26                      new Str (word), new Counter (1)));
27              else
28              {
29                  Association assoc = (Association) obj;
30                  Counter counter = (Counter) assoc.getValue ();
31                  counter.increment ();
32              }
33          }
34          out.println (table);
35      }
36  }
```

The running time of the **wordCounter** method depends on a number of factors, including the number of different keys, the frequency of occurrence of each key, and the distribution of the keys in the overall space of keys. Of course, the hash/scatter table implementation chosen has an effect, as does the size of the table used. For a reasonable set of keys we expect the hash function to do a good job of spreading the keys uniformly in the table. Provided a sufficiently large table is used, the average search and insertion time is bounded by a constant. Under these ideal conditions the running time should be $O(n)$, where n is the number of words in the input file.

Exercises

8.1   Suppose we know a priori that a given key is equally likely to be any integer between a and b.

  a.   When is the *division method of hashing* a good choice?

  b.   When is the *middle-square method of hashing* a good choice?

8.2   Compute (by hand) the hash value obtained by Program 8.3 for the strings `"ece.uw.ca"` and `"cs.uw.ca"`. **Hint**: Refer to Appendix C.

8.3   Canadian postal codes have the format LDL␣DLD, where L is always a letter (A–Z), D is always a digit (0–9), and ␣ is always a single space. For example, the postal code for the University of Waterloo is N2L␣3G1. Devise a suitable hash function for Canadian postal codes.

8.4   For each type of hash table listed in *a* through *e*, show the hash table obtained when we insert the keys

$$\{\texttt{"un"}, \texttt{"deux"}, \texttt{"trois"}, \texttt{"quatre"}, \texttt{"cinq"}, \texttt{"six"},$$

$$\texttt{"sept"}, \texttt{"huit"}, \texttt{"neuf"}, \texttt{"dix"}, \texttt{"onze"}, \texttt{"douze"}\}.$$

in the order given into a table of size $M = 16$ that is initially empty. Use the following table of hash values:

x	**Hash**(x) (octal)
`"un"`	016456
`"deux"`	0145446470
`"trois"`	016563565063
`"quatre"`	010440656345
`"cinq"`	0142505761
`"six"`^{2}	01625070
`"sept"`	0162446164
`"huit"`	0151645064
`"neuf"`	0157446446
`"dix"`	01455070
`"onze"`	0156577345
`"douze"`	014556647345

a. chained hash table

b. chained scatter table

c. open scatter table using *linear probing*

d. open scatter table using *quadratic probing*

e. open scatter table using *double hashing*. (Use Equation 8.6 as the secondary hash function.)

8.5 For each table obtained in Exercise 8.4, show the result when the key **"deux"** is withdrawn.

8.6 For each table considered in Exercise 8.4, derive an expression for the total memory space used to represent a table of size M that contains n items.

8.7 Consider a chained hash table of size M that contains n items. The performance of the table decreases as the load factor $\lambda = n/M$ increases. In order to keep the load factor below one, we propose to double the size of the array when $n = M$. However, in order to do so we must *rehash* all of the elements in the table. Explain why rehashing is necessary.

8.8 Give the sequence of M keys that fills a *chained scatter table* of size M in the *shortest* possible time. Find a tight, asymptotic bound on the minimum running time taken to fill the table.

8.9 Give the sequence of M keys that fills a *chained scatter table* of size M in the *longest* possible time. Find a tight, asymptotic bound on the minimum running time taken to fill the table.

8.10 Consider the chained hash table introduced shown in Program 8.8.

a. Rewrite the **insert** method so that it doubles the length of the array when $\lambda = 1$.

b. Rewrite the **withdraw** method so that it halves the length of the array when $\lambda = \frac{1}{2}$.

c. Show that the *average* time for both insert and withdraw operations is still $O(1)$.

8.11 Consider two sets of integers, $S = \{s_1, s_2, \ldots, s_m\}$ and $T = \{t_1, t_2, \ldots, t_n\}$.

a. Devise an algorithm that uses a hash table to test whether S is a subset of T. What is the average running time of your algorithm?

b. Two sets are *equivalent* if and only if both $S \subseteq T$ and $T \subseteq S$. Show that we can test whether two sets of integers are equivalent in $O(m + n)$ time (on average).

8.12 (This question should be attempted *after* reading Chapter 10.) Rather than use an array of linked lists, suppose we implement a hash table with an array of *binary search trees*.

a. What are the worst-case running times for **insert**, **find**, and **withdraw**?

b. What are the average running times for **insert**, **find**, and **withdraw**?

8.13 (This question should be attempted *after* reading Section 14.5.1.) Consider a scatter table with open addressing. Devise a probe sequence of the form

$$h_i(x) = (h(x) + c(i)) \bmod M,$$

where $c(i)$ is a *full-period pseudo-random number generator*. Why is such a sequence likely to be better than either linear probing or quadratic probing?

Programming Projects

8.1 Complete the implementation of the `ChainedHashTable` class declared in Program 8.8 by providing suitable definitions for the following methods: `isMember`, `compareTo`, `accept`, and `getEnumeration`. Write a test program and test your implementation.

8.2 Complete the implementation of the `ChainedScatterTable` class declared in Program 8.13 by providing suitable definitions for the following methods: `isFull`, `isMember`, `compareTo`, `accept`, and `getEnumeration`. Write a test program and test your implementation.

8.3 Complete the implementation of the `OpenScatterTable` class declared in Program 8.17 by providing suitable definitions for the following methods: `isFull`, `isMember`, `findInstance`, `compareTo`, `accept`, and `getEnumeration`. Write a test program and test your implementation.

8.4 The `withdraw` method defined in Program 8.9 was written under the assumption that linear probing is used. Therefore, it does not call explicitly the collision resolution method `c`. Rewrite the `withdraw` method so that it works correctly regardless of the collision resolution strategy used.

8.5 Consider an application that has the following profile: First, n symbols (character strings) are read in. As each symbol is read, it is assigned an ordinal number from 1 to n. Then a large number of operations are performed. In each operation we are given either a symbol or a number and we need to determine its mate. Design, implement, and test a data structure that provides both mappings in $O(1)$ time.

8.6 Spelling checkers are often implemented using hashing. However, the space required to store all words in a complete dictionary is usually prohibitive. An alternative solution is to use a very large array of bits. The array is initialized as follows: First, all of the bits are set to zero. Then for each word w in the dictionary, we set bit $h(w)$ to one, where $h(\cdot)$ is a suitable hash function.

To check the spelling in a given document, we hash the words in the document one-by-one and examine the corresponding bit of the array. If the bit is a zero, the word does not appear in the dictionary and we conclude that it is misspelled. Note that if the bit is a 1, the word may still be misspelled, but we cannot tell.

Design and implement a spelling checker. **Hint**: Use the `SetAsBitVector` class given in Chapter 12.

9 | Trees

In this chapter we consider one of the most important non-linear information structures—*trees*. A tree is often used to represent a *hierarchy*. This is because the relationships between the items in the hierarchy suggest the branches of a botanical tree.

For example, a tree-like *organization chart* is often used to represent the lines of responsibility in a business, as shown in Figure 9.1. The president of the company is shown at the top of the tree and the vice presidents are indicated below. Under the vice presidents we find the managers and below the managers the rest of the clerks. Each clerk reports to a manager, each manager reports to a vice president, and each vice president reports to the president.

It just takes a little imagination to see the tree in Figure 9.1. Of course, the tree is upside-down. However, this is the usual way the data structure is drawn. The president is called the *root* of the tree and the clerks are the *leaves*.

A tree is extremely useful for certain kinds of computations. For example, suppose we wish to determine the total salaries paid to employees by division or by department. The total of the salaries in division A can be found by computing the sum of the salaries paid in departments A1 and A2, plus the salary of the vice president of division A. Similarly, the total of the salaries paid in department A1 is the sum of the salaries of the manager of department A1 and of the two clerks below that manager.

Clearly, in order to compute all of the totals, it is necessary to consider the salary of every employee. Therefore, an implementation of this computation must *visit* all employees in the tree. An algorithm that systematically *visits* all items in a tree is called a *tree traversal*.

In this chapter we consider several different kinds of trees as well as several different tree-traversal algorithms. In addition, we show how trees can be used to represent arithmetic expressions and how we can evaluate an arithmetic expression by doing a tree traversal.

FIGURE 9.1
Representing a hierarchy using a tree.

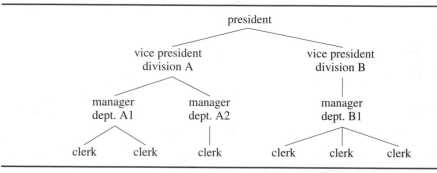

9.1 Basics

The following is a mathematical definition of a tree:

Definition 9.1 (Tree)
A tree T is a finite, non-empty set of nodes,

$$T = \{r\} \cup T_1 \cup T_2 \cup \cdots \cup T_n,$$

with the following properties:

1. *A designated node of the set, r, is called the* root *of the tree; and*
2. *The remaining nodes are partitioned into n ≥ 0 subsets, $T_1, T_2, \ldots, T_n$, each of which is a tree.*

For convenience, we will use the notation $T = \{r, T_1, T_2, \ldots, T_n\}$ to denote the tree T.

Notice that Definition 9.1 is *recursive*— a tree is defined in terms of itself! Fortunately, we do not have a problem with infinite recursion because every tree has a *finite* number of nodes and because in the base case a tree has $n = 0$ subtrees.

It follows from Definition 9.1 that the minimal tree is a tree composed of a single root node. For example, $T_a = \{A\}$ is such a tree. When there is more than one node, the remaining nodes are partitioned into subtrees. For example, $T_b = \{B, \{C\}\}$ is a tree that is composed of the root node B and the subtree $\{C\}$. Finally, the following is also a tree:

$$T_c = \{D, \{E, \{F\}\}, \{G, \{H, \{I\}\}, \{J, \{K\}, \{L\}\}, \{M\}\}\}. \tag{9.1}$$

How do T_a, T_b, and T_c resemble their arboreal namesake? The similarity becomes apparent when we consider the graphical representation of these trees shown in Figure 9.2. To draw such a pictorial representation of a tree, $T = \{r, T_1, T_2, \ldots, T_n\}$, the following recursive procedure is used: First, we first draw the root node r. Then, we draw each of the subtrees, $T_1, T_2, \ldots, T_n$, beside each other below the root. Finally, lines are drawn from r to the roots of each of the subtrees.

FIGURE 9.2
Examples of trees.

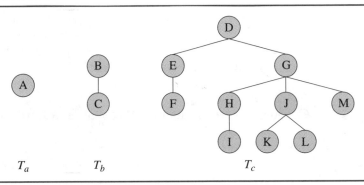

$$T_a \qquad T_b \qquad\qquad T_c$$

Of course, trees drawn in this fashion are upside-down. Nevertheless, this is the conventional way in which tree data structures are drawn. In fact, it is understood that when we speak of "up" and "down," we do so with respect to this pictorial representation. For example, when we move from a root to a subtree, we will say that we are moving *down* the tree.

The inverted pictorial representation of trees is probably due to the way that genealogical *lineal charts* are drawn. A *lineal chart* is a family tree that shows the descendants of some person. And it is from genealogy that much of the terminology associated with tree data structures is taken.

Terminology

Consider a tree $T = \{r, T_1, T_2, \ldots, T_n\}$, $n \geq 0$, as given by Definition 9.1.

- The *degree* of a node is the number of subtrees associated with that node. For example, the degree of tree T is n.
- A node of degree zero has no subtrees. Such a node is called a *leaf*.
- Each root r_i of subtree T_i of tree T is called a *child* of r. The term *grandchild* is defined in a similar manner.
- The root node r of tree T is the *parent* of all the roots r_i of the subtrees T_i, $1 < i \leq n$. The term *grandparent* is defined in a similar manner.
- Two roots r_i and r_j of distinct subtrees T_i and T_j of tree T are called *siblings*.

Clearly the terminology used for describing tree data structures is a curious mixture of the mathematical, the genealogical, and the botanical. There is still more terminology to be introduced, but in order to do that, we need the following definition:

Definition 9.2 (Path and Path Length)

Given a tree T containing the set of nodes R, a path *in T is defined as a non-empty sequence of nodes*

$$P = \{r_1, r_2, \ldots, r_k\},$$

where $r_i \in R$, for $1 \leq i \leq k$ such that the ith node in the sequence, r_i, is the parent *of the $(i + 1)$th node in the sequence r_{i+1}. The* length *of path P is $k - 1$.*

For example, consider again the tree T_c shown in Figure 9.2. This tree contains many different paths. In fact, if you count carefully, you should find that there are exactly 29 distinct paths in tree T_c. This includes the path of length zero, $\{D\}$; the path of length one, $\{E, F\}$; and the path of length three, $\{D, G, J, K\}$.

More Terminology

Consider a tree T containing the set of nodes R as given by Definition 9.1.

- The *level* or *depth* of a node $r_i \in R$ in a tree T is the length of the unique path in T from its root r to the node r_i. For example, the root of T is at level zero and the roots of the subtrees are of T are at level one.

- The *height of a node* $r_i \in R$ in a tree T is the length of the longest path from node r_i to a leaf. Therefore, the leaves are all at height zero.

- The *height of a tree* T is the height of its root node r.

- Consider two nodes r_i and r_j in a tree T. The node r_i is an *ancestor* of the node r_j if there exists a path in T from r_i to r_j. Notice that r_i and r_j may be the same node. That is, a node is its own ancestor. However, the node r_i is a *proper ancestor* if there exists a path p in T from r_i to r_j such that the length of the path p is non-zero.

- Similarly, node r_j is a *descendant* of the node r_i if there exists a path in T from r_i to r_j. And since r_i and r_j may be the same node, a node is its own descendant. The node r_j is a *proper descendant* if there exists a path p in T from r_i to r_j such that the length of the path p is non-zero.

Alternate Representations for Trees

Figure 9.3 shows an alternate representation of the tree T_c defined in Equation (9.1). In this case, the tree is represented as a set of nested regions in the plane. In fact, what we have is a *Venn diagram*, which corresponds to the view that a tree is a set of sets.

FIGURE 9.3
An alternate graphical representation for trees.

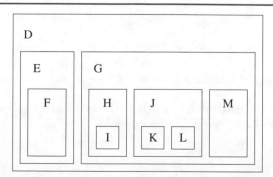

This hierarchical, set-within-a-set view of trees is also evoked by considering the nested structure of computer programs. For example, consider the following fragment of Java code:

```
class D {
    class E {
        class F {
        }
    }
    class G {
        class H {
            class I {}
        }
        class J {
            class K {}
            class L {}
        }
        class M {}
    }
}
```

The nesting structure of this program and the tree given in Equation (9.1) are *isomorphic*.[1] Therefore, it is not surprising that trees have an important role in the analysis and translation of computer programs.

9.2 *N*-ary Trees

In the preceding section we considered trees in which the nodes can have arbitrary degrees. In particular, the general case allows each of the nodes of a tree to have a different degree. In this section we consider a variation in which all of the nodes of the tree are required to have exactly the same degree.

Unfortunately, simply adding to Definition 9.1 the additional requirement that all of the nodes of the tree have the same degree does not work. It is not possible to construct a tree that has a finite number of nodes, all of which have the same degree N in any case except the trivial case of $N = 0$. In order to make it work, we need to introduce the notion of an empty tree as follows:

Definition 9.3 (*N*-ary Tree)
An N-ary tree T is a finite set of nodes *with the following properties:*

1. *Either the set is empty, $T = \varnothing$; or*
2. *The set consists of a root, R, and exactly N distinct N-ary trees. That is, the remaining nodes are partitioned into $N \geq 0$ subsets, $T_0, T_1, \ldots, T_{N-1}$, each of which is an N-ary tree such that $T = \{R, T_0, T_1, \ldots, T_{N-1}\}$.*

---

[1] Isomorphic is a fancy word that means being of identical or similar form, shape or structure.

According to Definition 9.3, an *N*-ary tree is either the empty tree, $\varnothing$, or it is a non-empty set of nodes that consists of a root and exactly *N* subtrees. Clearly, the empty set contains neither a root nor any subtrees. Therefore, the degree of each node of an *N*-ary tree is either zero or *N*.

There is a subtle, yet extremely important consequence of Definition 9.3 that often goes unrecognized. The empty tree, $T = \varnothing$, is a tree. That is, it is an object of the same type as a non-empty tree. Therefore, from the perspective of object-oriented program design, an empty tree must be an instance of some object class. It is inappropriate to use the `null` reference to represent an empty tree, since the `null` reference refers to nothing at all!

The empty trees are called *external nodes* because they have no subtrees and therefore appear at the extremities of the tree. Conversely, the non-empty trees are called *internal nodes*.

Figure 9.4 shows the following *tertiary* ($N = 3$) trees:

$$T_a = \{A, \varnothing, \varnothing, \varnothing\},$$
$$T_b = \{B, \{C, \varnothing, \varnothing, \varnothing\}, \varnothing, \varnothing\},$$
$$T_c = \{D, \{E, \{F, \varnothing, \varnothing, \varnothing\}, \varnothing, \varnothing\}, \{G, \{H, \{I, \varnothing, \varnothing, \varnothing\}, \varnothing, \varnothing\}, \{J, \{K, \varnothing, \varnothing, \varnothing\},$$
$$\{L, \varnothing, \varnothing, \varnothing\}, \varnothing\}, \{M, \varnothing, \varnothing, \varnothing\}\}, \varnothing\}.$$

FIGURE 9.4
Examples of *N*-ary trees.

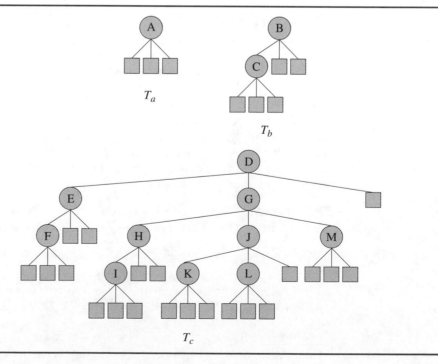

T_a

T_b

T_c

In the figure, square boxes denote the empty trees and circles denote non-empty nodes. Except for the empty trees, the tertiary trees shown in the figure contain the same sets of nodes as the corresponding trees shown in Figure 9.2.

Definitions 9.1 and 9.3 both define trees in terms of sets. In mathematics, elements of a set are normally unordered. Therefore, we might conclude that the relative ordering of the subtrees is not important. However, most practical implementations of trees define an implicit ordering of the subtrees. Consequently, it is usual to assume that the subtrees are ordered. As a result, the two tertiary trees, $T_1 = \{x, \{y, \varnothing, \varnothing, \varnothing\}, \varnothing, \varnothing\}$ and $T_2 = \{x, \varnothing\{y, \varnothing, \varnothing, \varnothing\}, \varnothing\}$, are considered to be distinct unequal trees. Trees in which the subtrees are ordered are called *ordered trees*. On the other hand, trees in which the order does not matter are called *oriented trees*. In this book, we will assume that all trees are ordered unless otherwise specified.

Figure 9.4 suggests that every *N*-ary tree contains a significant number of external nodes. The following theorem tells us precisely how many external nodes we can expect:

Theorem 9.1
An N-ary tree with $n \geq 0$ internal nodes contains $(N-1)n + 1$ external nodes.

Proof   Let the number of external nodes be *l*. Since every node except the root (empty or not) has a parent, there must be $(n + l - 1)/N$ parents in the tree since every parent has *N* children. Therefore, $n = (n + l - 1)/N$. Rearranging this gives $l = (N-1)n + 1$.

Since the external nodes have no subtrees, it is tempting to consider them to be the leaves of the tree. However, in the context of *N*-ary trees, it is customary to define a *leaf node* as an internal node that has only external subtrees. According to this definition, the trees shown in Figure 9.4 have exactly the same sets of leaves as the corresponding general trees shown in Figure 9.2.

Furthermore, since height is defined with respect to the leaves, by having the same leaves for both kinds of trees, the heights are also the same. The following theorem tells us something about the maximum size of a tree of a given height *h*:

Theorem 9.2
Consider an N-ary tree T of height $h \geq 0$. The maximum number of internal nodes in T is given by

$$\frac{N^{h+1} - 1}{N - 1}.$$

Proof   (By induction).

Base Case   Consider an *N*-ary tree of height zero. It consists of exactly one internal node and *N* empty subtrees. Clearly, the theorem holds for $h = 0$ since

$$\left.\frac{N^{h+1} - 1}{N - 1}\right|_{h=0} = 1.$$

Inductive Hypothesis   Suppose the theorem holds for $h = 0, 1, 2, \ldots, k$, for some $k \geq 0$. Consider a tree of height $k + 1$. Such a tree consists of a root and N subtrees, each of which contains at most $(N^{k+1} - 1)/(N - 1)$ nodes. Therefore, altogether the number of nodes is at most

$$N\left(\frac{N^{k+1} - 1}{N - 1}\right) + 1 = \frac{N^{k+2} - 1}{N - 1}. \tag{9.2}$$

That is, the theorem holds for $k + 1$. Therefore, by induction on k, the theorem is true for all values of h.

An interesting consequence of Theorems 9.1 and 9.2 is that the maximum number of external nodes in an N-ary tree of height h is given by

$$(N - 1)\left(\frac{N^{h+1} - 1}{N - 1}\right) + 1 = N^{h+1}.$$

The final theorem of this section addresses the maximum number of *leaves* in an N-ary tree of height h:

Theorem 9.3
Consider an N-ary tree T of height $h \geq 0$. The maximum number of leaf nodes in T is N^h.

Proof   (By induction).

Base Case   Consider an N-ary tree of height zero. It consists of exactly one internal node that has N empty subtrees. Therefore, the one node is a leaf. Clearly the theorem holds for $h = 0$ since $N^0 = 1$.

Inductive Hypothesis   Suppose the theorem holds for $h = 0, 1, 2, \ldots, k$, for some $k \geq 0$. Consider a tree of height $k + 1$. Such a tree consists of a root and N subtrees, each of which contains at most N^k leaf nodes. Therefore, altogether the number of leaves is at most $N \times N^k = N^{k+1}$. That is, the theorem holds for $k + 1$. Therefore, by induction on k, the theorem is true for all values of h.

9.3 Binary Trees

In this section we consider an extremely important and useful category of tree structure—*binary trees*. A binary tree is an N-ary tree for which N is two. Since a binary tree is an N-ary tree, all of the results derived in the preceding section apply to binary trees. However, binary trees have some interesting characteristics that arise from the restriction that N is two. For example, there is an interesting relationship between binary trees and the binary number system. Binary trees are also very useful for the representation of mathematical expressions involving the binary operations such as addition and multiplication.

Binary trees are defined as follows:

Definition 9.4 (Binary Tree)
A binary tree T is a finite set of nodes with the following properties:

1. *Either the set is empty, $T = \varnothing$; or*
2. *The set consists of a root, r, and exactly two distinct binary trees T_L and T_R,* $T = \{r, T_L, T_R\}$.

The tree T_L is called the left subtree *of T, and the tree T_R is called the* right subtree *of T.*

Binary trees are almost always considered to be *ordered trees*. Therefore, the two subtrees T_L and T_R are called the *left* and *right* subtrees, respectively. Consider the two binary trees shown in Figure 9.5. Both trees have a root with a single non-empty subtree. However, in one case it is the left subtree that is non-empty; in the other case it is the right subtree that is non-empty. Since the order of the subtrees matters, the two binary trees shown in Figure 9.5 are different.

We can determine some of the characteristics of binary trees from the theorems given in the preceding section by letting $N = 2$. For example, Theorem 9.1 tells us that a binary tree with $n \geq 0$ internal nodes contains $n + 1$ external nodes. This result is true regardless of the shape of the tree. Consequently, we expect that the storage overhead associated with the empty trees will be $O(n)$.

From Theorem 9.2 we learn that a binary tree of height $h \geq 0$ has at most $2^{h+1} - 1$ internal nodes. Conversely, the height of a binary tree with n internal nodes is at least $\lceil \log_2 n + 1 \rceil - 1$. That is, the height of a binary tree with n nodes is $\Omega(\log n)$.

Finally, according to Theorem 9.3, a binary tree of height $h \geq 0$ has at most 2^h leaves. Conversely, the height of a binary tree with l leaves is at least $\lceil \log_2 l \rceil$. Thus, the height of a binary tree with l leaves is $\Omega(\log l)$.

FIGURE 9.5
Two distinct binary trees.

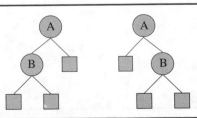

9.4 Tree Traversals

There are many different applications of trees. As a result, there are many different algorithms for manipulating them. However, many of the different tree algorithms have in common the characteristic that they systematically visit all nodes in the tree. That is, the algorithm walks through the tree data structure and performs some computation at each node in the tree. This process of walking through the tree is called a *tree traversal*.

There are essentially two different methods in which to visit systematically all nodes of a tree—*depth-first traversal* and *breadth-first traversal*. Certain depth-first traversal methods occur frequently enough that they are given names of their own: *preorder traversal*, *inorder traversal*, and *postorder traversal*.

The discussion that follows uses the tree in Figure 9.6 as an example. The tree shown in the figure is a general tree in the sense of Definition 9.1:

$$T = \{A, \{B, \{C\}\}, \{D, \{E, \{F\}, \{G\}\}, \{H, \{I\}\}\}\}. \tag{9.3}$$

However, we can also consider the tree in Figure 9.6 to be an *N*-ary tree (specifically, a binary tree if we assume the existence of empty trees at the appropriate positions):

$$T = \{A, \{B, \varnothing, \{C, \varnothing, \varnothing\}\}, \{D, \{E, \{F, \varnothing, \varnothing\}, \{G, \varnothing, \varnothing\}\}, \{H, \{I, \varnothing, \varnothing\}, \varnothing\}\}\}.$$

Preorder Traversal

The first depth-first traversal method we consider is called *preorder traversal*. Preorder traversal is defined recursively as follows. To do a preorder traversal of a general tree:

1. Visit the root first, and then
2. Do a preorder traversal each of the subtrees of the root one-by-one in the order given.

FIGURE 9.6
Sample tree.

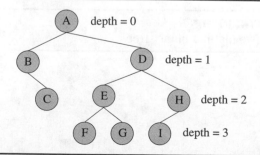

Preorder traversal gets its name from the fact that it visits the root first. In the case of a binary tree, the algorithm becomes:

1. Visit the root first, and then
2. Traverse the left subtree, and then
3. Traverse the right subtree.

For example, a preorder traversal of the tree shown in Figure 9.6 visits the nodes in the following order:

$$A, B, C, D, E, F, G, H, I.$$

Notice that the preorder traversal visits the nodes of the tree in precisely the same order in which they are written in Equation (9.3). A preorder traversal is often done when it is necessary to print a textual representation of a tree.

Postorder Traversal

The second depth first traversal method we consider is *postorder traversal*. In contrast with preorder traversal, which visits the root first, postorder traversal visits the root last. To do a postorder traversal of a general tree:

1. Do a postorder traversal each of the subtrees of the root one-by-one in the order given, and then
2. Visit the root.

To do a postorder traversal of a binary tree

1. Traverse the left subtree, and then
2. Traverse the right subtree, and then
3. Visit the root.

A postorder traversal of the tree shown in Figure 9.6 visits the nodes in the following order:

$$C, B, F, G, E, I, H, D, A.$$

Inorder Traversal

The third depth-first traversal method is *inorder traversal*. Inorder traversal only makes sense for binary trees. Whereas preorder traversal visits the root first and postorder traversal visits the root last, inorder traversal visits the root *in between* visiting the left and right subtrees:

1. Traverse the left subtree, and then
2. Visit the root, and then
3. Traverse the right subtree.

An inorder traversal of the tree shown in Figure 9.6 visits the nodes in the following order:

$$B, C, A, F, E, G, D, I, H.$$

Breadth-First Traversal

Whereas the depth-first traversals are defined recursively, *breadth-first traversal* is best understood as a non-recursive traversal. The breadth-first traversal of a tree visits the nodes in the order of their depth in the tree. Breadth-first traversal first visits all nodes at depth zero (i.e., the root), then all nodes at depth one, and so on. At each depth the nodes are visited from left to right.

A breadth-first traversal of the tree shown in Figure 9.6 visits the nodes in the following order:

$$A, B, D, C, E, H, F, G, I.$$

9.5 Expression Trees

Algebraic expressions such as

$$a/b + (c - d)e \qquad (9.4)$$

have an inherent tree-like structure. For example, Figure 9.7 is a representation of the expression in Equation (9.4). This kind of tree is called an *expression tree*.

The terminal nodes (leaves) of an expression tree are the variables or constants in the expression (a, b, c, d, and e). The non-terminal nodes of an expression tree are the operators ($+$, $-$, $\times$, and $\div$). Notice that the parentheses that appear in Equation (9.4) do not appear in the tree. Nevertheless, the tree representation has captured the intent of the parentheses since the subtraction is lower in the tree than the multiplication.

FIGURE 9.7
Tree representing the expression $a/b + (c - d)e$.

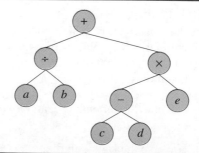

The common algebraic operators are either unary or binary. For example, addition, subtraction, multiplication, and division are all binary operations and negation is a unary operation. Therefore, the non-terminal nodes of the corresponding expression trees have either one or two non-empty subtrees. That is, expression trees are usually binary trees.

What can we do with an expression tree? Perhaps the simplest thing to do is to print the expression represented by the tree. Notice that an inorder traversal of the tree in Figure 9.7 visits the nodes in the order

$$a, \div, b, +, c, -, d, e.$$

Except for the missing parentheses, this is precisely the order in which the symbols appear in Equation (9.4)!

This suggests that an *inorder* traversal should be used to print the expression. Consider an inorder traversal that, when it encounters a terminal node, simply prints it out; and when it encounters a non-terminal node, it does the following:

1. Print a left parenthesis, and then
2. Traverse the left subtree, and then
3. Print the root, and then
4. Traverse the right subtree, and then
5. Print a right parenthesis.

Applying this procedure to the tree given in Figure 9.7, we get

$$((a \div b) + ((c - d) \times e)), \qquad (9.5)$$

which, despite the redundant parentheses, represents exactly the same expression as Equation (9.4).

Infix Notation
The algebraic expression in Equation (9.5) is written in the usual way such mathematical expressions are written. The notation used is called *infix notation* because each operator appears *in between* its operands. As we have seen, there is a natural relationship between infix notation and inorder traversal.

Infix notation is only possible for binary operations such as addition, subtraction, multiplication, and division. Writing an operator in between its operands is possible only when it has exactly two operands. In Chapter 6 we saw two alternative notations for algebraic expressions—*prefix* and *postfix*.

Prefix Notation
In prefix notation the operator is written before its operands. Therefore, in order to print the prefix expression from an expression tree, preorder traversal is done. That is, at

every non-terminal node we do the following:

1. Print the root, and then
2. Print a left parenthesis, and then
3. Traverse the left subtree, and then
4. Print a comma, and then
5. Traverse the right subtree, and then
6. Print a right parenthesis.

If we use this procedure to print the tree given in Figure 9.7, we get the prefix expression

$$+(\div(a, b), \times(-(c, d), e)). \qquad (9.6)$$

Although this notation may appear unfamiliar at first, consider the result obtained when we spell out the names of the operators:

```
plus (div (a,b), times (minus (c,d), e))
```

This is precisely the notation used in a typical programming language to invoke user-defined methods `plus`, `minus`, `times`, and `div`.

Postfix Notation

Since inorder traversal produces an infix expression and preorder traversal produces a prefix expression, it should not come as a surprise that postorder traversal produces a postfix expression. In a postfix expression, an operator always follows its operands. The beauty of postfix (and prefix) expressions is that parentheses are not necessary.

A simple postorder traversal of the tree in Figure 9.7 gives the postfix expression

$$a\, b \div c\, d - e \times +. \qquad (9.7)$$

In Section 6.1.3 we saw that a postfix expression is easily evaluated using a stack. So, given an expression tree, we can evaluate the expression by doing a postorder traversal to create the postfix expression and then using the algorithm given in Section 6.1.3 to evaluate the expression.

In fact, it is not really necessary to first create the postfix expression before computing its value. The expression can be evaluated by making use of an *evaluation stack* during the course of the traversal as follows: When a terminal node is visited, its value is pushed onto the stack. When a non-terminal node is visited, two values are popped from the stack, the operation specified by the node is performed on those values, and the result is pushed back onto the evaluation stack. When the traversal terminates, there will be one result in the evaluation stack and that result is the value of the expression.

Finally, we can take this one step further. Instead of actually evaluating the expression, the code to compute the value of the expression is emitted. Again, a postorder traversal is done. However, now instead of performing the computation as each node is visited, the code needed to perform the evaluation is emitted. This is precisely what a compiler does when it compiles an expression such as Equation (9.5) for execution.

9.6   Implementing Trees

In this section we consider the implementation of trees including general trees, N-ary trees, and binary trees. The implementations presented were developed in the context of the abstract data-type framework presented in Chapter 5. That is, the various types of trees are viewed as classes of *containers*, as shown in Figure 9.8.

Program 9.1 defines the **Tree** interface. The **Tree** interface extends the **Container** interface defined in Program 5.8.

FIGURE 9.8
Object class hierarchy.

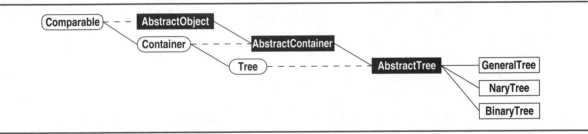

PROGRAM 9.1
Tree interface

```
1   public interface Tree
2       extends Container
3   {
4       Object getKey ();
5       Tree getSubtree (int i);
6       boolean isEmpty ();
7       boolean isLeaf ();
8       int getDegree ();
9       int getHeight ();
10      void depthFirstTraversal (PrePostVisitor visitor);
11      void breadthFirstTraversal (Visitor visitor);
12  }
```

The **Tree** interface adds the following methods to those inherited from the **Container** interface:

getKey   This method returns the object contained in the root node of a tree.

getSubtree   This method returns the *i*th subtree of the given tree.

isEmpty   This **boolean**-valued method returns **true** if the root of the tree is an empty tree—that is, an external node.

isLeaf   This **boolean**-valued method returns **true** if the root of the tree is a leaf node.

getDegree   This method returns the degree of the root node of the tree. By definition, the degree of an external node is zero.

getHeight   This method returns the height of the tree. By definition, the height of an empty tree is −1.

depthFirstTraversal and breadthFirstTraversal   These methods are like the **accept** method of the container class (see Section 5.2.4). Both of these methods perform a traversal. That is, all the nodes of the tree are visited systematically. The former takes a **PrePostVisitor** and the latter takes a **Visitor**. When a node is visited, the appropriate methods of the visitor are applied to that node.

9.6.1   Tree Traversals

Program 9.2 introduces the **AbstractTree** class. The **AbstractTree** class extends the **AbstractContainer** class introduced in Program 5.9 and it implements the **Tree** interface defined in Program 9.1. The **AbstractTree** class provides default implementations for both the **depthFirstTraversal** and **breadthFirstTraversal** methods. Both of these implementations call abstract methods such as **getKey** and **getSubtree**. In effect, they are *abstract algorithms*. An abstract algorithm describes behavior in the absence of implementation!

Depth-First Traversal
Program 9.2 defines the **depthFirstTraversal** method of the **AbstractTree** class. The traversal method takes one argument—any object that implements the **PrePostVisitor** interface defined in Program 9.3.

A **PrePostVisitor** is a visitor with four methods—**preVisit**, **inVisit**, **postVisit**, and **isDone**. During a depth-first traversal the **preVisit** and **postVisit** methods are each called once for every node in the tree. (The **inVisit** method is provided for binary trees and is discussed in Section 9.6.6.)

The depth-first traversal method first calls the **preVisit** method with the object in the root node. Then it calls recursively the **depthFirstTraversal** method for each subtree of the given node. After all of the subtrees have been visited, the **postVisit** method is called. Assuming that the **isEmpty**, **getKey**, and **getSubtree** methods

PROGRAM 9.2
`AbstractTree` class `depthFirstTraversal` method

```
1  public abstract class AbstractTree
2      extends AbstractContainer
3      implements Tree
4  {
5      public void depthFirstTraversal (PrePostVisitor visitor)
6      {
7          if (visitor.isDone ())
8              return;
9          if (!isEmpty ())
10         {
11             visitor.preVisit (getKey ());
12             for (int i = 0; i < getDegree (); ++i)
13                 getSubtree (i).depthFirstTraversal (visitor);
14             visitor.postVisit (getKey ());
15         }
16     }
17     // ...
18 }
```

PROGRAM 9.3
`PrePostVisitor` interface

```
1  public interface PrePostVisitor
2  {
3      void preVisit (Object object);
4      void inVisit (Object object);
5      void postVisit (Object object);
6      boolean isDone ();
7  }
```

all run in constant time, the total running time of the `depthFirstTraversal` method is

$$n(\mathcal{T}\langle \text{preVisit}\rangle + \mathcal{T}\langle \text{postVisit}\rangle) + O(n),$$

where n is the number of nodes in the tree, $\mathcal{T}\langle \text{preVisit}\rangle$ is the running time of `preVisit`, and $\mathcal{T}\langle \text{postVisit}\rangle$ is the running time of `postVisit`.

Preorder, Inorder, and Postorder Traversals

Preorder, inorder, and postorder traversals are special cases of the more general depth-first traversal described in the preceding section. Rather than implement each of these traversals directly, we make use of a design pattern, called *adapter*, which allows the single method to provide all of the needed functionality.

PROGRAM 9.4
`AbstractPrePostVisitor` class

```
1   public abstract class AbstractPrePostVisitor
2       implements PrePostVisitor
3   {
4       public void preVisit (Object object)
5           {}
6       public void inVisit (Object object)
7           {}
8       public void postVisit (Object object)
9           {}
10      public boolean isDone ()
11          { return false; }
12  }
```

Suppose we have an instance of the `PrintingVisitor` class (see Section 5.2.5). The `PrintingVisitor` class implements the `Visitor` interface. However, we cannot pass a `PrintingVisitor` instance to the `depthFirstTraversal` method shown in Program 9.2 because it expects an object that implements the `PrePostVisitor` interface.

The problem is that the interface implemented by the `PrintingVisitor` does not match the interface expected by the `depthFirstTraversal` method. The solution to this problem is to use an adapter. An *adapter* converts the interface provided by one class to the interface required by another. For example, if we want a preorder traversal, then the call to the `preVisit` (made by `depthFirstTraversal`) should be mapped to the `visit` method (provided by the `PrintingVisitor`). Similarly, a postorder traversal is obtained by mapping `postVisit` to `visit`.

Program 9.4 defines the `AbstractPrePostVisitor` class. This class implements the `PrePostVisitor` interface defined in Program 9.3. It provides trivial default implementations for all of the required methods.

Programs 9.5, 9.6, and 9.7 define three adapter classes—`PreOrder`, `InOrder`, and `PostOrder`. All three classes are similar: They all extend the `AbstractPrePostVisitor` class defined in Program 9.4, all have a single field that refers to a `Visitor`, and all have a constructor that takes a `Visitor`.

Each class provides a different interface mapping. For example, the `preVisit` method of the `PreOrder` class simply calls the `visit` method on the `visitor` field. Notice that the adapter provides no functionality of its own—it simply forwards method calls to the `visitor` instance as required.

The following code fragment illustrates how these adapters are used:

```
Visitor v = new PrintingVisitor ();
Tree t = new SomeTree ();
// ...
t.depthFirstTraversal (new PreOrder (v));
t.depthFirstTraversal (new InOrder (v));
t.depthFirstTraversal (new PostOrder (v));
```

PROGRAM 9.5
PreOrder class

```
1   public class PreOrder
2       extends AbstractPrePostVisitor
3   {
4       protected Visitor visitor;
5
6       public PreOrder (Visitor visitor)
7           { this.visitor = visitor; }
8
9       public void preVisit (Object object)
10          { visitor.visit (object); }
11
12      public boolean isDone ()
13          { return visitor.isDone (); }
14  }
```

PROGRAM 9.6
InOrder class

```
1   public class InOrder
2       extends AbstractPrePostVisitor
3   {
4       protected Visitor visitor;
5
6       public InOrder (Visitor visitor)
7           { this.visitor = visitor; }
8
9       public void inVisit (Object object)
10          { visitor.visit (object); }
11
12      public boolean isDone ()
13          { return visitor.isDone (); }
14  }
```

Breadth-First Traversal

Program 9.8 defines the **breadthFirstTraversal** method of the **AbstractTree** class. As defined in Section 9.4, a breadth-first traversal of a tree visits the nodes in the order of their depth in the tree and at each level the nodes are visited from left to right.

We already saw in Section 6.2.3 a non-recursive breadth-first traversal algorithm for N-ary trees. This algorithm makes use of a queue as follows: Initially, the root node of the given tree is enqueued, provided it is not the empty tree. Then the following steps

---

PROGRAM 9.7
PostOrder class

```
1   public class PostOrder
2       extends AbstractPrePostVisitor
3   {
4       protected Visitor visitor;
5
6       public PostOrder (Visitor visitor)
7           { this.visitor = visitor; }
8
9       public void postVisit (Object object)
10          { visitor.visit (object); }
11
12      public boolean isDone ()
13          { return visitor.isDone (); }
14  }
```

PROGRAM 9.8
AbstractTree class breadthFirstTraversal method

```
1   public abstract class AbstractTree
2       extends AbstractContainer
3       implements Tree
4   {
5       public void breadthFirstTraversal (Visitor visitor)
6       {
7           Queue queue = new QueueAsLinkedList ();
8           if (!isEmpty ())
9               queue.enqueue (this);
10          while (!queue.isEmpty () && !visitor.isDone ())
11          {
12              Tree head = (Tree) queue.dequeue ();
13              visitor.visit (head.getKey ());
14              for (int i = 0; i < head.getDegree (); ++i)
15              {
16                  Tree child = head.getSubtree (i);
17                  if (!child.isEmpty ())
18                      queue.enqueue (child);
19              }
20          }
21      }
22      // ...
23  }
```

---

are repeated until the queue is empty:

1. Remove the node at the head of the queue and call it **head**.
2. Visit the object contained in **head**.
3. Enqueue in order each non-empty subtree of **head**.

Notice that empty trees are never put into the queue. Furthermore, it should be obvious that each node of the tree is enqueued exactly once. Therefore, it is also dequeued exactly once. Consequently, the running time for the breadth-first traversal is $n\mathcal{T}\langle\texttt{visit}\rangle + O(n)$.

accept Method
The **AbstractTree** class replaces the functionality provided by the single method **accept** with two different kinds of traversal. Whereas the **accept** method is allowed to visit the nodes of a tree in any order, the tree traversals visit the nodes in two different, but well-defined orders. Consequently, we have chosen to provide a default implementation of the **accept** method that does a preorder traversal.

Program 9.9 shows the implementation of the **accept** method of the **Abstract-Tree** class. This method uses the **PreOrder** adapter to pass on a given visitor to the **depthFirstTraversal** method.

9.6.2 Tree Enumerations

This section describes the implementation of an enumeration that can be used to step through the contents of any tree instance. For example, suppose we have declared a variable **tree** that refers to a **BinaryTree**. Then we can view the **tree** instance as a container and print its contents as follows:

```
Tree tree = new BinaryTree ();
// ...
Enumeration e = tree.getEnumeration ();
while (e.hasMoreElements ())
{
    Object obj = e.nextElement ();
    System.out.println (obj);
}
```

Every concrete class that implements the **Container** interface must provide a **getEnumeration** method. This method returns an object that implements the **Enumeration** interface defined in Program 5.13. The enumeration can then be used to systematically visit the contents of the associated container.

We have already seen that when we systematically visit the nodes of a tree, we are doing a tree traversal. Therefore, the implementation of the enumeration must also do a tree traversal. However, there is a catch. A recursive tree traversal method such as **depthFirstTraversal** keeps track of where it is *implicitly* using the Java virtual

PROGRAM 9.9
AbstractTree class accept method

```
1   public abstract class AbstractTree
2       extends AbstractContainer
3       implements Tree
4   {
5       public void accept (Visitor visitor)
6           { depthFirstTraversal (new PreOrder (visitor)); }
7       // ...
8   }
```

PROGRAM 9.10
AbstractTree class getEnumeration method
and the TreeEnumeration class

```
1   public abstract class AbstractTree
2       extends AbstractContainer
3       implements Tree
4   {
5       public Enumeration getEnumeration ()
6           { return new TreeEnumeration (); }
7
8       protected class TreeEnumeration
9           implements Enumeration
10      {
11          protected Stack stack;
12
13          // ...
14      }
15      // ...
16  }
```

machine stack. However, when we implement an enumeration we must keep track of the state of the traversal *explicitly*. This section presents an enumeration implementation that does a preorder traversal of the tree and keeps track of the current state of the traversal using a stack from Chapter 6.

Program 9.10 introduces the inner class TreeEnumeration, which is declared within the AbstractTree class. The TreeEnumeration class implements the Enumeration interface defined in Program 5.13. The TreeEnumeration contains just one field—stack. As shown in Program 9.10, the getEnumeration method of the AbstractTree class returns a new instance of the TreeEnumeration class each time it is called.

PROGRAM 9.11
`AbstractTree TreeEnumeration` constructor

```
1   public abstract class AbstractTree
2       extends AbstractContainer
3       implements Tree
4   {
5       protected class TreeEnumeration
6           implements Enumeration
7       {
8           public TreeEnumeration ()
9           {
10              stack = new StackAsLinkedList ();
11              if (!isEmpty ())
12                  stack.push (AbstractTree.this);
13          }
14
15      }
16      // ...
17  }
```

Constructor

The code for the **TreeEnumeration** constructor method is given in Program 9.11. The constructor is quite simple. First, a new instance of the **StackAsLinkedList** class is created. (The linked-list implementation of stacks is described in Section 6.1.2.) Then the tree is pushed onto the stack (provided it is not the empty tree).

An empty stack can be created in constant time. In addition, the tree can be pushed onto the empty stack in constant time. Therefore, the running time of the constructor is $O(1)$.

hasMoreElements and nextElement Methods

Program 9.12 defines the two standard methods provided by enumerations, **hasMoreElements** and **nextElement**. The **hasMoreElements** method returns **true** as long as there are still more objects in the container that have not yet been visited. This is the case as long as there is something in the stack. Therefore, the implementation simply calls **isEmpty** to test whether the stack is empty. Clearly, the running time for **hasMoreElements** is $O(1)$.

The **nextElement** method returns the next object in the enumeration. In this case, the next object to be visited is at the root of the tree, which is at the top of the stack. Note, the stack will never contain an empty tree. Therefore, if the stack is not empty, then there is an item to visit. The **nextElement** method pops the top tree from the stack and then pushes its subtrees onto the stack provided that they are not empty. Notice that the order is important here. In a preorder traversal, the first subtree of a node is traversed before the second subtree. Therefore, the second subtree should appear in the stack *below* the first subtree. That is why subtrees are pushed in reverse order. The running time for **hasMoreElements** is $O(d)$, where d is the degree of the tree node found at the top of the stack.

PROGRAM 9.12
AbstractTree TreeEnumeration class hasMoreElements and
nextElement methods

```
1   public abstract class AbstractTree
2       extends AbstractContainer
3       implements Tree
4   {
5       protected class TreeEnumeration
6           implements Enumeration
7       {
8           public boolean hasMoreElements ()
9               { return !stack.isEmpty (); }
10
11          public Object nextElement ()
12          {
13              if (stack.isEmpty ())
14                  throw new NoSuchElementException ();
15
16              Tree top = (Tree) stack.pop ();
17              for (int i = top.getDegree () - 1; i >= 0; --i)
18              {
19                  Tree subtree = (Tree) top.getSubtree (i);
20                  if (!subtree.isEmpty ())
21                      stack.push (subtree);
22              }
23              return top.getKey ();
24          }
25          // ...
26      }
27      // ...
28  }
```

9.6.3 General Trees

This section outlines an implementation of general trees in the sense of Definition 9.1. The salient features of the definition are first, that the nodes of a general tree have arbitrary degrees; and second, that there is no such thing as an empty tree.

The recursive nature of Definition 9.1 has important implications when considering the implementation of such trees as containers. In effect, since a tree contains zero or more subtrees, when implemented as a container, we get a container that contains other containers!

Figure 9.9 shows the approach we have chosen for implementing general trees. This figure shows how the general tree T_c in Figure 9.2 can be stored in memory. The basic idea is that each node has associated with it a linked list of the subtrees of that node.

FIGURE 9.9
Representing general trees using linked lists.

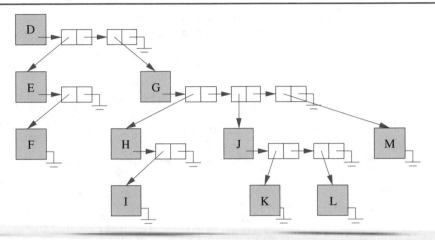

PROGRAM 9.13
GeneralTree fields

```
1   public class GeneralTree
2       extends AbstractTree
3   {
4       protected Object key;
5       protected int degree;
6       protected LinkedList list;
7
8       // ...
9   }
```

A linked list is used because there is no a priori restriction on its length. This allows each node to have an arbitrary degree. Furthermore, since there are no empty trees, we need not worry about representing them. An important consequence of this is that the implementation never makes use of the **null** reference!

Program 9.13 introduces the **GeneralTree** class, which is used to represent general trees as specified by Definition 9.1. The **GeneralTree** class extends the **AbstractTree** class introduced in Program 9.2.

Fields

The **GeneralTree** class definition comprises three fields—**key**, **degree**, and **list**. The first, **key**, represents the root node of the tree. The second, an integer **degree**, records the degree of the root node of the tree. The third, **list**, is an instance of the **LinkedList** class defined in Chapter 4. It is used to contain the subtrees of the given tree.

PROGRAM 9.14
GeneralTree class constructor and purge methods

```
1   public class GeneralTree
2       extends AbstractTree
3   {
4       protected Object key;
5       protected int degree;
6       protected LinkedList list;
7
8       public GeneralTree (Object key)
9       {
10          this.key = key;
11          degree = 0;
12          list = new LinkedList ();
13      }
14
15      public void purge ()
16      {
17          list.purge ();
18          degree = 0;
19      }
20      // ...
21  }
```

Constructor and purge Methods

Program 9.14 defines the GeneralTree constructor and purge methods. According to Definition 9.1, a general tree must contain at least one node—an empty tree is not allowed. Therefore, the constructor takes one argument, any Object instance. The constructor initializes the fields as follows: The key field is assigned the argument, the degree field is set to zero, and the list field is assigned an empty linked list. The running time of the constructor is clearly $O(1)$.

The purge method of a container normally empties the container. In this case, the container is a general tree, which is not allowed to be empty. Thus, the purge method shown in Program 9.14 discards the subtrees of the tree, but it does not discard the root. The running time of the purge method is clearly $O(1)$.

getKey and getSubtree Methods

Program 9.15 defines the various GeneralTree class methods for manipulating general trees. The getKey method is a field accessor that simply returns the object contained by the root node of the tree. Clearly, its running time is $O(1)$.

The getSubtree method takes as its argument an int, i, which must be between 0 and degree − 1, where degree is the degree of the root node of the tree. It returns the ith subtree of the given tree. The getSubtree method simply takes i steps down the linked list and returns the appropriate subtree. Assuming that i is valid, the worst-case running time for `getSubtree` is $O(d)$, where $d = $ `degree` is the degree of the root node of the tree.

`attachSubtree` and `detachSubtree` Methods
Program 9.15 also defines two methods for manipulating the subtrees of a general tree. The purpose of the `attachSubtree` method is to add the specified subtree to the root of a given tree. This method takes as its argument a `GeneralTree` instance, which is to be attached. The `attachSubtree` method simply appends to the linked list a pointer

PROGRAM 9.15
`GeneralTree` class `getKey`, `getSubtree`, `attachSubtree`, and `detachSubtree` methods

```
1   public class GeneralTree
2       extends AbstractTree
3   {
4       protected Object key;
5       protected int degree;
6       protected LinkedList list;
7
8       public Object getKey ()
9           { return key; }
10
11      public Tree getSubtree (int i)
12      {
13          if (i < 0 || i >= degree)
14              throw new IndexOutOfBoundsException ();
15          LinkedList.Element ptr = list.getHead ();
16          for (int j = 0; j < i; ++j)
17              ptr = ptr.getNext ();
18          return (GeneralTree) ptr.getDatum ();
19      }
20
21      public void attachSubtree (GeneralTree t)
22      {
23          list.append (t);
24          ++degree;
25      }
26
27      public GeneralTree detachSubtree (GeneralTree t)
28      {
29          list.extract (t);
30          --degree;
31          return t;
32      }
33      // ...
34  }
```

to the tree to be attached and then adds one to the **degree** variable. The running time for **attachSubtree** is $O(1)$.

Similarly, the **detachSubtree** method removes the specified subtree from the given tree. This method takes as its argument the **GeneralTree** instance that is to be removed. It removes the appropriate item from the linked list and then subtracts one from the **degree** variable. The running time for **detachSubtree** is $O(d)$ in the worst case, where $d = $ **degree**.

9.6.4 *N*-ary Trees

We now turn to the implementation of *N*-ary trees as given by Definition 9.3. According to this definition, an *N*-ary tree is either an empty tree or it is a tree comprised of a root and exactly *N* subtrees. The implementation follows the design pattern established in the preceding section. Specifically, we view an *N*-ary tree as a container.

Figure 9.10 illustrates the way in which *N*-ary trees can be represented. The figure gives the representation of the tertiary ($N = 3$) tree

$$\{A, \{B, \varnothing, \varnothing, \varnothing\}, \varnothing, \varnothing\}.$$

The basic idea is that each node has associated with it an array of length *N* of pointers to the subtrees of that node. An array is used because we assume that the *arity* of the tree, *N*, is known a priori.

Notice that we explicitly represent the empty trees. That is, a separate object instance is allocated for each empty tree. Of course, an empty tree contains neither root nor subtrees.

Program 9.16 introduces the the **NaryTree** class, which represents *N*-ary trees as specified by Definition 9.3. The class **NaryTree** extends the **AbstractTree** class introduced in Program 9.2.

FIGURE 9.10
Representing *N*-ary trees using pointer arrays.

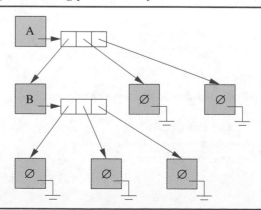

PROGRAM 9.16
`NaryTree` fields

```
1   public class NaryTree
2       extends AbstractTree
3   {
4       protected Object key;
5       protected int degree;
6       protected NaryTree[] subtree;
7
8       // ...
9   }
```

Fields
The implementation of the `NaryTree` class is very similar to that of the `GeneralTree` class. The `NaryTree` class definition also comprises three fields — `key`, `degree`, and `subtree`. The first, `key`, represents the root node of the tree. The second, an integer `degree`, records the degree of the root node of the tree. The third, `subtree`, is an array of `NaryTree`s. This array contains the subtrees of the given tree.

Constructors
The `NaryTree` class declares two constructors. Implementations for the two constructors are given in Program 9.17. The first constructor takes a single argument of type `int`, which specifies the degree of the tree. This constructor creates an empty tree. It does so by setting the `key` field to `null`, and by setting the `subtree` array to `null`. The running time of this constructor is $O(1)$.

The second constructor takes two arguments. The first specifies the degree of the tree and the second is any `Object` instance. This constructor creates a non-empty tree in which the specified object occupies the root node. According to Definition 9.3, every internal node in an N-ary tree must have exactly N subtrees. Therefore, this constructor creates and attaches N empty subtrees to the root node. The running time of this constructor is $O(N)$, since N empty subtrees are created and constructed and the constructor for an empty N-ary tree takes $O(1)$ time.

isEmpty Method
The purpose of the `isEmpty` method is to determine whether a given N-ary tree is the empty tree. The implementation of this method is given in Program 9.18. In this implementation, the `key` field is `null` if the tree is the empty tree. Therefore, `isEmpty` method simply tests the `key` field. Clearly, this is a constant-time operation.

getKey, attachKey, and detachKey Methods
Program 9.18 also defines three methods for manipulating the root of an N-ary tree. The first, `getKey`, is an accessor that returns the object contained in the root node of the tree. Clearly, this operation is not defined for the empty tree. If the tree is not empty, the running time of this method is $O(1)$.

PROGRAM 9.17
`NaryTree` constructors

```
1   public class NaryTree
2       extends AbstractTree
3   {
4       protected Object key;
5       protected int degree;
6       protected NaryTree[] subtree;
7
8       public NaryTree (int degree)
9       {
10          key = null;
11          this.degree = degree;
12          subtree = null;
13      }
14
15      public NaryTree (int degree, Object key)
16      {
17          this.key = key;
18          this.degree = degree;
19          subtree = new NaryTree[degree];
20          for (int i = 0; i < degree; ++i)
21              subtree [i] = new NaryTree (degree);
22      }
23      // ...
24  }
```

The purpose of **attachKey** is to insert the specified object into a given *N*-ary tree at the root node. This operation is only defined for an empty tree. The **attachKey** method takes as its argument an object to be inserted in the root node and assigns that object to the **key** field. Since the node is no longer empty, it must have exactly *N* subtrees. Therefore, *N* new empty subtrees are created and attached to the node. The running time is $O(N)$ since *N* subtrees are created, and the running time of the constructor for an empty *N*-ary tree takes $O(1)$.

Finally, **detachKey** is used to remove the object from the root of a tree. In order that the tree that remains still conforms to Definition 9.3, it is only permissible to remove the root from a leaf node. And on removal, the leaf node becomes an empty tree. The implementation given in Program 9.18 throws an exception if an attempt is made to remove the root from a non-leaf node. Otherwise, the node is a leaf, which means that its *N* subtrees are all empty. When the root is detached, the array of subtrees is also discarded. The running time of this method is clearly $O(1)$.

getSubtree, attachSubtree, and detachSubtree Methods
Program 9.19 defines the three methods for manipulating the subtrees of an *N*-ary tree. The **getSubtree** method takes as its argument an **int**, **i**, which must be between 0

PROGRAM 9.18
NaryTree methods

```
1   public class NaryTree
2       extends AbstractTree
3   {
4       protected Object key;
5       protected int degree;
6       protected NaryTree[] subtree;
7
8       public boolean isEmpty ()
9           { return key == null; }
10
11      public Object getKey ()
12      {
13          if (isEmpty ())
14              throw new InvalidOperationException ();
15          return key;
16      }
17
18      public void attachKey (Object object)
19      {
20          if (!isEmpty ())
21              throw new InvalidOperationException ();
22          key = object;
23          subtree = new NaryTree[degree];
24          for (int i = 0; i < degree; ++i)
25              subtree [i] = new NaryTree (degree);
26      }
27
28      public Object detachKey ()
29      {
30          if (!isLeaf ())
31              throw new InvalidOperationException ();
32          Object result = key;
33          key = null;
34          subtree = null;
35          return result;
36      }
37      // ...
38  }
```

PROGRAM 9.19
`NaryTree` methods

```
1   public class NaryTree
2       extends AbstractTree
3   {
4       protected Object key;
5       protected int degree;
6       protected NaryTree[] subtree;
7
8       public Tree getSubtree (int i)
9       {
10          if (isEmpty ())
11              throw new InvalidOperationException ();
12          return subtree [i];
13      }
14
15      public void attachSubtree (int i, NaryTree t)
16      {
17          if (isEmpty () || !subtree [i].isEmpty ())
18              throw new InvalidOperationException ();
19          subtree [i] = t;
20      }
21
22      NaryTree detachSubtree (int i)
23      {
24          if (isEmpty ())
25              throw new InvalidOperationException ();
26          NaryTree result = subtree [i];
27          subtree [i] = new NaryTree (degree);
28          return result;
29      }
30      // ...
31  }
```

---

and $N - 1$. It returns the `ith` subtree of the given tree. Note that this operation is only defined for a non-empty N-ary tree. Given that the tree is not empty, the running time is $O(1)$.

The **attachSubtree** method takes two arguments. The first is an integer `i` between 0 and $N - 1$. The second is an **NaryTree** instance. The purpose of this method is to make the N-ary tree specified by the second argument become the ith subtree of the given tree. It is only possible to attach a subtree to a non-empty node and it is only possible to attach a subtree in a place occupied by an empty subtree. If none of the exceptions are thrown, the running time of this method is simply $O(1)$.

The **detachSubtree** method takes a single argument `i`, which is an integer between 0 and $N - 1$. This method removes the `ith` subtree from a given N-ary tree and returns that subtree. Of course, it is only possible to remove a subtree from a non-empty tree. Since every non-empty node must have N subtrees, when a subtree is removed it is replaced by an empty tree. Clearly, the running time is $O(1)$ if we assume that no exceptions are thrown.

9.6.5 Binary Trees

This section presents an implementation of binary trees in the sense of Definition 9.4. A binary tree is essentially a N-ary tree, where $N = 2$. Therefore, it is possible to implement binary trees using the **NaryTree** class presented in the preceding section. However, because the **NaryTree** class implementation is a general implementation that can accommodate any value of N, it is somewhat less efficient in both time and space than an implementation that is designed specifically for the case $N = 2$. Since binary trees occur quite frequently in practice, it is important to have a good implementation.

Another consequence of restricting N to two is that we can talk of the left and right subtrees of a tree. Consequently the interface provided by a binary tree class is quite different from the general interface provided by an N-ary tree class.

Figure 9.11 shows how the binary tree given in Figure 9.6 is be represented. The basic idea is that each node of the tree contains two fields that refer to the subtrees of that node. Just as we did for N-ary trees, we represent explicitly the empty trees. Since an empty tree node contains neither root nor subtrees it is represented by a structure in which all fields are **null**.

FIGURE 9.11
Representing binary trees.

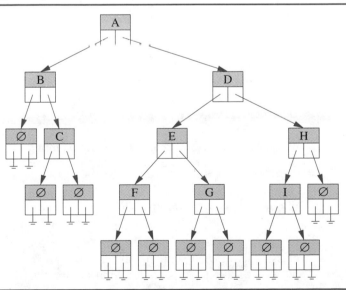

PROGRAM 9.20
`BinaryTree` fields

```
1   public class BinaryTree
2       extends AbstractTree
3   {
4       protected Object key;
5       protected BinaryTree left;
6       protected BinaryTree right;
7
8       // ...
9   }
```

The `BinaryTree` class is declared in Program 9.20. The `BinaryTree` class extends the `AbstractTree` class introduced in Program 9.2.

Fields
The `BinaryTree` class has three fields—`key`, `left`, and `right`. The first, `key`, represents the root node of the tree. The latter two represent the left and right subtrees of the given tree. All three fields are `null` if the node represents the empty tree. Otherwise, the tree must have a root and two subtrees. Consequently, all three fields are non-`null` in a non-empty node.

Constructors
Program 9.21 defines constructors for the `BinaryTree` class. The first one takes three arguments and assigns each of them to the corresponding field. Clearly the running time of this constructor is $O(1)$.

The second constructor, the no-arg constructor, creates an empty binary tree. It simply sets all three fields to `null`.

The third constructor takes as its argument any `Object`. The purpose of this constructor is to create a binary tree with the specified object as its root. Since every binary tree has exactly two subtrees, this constructor creates two empty subtrees and assigns them to the `left` and `right` fields.

purge Method
The `purge` method for the `BinaryTree` class is defined in Program 9.22. The purpose of the `purge` method is to make the tree empty. It does this by assigning `null` to all of the fields. Clearly, the running time of the `purge` method is $O(1)$.

9.6.6   Binary Tree Traversals

Program 9.23 defines the `depthFirstTraversal` method of the `BinaryTree` class. This method supports all three tree-traversal methods—preorder, inorder, and postorder. The implementation follows directly from the definitions given in Section

---

PROGRAM 9.21
BinaryTree constructors

```
1   public class BinaryTree
2       extends AbstractTree
3   {
4       protected Object key;
5       protected BinaryTree left;
6       protected BinaryTree right;
7
8       public BinaryTree (
9           Object key, BinaryTree left, BinaryTree right)
10      {
11          this.key = key;
12          this.left = left;
13          this.right = right;
14      }
15
16      public BinaryTree ()
17          { this (null, null, null); }
18
19      public BinaryTree (Object key)
20          { this (key, new BinaryTree (), new BinaryTree ()); }
21      // ...
22  }
```

PROGRAM 9.22
BinaryTree class purge method

```
1   public class BinaryTree
2       extends AbstractTree
3   {
4       protected Object key;
5       protected BinaryTree left;
6       protected BinaryTree right;
7
8       public void purge ()
9       {
10          key = null;
11          left = null;
12          right = null;
13      }
14      // ...
15  }
```

PROGRAM 9.23
BinaryTree class depthFirstTraversal method

```
1   public class BinaryTree
2       extends AbstractTree
3   {
4       protected Object key;
5       protected BinaryTree left;
6       protected BinaryTree right;
7
8       public void depthFirstTraversal (PrePostVisitor visitor)
9       {
10          if (!isEmpty ())
11          {
12              visitor.preVisit (key);
13              left.depthFirstTraversal (visitor);
14              visitor.inVisit (key);
15              right.depthFirstTraversal (visitor);
16              visitor.postVisit (key);
17          }
18      }
19      // ...
20  }
```

9.4. The traversal is implemented using recursion. That is, the method calls itself recursively to visit the subtrees of the given node. Note that the recursion terminates properly when an empty tree is encountered since the method does nothing in that case.

The traversal method takes as its argument any object that implements the **PrePost-Visitor** interface defined in Program 9.3. As each node is "visited" during the course of the traversal, the **preVisit**, **inVisit**, and **postVisit** methods of the visitor are invoked on the object contained in that node.

9.6.7 Comparing Trees

A problem that is relatively easy to solve is determining whether two trees are equivalent. Two trees are *equivalent* if they both have the same topology and if the objects contained in corresponding nodes are equal. Clearly, two empty trees are equivalent. Consider two non-empty binary trees $T_A = \{R_A, T_{AL}, T_{AR}\}$ and $T_B = \{R_B, T_{BL}, T_{BR}\}$. Equivalence of trees is given by

$$T_A \equiv T_B \iff R_A = R_B \wedge T_{AL} \equiv T_{BL} \wedge T_{AR} \equiv T_{BR}.$$

A simple, recursive algorithm suffices to test the equivalence of trees.

Since the `BinaryTree` class is ultimately derived from the `AbstractObject` class introduced in Program 5.2, it must provide a `compareTo` method to compare binary trees. Recall that the `compareTo` method is invoked by the `compare` method when the latter is used to compare two objects, say `obj1` and `obj2`, like this:

```
int result = obj1.compare (obj2);
```

The `compareTo` method returns a negative number if `obj1` < `obj2`, a positive number if `obj1` > `obj2`, and zero if `obj1` ≡ `obj2`.

So what we need is to define a *total order* relation on binary trees. Fortunately, it is possible to define such a relation for binary trees provided that the objects contained in the nodes of the trees are drawn from a totally ordered set.

Theorem 9.4
Consider two binary trees T_A and T_B and the relation $<$ given by

$$T_A < T_B \iff T_B \neq \varnothing \wedge (T_A = \varnothing \vee$$
$$T_A \neq \varnothing \wedge (R_A < R_B \vee$$
$$R_A = R_B \wedge (T_{AL} < T_{BL} \vee$$
$$T_{AL} = T_{BL} \wedge T_{AR} < T_{BR}))),$$

where T_A is either $\varnothing$ or $T_A = \{R, T_{AL}, T_{AR}\}$, and T_B is $T_B = \{R, T_{BL}, T_{BR}\}$. The relation $<$ is a total order.

Proof   The proof of Theorem 9.4 is straightforward albeit tedious. Essentially we need to show the following:

- For any two distinct trees T_A and T_B, such that $T_A \neq T_B$, either $T_A < T_B$ or $T_B < T_A$.
- For any three distinct trees T_A, T_B, and T_C, if $T_A < T_B$ and $T_B < T_C$, then $T_A < T_C$.

The details of the proof are left as an exercise for the reader (Exercise 9.10).

Program 9.24 gives an implementation of the `compareTo` method for the `Binary-Tree` class. This implementation is based on the total order relation $<$ defined in Theorem 9.4. The argument of the `compareTo` method can be any `Object` instance. However, normally that object will be another `BinaryTree` instance. Therefore, the cast on line 10 is normally successful.

The `compareTo` method compares the two binary trees `this` and `arg`. If they are both empty trees, `compareTo` returns zero. If `this` is empty and `arg` is not, `compareTo` returns -1; and if `arg` is empty and `this` is not, it returns 1.

Otherwise, both trees are non-empty. In this case, `compareTo` first compares their respective roots. We assume that the roots implement the `Comparable` interface

---

PROGRAM 9.24
BinaryTree class `compareTo` method

```
1   public class BinaryTree
2       extends AbstractTree
3   {
4       protected Object key;
5       protected BinaryTree left;
6       protected BinaryTree right;
7
8       protected int compareTo (Comparable object)
9       {
10          BinaryTree arg = (BinaryTree) object;
11          if (isEmpty ())
12              return arg.isEmpty () ? 0 : -1;
13          else if (arg.isEmpty ())
14              return 1;
15          else
16          {
17              int result = ((Comparable) getKey ()).compare (
18                  (Comparable) arg.getKey ());
19              if (result == 0)
20                  result = getLeft ().compareTo (arg.getLeft ());
21              if (result == 0)
22                  result = getRight ().compareTo (arg.getRight ());
23              return result;
24          }
25      }
26      // ...
27  }
```

---

defined in Program 5.1 and, therefore, we use the **compare** method to compare them. If the roots are equal, then the left subtrees are compared. Then, if the roots and the left subtrees are equal, the right subtrees are compared.

Clearly the worst-case running time occurs when comparing identical trees. Suppose there are exactly n nodes in each tree. Then, the running time of the **compareTo** method is $n\mathcal{T}\langle\text{isEQ}\rangle + O(n)$, where $\mathcal{T}\langle\text{isEQ}\rangle$ is the time needed to compare the objects contained in the nodes of the trees.

9.6.8 Applications

Section 6.1.3 shows how a stack can be used to compute the value of a postfix expression such as

$$a\,b \div c\,d - e \times +. \tag{9.8}$$

Suppose that instead of evaluating the expression we are interested in constructing the corresponding expression tree. Once we have an expression tree, we can use the methods described in Section 9.5 to print out the expression in prefix or infix notation. Thus, we have a means for translating expressions from one notation to another.

It turns out that an expression tree can be constructed from the postfix expression relatively easily. The algorithm to do this is a modified version of the algorithm for evaluating the expression. The symbols in the postfix expression are processed from left to right as follows:

1. If the next symbol in the expression is an operand, a tree composed of a single node labeled with that operand is pushed onto the stack.

2. If the next symbol in the expression is a binary operator, the top two trees in the stack correspond to its operands. Two trees are popped from the stack and a new tree is created that has the operator as its root and the two trees corresponding to the operands as its subtrees. Then the new tree is pushed onto the stack.

After all of the symbols of the expression have been processed in this fashion, the stack will contain a single tree, which is the desired expression tree. Figure 9.12 illustrates the use of a stack to construct the expression tree from the postfix expression given in Equation (9.8).

Implementation

Program 9.25 introduces the **ExpressionTree** class. This class provides a static method, called **parsePostfix**, which translates a postfix expression to an infix expression using the method previously described. This method reads an expression from the input stream one character at a time. The expression is assumed to be a syntactically valid postfix expression comprised of single-digit numbers, single-letter variables, and the binary operators +, -, *, and /.

Since only binary operators are allowed, the resulting expression tree is a binary tree. Consequently, the **ExpressionTree** class extends the **BinaryTree** class introduced in Program 9.20.

The main program loop, lines 13–25, reads characters from the input stream one at a time. If a letter or a digit is found, a new tree with the character as its root is created and pushed onto the stack (line 17). If an operator is found, a new tree is created with the operator as its root (line 20). Next, two trees are popped from the stack and attached to the new tree, which is then pushed onto the stack (lines 21–23).

When the **parsePostfix** method encounters the end-of-file, its main loop terminates. The resulting expression tree is popped from the stack and returned from the **parsePostfix** method.

Program 9.26 defines the **toString** method for the **ExpressionTree** class. This method can be used to print out the expression represented by the tree. The **toString** method constructs a string that represents the expression using a **PrePostVisitor**, which does a depth-first traversal and accumulates its result in a string buffer like this: At each non-terminal node of the expression tree, the depth-first traversal first calls **preVisit**, which appends a left parenthesis to the string buffer. In between the

FIGURE 9.12
Postfix to infix conversion using a stack of trees.

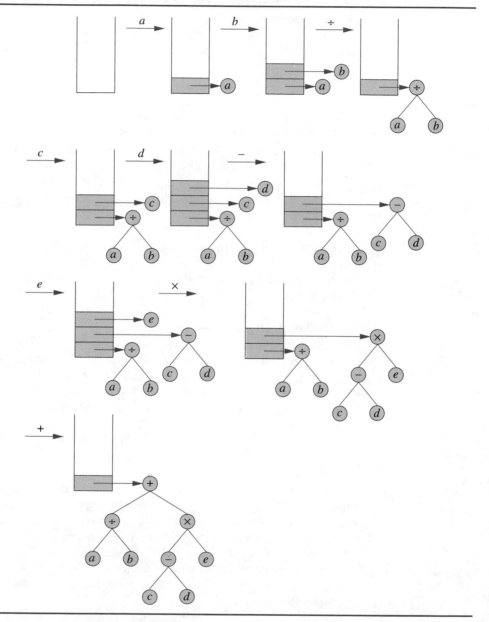

PROGRAM 9.25
Binary tree application—postfix to infix conversion

```
 1  public class ExpressionTree
 2      extends BinaryTree
 3  {
 4      public ExpressionTree (char c)
 5          { super (new Chr (c)); }
 6
 7      public static ExpressionTree parsePostfix (Reader in)
 8          throws IOException
 9      {
10          Stack stack = new StackAsLinkedList ();
11
12          int i;
13          while ((i = in.read ()) >= 0)
14          {
15              char c = (char) i;
16              if (Character.isLetterOrDigit (c))
17                  stack.push (new ExpressionTree (c));
18              else if (c == '+' || c == '-' || c == '*' || c =='/')
19              {
20                  ExpressionTree result = new ExpressionTree (c);
21                  result.attachRight((ExpressionTree) stack.pop());
22                  result.attachLeft ((ExpressionTree) stack.pop());
23                  stack.push (result);
24              }
25          }
26          return (ExpressionTree) stack.pop ();
27      }
28      // ...
29  }
```

traversals of the left and right subtrees, the **inVisit** method is called, which appends a textual representation of the object contained within the node to the string buffer. Finally, after traversing the right subtree, **postVisit** appends a right parenthesis to the string buffer. Given the input **ab/cd-e*+**, the program constructs the expression tree as shown in Figure 9.12, and then forms the infix expression

$$(((a)/(b))+(((c)-(d))*(e))).$$

The running time of the **parsePostfix** method depends upon the number of symbols in the input. The running time for one iteration of the main loop is $O(1)$. Therefore, the time required to construct the expression tree given n input symbols is $O(n)$. The **depthFirstTraversal** method visits each node of the expression tree exactly once

---

PROGRAM 9.26
Binary tree application—printing infix expressions

```
1   public class ExpressionTree
2       extends BinaryTree
3   {
4       public String toString ()
5       {
6           final StringBuffer buffer = new StringBuffer ();
7           PrePostVisitor visitor = new AbstractPrePostVisitor ()
8           {
9               public void preVisit (Object object)
10                  { buffer.append ("("); }
11              public void inVisit (Object object)
12                  { buffer.append (object); }
13              public void postVisit (Object object)
14                  { buffer.append (")"); }
15          };
16          depthFirstTraversal (visitor);
17          return buffer.toString ();
18      }
19      //...
20  }
```

---

and a constant amount of work is required to print a node. As a result, printing the infix expression is also $O(n)$, where n is the number of input symbols.

The output expression contains all of the input symbols plus the parentheses added by the **toString** method. It can be shown that a valid postfix expression that contains n symbols always has $(n-1)/2$ binary operators and $(n+1)/2$ operands (Exercise 9.9). Hence, the expression tree contains $(n-1)/2$ non-terminal nodes and since a pair of parentheses is added for each non-terminal node in the expression tree, the output string contains $2n-1 = O(n)$ symbols altogether. Therefore, the overall running time needed to translate a postfix expression comprised of n symbols to an infix expression is $O(n)$.

Exercises

9.1 For each tree shown in Figure 9.13, show the order in which the nodes are visited during the following tree traversals:

a. preorder traversal

b. inorder traversal (if defined)

c. postorder traversal

d. breadth-first traversal

FIGURE 9.13
Sample trees for Exercise 9.1.

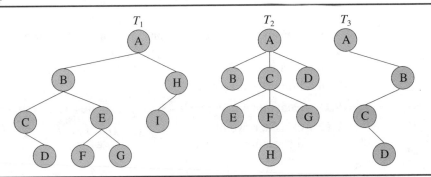

9.2 Write a visitor that prints the nodes of a general tree in the format of Equation (9.1).

9.3 Derive an expression for the total space needed to represent a tree of *n* internal nodes using each of the following classes:

a. `GeneralTree` introduced in Program 9.13

b. `NaryTree` introduced in Program 9.16

c. `BinaryTree` introduced in Program 9.20

9.4 A full node in a binary tree is a node with two non-empty subtrees. Let *l* be the number of leaf nodes in a binary tree. Show that the number of full nodes is $l - 1$.

9.5 The generic `depthFirstTraversal` method defined in Program 9.2 is a recursive method. Write a non-recursive depth-first traversal method that has exactly the same effect as the recursive version.

9.6 Program 9.26 defines a visitor that prints using *infix* notation the expression represented by an expression tree. Write a visitor that prints the same expression in *prefix* notation with the following format:

```
+(/(a,b),*(-(c,d),e)).
```

9.7 Repeat Exercise 9.6, but this time write a visitor that prints the expression in *postfix* notation with the following format:

```
ab/cd-e*+.
```

9.8 The visitor defined in Program 9.26 prints many redundant parentheses because it does not take into consideration the precedence of the operators. Rewrite the visitor so that it prints

```
a/b+(c-d)*e
```

rather than

$$(((a)/(b))+(((c)-(d))*(e))).$$

9.9 Consider postfix expressions involving only binary operators. Show that if such an expression contains n symbols, it always has $(n-1)/2$ operators and $(n+1)/2$ operands.

9.10 Prove Theorem 9.4.

9.11 Generalize Theorem 9.4 so that it applies to N-ary trees.

9.12 Consider two binary trees, $T_A = \{R_A, T_{AL}, T_{AR}\}$ and $T_B = \{R_B, T_{BL}, T_{BR}\}$, and the relation $\simeq$ given by

$$\begin{aligned}
T_A \simeq T_B \iff &((T_A = \varnothing \wedge T_B = \varnothing) \vee \\
&((T_A \neq \varnothing \wedge T_B \neq \varnothing) \wedge \\
&((T_{AL} \simeq T_{BL} \wedge T_{AR} \simeq T_{BR}) \vee \\
&(T_{AL} \simeq T_{BR} \wedge T_{AR} \simeq T_{BL}))).
\end{aligned}$$

If $T_A \simeq T_B$, the trees are said to be *isomorphic*. Devise an algorithm to test whether two binary trees are isomorphic. What is the running time of your algorithm?

Programming Projects

9.1 Devise an algorithm to compute the height of a tree. Write an implementation of your algorithm as the **getHeight** method of the **AbstractTree** class introduced in Program 9.2.

9.2 Devise an algorithm to count the number of internal nodes in a tree. Write an implementation of your algorithm as the **getCount** method of the **AbstractTree** class introduced in Program 9.2.

9.3 Devise an algorithm to count the number of leaves in a tree. Write an implementation of your algorithm as a method of the **AbstractTree** class introduced in Program 9.2.

9.4 Devise an abstract (generic) algorithm to compare trees. (See Exercise 9.11.) Write an implementation of your algorithm as the **compareTo** method of the **AbstractTree** class introduced in Program 9.2.

9.5 The **TreeEnumeration** class introduced in Program 9.10 does a *preorder* traversal of a tree.

   a. Write an enumeration class that does a *postorder* traversal.

   b. Write an enumeration class that does a *breadth-first* traversal.

   c. Write an enumeration class that does an *inorder* traversal. (In this case, assume that the tree is a **BinaryTree**.)

9.6 Complete the `GeneralTree` class introduced in Program 9.13 by providing suitable definitions for the following methods: `isEmpty`, `isLeaf`, `getDegree`, and `compareTo`. Write a test program and test your implementation.

9.7 Complete the `NaryTree` class introduced in Program 9.16 by providing suitable definitions for the following methods: `purge`, `isLeaf`, `getDegree`, and `compareTo`. Write a test program and test your implementation.

9.8 Complete the `BinaryTree` class introduced in Program 9.20 by providing suitable definitions for the following methods: `isEmpty`, `isLeaf`, `getDegree`, `getKey`, `attachKey`, `detachKey`, `getLeft`, `attachLeft`, `detachLeft`, `getRight`, `attachRight`, `detachRight`, and `getSubtree`. Write a test program and test your implementation.

9.9 Write a visitor that draws a picture of a tree on the screen.

9.10 Design and implement an algorithm that constructs an expression tree from an *infix* expression such as

$$a/b+(c-d)^{\wedge}e.$$

Hint: See Project 6.4.

10 | Search Trees

In the preceding chapter we considered trees in which the relative positions of the nodes in the tree are unconstrained. In other words, a given item may appear anywhere in the tree. Clearly, this allows us complete flexibility in the kind of tree that we may construct. And depending on the application, this may be precisely what we need. However, if we lose track of an item, in order to find it again it may be necessary to do a complete traversal of the tree (in the worst case).

In this chapter we consider trees that are designed to support efficient search operations. In order to make it easier to search, we constrain the relative positions of the items in the tree. In addition, we show that by constraining the *shape* of the tree, as well as the relative positions of the items in the tree, search operations can be made even more efficient.

10.1 Basics

A tree that supports efficient search, insertion, and withdrawal operations is called a *search tree*. In this context the tree is used to store a finite set of keys drawn from a totally ordered set of keys K. Each node of the tree contains one or more keys and all keys in the tree are unique; that is, no duplicate keys are permitted.

What makes a tree into a search tree is that the keys do not appear in arbitrary nodes of the tree. Instead, there is a *data-ordering criterion,* which determines where a given key may appear in the tree in relation to the other keys in that tree. The following sections present two related types of search trees, M-way search trees and binary search trees.

FIGURE 10.1
An *M*-way search tree.

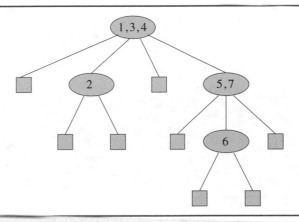

10.1.1 *M*-Way Search Trees

Definition 10.1 (*M*-way Search Tree)

An M-way search tree T is a finite set of keys. Either the set is empty, $T = \emptyset$; or the set consists of n M-way subtrees $T_0, T_1, \ldots, T_{n-1}$, and $n - 1$ keys, $k_1, k_2, \ldots, k_{n-1}$,

$$T = \{T_0, k_1, T_1, k_2, T_2, \ldots, k_{n-1}, T_{n-1}\},$$

where $2 \le n \le M$, such that the keys and nodes satisfy the following data-ordering properties:

1. *The keys in each node are distinct and ordered; that is, $k_i < k_{i+1}$ for $1 \le i \le n - 1$.*

2. *All of the keys contained in subtree T_{i-1} are less than k_i. The tree T_{i-1} is called the left subtree with respect to the key k_i.*

3. *All of the keys contained in subtree T_i are greater than k_i. The tree T_{i+1} is called the right subtree with respect to the key k_i.*

Figure 10.1 gives an example of an *M*-way search tree for $M = 4$. In this case, each of the non-empty nodes of the tree has between one and three keys and at most four subtrees. All keys in the tree satisfy the data-ordering properties. Specifically, the keys in each node are ordered and for each key in the tree, all keys in the left subtree with respect to the given key are less than the given key, and all keys in the right subtree with respect to the given key are larger than the given key. Finally, it is important to note that the topology of the tree is not determined by the particular set of keys it contains.

10.1.2 Binary Search Trees

Just as the binary tree is an important category of *N*-ary trees, the *binary search tree* is an important category of *M*-way search trees.

FIGURE 10.2
A binary search tree.

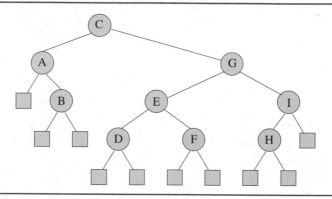

Definition 10.2 (Binary Search Tree)
A binary search tree T is a finite set of keys. Either the set is empty, $T = \emptyset$; or the set consists of a root r and exactly two binary search trees T_L and T_R, $T = \{r, T_L, T_R\}$, such that the following properties are satisfied:

1. *All keys contained in left subtree, T_L, are less than r.*
2. *All keys contained in the right subtree, T_R, are greater than r.*

Figure 10.2 shows an example of a binary search tree. In this case, since the nodes of the tree carry alphabetic rather than numeric keys, the ordering of the keys is alphabetic. That is, all keys in the left subtree of a given node precede alphabetically the root of that node, and all keys in the right subtree of a given node follow alphabetically the root of that node. The empty trees are shown explicitly as boxes in Figure 10.2. However, in order to simplify the graphical representation, the empty trees are often omitted from the diagrams.

10.2   Searching a Search Tree

The main advantage of a search tree is that the data-ordering criterion ensures that it is not necessary to do a complete tree traversal in order to locate a given item. Since search trees are defined recursively, it is easy to define a recursive search method.

Searching an *M*-way Tree
Consider the search for a particular item, say x, in an M-way search tree. The search always begins at the root. If the tree is empty, the search fails. Otherwise, the keys contained in the root node are examined to determine whether the object of the search is present. If it is, the search terminates successfully. If it is not, there are three possibilities: Either the object of the search, x, is less than k_1, in which case subtree T_0 is searched; or x is greater than k_{n-1}, in which case subtree T_{n-1} is searched; or there

exists an i such that $1 \leq i < n - 1$ for which $k_i < x < k_{i+1}$, in which case subtree T_i is searched.

Notice that when x is not found in a given node, only one of the n subtrees of that node is searched. Therefore, a complete tree traversal is not required. A successful search begins at the root and traces a downward path in the tree, which terminates at the node containing the object of the search. Clearly, the running time of a successful search is determined by the *depth* in the tree of the object of the search.

When the object of the search is not in the search tree, the search method described above traces a downward path from the root, which terminates when an empty subtree is encountered. In the worst case, the search path passes through the deepest leaf node. Therefore, the worst-case running time for an unsuccessful search is determined by the *height* of the search tree.

Searching a Binary Tree

The search method described above applies directly to binary search trees. As above, the search begins at the root node of the tree. If the object of the search, x, matches the root r, the search terminates successfully. If it does not, then if x is less than r, the left subtree is searched; otherwise x must be greater than r, in which case the right subtree is searched.

Figure 10.3 shows two binary search trees. The tree T_a is an example of a particularly bad search tree because it is not really very tree-like at all. In fact, it is topologically iso-morphic with a linear, linked list. In the worst case, a tree that contains n items has height $O(n)$. Therefore, in the worst case an unsuccessful search must visit $O(n)$ internal nodes.

On the other hand, tree T_b in 10.3 is an example of a particularly good binary search tree. This tree is an instance of a *perfect binary tree*.

FIGURE 10.3
Examples of search trees.

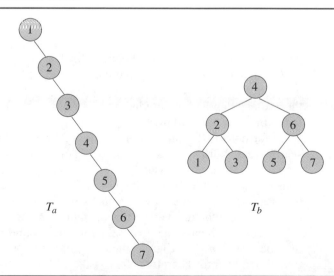

T_a $\qquad\qquad\qquad\qquad$ T_b

Definition 10.3 (Perfect Binary Tree)
A perfect binary tree of height $h \geq 0$ is a binary tree $T = \{r, T_L, T_R\}$ with the following properties:

1. *If $h = 0$, then $T_L = \varnothing$ and $T_R = \varnothing$.*
2. *Otherwise, $h > 0$, in which case both T_L and T_R are both perfect binary trees of height $h - 1$.*

It is fairly easy to show that a perfect binary tree of height h has exactly $2^{h+1} - 1$ internal nodes. Conversely, the height of a perfect binary tree with n internal nodes is $\log_2(n + 1)$. If we have a search tree that has the shape of a perfect binary tree, then every unsuccessful search visits exactly $h + 1$ internal nodes, where $h = \log_2(n + 1)$. Thus, the worst case for unsuccessful search in a perfect tree is $O(\log n)$.

10.3 Average-Case Analysis

10.3.1 Successful Search

When a search is successful, exactly $d + 1$ internal nodes are visited, where d is the depth in the tree of the object of the search. For example, if the object of the search is at the root that has depth zero, the search visits just one node—the root itself. Similarly, if the object of the search is at depth one, two nodes are visited, and so on. We will assume that it is equally likely for the object of the search to appear in any node of the search tree. In that case, the *average* number of nodes visited during a successful search is $\bar{d} + 1$, where $\bar{d}$ is the average of the depths of the nodes in a given tree. That is, given a binary search tree with $n > 0$ nodes,

$$\bar{d} = \frac{1}{n} \sum_{i=1}^{n} d_i,$$

where d_i is the depth of the ith node of the tree.

The quantity $\sum_{i=1}^{n} d_i$ is called the *internal path length*. The internal path length of a tree is simply the sum of the depths (levels) of all internal nodes in the tree. Clearly, the average depth of an internal node is equal to the internal path length divided by n, the number of nodes in the tree.

Unfortunately, for any given number of nodes n, there are many different possible search trees. Furthermore, the internal path lengths of the various possibilities are not equal. Therefore, to compute the average depth of a node in a tree with n nodes, we must consider all possible trees with n nodes. In the absence of any contrary information, we will assume that all trees having n nodes are equiprobable and then compute the average depth of a node in the average tree containing n nodes.

Let $I(n)$ be the average internal path length of a tree containing n nodes. Consider first the case of $n = 1$. Clearly, there is only one binary tree that contains one node—the tree of height zero. Therefore, $I(1) = 0$.

Now consider an arbitrary tree, $T_n(l)$, having $n \geq 1$ internal nodes altogether, l of which are found in its left subtree, where $0 \leq l < n$. Such a tree consists of a root, the left subtree with l internal nodes, and a right subtree with $n - l - 1$ internal nodes. The average internal path length for such a tree is the sum of the average internal path length of the left subtree, $I(l)$, plus that of the right subtree, $I(n - l - 1)$, plus $n - 1$, because the nodes in the two subtrees are one level lower in $T_n(l)$.

In order to determine the average internal path length for a tree with n nodes, we must compute the average of the internal path lengths of the trees $T_n(l)$ averaged over all possible sizes, l, of the (left) subtree, $0 \leq l < n$.

To do this we consider an ordered set of n distinct keys, $k_0 < k_1 < \cdots < k_{n-1}$. If we select the lth key, k_l, to be the root of a binary search tree, then there are l keys, $k_0, k_1, \ldots, k_{l-1}$, in its left subtree and $n - l - 1$ keys, $k_{l+1}, k_{l+2}, \ldots, k_{n-1}$, in its right subtree.

If we assume that it is equally likely for any of the n keys to be selected as the root, then all subtree sizes in the range $0 \leq l < n$ are equally likely. Therefore, the average internal path length for a tree with $n \geq 1$ nodes is

$$I(n) = \frac{1}{n} \sum_{i=0}^{n-1} \Big(I(i) + I(n - i - 1) + n - 1 \Big), \quad n > 1$$

$$= \frac{2}{n} \sum_{i=0}^{n-1} I(i) + n - 1.$$

Thus, in order to determine $I(n)$ we need to solve the recurrence

$$I(n) = \begin{cases} 0 & n = 1, \\ \dfrac{2}{n} \sum_{i=0}^{n-1} I(i) + n - 1 & n > 1. \end{cases} \tag{10.1}$$

To solve this recurrence we consider the case $n > 1$ and then multiply Equation (10.1) by n to get

$$nI(n) = 2 \sum_{i=0}^{n-1} I(i) + n^2 - n. \tag{10.2}$$

Since this equation is valid for any $n > 1$, by substituting $n - 1$ for n we can also write

$$(n - 1)I(n - 1) = 2 \sum_{i=0}^{n-2} I(i) + n^2 - 3n + 2, \tag{10.3}$$

which is valid for $n > 2$. Subtracting Equation (10.3) from Equation (10.2) gives

$$nI(n) - (n - 1)I(n - 1) = 2I(n - 1) + 2n - 2,$$

which can be rewritten as

$$I(n) = \frac{(n+1)I(n-1) + 2n - 2}{n}.$$ (10.4)

Thus, we have shown that the solution to the recurrence in Equation (10.1) is the same as the solution of the recurrence

$$I(n) = \begin{cases} 0 & n = 1, \\ 1 & n = 2, \\ ((n+1)I(n-1) + 2n - 2)/n & n > 2. \end{cases}$$ (10.5)

10.3.2 Solving the Recurrence—Telescoping

This section presents a technique for solving recurrence relations such as Equation (10.5) called *telescoping*. The basic idea is this: We rewrite the recurrence formula so that a similar functional form appears on both sides of the equal sign. For example, in this case, we consider $n > 2$ and divide both sides of Equation (10.5) by $n + 1$ to get

$$\frac{I(n)}{n+1} = \frac{I(n-1)}{n} + \frac{2}{n} - \frac{4}{n(n+1)}.$$

Since this equation is valid for any $n > 2$, we can write the following series of equations:

$$\frac{I(n)}{n+1} = \frac{I(n-1)}{n} + \frac{2}{n} - \frac{4}{n(n+1)}, \quad n > 2$$ (10.6)

$$\frac{I(n-1)}{n} = \frac{I(n-2)}{n-1} + \frac{2}{n-1} - \frac{4}{(n-1)n}, \quad n - 1 > 2$$

$$\frac{I(n-2)}{n-1} = \frac{I(n-3)}{n-2} + \frac{2}{n-2} - \frac{4}{(n-2)(n-1)}, \quad n - 2 > 2$$

$$\vdots$$

$$\frac{I(n-k)}{n-k+1} = \frac{I(n-k-1)}{n-k} + \frac{2}{n-k} - \frac{4}{(n-k)(n-k+1)}, \quad n - k > 2$$

$$\vdots$$

$$\frac{I(3)}{4} = \frac{I(2)}{3} + \frac{2}{3} - \frac{4}{3 \cdot 4}.$$ (10.7)

Each subsequent equation in this series is obtained by substituting $n - 1$ for n in the preceding equation. In principle, we repeat this substitution until we get an expression on the right-hand side involving the base case. In this example, we stop at $n - k - 1 = 2$.

Because Equation (10.6) has a similar functional form on both sides of the equal sign, when we add Equation (10.6) through Equation (10.7) together, most of the terms cancel leaving

$$\frac{I(n)}{n+1} = \frac{I(2)}{3} + 2\sum_{i=3}^{n}\frac{1}{i} - 4\sum_{i=3}^{n}\frac{1}{i(i+1)}, \quad n > 2$$

$$= 2\sum_{i=1}^{n}\frac{1}{i} - 4\sum_{i=1}^{n}\frac{1}{i(i+1)}$$

$$= 2H_n - 4n/(n+1),$$

where H_n is the nth *harmonic number*. In Section 2.1.8 we saw that $H_n \approx \ln n + \gamma$, where $\gamma \approx 0.577\,215$ is called *Euler's constant*. Thus, we get that the average internal path length of the average binary search tree with n internal nodes is

$$I(n) = 2(n+1)H_n - 4n$$

$$\approx 2(n+1)(\ln n + \gamma) - 4n.$$

Finally, we get to the point: The average depth of a node in the average binary search tree with n nodes is

$$\bar{d} = I(n)/n$$

$$= 2\left(\frac{n+1}{n}\right)H_n - 4$$

$$\approx 2\left(\frac{n+1}{n}\right)(\ln n + \gamma) - 4$$

$$= O(\log n).$$

10.3.3   Unsuccessful Search

All successful searches terminate when the object of the search is found. Therefore, all successful searches terminate at an internal node. In contrast, all unsuccessful searches terminate at an external node. In terms of the binary tree shown in Figure 10.2, a successful search terminates in one of the nodes, which are drawn as circles, and an unsuccessful search terminates in one of the boxes.

The preceding analysis shows that the average number of nodes visited during a successful search depends on the *internal path length*, which is simply the sum of the depths of all internal nodes. Similarly, the average number of nodes visited during an unsuccessful search depends on the *external path length*, which is the sum of the depths of all external nodes. Fortunately, there is a simple relationship between the internal path length and the external path length of a binary tree.

Theorem 10.1

Consider a binary tree T with n internal nodes and an internal path length of I. The external path length of T is given by

$$E = I + 2n.$$

In other words, Theorem 10.1 says that the *difference* between the internal path length and the external path length of a binary tree with n internal nodes is $E - I = 2n$.

Proof (By induction).

Base Case Consider a binary tree with one internal node and internal path length of zero. Such a tree has exactly two empty subtrees immediately below the root and its external path length is two. Therefore, the theorem holds for $n = 1$.

Inductive Hypothesis Assume that the theorem holds for $n = 1, 2, 3, \ldots, k$ for some $k \geq 1$. Consider an arbitrary tree, T_k, that has k internal nodes. According to Theorem 9.1, T_k has $k + 1$ external nodes. Let I_k and E_k be the internal and external path length of T_k, respectively. According to the inductive hypothesis, $E_k - I_k = 2k$.

Consider what happens when we create a new tree T_{k+1} by removing an external node from T_k and replacing it with an internal node that has two empty subtrees. Clearly, the resulting tree has $k + 1$ internal nodes. Furthermore, suppose the external node we remove is at depth d. Then the internal path length of T_{k+1} is $I_{k+1} = I_k + d$ and the external path length of T_{k+1} is $E_{k+1} = E_k - d + 2(d + 1) = E_k + d + 2$.

The difference between the internal path length and the external path length of T_{k+1} is

$$E_{k+1} - I_{k+1} = (E_k + d + 2) - (I_k + d)$$
$$= E_k - I_k + 2$$
$$= 2(k + 1).$$

Therefore, by induction on k, the difference between the internal path length and the external path length of a binary tree with n internal nodes is $2n$ for all $n \geq 1$.

Since the difference between the internal and external path lengths of any tree with n internal nodes is $2n$, then we can say the same thing about the *average* internal and external path lengths averaged over all search trees. Therefore, $E(n)$, the average external path length of a binary search tree, is given by

$$E(n) = I(n) + 2n$$
$$= 2(n + 1)H_n - 2n$$
$$\approx 2(n + 1)(\ln n + \gamma) - 2n.$$

A binary search tree with internal n nodes has $n+1$ external nodes. Thus, the average depth of an external node of a binary search tree with n internal nodes, $\bar{e}$, is given by

$$
\begin{aligned}
\bar{e} &= E(n)/(n+1) \\
&= 2H_n - 2n/(n+1) \\
&\approx 2(\ln n + \gamma) - 2n/(n+1) \\
&= O(\log n).
\end{aligned}
$$

These very nice results are the *raison d'être* for binary search trees. What they say is that the average number of nodes visited during either a successful or an unsuccessful search in the average binary search tree having n nodes is $O(\log n)$. We must remember, however, that these results are premised on the assumption that all possible search trees of n nodes are equiprobable. It is important to be aware that in practice this may not always be the case.

10.3.4 Traversing a Search Tree

In Section 9.4, the inorder traversal of a binary tree is defined as follows:

1. Traverse the left subtree, and then
2. Visit the root, and then
3. Traverse the right subtree.

It should not come as a surprise that when an *inorder traversal* of a binary search tree is done, the nodes of the tree are visited *in order*!

In an inorder traversal the root of the tree is visited after the entire left subtree has been traversed and in a binary search tree everything in the left subtree is less than the root. Therefore, the root is visited only after all keys less than the root have been visited.

Similarly, in an inorder traversal the root is visited before the right subtree is traversed and everything in the right subtree is greater than the root. Hence, the root is visited before all keys greater than the root are visited. Therefore, by induction, the keys in the search tree are visited in order.

Inorder traversal is not defined for arbitrary N-ary trees—it is only defined for the case of $N = 2$. Essentially this is because the nodes of N-ary trees contain only a single key. On the other hand, if a node of an M-way search tree has n subtrees, then it must contain $n - 1$ keys, such that $2 < n \leq M$. Therefore, we can define *inorder traversal of an M-way tree* as follows:

To traverse a node of an M-way tree having n subtrees,

1. Traverse T_0, and then
2. Visit k_1, and then
3. Traverse T_1, and then

4. Visit k_2, and then

5. Traverse T_2, and then

$\vdots$

2n − 2. Visit k_{n-1}, and then

2n − 1. Traverse T_{n-1}.

10.4 Implementing Search Trees

Since search trees are designed to support efficient searching, it is only appropriate that they implement the **SearchableContainer** interface. Recall from Section 5.2.7 that the searchable container interface includes the methods **find**, **isMember**, **insert**, and **withdraw**.

Program 10.1 defines the **SearchTree** interface. The **SearchTree** interface extends the **Tree** interface defined in Program 9.1 and the **SearchableContainer** interface defined in Program 5.14.

In addition, two more methods are defined—**findMin** and **findMax**. The **findMin** method returns the object contained in the search tree having the smallest key. Similarly, the **findMax** method returns the contained object having the largest key.

FIGURE 10.4
Object class hierarchy.

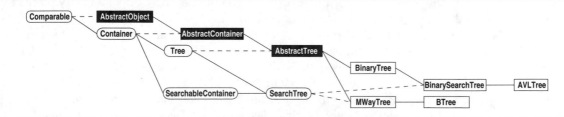

PROGRAM 10.1
SearchTree interface

```
1   public interface SearchTree
2       extends Tree, SearchableContainer
3   {
4       Comparable findMin ();
5       Comparable findMax ();
6   }
```

10.4.1   Binary Search Trees

The class **BinarySearchTree** introduced in Program 10.2 represents binary search trees. Since binary trees and binary search trees are topologically similar, the **Binary-SearchTree** class extends the **BinaryTree** introduced in Program 9.20. In addition, because it represents search trees, the **BinarySearchTree** class implements the **SearchTree** interface defined in Program 10.1.

Fields
The **BinarySearchTree** class inherits the three fields **key**, **left**, and **right** from the **BinaryTree** class. The first refers to any **Object** instance, and the latter two are **BinaryTree** instances, which are the subtrees of the given tree. All three fields are **null** if the node represents the empty tree. Otherwise, the tree must have a root and two subtrees. Therefore, all three fields are non-**null** in an internal node.

Program 10.3 defines the two methods **getLeftBST** and **getRightBST**, which return the left and right subtrees, respectively, of a given binary search tree. In the **BinaryTree** class the **left** and **right** fields are **BinaryTree**s. However, in a binary search tree, the subtrees will be instances of the **BinarySearchTree** class.

PROGRAM 10.2
BinarySearchTree class

```
1   public class BinarySearchTree
2       extends BinaryTree
3       implements SearchTree
4   {
5       // ...
6   }
```

PROGRAM 10.3
BinarySearchTree class **getLeftBST** and **getRightBST** methods

```
1    public class BinarySearchTree
2        extends BinaryTree
3        implements SearchTree
4    {
5        private BinarySearchTree getLeftBST ()
6            { return (BinarySearchTree) getLeft (); }
7
8        private BinarySearchTree getRightBST ()
9            { return (BinarySearchTree) getRight (); }
10       // ...
11   }
```

The `getLeftBST` and `getRightBST` methods cast the `left` and `right` fields to the appropriate type.

`find` Method

Program 10.4 gives the code for the `find` method of the `BinarySearchTree` class. The `find` method takes as its argument any `Comparable` object. The purpose of the method is to search the tree for an object that matches the argument. If a match is found, `find` returns the matching object. Otherwise, `find` returns `null`.

The recursive `find` method starts its search at the root and descends one level in the tree for each recursive call. At each level at most one object comparison is made (line 9). The worst-case running time for a search is

$$n\mathcal{T}\langle\text{compare}\rangle + O(n),$$

PROGRAM 10.4
BinarySearchTree class `find` and `findMin` methods

```
1   public class BinarySearchTree
2       extends BinaryTree
3       implements SearchTree
4   {
5       public Comparable find (Comparable object)
6       {
7           if (isEmpty ())
8               return null;
9           int diff = object.compare ((Comparable) getKey ());
10          if (diff == 0)
11              return (Comparable) getKey ();
12          else if (diff < 0)
13              return getLeftBST ().find (object);
14          else
15              return getRightBST ().find (object);
16      }
17
18      public Comparable findMin ()
19      {
20          if (isEmpty ())
21              return null;
22          else if (getLeftBST ().isEmpty ())
23              return (Comparable) getKey ();
24          else
25              return getLeftBST ().findMin();
26      }
27      // ...
28  }
```

---

where $\mathcal{T}\langle\texttt{compare}\rangle$ is the time to compare two objects and n is the number of internal nodes in the tree. The same asymptotic running time applies for both successful and unsuccessful searches.

The average running time for a successful search is $(\bar{d}+1)\mathcal{T}\langle\texttt{compare}\rangle + O(\bar{d})$, where $\bar{d} = 2(n+1)H_n/n - 4$ is the average depth of an internal node in a binary search tree. If $\mathcal{T}\langle\texttt{compare}\rangle = O(1)$, the average time of a successful search is $O(\log n)$.

The average running time for an unsuccessful search is $\bar{e}\mathcal{T}\langle\texttt{compare}\rangle + O(\bar{e})$, where $\bar{e} = 2H_n - 4n/(n+1)$ is the average depth of an external node in a binary search tree. If $\mathcal{T}\langle\texttt{compare}\rangle = O(1)$, the average time of an unsuccessful search is $O(\log n)$.

`findMin` Method

Program 10.4 also shows a recursive implementation of the `findMin` method of the `BinarySearchTree` class. It follows directly from the data-ordering property of search trees that to find the node containing the smallest key in the tree, we start at the root and follow the chain of left subtrees until we get to the node that has an empty left subtree. The key in that node is the smallest in the tree. Notice that no object comparisons are necessary to identify the smallest key in the tree.

The running time analysis of the `findMin` method follows directly from that of the `find` method. The worst-case running time of `findMin` is $O(n)$ and the average running time is $O(\log n)$, where n is the number of internal nodes in the tree.

10.4.2 Inserting Items in a Binary Search Tree

The simplest way to insert an item into a binary search tree is to pretend that the item is already in the tree and then follow the path taken by the `find` method to determine where the item would be. Assuming that the item is not already in the tree, the search will be unsuccessful and will terminate at an external, empty node. That is precisely where the item to be inserted is placed!

`insert` and `attachKey` Methods

The `insert` method of the `BinarySearchTree` class is defined in Program 10.6. This method takes as its argument the object that is to be inserted into the binary search tree. It is assumed in this implementation that duplicate keys are not permitted. That is, all of the keys contained in the tree are unique.

The `insert` method behaves like the `find` method until it arrives at an external, empty node. Once the empty node has been found, it is transformed into an internal node by calling the `attachKey` method. `attachKey` works as follows: The object being inserted is assigned to the `key` field and two new empty binary trees are attached to the node.

Notice that after the insertion is done, the `balance` method is called. However, as shown in Program 10.5, the `BinarySearchTree.balance` method does nothing. (Section 10.5 describes the class `AVLTree`, which is derived from the `Binary-SearchTree` class and which inherits the `insert` method but overrides the `balance` operation.)

The asymptotic running time of the `insert` method is the same as that of `find` for an unsuccessful search. That is, the worst-case running time is $n\mathcal{T}\langle\texttt{compare}\rangle + O(n)$ and

---

PROGRAM 10.5
BinarySearchTree class insert, attachKey, and balance methods

---

```
 1   public class BinarySearchTree
 2       extends BinaryTree
 3       implements SearchTree
 4   {
 5       public void insert (Comparable object)
 6       {
 7           if (isEmpty ())
 8               attachKey (object);
 9           else
10           {
11               int diff = object.compare ((Comparable) getKey ());
12               if (diff == 0)
13                   throw new IllegalArgumentException (
14                       "duplicate key");
15               if (diff < 0)
16                   getLeftBST ().insert (object);
17               else
18                   getRightBST ().insert (object);
19           }
20           balance ();
21       }
22
23       public void attachKey (Object object)
24       {
25           if (!isEmpty ())
26               throw new InvalidOperationException ();
27           key = object;
28           left = new BinarySearchTree ();
29           right = new BinarySearchTree ();
30       }
31
32       protected void balance ()
33           {}
34       // ...
35   }
```

---

the average-case running time is

$$\bar{e}\mathcal{T}\langle\text{compare}\rangle + O(\bar{e}),$$

where $\bar{e} = 2H_n - 2n/(n+1)$ is the average depth of an external node in a binary search tree with n internal nodes. When $\mathcal{T}\langle\text{compare}\rangle = O(1)$, the worst-case running time is $O(n)$ and the average case is $O(\log n)$.

10.4.3   Removing Items from a Binary Search Tree

When removing an item from a search tree, it is imperative that the tree that remains satisfies the data-ordering criterion. If the item to be removed is in a leaf node, then it is fairly easy to remove that item from the tree since doing so does not disturb the relative order of any of the other items in the tree.

For example, consider the binary search tree shown in Figure 10.5(a). Suppose we wish to remove the node labeled 4. Since node 4 is a leaf, its subtrees are empty. When we remove it from the tree, the tree remains a valid search tree, as shown in Figure 10.5 (b).

To remove a non-leaf node, we move it down in the tree until it becomes a leaf node since a leaf node is easily deleted. To move a node down we swap it with another node that is further down in the tree. For example, consider the search tree shown in Figure 10.6 (a). Node 1 is not a leaf since it has an empty left subtree but a non-empty right subtree. To remove node 1, we swap it with the smallest key in its right subtree, which in this case is node 2, Figure 10.6 (b). Since node 1 is now a leaf, it is easily deleted. Notice that the resulting tree remains a valid search tree, as shown in Figure 10.6 (c).

To move a non-leaf node down in the tree, we either swap it with the smallest key in the right subtree or with the largest one in the left subtree. At least one such swap is always possible, since the node is a non-leaf and therefore at least one of its subtrees is non-empty. If after the swap, the node to be deleted is not a leaf, then we push it further down the tree with yet another swap. Eventually, the node must reach the bottom of the tree where it can be deleted.

withdraw Method

Program 10.6 gives the code for the **withdraw** method of the **BinarySearchTree** class. The **withdraw** method takes as its argument the object instance to be removed

---

FIGURE 10.5
Removing a leaf node from a binary search tree.

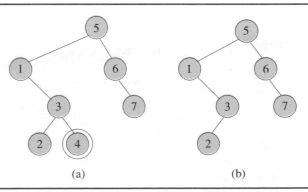

(a)   (b)

FIGURE 10.6
Removing a non-leaf node from a binary search tree.

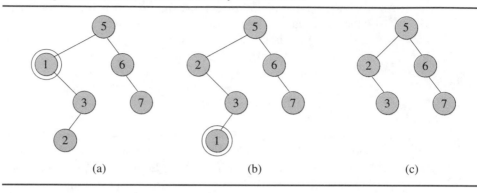

(a)   (b)   (c)

from the tree. The algorithm first determines the location of the object to be removed and then removes it according to the procedure just described.

10.5 AVL Search Trees

The problem with binary search trees is that whereas the average running times for search, insertion, and withdrawal operations are all $O(\log n)$, any one operation is still $O(n)$ in the worst case. This is so because we cannot say anything in general about the shape of the tree.

For example, consider the two binary search trees shown Figure 10.3. Both trees contain the same set of keys. The tree T_a is obtained by starting with an empty tree and inserting the keys in the following order:

$$1, 2, 3, 4, 5, 6, 7.$$

The tree T_b is obtained by starting with an empty tree and inserting the keys in this order:

$$4, 2, 6, 1, 3, 5, 7.$$

Clearly, T_b is a better tree search tree than T_a. In fact, since T_b is a *perfect binary tree*, its height is $\log_2(n + 1) - 1$. Therefore, all three operations—search, insertion, and withdrawal—have the same worst-case asymptotic running time, $O(\log n)$.

The reason that T_b is better than T_a is that it is the more *balanced* tree. If we could ensure that the search trees we construct are balanced, then the worst-case running time of search, insertion, and withdrawal, could be made logarithmic rather than linear. But under what conditions is a tree *balanced*?

If we say that a binary tree is balanced if the left and right subtrees of every node have the same height, then the only trees that are balanced are the perfect binary trees. A perfect binary tree of height h has exactly $2^{h+1} - 1$ internal nodes. Therefore, it is

PROGRAM 10.6
`BinarySearchTree` class `withdraw` method

```
1   public class BinarySearchTree
2       extends BinaryTree
3       implements SearchTree
4   {
5       public void withdraw (Comparable object)
6       {
7           if (isEmpty ())
8               throw new IllegalArgumentException (
9                   "object not found");
10          int diff = object.compare ((Comparable) getKey ());
11          if (diff == 0)
12          {
13              if (!getLeftBST ().isEmpty ())
14              {
15                  Comparable max = getLeftBST ().findMax ();
16                  key = max;
17                  getLeftBST ().withdraw (max);
18              }
19              else if (!getRightBST ().isEmpty ())
20              {
21                  Comparable min = getRightBST ().findMin ();
22                  key = min;
23                  getRightBST ().withdraw (min);
24              }
25              else
26                  detachKey ();
27          }
28          else if (diff < 0)
29              getLeftBST ().withdraw (object);
30          else
31              getRightBST ().withdraw (object);
32          balance ();
33      }
34      // ...
35  }
```

only possible to create perfect trees with *n* nodes for $n = 1, 3, 7, 15, 31, 63, \ldots$. Clearly, this is an unsuitable balance condition because it is not possible to create a balanced tree for every *n*.

What are the characteristics of a good *balance condition*?

1. A good balance condition ensures that the height of a tree with *n* nodes is $O(\log n)$.

2.   A good balance condition can be maintained efficiently. That is, the additional work necessary to balance the tree when an item is inserted or deleted is $O(1)$.

Adel'son-Vel'skiĭ and Landis[1] were the first to propose the following balance condition and show that it has the desired characteristics.

Definition 10.4 (AVL Balance Condition)
An empty binary tree is AVL balanced. A non-empty binary tree, $T = \{r, T_L, T_R\}$, is AVL balanced if both T_L and T_R are AVL balanced and

$$|h_L - h_R| \leq 1,$$

where h_L is the height of T_L and h_R is the height of T_R.

Clearly, all perfect binary trees are AVL balanced. What is not so clear is that heights of all trees that satisfy the AVL balance condition are logarithmic in the number of internal nodes.

Theorem 10.2
The height, h, of an AVL balanced tree with n internal nodes satisfies

$$\log_2(n + 1) + 1 \leq h \leq 1.440 \log(n + 2) - 0.328.$$

Proof   The lower bound follows directly from Theorem 9.2. It is in fact true for all binary trees regardless of whether they are AVL balanced.

To determine the upper bound, we turn the problem around and ask the question: What is the minimum number of internal nodes in an AVL balanced tree of height h?

Let T_h represent an AVL balanced tree of height h that has the smallest possible number of internal nodes, say N_h. Clearly, T_h must have at least one subtree of height $h - 1$ and that subtree must be T_{h-1}. To remain AVL balanced, the other subtree can have height $h - 1$ or $h - 2$. Since we want the smallest number of internal nodes, it must be T_{h-2}. Therefore, the number of internal nodes in T_h is $N_h = N_{h-1} + N_{h-2} + 1$, where $h \geq 2$.

Clearly, T_0 contains a single internal node, so $N_0 = 1$. Similarly, T_1 contains exactly two nodes, so $N_1 = 2$. Thus, N_h is given by the recurrence

$$N_h = \begin{cases} 1 & h = 0, \\ 2 & h = 1, \\ N_{h-1} + N_{h-2} + 1 & h \geq 2. \end{cases} \tag{10.8}$$

---

[1]Russian mathematicians G. M. Adel'son-Vel'skiĭ and E. M. Landis published this result in 1962.

The remarkable thing about Equation (10.8) is its similarity with the definition of *Fibonacci numbers* (Equation 3.4). In fact, it can easily be shown by induction that

$$N_h \geq F_{h+2} - 1$$

for all $h \geq 0$, where F_k is the kth Fibonacci number.

Base Cases

$$N_0 = 1, \quad F_2 = 1 \implies N_0 \geq F_2 - 1,$$
$$N_1 = 2, \quad F_3 = 2 \implies N_1 \geq F_3 - 1.$$

Inductive Hypothesis Assume that $N_h \geq F_{h+2} - 1$ for $h = 0, 1, 2, \ldots, k$. Then

$$\begin{aligned}
N_{h+1} &= N_h + N_{h-1} + 1 \\
&\geq F_{h+2} - 1 + F_{h+1} - 1 + 1 \\
&\geq F_{h+3} - 1 \\
&\geq F_{(h+1)+2} - 1.
\end{aligned}$$

Therefore, by induction on k, $N_h \geq F_{h+2} - 1$, for all $h \geq 0$.

According to Theorem 3.9, the Fibonacci numbers are given by

$$F_n = \frac{1}{\sqrt{5}}(\phi^n - \hat{\phi}^n),$$

where $\phi = (1 + \sqrt{5})/2$ and $\hat{\phi} = (1 - \sqrt{5})/2$. Furthermore, since $\hat{\phi} \approx -0.618$, $|\hat{\phi}^n/\sqrt{5}| < 1$. Therefore,

$$\begin{aligned}
N_h \geq F_{h+2} - 1 &\Rightarrow N_h \geq \phi^{h+2}/\sqrt{5} - 2 \\
&\Rightarrow \sqrt{5}(N_h + 2) \geq \phi^{h+2} \\
&\Rightarrow \log_\phi(\sqrt{5}(N_h + 2)) \geq h + 2 \\
&\Rightarrow h \leq \log_\phi(N_h + 2) + \log_\phi \sqrt{5} - 2 \\
&\Rightarrow h \leq 1.440 \log_2(N_h + 2) - 0.328.
\end{aligned}$$

This completes the proof of the upper bound.

So, we have shown that the AVL balance condition satisfies the first criterion of a good balance condition—balanced tree with n internal nodes is $\Theta(\log n)$. What remains to be shown is that the balance condition can be efficiently maintained. To see that it can, we need to look at an implementation.

PROGRAM 10.7
AVLTree fields

```
1   public class AVLTree
2       extends BinarySearchTree
3   {
4       protected int height;
5
6       // ...
7   }
```

10.5.1 Implementing AVL Trees

Having already implemented a binary search tree class, `BinarySearchTree`, we can make use of much of the existing code to implement an AVL tree class. Program 10.7 introduces the `AVLTree` class, which extends the `BinarySearchTree` class introduced in Program 10.2. The `AVLTree` class inherits most of its functionality from the binary tree class. In particular, it uses the inherited `insert` and `withdraw` methods! However, the inherited `balance`, `attachKey`, and `detachKey` methods are overridden and a number of new methods are declared.

Program 10.7 indicates that an additional field is added in the `AVLTree` class. This turns out to be necessary because we need to be able to determine quickly—that is, in $O(1)$ time—that the AVL balance condition is satisfied at a given node in the tree. In general, the running time required to compute the height of a tree containing n nodes is $O(n)$. Therefore, to determine whether the AVL balance condition is satisfied at a given node, it is necessary to completely traverse the subtrees of the given node. But this cannot be done in constant time.

To make it possible to verify the AVL balance condition in constant time, the field `height` has been added. Thus, every node in an `AVLTree` keeps track of its own height. In this way it is possible for the `getHeight` method to run in constant time—all it needs to do is to return the value of the `height` field. And this makes it possible to test whether the AVL balanced condition is satisfied at a given node in constant time.

Constructor
A no-arg constructor is shown in Program 10.8. This constructor creates an empty AVL tree. The `height` field is set to the value -1, which is consistent with the empty tree. Notice that according to Definition 10.4, the empty tree is AVL balanced. Therefore, the result is a valid AVL tree. Clearly, the running time of the constructor is $O(1)$.

getHeight, adjustHeight, and getBalanceFactor Methods
The `getHeight` method is implemented as an accessor that simply returns the value of the `height` field. Clearly the running time of this method is constant.

The purpose of `adjustHeight` is to recompute the height of a node and to update the `height` field. This method must be called whenever the height of one of the subtrees changes in order to ensure the `height` variable is always up to date. The `adjustHeight` method determines the height of a node by adding one to the height

PROGRAM 10.8
`AVLTree` class constructor, `getHeight`, `adjustHeight`, and
`getBalanceFactor` methods

```
1   public class AVLTree
2       extends BinarySearchTree
3   {
4       protected int height;
5
6       public AVLTree ()
7           { height = -1; }
8
9       public int getHeight ()
10          { return height; }
11
12      protected void adjustHeight ()
13      {
14          if (isEmpty ())
15              height = -1;
16          else
17              height = 1 + Math.max (
18                  left.getHeight (), right.getHeight ());
19      }
20
21      protected int getBalanceFactor ()
22      {
23          if (isEmpty ())
24              return 0;
25          else
26              return left.getHeight () - right.getHeight ();
27      }
28      // ...
29  }
```

of the highest subtree. Since the running time of the `getHeight` method is constant, so too is the running time of `adjustHeight`.

The `getBalanceFactor` method simply returns the difference between the heights of the left and right subtrees of a given AVL tree. By Definition 10.4, the empty node is AVL balanced. Therefore, the `getBalanceFactor` method returns zero for an empty tree. Again, since the running time of the `getHeight` method is constant, the running time of `getBalanceFactor` is also constant.

10.5.2   Inserting Items into an AVL Tree

Inserting an item into an AVL tree is a two-part process. First, the item is inserted into the tree using the usual method for insertion in binary search trees. After the item has been inserted, it is necessary to check that the resulting tree is still AVL balanced and to balance the tree when it is not.

Just as in a regular binary search tree, items are inserted into AVL trees by attaching them to the leaves. To find the correct leaf we pretend that the item is already in the tree and follow the path taken by the `find` method to determine where the item should go. Assuming that the item is not already in the tree, the search is unsuccessful and terminates an an external, empty node. The item to be inserted is placed in that external node.

Inserting an item in a given external node potentially affects the heights of all of the nodes along the *access path*, that is, the path from the root to that node. Of course, when an item is inserted in a tree, the height of the tree may increase by one. Therefore, to ensure that the resulting tree is still AVL balanced, the heights of all nodes along the access path must be recomputed and the AVL balance condition must be checked.

Sometimes increasing the height of a subtree does not violate the AVL balance condition. For example, consider an AVL tree $T = \{r, T_L, T_R\}$. Let h_L and h_R be the heights of T_L and T_R, respectively. Since T is an AVL tree, then $|h_L - h_R| \leq 1$. Now, suppose that $h_L = h_R + 1$. Then, if we insert an item into T_R, its height may increase by one to $h'_R = h_R + 1$. The resulting tree is still AVL balanced since $h_L - h'_R = 0$. In fact, this particular insertion actually makes the tree more balanced! Similarly if $h_L = h_R$ initially, an insertion in either subtree will not result in a violation of the balance condition at the root of T.

On the other hand, if $h_L = h_R + 1$ and an the insertion of an item into the left subtree T_L increases the height of that tree to $h'_L = h_L + 1$, the AVL balance condition is no longer satisfied because $h'_L - h_R = 2$. Therefore, it is necessary to change the structure of the tree to bring it back into balance.

Balancing AVL Trees

When an AVL tree becomes unbalanced, it is possible to bring it back into balance by performing an operation called a *rotation*. It turns out that there are only four cases to consider and each case has its own rotation.

Single Rotations

Figure 10.7 (a) shows an AVL balanced tree. For example, the balance factor for node A is zero, since its left and right subtrees have the same height; and the balance factor of node B is $+1$, since its left subtree has height $h + 1$ and its right subtree has height h.

Suppose we insert an item into A_L, the left subtree of A. The height of A_L can either increase or remain the same. In this case we assume that it increases. Then, as shown in Figure 10.7 (b), the resulting tree is no longer AVL balanced. Notice where the imbalance has been manifested—node A is balanced but node B is not.

Balance can be restored by reorganizing the two nodes A and B, and the three subtrees, A_L, A_R, and B_R, as shown in Figure 10.7 (c). This is called an *LL rotation*, because the first two edges in the insertion path from node B both go to the left.

There are three important properties of the LL rotation:

1. The rotation does not destroy the data-ordering property so the result is still a valid search tree. Subtree A_L remains to the left of node A, subtree A_R remains between nodes A and B, and subtree B_R remains to the right of node B.

FIGURE 10.7
Balancing an AVL tree with a single (LL) rotation.

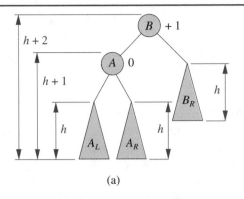

(a)

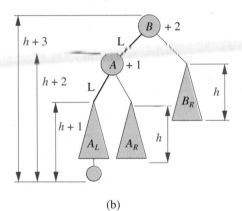

(b)

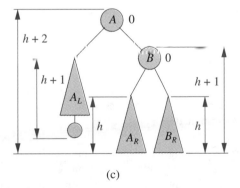

(c)

2.   After the rotation both A and B are AVL balanced. Both nodes A and B end up with zero balance factors.

3.   After the rotation, the tree has the same height it had originally. Inserting the item did not increase the overall height of the tree!

Notice that the LL rotation was called for because the root became unbalanced with a positive balance factor (i.e., its left subtree was too high) and the left subtree of the root also had a positive balance factor.

Not surprisingly, the left-right mirror image of the LL rotation is called an *RR rotation*. An RR rotation is called for when the root becomes unbalanced with a negative balance factor (i.e., its right subtree is too high) and the right subtree of the root also has a negative balance factor.

Double Rotations

The preceding cases have dealt with access paths LL and RR. Clearly two more cases remain to be implemented. Consider the case where the root becomes unbalanced with a positive balance factor but the left subtree of the root has a negative balance factor. This situation is shown in Figure 10.8 (b).

The tree can be restored by performing an RR rotation at node *A*, followed by an LL rotation at node *C*. The tree that results is shown in Figure 10.8 (c). The LL and RR rotations are called *single rotations*. The combination of the two single rotations is called a *double rotation* and is given the name *LR rotation* because the first two edges in the insertion path from node *C* both go left and then right.

Obviously, the left-right mirror image of the LR rotation is called an *RL rotation*. An RL rotation is called for when the root becomes unbalanced with a negative balance factor but the right subtree of the root has a positive balance factor. Double rotations have the same properties as the single rotations: The result is a valid, AVL-balanced search tree and the height of the result is the same as that of the initial tree.

Clearly the four rotations, LL, RR, LR, and RL, cover all possible ways in which any one node can become unbalanced. But how many rotations are required to balance a tree when an insertion is done? The following theorem addresses this question:

Theorem 10.3

When an AVL tree becomes unbalanced after an insertion, exactly one single or double rotation is required to balance the tree.

Proof   When an item, *x*, is inserted into an AVL tree, *T*, that item is placed in an external node of the tree. The only nodes in *T* whose heights may be affected by the insertion of *x* are those nodes that lie on the access path from the root of *T* to *x*. Therefore, the only nodes at which an imbalance can appear are those along the access path. Furthermore, when a node is inserted into a tree, either the height of the tree remains the same or the height of the tree increases by one.

Consider some node *c* along the access path from the root of *T* to *x*. When *x* is inserted, the height of *c* either increases by one, or remains the same. If the height of *c* does not change, then no rotation is necessary at *c* or at any node above *c* in the access path.

If the height of *c* increases then there are two possibilities: Either *c* remains balanced or an imbalance appears at *c*. If *c* remains balanced, then no rotation is necessary at *c*. However, a rotation may be needed somewhere above *c* along the access path.

On the other hand, if *c* becomes unbalanced, then a single or a double rotation must be performed at *c*. After the rotation is done, the height of *c* is the same as it was before the insertion. Therefore, no further rotation is needed above *c* in the access path.

FIGURE 10.8
Balancing an AVL tree with a double (LR) rotation.

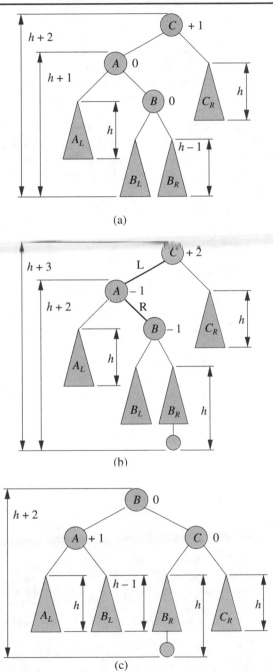

Theorem 10.3 suggests the following method for balancing an AVL tree after an insertion: Begin at the node containing the item that was just inserted and move back along the access path toward the root. For each node determine its height and check the balance condition. If the height of the current node does not increase, then the tree is AVL balanced and no further nodes need be considered. If the node has become unbalanced, a rotation is needed to balance it. After the rotation, the height of the node remains unchanged, the tree is AVL balanced and no further nodes need be considered. Otherwise, the height of the node increases by one, but no rotation is needed and we proceed to the next node on the access path.

Implementation

Program 10.9 gives the code for the **doLLRotation** method of the **AVLTree** class. This code implements the LL rotation shown in Figure 10.7. The purpose of the **doLLRotation** method is to perform an LL rotation at the root of a given AVL tree instance.

The rotation is simply a sequence of variable manipulations followed by two height adjustments. Notice the rotation is done in such a way so that the given **AVLTree**

PROGRAM 10.9
AVLTree class doLLRotation method

```
 1   public class AVLTree
 2       extends BinarySearchTree
 3   {
 4       protected int height;
 5
 6       protected void doLLRotation ()
 7       {
 8           if (isEmpty ())
 9               throw new InvalidOperationException ();
10           BinaryTree tmp = right;
11           right = left;
12           left = right.left;
13           right.left = right.right;
14           right.right = tmp;
15
16           Object tmpObj = key;
17           key = right.key;
18           right.key = tmpObj;
19
20           getRightAVL ().adjustHeight ();
21           adjustHeight ();
22       }
23       // ...
24   }
```

---

instance remains the root of the tree. This is done so that if the tree has a parent, it is not necessary to modify the contents of the parent.

The **AVLTree** class also requires a **doRRRotation** method to implement an RR rotation. The implementation of that method follows directly from Program 10.9. Clearly, the running time for the single rotations is $O(1)$.

Program 10.10 gives the implementation for the **doLRRotation** method of the **AVLTree** class. This double rotation is trivially implemented as a sequence of two single rotations. As above, the method for the complementary rotation is easily derived from the given code. The running time for each of the double rotation methods is also $O(1)$.

When an imbalance is detected, it is necessary to correct the imbalance by doing the appropriate rotation. The code given in Program 10.11 takes care of this. The **balance** method tests for an imbalance by calling the **getBalanceFactor** method. The balance test itself takes constant time. If the node is balanced, only a constant-time height adjustment is needed.

Otherwise, the **balance** method of the **AVLTree** class determines which of the four cases has occurred, and invokes the appropriate rotation to correct the imbalance. To determine which case has occurred, the **balance** method calls the **getBalanceFactor** method at most twice. Therefore, the time for selecting the case is constant. In all, only one rotation is done to correct the imbalance. Therefore, the running time of this method is $O(1)$.

The **insert** method for AVL trees is inherited from the **BinarySearchTree** class (see Program 10.5). The **insert** method calls **attachKey** to do the actual insertion. The **attachKey** method is overridden in the **AVLTree** class as shown in Program 10.12.

PROGRAM 10.10
AVLTree class **doLRRotation** method

```
1  public class AVLTree
2      extends BinarySearchTree
3  {
4      protected int height;
5
6      protected void doLRRotation ()
7      {
8          if (isEmpty ())
9              throw new InvalidOperationException ();
10         getLeftAVL ().doRRRotation ();
11         doLLRotation ();
12     }
13     // ...
14 }
```

PROGRAM 10.11
AVLTree class balance method

```
1   public class AVLTree
2       extends BinarySearchTree
3   {
4       protected int height;
5
6       protected void balance ()
7       {
8           adjustHeight ();
9           if (getBalanceFactor () > 1)
10          {
11              if (getLeftAVL ().getBalanceFactor () > 0)
12                  doLLRotation ();
13              else
14                  doLRRotation ();
15          }
16          else if (getBalanceFactor () < -1)
17          {
18              if (getRightAVL ().getBalanceFactor () < 0)
19                  doRRRotation ();
20              else
21                  doRLRotation ();
22          }
23      }
24      // ...
25  }
```

The very last thing that the **insert** method does is to call the **balance** method, which has also been overridden as shown in Program 10.11. As a result, the **insert** method adjusts the heights of the nodes along the insertion path and does a rotation when an imbalance is detected. Since the height of an AVL tree is guaranteed to be $O(\log n)$, the time for insertion is simply $O(\log n)$.

10.5.3 Removing Items from an AVL Tree

The method for removing items from an AVL tree is inherited from the **Binary-SearchTree** class in the same way as AVL insertion. (See Program 10.6.) All of the differences are encapsulated in the **detachKey** and **balance** methods. The **balance** method was previously discussed. The **detachKey** method is defined in Program 10.13.

PROGRAM 10.12
AVLTree class attachKey method

```
1   public class AVLTree
2       extends BinarySearchTree
3   {
4       protected int height;
5
6       public void attachKey (Object object)
7       {
8           if (!isEmpty ())
9               throw new InvalidOperationException ();
10          key = object;
11          left = new AVLTree ();
12          right = new AVLTree ();
13          height = 0;
14      }
15      // ...
16  }
```

PROGRAM 10.13
AVLTree class detachKey method

```
1   public class AVLTree
2       extends BinarySearchTree
3   {
4       protected int height;
5
6       public Object detachKey ()
7       {
8           height = -1;
9           return super.detachKey ();
10      }
11      // ...
12  }
```

10.6 *M*-Way Search Trees

As defined in Section 10.1.1, an internal node of an *M*-way search tree contains n subtrees and $n-1$ keys, where $2 \leq n \leq M$, for some fixed value of $M \geq 2$. The preceding sections give implementations for the special case in which the fixed value of $M = 2$ is assumed (binary search trees). In this section we consider the implementation of *M*-way search trees for *arbitrary*, larger values of $M \gg 2$.

Why are we interested in larger values of M? Suppose we have a very large data set—so large that we cannot get it all into the main memory of the computer at the same time. In this situation we implement the search tree in secondary storage, that is, on disk. The unique characteristics of disk-based storage *vis-à-vis* memory-based storage make it necessary to use larger values of M in order to implement search trees efficiently.

The typical disk access time is 1–10 ms, whereas the typical main memory access time is 10–100 ns. Thus, main memory accesses are between 10 000 and 1 000 000 times faster than typical disk accesses. Therefore, to maximize performance, it is imperative that the total number of disk accesses be minimized.

In addition, disks are block-oriented devices. Data are transfered between main memory and disk in large blocks. The typical block sizes are between 512 bytes and 4096 bytes. Consequently, it makes sense to organize the data structure to take advantage of the ability to transfer entire blocks of data efficiently.

By choosing a suitably large value for M, we can arrange that one node of an M-way search tree occupies an entire disk block. If every internal node in the M-way search tree has exactly M children, we can use Theorem 9.2 to determine the height of the tree:

$$h \geq \lceil \log_M((M-1)n + 1) \rceil - 1, \tag{10.9}$$

where n is the number of internal nodes in the search tree. A node in an M-way search tree that has M children contains exactly $M - 1$ keys. Therefore, altogether there are $K = (M-1)n$ keys and Equation (10.9) becomes $h \geq \lceil \log_M(K+1) \rceil - 1$. Ideally the search tree is well balanced and the inequality becomes an equality.

For example, consider a search tree that contains $K = 2\,097\,151$ keys. Suppose the size of a disk block is such that we can fit a node of size $M = 128$ in it. Since each node contains at most 127 keys, at least 16 513 nodes are required. In the best case, the height of the M-way search tree is only two and at most three disk accesses are required to retrieve any key! This is a significant improvement over a binary tree, the height of which is at least 20.

10.6.1 Implementing M-Way Search Trees

In order to illustrate the basic ideas, this section describes an implementation of M-way search trees in main memory. According to Definition 10.1, each internal node of an M-way search tree has n subtrees, where n is at least two and at most M. Furthermore, if a node has n subtrees, it must contain $n - 1$ keys.

Figure 10.9 shows how we can implement a single node of an M-way search tree. The idea is that we use two arrays in each node—the first holds the keys and the second contains pointers to the subtrees. Since there are at most M subtrees but only $M - 1$ keys, the first element of the array of keys is not used.

Implementation

Program 10.14 introduces the **MWayTree** class. The **MWayTree** class extends the **AbstractTree** class introduced in Program 9.2 and it implements the **Searchable-Container** interface defined in Program 5.14. The two fields, **key** and **subtree**,

FIGURE 10.9
Representing a node of an *M*-way search tree.

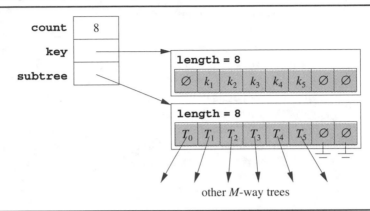

other *M*-way trees

PROGRAM 10.14
MWayTree fields, constructor, and getM method

```
1   public class MWayTree
2       extends AbstractTree
3       implements SearchTree
4   {
5       protected Comparable key[];
6       protected MWayTree subtree[];
7
8       public MWayTree (int m)
9       {
10          if (m < 2)
11              throw new IllegalArgumentException("invalid degree");
12          key = new Comparable [m];
13          subtree = new MWayTree [m];
14      }
15
16      int getM ()
17          { return subtree.length; }
18      // ...
19  }
```

correspond to the components of a node shown in Figure 10.9. (Remember, the **count** field is inherited from the **AbstractContainer** base class introduced in Program 5.9.)

The first field, **key**, is an array of **Comparable** object instances. It is used to record the keys contained in the node. The second field, **subtree**, is an array of **MWayTree** instances, which are the subtrees of the given node.

The inherited **count** field keeps track of the number of keys contained in the node. Recall that a node containing **count** keys has **count** + 1 subtrees. We have chosen to keep track of the number of keys of a node rather than the number of subtrees because it simplifies the coding of the algorithms by eliminating some of the special cases.

Constructor and `getM` Methods

Program 10.14 defines the constructor and `getM` methods of the `MWayTree` class. The constructor takes a single, integer-valued argument that specifies the desired value of M. Provided M is greater than or equal to two, the constructor creates two arrays of length M. Note that a node in an M-way tree contains at most $M - 1$ keys. In the implementation shown, `key[0]` is never used. Because the constructor allocates arrays of length M, its worst-case running time is $O(M)$.

The `getM` method shown in Program 10.14 returns the value of M. That is, it returns the maximum number of subtrees that a node is allowed to have. This is simply given by the `length` of the `subtree` array. The running time of the `getM` method is clearly $O(1)$.

Inorder Traversal

Whereas inorder traversal of an N-ary tree is *not* defined for $N > 2$, inorder traversal *is* defined for an M-way search tree: By definition, the inorder traversal of a search tree visits all keys contained in the search tree *in order*.

Program 10.15 is an implementation of the algorithm for depth-first traversal of an M-way search tree given in Section 10.3.4. The keys contained in a given node are visited (by calling the `inVisit` method of the visitor) *in between* the appropriate subtrees of that node. That is, key k_i is visited *in between* subtrees T_{i-1} and T_i.

In addition, the `postVisit` method is called on k_{i-1} *after* subtree T_{i-1} has been visited, and the `preVisit` method is called on k_{i+1} before subtree T_i is visited.

It is clear that the amount of work done at each node during the course of a depth-first traversal is proportional to the number of keys contained in that node. Therefore, the total running time for the depth-first traversal is $K(\mathcal{T}\langle \texttt{preVisit} \rangle + \mathcal{T}\langle \texttt{inVisit} \rangle + \mathcal{T}\langle \texttt{postVisit} \rangle) + O(K)$, where K is the number of keys contained in the search tree.

10.6.2 Finding Items in an M-Way Search Tree

Two algorithms for finding items in an M-way search tree are described in this section. The first is a naïve implementation using linear search. The second version improves on the first by using a binary search.

Linear Search

Program 10.16 gives the naïve version of the `find` method of the `MWayTree` class. The `find` method takes a `Comparable` object and locates the item in the search tree that matches the given object.

Consider the execution of the `find` method for a node T of an M-way search tree. Suppose the object of the search is x. Clearly, the search fails when $T = 0$ (lines 10–11). In this case, `null` is returned.

Suppose $T = \{T_0, k_1, T_1, k_2, T_2, \ldots, k_{n-1}, T_{n-1}\}$. The linear search on lines 13–20 considers the keys $k_{n-1}, k_{n-2}, k_{n-3}, \ldots, k_1$, in that order. If a match is found, the matching object is returned immediately (lines 16–17).

PROGRAM 10.15
MWayTree class depthFirstTraversal method

```
 1  public class MWayTree
 2      extends AbstractTree
 3      implements SearchTree
 4  {
 5      protected Comparable key[];
 6      protected MWayTree subtree[];
 7
 8      public void depthFirstTraversal (PrePostVisitor visitor)
 9      {
10          if (!isEmpty ())
11          {
12              for (int i = 0; i <= count + 1; ++i)
13              {
14                  if (i >= 2)
15                      visitor.postVisit (key [i - 1]);
16                  if (i >= 1 && i <= count)
17                      visitor.inVisit (key [i]);
18                  if (i <= count - 1)
19                      visitor.preVisit (key [i + 1]);
20                  if (i <= count)
21                      subtree [i].depthFirstTraversal (visitor);
22              }
23          }
24      }
25      // ...
26  }
```

Otherwise, when the main loop terminates there are three possibilities: $i = 0$ and $x < k_{i+1}$, $1 \le i \le n - 2$ and $k_i < x < k_{i+1}$; or $i = n - 1$ and $k_i < x$. In all three cases, the appropriate subtree in which to continue the search is T_i (line 21).

Clearly the running time of Program 10.16 is determined by the main loop. In the worst case, the loop is executed $M - 1$ times. Therefore, at each node in the search path at most $M - 1$ object comparisons are done.

Consider an unsuccessful search in an M-way search tree. The running time of the **find** method is

$$(M - 1)(h + 1)\mathcal{T}\langle\text{compare}\rangle + O(Mh)$$

in the worst case, where h is the height of the tree and $\mathcal{T}\langle\text{compare}\rangle$ is the time required to compare two objects. Clearly, the time for a successful search has the same asymptotic bound. If the tree is balanced and $\mathcal{T}\langle\text{compare}\rangle = O(1)$, then the running time of Program 10.16 is $O(M \log_M K)$, where K is the number of keys in the tree.

PROGRAM 10.16
MWayTree class `find` method (linear search)

```
1   public class MWayTree
2       extends AbstractTree
3       implements SearchTree
4   {
5       protected Comparable key[];
6       protected MWayTree subtree[];
7
8       public Comparable find (Comparable object)
9       {
10          if (isEmpty ())
11              return null;
12          int i;
13          for (i = count; i > 0; --i)
14          {
15              int diff = object.compare (key [i]);
16              if (diff == 0)
17                  return key [i];
18              if (diff > 0)
19                  break;
20          }
21          return subtree [i].find (object);
22      }
23      // ...
24  }
```

Binary Search

We can improve the performance of the M-way search tree search algorithm by recognizing that since the keys are kept in a sorted array, we can do a binary search rather than a linear search. Program 10.17 gives an alternate implementation for the `find` method of the MWayTree class. This method makes use of the `findIndex` method, which does the actual binary search.

The `findIndex` method has as its argument a `Comparable` object, say x, and returns an `int` in the range between 0 and $n - 1$, where n is the number of subtrees of the given node. The result is the largest integer i, if it exists, such that $x \geq k_i$ where k_i is the ith key. Otherwise, it returns the value 0.

`findIndex` determines its result by doing a binary search. In the worst case, $\lceil \log_2(M - 1) \rceil + 1$ iterations of the main loop (lines 14–21) are required to determine the correct index. One object comparison is done before the loop (line 10) and one comparison is done in each loop iteration (line 17). Therefore, the running time of the `findIndex` method is

$$(\lceil \log_2(M - 1) \rceil + 2)\mathcal{T}\langle \text{compare} \rangle + O(\log_2 M).$$

If $\mathcal{T}\langle \text{compare} \rangle = O(1)$, this simplifies to $O(\log M)$.

PROGRAM 10.17
MWayTree class findIndex and find methods (binary search)

```
1   public class MWayTree
2       extends AbstractTree
3       implements SearchTree
4   {
5       protected Comparable key[];
6       protected MWayTree subtree[];
7
8       protected int findIndex (Comparable object)
9       {
10          if (isEmpty () || object.isLT (key [1]))
11              return 0;
12          int left = 1;
13          int right = count;
14          while (left < right)
15          {
16              int middle = (left + right + 1) / 2;
17              if (object.isLT (key [middle]))
18                  right = middle - 1;
19              else
20                  left = middle;
21          }
22          return left;
23      }
24
25      public Comparable find (Comparable object)
26      {
27          if (isEmpty ())
28              return null;
29          int index = findIndex (object);
30          if (index != 0 && object.isEQ (key [index]))
31              return key [index];
32          else
33              return subtree [index].find (object);
34      }
35      // ...
36  }
```

The **find** method of the **MWayTree** class does the actual search. It calls **findIndex** to determine largest integer i, if it exists, such that $x \geq k_i$ where k_i is the ith key (line 29). If it turns out that $x = k_i$, then the search is finished (lines 30–31). Otherwise, **find** calls itself recursively to search subtree T_i (line 33).

Consider a search in an M-way search tree. The running time of the second version of **find** is

$$(h + 1)(\lceil \log_2(M - 1)\rceil + 2)\mathcal{T}\langle \text{compare}\rangle + O(h \log M),$$

where h is the height of the tree and regardless of whether the search is successful. If the tree is balanced and $\mathcal{T}\langle \text{compare}\rangle = O(1)$, then the running time of Program 10.17 is simply $O((\log_2 M)(\log_M K))$, where K is the number of keys in the tree.

10.6.3 Inserting Items into an M-Way Search Tree

The method for inserting items in an M-way search tree follows directly from the algorithm for insertion in a binary search tree given in Section 10.4.2. The added wrinkle in an M-way tree is that an internal node may contain between 1 and $M - 1$ keys, whereas an internal node in a binary tree must contain exactly one key.

Program 10.18 gives the implementation of the **insert** method of the **MWayTree** class. This method takes as its argument the object to be inserted into the search tree.

The general algorithm for insertion is to search for the item to be inserted and then to insert it at the point where the search terminates. If the search terminates at an external node, that node is transformed to an internal node of the form $\{\varnothing, x, \varnothing\}$, where x is the key just inserted (lines 10–16).

If the search terminates at an internal node, we insert the new item into the sorted list of keys at the appropriate offset. Inserting the key x in the array of keys moves all keys larger than x and the associated subtrees to the right one position (lines 23–33). The hole in the list of subtrees is filled with an empty tree (line 31).

The preceding section gives the running time for a search in an M-way search tree as

$$(h + 1)(\lceil \log_2(M - 1)\rceil + 2)\mathcal{T}\langle \text{compare}\rangle + O(h \log M),$$

where h is the height of the tree. The additional time required to insert the item into the node once the correct node has been located is $O(M)$. Therefore, the total running time for the **insert** algorithm given in Program 10.18 is

$$(h + 1)(\lceil \log_2(M - 1)\rceil + 2)\mathcal{T}\langle \text{compare}\rangle + O(h \log M) + O(M).$$

10.6.4 Removing Items from an M-Way Search Tree

The algorithm for removing items from an M-way search tree follows directly from the algorithm for removing items from a binary search tree given in Section 10.4.3. The

PROGRAM 10.18
`MWayTree` class `insert` method

```
1   public class MWayTree
2       extends AbstractTree
3       implements SearchTree
4   {
5       protected Comparable key[];
6       protected MWayTree subtree[];
7
8       public void insert (Comparable object)
9       {
10          if (isEmpty ())
11          {
12              subtree [0] = new MWayTree (getM ());
13              key [1] = object;
14              subtree [1] = new MWayTree (getM ());
15              count = 1;
16          }
17          else
18          {
19              int index = findIndex (object);
20              if (index != 0 && object.isEQ (key [index]))
21                  throw new IllegalArgumentException (
22                      "duplicate key");
23              if (!isFull ())
24              {
25                  for (int i = count; i > index; --i)
26                  {
27                      key [i + 1] = key [i];
28                      subtree [i + 1] = subtree [i];
29                  }
30                  key [index + 1] = object;
31                  subtree [index + 1] = new MWayTree (getM ());
32                  ++count;
33              }
34              else
35                  subtree [index].insert (object);
36          }
37      }
38      // ...
39  }
```

```
1   public class MWayTree
2       extends AbstractTree
3       implements SearchTree
4   {
5       protected Comparable key[];
6       protected MWayTree subtree[];
7
8       public void withdraw (Comparable object)
9       {
10          if (isEmpty ()) throw new IllegalArgumentException (
11              "object not found");
12          int index = findIndex (object);
13          if (index != 0 && object.isEQ (key [index]))
14          {
15              if (!subtree [index - 1].isEmpty ())
16              {
17                  Comparable max = subtree [index - 1].findMax ();
18                  key [index] = max;
19                  subtree [index - 1].withdraw (max);
20              }
21              else if (!subtree [index].isEmpty ())
22              {
23                  Comparable min = subtree [index].findMin ();
24                  key [index] = min;
25                  subtree [index].withdraw (min);
26              }
27              else
28              {
29                  --count;
30                  int i;
31                  for (i = index; i <= count; ++i)
32                  {   key [i] = key [i + 1];
33                      subtree [i] = subtree [i + 1];
34                  }
35                  key [i] = null;
36                  subtree [i] = null;
37                  if (count == 0)
38                      subtree [0] = null;
39              }
40          }
41          else
42              subtree [index].withdraw (object);
43      }
44      // ...
45  }
```

basic idea is that the item to be deleted is pushed down the tree from its initial position to a node from which it can be easily deleted. Clearly, items are easily deleted from leaf nodes. In addition, consider an internal node of an M-way search tree of the form

$$T = \{T_0, k_1, T_1, \ldots, T_{i-1}, k_i, T_i, \ldots, k_{n-1}, T_{n-1}\}.$$

If both T_{i-1} and T_i are empty trees, then the key k_i can be deleted from T by removing both k_i and T_i, say. If T_{i-1} is non-empty, k_i can be pushed down the tree by swapping it with the largest key in T_{i-1}; and if T_i is non-empty, k_i can be pushed down the tree by swapping it with the smallest key in T_i.

Program 10.19 gives the code for the **withdraw** method of the **MWayTree** class. The general form of the algorithm follows that of the **withdraw** method for the **BinarySearchTree** class (Program 10.6).

10.7 B-Trees

Just as AVL trees are balanced binary search trees, *B-trees* are balanced M-way search trees.[2] By imposing a *balance condition*, the shape of an AVL tree is constrained in a way that guarantees that the search, insertion, and withdrawal operations are all $O(\log n)$, where n is the number of items in the tree. The shapes of B-trees are constrained for the same reasons and with the same effect.

Definition 10.5 (B-Tree)
A B-tree of order M is either the empty tree or it is an M-way search tree T with the following properties:

1. *The root of T has at least two subtrees and at most M subtrees.*
2. *All internal nodes of T (other than its root) have between $\lceil M/2 \rceil$ and M subtrees.*
3. *All external nodes of T are at the same level.*

A B-tree of order one is clearly impossible. Hence, B-trees of order M are really only defined for $M \geq 2$. However, in practice we expect that M is large for the same reasons that motivate M-way search trees—large databases in secondary storage.

Figure 10.10 gives an example of a B-tree of order $M = 3$. By Definition 10.5, the root of a B-tree of order three has either two or three subtrees and the internal nodes also have either two or three subtrees. Furthermore, all the external nodes, which are shown as small boxes in Figure 10.10, are at the same level.

It turns out that the balance conditions imposed by Definition 10.5 are good in the same sense as the AVL balance conditions. That is, the balance condition guarantees

---

[2] Obviously since B-trees are M-way trees, the "B" in *B-tree* does not stand for *binary*. B-trees were invented by R. Bayer and E. McCright in 1972, so the "B" either stands for *balanced* or *Bayer*—take your pick.

FIGURE 10.10
A B-tree of order 3.

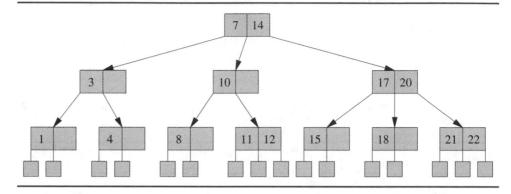

that the height of B-trees is logarithmic in the number of keys in the tree, and the time required for insertion and deletion operations remains proportional to the height of the tree even when balancing is required.

Theorem 10.4

The minimum number of keys in a B-tree of order $M \geq 2$ and height $h \geq 0$ is $n_h = 2\lceil M/2 \rceil^h - 1$.

Proof   Clearly, a B-tree of height zero contains at least one node. Consider a B-tree of order M and height $h > 0$. By Definition 10.5, each internal node (except the root) has at least $\lceil M/2 \rceil$ subtrees. This implies that the minimum number of keys contained in an internal node is $\lceil M/2 \rceil - 1$. The minimum number of keys at level zero is 1; at level one, $2(\lceil M/2 \rceil - 1)$; at level two, $2\lceil M/2 \rceil(\lceil M/2 \rceil - 1)$; at level three, $2\lceil M/2 \rceil^2(\lceil M/2 \rceil - 1)$; and so on.

Therefore, the minimum number of keys in a B-tree of height $h > 0$ is given by the summation

$$n_h = 1 + 2(\lceil M/2 \rceil - 1)\sum_{i=0}^{h-1}\lceil M/2 \rceil^i$$

$$= 1 + 2(\lceil M/2 \rceil - 1)\left(\frac{\lceil M/2 \rceil^h - 1}{\lceil M/2 \rceil - 1}\right)$$

$$= 2\lceil M/2 \rceil^h - 1.$$

A corollary of Theorem 10.4 is that the height, h, of a B-tree containing n keys is given by

$$h \leq \log_{\lceil M/2 \rceil}((n + 1)/2).$$

Thus, we have shown that a B-tree satisfies the first criterion of a good balance condition—the height of B-tree with n internal nodes is $O(\log n)$. What remains to be shown is that the balance condition can be efficiently maintained during insertion and withdrawal operations. To see that it can, we need to look at an implementation.

10.7.1 Implementing B-Trees

Having already implemented the *M*-way search tree class, `MWayTree`, we can make use of much of the existing code to implement a B-tree class. Program 10.20 introduces the `BTree` class, which extends the class `MWayTree` class introduced in Program 10.14. With the exception of the two methods that modify the tree, `insert` and `withdraw`, the `BTree` class inherits all its functionality from the *M*-way tree class. Of course, the `insert` and `withdraw` methods need to be redefined in order to ensure that every time the tree is modified the tree that results is a B-tree.

Fields

To simplify the implementation of the algorithms, a `parent` field has been added. The `parent` field refers to the `BTree` node, which is the parent of the given node. Whereas the `subtree` field of the `MWayTree` class allows an algorithm to move down the tree, the `parent` field admits movement up the tree. Since the root of a tree has no parent, the `parent` field of the root node is assigned the value `null`.

Constructor and `attachSubtree` Methods

Program 10.20 defines a constructor that takes a single `int` argument *M* and creates an empty B-tree of order *M*. By default, the `parent` field is `null`.

PROGRAM 10.20
`BTree` fields, constructor, and `attachSubtree` method

```
1  public class BTree
2      extends MWayTree
3  {
4      protected BTree parent;
5
6      public BTree (int m)
7          { super (m); }
8
9      public void attachSubtree (int i, MWayTree arg)
10     {
11         BTree btree = (BTree) arg;
12         subtree [i] = btree;
13         btree.parent = this;
14     }
15     // ...
16 }
```

The **attachSubtree** method is used to attach a new subtree to a given node. The **attachSubtree** routine takes an integer, i, and an M-way tree (which must be a B-tree instance), and makes it the ith subtree of the given node. Notice that this method also modifies the **parent** field in the attached node.

10.7.2 Inserting Items into a B-Tree

The algorithm for insertion into a B-tree begins as do all of the other search tree insertion algorithms: To insert item x, we begin at the root and conduct a search for the item. Assuming the item is not already in the tree, the unsuccessful search will terminate at a leaf node. This is the point in the tree at which the x is inserted.

If the leaf node has fewer than $M - 1$ keys in it, we simply insert the item in the leaf node and we are done. For example, consider a leaf node with $n < M$ subtrees and $n - 1$ keys of the form

$$T = \{T_0, k_1, T_1, k_2, T_2, \ldots, k_{n-1}, T_{n-1}\}.$$

For every new key inserted in the node, a new subtree is required too. In this case because T is a leaf, all its subtrees are empty trees. Therefore, when we insert item x, we really insert the pair of items $(x, \varnothing)$. Suppose the key to be inserted falls between k_i and k_{i+1}, that is, $k_i < x < k_{i+1}$. When we insert the pair $(x, \varnothing)$ into T we get the new leaf T' given by

$$T' = \{T_0, k_1, T_1, k_2, T_2, \ldots, k_i, T_i, x, 0, k_{i+1}, T_{i+1}, \ldots, k_{n-1}, T_{n-1}\}.$$

What happens when the leaf is full? That is, suppose we wish to insert the pair $(x, \varnothing)$ into a node T that already has $M - 1$ keys. Inserting the pair in its correct position gives a result of the form

$$T' = \{T_0, k_1, T_1, k_2, T_2, \ldots, k_M, T_M\}.$$

However, this is not a valid node in a B-tree of order M because it has $M + 1$ subtrees and M keys. The solution is to split node T' in half as follows:

$$T'_L = \{T_0, k_1, T_1, \ldots, k_{\lceil M/2 \rceil - 1}, T_{\lceil M/2 \rceil - 1}\}$$
$$T'_R = \{T_{\lceil M/2 \rceil}, k_{\lceil M/2 \rceil + 1}, T_{\lceil M/2 \rceil + 1}, \ldots, k_M, T_M\}.$$

Note that T'_L is a valid B-tree node because it contains $\lceil M/2 \rceil$ subtrees and $\lceil M/2 \rceil - 1$ keys. Similarly, T'_R is a valid B-tree node because it contains $\lceil (M + 1)/2 \rceil$ subtrees and $\lceil (M + 1)/2 \rceil - 1$ keys. Note that there is still a key left over, namely $k_{\lceil M/2 \rceil}$.

There are now two cases to consider—either T is the root or it is not. Suppose T is not the root. Where we once had the single node T, we now have the two nodes, T'_L and T'_R, and the left-over key, $k_{\lceil M/2 \rceil}$. This situation is resolved as follows: First, T'_L replaces T in the parent of T. Next, we take the pair $(k_{\lceil M/2 \rceil}, T'_R)$ and recursively insert it in the parent of T.

Figure 10.11 illustrates this case for a B-tree of order three. Inserting the key 6 in the tree causes the leaf node to overflow. The leaf is split in two. The left half contains key 5; and the right, key 7; and key 6 is left over. The two halves are reattached to the parent in the appropriate place with the left-over key between them.

16

e two new nodes are inserted in
up the tree to the root. What do
also split. However, since there
a new root is inserted above the
es and one key, as allowed by

ler three. Inserting the key 3 in
af and reattaching it causes the
eattaching it causes the grand-
root is split and a new root is

en the root node splits. Further-
attached under the new root.
pth, as required by Definition

FIGURE 10.12
Inserting items into a B-tree (insert 3).

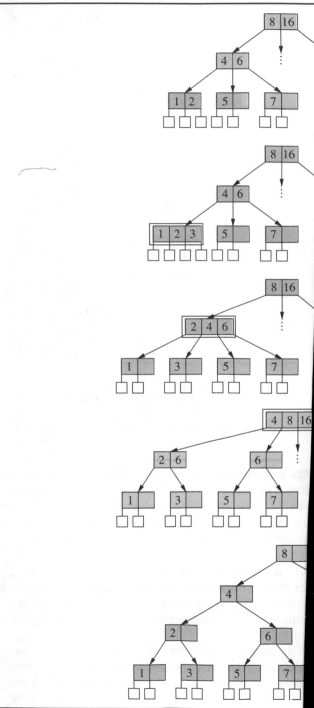

Implementation

Insertion in a B-tree is a two-pass process. The first pass moves down the tree from the root in order to locate the leaf in which the insertion is to begin. This part of the algorithm is quite similar to the **find** method given in Program 10.17. The second pass moves from the bottom of the tree back up to the root, splitting nodes and inserting them further up the tree as needed. Program 10.21 gives the code for the first (downward) pass (**insert** method) and Program 10.22 gives the code for the second (upward) pass (**insertPair** method).

In the implementation shown, the downward pass starts at the root node and descends the tree until it arrives at an external node. If the external node has no parent, it must be the root and, therefore, the tree is empty. In this case, the root becomes an internal

---

PROGRAM 10.21
BTree class insert method

```
1   public class BTree
2       extends MWayTree
3   {
4       protected MWayTree parent;
5
6       public void insert (Comparable object)
7       {
8           if (isEmpty ())
9           {
10              if (parent == null)
11              {
12                  attachSubtree (0, new BTree (getM ()));
13                  key [1] = object;
14                  attachSubtree (1, new BTree (getM ()));
15                  count = 1;
16              }
17              else
18                  parent.insertPair (object, new BTree (getM ()));
19          }
20          else
21          {
22              int index = findIndex (object);
23              if (index != 0 && object.isEQ (key [index]))
24                  throw new IllegalArgumentException (
25                      "duplicate key");
26              subtree [index].insert (object);
27          }
28      }
29      // ...
30  }
```

PROGRAM 10.22
BTree class insertPair method

```
1   public class BTree
2       extends MWayTree
3   {
4       protected BTree parent;
5
6       protected void insertPair (Comparable object, BTree child)
7       {
8           int index = findIndex (object);
9           if (!isFull ())
10          {
11              insertKey (index + 1, object);
12              insertSubtree (index + 1, child);
13              ++count;
14          }
15          else
16          {
17              Comparable extraKey = insertKey (index + 1, object);
18              BTree extraTree = insertSubtree (index + 1, child);
19              if (parent == null)
20              {
21                  BTree left = new BTree (getM ());
22                  BTree right = new BTree (getM ());
23                  left.attachLeftHalfOf (this);
24                  right.attachRightHalfOf (this);
25                  right.insertPair (extraKey, extraTree);
26                  attachSubtree (0, left);
27                  key [1] = key [(getM () + 1)/2];
28                  attachSubtree (1, right);
29                  count = 1;
30              }
31              else
32              {
33                  count = (getM () + 1)/2 - 1;
34                  BTree right = new BTree (getM ());
35                  right.attachRightHalfOf (this);
36                  right.insertPair (extraKey, extraTree);
37                  parent.insertPair (key [(getM () + 1)/2], right);
38              }
39          }
40      }
41      // ...
42  }
```

---

node containing a single key and two empty subtrees (lines 12–14). Otherwise, we have arrived at an external node in a non-empty tree and the second pass begins by calling `insertPair` to insert the pair $(x, \varnothing)$ in the parent.

The upward pass of the insertion algorithm is done by the recursive `insertPair` method shown in Program 10.22. The `insertPair` method takes two arguments. The first, `object`, is a `Comparable` object and the second, `child`, is a `BTree`. It is assumed that all of the keys in `child` are strictly greater than `object`.

The `insertPair` method calls `findIndex` to determine the position in the array of keys at which pair (`object`, `child`) should be inserted (line 8). If this node is full (line 9), the `insertKey` is called to insert the given key at the specified position in the `key` array (line 11) and `insertSubtree` is called to insert the given tree at the specified position in the `subtree` array (line 12).

In the event that the node is full, the `insertKey` method returns the key that falls off the right end of the array. This is assigned to `extraKey` (line 17). Similarly, the `insertSubtree` method returns the tree that falls off the right end of the array. This is assigned to `extraTree` (line 18).

The node has now overflowed and it is necessary to balance the B-tree. If the node overflows and it is the root (line 19), then two new B-trees, `left` and `right`, are created (lines 21–22). The first $\lceil M/2 \rceil - 1$ keys and $\lceil M/2 \rceil$ subtrees of the given node are moved to the `left` tree by the `attachLeftHalfOf` method (line 23); and the last $\lceil (M+1)/2 \rceil - 2$ keys and $\lceil (M+1)/2 - 1 \rceil$ subtrees of the given node are moved to the `right` tree by the `attachRightHalfOf` method (line 24). Then, the pair (`extraKey`,`extraTree`) is inserted into the `right` tree (line 25).

The left-over key is the one in the middle of the array, that is, $k_{\lceil M/2 \rceil}$. Finally, the root node is modified so that it contains the two new subtrees and the single left-over key (lines 26–29).

If the node overflows and it is not the root, then one new B-tree is created, `right` (line 34). The last $\lceil (M+1)/2 \rceil - 2$ keys and $\lceil (M+1)/2 - 1 \rceil$ subtrees of the given node are moved to the `left` tree by the `attachRightHalfOf` method (line 35) and the pair (`extraKey`, `extraTree`) is inserted in the `right` tree (line 36). The first $\lceil M/2 \rceil - 1$ keys and $\lceil M/2 \rceil$ subtrees of the given node remain attached to it.

Finally, the `insertPair` method calls itself recursively to insert the left over key, $k_{\lceil M/2 \rceil}$, and the new B-tree, `right`, into the parent of this (line 37). This is the place where the `parent` field is needed!

Running Time Analysis

The running time of the downward pass of the insertion algorithm is identical to that of an unsuccessful search (assuming the item to be inserted is not already in the tree). That is, for a B-tree of height h, the worst-case running time of the downward pass is

$$(h + 1)(\lceil \log_2(M - 1) \rceil + 2)\mathcal{T}\langle \text{compare} \rangle + O(h \log M).$$

The second pass of the insertion algorithm does the insertion and balances the tree if necessary. In the worst case, all of the nodes in the insertion path up to the root need to be balanced. Each time the `insertPair` method is invoked, it calls `findIndex`, which has running time $(\lceil \log_2(M-1) \rceil + 2)\mathcal{T}\langle \text{compare} \rangle + O(\log M)$ in the worst case. The additional time required to balance a node is $O(M)$. Therefore, the worst-case running time of the upward pass is

$$(h + 1)(\lceil \log_2(M - 1)\rceil + 2)\mathcal{T}\langle\texttt{compare}\rangle + O(hM).$$

Therefore, the total running time for insertion is

$$2(h + 1)(\lceil \log_2(M - 1)\rceil + 2)\mathcal{T}\langle\texttt{compare}\rangle + O(hM).$$

According to Theorem 10.4, the height of a B-tree is $h \leq \log_{\lceil M/2\rceil}((n + 1)/2)$, where n is the number of keys in the B-tree. If we assume that two keys can be compared in constant time, that is, $\mathcal{T}\langle\texttt{compare}\rangle = O(1)$, then the running time for insertion in a B-tree is simply $O(M \log n)$.

10.7.3   Removing Items from a B-Tree

The algorithm for removing items from a B-tree is similar to the algorithm for removing items from an AVL tree. That is, once the item to be removed has been found, it is pushed down the tree to a leaf node where it can be easily deleted. When an item is deleted from a node it is possible that the number of keys remaining is less than $\lceil M/2\rceil - 1$. In this case, balancing is necessary.

The algorithm of balancing after deletion is like the balancing after insertion in that it progresses from the leaf node up the tree toward the root. Given a node T that has $\lceil M/2\rceil - 2$ keys, there are four cases to consider.

In the first case, T is the root. If no keys remain, T becomes the empty tree. Otherwise, no balancing is needed because the root is permitted to have as few as two subtrees and one key. For the remaining cases T is not the root.

In the second case, T has $\lceil M/2\rceil - 2$ keys and it also has a sibling immediately on the left with at least $\lceil M/2\rceil$ keys. The tree can be balanced by doing an LL rotation as shown in Figure 10.13. Notice that after the rotation, both siblings have at least $\lceil M/2\rceil - 1$ keys. Furthermore, the heights of the siblings remain unchanged. Therefore, the resulting tree is a valid B-tree.

The third case is the left-right mirror of the second case. That is, T has $\lceil M/2\rceil - 2$ keys and it also has a sibling immediately on the right with a least $\lceil M/2\rceil$ keys. In this case, the tree can be balanced by doing an RR rotation.

In the fourth and final case, T has $\lceil M/2\rceil - 2$ keys, and its immediate sibling(s) have $\lceil M/2\rceil - 1$ keys. In this case, the sibling(s) cannot give up a key in a rotation because they already have the minimum number of keys. The solution is to *merge* T with one of its siblings as shown in Figure 10.14.

The merged node contains $\lceil M/2\rceil - 2$ keys from T, $\lceil M/2\rceil - 1$ keys from the sibling, and one key from the parent (the key x in Figure 10.14). The resulting node contains $2\lceil M/2\rceil - 2$ keys altogether, which is $M - 2$ if M is even and $M - 1$ if M is odd. Either way, the resulting node contains no more than $M - 1$ keys and is a valid B-tree node. Notice that in this case a key has been removed from the parent of T. Therefore, it may be necessary to balance the parent. Balancing the parent may necessitate balancing the grandparent, and so on, up the tree to the root.

FIGURE 10.13
LL rotation in a B-tree.

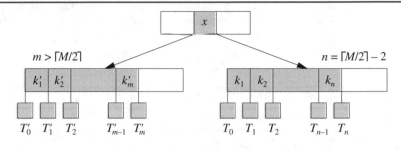

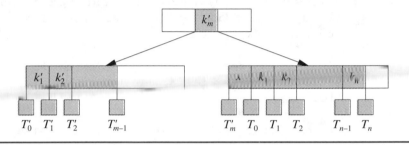

FIGURE 10.14
Merging nodes in a B-tree.

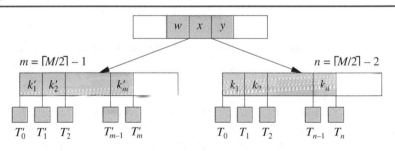

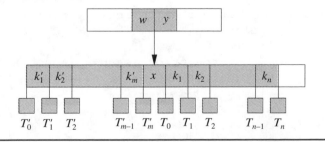

10.8 Applications

There are many applications for search trees. The principal characteristic of such applications is that a database of keyed information needs to be frequently accessed and the access pattern is either unknown or known to be random. For example, *dictionaries* are often implemented using search trees. A dictionary is essentially a container that

---

PROGRAM 10.23
Application of search trees—word translation

```
1   public class Algorithms
2   {
3       public static void translate (Reader dictionary,
4           Reader inputText, PrintWriter outputText)
5           throws IOException
6       {
7           SearchTree searchTree = new AVLTree();
8           StreamTokenizer tin = new StreamTokenizer(dictionary);
9           for (;;)
10          {
11              if (tin.nextToken() == StreamTokenizer.TT_EOF)
12                  break;
13              Comparable key = new Str (tin.sval);
14
15              if (tin.nextToken() == StreamTokenizer.TT_EOF)
16                  break;
17              String value = tin.sval;
18
19              searchTree.insert (new Association (key, value));
20          }
21
22          tin = new StreamTokenizer (inputText);
23          while (tin.nextToken () != StreamTokenizer.TT_EOF)
24          {
25              Comparable word = new Str (tin.sval);
26              Object obj = searchTree.find (new Association(word));
27              if (obj == null)
28                  outputText.println (''?'');
29              else
30              {
31                  Association assoc = (Association) obj;
32                  outputText.println (assoc.getValue ());
33              }
34          }
35      }
36  }
```

contains ordered key/value pairs. The keys are words in a source language and, depending on the application, the values may be the definitions of the words or the translation of the word in a target language.

This section presents a simple application of search trees. Suppose we are required to translate the words in an input file one-by-one from some source language to another target language. In this example, the translation is done one word at a time. That is, no natural language syntactic or semantic processing is done.

In order to implement the translator we assume that there exists a text file, which contains pairs of words. The first element of the pair is a word in the source language and the second element is a word in the target language. To translate a text, we first read the words and the associated translations and build a search tree. The translation is created one word at a time by looking up each word in the text.

Program 10.23 gives an implementation of the translator. The **translate** method uses a search tree to hold the pairs of words. In this case, an AVL tree is used. However, this implementation works with all of the search tree types described in this chapter (e.g., **BinarySearchTree**, **AVLTree**, **MWayTree**, and **BTree**).

The **translate** method reads pairs of strings from the input stream (lines 11–17). The **Association** class defined in Section 5.2.8 is used to contain the key/value pairs. A new instance is created for each key/value pair, which is then inserted into the search tree (line 19). The process of building the search tree terminates when the end-of-file is encountered.

During the translation phase, the **translate** method reads words one at a time from the input stream and writes the translation of each word on the output stream. Each word is looked up as it is read (lines 25–26). If no key matches the given word, the word is printed followed by a question mark (lines 27–28). Otherwise, the value associated with the matching key is printed (lines 31–32).

Exercises

10.1 For each of the following key sequences, determine the binary search tree obtained when the keys are inserted one-by-one in the order given into an initially empty tree:

a. 1, 2, 3, 4, 5, 6, 7

b. 4, 2, 1, 3, 6, 5, 7

c. 1, 6, 7, 2, 4, 3, 5

10.2 For each of the binary search trees obtained in Exercise 10.1, determine the tree obtained when the root is withdrawn.

10.3 Repeat Exercises 10.1 and 10.2 for AVL trees.

10.4 Derive an expression for the total space needed to represent a tree of n internal nodes using each of the following classes:

a. **BinarySearchTree** introduced in Program 10.2

b. **AVLTree** introduced in Program 10.7

    c. `MWayTree` introduced in Program 10.14

    d. `BTree` introduced in Program 10.20

    Hint: For the `MWayTree` and `BTree` assume that the tree contains k keys, where $k \geq n$.

10.5 To delete a non-leaf node from a binary search tree, we swap it either with the smallest key in its right subtree or with the largest key in its left subtree and then recursively delete it from the subtree. In a tree of n nodes, what is the maximum number of swaps needed to delete a key?

10.6 Devise an algorithm to compute the internal path length of a tree. What is the running time of your algorithm?

10.7 Devise an algorithm to compute the external path length of a tree. What is the running time of your algorithm?

10.8 Suppose that you are given a sorted sequence of n keys, $k_0 \leq k_1 \leq \cdots \leq k_{n-1}$, to be inserted into a binary search tree.

    a. What is the minimum height of a binary tree that contains n nodes?

    b. Devise an algorithm to insert the given keys into a binary search tree so that the height of the resulting tree is minimized.

    c. What is the running time of your algorithm?

10.9 Devise an algorithm to construct an AVL tree of a given height h that contains the minimum number of nodes. The tree should contain the keys $1, 2, 3, \ldots, N_h$, where N_h is given by Equation (10.8).

10.10 Consider what happens when we insert the keys $1, 2, 3, \ldots, 2^{h+1} - 1$ one-by-one in the order given into an initially empty AVL tree for $h \geq 0$. Prove that the result is always a perfect tree of height h.

10.11 The `find` method defined in Program 10.4 is recursive. Write a non-recursive method to find a given item in a binary search tree.

10.12 Repeat Exercise 10.11 for the `findMin` method defined in Program 10.4

10.13 Devise an algorithm to select the kth key in a binary search tree. For example, given a tree with n nodes, $k = 0$ selects the smallest key, $k = n - 1$ selects the largest key, and $k = \lceil n/2 \rceil - 1$ selects the median key.

10.14 Devise an algorithm to test whether a given binary search tree is AVL balanced. What is the running time of your algorithm?

10.15 Devise an algorithm that takes two values, a and b such that $a \leq b$, and that visits all keys x in a binary search tree such that $a \leq x \leq b$. The running time of your algorithm should be $O(N + \log n)$, where N is the number of keys visited and n is the number of keys in the tree.

10.16 Devise an algorithm to merge the contents of two binary search trees into one. What is the running time of your algorithm?

10.17 (This question should be attempted *after* reading Chapter 11.) Prove that a *complete binary tree* (Definition 11.12) is AVL balanced.

10.18 Do Exercise 8.12.

10.19 For each of the following key sequences, determine the 3-way search tree obtained when the keys are inserted one-by-one in the order given into an initially empty tree:

a. 0, 1, 2, 3, 4, 5, 6, 7, 8, 9

b. 3, 1, 4, 5, 9, 2, 6, 8, 7, 0

c. 2, 7, 1, 8, 4, 5, 9, 0, 3, 6

10.20 Repeat Exercise 10.19 for B-trees of order 3.

Programming Projects

10.1 Complete the implementation of the **BinarySearchTree** class introduced in Program 10.2 by providing suitable definitions for the following methods: isMember and findMin. You must also have a complete implementation of the base class **BinaryTree**. (See Project 9.8.) Write a test program and test your implementation.

10.2 Complete the implementation of the **AVLTree** class introduced in Program 10.7 by providing suitable definitions for the following methods: **getLeft**, **getRight**, **doRRRotation**, and **doRLRotation**. You must also have a complete implementation of the base class **BinarySearchTree**. (See Project 10.1.) Write a test program and test your implementation.

10.3 Complete the implementation of the **MWayTree** class introduced in Program 10.14 by providing suitable definitions for the following methods: **purge**, **getCount**, **isEmpty**, **isLeaf**, **getDegree**, **getKey**, **getSubtree**, **isMember**, **findMin**, **findMax**, **breadthFirstTraversal**, and **getEnumeration**. Write a test program and test your implementation.

10.4 Complete the implementation of the **BTree** class introduced in Program 10.20 by providing suitable definitions for the following methods: **insertKey**, **insertSubtree**, **attachLeftHalfOf**, **attachRightHalfOf**, and **withdraw**. You must also have a complete implementation of the base class **MWayTree**. (See Project 10.3.) Write a test program and test your implementation.

10.5 The binary search tree **withdraw** method shown in Program 10.6 is biased in the following way: If the key to be deleted is in a non-leaf node with two non-empty subtrees, the key is swapped with the maximum key in the left subtree and then recursively deleted from the left subtree. Following a long series of insertions and deletions, the search tree will tend to have more nodes in the right subtrees and fewer nodes in the left subtrees. Devise and conduct an experiment that demonstrates this phenomenon.

10.6 Consider the implementation of AVL trees. In order to check the AVL balance condition in constant time, we record in each node the height of that node. An alternative to keeping track of the height information explicitly is to record in each node the *difference* in the heights of its two subtrees. In an AVL balanced tree, this difference is either -1, 0 or $+1$. Replace the `height` field of the AVL class defined in Program 10.7 with one called `diff` and rewrite the various methods accordingly.

10.7 The *M*-way tree implementation given in Section 10.6.1 is an *internal* data structure—it is assumed that all nodes reside in the main memory. However, the motivation for using an *M*-way tree is that it is an efficient way to organize an *external* data structure—one that is stored on disk. Design, implement, and test an external *M*-way tree implementation.

11 | Heaps and Priority Queues

In this chapter we consider priority queues. A priority queue is essentially a list of items in which each item has associated with it a *priority*. In general, different items may have different priorities, and we speak of one item having a higher priority than another. Given such a list we can determine which is the highest (or the lowest) priority item in the list. Items are inserted into a priority queue in any, arbitrary order. However, items are withdrawn from a priority queue in order of their priorities starting with the highest priority item first.

For example, consider the software that manages a printer. In general, it is possible for users to submit documents for printing much more quickly than it is possible to print them. A simple solution is to place the documents in a *FIFO* queue (Chapter 6). In a sense this is fair, because the documents are printed on a first-come, first-served basis.

However, a user who has submitted a short document for printing will experience a long delay when much longer documents are already in the queue. An alternative solution is to use a priority queue in which the shorter a document, the higher its priority. By printing the shortest documents first, we reduce the level of frustration experienced by the users. In fact, it can be shown that printing documents in order of their length minimizes the average time a user waits for her document.

Priority queues are often used in the implementation of algorithms. Typically the problem to be solved consists of a number of subtasks, and the solution strategy involves prioritizing the subtasks and then performing those subtasks in the order of their priorities. For example, in Chapter 14 we show how a priority queue can improve the performance of backtracking algorithms, in Chapter 15 we will see how a priority queue can be used in sorting, and in Chapter 16 several graph algorithms that use a priority queue are discussed.

11.1 Basics

A priority queue is a container that provides the following three operations:

enqueue is used to put objects into the container;

findMin returns the smallest object in the container; and

dequeueMin removes the smallest object from the container.

A priority queue is used to store a finite set of keys drawn from a totally ordered set of keys K. As distinct from search trees, duplicate keys *are* allowed in priority queues.

Program 11.1 defines the **PriorityQueue** interface. The **PriorityQueue** interface extends the **Container** interface defined in Program 5.8. In addition to the inherited methods, the **PriorityQueue** interface comprises the three methods listed above.

Program 11.2 defines the **MergeablePriorityQueue** interface. The **MergeablePriorityQueue** interface extends the **PriorityQueue** interface defined in Program 11.1. A *mergeable priority queue* is one that provides the ability to merge efficiently two priority queues into one. Of course it is always possible to merge two priority queues by dequeuing the elements of one queue and enqueueing them in the other. However, the mergeable priority queue implementations we will consider allow more efficient merging than this.

It is possible to implement the required functionality using data structures that we have already considered. For example, a priority queue can be implemented simply as

PROGRAM 11.1
PriorityQueue interface

```
1  public interface PriorityQueue
2      extends Container
3  {
4      void enqueue (Comparable object);
5      Comparable findMin ();
6      Comparable dequeueMin ();
7  }
```

PROGRAM 11.2
MergeablePriorityQueue interface

```
1  public interface MergeablePriorityQueue
2      extends PriorityQueue
3  {
4      void merge (MergeablePriorityQueue queue);
5  }
```

a list. If an *unsorted list* is used, enqueueing can be accomplished in constant time. However, finding the minimum and removing the minimum each require $O(n)$ time where n is the number of items in the queue. On the other hand, if a *sorted list* is used, finding the minimum and removing it is easy—both operations can be done in constant time. However, enqueueing an item in a sorted list requires $O(n)$ time.

Another possibility is to use a search tree. For example, if an *AVL tree* is used to implement a priority queue, then all three operations can be done in $O(\log n)$ time. However, search trees provide more functionality than we need. Search trees support finding the largest item with **findMax**, deletion of arbitrary objects with **withdraw**, and the ability to visit in order all of the contained objects via **depthFirstTraversal**. All these operations can be done as efficiently as the priority queue operations. Because search trees support more methods than we really need for priority queues, it is reasonable to suspect that there are more efficient ways to implement priority queues. And indeed there are!

A number of different priority queue implementations are described in this chapter. All the implementations have one thing in common—they are all based on a special kind of tree called a *min heap* or simply a *heap*.

Definition 11.1 ((Min) Heap)
A (Min) Heap is a tree,

$$T = \{R, T_0, T_1, T_2, \ldots, T_{n-1}\},$$

with the following properties:

1. *Every subtree of T is a heap, and*
2. *The root of T is less than or equal to the root of every subtree of T. That is, $R \leq R_i$ for all i, $0 \leq i < n$, where R_i is the root of T_i.*

According to Definition 11.1, the key in each node of a heap is less than or equal to the roots of all subtrees of that node. Therefore, by induction, the key in each node is less than or equal to all of the keys contained in the subtrees of that node. Note, however, that the definition says nothing about the relative ordering of the keys in the subtrees of a given node. For example, in a binary heap either the left or the right subtree of a given node may have the larger key.

11.2 Binary Heaps

A binary heap is a heap-ordered binary tree that has a very special shape called a *complete tree*. As a result of its special shape, a binary heap can be implemented using an array as the underlying foundational data structure. Array subscript calculations are used to find the parent and the children of a given node in the tree. And since an array is used, the storage overhead associated with the subtree fields contained in the nodes of the trees is eliminated.

11.2.1 Complete Trees

The preceding chapter introduces the idea of a *perfect tree* (see Definition 10.3). Complete trees and perfect trees are closely related, yet quite distinct. As pointed out in the preceding chapter, a perfect binary tree of height h has exactly $n = 2^{h+1} - 1$ internal nodes. Since the only permissible values of n are

$$0, 1, 3, 7, 15, 31, \ldots, 2^{h+1} - 1, \ldots,$$

there is no *perfect* binary tree that contains, say 2, 4, 5, or 6 nodes.

However, we want a data structure that can hold an arbitrary number of objects so we cannot use a perfect binary tree. Instead, we use a *complete binary tree*, which is defined as follows:

Definition 11.2 (Complete Binary Tree)
A complete binary tree of height $h \geq 0$, is a binary tree $\{R, T_L, T_R\}$ with the following properties:

1. *If $h = 0$, $T_L = \varnothing$ and $T_R = \varnothing$.*
2. *For $h > 0$ there are two possibilities:*
    (a) *T_L is a perfect binary tree of height $h - 1$ and T_R is a complete binary tree of height $h - 1$, or*
    (b) *T_L is a complete binary tree of height $h - 1$ and T_R is a perfect binary tree of height $h - 2$.*

Figure 11.1 shows an example of a complete binary tree of height four. Notice that the left subtree of node 1 is a complete binary tree of height three, and the right subtree is a perfect binary tree of height two. This corresponds to case 2 (b) of Definition 11.2. Similarly, the left subtree of node 2 is a perfect binary tree of height two, and the

FIGURE 11.1
A complete binary tree.

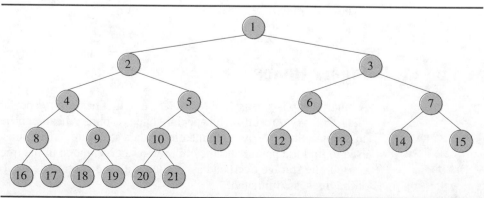

right subtree is a complete binary tree of height two. This corresponds to case 2 (a) of Definition 11.2.

Is there a complete binary with exactly n nodes for every integer $n > 0$? The following theorem addresses this question indirectly by defining the relationship between the height of a complete tree and the number of nodes it contains.

Theorem 11.1
A complete binary tree of height $h \geq 0$ contains at least 2^h and at most $2^{h+1} - 1$ nodes.

Proof First, we prove the lower bound by induction. Let m_h be the *minimum* number of nodes in a complete binary tree of height h. To prove the lower bound we must show that $m_h = 2^h$.

Base Case There is exactly one node in a tree of height zero. Therefore, $m_0 = 1 = 2^0$.

Inductive Hypothesis Assume that $m_h = 2^h$ for $h = 0, 1, 2, \ldots, k$, for some $k \geq 0$. Consider the complete binary tree of height $k + 1$ that has the smallest number of nodes. Its left subtree is a complete tree of height k having the smallest number of nodes and its right subtree is a perfect tree of height $k - 1$.

From the inductive hypothesis, there are 2^k nodes in the left subtree and there are exactly $2^{(k-1)+1} - 1$ nodes in the perfect right subtree. Thus,

$$m_{k+1} = 1 + 2^k + 2^{(k-1)+1} - 1$$
$$= 2^{k+1}.$$

Therefore, by induction $m_h = 2^h$ for all $h \geq 0$, which proves the lower bound.

Next, we prove the upper bound by induction. Let M_h be the *maximum* number of nodes in a complete binary tree of height h. To prove the upper bound we must show that $M_h = 2^{h+1} - 1$.

Base Case There is exactly one node in a tree of height zero. Therefore, $M_0 = 1 = 2^1 - 1$.

Inductive Hypothesis Assume that $M_h = 2^{h+1} - 1$ for $h = 0, 1, 2, \ldots, k$, for some $k \geq 0$. Consider the complete binary tree of height $k + 1$ that has the largest number of nodes. Its left subtree is a perfect tree of height k and its right subtree is a complete tree of height k having the largest number of nodes.

There are exactly $2^{k+1} - 1$ nodes in the perfect left subtree. From the inductive hypothesis, there are $2^{k+1} - 1$ nodes in the right subtree. Thus,

$$M_{k+1} = 1 + 2^{k+1} - 1 + 2^{k+1} - 1$$
$$= 2^{(k+1)+1} - 1.$$

Therefore, by induction $M_h = 2^{h+1} - 1$ for all $h \geq 0$, which proves the upper bound.

It follows from Theorem 11.1 that there exists exactly one complete binary tree that contains exactly n internal nodes for every integer $n \geq 0$. It also follows from Theorem 11.1 that the height of a complete binary tree containing n internal nodes is $h = \lfloor \log_2 n \rfloor$.

Why are we interested in complete trees? As it turns out, complete trees have some useful characteristics. For example, in the preceding chapter we saw that the internal path length of a tree—that is, the sum of the depths of all the internal nodes—determines the average time for various operations. A complete binary tree has the nice property of having the smallest possible internal path length:

Theorem 11.2

The internal path length of a binary tree with n nodes is at least as big as the internal path length of a complete binary tree with n nodes.

Proof Consider a binary tree with n nodes that has the smallest possible internal path length. Clearly, there can only be one node at depth zero—the root. Similarly, at most two nodes can be at depth one; at most four nodes can be at depth two; and so on. Therefore, the internal path length of a tree with n nodes is always at least as large as the sum of the first n terms in the series

$$\underbrace{0}_{1}, \underbrace{1, 1}_{2}, \underbrace{2, 2, 2, 2}_{4}, \underbrace{3, 3, 3, 3, 3, 3, 3, 3}_{8}, 4, \dots.$$

But this summation is precisely the internal path length of a complete binary tree!

Since the depth of the average node in a tree is obtained by dividing the internal path length of the tree by n, Theorem 11.2 tells us that complete trees are the best possible in the sense that the average depth of a node in a complete tree is the smallest possible. But how small is small? That is, does the average depth grow logarithmically with n? The following theorem addresses this question:

Theorem 11.3

The internal path length *of a complete binary tree with n nodes is*

$$\sum_{i=1}^{n} \lfloor \log_2 i \rfloor = (n + 1) \lfloor \log_2(n + 1) \rfloor - 2^{\lfloor \log_2(n+1) \rfloor + 1} + 2.$$

Proof The proof of Theorem 11.3 is left as an exercise for the reader (Exercise 11.6).

From Theorem 11.3 we may conclude that the internal path length of a complete tree is $O(n \log n)$. Consequently, the depth of the average node in a complete tree is $O(\log n)$.

Complete N-ary Trees

The definition for complete binary trees can be easily extended to trees with arbitrary fixed degree $N \geq 2$ as follows:

Definition 11.3 (Complete *N*-ary Tree)

A complete N-ary tree of height $h \geq 0$ is an N-ary tree $\{R, T_0, T_1, T_2, \ldots, T_{N-1}\}$ with the following properties:

1. If $h = 0$, $T_i = \varnothing$ for all i, $0 \leq i < N$.

2. *For $h > 0$ there exists a j, $0 \leq j < N$ such that*

   (a) *T_i is a perfect binary tree of height $h - 1$ for all i : $0 \leq i < j$;*

   (b) *T_j is a complete binary tree of height $h - 1$; and*

   (c) *T_i is a perfect binary tree of height $h - 2$ for all i : $j < i < N$.*

Note that although it is expressed in somewhat different terms, the definition of a complete *N*-ary tree is consistent with the definition of a binary tree for $N = 2$. Figure 11.2 shows an example of a complete ternary ($N = 3$) tree.

Informally, a complete tree is a tree in which all levels are full except for the bottom level and the bottom level is filled from left to right. For example in Figure 11.2, the first three levels are full. The fourth level, which comprises nodes 14–21, is partially full and has been filled from left to right.

The main advantage of using complete binary trees is that they can be easily stored in an array. Specifically, consider the nodes of a complete tree numbered consecutively in *level-order* as they are in Figures 11.1 and 11.2. There is a simple formula that relates the number of a node with the number of its parent and the numbers of its children.

Consider the case of a complete binary tree. The root node is node 1 and its children are nodes 2 and 3. In general, the children of node i are $2i$ and $2i + 1$. Conversely, the parent of node i is $\lfloor i/2 \rfloor$. Figure 11.3 illustrates this idea by showing how the complete binary tree shown in Figure 11.1 is mapped into an array.

A remarkable characteristic of complete trees is that filling the bottom level from left to right corresponds to adding elements at the end of the array! Thus, a complete tree containing n nodes occupies the first n consecutive array positions.

The array subscript calculations given above can be easily generalized to complete *N*-ary trees. Assuming that the root occupies position 1 of the array, its N children occupy positions $2, 3, \ldots, N + 1$. In general, the children of node i occupy positions

$$N(i - 1) + 2, N(i - 1) + 3, N(i - 1) + 4, \ldots, Ni + 1,$$

FIGURE 11.2
A complete ternary tree.

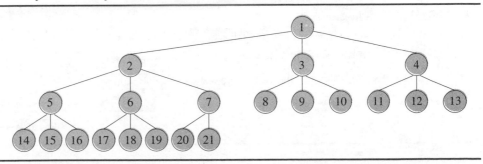

FIGURE 11.3
Array representation of a complete binary tree.

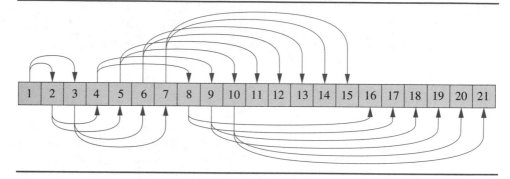

and the parent of node i is found at

$$\lceil (i - 1)/N \rceil.$$

11.2.2 Implementation

A binary heap is a heap-ordered complete binary tree that is implemented using an array. In a heap the smallest key is found at the root and since the root is always found in the first position of the array, finding the smallest key is a trivial operation in a binary heap.

In this section we describe the implementation of a priority queue as a binary heap. As shown in Figure 11.4, we define a concrete class called **BinaryHeap** for this purpose.

Program 11.3 introduces the **BinaryHeap** class. The **BinaryHeap** class extends the **AbstractContainer** class introduced in Program 5.9 and it implements the **PriorityQueue** interface defined in Program 11.1.

FIGURE 11.4
Object class hierarchy.

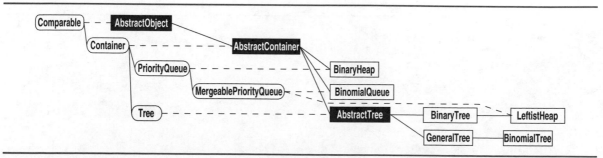

PROGRAM 11.3
BinaryHeap fields

```
1   public class BinaryHeap
2       extends AbstractContainer
3       implements PriorityQueue
4   {
5       protected Comparable[] array;
6
7       // ...
8   }
```

Fields

The BinaryHeap class has a rather simple implementation. In particular, it requires only a single field, array, which is declared as an array of Comparable objects. This array is used to hold the objects that are contained in the binary tree. When there are n items in the heap, those items occupy array positions $1, 2, \ldots, n$.

Constructor and purge Methods

Program 11.4 defines the BinaryHeap constructor. The constructor takes a single argument of type int, which specifies the maximum capacity of the binary heap. The constructor allocates an array of the specified size *plus one*. This is done because array position zero will not be used. The running time of the constructor is $O(n)$, where n is the maximum length of the priority queue.

PROGRAM 11.4
BinaryHeap class constructor and purge methods

```
1   public class BinaryHeap
2       extends AbstractContainer
3       implements PriorityQueue
4   {
5       protected Comparable[] array;
6
7       public BinaryHeap (int length)
8           { array = new Comparable[length + 1]; }
9
10      public void purge ()
11      {
12          while (count > 0)
13              array [count--] = null;
14      }
15      // ...
16  }
```

The purpose of the **purge** method is to make the priority queue empty. The **purge** method assigns the value **null** to the array positions one-by-one. Clearly the worst-case running time for the **purge** method is $O(n)$, where n is the maximum length of the priority queue.

11.2.3 Putting Items into a Binary Heap

There are two requirements that must be satisfied when an item is inserted in a binary heap. First, the resulting tree must have the correct shape. Second, the tree must remain heap-ordered. Figure 11.5 illustrates the way in which this is done.

Since the resulting tree must be a complete tree, there is only one place in the tree where a node can be added. That is, since the bottom level must be filled from left to right, the node must be added at the next available position in the bottom level of the tree as shown in Figure 11.5 (a).

In this example, the new item to be inserted has the key 2. Note that we cannot simply drop the new item into the next position in the complete tree because the resulting tree is no longer heap ordered. Instead, the hole in the heap is moved toward the root by moving items down in the heap as shown in Figure 11.5 (b) and (c). The process of moving items down terminates either when we reach the root of the tree or when the hole has been moved up to a position in which when the new item is inserted the result is a heap.

Program 11.5 gives the code for inserting an item in a binary heap. The **enqueue** method of the **BinaryHeap** class takes as its argument the item to be inserted in the heap. If the priority queue is full an exception is thrown. Otherwise, the item is inserted as described above.

FIGURE 11.5
Inserting an item into a binary heap.

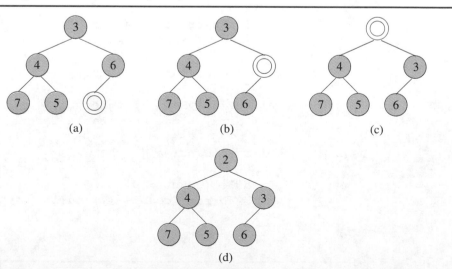

PROGRAM 11.5
BinaryHeap class enqueue method

```
1  public class BinaryHeap
2      extends AbstractContainer
3      implements PriorityQueue
4  {
5      protected Comparable[] array;
6
7      public void enqueue (Comparable object)
8      {
9          if (count == array.length - 1)
10             throw new ContainerFullException ();
11         ++count;
12         int i = count;
13         while (i > 1 && array [i/2].isGT (object))
14         {
15             array [i] = array [i / 2];
16             i /= 2;
17         }
18         array [i] = object;
19     }
20     // ...
21 }
```

The implementation of the algorithm is actually remarkably simple. Lines 13–17 move the hole in the heap up by moving items down. When the loop terminates, the new item can be inserted at position i. Therefore, the loop terminates either at the root, $i = 1$, or when the key in the parent of i, which is found at position $\lfloor i/2 \rfloor$, is smaller than the item to be inserted.

Notice too that a good optimizing compiler will recognize that the subscript calculations involve only division by two. Therefore, the divisions can be replaced by bitwise right shifts, which usually run much more quickly.

Since the depth of a complete binary tree with n nodes is $\lfloor \log_2 n \rfloor$, the worst-case running time for the **enqueue** operation is

$$\lfloor \log_2 n \rfloor \mathcal{T} \langle \text{isGT} \rangle + O(\log n),$$

where $\mathcal{T} \langle \text{isGT} \rangle$ is the time required to compare two objects. If $\mathcal{T} \langle \text{isGT} \rangle = O(1)$, the **enqueue** operation is simply $O(\log n)$ in the worst case.

11.2.4 Removing Items from a Binary Heap

The **dequeueMin** method removes from a priority queue the item having the smallest key. In order to remove the smallest item, it first needs to be located. Therefore, the **dequeueMin** operation is closely related to **findMin**.

The smallest item is always at the root of a min heap. Therefore, the `findMin` operation is trivial. Program 11.6 gives the code for the `findMin` method of the `BinaryHeap` class. Assuming that no exception is thrown, the running time of `findMin` is clearly $O(1)$.

Since the bottom row of a complete tree is filled from left to right as items are added, it follows that the bottom row must be emptied from right to left as items are removed. So we have a problem: The datum to be removed from the heap by `dequeueMin` is in the root, but the node to be removed from the heap is in the bottom row.

Figure 11.6 (a) illustrates the problem. The `dequeueMin` operation removes the key 2 from the heap, but it is the node containing key 6 that must be removed from the tree to make it into a complete tree again. When key 2 is removed from the root, a hole is created in the tree as shown in Figure 11.6 (b).

The trick is to move the hole down in the tree to a point where the left-over key, in this case the key 6, can be reinserted into the tree. To move a hole down in the tree, we consider the children of the empty node and move up the smallest key. Moving up the smallest key ensures that the result will be a min heap.

The process of moving up continues until either the hole has been pushed down to a leaf node, or until the hole has been pushed to a point where the left-over key can be inserted into the heap. In the example shown in Figure 11.6 (b)–(c), the hole is pushed from the root node to a leaf node, where the key 6 is ultimately placed as shown in Figure 11.6 (d).

Program 11.7 gives the code for the `dequeueMin` method of the `BinaryHeap` class. This method implements the deletion algorithm described above. The main loop (lines 15–25) moves the hole in the tree down by moving up the child with the smallest key until either a leaf node is reached or until the hole has been moved down to a point where the last element of the array can be reinserted.

In the worst case, the hole must be pushed from the root to a leaf node. Each iteration of the loop makes at most two object comparisons and moves the hole down one level.

PROGRAM 11.6
`BinaryHeap` class `findMin` method

```
1   public class BinaryHeap
2       extends AbstractContainer
3       implements PriorityQueue
4   {
5       protected Comparable[] array;
6
7       public Comparable findMin ()
8       {
9           if (count == 0)
10              throw new ContainerEmptyException ();
11          return array [1];
12      }
13      // ...
14  }
```

FIGURE 11.6
Removing an item from a binary heap.

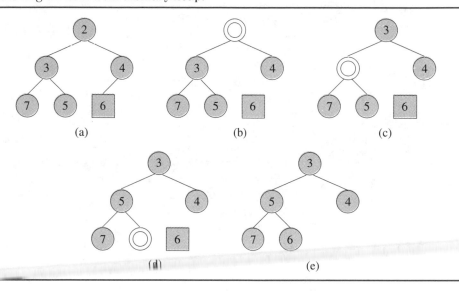

Therefore, the running time of the **dequeueMin** operation is

$$\lfloor \log_2 n \rfloor (\mathcal{T}\langle \text{isLT} \rangle + \mathcal{T}\langle \text{isLE} \rangle) + O(\log n),$$

where $n = $ **count** is the number of items in the heap. If $\mathcal{T}\langle \text{isLT} \rangle = O(1)$ and $\mathcal{T}\langle \text{isLE} \rangle = O(1)$, the **dequeueMin** operation is simply $O(\log n)$ in the worst case.

11.3 Leftist Heaps

A leftist heap is a heap-ordered binary tree that has a very special shape called a *leftist tree*. One of the nice properties of leftist heaps is that is possible to merge two leftist heaps efficiently. As a result, leftist heaps are suited for the implementation of mergeable priority queues.

11.3.1 Leftist Trees

A *leftist tree* is a tree that tends to "lean" to the left. The tendency to lean to the left is defined in terms of the shortest path from the root to an external node. In a leftist tree, the shortest path to an external node is always found on the right.

Every node in binary tree has associated with it a quantity called its *null path length*, which is defined as follows:

PROGRAM 11.7
BinaryHeap class dequeueMin method

```
1   public class BinaryHeap
2       extends AbstractContainer
3       implements PriorityQueue
4   {
5       protected Comparable[] array;
6
7       public Comparable dequeueMin ()
8       {
9           if (count == 0)
10              throw new ContainerEmptyException ();
11          Comparable result = array [1];
12          Comparable last = array [count];
13          --count;
14          int i = 1;
15          while (2 * i < count + 1)
16          {
17              int child = 2 * i;
18              if (child + 1 < count + 1
19                  && array [child + 1].isLT (array [child]))
20                  child += 1;
21              if (last.isLE (array [child]))
22                  break;
23              array [i] = array [child];
24              i = child;
25          }
26          array [i] = last;
27          return result;
28      }
29      // ...
30  }
```

Definition 11.4 (Null Path and Null Path Length)
Consider an arbitrary node x in some binary tree T. The null path *of node x is the shortest path in T from x to an external node of T.*

The null path length *of node x is the length of its null path.*

Sometimes it is convenient to talk about the null path length of an entire tree rather than of a node:

Definition 11.5 (Null Path Length of a Tree)
The null path length *of an empty tree is zero and the null path length of a non-empty binary tree $T = \{R, T_L, T_R\}$ is the null path length of its root R.*

When a new node or subtree is attached to a given tree, it is usually attached in place of an external node. Since the null path length of a tree is the length of the shortest path from the root of the tree to an external node, the null path length gives a lower bound on the cost of insertion. For example, the running time for insertion in a binary search tree, Program 10.4, is at least

$$dT\langle \text{compare}\rangle + \Omega(d),$$

where d is the null path length of the tree.

A *leftist tree* is a tree in which the shortest path to an external node is always on the right. This informal idea is defined more precisely in terms of the null path lengths as follows:

Definition 11.6 (Leftist Tree)
A leftist tree *is a binary tree T with the following properties:*

1. *Either $T = \emptyset$; or*
2. *$T = \{R, T_L, T_R\}$, where both T_L and T_R are leftist trees that have null path lengths d_L and d_R, respectively, such that*

$$d_L \geq d_R.$$

Figure 11.7 shows an example of a leftist heap. A leftist heap is simply a heap-ordered leftist tree. The null path length of the node is shown to the right of each node in Figure 11.7. The figure clearly shows that it is not necessarily the case in a leftist tree that the number of nodes to the left of a given node is greater than the number to the right. However, it is always the case that the null path length on the left is greater than or equal to the null path length on the right for every node in the tree.

FIGURE 11.7
A leftist heap.

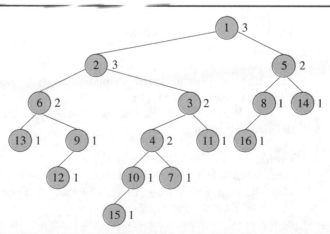

The reason for our interest in leftist trees is illustrated by the following theorems:

Theorem 11.4
Consider a leftist tree T that contains n internal nodes. The path leading from the root of T downward to the rightmost external node contains at most $\lfloor \log_2(n + 1) \rfloor$ nodes.

Proof Assume that T has null path length d. Then T must contain at least 2^{d-1} leaves. Otherwise, there would be a shorter path than d from the root of T to an external node.

A binary tree with exactly l leaves has exactly $l - 1$ non-leaf internal nodes. Since T has at least 2^{d-1} leaves, it must contain at least $n \geq 2^d - 1$ internal nodes altogether. Therefore, $d \leq \log_2(n + 1)$.

Since T is a leftist tree, the shortest path to an external node must be the path on the right. Thus, the length of the path to the rightmost external is at most $\lfloor \log_2(n + 1) \rfloor$.

There is an interesting dichotomy between AVL balanced trees and leftist trees. The shape of an AVL tree satisfies the AVL balance condition, which stipulates that the difference in the heights of the left and right subtrees of every node may differ by at most one. The effect of AVL balancing is to ensure that the height of the tree is $O(\log n)$.

On the other hand, leftist trees have an "imbalance condition," which requires the null path length of the left subtree to be greater than or equal to that of the right subtree. The effect of the condition is to ensure that the length of the right path in a leftist tree is $O(\log n)$. Therefore, by devising algorithms for manipulating leftist heaps that only follow the right path of the heap, we can achieve running times that are logarithmic in the number of nodes.

The dichotomy also extends to the structure of the algorithms. For example, an imbalance sometimes results from an insertion in an AVL tree. The imbalance is rectified by doing rotations. Similarly, an insertion into a leftist tree may result in a violation of the "imbalance condition." That is, the null path length of the right subtree of a node may become greater than that of the left subtree. Fortunately, it is possible to restore the proper condition simply by swapping the left and right subtrees of that node.

11.3.2 Implementation

This section presents an implementation of leftist heaps that is based on the binary tree implementation described in Section 9.6.5. Program 11.8 introduces the **LeftistHeap** class. The **LeftistHeap** class extends the **BinaryTree** class introduced in Program 9.20 and it implements the **MergeablePriorityQueue** interface defined in Program 11.2.

Fields
Since a leftist heap is a heap-ordered binary tree, it inherits from the **BinaryTree** base class the three fields: **key**, **left**, and **right**. The **key** refers to the object contained in the given node and the **left** and **right** fields refer to the left and right subtrees of the given node, respectively. In addition, the field **nullPathLength** records the

PROGRAM 11.8
LeftistHeap fields

```
1  public class LeftistHeap
2        extends BinaryTree
3        implements MergeablePriorityQueue
4  {
5        protected int nullPathLength;
6
7        // ...
8  }
```

null path length of the given node. By recording the null path length in the node, it is possible to check the leftist heap balance condition in constant time.

11.3.3 Merging Leftist Heaps

In order to merge two leftist heaps, say h1 and h2, declared as follows:

```
MergeablePriorityQueue h1 = new LeftistHeap ();
MergeablePriorityQueue h2 = new LeftistHeap ();
```

we invoke the **merge** method like this:

```
h1.merge (h2);
```

The effect of the **merge** method is to take all of the nodes from **h2** and to attach them to **h1**, thus leaving **h2** as the empty heap.

In order to achieve a logarithmic running time, it is important for the **merge** method to do all its work on the right sides of **h1** and **h2**. It turns out that the algorithm for merging leftist heaps is actually quite simple.

To begin with, if **h1** is the empty heap, then we can simply swap the contents of **h1** and **h2**. Otherwise, let us assume that the root of **h2** is larger than the root of **h1**. Then we can merge the two heaps by recursively merging **h2** with the *right* subheap of **h1**. After doing so, it may turn out that the right subheap of **h1** now has a larger null path length than the left subheap. This we rectify by swapping the left and right subheaps so that the result is again leftist. On the other hand, if **h2** initially has the smaller root, we simply exchange the roles of **h1** and **h2** and proceed as above.

Figure 11.8 illustrates the merge operation. In this example, we wish to merge the two trees T_1 and T_2 shown in Figure 11.8 (a). Since T_2 has the larger root, it is recursively merged with the right subtree of T_1. The result of that merge replaces the right subtree of T_1, as shown in Figure 11.8 (b). Since the null path length of the right subtree is now greater than that of the left, the subtrees of T_1 are swapped, resulting in the leftist heap shown in Figure 11.8 (c).

Program 11.9 gives the code for the **merge** method of the **LeftistHeap** class. The **merge** method uses two other methods, **swapContents** and **swapSubtrees**.

FIGURE 11.8
Merging leftist heaps.

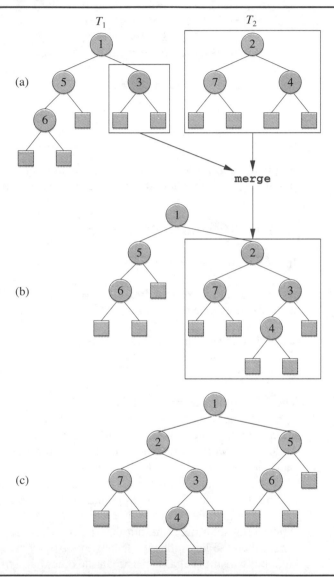

The **swapContents** method takes as its argument a leftist heap, and exchanges all of
the contents (key and subtrees) of **this** heap with the given one. The **swapSubtrees**
method exchanges the left and right subtrees of **this** node. The implementation of
these routines is trivial and is left as a project for the reader (Project 11.3). Clearly, the
worst-case running time for each of these routines is $O(1)$.

The **merge** method only visits nodes on the rightmost paths of the trees being
merged. Suppose we are merging two trees, say T_1 and T_2, with null path lengths d_1

PROGRAM 11.9
LeftistHeap class merge method

```
1   public class LeftistHeap
2       extends BinaryTree
3       implements MergeablePriorityQueue
4   {
5       protected int nullPathLength;
6
7       public void merge (MergeablePriorityQueue queue)
8       {
9           LeftistHeap arg = (LeftistHeap) queue;
10          if (isEmpty ())
11              swapContents (arg);
12          else if (!arg.isEmpty ())
13          {
14              if ( ((Comparable) getKey ()).isGT (
15                      ((Comparable) arg.getKey ())) )
16                  swapContents (arg);
17              getRightHeap ().merge (arg);
18              if (getLeftHeap ().nullPathLength <
19                      getRightHeap ().nullPathLength)
20                  swapSubtrees ();
21              nullPathLength = 1 + Math.min (
22                      getLeftHeap ().nullPathLength,
23                      getRightHeap ().nullPathLength);
24          }
25      }
26      // ...
27  }
```

and d_2, respectively. Then the running time of the **merge** method is

$$(d_1 - 1 + d_2 - 1)\mathcal{T}\langle \texttt{isGT} \rangle + O(d_1 + d_2),$$

where $\mathcal{T}\langle \texttt{isGT} \rangle$ is the time required to compare two keys. If we assume that the time to compare two keys is a constant, then we get $O(\log n_1 + \log n_2)$, where n_1 and n_2 are the number of internal nodes in trees T_1 and T_2, respectively.

11.3.4 Putting Items into a Leftist Heap

The **enqueue** method of the **LeftistHeap** class is used to put items into the heap. **enqueue** is easily implemented using the **merge** operation. That is, to enqueue an item

---

PROGRAM 11.10
LeftistHeap class enqueue method

```
1   public class LeftistHeap
2       extends BinaryTree
3       implements MergeablePriorityQueue
4   {
5       protected int nullPathLength;
6
7       public void enqueue (Comparable object)
8           { merge (new LeftistHeap (object)); }
9       // ...
10  }
```

---

in a given heap, we simply create a new heap containing the one item to be enqueued and merge it with the given heap. The algorithm to do this is shown in Program 11.10.

The expression for the running time for the **insert** operation follows directly from that of the **merge** operation. That is, the time required for the **insert** operation in the worst case is

$$(d - 1)\mathcal{T}\langle \texttt{isGT} \rangle + O(d),$$

where d is the null path length of the heap into which the item is inserted. If we assume that two keys can be compared in constant time, the running time for **insert** becomes simply $O(\log n)$, where n is the number of nodes in the tree into which the item is inserted.

11.3.5 Removing Items from a Leftist Heap

The **findMin** method locates the item with the smallest key in a given priority queue and the **dequeueMin** method removes it from the queue. Since the smallest item in a heap is found at the root, the **findMin** operation is easy to implement. Program 11.11 shows how it can be done. Clearly, the running time of the **findMin** operation is $O(1)$.

Since the smallest item in a heap is at the root, the **dequeueMin** operation must delete the root node. Since a leftist heap is a binary heap, the root has at most two children. In general when the root is deleted, we are left with two non-empty leftist heaps. Since we already have an efficient way to merge leftist heaps, the solution is to simply merge the two children of the root to obtain a single heap again! Program 11.12 shows how the **dequeueMin** operation of the **LeftistHeap** class can be implemented.

The running time of Program 11.12 is determined by the time required to merge the two children of the root (line 17) since the rest of the work in **dequeueMin** can be done in constant time. Consider the running time to delete the root of a leftist heap T

PROGRAM 11.11
LeftistHeap class findMin method

```
1   public class LeftistHeap
2       extends BinaryTree
3       implements MergeablePriorityQueue
4   {
5       protected int nullPathLength;
6
7       public Comparable findMin ()
8       {
9           if (isEmpty ())
10              throw new ContainerEmptyException ();
11          return (Comparable) getKey ();
12      }
13      // ...
14  }
```

PROGRAM 11.12
LeftistHeap class dequeueMin method

```
1   public class LeftistHeap
2       extends BinaryTree
3       implements MergeablePriorityQueue
4   {
5       protected int nullPathLength;
6
7       public Comparable dequeueMin ()
8       {
9           if (isEmpty ())
10              throw new ContainerEmptyException ();
11
12          Comparable result = (Comparable) getKey ();
13          LeftistHeap oldLeft = getLeftHeap ();
14          LeftistHeap oldRight = getRightHeap ();
15
16          purge ();
17          swapContents (oldLeft);
18          merge (oldRight);
19
20          return result;
21      }
22      // ...
23  }
```

with n internal nodes. The running time to merge the left and right subtrees of T is

$$(d_L - 1 + d_R - 1)\mathcal{T}\langle \texttt{isGT} \rangle + O(d_L + d_R),$$

where d_L and d_R are the null path lengths of the left and right subtrees T, respectively. In the worst case, $d_R = 0$ and $d_L = \lfloor \log_2 n \rfloor$. If we assume that $\mathcal{T}\langle \texttt{isGT} \rangle = O(1)$, the running time for **dequeueMin** is $O(\log n)$.

11.4 Binomial Queues

A binomial queue is a priority queue that is implemented not as a single tree but as a collection of heap-ordered trees. A collection of trees is called a *forest*. Each of the trees in a binomial queue has a very special shape called a binomial tree. Binomial trees are general trees. That is, the maximum degree of a node is not fixed.

The remarkable characteristic of binomial queues is that the merge operation is similar in structure to binary addition. That is, the collection of binomial trees that make up the binomial queue is like the set of bits that make up the binary representation of a non-negative integer. Furthermore, the merging of two binomial queues is done by adding the binomial trees that make up that queue in the same way that the bits are combined when adding two binary numbers.

11.4.1 Binomial Trees

A binomial tree is a general tree with a very special shape:

Definition 11.7 (Binomial Tree)
The binomial tree of order $k \geq 0$ with root R is the tree B_k, defined as follows:

1. *If $k = 0$, $B_k = B_0 = \{R\}$. That is, the binomial tree of order zero consists of a single node, R.*
2. *If $k > 0$, $B_k = \{R, B_0, B_1, \ldots, B_{k-1}\}$. That is, the binomial tree of order $k > 0$ comprises the root R, and k binomial subtrees, $B_0, B_1, \ldots, B_{k-1}$.*

Figure 11.9 shows the first five binomial trees, B_0–B_4. It follows directly from Definition 11.7 that the root of B_k, the binomial tree of order k, has degree k. Since k may be arbitrarily large, so too can be the degree of the root. Furthermore, the root of a binomial tree has the largest fanout of any of the nodes in that tree.

The number of nodes in a binomial tree of order k is a function of k:

Theorem 11.5
The binomial tree of order k, B_k, contains 2^k nodes.

Proof (By induction). Let n_k be the number of nodes in B_k, a binomial tree of order k.

FIGURE 11.9
Binomial trees $B_0, B_1, \ldots, B_4$.

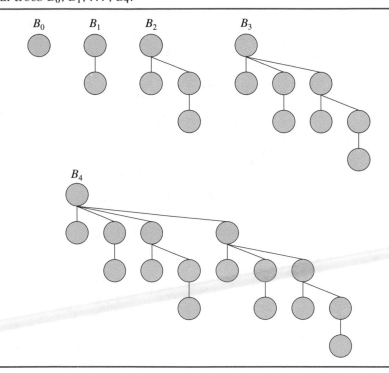

Base Case By definition, B_0 consists of a single node. Therefore, $n_0 = 1 = 2^0$.

Inductive Hypothesis Assume that $n_k = 2^k$ for $k = 0, 1, 2, \ldots, l$, for some $l \geq 0$. Consider the binomial tree of order $l + 1$:

$$B_{l+1} = \{R, B_0, B_1, B_2, \ldots, B_l\}.$$

Therefore, the number of nodes in B_{l+1} is given by

$$n_{l+1} = 1 + \sum_{i=0}^{l} n_i$$

$$= 1 + \sum_{i=0}^{l} 2^i$$

$$= 1 + \frac{2^{l+1} - 1}{2 - 1}$$

$$= 2^{l+1}.$$

Therefore, by induction on l, $n_k = 2^k$ for all $k \geq 0$.

It follows from Theorem 11.5 that binomial trees only come in sizes that are a power of two. That is, $n_k \in \{1, 2, 4, 8, 16, \ldots\}$. Furthermore, for a given power of two, there is exactly one shape of binomial tree.

Theorem 11.6
The height of B_k, the binomial tree of order k, is k.

Proof (By induction). Let h_k be the height of B_k, a binomial tree of order k.

Base Case By definition, B_0 consists of a single node. Therefore, $h_0 = 0$.

Inductive Hypothesis Assume that $h_k = k$ for $k = 0, 1, 2, \ldots, l$, for some $l \geq 0$. Consider the binomial tree of order $l + 1$:

$$B_{l+1} = \{R, B_0, B_1, B_2, \ldots, B_l\}.$$

Therefore, the height B_{l+1} is given by

$$
\begin{aligned}
h_{l+1} &= 1 + \max_{0 \leq i \leq l} h_i \\
&= 1 + \max_{0 \leq i \leq l} i \\
&= l + 1.
\end{aligned}
$$

Therefore, by induction on l, $h_k = k$ for all $k \geq 0$.

Theorem 11.6 tells us that the height of a binomial tree of order k is k and Theorem 11.5 tells us that the number of nodes is $n_k = 2^k$. Therefore, the height of B_k is exactly $O(\log n)$.

Figure 11.10 shows that there are two ways to think about the construction of binomial trees. The first way follows directly from Definition 11.7. That is, binomial B_k consists of a root node to which the k binomial trees $B_0, B_1, \ldots, B_{k-1}$ are attached as shown in Figure 11.10 (a).

Alternatively, we can think of B_k as being composed of two binomial trees of order $k - 1$. For example, Figure 11.10 (b) shows that B_4 is made up of two instances of B_3. In general, suppose we have two trees of order $k - 1$, say B_{k-1}^1 and B_{k-1}^2, where $B_{k-1}^1 = \{R^1, B_0^1, B_1^1, B_2^1, \ldots, B_{k-2}^1\}$. Then we can construct a binomial tree of order k by combining the trees to get

$$B_k = \{R^1, B_0^1, B_1^1, B_2^1, \ldots, B_{k-2}^1, B_{k-1}^2\}.$$

Why do we call B_k a *binomial* tree? It is because the number of nodes at a given depth in the tree is determined by the *binomial coefficient*. And the binomial coefficient derives its name from the *binomial theorem*. And the binomial theorem tells us how to compute the nth power of a *binomial*. And a binomial is an expression that consists of two terms, such as $x + y$. That is why it is called a binomial tree!

FIGURE 11.10
Two views of binomial tree B_4.

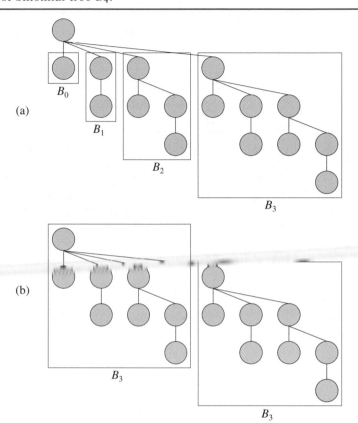

(a)

B_0

B_1

B_2

B_3

(b)

B_3

B_3

B_3

Theorem 11.7 (Binomial Theorem)
The nth power of the binomial $x + y$ for $n \geq 0$ is given by

$$(x + y)^n = \sum_{i=0}^{n} \binom{n}{i} x^i y^{n-i},$$

where $\binom{n}{i} = \dfrac{n!}{i!(n-i)!}$ *is called the* binomial coefficient.

Proof The proof of the binomial theorem is left as an exercise for the reader (Exercise 11.15).[1]

---

[1] Isaac Newton discovered the binomial theorem in 1676 but did not publish a proof. Leonhard Euler attempted a proof in 1774. Karl Friedrich Gauss produced the first correct proof in 1812.

The following theorem gives the expression for the number of nodes at a given depth in a binomial tree:

Theorem 11.8
The number of nodes at level l in B_k, the binomial tree of order k, where $0 \leq l \leq k$, is given by the binomial coefficient $\binom{k}{l}$.

Proof   (By induction). Let $n_k(l)$ be the number of nodes at level l in B_k, a binomial tree of order k.

Base Case   Since B_0 contains a single node, there is only one level in the tree, $l = 0$, and exactly one node at that level. Therefore, $n_0(0) = 1 = \binom{0}{0}$.

Inductive Hypothesis   Assume that $n_k(l) = \binom{k}{l}$ for $k = 0, 1, 2, \ldots, h$, for some $h \geq 0$. The binomial tree of order $h + 1$ is composed of two binomial trees of height h, one attached under the root of the other. Hence, the number of nodes at level l in B_{h+1} is equal to the number of nodes at level l in B_h plus the number of nodes at level $l - 1$ in B_h:

$$
\begin{aligned}
n_{h+1}(l) &= n_h(l) + n_h(l - 1) \\
&= \binom{h}{l} + \binom{h}{l - 1} \\
&= \frac{h!}{(h - l)!l!} + \frac{h!}{(h - (l - 1))!(l - 1)!} \\
&= \frac{h!(h + 1 - l)}{(h + 1 - l)(h - l)!l!} + \frac{h!l}{(h + 1 - l))!l(l - 1)!} \\
&= \frac{h!(h + 1 - l) + h!l}{(h + 1 - l)!l!} \\
&= \frac{(h + 1)!}{(h + 1 - l)!l!} \\
&= \binom{h + 1}{l}.
\end{aligned}
$$

Therefore, by induction on h, $n_k(l) = \binom{k}{l}$.

11.4.2   Binomial Queues

If binomial trees only come in sizes that are powers of two, how do we implement a container that holds an arbitrary number number of items n using binomial trees? The answer is related to the binary representation of the number n. Every non-negative integer n can be expressed in binary form as

$$
n = \sum_{i=0}^{\lfloor \log_2 n \rfloor} b_i 2^i, \tag{11.1}
$$

where $b_i \in \{0, 1\}$ is the ith *binary digit* or *bit* in the representation of n. For example, $n = 27$ is expressed as the binary number 11011_2 because $27 = 16 + 8 + 2 + 1$.

To make a container that holds exactly n items we use a collection of binomial trees. A collection of trees is called a *forest*. The forest contains binomial tree B_i if the ith bit in the binary representation of n is a one. That is, the forest F_n, which contains exactly n items, is given by

$$F_n = \{B_i : b_i = 1\},$$

where b_i is determined from Equation 11.1. For example, the forest that contains 27 items is $F_{27} = \{B_4, B_3, B_1, B_0\}$.

The analogy between F_n and the binary representation of n carries over to the merge operation. Suppose we have two forests, say F_n and F_m. Since F_n contains n items and F_m contains m items, the combination of the two contains $n + m$ items. Therefore, the resulting forest is F_{n+m}.

For example, consider $n = 27$ and $m = 10$. In this case, we need to merge $F_{27} = \{B_4, B_3, B_1, B_0\}$ with $F_{10} = \{B_3, B_1\}$. Recall that two binomial trees of order k can be combined to obtain a binomial tree of order $k + 1$. For example, $B_1 + B_1 = B_2$. But this is just like adding binary digits. In binary notation, the sum $27 + 10$ is calculated like this.

$$
\begin{array}{cccccc}
 & 1 & 1 & 0 & 1 & 1 \\
+ & & 1 & 0 & 1 & 0 \\
\hline
1 & 0 & 0 & 1 & 0 & 1 \\
\end{array}
$$

The merging of F_{27} and F_{20} is done in the same way:

	B_4	B_3	$\varnothing$	B_1	B_0	F_{27}
$+$		B_3	$\varnothing$	B_1	$\varnothing$	F_{10}
B_5	$\varnothing$	$\varnothing$	B_2	$\varnothing$	B_0	F_{37}

Therefore, the result is $F_{37} = \{B_5, B_2, B_0\}$.

11.4.3 Implementation

Heap-Ordered Binomial Trees

Since binomial trees are simply general trees with a special shape, we can make use of the `GeneralTree` class presented in Section 9.6.3 to implement the `BinomialTree` class. (See Figure 11.4.)

Program 11.13 introduces the `BinomialQueue` class and the inner class `BinomialTree`. The `BinomialTree` class extends the GeneralTree class introduced in Program 9.13.

No new fields are declared in the `BinomialTree` class. Remember that the implementation of the `GeneralTree` class uses a linked list to contain the pointers to the subtrees, since the degree of a node in a general tree may be arbitrarily large. Also, the

---

PROGRAM 11.13
BinomialTree class

```
1   public class BinomialQueue
2       extends AbstractContainer
3       implements MergeablePriorityQueue
4   {
5       protected LinkedList treeList;
6
7       protected static class BinomialTree
8           extends GeneralTree
9       {
10          // ...
11      }
12      // ...
13  }
```

GeneralTree class already keeps track of the degree of a node in its **degree** field. Since the degree of the root node of a binomial tree of order k is k, it is not necessary to keep track of the order explicitly. The **degree** variable serves this purpose nicely.

Adding Binomial Trees

Recall that we can combine two binomial trees of the same order, say k, into a single binomial tree of order $k + 1$. Each of the two trees to be combined is heap-ordered. Since the smallest key is at the root of a heap-ordered tree, we know that the root of the result must be the smaller root of the two trees that are to be combined. Therefore, to combine the two trees, we simply attach the tree with the larger root under the root of the tree with the smaller root. For example, Figure 11.11 illustrates how two heap-ordered binomial trees of order two are combined into a single heap-ordered tree of order three.

The **add** method defined in Program 11.14 provides the means to combine two binomial trees of the same order. The **add** method takes a **BinomialTree** and attaches the specified tree to **this** node. This is only permissible when both trees have the same order.

In order to ensure that the resulting binomial tree is heap ordered, the roots of the trees are compared. If necessary, the contents of the nodes are exchanged using **swapContents** (lines 15–16) before the subtree is attached (line 17). Assuming that **swapContents** and **attachSubtree** both run in constant time, the worst-case running time of the **add** method is $\mathcal{T}\langle\text{isGT}\rangle + O(1)$. That is, exactly one comparison and a constant amount of additional work are needed to combine two binomial trees.

Binomial Queues

A binomial queue is a mergeable priority queue implemented as a forest of binomial trees. In this section we present a linked-list implementation of the forest. That is, the forest is represented using a linked list of binomial trees.

FIGURE 11.11
Adding binomial trees.

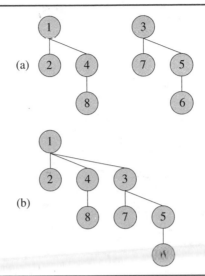

(a)

(b)

PROGRAM 11.14
BinomialTree class add method

```
1   public class BinomialQueue
2       extends AbstractContainer
3       implements MergeablePriorityQueue
4   {
5       protected LinkedList treeList;
6
7       protected static class BinomialTree
8           extends GeneralTree
9       {
10          protected void add (BinomialTree tree)
11          {
12              if (degree != tree.degree)
13                  throw new IllegalArgumentException (
14                      "incompatible degrees");
15              if ( ((Comparable) getKey ()).isGT (
16                      ((Comparable) tree.getKey ())) )
17                  swapContents (tree);
18              attachSubtree (tree);
19          }
20      }
21      // ...
22  }
```

PROGRAM 11.15
BinomialQueue fields

```
1   public class BinomialQueue
2       extends AbstractContainer
3       implements MergeablePriorityQueue
4   {
5       protected LinkedList treeList;
6
7       public BinomialQueue ()
8           { treeList = new LinkedList (); }
9       // ...
10  }
```

Program 11.15 introduces the BinomialQueue class. The BinomialQueue class extends the AbstractContainer class introduced in Program 5.9 and it implements the MergeablePriorityQueue interface defined in Program 11.12.

Fields

The BinomialQueue class definition contains the single field treeList, which is an instance of the LinkedList class introduced in Program 4.13. The binomial trees contained in the linked list are stored in increasing *order*. That is, the binomial tree at the head of the list has the smallest order, and the binomial tree at the tail has the largest order.

addTree and removeTree

The addTree and removeTree methods of the BinomialQueue class facilitate the implementation of the various priority queue operations. These methods are defined in Program 11.16. The addTree method takes a BinomialTree and appends that tree to treeList. addTree also adjusts the count in order to keep track of the number of items in the priority queue. It is assumed that the order of the tree that is added is larger than all others in the list and, therefore, that it belongs at the end of the list. The running time of addTree is clearly $O(1)$.

The removeTree method takes a binomial tree and removes it from the list. It is assumed that the specified tree is actually in the list. removeTree also adjusts the count as required. The running time of removeTree depends on the position of the tree in the list. A binomial queue that contains exactly n items altogether has at most $\lceil \log_2(n + 1) \rceil$ binomial trees. Therefore, the running time of removeTree is $O(\log n)$ in the worst case.

findMinTree and findMin Methods

A binomial queue that contains n items consists of at most $\lceil \log_2(n + 1) \rceil$ binomial trees. Each of these binomial trees is heap ordered. In particular, the smallest key in each binomial tree is at the root of that tree. So, we know that the smallest key in the queue is found at the root of one of the binomial trees, but we do not know which tree it is.

PROGRAM 11.16
BinomialQueue class addTree and removeTree methods

```
1  public class BinomialQueue
2      extends AbstractContainer
3      implements MergeablePriorityQueue
4  {
5      protected LinkedList treeList;
6
7      protected void addTree (BinomialTree tree)
8      {
9          treeList.append (tree);
10         count += tree.getCount ();
11     }
12
13     protected void removeTree (BinomialTree tree)
14     {
15         treeList.extract (tree);
16         count -= tree.getCount ();
17     }
18     // ...
19 }
```

The **findMinTree** method is used to determine which of the binomial trees in the queue has the smallest root. As shown in Program 11.17, the **findMinTree** simply traverses the entire linked list to find the tree with the smallest key at its root. Since there are at most $\lceil \log_2(n + 1) \rceil$ binomial trees, the worst-case running time of **findMinTree** is

$$(\lceil \log_2(n + 1) \rceil - 1)\mathcal{T}\langle \text{isLT} \rangle + O(\log n).$$

Program 11.17 also defines the **findMin** method, which returns the smallest key in the priority queue. The **findMin** method uses **findMinTree** to locate the tree with the smallest key at its root and returns that key. Clearly, the asymptotic running time of **findMin** is the same as that of **findMinTree**.

11.4.4 Merging Binomial Queues

Merging two binomial queues is like doing binary addition. For example, consider the addition of F_{27} and F_{10}:

	B_4	B_3	$\varnothing$	B_1	B_0	F_{27}
+		B_3	$\varnothing$	B_1	$\varnothing$	F_{10}
B_5	$\varnothing$	$\varnothing$	B_2	$\varnothing$	B_0	F_{37}

PROGRAM 11.17
BinomialQueue class findMinTree and findMin methods

```
1   public class BinomialQueue
2       extends AbstractContainer
3       implements MergeablePriorityQueue
4   {
5       protected LinkedList treeList;
6
7       protected BinomialTree findMinTree ()
8       {
9           BinomialTree minTree = null;
10          for (LinkedList.Element ptr = treeList.getHead ();
11              ptr != null; ptr = ptr.getNext ())
12          {
13              BinomialTree tree = (BinomialTree) ptr.getDatum ();
14              if (minTree == null ||
15                      ((Comparable) tree.getKey ()).isLT (
16                      ((Comparable) minTree.getKey ())) )
17                  minTree = tree;
18          }
19          return minTree;
20      }
21
22      public Comparable findMin ()
23      {
24          if (count == 0)
25              throw new ContainerEmptyException ();
26          return (Comparable) findMinTree ().getKey ();
27      }
28      // ...
29  }
```

The usual algorithm for addition begins with the least significant "bit." Since F_{27} contains a B_0 tree and F_{10} does not, the result is simply the B_0 tree from F_{27}.

In the next step, we add the B_1 from F_{27} and the B_1 from F_{10}. Combining the two B_1s we get a B_2, which we *carry* to the next column. Since there are no B_1s left, the result does not contain any. The addition continues in a similar manner until all columns have been added up.

Program 11.18 gives an implementation of this addition algorithm. The **merge** method of the **BinomialQueue**class takes a **BinomialQueue** and adds its subtrees to **this** binomial queue.

Each iteration of the main loop of the algorithm (lines 16–42) computes the ith "bit" of the result—the ith bit is a binomial tree of order i. At most three terms need to be

```
1   public class BinomialQueue
2       extends AbstractContainer
3       implements MergeablePriorityQueue
4   {
5       protected LinkedList treeList;
6
7       public void merge (MergeablePriorityQueue queue)
8       {
9           BinomialQueue arg = (BinomialQueue) queue;
10          LinkedList oldList = treeList;
11          treeList = new LinkedList ();
12          count = 0;
13          LinkedList.Element p = oldList.getHead ();
14          LinkedList.Element q = arg.treeList.getHead();
15          BinomialTree carry = null;
16          for (int i = 0; p!=null || q!=null || carry!=null; ++i)
17          {
18              BinomialTree a = null;
19              if (p != null)
20              {
21                  BinomialTree tree = (BinomialTree) p.getDatum ();
22                  if (tree.getDegree () == i)
23                  {
24                      a = tree;
25                      p = p.getNext ();
26                  }
27              }
28              BinomialTree b = null;
29              if (q != null)
30              {
31                  BinomialTree tree = (BinomialTree) q.getDatum ();
32                  if (tree.getDegree () == i)
33                  {
34                      b = tree;
35                      q = q.getNext ();
36                  }
37              }
38              BinomialTree sum = sum (a, b, carry);
39              if (sum != null)
40                  addTree (sum);
41              carry = carry (a, b, carry);
42          }
43          arg.purge ();
44      }
45      // ...
46  }
```

PROGRAM 11.19
BinomialQueue class sum and carry methods

```
1  public class BinomialQueue
2      extends AbstractContainer
3      implements MergeablePriorityQueue
4  {
5      protected LinkedList treeList;
6
7      protected BinomialTree sum (
8          BinomialTree a, BinomialTree b, BinomialTree c)
9      {
10         if (a != null && b == null && c == null)
11             return a;
12         else if (a == null && b != null && c == null)
13             return b;
14         else if (a == null && b == null && c != null)
15             return c;
16         else if (a != null && b != null && c != null)
17             return c;
18         else
19             return null;
20     }
21
22     protected BinomialTree carry (
23         BinomialTree a, BinomialTree b, BinomialTree c)
24     {
25         if (a != null && b != null && c == null)
26             { a.add (b); return a; }
27         else if (a != null && b == null && c != null)
28             { a.add (c); return a; }
29         else if (a == null && b != null && c != null)
30             { b.add (c); return b; }
31         else if (a != null && b != null && c != null)
32             { a.add (b); return a; }
33         else
34             return null;
35     }
36     // ...
37 }
```

---

considered: the carry from the preceding iteration and two B_is, one from each of the queues that are being merged.

Two methods, **sum** and **carry**, compute the result required in each iteration. Program 11.19 defines both **sum** and **carry**. Notice that the **sum** method simply selects and returns one of its arguments. Therefore, the running time for **sum** is clearly $O(1)$.

In the worst case, the **carry** method calls the **add** method to combine two **Binomial-Trees** into one. Therefore, the worst-case running time for **carry** is

$$\mathcal{T}\langle \texttt{isGT} \rangle + O(1).$$

Suppose the **merge** method of Program 11.18 is used to combine a binomial queue with n items with another that contains m items. Since the resulting priority queue contains $n + m$ items, there are at most $\lceil \log_2(n + m + 1) \rceil$ binomial trees in the result. Thus, the worst-case running time for the **merge** operation is

$$\lceil \log_2(n + m + 1) \rceil \mathcal{T}\langle \texttt{isGT} \rangle + O(\log(n + m)).$$

11.4.5 Putting Items into a Binomial Queue

With the **merge** method at our disposal, the **enqueue** operation is easy to implement. To enqueue an item in a given binomial queue, we create another binomial queue that contains just the one item to be enqueued and merge that queue with the original one.

Program 11.20 shows how easily this can be done. Creating the empty queue (line 9) takes a constant amount of time. Creating the binomial tree B_0 with the one object at its root (line 10) can also be done in constant time. Finally, the time required to merge the two queues is

$$\lceil \log_2(n + 2) \rceil \mathcal{T} \langle \texttt{isGT} \rangle + O(\log n),$$

where n is the number of items originally in the queue.

11.4.6 Removing an Item from a Binomial Queue

A binomial queue is a forest of heap-ordered binomial trees. Therefore, to dequeue the smallest item from the queue, we must withdraw the root of one of the binomial trees. But what do we do with the rest of the tree once its root has been removed?

The solution lies in realizing that the collection of subtrees of the root of a binomial tree is a forest! For example, consider the binomial tree of order k,

$$B_k = \{R, B_0, B_1, B_2, \ldots, B_{k-1}\}.$$

PROGRAM 11.20
BinomialQueue class enqueue method

```
1   public class BinomialQueue
2       extends AbstractContainer
3       implements MergeablePriorityQueue
4   {
5       protected LinkedList treeList;
6
7       public void enqueue (Comparable object)
8       {
9           BinomialQueue queue = new BinomialQueue ();
10          queue.addTree (new BinomialTree (object));
11          merge (queue);
12      }
13      // ...
14  }
```

Taken all together, its subtrees form the binomial queue F_{2^k-1}:

$$F_{2^k-1} = \{B_0, B_1, B_2, \ldots, B_{k-1}\}.$$

Therefore, to delete the smallest item from a binomial queue, we first identify the binomial tree with the smallest root and remove that tree from the queue. Then, we consider all subtrees of the root of that tree as a binomial queue and merge that queue back into the original one. Program 11.21 shows how this can be coded.

The **dequeueMin** method begins by calling **findMinTree** to find the tree with the smallest root and then removing that tree using **removeTree** (lines 12–13). The time required to find the appropriate tree and to remove it is

$$(\lceil \log_2(n + 1) \rceil - 1)\mathcal{T}\langle \texttt{isLT} \rangle + O(\log n),$$

where n is the number of items in the queue.

A new binomial queue is created on line 15. All of the children of the root of the minimum tree are detached from the tree and added to the new binomial queue (lines 16–21). In the worst case, the minimum tree is the one with the highest order—that is, $B_{\lfloor \log_2 n \rfloor}$—and the root of that tree has $\lfloor \log_2 n \rfloor$ children. Therefore, the running time of the loop on lines 16–21 is $O(\log n)$.

The new queue is then merged with the original one (line 22). Since the resulting queue contains $n - 1$ keys, the running time for the **merge** operation in this case is

$$\lceil \log_2 n \rceil \mathcal{T}\langle \texttt{isGT} \rangle + O(\log n).$$

PROGRAM 11.21
BinomialQueue class dequeueMin method

```
1   public class BinomialQueue
2       extends AbstractContainer
3       implements MergeablePriorityQueue
4   {
5       protected LinkedList treeList;
6
7       public Comparable dequeueMin ()
8       {
9           if (count == 0)
10              throw new ContainerEmptyException ();
11
12          BinomialTree minTree = findMinTree ();
13          removeTree (minTree);
14
15          BinomialQueue queue = new BinomialQueue ();
16          while (minTree.getDegree () > 0)
17          {
18              BinomialTree child =
19                  (BinomialTree) minTree.getSubtree (0);
20              minTree.detachSubtree (child);
21              queue.addTree (child);
22          }
23          merge (queue);
24
25          return (Comparable) minTree.getKey ();
26      }
27      // ...
28  }
```

11.5 Applications

11.5.1 Discrete Event Simulation

One of the most important applications of priority queues is in *discrete event simulation*. Simulation is a tool that is used to study the behavior of complex systems. The first step in simulation is *modeling*. We construct a mathematical model of the system we wish to study, then we write a computer program to evaluate the model. In a sense the behavior of the computer program mimics the system we are studying.

The systems studied using *discrete event simulation* have the following characteristics: The system has a *state* that evolves or changes with time. Changes in state occur

---

FIGURE 11.12
A simple queueing system.

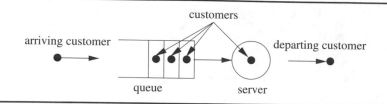

at distinct points in simulation time. A state change moves the system from one state to another instantaneously. State changes are called *events*.

For example, suppose we wish to study the service received by customers in a bank. Suppose a single teller is serving customers. If the teller is not busy when a customer arrives at the bank, then that customer is immediately served. On the other hand, if the teller is busy when another customer arrives, that customer joins a queue and waits to be served.

We can model this system as a discrete event process, as shown in Figure 11.12. The state of the system is characterized by the state of the server (the teller), which is either busy or idle, and by the number of customers in the queue. The events that cause state changes are the arrival of a customer and the departure of a customer.

If the server is idle when a customer arrives, the server immediately begins to serve the customer and therefore changes its state to busy. If the server is busy when a customer arrives, that customer joins the queue.

When the server finishes serving the customer, that customer departs. If the queue is not empty, the server immediately commences serving the next customer. Otherwise, the server becomes idle.

How do we keep track of which event to simulate next? Each event (arrival or departure) occurs at a discrete point in *simulation time*. In order to ensure that the simulation program is correct, it must compute the events in order. This is called the *causality constraint*—events cannot change the past.

In our model, when the server begins to serve a customer we can compute the departure time of that customer. So, when a customer arrives at the server we *schedule* an event in the future, which corresponds to the departure of that customer. In order to ensure that events are processed in order, we keep them in a priority queue in which the time of the event is its priority. Since we always process the pending event with the smallest time next and since an event can schedule new events only in the future, the causality constraint will not be violated.

11.5.2 Implementation

This section presents the simulation of a system composed of a single queue and server as shown in Figure 11.12. Program 11.22 defines the class **Event**, which represents

PROGRAM 11.22
Event class

```
1   public class Simulation
2   {
3       static class Event
4           extends Association
5       {
6           public static final int arrival = 0;
7           public static final int departure = 1;
8
9           Event (int type, double time)
10              { super (new Dbl (time), new Int (type)); }
11
12          double getTime ()
13              { return ((Dbl) getKey ()).doubleValue (); }
14
15          int getType ()
16              { return ((Int) getValue ()).intValue (); }
17      }
18      // ...
19  }
```

events in the simulation. There are two parts to an event, a *type* (either **arrival** or **departure**), and a *time*.

Since events will be put into a priority queue, the **Event** class is derived from the **Association** class introduced in Section 5.2.8. An association is an ordered pair composed of a key and a value. In the case of the **Event** class, the key is the *time* of the event and the value is the *type* of the event. Therefore, the events in a priority queue are prioritized by their times.

Program 11.23 defines the **run** method, which implements the discrete event simulation. This method takes one argument, **timeLimit**, which specifies the total amount of time to be simulated.

The **Simulation** class contains a single field, called **eventList**, which is a priority queue. This priority queue is used to hold the events during the course of the simulation.

The state of the system being simulated is represented by the two variables **serverBusy** and **numberInQueue**. The first is a **boolean** value that indicates whether the server is busy. The second keeps track of the number of customers in the queue.

In addition to the state variables, there are two instances of the class **ExponentialRV**. The class **ExponentialRV** is a random number generator defined in Section 14.5.1. It implements the **RandomVariable** interface defined in Program 14.14. This interface defines a method called **nextDouble**, which is used to sample the random number generator. Every time **nextDouble** is called, a different (random) result is returned. The random values are exponentially distributed around a mean value,

PROGRAM 11.23

Application of priority queues—discrete event simulation

```
1   public class Simulation
2   {
3       PriorityQueue eventList = new LeftistHeap ();
4
5       public void run (double timeLimit)
6       {
7           boolean serverBusy = false;
8           int numberInQueue = 0;
9           RandomVariable serviceTime = new ExponentialRV (100.);
10          RandomVariable interArrivalTime =
11              new ExponentialRV (100.);
12          eventList.enqueue (new Event (Event.arrival, 0));
13          while (!eventList.isEmpty ())
14          {
15              Event event = (Event) eventList.dequeueMin ();
16              double t = event.getTime ();
17              if (t > timeLimit)
18                  { eventList.purge (); break; }
19              switch (event.getType ())
20              {
21              case Event.arrival:
22                  if (!serverBusy)
23                  {
24                      serverBusy = true;
25                      eventList.enqueue (new Event(Event.departure,
26                          t + serviceTime.nextDouble ()));
27                  }
28                  else
29                      ++numberInQueue;
30                  eventList.enqueue (new Event (Event.arrival,
31                      t + interArrivalTime.nextDouble ()));
32                  break;
33              case Event.departure:
34                  if (numberInQueue == 0)
35                      serverBusy = false;
36                  else
37                  {
38                      --numberInQueue;
39                      eventList.enqueue (new Event(Event.departure,
40                          t + serviceTime.nextDouble ()));
41                  }
42                  break
43              }
44          }
45      }
46      // ...
47  }
```

which is specified in the constructor. For example, in this case both `serviceTime` and `interArrivalTime` produce random distributions with the mean value of 100 (lines 9–11).

It is assumed that the `eventList` priority queue is initially empty. The simulation begins by enqueueing a customer arrival at time zero (line 12). The `while` loop (lines 13–44) constitutes the main simulation loop. This loop continues as long as the `eventList` is not empty, that is, as long as there is an event to be simulated.

Each iteration of the simulation loop begins by dequeuing the next event in the event list (line 15). If the time of that event exceeds `timeLimit`, the event is discarded, the `eventList` is purged, and the simulation is terminated. Otherwise, the simulation proceeds.

The simulation of an event depends on the type of that event. The `switch` statement (line 19) invokes the appropriate code for the given event. If the event is a customer arrival and the server is not busy, `serverBusy` is set to `true` and the `serviceTime` random number generator is sampled to determine the amount of time required to service the customer. A customer departure is scheduled at the appropriate time in the future (lines 24–26). On the other hand, if the server is already busy when the customer arrives, we add one to the `numberInQueue` variable (line 29).

Another customer arrival is scheduled after every customer arrival. The `interArrivalTime` random number generator is sampled, and the arrival is scheduled at the appropriate time in the future (lines 30–31).

If the event is a customer departure and the queue is empty, the server becomes idle (lines 34–35). When a customer departs and there are still customers in the queue, the next customer in the queue is served. Therefore, `numberInQueue` is decreased by one and the `serviceTime` random number generator is sampled to determine the amount of time required to service the next customer. A customer departure is scheduled at the appropriate time in the future (lines 38–40).

Clearly the execution of the `Simulation` method given in Program 11.23 mimics the modeled system. Of course, the program given produces no output. For it to be of any practical value, the simulation program should be instrumented to allow the user to study its behavior. For example, the user may be interested in knowing statistics such as the average queue length and the average waiting time that a customer waits for service. And such instrumentation can be easily incorporated into the given framework.

Exercises

11.1 For each of the following key sequences, determine the binary heap obtained when the keys are inserted one-by-one in the order given into an initially empty heap:

a. 0, 1, 2, 3, 4, 5, 6, 7, 8, 9

b. 3, 1, 4, 1, 5, 9, 2, 6, 5, 4

c. 2, 7, 1, 8, 2, 8, 1, 8, 2, 8

11.2 For each of the binary heaps obtained in Exercise 11.1, determine the heap obtained after three consecutive `dequeueMin` operations.

11.3 Repeat Exercises 11.1 and 11.2 for a leftist heap.

11.4 Show the result obtained by inserting the keys $1, 2, 3, \ldots, 2^h$ one-by-one in the order given into an initially empty binomial queue.

11.5 A *full* binary tree is a tree in which each node is either a leaf or a *full node* (see Exercise 9.4). Consider a *complete* binary tree with n nodes.

   a. For what values of n is a complete binary tree a *full* binary tree?

   b. For what values of n is a complete binary a *perfect* binary tree?

11.6 Prove by induction Theorem 11.3.

11.7 Devise an algorithm to determine whether a given binary tree is a heap. What is the running time of your algorithm?

11.8 Devise an algorithm to find the *largest* item in a binary *min* heap. **Hint**: First, show that the largest item must be in one of the leaves. What is the running time of your algorithm?

11.9 Suppose we are given an arbitrary array of n keys to be inserted into a binary heap all at once. Devise an $O(n)$ algorithm to do this. **Hint**: See Section 15.5.2.

11.10 Devise an algorithm to determine whether a given binary tree is a leftist tree. What is the running time of your algorithm?

11.11 Prove that a complete binary tree is a leftist tree.

11.12 Suppose we are given an arbitrary array of n keys to be inserted into a leftist heap all at once. Devise an $O(n)$ algorithm to do this. **Hint**: See Exercises 11.9 and 11.11.

11.13 Consider a complete binary tree with its nodes numbered as shown in Figure 11.1. Let K be the number of a node in the tree. Then the binary representation of K is

$$K = \sum_{i=0}^{k} b_i 2^i,$$

where $k = \lfloor \log_2 K \rfloor$.

   a. Show that the path from the root to a given node K passes through the following nodes:

$$b_k$$
$$b_k b_{k-1}$$
$$b_k b_{k-1} b_{k-2}$$
$$\vdots$$
$$b_k b_{k-1} b_{k-2} \ldots b_2 b_1$$
$$b_k b_{k-1} b_{k-2} \ldots b_2 b_1 b_0.$$

b. Consider a complete binary tree with n nodes. The nodes on the path from the root to the nth are *special*. Show that every non-special node is the root of a perfect tree.

11.14 The `enqueue` algorithm for the `BinaryHeap` class does $O(\log n)$ object comparisons in the worst case. In effect, this algorithm does a linear search from a leaf to the root to find the point at which to insert a new key. Devise an algorithm that does a binary search instead. Show that the number of comparisons required becomes $O(\log \log n)$. **Hint**: See Exercise 11.13.

11.15 Prove Theorem 11.7.

11.16 Do Exercise 10.17.

Programming Projects

11.1 Design and implement a sorting algorithm using one of the priority queue implementations described in this chapter.

11.2 Complete the `BinaryHeap` class introduced in Program 11.3 by providing suitable definitions for the following methods: `compareTo`, `isFull`, `accept`, and `getEnumeration`. Write a test program and test your implementation.

11.3 Complete the `LeftistHeap` class introduced in Program 11.8 by providing suitable definitions for the following methods: `LeftistHeap` (constructor), `getLeftHeap`, `getRightHeap`, `swapContents`, and `swapSubtrees`. You will require a complete implementation of the base class `BinaryTree`. (See Project 9.8.) Write a test program and test your implementation.

11.4 Complete the implementation of the `BinomialTree` class introduced in Program 11.13 by providing suitable definitions for the following methods: `BinomialTree` (constructor), `getCount`, and `swapContents`. You must also have a complete implementation of the base class `GeneralTree`. (See Project 9.6.) Write a test program and test your implementation

11.5 Complete the implementation of the `BinomialQueue` class introduced in Program 11.15 by providing suitable definitions for the following methods: `BinomialQueue` (constructor), `purge`, `compareTo`, `accept`, and `getEnumeration`. You must also have a complete implementation of the `BinomialTree` class. (See Project 11.4.) Write a test program and test your implementation.

11.6 The binary heap described in this chapter uses an array as the underlying foundational data structure. Alternatively we may base an implementation on the `BinaryTree` class described in Chapter 9. Implement a priority queue class that extends the `BinaryTree` class (Program 9.20) and implements the `PriorityQueue` interface (Program 11.1).

11.7 Implement a priority queue class using the binary search tree class from Chapter 10. Specifically, extend the `BinarySearchTree` class (Program 10.2) and implement the **PriorityQueue** interface (Program 11.1). You will require a complete implementation of the base class **BinarySearchTree**. (See Project 10.1.) Write a test program and test your implementation.

11.8 Devise and implement an algorithm to multiply two polynomials:

$$\left(\sum_{i=0}^{n} a_i x^i\right) \times \left(\sum_{j=0}^{m} b_j x^j\right).$$

Generate the terms of the result in order by putting intermediate product terms into a priority queue. That is, use the priority queue to group terms with the same exponent. **Hint**: See also Project 7.4.

12 | Sets, Multisets, and Partitions

In mathematics a *set* is a collection of elements, especially a collection having some feature or features in common. The set may have a finite number of elements, such as the set of prime numbers less than 100; or it may have an infinite number of elements, such as the set of right triangles. The *elements* of a set may be anything at all—from simple integers to arbitrarily complex objects. However, all elements of a set are distinct—a set may contain only one instance of a given element.

For example, {}, {a}, {a, b, c, d}, and {d, e} are all sets, the elements of which are drawn from $U = \{a, b, c, d, e\}$. The set of all possible elements, U, is called the *universal set*. Note also that the elements comprising a given set are not ordered. Thus, {a, b, c} and {b, c, a} are the same set.

There are many possible operations on sets. In this chapter we consider the most common operations for *combining sets*—union, intersection, difference:

union The *union* or (*conjunction*) of sets S and T, written $S \cup T$, is the set comprised of all elements of S together with all elements of T. Since a set cannot contain duplicates, if the same item is an element of both S and T, only one instance of that item appears in $S \cup T$. If $S = \{a, b, c, d\}$ and $T = \{d, e\}$, then $S \cup T = \{a, b, c, d, e\}$.

intersection The *intersection* (or *disjunction*) of sets S and T is written $S \cap T$. The elements of $S \cap T$ are those items that are elements of *both* S and T. If $S = \{a, b, c, d\}$ and $T = \{d, e\}$, then $S \cap T = \{d\}$.

difference The *difference* (or *subtraction*) of sets S and T, written $S - T$, contains those elements of S that are *not also* elements of T. That is, the result $S - T$ is obtained by taking the set S and removing from it those elements that are also found in T. If $S = \{a, b, c, d\}$ and $T = \{d, e\}$, then $S - T = \{a, b, c\}$.

Figure 12.1 illustrates the basic set operations using a *Venn diagram*. A Venn diagram represents the membership of sets by regions of the plane. In Figure 12.1 the two

391

FIGURE 12.1
Venn diagram illustrating the basic set operations.

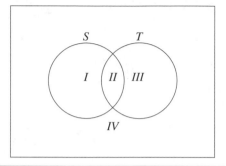

sets S and T divide the plane into the four regions labeled I–IV. The following table illustrates the basic set operations by enumerating the regions that comprise each set.

Set	Region(s) of Figure 12.1
U	I, II, III, IV
S	I, II
S'	III, IV
T	II, III
$S \cup T$	I, II, III
$S \cap T$	II
$S - T$	I
$T - S$	III

12.1 Basics

In this chapter we consider sets which elements are integers. By using integers as the universe rather than arbitrary objects, certain optimizations are possible. For example, we can use a bit-vector of length N to represent a set whose universe is $\{0, 1, \ldots, N-1\}$. Of course, using integers as the universe does not preclude the use of more complex objects, provided there is a one-to-one mapping between those objects and the elements of the universal set.

A crucial requirement of any set representation scheme is that it supports the common set operations including *union*, *intersection*, and set *difference*. We also need to compare sets and, specifically, to determine whether a given set is a subset of another.

12.1.1 Implementing Sets

As previously discussed, this chapter addresses the implementation of sets of integers. A set is a collection of elements. Naturally, we want to insert and withdraw objects

FIGURE 12.2
Object class hierarchy.

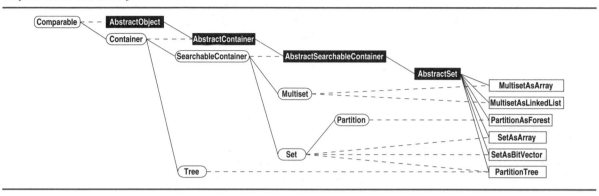

PROGRAM 12.1
`Set` interface

```
1  public interface Set
2        extends SearchableContainer
3  {
4        Set union (Set set);
5        Set intersection (Set set);
6        Set difference (Set set);
7        boolean isEQ (Set set);
8        boolean isSubset (Set set);
9  }
```

---

from the collection and to test whether a given object is a member of the collection. Therefore, we consider sets as being derived from the **SearchableContainer** class defined in Chapter 5. (See Figure 12.2.) In general, a searchable container can hold arbitrary objects. However, in this chapter we will assume that the elements of a set are integers.

Program 12.1 defines the **Set** interface. The **Set** interface extends the **SearchableContainer** interface defined in Program 5.14. Five new methods are declared—**union**, **intersection**, **difference**, **isEQ**, and **isSubset**. These methods correspond to the various set operations previously discussed.

Program 12.2 defines the **AbstractSet** class. The **AbstractSet** class extends the **AbstractSearchableContainer** class introduced in Program 5.15 and it implements the **Set** interface defined in Program 12.1. As shown in Figure 12.2, all of the concrete set classes discussed in this chapter are derived from the **AbstractSet** class.

The **AbstractSet** class defines a field called **universeSize**. This field is used to record the size of the universal set. The constructor for the **AbstractSet** class

---

PROGRAM 12.2
AbstractSet class

```
1    public abstract class AbstractSet
2        extends AbstractSearchableContainer
3    {
4        protected int universeSize;
5
6        public AbstractSet (int universeSize)
7            { this .universeSize = universeSize; }
8
9        protected abstract void insert (int i);
10       protected abstract void withdraw (int i);
11       protected abstract boolean isMember (int i);
12
13       public void insert (Comparable object)
14           { insert (((Int) object).intValue ()); }
15
16       public void withdraw (Comparable object)
17           { withdraw (((Int) object).intValue ()); }
18
19       public boolean isMember (Comparable object)
20           { return isMember (((Int) object).intValue ()); }
21   }
```

---

is given in Program 12.2. It takes a single argument, $N =$ universeSize, which specifies that the universal set will be $\{0, 1, \ldots, N - 1\}$.

The items *contained* in a set are integers. Therefore, the AbstractSet class defines abstract methods called as insert, isMember, and withdraw, that take int arguments.

However, the methods of the SearchableContainer interface, such as insert, isMember, and withdraw, expect their arguments to be Comparable objects. For this reason, the AbstractSet class provides a default implementation for each such method, which converts its argument to an int and then invokes the like-named abstract method that takes an int argument.

12.2 Array and Bit-Vector Sets

In this section we consider finite sets over a finite universe. Specifically, the universe we consider is $\{0, 1, \ldots, N - 1\}$, the set of integers in the range from zero to $N - 1$, for some fixed and relatively small value of N.

Let $U = \{0, 1, \ldots, N - 1\}$ be the universe. Every set that we wish to represent is a subset of U. The set of all subsets of U is called the *power set* of U and is written 2^U.

PROGRAM 12.3
SetAsArray fields

```
1   public class SetAsArray
2       extends AbstractSet
3       implements Set
4   {
5       protected boolean[] array;
6
7       // ...
8   }
```

Thus, the sets that we wish to represent are the *elements* of 2^U. The number of elements in the set U, written $|U|$, is N. Similarly, $|2^U| = 2^{|U|} = 2^N$. This observation should be obvious: For each element of the universal set U there are only two possibilities: Either it is, or it is not, a member of the given set.

This suggests a relatively straightforward representation of the elements of 2^U — an array of boolean values, one for each element of the universal set. By using array subscripts in U, we can represent the set implicitly. That is, i is a member of the set if the ith array element is true.

Program 12.3 introduces the class **SetAsArray**. The **SetAsArray** class extends the **AbstractSet** class defined in Program 12.2. This class uses an array of length $N =$ **numberOfItems** to represent the elements of 2^U where $U = \{0, 1, \ldots, N - 1\}$.

Basic Operations

Program 12.4 defines the constructor for the **SetAsArray** class as well as the three basic operations—**insert**, **isMember**, and **withdraw**. The constructor takes a single argument $N =$ **numberOfItems**, which defines the universe and, consequently, the size of the array of **boolean** values. The constructor creates the empty set by initializing all elements of the **boolean** array to **false**. Clearly, the running time of the constructor is $O(N)$.

The **insert** method is used to put an item into the set. The method takes an **int** argument that specifies the item to be inserted. Then the corresponding element of **array** is set to **true** to indicate that the item has been added to the set. The running time of the **insert** operation is $O(1)$.

The **isMember** method is used to test whether a given item is an element of the set. The semantics are somewhat subtle. Since a set does not actually keep track of the specific object instances that are inserted, the membership test is based on the *value* of the argument. The method simply returns the value of the appropriate element of the **array**. The running time of the **isMember** operation is $O(1)$.

The **withdraw** method is used to take an item out of a set. The withdrawal operation is the opposite of insertion. Instead of setting the appropriate array element to **true**, it is set to **false**. The running time of **withdraw** is identical to that of **insert**, viz., is $O(1)$.

PROGRAM 12.4
`SetAsArray` class constructor, `insert`, `withdraw`, and `isMember` methods

```
1   public class SetAsArray
2       extends AbstractSet
3       implements Set
4   {
5       protected boolean[] array;
6
7       public SetAsArray (int n)
8       {
9           super (n);
10          array = new boolean [universeSize];
11          for (int item = 0; item < universeSize; ++item)
12              array [item] = false;
13      }
14
15      protected void insert (int item)
16          { array [item] = true; }
17
18      protected boolean isMember (int item)
19          { return array [item]; }
20
21      protected void withdraw (int item)
22          { array [item] = false; }
23      // ...
24  }
```

Union, Intersection, and Difference

Program 12.5 defines the three methods, `union`, `intersection`, and `difference`. These methods correspond to $\cup$, $\cap$, and $-$, respectively.

The set union operator takes one argument, which is assumed to be a `SetAsArray` instance. It computes the `SetAsArray` obtained from the union of `this` and `set`. The implementation given requires that the sets be compatible. Two sets are deemed to be compatible if they have the same universe. The result also has the same universe. Consequently, the `boolean` array in all three sets has the same length, N. The set union method creates a result array of the required size and then computes the elements of the array as required. The ith element of the result is `true` if either the ith element of `s` or the ith element of `t` is `true`. Thus, set union is implemented using the `boolean` *or* operator, `||`.

The set intersection method is almost identical to set union, except that the elements of the result are computed using the `boolean` *and* operator. The set difference method is also very similar. In this case, an item is an element of the result only if it is a member of `this` and not a member of `set`.

PROGRAM 12.5
SetAsArray class union, intersection, and difference methods

```
1   public class SetAsArray
2       extends AbstractSet
3       implements Set
4   {
5       protected boolean[] array;
6
7       public Set union (Set set)
8       {
9           SetAsArray arg = (SetAsArray) set;
10          if (universeSize != arg.universeSize)
11              throw new IllegalArgumentException (
12                  "mismatched sets");
13          SetAsArray result = new SetAsArray (universeSize);
14          for (int i = 0; i < universeSize; ++i)
15              result.array [i] = array [i] || arg.array [i];
16          return result;
17      }
18
19      public Set intersection (Set set)
20      {
21          SetAsArray arg = (SetAsArray) set;
22          if (universeSize != arg.universeSize)
23              throw new IllegalArgumentException (
24                  "mismatched sets");
25          SetAsArray result = new SetAsArray (universeSize);
26          for (int i = 0; i < universeSize; ++i)
27              result.array [i] = array [i] && arg.array [i];
28          return result;
29      }
30
31      public Set difference (Set set)
32      {
33          SetAsArray arg = (SetAsArray) set;
34          if (universeSize != arg.universeSize)
35              throw new IllegalArgumentException (
36                  "mismatched sets");
37          SetAsArray result = new SetAsArray (universeSize);
38          for (int i = 0; i < universeSize; ++i)
39              result.array [i] = array [i] && !arg.array [i];
40          return result;
41      }
42      // ...
43  }
```

Because all three methods are almost identical, their running times are essentially the same. That is, the running time of the set union, intersection, and difference operations is $O(N)$, where $N =$ `numberOfItems`.

Comparing Sets

There is a special family of operators for comparing sets. Consider two sets, say S and T. We say that S is a *subset* of T, written $S \subseteq T$, if every element of S is also an element of T. If there is at least one element of T that is not also an element of S, we say that S is a *proper subset* of T, written $S \subset T$. We can also reverse the order in which the expressions are written to get $T \supset S$ or $T \supseteq S$, which indicates that T is a (proper) *superset* of S.

The set comparison operators follow the rule that if $S \subseteq T$ and $T \subseteq S$ then $S \equiv T$, which is analogous to a similar property of numbers: $x \leq y \wedge y \leq x \Longleftrightarrow x = y$. However, set comparison is unlike numeric comparison in that there exist sets S and T for which neither $S \subseteq T$ nor $T \subseteq S$! For example, clearly this is the case for $S = \{1, 2\}$ and $T = \{2, 3\}$. Mathematically, the relation $\subseteq$ is called a *partial order* because there exist some pairs of sets for which neither $S \subseteq T$ nor $T \subseteq S$ holds; whereas the relation $\leq$ (among integers, say) is a total order.

Program 12.6 defines the methods `isEQ` and `isSubset`, each of which take an argument that is assumed to be a `SetAsArray` instance. The former tests for equality and the latter determines whether the relation $\subseteq$ holds between `this` and `set`. Both operators return a `boolean` result. The worst-case running time of each of these operations is clearly $O(N)$.

A complete repertoire of comparison methods would also include methods to compute $\subset$, $\supset$, $\supseteq$, and $\neq$. These operations follow directly from the implementation shown in Program 12.6 (Exercise 12.2).

12.2.1 Bit-Vector Sets

The Java Virtual Machine does not support the `boolean` type directly. As a result, the Java compiler converts every `boolean` variable to an `int`. Thus, a Java `boolean` occupies four bytes. However, since there are only the two values `true` and `false`, a single bit is sufficient to hold a `boolean` value. Therefore, we can realize a significant reduction in the memory space required to represent a set if we use an array of bits. Furthermore, by using bitwise operations to implement the basic set operations such as union and intersection, we can achieve a commensurate reduction in execution time. Unfortunately, these improvements are not free—the operations `insert`, `isMember`, and `withdraw` all slow down by a constant factor.

Since Java does not directly support arrays of bits, we will simulate an array of bits using an array of `int`s. Program 12.7 illustrates how this can be done. The constant `intBits` is defined as the number of bits in a single `int`.

Basic Operations

Program 12.8 defines the constructor for the `SetAsBitVector` class as well as the three basic operations—`insert`, `isMember`, and `withdraw`. The constructor takes

```
1   public class SetAsArray
2       extends AbstractSet
3       implements Set
4   {
5       protected boolean[] array;
6
7       public boolean isEQ (Set set)
8       {
9           SetAsArray arg = (SetAsArray) set;
10          if (universeSize != arg.universeSize)
11              throw new IllegalArgumentException (
12                  "mismatched sets");
13          for (int item = 0; item < universeSize; ++item)
14              if (array [item] != arg.array [item])
15                  return false;
16          return true;
17      }
18
19      public boolean isSubset (Set set)
20      {
21          SetAsArray arg = (SetAsArray) set;
22          if (universeSize != arg.universeSize)
23              throw new IllegalArgumentException (
24                  "mismatched sets");
25          for (int item = 0; item < universeSize; ++item)
26              if (array [item] && !arg.array [item])
27                  return false;
28          return true;
29      }
30      // ...
31  }
```

```
1   public class SetAsBitVector
2       extends AbstractSet
3       implements Set
4   {
5       protected int[] vector;
6
7       protected static final int intBits = 32;
8       // ...
9   }
```

PROGRAM 12.8
SetAsBitVector class constructor, insert, withdraw, and isMember
methods

```
1   public class SetAsBitVector
2       extends AbstractSet
3       implements Set
4   {
5       protected int[] vector;
6
7       public SetAsBitVector (int n)
8       {
9           super (n);
10          vector  = new int [(n + intBits - 1) / intBits];
11          for (int i = 0; i < vector.length; ++i)
12              vector [i] = 0;
13      }
14
15      protected void insert (int item)
16      {
17          vector [item / intBits] |= 1 << item % intBits;
18      }
19
20      protected void withdraw (int item)
21      {
22          vector [item / intBits] &= ~(1 << item % intBits);
23      }
24
25      protected boolean isMember (int item)
26      {
27          return (vector [item / intBits] &
28              (1 << item % intBits)) != 0;
29      }
30      // ...
31  }
```

a single argument $N =$ numberOfItems, which specifies the universe and, consequently, the number of bits needed in the bit array. The constructor creates an array of ints of length $\lceil N/w \rceil$, where $w =$ intBits is the number of bits in an int, and sets the elements of the array to zero. The running time of the constructor is $O(\lceil N/w \rceil) = O(N)$.

To insert an item into the set, we need to change the appropriate bit in the array of bits to one. The ith bit of the bit array is bit $i \bmod w$ of word $\lfloor i/w \rfloor$. Thus, the insert method is implemented using a *bitwise or* operation to change the ith bit to one as shown in Program 12.8. Even though it is slightly more complicated than the corresponding operation for the `SetAsArray` class, the running time for this operation is still $O(1)$. Since $w = $ `intBits` is a power of two, it is possible to replace the division and modulo operations, `/` and `%`, with shifts and masks like this:

```
vector [item >> shift] |= 1 << (item & mask);
```

for a suitable definition of the constants `shift` and `mask`. Depending on the compiler and machine architecture, doing so may improve the performance of the `insert` operation by a constant factor. Of course, its asymptotic performance is still $O(1)$.

To withdraw an item from the set, we need to clear the appropriate bit in the array of bits, and to test whether an item is a member of the set, we test the corresponding bit. The `isMember` and `withdraw` methods in Program 12.8 show how this can be done. Like `insert`, both these methods have constant worst-case running times.

Union, Intersection, and Difference

The implementations of the union, intersection, and difference methods for operands of type `SetAsBitVector` are shown in Program 12.9. The code is quite similar to that for the `SetAsArray` class given in Program 12.5. Instead of using the boolean operators `&&`, `||`, and `!`, we have used the bitwise operators `&`, `|`, and `~`. By using the bitwise operators, $w = $ `intBits` bits of the result are computed in each iteration of the loop. Therefore, the number of iterations required is $\lceil N/w \rceil$ instead of N. The worst-case running time of each of these operations is $O(\lceil N/w \rceil) = O(N)$.

Notice that the asymptotic performance of these `SetAsBitVector` class operations is the same as the asymptotic performance of the `SetAsArray` class operations. That is, both of them are $O(N)$. Nevertheless, the `SetAsBitVector` class operations are faster. In fact, the bit-vector approach is asymptotically faster than the array approach by the factor w.

12.3 Multisets

A *multiset* is a set in which an item may appear more than once. That is, whereas duplicates are not permitted in a regular set, they are permitted in a multiset. Multisets are also known simply as *bags*.

Sets and multisets are in other respects quite similar: Both support operations to insert and withdraw items; both provide a means to test the membership of a given item; and both support the basic set operations of union, intersection, and difference. As a result, the `Multiset` interface is essentially the same as the `Set` interface as shown in Program 12.10.

12.3.1 Array Implementation

A regular set may contain either zero or one instance of a particular item. As shown in the preceding section, if the number of possible items is not excessive, we may use an

PROGRAM 12.9
SetAsBitVector class union, intersection, and difference methods

```
1    public class SetAsBitVector
2        extends AbstractSet
3        implements Set
4    {
5        protected int[] vector;
6
7        public Set union (Set set)
8        {
9            SetAsBitVector arg = (SetAsBitVector) set;
10           if (universeSize != arg.universeSize)
11               throw new IllegalArgumentException (
12                   "mismatched sets");
13           SetAsBitVector result = new SetAsBitVector(universeSize);
14           for (int i = 0; i < vector.length; ++i)
15               result.vector [i] = vector [i] | arg.vector [i];
16           return result;
17       }
18
19       public Set intersection (Set set)
20       {
21           SetAsBitVector arg = (SetAsBitVector) set;
22           if (universeSize != arg.universeSize)
23               throw new IllegalArgumentException (
24                   "mismatched sets");
25           SetAsBitVector result = new SetAsBitVector(universeSize);
26           for (int i = 0; i < vector.length; ++i)
27               result.vector [i] = vector [i] & arg.vector [i];
28           return result;
29       }
30
31       public Set difference (Set set)
32       {
33           SetAsBitVector arg = (SetAsBitVector) set;
34           if (universeSize != arg.universeSize)
35               throw new IllegalArgumentException (
36                   "mismatched sets");
37           SetAsBitVector result = new SetAsBitVector(universeSize);
38           for (int i = 0; i < vector.length; ++i)
39               result.vector [i] = vector [i] & ~arg.vector [i];
40           return result;
41       }
42       // ...
43   }
```

PROGRAM 12.10
`Multiset` interface

```
1   public interface Multiset
2       extends SearchableContainer
3   {
4       Multiset union (Multiset set);
5       Multiset intersection (Multiset set);
6       Multiset difference (Multiset set);
7       boolean isEQ (Multiset set);
8       boolean isSubset (Multiset set);
9   }
```

PROGRAM 12.11
`MultisetAsArray` class

```
1   public class MultisetAsArray
2       extends AbstractSet
3       implements Multiset
4   {
5       protected int[] array;
6
7       // ...
8   }
```

---

array of `boolean` variables to keep track of the number of instances of a particular item in a regular set. The natural extension of this idea for a multiset is to keep a separate count of the number of instances of each item in the multiset.

Program 12.11 introduces the `MultisetAsArray` class. The `MultisetAsArray` class extends the `AbstractSet` class defined in Program 12.2 and it implements the `Multiset` interface defined in Program 12.10. The multiset is implemented using an array of $N =$ `numberOfItems` counters. Each counter is an `int` in this case.

Basic Operations

Program 12.12 defines the constructor for the `MultisetAsArray` class as well as the three basic operations—`insert`, `isMember`, and `withdraw`. The constructor takes a single argument, $N =$ `numberOfItems`, and initializes an array of length N counters all to zero. The running time of the constructor is $O(N)$.

PROGRAM 12.12
`MultisetAsArray` class constructor, `insert`, `withdraw`,
and `isMember` methods

```
1   public class MultisetAsArray
2       extends AbstractSet
3       implements Multiset
4   {
5       protected int[] array;
6
7       public MultisetAsArray (int n)
8       {
9           super (n);
10          array = new int[universeSize];
11          for (int item = 0; item < universeSize; ++item)
12              array [item] = 0;
13      }
14
15      protected void insert (int item)
16          { ++array [item]; }
17
18      protected void withdraw (int item)
19      {
20          if (array [item] > 0)
21              --array [item];
22      }
23
24      protected boolean isMember (int item)
25          { return array [item] > 0; }
26      // ...
27  }
```

To insert an item, we simply increase the appropriate counter; to delete an item, we decrease the counter; and to test whether an item is in the set, we test whether the corresponding counter is greater than zero. In all cases the operation can be done in constant time.

Union, Intersection, and Difference

Because multisets permit duplicates but sets do not, the definitions of union, intersection, and difference are slightly modified for multisets. The *union* of multisets S and T, written $S \cup T$, is the multiset composed of all elements of S together with all elements of T. Since a multiset may contain duplicates, it does not matter whether the same element appears in S and T.

The subtle difference between union of sets and union of multisets gives rise to an interesting and useful property. If S and T are regular sets,

$$\min(|S|, |T|) \le |S \cup T| \le |S| + |T|.$$

On the other hand, if S and T are *multisets*,

$$|S \cup T| = |S| + |T|.$$

The *intersection* of sets S and T is written $S \cap T$. The elements of $S \cap T$ are those items that are elements of *both* S and T. If a given element appears more than once in S or T (or both), the intersection contains m copies of that element, where m is the smaller of the number of times the element appears in S or T. For example, if $S = \{0, 1, 1, 2, 2, 2\}$ and $T = \{1, 2, 2, 3\}$, the intersection is $S \cap T = \{1, 2, 2\}$.

The *difference* of sets S and T, written $S - T$, contains those elements of S that are *not also* elements of T. That is, the result $S - T$ is obtained by taking the set S and removing from it those elements that are also found in T.

Program 12.13 gives the implementations of the union, intersection, and difference methods of **MultisetAsArray** class. This code is quite similar to that of the **SetAsArray** class (Program 12.5) and the **SetAsBitVector** class (Program 12.8). The worst-case running time of each of these operations is $O(N)$.

Instead of using the **boolean** operators &&, ||, and !, we have used + (integer addition), **Math.min** and – (integer subtraction). The following table summarizes the operators used in the various set and multiset implementations.

Operation	SetAsArray	SetAsBitVector	MultisetAsArray
		Class	
union	||	|	+
intersection	&&	&	Math.min
difference	&& and !	& and ~	<= and –

12.3.2 Linked-List Implementation

The array implementation of multisets is really only practical if the number of items in the universe, $N = |U|$, is not too large. If N is large, then it is impractical, or at least extremely inefficient, to use an array of N counters to represent the multiset. This is especially so if the number of elements in the multisets is significantly less than N.

If we use a linked list of elements to represent a multiset S, the space required is proportional to the size of the multiset, $|S|$. When the size of the multiset is significantly less than the size of the universe, $|S| \ll |U|$, it is more efficient in terms of both time and space to use a linked list.

PROGRAM 12.13
MultisetAsArray class union, intersection, and difference methods

```
1   public class MultisetAsArray
2       extends AbstractSet
3       implements Multiset
4   {
5       protected int[] array;
6
7       public Multiset union (Multiset set)
8       {
9           MultisetAsArray arg = (MultisetAsArray) set;
10          if (universeSize != arg.universeSize)
11              throw new IllegalArgumentException (
12                  "mismatched sets");
13          MultisetAsArray result =
14              new MultisetAsArray (universeSize);
15          for (int i = 0; i < universeSize; ++i)
16              result.array [i] = array [i] + arg.array [i];
17          return result;
18      }
19
20      public Multiset intersection (Multiset set)
21      {
22          MultisetAsArray arg = (MultisetAsArray) set;
23          if (universeSize != arg.universeSize)
24              throw new IllegalArgumentException (
25                  "mismatched sets");
26          MultisetAsArray result =
27              new MultisetAsArray (universeSize);
28          for (int i = 0; i < universeSize; ++i)
29              result.array [i] = Math.min (
30                  array [i], arg.array [i]);
31          return result;
32      }
33
34      public Multiset difference (Multiset set)
35      {   MultisetAsArray arg = (MultisetAsArray) set;
36          if (universeSize != arg.universeSize)
37              throw new IllegalArgumentException (
38                  "mismatched sets");
39          MultisetAsArray result =
40              new MultisetAsArray (universeSize);
41          for (int i = 0; i < universeSize; ++i)
42              if (arg.array [i] <= array [i])
43                  result.array [i] = array [i] - arg.array [i];
44          return result;
45      }
46      // ...
47  }
```

PROGRAM 12.14
`MultisetAsLinkedList` fields

```
1   public class MultisetAsLinkedList
2        extends AbstractSet
3        implements Multiset
4   {
5        protected LinkedList list;
6
7        // ...
8   }
```

Program 12.14 introduces the `MultisetAsLinkedList` class. The `Multiset-AsLinkedList` extends the `AbstractSet` class defined in Program 12.2 and it implements the `Multiset` interface defined in Program 12.10. In this case a linked list of `Int`s is used to record the contents of the multiset.

How should the elements of the multiset be stored in the list? Perhaps the simplest way is to store the elements in the list in no particular order. Doing so makes the `insert` operation efficient—it can be done in constant time. Furthermore, the `isMember` and `withdraw` operations both take $O(n)$ time, where n is the number of items in the multiset, *regardless of the order of the items in the linked list*.

Consider now the union, intersection, and difference of two multisets, say S and T. If the linked list is unordered, the worst-case running time for the union operation is $O(m + n)$, where $m = |S|$ and $n = |T|$. Unfortunately, intersection, and difference are both $O(mn)$.

If, on the other hand, we use a *sorted* linked list, union, intersection, and difference can all be done in $O(m + n)$ time. The trade-off is that the insertion becomes an $O(n)$ operation rather than a $O(1)$. The `MultisetAsLinkedList` implementation presented in this section records the elements of the multiset in a *sorted* linked list.

Union

The union operation for `MultisetAsLinkedList` class requires the merging of two sorted, linked lists as shown in Program 12.15. We have assumed that the smallest element contained in a multiset is found at the head of the linked list and the largest is at the tail.

The `union` method computes its result as follows: The main loop of the program (lines 17–30) traverses the linked lists of the two operands, in each iteration appending the smallest remaining element to the result. Once one of the lists has been exhausted, the remaining elements in the other list are simply appended to the result (lines 31–34). The total running time for the `union` method is $O(m + n)$, where $m = |$`this`$|$ and $n = |$`set`$|$.

Intersection

The implementation of the intersection operator for the `MultisetAsLinkedList` class is similar to that of union. However, instead of merging two sorted, linked lists to construct a third, we compare the elements of two lists and append an item to the

PROGRAM 12.15
MultisetAsLinkedList class union method

```
1   public class MultisetAsLinkedList
2       extends AbstractSet
3       implements Multiset
4   {
5       protected LinkedList list;
6
7       public Multiset union (Multiset set)
8       {
9           MultisetAsLinkedList arg = (MultisetAsLinkedList) set;
10          if (universeSize != arg.universeSize)
11              throw new IllegalArgumentException (
12                  "mismatched sets");
13          MultisetAsLinkedList result =
14              new MultisetAsLinkedList (universeSize);
15          LinkedList.Element p = list.getHead ();
16          LinkedList.Element q = arg.list.getHead ();
17          while (p != null && q != null)
18          {
19              if (((Int) p.getDatum ()).isLE (
20                  (Int) q.getDatum ()))
21              {
22                  result.list.append (p.getDatum ());
23                  p = p.getNext ();
24              }
25              else
26              {
27                  result.list.append (q.getDatum ());
28                  q = q.getNext ();
29              }
30          }
31          for ( ; p != null; p = p.getNext ())
32              result.list.append (p.getDatum ());
33          for ( ; q != null; q = q.getNext ())
34              result.list.append (q.getDatum ());
35          return result;
36      }
37      // ...
38  }
```

PROGRAM 12.16
MultisetAsLinkedList class intersection method

```
 1  public class MultisetAsLinkedList
 2      extends AbstractSet
 3      implements Multiset
 4  {
 5      protected LinkedList list;
 6
 7      public Multiset intersection (Multiset set)
 8      {
 9          MultisetAsLinkedList arg = (MultisetAsLinkedList) set;
10          if (universeSize != arg.universeSize)
11              throw new IllegalArgumentException (
12                  "mismatched sets");
13          MultisetAsLinkedList result =
14              new MultisetAsLinkedList (universeSize);
15          LinkedList.Element p = list.getHead ();
16          LinkedList.Element q = arg.list.getHead ();
17          while (p != null && q != null)
18          {
19              int diff = ((Int) p.getDatum ()).compare (
20                  (Int) q.getDatum ());
21              if (diff == 0)
22                  result.list.append (p.getDatum ());
23              if (diff <= 0)
24                  p = p.getNext ();
25              if (diff >= 0)
26                  q = q.getNext ();
27          }
28          return result;
29      }
30      // ...
31  }
```

third only when it appears in both of the input lists. The **intersection** method is shown in Program 12.16.

The main loop of the program traverses the linked lists of both input operands at once using two variables (lines 17–27). If the next element in each list is the same, that element is appended to the result and both variables are advanced. Otherwise, only one of the variables is advanced—the one pointing to the smaller element.

The number of iterations of the main loop actually done depends on the contents of the respective linked lists. The best case occurs when both lists are identical. In this case, the number of iterations is m, where $m = |\text{this}| = |\text{set}|$. In the worst case, the number of iterations done is $m + n$. Therefore, the running time of the **intersection** method is $O(m + n)$.

12.4 Partitions

Consider the finite universal set $U = \{0, 1, \ldots, N - 1\}$. A *partition* of U is a finite set of sets $P = \{S_1, S_2, \ldots, S_p\}$ with the following properties:

1. The sets $S_1, S_2, \ldots, S_p$ are pairwise *disjoint*. That is, $S_i \cap S_j = \emptyset$ for all values of i and j such that $1 \leq i < j \leq p$.

2. The sets $S_1, S_2, \ldots, S_p$ *span* the universe U. That is,

$$\bigcup_{i=1}^{p} S_i = S_1 \cup S_2 \cup \cdots \cup S_p$$

$$= U.$$

For example, consider the universe $U = \{1, 2, 3\}$. There are exactly five partitions of U:

$$P_0 = \big\{\{1\}, \{2\}, \{3\}\big\},$$
$$P_1 = \big\{\{1\}, \{2, 3\}\big\},$$
$$P_2 = \big\{\{2\}, \{1, 3\}\big\},$$
$$P_3 = \big\{\{3\}, \{1, 2\}\big\}, \text{ and}$$
$$P_4 = \big\{\{1, 2, 3\}\big\}.$$

In general, given a universe U of size $n > 0$—that is, $|U| = n$—there are $\sum_{m=0}^{n} \{{n \atop m}\}$ partitions of U, where $\{{n \atop m}\}$ is the so-called *Stirling number of the second kind*, which denotes the number of ways to partition a set of n elements into m nonempty disjoint subsets.[1]

Applications that use partitions typically start with an initial partition and refine that partition either by joining or by splitting elements of the partition according to some application-specific criterion. The result of such a computation is the partition obtained when no more elements can be split or joined.

In this chapter we will consider only applications that begin with the initial partition of U in which each item in U is in a separate element of the partition. Thus, the initial partition consists of $|U|$ sets, each of size one (like P_0 above). Furthermore, we restrict the applications in that we only allow elements of a partition to be joined—we do not allow elements to be split.

---

[1] *Stirling numbers of the second kind* are given by the formula

$$\left\{ {n \atop m} \right\} = \begin{cases} 1 & n = 1, \\ 1 & n = m, \\ m\left\{ {n-1 \atop m} \right\} + \left\{ {n-1 \atop m-1} \right\} & \text{otherwise,} \end{cases}$$

where $n > 0$ and $1 \leq m \leq n$.

The two operations to be performed on partitions are:

Find Given an item in the universe, say $i \in U$, find the element of the partition that contains i. That is, find $S_j \in P$ such that $i \in S_j$.

Join Given two distinct elements of a partition P, say $S_i \in P$ and $S_j \in P$ such that $i \neq j$, create a new partition P' by removing the two elements S_i and S_j from P and replacing them with a single element $S_i \cup S_j$.

For example, consider the partition $P = \{S_1, S_2, S_3\} = \{\{1\}, \{2, 3\}, \{4\}\}$. The result of the operation *find*(3) is the set $S_2 = \{2, 3\}$ because 3 is a member of S_2. Furthermore, when we *join* sets S_1 and S_3, we get the partition $P' = \{\{1, 4\}, \{2, 3\}\}$.

Representing Partitions

Program 12.17 defines the **Partition** interface. The **Partition** interface extends the **Set** interface defined in Program 12.1. Since a partition is a set of sets, it makes sense to derive **Partition** from **Set**. The two methods, **find** and **join**, correspond to the partition operations previously described.

The elements of a partition are also sets. Consequently, the objects contained in a **Partition** also implement the **Set** interface. The **find** method of the **Partition** class expects as its argument an **int** and returns the **Set** that contains the specified item.

The **join** method takes two arguments, both of them references to **Set**s. The two arguments are expected to be distinct elements of the partition. The effect of the **join** operation is to remove the specified sets from the partition and replace them with a **Set** that represents the *union* of the two.

12.4.1 Implementing a Partition Using a Forest

A partition is a set of sets. Consequently, there are two related issues to consider when developing an approach for representing partitions:

1. How are the individual elements or parts of the partition represented?
2. How are the elements of a partition combined into the whole?

PROGRAM 12.17
Partition interface

```
1  public interface Partition
2      extends Set
3  {
4      Set find (int item);
5      void join (Set set1, Set set2);
6  }
```

FIGURE 12.3
Representing a partition as a forest.

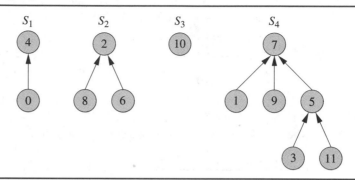

This section presents an approach in which each element of a partition is a tree. Therefore, the whole partition is a *forest*.

For example, Figure 12.3 shows how the partition

$$P = \{S_1, S_2, S_3, S_4\}$$
$$= \{\{0, 4\}, \{2, 6, 8\}, \{10\}, \{1, 3, 5, 7, 9, 11\}\}$$

can be represented using a forest. Notice that each element of the universal set $U = \{0, 1, \ldots, 11\}$ appears in exactly one node of exactly one tree.

The trees in Figure 12.3 have some very interesting characteristics. The first characteristic concerns the shapes of the trees: The nodes of the trees have arbitrary degrees. The second characteristic concerns the positions of the keys: There are no constraints on the positions of the keys in a tree. The final characteristic has to do with the way the tree is represented: Instead of pointing to its children, each node of the tree points to its parent!

Since there is no particular order to the nodes in the trees, it is necessary to keep track of the position of each node explicitly. Figure 12.4 shows how this can be done using an array. (This figure shows the same partition as in Figure 12.3.) The array contains a node for each element of the universal set U. Specifically, the ith array element holds the node that contains item i. Having found the desired node, we can follow the chain of parent pointers to find the root of the corresponding tree.

Implementation

Program 12.18 declares two classes—**PartitionAsForest** and the inner class **PartitionTree**. The latter is used to represent the individual elements or parts of a partition and the former encapsulates all of the parts that make up a given partition.

The **PartitionTree** class extends the **AbstractSet** class defined in Program 12.2 and it implements the **Tree** interface defined in Program 9.1. Since we are representing the parts of a partition using trees, it makes sense that they implement the **Tree** interface. On the other hand, since a partition is a set of sets, we must derive the parts of a partition from the **AbstractSet** class.

FIGURE 12.4
Finding the elements of a partition.

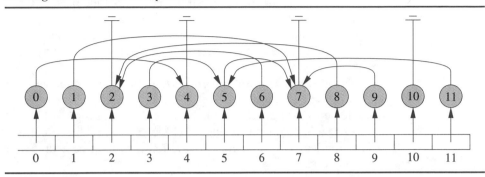

PROGRAM 12.18
`PartitionAsForest` and `PartitionTree` fields

```
1   public class PartitionAsForest
2       extends AbstractSet
3       implements Partition
4   {
5       protected PartitionTree[] array;
6
7       protected class PartitionTree
8           extends AbstractSet
9           implements Set, Tree
10      {
11          protected int item;
12          protected PartitionTree parent;
13          protected int rank;
14
15          public PartitionTree (int item)
16          {
17              super (PartitionAsForest.this.universeSize);
18              this.item = item;
19              parent = null;
20              rank = 0;
21              count = 1;
22          }
23          // ...
24      }
25      // ...
26  }
```

The **PartitionTree** class has three fields—**item**, **parent**, and **rank**. Each instance of this class represents one node of a tree. The **parent** field refers to the parent of a given node and the **item** field records the element of the universal set that the given node represents. The remaining variable, **rank**, is optional. Although it is not required in order to provide the basic functionality, as shown below, the **rank** variable can be used in the implementation of the **join** operation to improve the performance of subsequent **find** operations.

The **PartitionAsForest** class represents a complete partition. The **PartitionAsForest** class extends the **AbstractSet** class defined in Program 12.2 and it implements the **Partition** interface defined in Program 12.17. The **PartitionAsForest** class contains a single field, **array**, which is an array **PartitionTree**s. The *i*th element of the array always refers to the tree node that contains element *i* of the universe.

Constructor

Program 12.18 gives the code for the **PartitionTree** constructor. The constructor creates a tree comprised of a single node. It takes an argument that specifies the element of the universal set that the node is to represent. The **parent** field is set to **null** to indicate that the node has no parent. Consequently, the node is a root node. Finally, the **rank** field is initialized to zero. The running time of the constructor is $O(1)$.

Program 12.19 shows the constructor for the **PartitionAsForest** class. The constructor takes a single argument N, which specifies that the universe will be $U = \{0, 1, \ldots, N-1\}$. It creates an initial partition of the universe consisting of N parts. Each part contains one element of the universal set and, therefore, comprises a one-node tree.

PROGRAM 12.19
PartitionAsForest constructors

```
1   public class PartitionAsForest
2       extends AbstractSet
3       implements Partition
4   {
5       protected PartitionTree[] array;
6
7       public PartitionAsForest (int n)
8       {
9           super (n);
10          array = new PartitionTree [universeSize];
11          for (int item = 0; item < universeSize; ++item)
12              array [item] = new PartitionTree (item);
13          count = universeSize;
14      }
15      // ...
16  }
```

---

find and join Methods

Two elements of the universe are in the same part of the partition if and only if they share the same root node. Since every tree has a unique root, it makes sense to use the root node as the "handle" for that tree. Therefore, the *find* operation takes an element of the universal set and returns the root node of the tree that contains that element. And because of way in which the trees are represented, we can follow the chain of parent pointers to find the root node.

Program 12.20 gives the code for the find method of the **PartitionAsForest** class. The find method takes as its argument an int and returns a Set. The argument specifies the item of the universe that is the object of the search.

The find operation begins at the node array[item] and follows the chain of parent fields to find the root node of the tree that contains the specified item. The result of the method is the root node.

The running time of the find operation is $O(d)$, where d is the depth in the tree of the node from which the search begins. If we don't do anything special to prevent it, the worst-case running time is $O(N)$, where N is the size of the universe. The best performance is achieved when every non-root node points to the root node. In this case, the running time is $O(1)$.

Another advantage of having the parent field in each node is that the *join* operation can be implemented easily and efficiently. For example, suppose we wish to *join* the two sets S_1 and S_2 shown in Figure 12.3. Although there are many possible representations for $S_1 \cup S_2$, it turns out that there are two simple alternatives that can be obtained in constant time. These are shown in Figure 12.5. In the first alternative, the root of S_2 is made a child of the root of S_1. This can be done in constant time simply by making the parent field of the root of S_2 refer to the root of S_1. The second alternative is essentially the same as the first except the roles of S_1 and S_2 are exchanged.

PROGRAM 12.20
PartitionAsForest class find method

```
1   public class PartitionAsForest
2       extends AbstractSet
3       implements Partition
4   {
5       protected PartitionTree[] array;
6
7       public Set find (int item)
8       {
9           PartitionTree ptr = array [item];
10          while (ptr.parent != null)
11              ptr = ptr.parent;
12          return ptr;
13      }
14      // ...
15  }
```

FIGURE 12.5
Alternatives for joining elements of a partition.

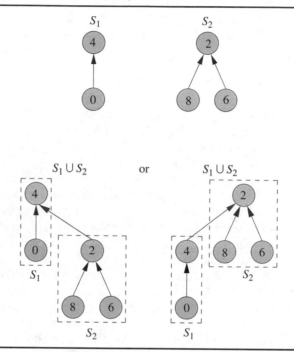

Program 12.21 gives the simplest possible implementation for the **join** operation. The **join** method of the **PartitionAsForest** class takes two arguments—both of them references to **Set**s. Both arguments are required to be references to distinct **PartitionTree** instances that are contained in the given partition. Furthermore, both of them are required to be root nodes. Therefore, the sets that the arguments represent are *disjoint*. The method **checkArguments** makes sure that the arguments satisfy these conditions.

The **join** operation is trivial and executes in constant time: It simply makes one node the parent of the other. In this case, we have arbitrarily chosen that the node specified by the first argument will always become the parent.

12.4.2   Collapsing Find

Unfortunately, using the **join** algorithm given in Program 12.21 can result in particularly bad trees. For example, Figure 12.6 shows the worst possible tree that can be obtained. Such a tree is bad because its height is $O(N)$. In such a tree both the worst-case and the average-case running time for the **find** operation is $O(N)$.

There is an interesting trick we can play that can improve matters significantly. Recall that the find operation starts from a given node and locates the root of the tree

PROGRAM 12.21
PartitionAsForest class simple join method

```
1   public class PartitionAsForest
2       extends AbstractSet
3       implements Partition
4   {
5       protected PartitionTree[] array;
6
7       protected void checkArguments (
8           PartitionTree s, PartitionTree t)
9       {
10          if (!isMember (s) || s.parent != null ||
11              !isMember (t) || t.parent != null || s == t)
12              throw new IllegalArgumentException (
13                  "incompatible sets");
14      }
15
16      public void join (Set s, Set t)
17      {
18          PartitionTree p = (PartitionTree) s;
19          PartitionTree q = (PartitionTree) t;
20          checkArguments (p, q);
21          q.parent = p;
22          --count;
23      }
24      // ...
25  }
```

containing that node. If, having found the root, we replace the parent of the given node with the root, the next time we do a find it will be more efficient.

In fact, we can go one step further and replace the parent of every node along the search path to the root. This is called a *collapsing find* operation. Doing so does not change the asymptotic complexity of the find operation. However, a subsequent find operation that begins at any point along the search path to the root will run in constant time!

Program 12.22 gives the code for a collapsing version of the find operation. The find method first determines the root node as before. Then, a second pass is made up the chain from the initial node to the root, during which the parent of each node is assigned the root. Clearly, this version of find is slower than the one given in Program 12.20 because it makes two passes up the chain rather than one. However, the running time of this version of find is still $O(d)$, where d is the depth of the node from which the search begins.

Figure 12.7 illustrates the effect of a collapsing find operation. After the find, all nodes along the search path are attached directly to the root. That is, they have had

FIGURE 12.6
A degenerate tree.

PROGRAM 12.22
`PartitionAsForest` class collapsing `find` method

```
public class PartitionAsForestV2
    extends PartitionAsForest
{
    public Set find (int item)
    {
        PartitionTree root = array [item];
        while (root.parent != null)
            root = root.parent;
        PartitionTree ptr = array [item];
        while (ptr.parent != null)
        {
            PartitionTree tmp = ptr.parent;
            ptr.parent = root;
            ptr = tmp;
        }
        return root;
    }
    // ...
}
```

FIGURE 12.7
Example of collapsing find.

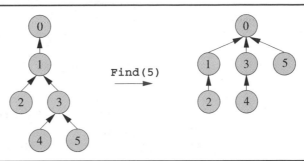

their depths decreased to one. As a side-effect, any node that is in the subtree of a node along the search path may have its depth decreased by the collapsing find operation. The depth of a node is never increased by the find operation. Eventually, if we do enough collapsing find operations, it is possible to obtain a tree of height one in which all the non-root nodes point directly at the root.

12.4.3 Union by Size

Although using collapsing find does mitigate the negative effects of poor trees, a better approach is to avoid creating bad trees in the first place. As shown in Figure 12.5, when we join to trees we have a choice—which node we should choose to be the root of the new tree. A simple but effective choice is to attach the smaller tree under the root of the larger one. In this case, the smaller tree is the one that has fewer nodes. This is the so-called *union-by-size* join algorithm. Program 12.23 shows how this can be done.

The implementation uses the `count` field of the `Container` class, from which `PartitionTree` is derived, to keep track of the number of items contained in the tree. (Since each node contains one item from the universal set, the number of items contained in a tree is equal to the number of nodes in that tree.) The algorithm simply selects the tree with the largest number of nodes to become the root of the result and attaches the root of the smaller tree under that of the larger one. Clearly, the running time of the union-by-size version of `join` is $O(1)$.

The following theorem shows that when using the union-by-size join operation, the heights of the resulting trees grow logarithmically.

Theorem 12.1
Consider an initial partition P of the universe $U = \{0, 1, \ldots, N - 1\}$ composed of N sets of size 1. Let S be an element of the partition obtained from P after some sequence of union-by-size join operations, such that $|S| = n$ for some $n \geq 1$. Let T be the tree representing the set S. The height of tree T satisfies the inequality

$$h \leq \lfloor \log_2 n \rfloor.$$

PROGRAM 12.23
PartitionAsForest class union-by-size `join` method

```
1   public class PartitionAsForestV2
2       extends PartitionAsForest
3   {
4       public void join (Set s, Set t)
5       {
6           PartitionTree p = (PartitionTree) s;
7           PartitionTree q = (PartitionTree) t;
8           checkArguments (p, q);
9           if (p.getCount () > q.getCount ())
10          {
11              q.parent = p;
12              p.setCount (p.getCount () + q.getCount ());
13          }
14          else
15          {
16              p.parent = q;
17              q.setCount (p.getCount () + q.getCount ());
18          }
19          --count;
20      }
21      // ...
22  }
```

Proof (By induction).

Base Case Since a tree composed of a single node has height zero, the theorem clearly holds for $n = 1$.

Inductive Hypothesis Suppose the theorem holds for trees containing n nodes for $n = 1, 2, \ldots, k$ for some $k \geq 1$. Consider a union-by-size join operation that produces a tree containing $k + 1$ nodes. Such a tree is obtained by joining a tree T_l having $l \leq k$ nodes with another tree T_m that has $m \leq k$ nodes, such that $l + m = k + 1$.

Without loss of generality, suppose $1 \leq l \leq (k + 1)/2$. As a result, l is less than or equal to m. Therefore, the union-by-size algorithm will attach T_l under the root of T_m. Let h_l and h_m be the heights of T_l and T_r respectively. The height of the resulting tree is $\max(h_l + 1, h_m)$. According to the inductive hypothesis, the height of T_m is given by

$$
\begin{aligned}
h_m &\leq \lfloor \log_2 m \rfloor \\
&\leq \lfloor \log_2(k + 1 - l) \rfloor \\
&\leq \lfloor \log_2(k + 1) \rfloor.
\end{aligned}
$$

Similarly, the quantity $h_l + 1$ is bounded by

$$h_l + 1 \leq \lfloor \log_2 l \rfloor + 1$$

$$\leq \lfloor \log_2((k+1)/2) \rfloor + 1$$

$$\leq \lfloor \log_2(k+1) \rfloor.$$

Therefore, the height of the tree containing $k + 1$ nodes is no greater than $\max(h_l + 1, h_m) = \lfloor \log_2(k+1) \rfloor$. By induction on k, the theorem holds for all values of $n \geq 1$.

Note that Theorem 12.1 and its proof does not require that we use the collapsing find algorithm of Section 12.4.2. That is, the height of a tree containing n nodes is guaranteed to be $O(\log n)$ when the simple find is used. Of course, there is nothing precluding the use of the collapsing find in conjunction with the union-by-size join method. And doing so only makes things better.

12.4.4 Union by Height or Rank

The union-by-size join algorithm just described controls the heights of the trees indirectly by basing the join algorithm on the sizes of the trees. If we explicitly keep track of the height of a node in the node itself, we can accomplish the same thing.

Program 12.24 gives an implementation of the `join` method that always attaches the shorter tree under the root of the taller one. This method assumes that the **rank** field is used to keep track of the height of a node. (The reason for calling it **rank** rather than **height** will become evident shortly.)

The only time the height of node increases is when joining two trees that have the same height. In this case, the height of the root increases by exactly one. If the two trees being joined have different heights, attaching the shorter tree under the root of the taller one has no effect on the height of the root.

Unfortunately, there is a slight complication if we combine union-by-height with the collapsing find. Since the collapsing find works by moving nodes closer to the root, it affects potentially the height of any node moved. It is not at all clear how to recompute efficiently the heights that have changed. The solution is not to do it at all!

If we don't recompute the heights during the collapsing find operations, then the height fields will no longer be exact. Nevertheless, the quantities remain useful estimates of the heights of nodes. We call the estimated height of a node its *rank*, and the join algorithm, which uses rank instead of height, is called *union by rank*.

Fortunately, Theorem 12.1 applies equally well when when union-by-rank is used. That is, the height of a tree that contains n nodes is $O(\log n)$. Thus, the worst-case running time for the **find** operation grows logarithmically with n. And as before, collapsing find only makes things better.

PROGRAM 12.24
`PartitionAsForest` class union-by-rank `join` method

```
1   public class PartitionAsForestV3
2       extends PartitionAsForestV2
3   {
4       public void join (Set s, Set t)
5       {
6           PartitionTree p = (PartitionTree) s;
7           PartitionTree q = (PartitionTree) t;
8           checkArguments (p, q);
9           if (p.rank > q.rank)
10              q.parent = p;
11          else
12          {
13              p.parent = q;
14              if (p.rank == q.rank)
15                  q.rank += 1;
16          }
17          --count;
18      }
19      // ...
20  }
```

12.5 Applications

One of the most important applications of partitions involves the processing of equivalence relations. Equivalence relations arise in many interesting contexts. For example, two nodes in an electric circuit are electrically equivalent if there is a conducting path (a wire) connecting the two nodes. In effect, the wires establish an electrical equivalence relation over the nodes of a circuit.

A similar relation arises among the classes in a Java program. Consider the following Java code fragment:

```
interface I {}
class A implements I {}
class B implements I {}
class C extends A {}
class D extends B {}
```

The three classes **A**, **B**, **C**, and **D** are equivalent in the sense that they all implement the same interface **I**. In effect, the class declarations establish an equivalence relation over the classes in a Java program.

Definition 12.1(Equivalence Relation)

An equivalence relation *over a universal set U is a relation $\equiv$ with the following properties:*

1. *The relation $\equiv$ is* reflexive. *That is, for every $x \in U$, $x \equiv x$.*
2. *The relation $\equiv$ is* symmetric. *That is, for every pair $x \in U$ and $y \in U$, if $x \equiv y$ then $y \equiv x$.*
3. *The relation $\equiv$ is* transitive. *That is, for every triple $x \in U$, $y \in U$, and $z \in U$, if $x \equiv y$ and $y \equiv z$ then $x \equiv z$.*

An important characteristic of an equivalence relation is that it partitions the elements of the universal set U into a set of *equivalence classes*. That is, U is partitioned into $P = \{S_1, S_2, \ldots, S_p\}$, such that for every pair $x \in U$ and $y \in U$, $x \equiv y$ if and only if x and y are in the same element of the partition. That is, $x \equiv y$ if there exists a value of i such that $x \in S_i \wedge y \in S_i$.

For example, consider the universe $U = \{0, 1, \ldots, 9\}$, and the equivalence relation $\equiv$ defined over U defined as follows:

$$0 \equiv 0, 1 \equiv 1, 1 \equiv 2, 2 \equiv 2, 3 \equiv 3, 3 \equiv 4, 3 \equiv 5, 4 \equiv 4, 4 \equiv 5, 5 \equiv 5,$$
$$6 \equiv 6, 6 \equiv 7, 6 \equiv 8, 6 \equiv 9, 7 \equiv 7, 7 \equiv 8, 7 \equiv 9, 8 \equiv 8, 8 \equiv 9, 9 \equiv 9. \quad (12.1)$$

This relation results in the following partition of U:

$$\{ \{0\}, \{1, 2\}, \{3, 4, 5\}, \{6, 7, 8, 9\} \} .$$

The list of equivalences in Equation 12.1 contains many redundancies. Since we know that the relation $\equiv$ is reflexive, symmetric, and transitive, it is possible to infer the complete relation from the following list:

$$1 \equiv 2, 3 \equiv 4, 3 \equiv 5, 6 \equiv 7, 6 \equiv 8, 6 \equiv 9.$$

The problem of finding the set of equivalence classes from a list of equivalence pairs is easily solved using a partition. Program 12.25 shows how it can be done using the `PartitionAsForest` class defined in Section 12.4.1.

The algorithm first gets a positive integer **n** from the input and creates a partition, **p**, of the universe $U = \{0, 1, \ldots, n-1\}$ (lines 7–12). As explained in Section 12.4.1, the initial partition comprises **n** disjoint sets of size one. That is, each element of the universal set is in a separate element of the partition.

Each iteration of the main loop processes one equivalence pair (lines 18–23). An equivalence pair consists of two numbers, **i** and **j**, such that $i \in U$ and $j \in U$. The *find* operation is used to determine the sets **s** and **t** in partition **p** that contain elements **i** and **j**, respectively (lines 24–25).

If **s** and **t** are not the same set, then the disjoint sets are united using the *join* operation (lines 26–27). Otherwise, **i** and **j** are already in the same set and the equivalence pair is redundant (line 29). After all of the pairs have been processed, the final partition is printed (line 31).

PROGRAM 12.25
Application of disjoint sets—finding equivalence classes

```
1   public class Algorithms
2   {
3       public static void equivalenceClasses (
4           Reader in, PrintWriter out)
5           throws IOException
6       {
7           StreamTokenizer tin = new StreamTokenizer (in);
8           tin.parseNumbers ();
9           if (tin.nextToken () != StreamTokenizer.TT_NUMBER)
10              throw new DomainException ("invalid input");
11          int n = (int) tin.nval;
12          partition p = new PartitionAsForest (n);
13
14          int i;
15          int j;
16          for (;;)
17          {
18              if (tin.nextToken () != StreamTokenizer.TT_NUMBER
19                  break;
20              i = (int) tin.nval;
21              if (tin.nextToken () != StreamTokenizer.TT_NUMBER
22                  break;
23              j = (int) tin.nval;
24              Set s = p.find (i);
25              Set t = p.find (j);
26              if (s !=t);
27                  p.join (s, t);
28              else
29                  out.println ("redundant pair: " + i + ", " + j);
30          }
31          out.println (p);
32      }
33  }
```

Exercises

12.1   For each of the following implementations, derive an expression for the total memory space required to represent a set that contains n elements drawn from the universe $U = \{0, 1, \ldots, N - 1\}$.

    a. `SetAsArray` (Program 12.3)

    b. `SetAsBitVector` (Program 12.7)

    c. `MultisetAsArray` (Program 12.11)

    d. `MultisetAsLinkedList` (Program 12.14)

12.2 In addition to $=$ and $\subseteq$, a complete repertoire of set operators includes $\subset$, $\supset$, $\supseteq$, and $\neq$. For each of the set implementations listed in Exercise 12.1, show how to implement the remaining operators.

12.3 The *symmetric difference* of two sets S and T, written $S\Delta T$, is given by

$$S\Delta T = (S \cup T) - (S \cap T).$$

For each of the set implementations listed in Exercise 12.1, devise an algorithm to compute symmetric difference. What is the running time of your algorithm?

12.4 The *complement* of a set S over universe U, written S', is given by

$$S' = U - S.$$

Devise an algorithm to compute the complement of a set represented as a bit vector. What is the running time of your algorithm?

12.5 Devise an algorithm to sort a list of integers using a multiset. What is the running time of your algorithm? **Hint**: See Section 15.8.1.

12.6 Consider a multiset implemented using linked lists. When the multiset contains duplicate items, each of those items occupies a separate list element. An alternative is to use a linked list of ordered pairs of the form (i, n_i), where i is an element of the universal set U and n_i is a non-negative integer that counts the number of instances of the element i in the multiset.

Derive an expression for the total memory space required to represent a multiset that contains n instances of m distinct elements drawn from the universe $U = \{0, 1, \ldots, N - 1\}$.

12.7 Consider a multiset implemented as described in Exercise 12.6. Devise algorithms for set union, intersection, and difference. What are the running times of your algorithms?

12.8 Consider the initial partition $P = \{\{0\}, \{1\}, \{2\}, \ldots, \{9\}\}$. For each of the methods of computing the union listed in **a** through **d**, show the result of the following sequence *join* operations: $join(0, 1)$, $join(2, 3)$, $join(2, 4)$, $join(2, 5)$, $join(6, 7)$, $join(8, 9)$, $join(6, 8)$, $join(0, 6)$, $join(0, 2)$.

  a. simple union
  b. union by size
  c. union by height
  d. union by rank

12.9 For each final partition obtained in Exercise 12.8, show the result of performing a *collapsing find* operation for item 9.

12.10 Consider the initial partition P of the universe $U = \{0, 1, \ldots, N-1\}$ composed of N sets [22].

  a. Show that $N - 1$ join operations can be performed before the number of elements in the partition is reduced to one.

b. Show that if n join operations are done $(0 \leq n < N)$, the size of the largest element of the partition is at most $n + 1$.

c. A *singleton* is an element of a partition that contains only one element of the universal set. Show that when n join operations are done $(0 \leq n < N)$, at least $\max \{N - 2n, 0\}$ singletons are left.

d. Show that if less than $\lceil N/2 \rceil$ join operations are done, at least one singleton is left.

Programming Projects

12.1 Complete the **SetAsArray** class introduced in Program 12.3 by providing suitable definitions for the following methods: **purge, isEmpty, isFull, getCount, accept**, and **getEnumeration**. Write a test program and test your implementation.

12.2 Complete the **SetAsBitVector** class introduced in Program 12.7 by providing suitable definitions for the following methods: **purge, isEmpty, isFull, getCount, accept**, and **getEnumeration**. Write a test program and test your implementation.

12.3 Rewrite the **insert, withdraw**, and **isMember** methods of the **SetAsBitVector** implementation so that they use bitwise shift and mask operations rather than division and modulo operations. Compare the running times of the modified methods with the original ones and explain your observations.

12.4 Complete the **MultisetAsArray** class introduced in Program 12.11 by providing suitable definitions for the following methods: **purge, getCount, accept**, and **getEnumeration**. Write a test program and test your implementation.

12.5 Complete the **MultisetAsLinkedList** class introduced in Program 12.14 by providing suitable definitions for the following methods: **purge, isEmpty, isFull, getCount, compareTo, accept**, and **getEnumeration**. Write a test program and test your implementation.

12.6 Design and implement a multiset class in which the contents of the set are represented by a linked list of ordered pairs of the form (i, n_i), where i is an element of the universal set U and n_i is a non-negative integer that counts the number of instances of the element i in the multiset. (See Exercise 12.6 and 12.7.)

12.7 Write a program to compute the number of ways in which a set of n elements can be partitioned. That is, compute $\sum_{m=0}^{n} \left\{ {n \atop m} \right\}$, where

$$\left\{ {n \atop m} \right\} = \begin{cases} 1 & n = 1, \\ 1 & n = m, \\ m \left\{ {n-1 \atop m} \right\} + \left\{ {n-1 \atop m-1} \right\} & \text{otherwise.} \end{cases}$$

Hint: See Section 14.4.2.

13 | Garbage Collection and the Other Kind of Heap

A Java object is an instance of a class or an array. Every object instance in a Java program occupies some memory. The manner in which a Java object is represented in memory is left up to the implementor of the Java virtual machine and can vary from one implementation to another. However, in the typical Java virtual machine, object data occupy contiguous memory locations.

The region of memory in which objects are allocated dynamically is often called *a heap*. In Chapter 11 we considered *heaps* and *heap-ordered trees* in the context of priority queue implementations. Unfortunately, the only thing that the heaps of Chapter 11 and the heap considered here have in common is the name. Although it may be possible to use a heap (in the sense of Definition 11.1) to manage a region of memory, typical implementations do not. In this context the technical meaning of the term *heap* is closer to its dictionary definition—"a pile of many things."

The amount of memory required to represent a Java object is determined by the number and the types of its fields. For example, fields of the primitive types—`boolean`, `char`, `byte`, `short`, `int`, and `float`—typically occupy a single, 32-bit word, whereas `long` and `double` both require two words of storage. A field that refers to an object or to an interface typically requires only one word.

In addition to the memory required for the fields of an object, there is usually some fixed, constant amount of extra storage set aside in every object. This extra storage carries information used by the Java virtual machine to make sure that object is used correctly and to aid the process of garbage collection.

Every object in a Java program is created explicitly by invoking the **new** operator. Invoking the **new** operator causes the Java virtual machine to perform the following steps:

1. An unused region of memory large enough to hold an instance of the desired class is found.
2. All of the fields of the object are assigned their default initial values.

3. The appropriate constructor is run to initialize the object instance.

4. A reference to the newly created object is returned.

13.1 What Is Garbage?

Although Java provides the means to create an object, the language does not provide the means to destroy an object *explicitly*. As long as a program contains a reference to some object instance, the Java virtual machine is required to ensure that the object exists. If the Java language provided the means to destroy objects, it would be possible for a program to destroy an object even when a reference to that object still existed. This situation is unsafe because the program could attempt later to invoke a method on the destroyed object, leading to unpredictable results.

The situation that arises when a program contains a reference (or pointer) to a destroyed object is called a *dangling reference* (or dangling pointer). By disallowing the explicit destruction of objects, Java eliminates the problem of dangling references.

Languages that support the explicit destruction of objects typically require the program to keep track of all the objects it creates and destroy them explicitly when they are no longer needed. If a program somehow loses track of an object it has created then that object cannot be destroyed. And if the object is never destroyed, the memory occupied by that object cannot be used again by the program.

A program that loses track of objects before it destroys them suffers from a *memory leak*. If we run a program that has a memory leak for a very long time, it is quite possible that it will exhaust all available memory and eventually fail because no new objects can be created.

It would seem that by disallowing the explicit destruction of objects, a Java program is doomed to eventual failure due to memory exhaustion. Indeed this would be the case, were it not for the fact that the Java language specification requires the Java virtual machine to be able to find unreferenced objects and to reclaim the memory locations allocated to those objects. An unreferenced object is called *garbage* and the process of finding all unreferenced objects and reclaiming the storage is called *garbage collection*.

Just as the Java language does not specify precisely how objects are to be represented in the memory of a virtual machine, the language specification also does not stipulate how the garbage collection is to be implemented or when it should be done. Garbage collection is usually invoked when the total amount of memory allocated to a Java program exceeds some threshold. Typically, the program is suspended while the garbage collection is done.

In the analyses presented in the preceding chapters we assume that the running time of the **new** operator is a fixed constant, τ_{new}, and we completely ignore the garbage collection overhead. In reality, neither assumption is valid. Even if sufficient memory is available, the time required by the Java virtual machine to locate an unused region of memory depends very much on the data structures used to keep track of the memory regions allocated to a program as well as on the way in which a program uses the objects it creates. Furthermore, invoking the **new** operator may trigger the garbage collection process. The running time for garbage collection can be a significant fraction of the total running time of a program.

13.1.1 Reduce, Reuse, Recycle

Modern societies produce an excessive amount of waste. The costs of doing so include the direct costs of waste disposal as well as the damage to the environment caused by the manufacturing, distribution, and ultimate disposal of products. The slogan "*reduce, reuse, recycle*," prescribes three strategies for reducing the environmental costs associated with waste materials.

These strategies apply equally well to Java programs! A Java program that creates excessive garbage may require more frequent garbage collection than a program that creates less garbage. Since garbage collection can take a significant amount of time to do, it makes sense to use strategies that decrease the cost of garbage collection.

Reduce A Java program that does not create any object instances or arrays does not create garbage. Similarly, a program that creates all the objects it needs at the beginning of its execution and uses the same objects until it terminates also does not create garbage. By reducing the number of objects a program creates dynamically during its execution, we can reduce or even eliminate the need for garbage collection.

Reuse Sometimes, a Java program will create many objects that are used only once. For example, a program may create an object in the body of a loop that is used to hold "temporary" information that is only required for the particular iteration of the loop in which it is created. Consider the following:

```
for (int i = 0; i < 1000000; ++i)
{
    SomeClass obj = new SomeClass (i);
    System.out.println (obj);
}
```

This creates a million instances of the `SomeClass` class and prints them out. If the `SomeClass` class implements a `setInt` method, we can reuse an a single object instance like this:

```
SomeClass obj = new SomeClass ();
for (int i = 0; i < 1000000; ++i)
{
    obj.setInt (i);
    System.out.println (obj);
}
```

Clearly, by reusing a single object instance, we have dramatically reduced the amount of garbage produced.

Recycle Recycling of objects is a somewhat more complex strategy for reducing the overhead associated with garbage collection. Instead of leaving an unused object around for the garbage collector to find, it is put into a container of unused objects. When a new object is needed, the container is searched first to see if an unused one already exists. Because a container always refers to the objects it contains, those objects are never garbage collected.

The recycling strategy can indeed reduce garbage collection overhead. However, it puts the burden back on the programmer to explicitly put unused objects into the container (avoid memory leaks) and to make sure objects put into the container are really unused (avoid dangling references). Because the recycling strategy undermines some of the benefits of garbage collection, it should be used with great care.

13.1.2   Helping the Garbage Collector

The preceding section presents strategies for avoiding garbage collection. However, there are times when garbage collection is actually desirable. Imagine a program that requires a significant amount of memory. Suppose the amount of memory required is very close to the amount of memory available for use by the Java virtual machine. The performance of such a program is going to depend on the ability of the garbage collector to find and reclaim as much unused storage as possible. Otherwise, the garbage collector will run too often. In this case, it pays to help out the garbage collector.

How can we help out the garbage collector? Since the garbage collector collects only unreferenced objects it is necessary to eliminate all references to objects that are no longer needed. This is done by assigning the value **null** to every variable that refers to an object that is no longer needed. Consequently, helping the garbage collector requires a program to do a bit more work.

13.2   Reference Counting Garbage Collection

The difficulty in garbage collection is not the actual process of collecting the garbage—it is the problem of finding the garbage in the first place. An object is considered to be garbage when no references to that object exist. But how can we tell when no references to an object exist?

A simple expedient is to keep track in each object of the total number of references to that object. That is, we add a special field to each object called a *reference count*. The idea is that the reference count field is not accessible to the Java program. Instead, the reference count field is updated by the Java virtual machine itself.

Consider the statement

```
Object p = new Integer (57);
```

which creates a new instance of the **Integer** class. Only a single variable, **p**, refers to the object. Thus, its reference count should be one as shown in Figure 13.1 (a).

FIGURE 13.1
Objects with reference counters.

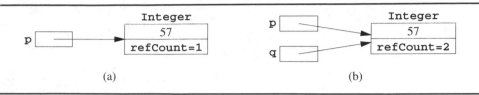

(a)   (b)

Now consider the following sequence of statements:

```
Object p = new Integer (57);
Object q = p;
```

This sequence creates a single **Integer** instance. Both **p** and **q** refer to the same object. Therefore, its reference count should be two as shown in Figure 13.1 (b).

In general, every time one reference variable is assigned to another, it may be necessary to update several reference counts. Suppose **p** and **q** are both reference variables. The assignment

```
p = q;
```

would be implemented by the Java virtual machine as follows:

```
if (p != q)
{
    if (p != null)
        --p.refCount;
    p = q;
    if (p != null)
        ++p.refCount;
}
```

For example suppose **p** and **q** are initialized as follows:

```
Object p = new Integer (57);
Object q = new Integer (99);
```

As shown in Figure 13.2 (a), two **Integer** objects are created, each with a reference count of one. Now, suppose we assign **q** to **p** using the code sequence given above. Figure 13.2 (b) shows that after the assignment, both **p** and **q** refer to the same object—its reference count is two. And the reference count on **Integer(57)** has gone to zero, which indicates that it is garbage.

FIGURE 13.2

Reference counts before and after the assignment 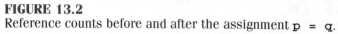.

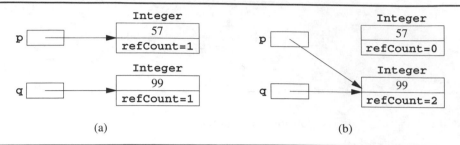

The costs of using reference counts are twofold: First, every object requires the special reference count field. Typically, this means an extra word of storage must be allocated in each object. Second, every time one reference is assigned to another, the reference counts must be adjusted as above. This increases significantly the time taken by assignment statements.

The advantage of using reference counts is that garbage is easily identified. When it becomes necessary to reclaim the storage from unused objects, the garbage collector needs only to examine the reference count fields of all objects that have been created by the program. If the reference count is zero, the object is garbage.

It is not necessary to wait until there is insufficient memory before initiating the garbage collection process. We can reclaim memory used by an object immediately when its reference goes to zero. Consider what happens if we implement the Java assignment `p = q` in the Java virtual machine as follows:

```
if (p != q)
{
    if (p != null)
        if (--p.refCount == 0)
          heap.release (p);
    p = q;
    if (p != null)
        ++p.refCount;
}
```

Notice that the **release** method is invoked immediately when the reference count of an object goes to zero, that is, when it becomes garbage. In this way, garbage may be collected incrementally as it is created.

13.2.1 When Objects Refer to Other Objects

The **Integer** objects considered in the preceding examples are very simple objects—they contain no references to other objects. Reference counting is an ideal strategy for garbage collecting such objects. But what about objects that refer to other objects? For

FIGURE 13.3
Reference counting when objects refer to other objects.

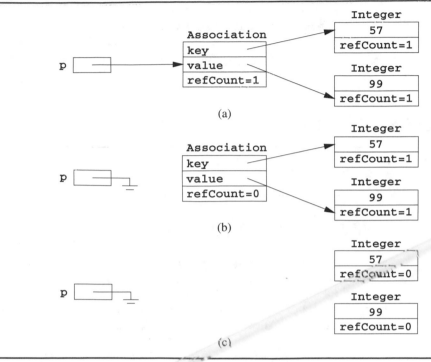

(a)

(b)

(c)

example, consider the **Association** class described in Chapter 5, which represents a (key, value) pair. We can still use reference counting, provided we count all references to an object *including references from other objects.*

Figure 13.3 (a) illustrates the contents memory following the execution of this statement:

```
Object p = new Association(
    new Integer (57), new Integer (99));
```

The reference count of the **Association** is one, because the variable **p** refers to it. Similarly, the reference counts of the two **Integer** instances are one, because the **Association** refers to both of them.

Suppose we assign the value null to the variable **p**. As shown in Figure 13.3 (b), the reference count of the association becomes zero—it is now garbage. However, the **Association** instance continues to exist until it is garbage collected. And because it still exists, it still refers to the **Integer** objects.

Figure 13.3 (c) shows that the garbage collection process adjusts the reference counts on the objects to which the association refers only when the association is garbage collected. The two **Integer** objects are now unreferenced and can be garbage collected as well.

FIGURE 13.4
Why reference counting fails.

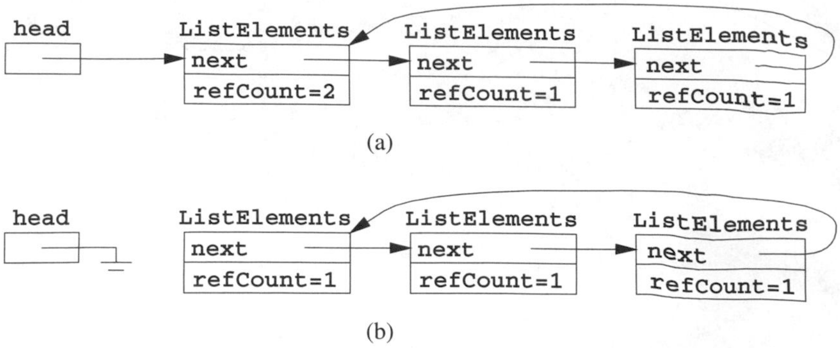

(a)

(b)

13.2.2 Why Reference Counting Does Not Work

So far, reference counting looks like a good idea. However, reference counting does not always work. Consider a circular, singly-linked list such as the one shown in Figure 13.4 (a). In the figure, the variable **head** refers to the head of the linked list and the last element of the linked list also refers to the head. Therefore, the reference count on the first list element is two, whereas the remaining list elements each have a reference count of one.

Consider what happens when we assign the value **null** to the **head** variable. This results in the situation shown in Figure 13.4 (b). The reference count on the first list element has been decreased by one because the **head** variable no longer refers to it. However, its reference count is not zero, because the tail of the list still refers to the head.

We now have a problem. The reference counts on all the list elements are non-zero. Therefore, they are not considered to be garbage by a reference-counting garbage collector. On the other hand, no external references to the linked-list elements remain. Therefore, the list elements are indeed garbage.

This example illustrates the Achilles' heel of reference counting—circular data structures. In general, reference counting will fail to work whenever the data structure contains a cycle of references. Java does not prevent the creation of cyclic structures. Therefore, reference counting by itself is not a suitable garbage collection scheme for arbitrary objects. Nevertheless, it is an extremely useful technique for dealing with simple objects that don't refer to other objects, such as **Integer**s and **String**s.

13.3 Mark-and-Sweep Garbage Collection

This section presents the *mark-and-sweep* garbage collection algorithm. The mark-and-sweep algorithm was the first garbage collection algorithm to be developed that is able to reclaim cyclic data structures.[1] Variations of the mark-and-sweep algorithm continue to be among the most commonly used garbage collection techniques.

When using mark-and-sweep, unreferenced objects are not reclaimed immediately. Instead, garbage is allowed to accumulate until all available memory has been exhausted. When that happens, the execution of the program is suspended temporarily while the mark-and-sweep algorithm collects all the garbage. Once all unreferenced objects have been reclaimed, the normal execution of the program can resume.

The mark-and-sweep algorithm is called a *tracing* garbage collector because it *traces out* the entire collection of objects that are directly or indirectly accessible by the program. The objects that a program can access directly are those objects that are referenced by local variables on the processor stack as well as by any static variables that refer to objects. In the context of garbage collection, these variables are called the *roots*. An object is indirectly accessible if it is referenced by a field in some other (directly or indirectly) accessible object. An accessible object is said to be *live*. Conversely, an object that is not *live* is garbage.

The mark-and-sweep algorithm consists of two phases: In the first phase, it finds and marks all accessible objects. The first phase is called the *mark* phase. In the second phase, the garbage collection algorithm scans through the heap and reclaims all of the unmarked objects. The second phase is called the *sweep* phase. The algorithm can be expressed as follows:

```
for each root variable r
    mark (r);
sweep ();
```

In order to distinguish the live objects from garbage, we record the state of an object in each object. That is, we add a special **boolean** field to each object called, say, **marked**. By default, all objects are unmarked when they are created. Thus, the **marked** field is initially **false**.

An object **p** and all of the objects indirectly accessible from **p** can be marked by using the following recursive **mark** method:

```
void mark (Object p)
{
    if (!p.marked)
    {
        p.marked = true;
        for each Object q   referenced by p
            mark (q);
    }
}
```

---

[1]Mark-and-sweep garbage collection is described by John McCarthy in a paper on the LISP language published in 1960.

Notice that this recursive **mark** algorithm does nothing when it encounters an object that has already been marked. Consequently, the algorithm is guaranteed to terminate. And it terminates only when all accessible objects have been marked.

In its second phase, the mark-and-sweep algorithm scans through all of the objects in the heap, in order to locate all unmarked objects. The storage allocated to the unmarked objects is reclaimed during the scan. At the same time, the **marked** field on every live object is set back to **false** in preparation for the next invocation of the mark-and-sweep garbage collection algorithm:

```
void sweep ()
{
    for each Object p  in the heap
    {
        if (p.marked)
            p.marked = false
        else
            heap.release (p);
    }
}
```

Figure 13.5 illustrates the operation of the mark-and-sweep garbage collection algorithm. Figure 13.5 (a) shows the conditions before garbage collection begins. In this example, there is a single root variable. Figure 13.5 (b) shows the effect of the *mark* phase of the algorithm. At this point, all live objects have been marked. Finally, Figure 13.5 (c) shows the objects left after the *sweep* phase has been completed. Only live objects remain in memory and the **marked** fields have all been set to **false** again.

Because the mark-and-sweep garbage collection algorithm traces out the set of objects accessible from the roots, it is able to correctly identify and collect garbage even in the presence of reference cycles. This is the main advantage of mark-and-sweep over the reference-counting technique presented in the preceding section. A secondary benefit of the mark-and-sweep approach is that the normal manipulations of reference variables incur no overhead.

The main disadvantage of the mark-and-sweep approach is the fact that normal program execution is suspended while the garbage collection algorithm runs. In particular, this can be a problem in a program that interacts with a human user or that must satisfy real-time execution constraints. For example, an interactive application that uses mark-and-sweep garbage collection becomes unresponsive periodically.

13.3.1   The Fragmentation Problem

Fragmentation is a phenomenon that occurs in a long-running program that has undergone garbage collection several times. The problem is that objects tend to become spread out in the heap. Live objects end up being separated by many, small unused memory regions. The problem in this situation is that it may become impossible to allocate memory for an object. Although there may indeed be sufficient unused memory, the

FIGURE 13.5
Mark-and-sweet garbage collection.

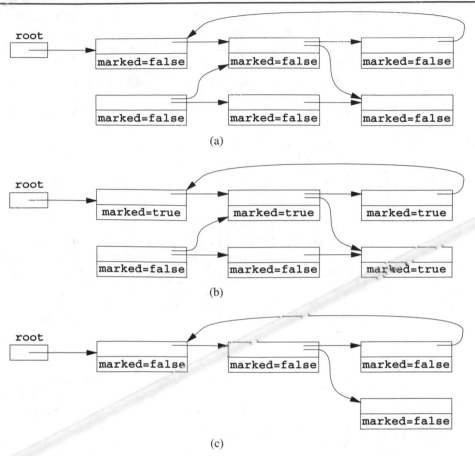

(a)

(b)

(c)

unused memory is not contiguous. Since objects typically occupy consecutive memory locations, it is impossible to allocate storage.

The mark-and-sweep algorithm does not address fragmentation. Even after reclaiming the storage from all garbage objects, the heap may still be too fragmented to allocate the required amount of space. The next section presents an alternative to the mark-and-sweep algorithm that also *defragments* (or *compacts*) the heap.

13.4   Stop-and-Copy Garbage Collection

The section describes a garbage collection approach that collects garbage *and* defragments the heap, called *stop-and-copy*. When using the stop-and-copy garbage collection algorithm, the heap is divided into two separate regions. At any point in time, all dynamically allocated object instances reside in only one of the two regions—the *active* region. The other, *inactive* region is unoccupied.

When the memory in the active region is exhausted, the program is suspended and the garbage-collection algorithm is invoked. The stop-and-copy algorithm copies all of the live objects from the active region to the inactive region. As each object is copied, all references contained in that object are updated to reflect the new locations of the referenced objects.

After the copying is completed, the active and inactive regions exchange their roles. Since the stop-and-copy algorithm copies only the live objects, the garbage objects are left behind. In effect, the storage occupied by the garbage is reclaimed all at once when the active region becomes inactive.

As the stop-and-copy algorithm copies the live objects from the active region to the inactive region, it stores the objects in contiguous memory locations. Thus, the stop-and-copy algorithm automatically defragments the heap. This is the main advantage of the stop-and-copy approach over the mark-and-sweep algorithm described in the preceding section.

The costs of the stop-and-copy algorithm are twofold: First, the algorithm requires that *all* live objects be copied every time garbage collection is invoked. If an application program has a large memory footprint, the time required to copy all objects can be quite significant. A second cost associated with stop-and-copy is the fact that it requires twice as much memory as the program actually uses. When garbage collection is finished, at least half of the memory space is unused.

13.4.1 The Copy Algorithm

The stop-and-copy algorithm divides the heap into two regions— an active region and an inactive region. For convenience, we can view each region as a separate heap and we will refer to them as **activeHeap** and **inactiveHeap**. When the stop-and-copy algorithm is invoked, it copies all live objects from the **activeHeap** to the **inactiveHeap**. It does so by invoking the **copy** method given below starting at each root:

```
for each root variable r
    r = copy (r, inactiveHeap);
swap (activeHeap, inactiveHeap);
```

The **copy** method is complicated by the fact that it needs to update all object references contained in the objects as it copies those objects. In order to facilitate this, we record in every object a reference to its copy. That is, we add a special field to each object called **forward**, which is a reference to the copy of this object.

The recursive **copy** method given below copies a given object and all objects indirectly accessible from the given object to the destination heap. When the **forward** field of an object is **null**, it indicates that the given object has not yet been copied. In this case, the method creates a new instance of the object class in the destination heap. Then, the fields of the object are copied one-by-one. If the field is a primitive type, the value of that field is copied. However, if the field refers to another object, the **copy** method calls itself recursively to copy that object.

```
Object copy (Object p, Heap destination)
{
    if (p == null)
        return null;
    if (p.forward == null)
    {
        q = destination.newInstance (p.class);
        p.forward = q;
        for each field f  in p
        {
            if (f is a primitive type)
                q.f = p.f;
            else
                q.f = copy (p.f, destination);
        }
        q.forward = null;
    }
    return p.forward;
}
```

If the **copy** method is invoked for an object whose **forward** field is non-**null**, that object has already been copied and the **forward** field refers to the copy of that object in the destination heap. In that case, the **copy** method simply returns a reference to the previously copied object.

Figure 13.6 traces the execution of the stop-and-copy garbage collection algorithm. When the algorithm is invoked and before any objects have been copied, the **forward** field of every object in the active region is **null** as shown in Figure 13.6 (a). In Figure 13.6 (b), a copy of object A, called A', has been created in the inactive region, and the **forward** field of A refers to A'.

Since A refers to B, the next object copied is object B. As shown in Figure 13.6 (c), fragmentation is eliminated by allocating storage for B' immediately next to A'. Next, object C is copied. Notice that C refers to A, but A has already been copied. Object C' obtains its reference to A' from the **forward** field of A, as shown in Figure 13.6 (d).

After all of the live objects have been copied from the active region to the inactive region, the regions exchange their roles. As shown in Figure 13.6 (e), all of the garbage has been collected and the heap is no longer fragmented.

13.5 Mark-and-Compact Garbage Collection

The mark-and-sweep algorithm described in Section 13.3 has the unfortunate tendency to fragment the heap. The stop-and-copy algorithm described in Section 13.4 avoids fragmentation at the expense of doubling the size of the heap. This section describes the *mark-and-compact* approach to garbage collection, which eliminates fragmentation without the space penalty of stop-and-copy.

FIGURE 13.6
Stop-and-copy garbage collection.

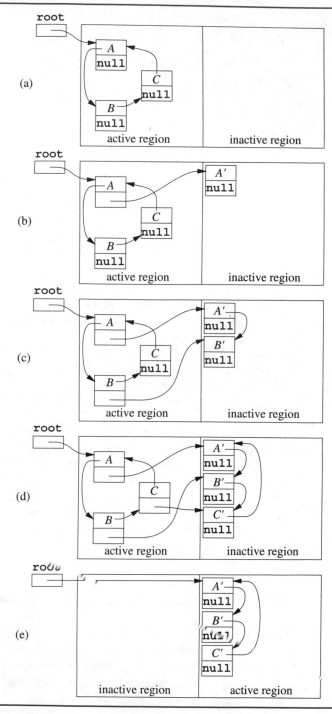

The mark-and-compact algorithm consists of two phases: In the first phase, it finds and marks all live objects. The first phase is called the *mark* phase. In the second phase, the garbage collection algorithm compacts the heap by moving all live objects into contiguous memory locations. The second phase is called the *compaction* phase. The algorithm can be expressed as follows:

```
for each root variable r
    mark (r);
compact ();
```

13.5.1 Handles

The Java virtual machine specification does not prescribe how reference variables are implemented. A common approach is for a reference variable to be implemented as an index into an array of object *handles*. Every object instance has its own handle. The handle for an object typically contains a reference to a **Class** instance that describes the type of the object and a pointer to the region in the heap where the object data reside.

The advantage of using handles is that when the position in the heap of an object is changed, only the handle for that object needs to be modified. All other references to that object are unaffected because such references actually refer to the handle. The cost of using handles is that the handle must be dereferenced every time an object is accessed.

The mark-and-compact algorithm uses the handles in two ways: First, the **marked** flags that are set during the mark operation are stored in the handles rather than in the objects themselves. Second, compaction is greatly simplified because when an object is moved only its handle needs to be updated—all other objects are unaffected.

Figure 13.7 illustrates how object references are implemented using handles. Figure 13.7 (a) shows a circular, singly-linked list as it is usually drawn, while Figure 13.7 (b) shows how the list is represented when using handles. Each reference variable actually contains an index into the array of handles. For example, the **head** variable selects the handle at offset 2 and that handle points to linked-list element *A*. Similarly, the **next** field of list element *A* selects the handle at offset 5, which refers to list element *B*. Notice that when an object is moved, only its handle needs to be modified.

The handle is a convenient place in which to record information used by the garbage collection algorithm. For example, we add a **boolean** field to each handle, called **marked**. The **marked** field is used to mark live objects as follows:

```
void mark (Object p)
{
    if (!handle[p].marked)
    {
        handle[p].marked = true;
        for each Object q   referenced by p
            mark (q);
    }
}
```

FIGURE 13.7
Representing object references using handles.

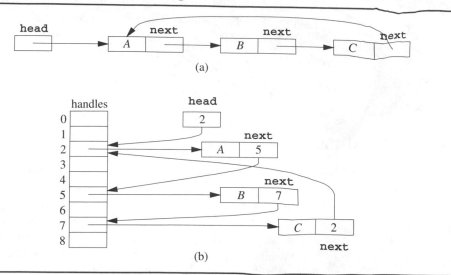

(a)

(b)

Notice that this version of the **mark** method marks the object handles rather than the objects themselves.

Once all of the live objects in the heap have been identified, the heap needs to be defragmented. Perhaps the simplest way to defragment the heap is to *slide* the objects in the heap all to one end, removing the unused memory locations separating them. The following version of the **compact** method does just this:

```
void compact ()
{
    long offset = 0;
    for each Object p   in the heap
    {
        if (handle[p].marked)
        {
            handle[p].object = heap.move (p, offset);
            handle[p].marked = false;
            offset += sizeof (p);
        }
    }
}
```

This algorithm makes a single pass through the objects in the heap, moving the live objects toward the lower heap addresses as it goes. The **compact** method only modifies the object handles—object data remain unchanged. This algorithm also illustrates an important characteristic of the sliding compaction algorithm—the relative positions of the objects in the heap remain unchanged after the compaction operation. Also, when the compaction method has finished, the **marked** fields have all been set back to **false** in preparation for the next garbage collection operation.

Exercises

13.1 Let M be the size of the heap and let f be the fraction of the heap occupied by live data. Estimate the running time of the **mark** method of the *mark-and-sweep* garbage collection scheme as a function of f and M.

13.2 Repeat Exercise 13.1 for the *stop-and-copy* garbage collection scheme.

13.3 Repeat Exercise 13.1 for the *stop-and-compact* garbage collection scheme.

13.4 Using your answers to Exercises 13.1, 13.2, and 13.3, show that running time of garbage collection decreases as the amount of storage recovered increases.

13.5 The efficiency of a garbage collection scheme is the rate at which memory is reclaimed. Using your answers to Exercises 13.1 and 13.2, compare the efficiency of *mark-and-sweep* with that of *stop-and-copy*.

13.6 Devise a *non-recursive* algorithm for the **mark** method of the *mark-and-sweep* garbage collection scheme.

13.7 Repeat Exercise 13.6 for the **copy** method of the *stop-and-copy* garbage collection scheme.

13.8 Repeat Exercise 13.6 for the **mark** method of the *mark-and-compact* garbage collection scheme.

13.9 Consider the use of *handles* for representing object references. Is it correct to assume that the order in which objects appear in the heap is the same as the order in which the corresponding handles appear in the array of handles? How does this affect *compaction* of the heap?

13.10 Consider the **compact** method of the *mark-and-compact* garbage collection scheme. The algorithm visits the objects in the heap in the order in which they appear in the heap, rather than in the order in which the corresponding handles appear in the array of handles. Why is this necessary?

13.11 The **compact** method of the *mark-and-compact* garbage collection scheme slides the objects in the heap all to one end, but leaves the handles where they are. As a result, the handle array becomes *fragmented*. What modifications are necessary in order to compact the handle array as well as the heap?

Programming Projects

13.1 Devise and conduct a set of experiments to measure garbage collection overhead. For example, write a program that creates a specified number of garbage objects as quickly as possible. Determine the number of objects needed to trigger garbage collection. Measure the running time of your program when no garbage collection is performed and compare it to the running time observed when garbage collection is invoked.

13.2   Java does not provide the means for accessing memory directly. Consequently, it is not possible to implement the Java heap in Java (without using **native** methods). Nevertheless, we can *simulate* a heap using a Java array of **int**s. Write a Java class that manages an array of **int**s. Your class should implement the following interface:

```
public interface Heap
{
    int acquire (int size);
    int release (int offset);
    int fetch (int offset);
    void store (int offset, int value);
}
```

The **acquire** method allocates a region of **size** consecutive **int**s in the array and returns the offset of the first byte in the region. The **release** method releases a region of **int**s at the specified offset, which was obtained previously using **acquire**. The **fetch** method is used to read a value from the array at the given offset and the **store** method writes a value into the array at the given offset.

13.3   Using an array of **int**s, simulate the *mark-and-sweep* garbage collection as follows:

   a.   Write a class that implements the **Handle** interface given here:

```
public interface Handle
{
    int getSize ();
    int fetchInt (int offset);
    Handle fetchReference (int offset);
    storeInt (int offset, int value);
    storeReference (int offset, Handle h);
}
```

A handle refers to an object that contains either **int**s or other handles. The size of an object is the total number of **int**s and handles it contains. The various store and fetch methods are used to insert and remove items from the object to which this handle refers.

   b.   Write a class that implements the **Heap** interface given here:

```
public interface Heap
{
    Handle acquire (int size);
    void release (Handle h);
    void collectGarbage ();
}
```

The **acquire** method allocates a handle and space in the heap for an object of the given size. The **release** method releases the given handle but does not reclaim the associated heap space. The **collectGarbage** method performs the actual garbage collection operation.

13.4 Using the approach described in Project 13.3, implement a simulation of *mark-and-compact* garbage collection.

13.5 Using the approach described in 13.3, implement a simulation of *reference-counting* garbage collection.

14 | Algorithmic Patterns and Problem Solvers

This chapter presents a number of different algorithmic patterns. Each pattern addresses a category of problems and describes a core solution strategy for that category. Given a problem to be solved, we may find that there are several possible solution strategies. We may also find that only one strategy applies or even that none of them do. A good programmer is one who is proficient at examining the problem to be solved and identifying the appropriate algorithmic technique to use. The following algorithmic patterns are discussed in this chapter:

Direct solution strategies Brute-force algorithms and greedy algorithms.

Backtracking strategies Simple backtracking and branch-and-bound algorithms.

Top-down solution strategies Divide-and-conquer algorithms.

Bottom-up solution strategies Dynamic programming.

Randomized strategies Monte Carlo algorithms and simulated annealing.

14.1 Brute-Force and Greedy Algorithms

In this section we consider two closely related algorithm types—brute-force and greedy. *Brute-force algorithms* are distinguished not by their structure or form, but by the way in which the problem to be solved is approached. A brute-force algorithm solves a problem in the most simple, direct, or obvious way. As a result, such an algorithm can end up doing far more work to solve a given problem than a more clever or sophisticated algorithm might do. On the other hand, a brute-force algorithm is often easier to implement than a more sophisticated one and, because of this simplicity, sometimes it can be more efficient.

Often a problem can be viewed as a sequence of decisions to be made. For example, consider the problem of finding the best way to place electronic components on a circuit board. To solve this problem we must decide where on the board to place each component. Typically, a brute-force algorithm solves such a problem by exhaustively enumerating all possibilities. That is, for every decision we consider each possible outcome.

A greedy algorithm is one that makes the sequence of decisions (in some order) such that once a given decision has been made, that decision is never reconsidered. For example, if we use a greedy algorithm to place the components on the circuit board, once a component has been assigned a position it is never again moved. Greedy algorithms can run significantly faster than brute force ones. Unfortunately, it is not always the case that a greedy strategy leads to the correct solution.

14.1.1 Example—Counting Change

Consider the problem a cashier solves every time he or she counts out some amount of currency. The cashier has at his or her disposal a collection of notes and coins of various denominations and is required to count out a specified sum using the smallest possible number of pieces.

The problem can be expressed mathematically as follows: Let there be n pieces of money (notes or coins), $P = \{p_1, p_2, \ldots, p_n\}$, and let d_i be the denomination of p_i. For example, if p_i is a dime, then $d_i = 10$. To count out a given sum of money A, we find the smallest subset of P, say $S \subseteq P$, such that $\sum_{p_i \in S} d_i = A$.

One way to represent the subset S is to use n variables $X = \{x_1, x_2, \ldots, x_n\}$, such that

$$x_i = \begin{cases} 1 & p_i \in S, \\ 0 & p_i \notin S. \end{cases}$$

Given $\{d_1, d_2, \ldots, d_n\}$, our *objective* is to minimize

$$\sum_{i=1}^{n} x_i$$

subject to the constraint

$$\sum_{i=1}^{n} d_i x_i = A.$$

Brute-Force Algorithm

Since each of the elements of $X = \{x_1, x_2, \ldots, x_n\}$ is either a zero or a one, there are 2^n possible values for X. A brute-force algorithm to solve this problem finds the best solution by enumerating all possible values of X.

For each possible value of X we check first whether the constraint $\sum_{i=1}^{n} d_i x_i = A$ is satisfied. A value that satisfies the constraint is called a *feasible solution*. The solution to the problem is the feasible solution that minimizes $\sum_{i=1}^{n} x_i$, which is called the *objective function*.

Since there are 2^n possible values of X, the running time of a brute-force solution is $\Omega(2^n)$. The running time needed to determine whether a possible value is a feasible solution is $O(n)$ and the time required to evaluate the objective function is also $O(n)$. Therefore, the running time of the brute-force algorithm is $O(n2^n)$.

Greedy Algorithm

A cashier does not really consider all possible ways in which to count out a given sum of money. Instead, he or she counts out the required amount beginning with the largest denomination and proceeding to the smallest denomination.

For example, suppose we have ten coins: five pennies, two nickels, two dimes, and one quarter—that is, $\{d_1, d_2, \ldots, d_{10}\} = \{1, 1, 1, 1, 1, 5, 5, 10, 10, 25\}$. To count out 32 cents, we start with a quarter, then add a nickel followed by two pennies. This is a greedy strategy because once a coin has been counted out, it is never taken back. Furthermore, the solution obtained is the correct solution because it uses the fewest number of coins.

If we assume that the pieces of money (notes and coins) are sorted by their denomination, the running time for the greedy algorithm is $O(n)$. This is significantly better than that of the brute-force algorithm previously given.

Does this greedy algorithm always produce the correct answer? Unfortunately it does not. Consider what happens if we introduce a 15-cent coin. Suppose we are asked to count out 20 cents from the following set of coins: $\{1, 1, 1, 1, 1, 10, 10, 15\}$. The greedy algorithm selects 15 followed by five ones—six coins in total. Of course, the correct solution requires only two coins. The solution found by the greedy strategy is a feasible solution, but it does not minimize the objective function.

14.1.2 Example—The 0/1 Knapsack Problem

The *0/1 knapsack problem* is closely related to the change counting problem discussed in the preceding section: We are given a set of *n* items from which we are to select some number of items to be carried in a knapsack. Each item has both a *weight* and a *profit*. The objective is to choose the set of items that fits in the knapsack and maximizes the profit.

Let w_i be the weight of the *i*th item, p_i be the profit accrued when the *i*th item is carried in the knapsack, and C be the capacity of the knapsack. Let x_i be a variable the value of which is either zero or one. The variable x_i has the value one when the *i*th item is carried in the knapsack.

Given $\{w_1, w_2, \ldots, w_n\}$ and $\{p_1, p_2, \ldots, p_n\}$, our *objective* is to maximize

$$\sum_{i=1}^{n} p_i x_i$$

subject to the constraint

$$\sum_{i=1}^{n} w_i x_i \leq C.$$

Clearly, we can solve this problem by exhaustively enumerating the feasible solutions and selecting the one with the highest profit. However, since there are 2^n possible solutions, the running time required for the brute-force solution becomes prohibitive as n gets large.

An alternative is to use a greedy solution strategy, which solves the problem by putting items into the knapsack one-by-one. This approach is greedy because once an item has been put into the knapsack, it is never removed.

How do we select the next item to be put into the knapsack? There are several possibilities:

Greedy by Profit At each step select from the remaining items the one with the highest profit (provided the capacity of the knapsack is not exceeded). This approach tries to maximize the profit by choosing the most profitable items first.

Greedy by Weight At each step select from the remaining items the one with the least weight (provided the capacity of the knapsack is not exceeded). This approach tries to maximize the profit by putting as many items into the knapsack as possible.

Greedy by Profit Density At each step select from the remaining items the one with the largest *profit density*, p_i/w_i (provided the capacity of the knapsack is not exceeded). This approach tries to maximize the profit by choosing items with the largest profit per unit of weight.

Although all three approaches generate feasible solutions, we cannot guarantee that any of them will always generate the optimal solution. In fact, it is even possible that none of them does! Table 14.1 gives an example where this is the case.

The bottom line about greedy algorithms is this: Before using a greedy algorithm you must make sure that it always gives the correct answer. Fortunately, in many cases this is true.

TABLE 14.1
0/1 Knapsack Problem Example ($C = 100$)

				Greedy by			
i	w_i	p_i	p_i/w_i	Profit	Weight	Density	Optimal Solution
1	100	40	0.4	1	0	0	0
2	50	35	0.7	0	0	1	1
3	45	18	0.4	0	1	0	1
4	20	4	0.2	0	1	1	0
5	10	10	1.0	0	1	1	0
6	5	2	0.4	0	1	1	1
		Total weight		100	80	85	100
		Total profit		40	34	51	55

14.2 Backtracking Algorithms

In this section we consider *backtracking algorithms*. As in the preceding section, we view the problem to be solved as a sequence of decisions. A backtracking algorithm systematically considers all possible outcomes for each decision. In this sense, backtracking algorithms are like the brute-force algorithms discussed in the preceding section. However, backtracking algorithms are distinguished by the way in which the space of possible solutions is explored. Sometimes a backtracking algorithm can detect that an exhaustive search is unnecessary and, therefore, it can perform much better.

14.2.1 Example—Balancing Scales

Consider the set of *scales* shown in Figure 14.1. Suppose we are given a collection of n weights, $\{w_1, w_2, \ldots, w_n\}$, and we are required to place *all* of the weights onto the scales so that they are balanced.

The problem can be expressed mathematically as follows: Let x_i represent the pan in which weight w_i is placed such that

$$x_i = \begin{cases} 0 & w_i \text{ is placed in the left pan,} \\ 1 & w_i \text{ is placed in the right pan.} \end{cases}$$

The scales are balanced when the sum of the weights in the left pan equals the sum of the weights in the right pan,

$$\sum_{i=1}^{n} w_i x_i = \sum_{i=1}^{n} w_i (1 - x_i).$$

Given an arbitrary set of n weights, there is no guarantee that a solution to the problem exists. A solution always exists if, instead of balancing the scales, the goal is to minimize the difference between the total weights in the left and right pans. Thus,

FIGURE 14.1
A set of scales.

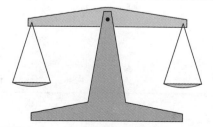

given $\{w_1, w_2, \ldots, w_n\}$, our *objective* is to *minimize* δ, where

$$\delta = \left| \sum_{i=1}^{n} w_i x_i - \sum_{i=1}^{n} w_i (1 - x_i) \right|$$

subject to the constraint that *all* of the weights are placed on the scales.

Given a set of scales and collection of weights, we might solve the problem by trial-and-error: Place all of the weights onto the pans one-by-one. If the scales balance, a solution has been found. If not, remove some number of the weights and place them back on the scales in some other combination. In effect, we search for a solution to the problem by first trying one solution and then backing-up to try another.

Figure 14.2 shows the *solution space* for the scales balancing problem. In this case the solution space takes the form of a tree: Each node of the tree represents a *partial solution* to the problem. At the root (node A) no weights have been placed yet and the scales are balanced. Let δ be the difference between the sum of the weights currently placed in the left and right pans. Therefore, $\delta = 0$ at node A.

Node B represents the situation in which weight w_1 has been placed in the left pan. The difference between the pans is $\delta = -w_1$. Conversely, node C represents the situation in which the weight w_1 has been placed in the right pan. In this case $\delta = +w_1$. The complete solution tree has depth n and 2^n leaves. Clearly, the solution is the leaf node having the smallest $|\delta|$ value.

In this case (as in many others) the solution space is a tree. In order to find the best solution a backtracking algorithm visits all of the nodes in the solution space. That is, it does a tree *traversal*. Section 9.4 presents the two most important tree traversals—*depth-first* and *breadth-first*. Both kinds can be used to implement a backtracking algorithm.

FIGURE 14.2
Solution space for the scales balancing problem.

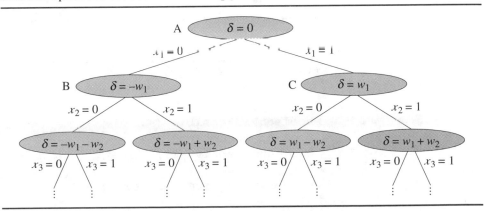

14.2.2   Representing the Solution Space

This section presents an interface for the nodes of a solution space. By using an interface, we hide the details of the specific problem to be solved from the backtracking algorithm. In so doing, it is possible to implement completely generic backtracking problem solvers.

Although a backtracking algorithm behaves as if it is traversing a solution tree, it is important to realize that it is not necessary to have the entire solution tree constructed at once. Instead, the backtracking algorithm creates the nodes dynamically as it explores the solution space.

Program 14.1 defines the **Solution** interface. The **Solution** interface extends the **Comparable** interface defined in Program 5.1 and it extends the **Cloneable** interface defined in **java.lang**. Each instance of a class that implements the **Solution** interface represents a single node in the solution space.

The **Solution** interface extends the **Comparable** interface. Consequently, instances of the **Solution** class can be inserted in the various containers discussed in the preceding chapters. The **Solution** interface adds the following methods:

isFeasible This method returns **true** if the solution instance is a feasible solution to the given problem. A solution is feasible if it satisfies the problem constraints.

isComplete This method returns **true** if the solution instance represents a complete solution. A solution is complete when all possible decisions have been made.

getObjective This method returns the value of the objective function for the given solution instance.

getBound This method returns a value that is a lower bound (if it exists) on the objective function for the given solution instance as well as all solutions that can

---

PROGRAM 14.1
Solution interface

```
1  public interface Solution
2      extends Comparable, Cloneable
3  {
4      boolean isFeasible ();
5      boolean isComplete ();
6      int getObjective ();
7      int getBound ();
8      Enumeration getSuccessors ();
9  }
```

possibly be derived from that instance. This is a hook provided to facilitate the implementation of *branch-and-bound* backtracking, which is described in Section 14.2.4.

getSuccessors This method returns an **Enumeration** that enumerates all of the successors (i.e., the children) of the given solution instance. It is assumed that the children of the given node are created *dynamically*.

14.2.3 Abstract Backtracking Solvers

The usual way to implement a backtracking algorithm is to write a method that traverses the solution space. This section presents an alternate, object-oriented approach that is based on the notion of an *abstract solver*.

Think of a solver as an abstract machine, the sole purpose of which is to search a given solution space for the best possible solution. A machine is an object. Therefore, it makes sense that we represent it as an instance of some class.

Program 14.2 defines the **Solver** interface. The **Solver** interface consists of the single method **solve**. This method takes as its argument a **Solution** that is the node in the solution space from which to begin the search. The **solve** method returns a reference to the best solution found.

Abstract Solvers

Program 14.3 defines the **AbstractSolver** class. The **AbstractSolver** class implements the **Solver** interface defined in Program 14.2. The **AbstractSolver** class contains two fields, **bestSolution** and **bestObjective**, two concrete methods, **updateBest** and **solve**, and the abstract method **search**. Since **search** is an abstract method, its implementation must be given in a derived class.

The **solve** method does not search the solution space itself—it merely sets things up for the **search** method. It is the **search** method, which is provided by a derived class, that does the actual searching. When **search** returns it is expected that the **bestSolution** field will refer to the best solution and that **bestObjective** will be the value of the objective function for the best solution.

The **updateBest** method is meant to be called by the **search** method as it explores the solution space. As each complete solution is encountered, the **updateBest** method is called to keep track of the solution that *minimizes* the objective function.

PROGRAM 14.2
Solver interface

```
1  public interface Solver
2  {
3      Solution solve (Solution initial);
4  }
```

PROGRAM 14.3
`AbstractSolver` class

```
1   public abstract class AbstractSolver
2       implements Solver
3   {
4       protected Solution bestSolution;
5       protected int bestObjective;
6
7       protected abstract void search (Solution initial);
8
9       public Solution solve (Solution initial)
10      {
11          bestSolution = null;
12          bestObjective = Integer.MAX_VALUE;
13          search (initial);
14          return bestSolution;
15      }
16
17      public void updateBest (Solution solution)
18      {
19          if (solution.isComplete () && solution.isFeasible ()
20              && solution.getObjective () < bestObjective)
21          {
22              bestSolution = solution;
23              bestObjective = solution.getObjective ();
24          }
25      }
26  }
```

Depth-First Solver

This section presents a backtracking solver that finds the best solution to a given problem by performing depth-first traversal of the solution space. Program 14.4 defines the `DepthFirstSolver` class. The `DepthFirstSolver` class extends the `AbstractSolver` class defined in Program 14.3. It provides an implementation for the `search` method.

The `search` method does a complete, depth-first traversal of the solution space.[1] Note that the implementation does not depend on the characteristics of the problem being solved. In this sense the solver is a generic, *abstract solver* and can be used to solve any problem that has a tree-structured solution space!

Since the `search` method in Program 14.4 visits all of the nodes in the solution space, it is essentially a *brute-force* algorithm. And because the recursive method backs up and then tries different alternatives, it is called a *backtracking* algorithm.

---

[1]The reader may find it instructive to compare Program 14.4 with Program 9.2 and Program 16.8.

PROGRAM 14.4
DepthFirstSolver class

```
1   public class DepthFirstSolver
2       extends AbstractSolver
3   {
4       protected void search (Solution solution)
5       {
6           if (solution.isComplete ())
7               updateBest (solution);
8           else
9           {
10              Enumeration i = solution.getSuccessors ();
11              while (i.hasMoreElements ())
12              {
13                  Solution successor = (Solution) i.nextElement ();
14                  search (successor);
15              }
16          }
17      }
18  }
```

Breadth-First Solver

If we can find the optimal solution by doing a depth-first traversal of the solution space, then we can find the solution with a breadth-first traversal too. As defined in Section 9.4, a breadth-first traversal of a tree visits the nodes in the order of their depth in the tree. That is, first the root is visited, then the children of the root are visited, then the grandchildren are visited, and so on.

The **BreadthFirstSolver** class is defined in Program 14.5. The **Breadth-FirstSolver** class extends the **AbstractSolver** class defined in Program 14.3. It simply provides an implementation for the **search** method.

The **search** method implements a non-recursive, breadth-first traversal algorithm that uses a queue to keep track of nodes to be visited. The initial solution is enqueued first. Then the following steps are repeated until the queue is empty:

1. Dequeue the first solution in the queue.
2. If the solution is complete, call the **updateBest** method to keep track of the solution that minimizes the objective function.
3. Otherwise the solution is not complete. Enqueue all its successors.

Clearly, this algorithm does a complete traversal of the solution space.[2]

---

[2]The reader may find it instructive to compare Program 14.5 with Program 9.8 and Program 16.9.

PROGRAM 14.5
BreadthFirstSolver class

```
 1  public class BreadthFirstSolver
 2      extends AbstractSolver
 3  {
 4      protected void search (Solution initial)
 5      {
 6          Queue queue = new QueueAsLinkedList ();
 7          queue.enqueue (initial);
 8          while (!queue.isEmpty ())
 9          {
10              Solution solution = (Solution) queue.dequeue ();
11              if (solution.isComplete ())
12                  updateBest (solution);
13              else
14              {
15                  Enumeration i = solution.getSuccessors ();
16                  while (i.hasMoreElements ())
17                  {
18                      Solution successor =
19                          (Solution) i.nextElement ();
20                      queue.enqueue (successor);
21                  }
22              }
23          }
24      }
25  }
```

14.2.4 Branch-and-Bound Solvers

The depth-first and breadth-first backtracking algorithms described in the preceding sections both naïvely traverse the entire solution space. However, sometimes we can determine that a given node in the solution space does not lead to the optimal solution—either because the given solution and all its successors are infeasible or because we have already found a solution that is guaranteed to be better than any successor of the given solution. In such cases, the given node and its successors need not be considered. In effect, we can *prune* the solution tree, thereby reducing the number of solutions to be considered.

For example, consider the scales balancing problem described in Section 14.2.1. Consider a partial solution P_k in which we have placed k weights onto the pans ($0 \leq k < n$) and, therefore, $n - k$ weights remain to be placed. The difference between the weights of the left and right pans is given by

$$\delta = \sum_{i=1}^{k} w_i x_i - \sum_{i=1}^{k} w_i (1 - x_i),$$

and the sum of the weights still to be placed is

$$r = \sum_{i=k+1}^{n} w_i.$$

Suppose that $|\delta| > r$. That is, the total weight remaining is less than the difference between the weights in the two pans. Then, the best possible solution that we can obtain without changing the positions of the weights that have already been placed is $\widehat{\delta} = |\delta| - r$. The quantity $\widehat{\delta}$ is a *lower bound* on the value of the objective function for all solutions in the solution tree below the given partial solution P_k.

In general, during the traversal of the solution space we may have already found a complete, feasible solution for which the objective function is *less* than $\widehat{\delta}$. In that case, there is no point in considering any of the solutions below P_k. That is, we can *prune* the subtree rooted at node P_k from the solution tree. A backtracking algorithm that prunes the search space in this manner is called a *branch-and-bound* algorithm.

Depth-First, Branch-and-Bound Solver

Only a relatively minor modification of the simple, depth-first solver shown in Program 14.4 is needed to transform it into a branch-and-bound solver. Program 14.6 defines the DepthFirstBranchAndBoundSolver class.

PROGRAM 14.6
DepthFirstBranchAndBoundSolver class

```
1   public class DepthFirstBranchAndBoundSolver
2       extends AbstractSolver
3   {
4       protected void search (Solution solution)
5       {
6           if (solution.isComplete ())
7               updateBest (solution);
8           else
9           {
10              Enumeration i = solution.getSuccessors ();
11              while (i.hasMoreElements ())
12              {
13                  Solution successor = (Solution) i.nextElement ();
14                  if (successor.isFeasible () &&
15                          successor.getBound () < bestObjective)
16                      search (successor);
17              }
18          }
19      }
20  }
```

The only difference between the simple, depth-first solver and the branch-and-bound version is the `if` statement on lines 14–15. As each node in the solution space is visited two tests are done: First, the `isFeasible` method is called to check whether the given node represents a feasible solution. Next, the `getBound` method is called to determine the lower bound on the best possible solution in the given subtree. The second test determines whether this bound is less than the value of the objective function of the best solution already found. The recursive call to explore the subtree is only made if both tests succeed. Otherwise, the subtree of the solution space is pruned.

The degree to which the solution space may be pruned depends strongly on the nature of the problem being solved. In the worst case, no subtrees are pruned and the branch-and-bound method visits all of the nodes in the solution space. The branch-and-bound technique is really just a *heuristic*—sometimes it works and sometimes it does not.

It is important to understand the trade-off being made: The solution space is being pruned at the added expense of performing the tests as each node is visited. The technique is successful only if the savings that accrue from pruning exceed the additional execution time arising from the tests.

14.2.5   Example—The 0/1 Knapsack Problem Again

Consider again the 0/1 knapsack problem described in Section 14.1.2. We are given a set of n items from which we are to select some number of items to be carried in a knapsack. The solution to the problem has the form $\{x_1, x_2, \ldots, x_n\}$, where x_i is one if the ith item is placed in the knapsack and zero otherwise. Each item has both a *weight*, w_i, and a *profit*, p_i. The goal is to maximize the total profit,

$$\sum_{i=1}^{n} p_i x_i,$$

subject to the knapsack capacity constraint

$$\sum_{i=1}^{n} w_i x_i \leq C.$$

A partial solution to the problem is one in which only the first k items have been considered. That is, the solution has the form $S_k = \{x_1, x_2, \ldots, x_k\}$, where $1 \leq k < n$. The partial solution S_k is feasible if and only if

$$\sum_{i=1}^{k} w_i x_i \leq C. \tag{14.1}$$

Clearly if S_k is infeasible, then every possible complete solution containing S_k is also infeasible.

If S_k is feasible, the total profit of any solution containing S_k is bounded by

$$\sum_{i=1}^{k} p_i x_i + \sum_{i=k+1}^{n} p_i. \tag{14.2}$$

That is, the bound is equal the *actual* profit accrued from the k items already considered plus the sum of the profits of the remaining items.

Clearly, the 0/1 knapsack problem can be solved using a backtracking algorithm. Furthermore, by using Equation (14.1) and (14.2) a branch-and-bound solver can potentially prune the solution space, thereby arriving at the solution more quickly.

For example, consider the 0/1 knapsack problem with $n = 6$ items given in Table 14.1. There are $2^n = 64$ possible solutions and the solution space contains $2^{n+1} - 1 = 127$ nodes. The simple **DepthFirstSolver** given in Program 14.4 visits all 127 nodes and generates all 64 solutions because it does a complete traversal of the solution tree. The **BreadthFirstSolver** of Program 14.5 behaves similarly. On the other hand, the **DepthFirstBranchAndBoundSolver** shown in Program 14.6 visits only 67 nodes and generates only 27 complete solutions. In this case, the branch-and-bound technique prunes almost half of the nodes from the solution space!

14.3 Top-Down Algorithms: Divide and Conquer

In this section we discuss a top-down algorithmic paradigm called *divide and conquer*. To solve a given problem, it is subdivided into one or more subproblems, each of which is similar to the given problem. Each of the subproblems is solved independently. Finally, the solutions to the subproblems are combined in order to obtain the solution to the original problem.

Divide-and-conquer algorithms are often implemented using recursion. However, not all recursive methods are divide-and-conquer algorithms. Generally, the subproblems solved by a divide-and-conquer algorithm are *non-overlapping*.

14.3.1 Example—Binary Search

Consider the problem of finding the position of an item in a sorted list. That is, given the sorted sequence $S = \{a_1, a_2, \ldots, a_n\}$ and an item x, find i (if it exists) such that $a_i = x$. The usual solution to this problem is *binary search*.

Binary search is a divide-and-conquer strategy. The sequence S is split into two subsequences, $S_L = \{a_1, a_2, \ldots, a_{\lfloor n/2 \rfloor}\}$ and $S_R = \{a_{\lfloor n/2 \rfloor + 1}, a_{\lfloor n/2 \rfloor + 1}, \ldots, a_n\}$. The original problem is split into two subproblems: Find x in S_L or S_R. Of course, since the original list is sorted, we can quickly determine the list in which x must appear. Therefore, we only need to solve one subproblem.

Program 14.7 defines the method **binarySearch**, which takes four arguments, **array**, **x**, **i**, and **n**. This method looks for the position in **array** at which item **x** is found. Specifically, it considers the following elements of the array:

$$\texttt{array[i]}, \texttt{array[i + 1]}, \texttt{array[i + 2]}, \ldots, \texttt{array[i + n - 1]}.$$

The running time of the algorithm is clearly a function of n, the number of elements to be searched. Although Program 14.7 works correctly for arbitrary values of n, it is much easier to determine the running time if we assume that n is a power of two. In

---

PROGRAM 14.7
Divide-and-conquer example—binary search

```
1   public class Example
2   {
3       public static int binarySearch (
4           Comparable[] array, Comparable target, int i, int n)
5       {
6           if (n == 0)
7               throw new IllegalArgumentException ("empty array");
8           if (n == 1)
9           {
10              if (array [i].isEQ (target))
11                  return i;
12              throw new IllegalArgumentException (
13                  "target not found");
14          }
15          else
16          {
17              int j = i + n / 2;
18              if (array [j].isLE (target))
19                  return binarySearch (array, target, j, n - n/2);
20              else
21                  return binarySearch (array, target, i, n/2);
22          }
23      }
24  }
```

---

this case, the running time is given by the recurrence

$$T(n) = \begin{cases} O(1) & n \leq 1, \\ T(n/2) + O(1) & n > 1. \end{cases} \tag{14.3}$$

Equation (14.3) is easily solved using repeated substitution:

$$\begin{aligned} T(n) &= T(n/2) + 1 \\ &= T(n/4) + 2 \\ &= T(n/8) + 3 \\ &\quad\vdots \\ &= T(n/2^k) + k. \end{aligned}$$

Setting $n/2^k = 1$ gives $T(n) = \log n + 1 = O(\log n)$.

14.3.2 Example—Computing Fibonacci Numbers

The Fibonacci numbers are given by following recurrence:

$$F_n = \begin{cases} 0 & n = 0, \\ 1 & n = 1, \\ F_{n-1} + F_{n-2} & n \geq 2. \end{cases} \tag{14.4}$$

Section 3.4.3 presents a recursive method to compute the Fibonacci numbers by implementing directly Equation (14.4). (See Program 3.4.) The running time of that program is shown to be $T(n) = \Omega((3/2)^n)$.

In this section we present a divide-and-conquer style of algorithm for computing Fibonacci numbers. We make use of the following identities:

$$F_{2k-1} = (F_k)^2 + (F_{k-1})^2$$
$$F_{2k} = (F_k)^2 + 2F_k F_{k-1}$$

for $k \geq 1$. (See Exercise 3.6.) Thus, we can rewrite Equation (14.4) as

$$F_n = \begin{cases} 0 & n = 0, \\ 1 & n = 1, \\ (F_{\lceil n/2 \rceil})^2 + (F_{\lceil n/2 \rceil - 1})^2 & n \geq 2 \text{ and } n \text{ is odd,} \\ (F_{\lceil n/2 \rceil})^2 + 2F_{\lceil n/2 \rceil}F_{\lceil n/2 \rceil - 1} & n \geq 2 \text{ and } n \text{ is even.} \end{cases} \tag{14.5}$$

PROGRAM 14.8
Divide-and-conquer example—computing Fibonacci numbers

```
1   public class Example
2   {
3       public static int fibonacci (int n)
4       {
5           if (n == 0 || n == 1)
6               return n;
7           else
8           {
9               int a = fibonacci ((n + 1) / 2);
10              int b = fibonacci ((n + 1) / 2 - 1);
11              if (n % 2 == 0)
12                  return a * (a + 2 * b);
13              else
14                  return a * a + b * b;
15          }
16      }
17  }
```

Program 14.8 defines the method `fibonacci`, which implements directly Equation (14.5). Given $n > 1$, it computes F_n by calling itself recursively to compute $F_{\lceil n/2 \rceil}$ and $F_{\lceil n/2 \rceil - 1}$ and then combines the two results as required.

To determine a bound on the running time of the `fibonacci` method in Program 14.8, we assume that $T(n)$ is a non-decreasing function. That is, $T(n) \geq T(n - 1)$ for all $n \geq 1$. Therefore, $T(\lceil n/2 \rceil) \geq T(\lceil n/2 \rceil - 1)$. Although the program works correctly for all values of n, it is convenient to assume that n is a power of 2. In this case, the running time of the method is upper-bounded by $T(n)$, where

$$T(n) = \begin{cases} O(1) & n \leq 1, \\ 2T(n/2) + O(1) & n > 1. \end{cases} \tag{14.6}$$

Equation (14.6) is easily solved using repeated substitution:

$$\begin{aligned} T(n) &= 2T(n/2) + 1 \\ &= 4T(n/4) + 1 + 2 \\ &= 8T(n/8) + 1 + 2 + 4 \\ &\vdots \\ &= 2^k T(n/2^k) + \sum_{i=0}^{k-1} 2^i \\ &\vdots \\ &= nT(1) + n - 1 \quad (n = 2^k). \end{aligned}$$

Thus, $T(n) = 2n - 1 = O(n)$.

14.3.3 Example—Merge Sorting

Sorting algorithms and sorters are covered in detail in Chapter 15. In this section we consider a divide-and-conquer sorting algorithm—*merge sort*. Given an array of n items in arbitrary order, the objective is to rearrange the elements of the array so that they are ordered from the smallest element to the largest one.

The merge sort algorithm sorts a sequence of length $n > 1$ by splitting it into two subsequences—one of length $\lfloor n/2 \rfloor$, the other of length $\lceil n/2 \rceil$. Each subsequence is sorted and then the two sorted sequences are merged into one.

Program 14.9 defines the method `mergeSort`, which takes three arguments, `array`, `i`, and `n`. The method sorts the following `n` elements:

$$\texttt{array[i]}, \texttt{array[i + 1]}, \texttt{array[i + 2]}, \ldots, \texttt{array[i + n - 1]}.$$

The `mergeSort` method calls itself as well as the `merge` method. The purpose of the `merge` method is to merge two sorted sequences, one of length $\lfloor n/2 \rfloor$, the other of

PROGRAM 14.9
Divide-and-conquer example—merge sorting

```
1   public class Example
2   {
3       public static void mergeSort (
4           Comparable[] array, int i, int n)
5       {
6           if (n > 1)
7           {
8               mergeSort (array, i, n / 2);
9               mergeSort (array, i + n / 2, n - n / 2);
10              merge (array, i, n / 2, n - n / 2);
11          }
12      }
13  }
```

length $\lceil n/2 \rceil$, into a single sorted sequence of length n. This can easily be done in $O(n)$ time. (See Program 15.15.)

The running time of the mergeSort method depends on the number of items to be sorted, n. Although Program 14.9 works correctly for arbitrary values of n, it is much easier to determine the running time if we assume that n is a power of two. In this case, the running time is given by the recurrence

$$T(n) = \begin{cases} O(1) & n \leq 1, \\ 2T(n/2) + O(n) & n > 1. \end{cases} \qquad (14.7)$$

Equation (14.7) is easily solved using repeated substitution:

$$\begin{aligned} T(n) &= 2T(n/2) + n \\ &= 4T(n/4) + 2n \\ &= 8T(n/8) + 3n \\ &\vdots \\ &= 2^k T(n/2^k) + kn. \end{aligned}$$

Setting $n/2^k = 1$ gives $T(n) = n + n \log n = O(n \log n)$.

14.3.4 Running Time of Divide-and-Conquer Algorithms

A number of divide-and-conquer algorithms are presented in the preceding sections. Because these algorithms have a similar form, the recurrences that give the running

TABLE 14.2
Running Times of Divide-and-Conquer Algorithms

Program	Recurrence	Solution
Program 14.7	$T(n) = T(n/2) + O(1)$	$O(\log n)$
Program 14.8	$T(n) = 2T(n/2) + O(1)$	$O(n)$
Program 14.9	$T(n) = 2T(n/2) + O(n)$	$O(n \log n)$

times of the algorithms are also similar in form. Table 14.2 summarizes the running times of Program 14.7, 14,8, and 14.9.

In this section we develop a general recurrence that characterizes the running times of many divide-and-conquer algorithms. Consider the form of a divide-and-conquer algorithm to solve a given problem. Let n be a measure of the size of the problem. Since the divide-and-conquer paradigm is essentially recursive, there must be a base case. That is, there must be some value of n, say n_0, for which the solution to the problem is computed directly. We assume that the worst-case running time for the base case is bounded by a constant.

To solve an arbitrarily large problem using divide-and-conquer, the problem is *divided* into a number of smaller problems, each of which is solved independently. Let a be the number of smaller problems to be solved ($a \in \mathbb{Z}$, $a \geq 1$). The size of each of these problems is some fraction of the original problem, typically either $\lceil n/b \rceil$ or $\lfloor n/b \rfloor$ ($b \in \mathbb{Z}$, $b \geq 1$).

The solution to the original problem is constructed from the solutions to the smaller problems. The running time required to do this depends on the problem to be solved. In this section we consider polynomial running times. That is, $O(n^k)$ for some integer $k \geq 0$.

For the assumptions stated above, the running time of a divide-and-conquer algorithm is given by

$$T(n) = \begin{cases} O(1) & n \leq n_0, \\ aT(\lceil n/b \rceil) + O(n^k) & n > n_0. \end{cases} \tag{14.8}$$

In order to make it easier to find the solution to Equation (14.8), we drop the $O(\cdot)$s as well as the $\lceil \cdot \rceil$ from the recurrence. We can also assume (without loss of generality) that $n_0 = 1$. As a result, the recurrence becomes

$$T(n) = \begin{cases} 1 & n = 1, \\ aT(n/b) + n^k & n > 1. \end{cases}$$

Finally, we assume that n is a power of b. That is, $n = b^m$ for some integer $m \geq 0$. Consequently, the recurrence formula becomes

$$T(b^m) = \begin{cases} 1 & m = 0, \\ T(b^m) = aT(b^{m-1}) + b^{mk} & m > 0. \end{cases} \tag{14.9}$$

We solve Equation (14.9) as follows: Divide both sizes of the recurrence by a^m and then *telescope*:

$$\frac{T(b^m)}{a^m} = \frac{T(b^{m-1})}{a^{m-1}} + \left(\frac{b^k}{a}\right)^m \tag{14.10}$$

$$\frac{T(b^{m-1})}{a^{m-1}} = \frac{T(b^{m-2})}{a^{m-2}} + \left(\frac{b^k}{a}\right)^{m-1}$$

$$\frac{T(b^{m-2})}{a^{m-2}} = \frac{T(b^{m-3})}{a^{m-3}} + \left(\frac{b^k}{a}\right)^{m-2}$$

$$\vdots$$

$$\frac{T(b)}{a} = T(1) + \left(\frac{b^k}{a}\right). \tag{14.11}$$

Adding Equation (14.10) through Equation (14.11), substituting $T(1) = 1$, and multiplying both sides by a^m gives

$$T(n) = a^m \sum_{i=0}^{m} \left(\frac{b^k}{a}\right)^i. \tag{14.12}$$

In order to evaluate the summation in Equation (14.11) we must consider three cases:

Case 1 $(a > b^k)$ In this case, the term b^k/a falls between zero and one. Consider the *infinite* geometric series summation:

$$\sum_{i=0}^{\infty} \left(\frac{b^k}{a}\right)^i = \frac{a}{a - b^k} = C.$$

Since the infinite series summation approaches a finite constant C and since each term in the series is positive, the *finite* series summation in Equation (14.11) is bounded from above by C:

$$\sum_{i=0}^{m} \left(\frac{b^k}{a}\right)^i < C.$$

Substituting this result into Equation (14.11) and making use of the fact that $n = b^m$, and therefore $m = \log_b n$, gives

$$T(n) \leq Ca^m$$
$$= O(a^m)$$
$$= O(a^{\log_b n})$$
$$= O(a^{\log_a n \log_b a})$$
$$= O(n^{\log_b a}).$$

Case 2 ($a = b^k$)   In this case the term b^k/a is exactly one. Therefore, the series summation in Equation (14.11) is simply

$$\sum_{i=0}^{m} \left(\frac{b^k}{a}\right)^i = m + 1.$$

Substituting this result into Equation (14.11) and making use of the fact that $n = b^m$ and $a = b^k$ gives

$$
\begin{aligned}
T(n) &= (m + 1)a^m \\
&= O(ma^m) \\
&= O(m(b^k)^m) \\
&= O((b^m)^k m) \\
&= O(n^k \log_b n).
\end{aligned}
$$

Case 3 ($a < b^k$)   In this case the term b^k/a is greater than one and we make use of the general formula for a finite geometric series summation (see Section 2.2.4) to evaluate the summation:

$$\sum_{i=0}^{m} \left(\frac{b^k}{a}\right)^i = \frac{(b^k/a)^{m+1} - 1}{b^k/a - 1}.$$

Substituting this result in Equation (14.11) and simplifying gives:

$$
\begin{aligned}
T(n) &= a^m \left(\frac{(b^k/a)^{m+1} - 1}{b^k/a - 1}\right) \\
&= a^m \left(\frac{(b^k/a)^m - a/b^k}{1 - a/b^k}\right) \\
&= O(a^m (b^k/a)^m) \\
&= O(b^{km}) \\
&= O(n^k).
\end{aligned}
$$

Summary   For many divide-and-conquer algorithms the running time is given by the general recurrence shown in Equation (14.8). Solutions to the recurrence depend on the relative values of the constants a, b, and k. Specifically, the solutions satisfy the following bounds:

$$T(n) = \begin{cases} O(n^{\log_b a}) & a > b^k, \\ O(n^k \log_b n) & a = b^k, \\ O(n^k) & a < b^k. \end{cases} \qquad (14.13)$$

Table 14.3 shows how to apply Equation (14.13) to find the running times of the divide-and-conquer algorithms described in the preceding sections. Comparing the

TABLE 14.3
Computing Running Times Using Equation (14.13)

Program	Recurrence	a	b	k	Case	Solution
Program 14.7	$T(n) = T(n/2) + O(1)$	1	2	0	$a = b^k$	$O(n^0 \log_2 n)$
Program 14.8	$T(n) = 2T(n/2) + O(1)$	2	2	0	$a > b^k$	$O(n^{\log_2 2})$
Program 14.9	$T(n) = 2T(n/2) + O(n)$	2	2	1	$a = b^k$	$O(n^1 \log_2 n)$

solutions in Table 14.3 with those given in Table 14.2 shows that the results obtained using the general formula agree with the analyses done in the preceding sections.

14.3.5 Example—Matrix Multiplication

Consider the problem of computing the product of two matrices. That is, given two $n \times n$ matrices, A and B, compute the $n \times n$ matrix $C = A \times B$, the elements of which are given by

$$c_{i,j} = \sum_{k=0}^{n-1} a_{i,k} b_{k,j}. \tag{14.14}$$

Section 4.2.7 shows that the direct implementation of Equation (14.14) results in an $O(n^3)$ running time. In this section we show that the use of a divide-and-conquer strategy results in a slightly better asymptotic running time.

To implement a divide-and-conquer algorithm we must break the given problem into several subproblems that are similar to the original one. In this instance we view each of the $n \times n$ matrices as a 2×2 matrix, the elements of which are $(\frac{n}{2}) \times (\frac{n}{2})$ submatrices. Thus, the original matrix multiplication, $C = A \times B$ can be written as

$$\begin{bmatrix} C_{1,1} & C_{1,2} \\ C_{2,1} & C_{2,2} \end{bmatrix} = \begin{bmatrix} A_{1,1} & A_{1,2} \\ A_{2,1} & A_{2,2} \end{bmatrix} \times \begin{bmatrix} B_{1,1} & B_{1,2} \\ B_{2,1} & B_{2,2} \end{bmatrix},$$

where each $A_{i,j}$, $B_{i,j}$, and $C_{i,j}$ is an $(\frac{n}{2}) \times (\frac{n}{2})$ matrix.

From Equation (14.14) we get that the result submatrices can be computed as follows:

$$C_{1,1} = A_{1,1} \times B_{1,1} + A_{1,2} \times B_{2,1}$$
$$C_{1,2} = A_{1,1} \times B_{1,2} + A_{1,2} \times B_{2,2}$$
$$C_{2,1} = A_{2,1} \times B_{1,1} + A_{2,2} \times B_{2,1}$$
$$C_{2,2} = A_{2,1} \times B_{1,2} + A_{2,2} \times B_{2,2}.$$

Here the symbols $+$ and $\times$ are taken to mean addition and multiplication (respectively) of $(\frac{n}{2}) \times (\frac{n}{2})$ matrices.

In order to compute the original $n \times n$ matrix multiplication we must compute eight $(\frac{n}{2}) \times (\frac{n}{2})$ matrix products (*divide*) followed by four $(\frac{n}{2}) \times (\frac{n}{2})$ matrix sums (*conquer*).

Since matrix addition is an $O(n^2)$ operation, the total running time for the multiplication operation is given by the recurrence:

$$T(n) = \begin{cases} O(1) & n = 1, \\ 8T(n/2) + O(n^2) & n > 1. \end{cases} \qquad (14.15)$$

Note that Equation (14.15) is an instance of the general recurrence given in Equation (14.8). In this case, $a = 8$, $b = 2$, and $k = 2$. We can obtain the solution directly from Equation (14.13). Since $a > b^k$, the total running time is $O(n^{\log_b a}) = O(n^{\log_2 8}) = O(n^3)$. But this no better than the original, direct algorithm!

Fortunately, it turns out that one of the eight matrix multiplications is redundant. Consider the following series of seven $(\frac{n}{2}) \times (\frac{n}{2})$ matrices:

$$M_0 = (A_{1,1} + A_{2,2}) \times (B_{1,1} + B_{2,2})$$
$$M_1 = (A_{1,2} - A_{2,2}) \times (B_{2,1} + B_{2,2})$$
$$M_2 = (A_{1,1} - A_{2,1}) \times (B_{1,1} + B_{1,2})$$
$$M_3 = (A_{1,1} + A_{1,2}) \times B_{2,2}$$
$$M_4 = A_{1,1} \times (B_{1,2} - B_{2,2})$$
$$M_5 = A_{2,2} \times (B_{2,1} - B_{1,1})$$
$$M_6 = (A_{2,1} + A_{2,2}) \times B_{1,1}.$$

Each equation above has only one multiplication. Ten additions and seven multiplications are required to compute M_0 through M_6. Given M_0 through M_6, we can compute the elements of the product matrix C as follows:

$$C_{1,1} = M_0 + M_1 - M_3 + M_5$$
$$C_{1,2} = M_3 + M_4$$
$$C_{2,1} = M_5 + M_6$$
$$C_{2,2} = M_0 - M_2 + M_4 - M_6.$$

Altogether this approach requires seven $(\frac{n}{2}) \times (\frac{n}{2})$ matrix multiplications and 18 $(\frac{n}{2}) \times (\frac{n}{2})$ additions. Therefore, the worst-case running time is given by the following recurrence:

$$T(n) = \begin{cases} O(1) & n = 1, \\ 7T(n/2) + O(n^2) & n > 1. \end{cases} \qquad (14.16)$$

As above, Equation (14.16) is an instance of the general recurrence given in Equation (14.8), and we obtain the solution directly from Equation (14.13). In this case, $a = 7$, $b = 2$, and $k = 2$. Therefore, $a > b^k$ and the total running time is

$$O(n^{\log_b a}) = O(n^{\log_2 7}).$$

Note that $\log_2 7 \approx 2.807\,355$. Consequently, the running time of the divide-and-conquer matrix multiplication strategy is $O(n^{2.8})$, which is better (asymptotically) than the straightforward $O(n^3)$ approach.

14.4 Bottom-Up Algorithms: Dynamic Programming

In this section we consider a bottom-up algorithmic paradigm called *dynamic programming*. In order to solve a given problem, a series of subproblems is solved. The series of subproblems is devised carefully in such a way that each subsequent solution is obtained by combining the solutions to one or more of the subproblems that have already been solved. All intermediate solutions are kept in a table in order to prevent unnecessary duplication of effort.

14.4.1 Example—Generalized Fibonacci Numbers

Consider the problem of computing the *generalized Fibonacci numbers*. The generalized Fibonacci numbers of order $k \geq 2$ are given by

$$F_n^{(k)} = \begin{cases} 0 & 0 \leq n < k - 1, \\ 1 & n = k - 1, \\ \sum_{i=1}^{k} F_{n-i}^{(k)} & n \geq k. \end{cases} \qquad (14.17)$$

Notice that the "normal" Fibonacci numbers considered in Section 3.4.3 are the same as the generalized Fibonacci numbers of order 2.

If we write a recursive method that implements directly Equation (14.17), we get an algorithm with exponential running time. For example, in Section 3.4.3 it is shown that the time to compute the second-order Fibonacci numbers is $T(n) = \Omega((3/2)^n)$.

The problem with the direct recursive implementation is that it does far more work than is needed because it solves the same subproblem many times. For example, to compute $F_{10}^{(2)}$ it is necessary to compute both $F_9^{(2)}$ and $F_8^{(2)}$. However, in computing $F_9^{(2)}$ it is also necessary to compute $F_8^{(2)}$, and so on.

An alternative to the top-down recursive implementation is to do the calculation from the bottom up. In order to do this we compute the series of sequences

$$S_0 = \{F_0^{(k)}\}$$
$$S_1 = \{F_0^{(k)}, F_1^{(k)}\}$$
$$\vdots$$
$$S_n = \{F_0^{(k)}, F_1^{(k)}, \ldots, F_n^{(k)}\}.$$

Notice that we can compute S_{i+1} from the information contained in S_i simply by using Equation (14.17).

Program 14.10 defines the method `fibonacci`, which takes two integer arguments n and k and computes the nth Fibonacci number of order k using the approach described above. This algorithm uses an array to represent the series of sequences $S_0, S_1, \ldots, S_n$. As each subsequent Fibonacci number is computed it is added to the end of the array.

PROGRAM 14.10
Dynamic programming example—computing generalized Fibonacci numbers

---

```
1   public class Example
2   {
3       public static int fibonacci (int n, int k)
4       {
5           if (n < k - 1)
6               return 0;
7           else if (n == k - 1)
8               return 1;
9           else
10          {
11              int [] f = new int [n + 1];
12              for (int i = 0; i < k - 1; ++i)
13                  f [i] = 0;
14              f [k - 1] = 1;
15              for (int i = k; i <= n; ++i)
16              {
17                  int sum = 0;
18                  for (int j = 1; j <= k; ++j)
19                      sum += f [i - j];
20                  f [i] = sum;
21              }
22              return f [n];
23          }
24      }
25  }
```

The worst-case running time of the **fibonacci** method given in Program 14.10 is a function of both n and k:

$$T(n, k) = \begin{cases} O(1) & 0 \leq n < k, \\ O(kn) & n \geq k. \end{cases}$$

14.4.2   Example—Computing Binomial Coefficients

Consider the problem of computing the *binomial coefficient*

$$\binom{n}{m} = \frac{n!}{(n - m)!m!},$$ (14.18)

given non-negative integers n and m. (See Theorem 11.7.)

The problem with implementing directly Equation (14.18) is that the factorials grow quickly with increasing n and m. For example, $13! = 6\,227\,020\,800 > 2^{31}$. Therefore, it is not possible to represent $n!$ for $n \geq 13$ using 32-bit integers. Nevertheless it is possible to represent the binomial coefficients $\binom{n}{m}$ up to $n = 33$ without overflowing. For example, $\binom{33}{16} = 1\,166\,803\,110 < 2^{31}$.

Consider the following *recursive* definition of the binomial coefficients:

$$
\binom{n}{m} = \begin{cases} 1 & m = 0, \\ 1 & n = m, \\ \binom{n-1}{m} + \binom{n-1}{m-1} & \text{otherwise.} \end{cases} \tag{14.19}
$$

This formulation does not require the computation of factorials. In fact, the only computation needed is addition.

If we implement Equation (14.19) directly as a recursive method, we get a method whose running time is given by

$$
T(n, m) = \begin{cases} O(1) & m = 0, \\ O(1) & n = m, \\ T(n-1, m) + T(n-1, m-1) + O(1) & \text{otherwise,} \end{cases}
$$

which is very similar to Equation (14.19). In fact, we can show that $T(n, m) = \Omega(\binom{n}{m})$, which (by Equation 14.18) is not a very good running time at all! Again the problem with the direct recursive implementation is that it does far more work than is needed because it solves the same subproblem many times.

An alternative to the top-down recursive implementation is to do the calculation from the bottom up. In order to do this we compute the series of sequences

$$
S_0 = \left\{ \binom{0}{0} \right\}
$$

$$
S_1 = \left\{ \binom{1}{0}, \binom{1}{1} \right\}
$$

$$
S_2 = \left\{ \binom{2}{0}, \binom{2}{1}, \binom{2}{2} \right\}
$$

$$
\vdots
$$

$$
S_n = \left\{ \binom{n}{0}, \binom{n}{1}, \binom{n}{2}, \ldots, \binom{n}{n} \right\}.
$$

Notice that we can compute S_{i+1} from the information contained in S_i simply by using Equation (14.19). Table 14.4 shows the sequence in tabular form—the ith row of the table corresponds the sequence S_i. This tabular representation of the binomial coefficients is known as *Pascal's triangle*.[3]

---

[3] The table is named in honor of *Blaise Pascal*, who published a treatise on the subject in 1653.

TABLE 14.4
Pascal's Triangle

n	$\binom{n}{0}$	$\binom{n}{1}$	$\binom{n}{2}$	$\binom{n}{3}$	$\binom{n}{4}$	$\binom{n}{5}$	$\binom{n}{6}$	$\binom{n}{7}$
0	1							
1	1	1						
2	1	2	1					
3	1	3	3	1				
4	1	4	6	4	1			
5	1	5	10	10	5	1		
6	1	6	15	20	15	6	1	
7	1	7	21	35	35	21	7	1

Program 14.11 defines the method **binom**, which takes two integer arguments n and m and computes the binomial coefficient $\binom{n}{m}$ by computing Pascal's triangle. According to Equation (14.19), each subsequent row depends only on the preceding row—it is only necessary to keep track of one row of data. The implementation shown uses an array of length n to represent a row of Pascal's triangle. Consequently, instead of a table of size $O(n^2)$, the algorithm gets by with $O(n)$ space. The implementation has been coded carefully so that the computation can be done in place. That is, the elements of S_{i+1} are computed in reverse so that they can be written over the elements of S_i that are no longer needed.

The worst-case running time of the **binom** method given in Program 14.11 is clearly $O(n^2)$.

PROGRAM 14.11
Dynamic programming example—computing binomial coefficients

```
1   public class Example
2   {
3       public static int binom (int n, int m)
4       {
5           int[] b = new int [n + 1];
6           b [0] = 1;
7           for (int i = 1; i <= n; ++i)
8           {
9               b [i] = 1;
10              for (int j = i - 1; j > 0; --j)
11                  b [j] += b [j - 1];
12          }
13          return b [m];
14      }
15  }
```

14.4.3 Application: Typesetting Problem

Consider the problem of typesetting a paragraph of justified text. A paragraph can be viewed as a sequence of $n > 0$ words, $\{w_1, w_2, \ldots, w_n\}$. The objective is to determine how to break the sequence into individual lines of text of the appropriate size. Each word is separated from the next by some amount of space. By stretching or compressing the space between the words, the left and right ends of consecutive lines of text are made to line up. A paragraph looks best when the amount of stretching or compressing is minimized.

We can formulate the problem as follows: Assume that we are given the lengths of the words, $\{l_1, l_2, \ldots, l_n\}$, and that the desired length of a line is D. Let $W_{i,j}$ represent the sequence of words from w_i to w_j (inclusive). That is,

$$W_{i,j} = \{w_i, w_{i+1}, \ldots, w_j\},$$

for $1 \leq i \leq j \leq n$.

Let $L_{i,j}$ be the sum of the lengths of the words in the sequence $W_{i,j}$. That is,

$$L_{i,j} = \sum_{k=i}^{j} l_k.$$

The *natural length* for the sequence $W_{i,j}$ is the sum of the lengths of the words, $L_{i,j}$, plus the normal amount of space between those words. Let s be the normal size of the space between two words. Then the natural length of $W_{i,j}$ is $L_{i,j} + (j - i)s$. Note that we can also define $L_{i,j}$ *recursively* as follows:

$$L_{i,j} = \begin{cases} l_i & i = j, \\ L_{i,j-1} + l_j & i < j. \end{cases} \tag{14.20}$$

In general, when we typeset the sequence $W_{i,j}$ all on a single line, we need to stretch or compress the spaces between the words so that the length of the line is the desired length D. Therefore, the amount of stretching or compressing is given by the difference $D - (L_{i,j} + (j - i)s)$. However, if the sum of the lengths of the words, $L_{i,j}$, is longer than the desired line length D, it is not possible to typeset the sequence on a single line.

Let $P_{i,j}$ be the *penalty* associated with typesetting the sequence $L_{i,j}$ on a single line. Then,

$$P_{i,j} = \begin{cases} |D - L_{i,j} - (j - i)s| & D \geq L_{i,j}, \\ \infty & D < L_{i,j}. \end{cases} \tag{14.21}$$

This definition of penalty is consistent with the stated objectives: The penalty increases as the difference between the natural length of the sequence and the desired length increases and the infinite penalty disallows lines that are too long.

Finally, we define the quantity $C_{i,j}$ for $1 \leq i \leq j \leq n$ as the minimum total penalty required to typeset the sequence $W_{i,j}$. In this case, the text may be all on one line or it may be split over more than one line. The quantity $C_{i,j}$ is given by

$$C_{i,j} = \begin{cases} P_{i,j} & i = j, \\ \min\{P_{i,j}, \min_{i \leq k < j} (P_{i,k} + C_{k+1,j})\} & \text{otherwise.} \end{cases} \quad (14.22)$$

We obtain Equation (14.22) as follows: When $i = j$ there is only one word in the paragraph. The minimum total penalty associated with typesetting the paragraph in this case is just the penalty that results from putting the one word on a single line.

In the general case, there is more than one word in the sequence $W_{i,j}$. In order to determine the optimal way in which to typeset the paragraph we consider the cost of putting the first k words of the sequence on the first line of the paragraph, $P_{i,k}$, plus the minimum total cost associated with typesetting the rest of the paragraph $C_{k+1,j}$. The value of k that minimizes the total cost also specifies where the line break should occur.

Example

Suppose we are given a sequence of $n = 5$ words, $W = \{w_1, w_2, w_3, w_4, w_5\}$ having lengths $\{10, 10, 10, 12, 50\}$, respectively, which are to be typeset in a paragraph of width $D = 60$. Assume that the normal width of an inter-word space is $s = 10$.

We begin by computing the lengths of all subsequences of W using Equation (14.20). The lengths of all $n(n - 1)/2$ subsequences of W are tabulated in Table 14.5.

Given $L_{i,j}$, D, and s, it is a simple matter to apply Equation (14.21) to obtain the one-line penalties, $P_{i,j}$, which measure the amount of stretching or compressing needed to set all words in a given subsequence on a single line. These are tabulated in Table 14.6.

Given the one-line penalties $P_{i,j}$, we can use Equation (14.22) to find for each subsequence of W the minimum total penalty, $C_{i,j}$, associated with forming a paragraph from the words in that subsequence. These are tabulated in Table 14.6.

The $C_{1,5}$ entry in Table 14.6 gives the minimum total cost of typesetting the entire paragraph. The value 22 was obtained as follows:

$$\begin{aligned} C_{1,5} &= \min\{P_{1,1} + C_{2,5}, P_{1,2} + C_{3,5}, P_{1,3} + C_{4,5}, P_{1,4} + C_{5,5}, P_{1,5}\} \\ &= P_{1,4} + C_{5,5} \\ &= 12 + 10. \end{aligned}$$

TABLE 14.5
Typesetting Problem

i	l_i	$j = 1$	2	3	4	5
1	10	10	20	30	42	92
2	10		10	20	32	82
3	10			10	22	72
4	12				12	62
5	50					50

(header spanning columns $j = 1$ through 5: $L_{i,j}$)

TABLE 14.6
Penalties

i	$P_{i,j}$					$C_{i,j}$				
	$j=1$	2	3	4	5	$j=1$	2	3	4	5
1	50	30	10	12	∞	50	30	10	12	22
2		50	30	8	∞		50	30	8	18
3			50	28	∞			50	28	38
4				48	∞				48	58
5					10					10

This indicates that the optimal solution is to set words w_1, w_2, w_3, and w_4 on the first line of the paragraph and leave w_5 by itself on the last line of the paragraph. Figure 14.3 illustrates this result.

This formulation of the typesetting problem seems like overkill. Why not just typeset the lines of text one-by-one, minimizing the penalty for each line as we go? In other words, why don't we just use a greedy strategy? Unfortunately, the obvious greedy solution strategy *does not work*!

For example, the greedy strategy begins by setting the first line of text. To do so it must decide how many words to put on that line. The obvious thing to do is to select the value of k for which $P_{1,k}$ is the smallest. From Table 14.6 we see that $P_{1,3} = 10$ has the smallest penalty. Therefore, the greedy approach puts three words on the first line as shown in Figure 14.3.

FIGURE 14.3
Typesetting a paragraph.

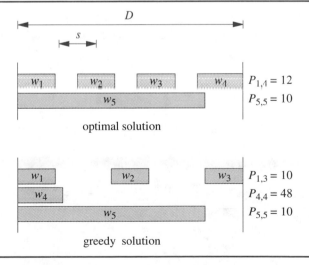

PROGRAM 14.12
Dynamic programming example—typesetting a paragraph

```java
public class Example
{
    public static void typeset (int[] l, int D, int s)
    {
        int n = l.length;
        int[][] L = new int [n][n];
        for (int i = 0; i < n; ++i)
        {
            L [i][i] = l [i];
            for (int j = i + 1; j < n; ++j)
                L [i][j] = L [i][j - 1] + l [j];
        }
        int[][] P = new int [n][n];
        for (int i = 0; i < n; ++i)
            for (int j = i; j < n; ++j)
            {
                if (L [i][j] < D)
                    P [i][j] = Math.abs (D - L[i][j] - (j-i)*s);
                else
                    P [i][j] = Integer.MAX_VALUE;
            }
        int[][] c = new int [n][n];
        for (int j = 0; j < n; ++j)
        {
            c [j][j] = P [j][j];
            for (int i = j - 1; i >= 0; --i)
            {
                int min = P [i][j];
                for (int k = i; k < j; ++k)
                {
                    int tmp = P [i][k] + c [k + 1][j];
                    if (tmp < min)
                        min = tmp;
                }
                c [i][j] = min;
            }
        }
    }
}
```

Since the remaining two words do not both fit on a single line, they are set on separate lines. The total of the penalties for the paragraph typeset using the greedy algorithm is $P_{1,3} + P_{4,4} + P_{5,5} = 68$. Clearly, the solution is not optimal (nor is it very pleasing esthetically).

Implementation

Program 14.12 defines the method **typeset**, which takes three arguments. The first, **l**, is an array of n integers that gives the lengths of the words in the sequence to be typeset. The second, **D**, specifies the desired paragraph width and the third, **s**, specifies the normal inter-word space.

The method first computes the lengths, $L_{i,j}$, of all possible subsequences (lines 6–12). This is done by using the dynamic programming paradigm to evaluate the recursive definition of $L_{i,j}$ given in Equation (14.20). The running time for this computation is clearly $O(n^2)$.

The next step computes the one-line penalties $P_{i,j}$ as given by Equation (14.21) (lines 13–21). This calculation is a straightforward one and its running time is also $O(n^2)$.

Finally, the minimum total costs, $C_{i,j}$, of typesetting each subsequence are determined for all possible subsequences (lines 22–37). Again we make use of the dynamic programming paradigm to evaluate the recursive definition of $C_{i,j}$ given in Equation (14.22). The running time for this computation is $O(n^3)$. As a result, the overall running time required to determine the best way to typeset a paragraph of n words is $O(n^3)$.

14.5 Randomized Algorithms

In this section we discuss algorithms that behave randomly. By this we mean that there is an element of randomness in the way that the algorithm solves a given problem. Of course, if an algorithm is to be of any use, it must find a solution to the problem at hand, so it cannot really be completely random.

Randomized algorithms are said to be methods of last resort. This is because they are used often when no other feasible solution technique is known. For example, randomized methods are used to solve problems for which no closed-form, analytic solution is known. They are also used to solve problems for which the solution space is so large that an exhaustive search is infeasible.

To implement a randomized algorithm we require a source of randomness. The usual source of randomness is a random number generator. Therefore, before presenting randomized algorithms, we first consider the problem of computing random numbers.

14.5.1 Generating Random Numbers

In this section we consider the problem of generating a sequence of *random numbers* on a computer. Specifically, we desire an infinite sequence of statistically independent random numbers uniformly distributed between zero and one. In practice, because the sequence is generated algorithmically using finite-precision arithmetic, it is neither infinite nor truly random. Instead, we say that an algorithm is "good enough" if the sequence it generates satisfies almost any statistical test of randomness. Such a sequence is said to be *pseudo-random*.

The most common algorithms for generating pseudo-random numbers are based on the *linear congruential* random number generator invented by Lehmer. Given a positive integer m called the *modulus* and an initial *seed* value X_0 ($0 \le X_0 < m$), Lehmer's algorithm computes a sequence of integers between 0 and $m - 1$. The elements of the sequence are given by

$$X_{i+1} = (aX_i + c) \bmod m, \qquad (14.23)$$

where a and c are carefully chosen integers such that $2 \le a < m$ and $0 \le c < m$.

For example, the parameters $a = 13$, $c = 1$, $m = 16$, and $X_0 = 0$ produce the sequence

$$0, 1, 14, 7, 12, 13, 10, 3, 8, 9, 6, 15, 4, 5, 2, 11, 0, \ldots.$$

The first m elements of this sequence are distinct and appear to have been drawn at random from the set $\{0, 1, 2, \ldots, 15\}$. However since $X_m = X_0$ the sequence is cyclic with *period m*.

Notice that the elements of the sequence alternate between odd and even integers. This follows directly from Equation (14.23) and the fact that $m = 16$ is a multiple of 2. Similar patterns arise when we consider the elements as binary numbers:

$$0000, 0001, 1110, 0111, 1100, 1101, 1010, 0011, 1000, \ldots.$$

The least significant two bits are cyclic with period four and the least significant three bits are cyclic with period eight! (These patterns arise because $m = 16$ is also a multiple of 4 and 8.) The existence of such patterns makes the sequence *less random*. This suggests that the best choice for the modulus m is a prime number.

Not all parameter values result in a period of m. For example, changing the multiplier a to 11 produces the sequence

$$0, 1, 12, 5, 8, 9, 4, 13, 0, \ldots,$$

the period of which is only $m/2$. In general because each subsequent element of the sequence is determined solely from its predecessor and because there are m possible values, the longest possible period is m. Such a generator is called a *full period* generator.

In practice the *increment c* is often set to zero. In this case, Equation (14.23) becomes

$$X_{i+1} = aX_i \bmod m. \qquad (14.24)$$

This is called a *multiplicative linear congruential* random number generator. (For $c \neq 0$ it is called a *mixed linear congruential* generator.)

In order to prevent the sequence generated by Equation (14.24) from collapsing to zero, the modulus m must be prime and X_0 cannot be zero. For example, the parameters $a = 6$, $m = 13$, and $X_0 = 1$ produce the sequence

$$1, 6, 10, 8, 9, 2, 12, 7, 3, 5, 4, 11, 1, \ldots.$$

Notice that the first 12 elements of the sequence are distinct. Since a multiplicative congruential generator can never produce a zero, the maximum possible period is $m - 1$. Therefore, this is a full period generator.

As the final step of the process, the elements of the sequence are *normalized* by division by the modulus:

$$U_i = X_i/m.$$

In so doing, we obtain a sequence of random numbers that fall between zero and one. Specifically, a mixed congruential generator ($c \neq 0$) produces numbers in the interval $[0, 1)$, whereas a multiplicative congruential generator ($c = 0$) produces numbers in the interval $(0, 1)$.

The Minimal Standard Random Number Generator

A great deal of research has gone into the question of finding an appropriate set of parameters to use in Lehmer's algorithm. A good generator has the following characteristics:

- It is a *full period* generator.
- The generated sequence passes statistical tests of *randomness*.
- The generator can be implemented efficiently using 32-bit integer arithmetic.

The choice of modulus depends on the arithmetic precision used to implement the algorithm. A signed 32-bit integer can represent values between -2^{31} and $2^{31} - 1$. Fortunately, the quantity $2^{31} - 1 = 2\,147\,483\,647$ is a prime number![4] Therefore, it is an excellent choice for the modulus m.

Because Equation (14.24) is slightly simpler than Equation (14.23), we choose to implement a multiplicative congruential generator ($c = 0$). The choice of a suitable multiplier is more difficult. However, a popular choice is $a = 16\,807$ because it satisfies all three criteria given above: It results in a full period random number generator; the generated sequence passes a wide variety of statistical tests for randomness; and it is possible to compute Equation (14.24) using 32-bit arithmetic without overflow.

The algorithm is derived as follows: First, let $q = m$ div a and $r = m$ mod a.[5] In this case, $q = 127\,773$, $r = 2\,836$, and $r < q$.

---

[4] Prime numbers of the form $2^p - 1$ are known as *Mersenne primes*.
[5] For convenience, we use the notation m div a to denote $\lfloor m/a \rfloor$.

Next, we rewrite Equation (14.24) as follows:

$$\begin{aligned} X_{i+1} &= aX_i \bmod m \\ &= aX_i - m(aX_i \text{ div } m) \\ &= aX_i - m(X_i \text{ div } q) + m(X_i \text{ div } q - aX_i \text{ div } m). \end{aligned}$$

This somewhat complicated formula can be simplified if we let $\delta(X_i) = X_i \text{ div } q - aX_i \text{ div } m$:

$$\begin{aligned} X_{i+1} &= aX_i - m(X_i \text{ div } q) + m\delta(X_i) \\ &= a\big(q(X_i \text{ div } q) + X_i \bmod q\big) - m(X_i \text{ div } q) + m\delta(X_i) \\ &= a(X_i \bmod q) + (aq - m)(X_i \text{ div } q) + m\delta(X_i). \end{aligned}$$

Finally, we make use of the fact that $m = aq - r$ to get

$$X_{i+1} = a(X_i \bmod q) - r(X_i \text{ div } q) + m\delta(X_i). \tag{14.25}$$

Equation (14.25) has several nice properties: Both $a(X_i \bmod q)$ and $r(X_i \text{ div } q)$ are positive integers between 0 and $m - 1$. Therefore, the difference $(X_i \bmod q) - r(X_i \text{ div } q)$ can be represented using a signed 32-bit integer without overflow. Finally, $\delta(X_i)$ is either a zero or a one. Specifically, it is zero when the sum of the first two terms in Equation (14.25) is positive and it is one when the sum is negative. As a result, it is not necessary to compute $\delta(X_i)$—a simple test suffices to determine whether the third term is 0 or m.

Implementation

We now describe the implementation of a random number generator based on Equation (14.25). Program 14.13 defines the **RandomNumberGenerator** class. This class has only **static** fields and methods. In addition, the constructor is declared **private** to prevent instantiation. Because there can only be one instance of a static field, the implementation of the **RandomNumberGenerator** class is an example of the *singleton* design pattern.

The **setSeed** method is used to specify the initial seed, X_0. The seed must fall between 0 and $m - 1$. If it does not, an exception is thrown.

The **nextDouble** method generates the elements of the random sequence. Each subsequent call returns the next element of the sequence. The implementation follows directly from Equation (14.25). Notice that the return value is normalized. Therefore, the values computed by the **nextDouble** method are uniformly distributed on the interval $(0, 1)$.

14.5.2 Random Variables

In this section we introduce the notion of an abstract *random variable*. In this context, a random variable is an object that behaves like a random number generator in that it produces a pseudo-random number sequence. The distribution of the values produced depends on the class of random variable used.

Program 14.14 defines the **RandomVariable** interface. The **RandomVariable** interface provides the single method **nextDouble**. Given an instance, say **rv**,

PROGRAM 14.13
RandomNumberGenerator class

```
1   public final class RandomNumberGenerator
2   {
3       private static int seed = 1;
4
5       private static final int a = 16807;
6       private static final int m = 2147483647;
7       private static final int q = 127773;
8       private static final int r = 2836;
9
10      private RandomNumberGenerator ()
11          {}
12
13      public static void setSeed (int s)
14      {
15          if (s < 1 || s >= m)
16              throw new IllegalArgumentException ("invalid seed");
17          seed = s;
18      }
19
20      public static double nextDouble ()
21      {
22          seed = a * (seed % q) - r * (seed / q);
23          if (seed < 0)
24              seed += m;
25          return (double) seed / (double) m;
26      }
27      // ...
28  }
```

of a class that implements the RandomVariable interface, repeated calls of the form

```
rv.nextDouble ();
```

are expected to return successive elements of a pseudo-random sequence.

PROGRAM 14.14
RandomVariable interface

```
1   public interface RandomVariable
2   {
3       double nextDouble ();
4   }
```

PROGRAM 14.15
SimpleRV class

```
1   public class SimpleRV
2       implements RandomVariable
3   {
4       public double nextDouble ()
5           { return RandomNumberGenerator.nextDouble (); }
6   }
```

A Simple Random Variable

Program 14.15 defines the SimpleRV class. The SimpleRV class implements the RandomVariable interface defined in Program 14.14. This class generates random numbers uniformly distributed in the interval (0, 1).

The implementation of the SimpleRV class is trivial because the RandomNumberGenerator class generates the desired distribution of random numbers. Consequently, the nextDouble method simply calls RandomNumberGenerator.nextDouble.

Uniformly Distributed Random Variables

Program 14.16 defines the UniformRV class. This class generates random numbers that are uniformly distributed in an arbitrary interval (u, v), where $u < v$. The parameters u and v are specified in the constructor.

The UniformRV class is also quite simple. Given that the RandomNumberGenerator class generates a sequence random numbers U_i uniformly distributed on the

---

PROGRAM 14.16
UniformRV class

```
1   public class UniformRV
2       implements RandomVariable
3   {
4       protected double u = 0.0;
5       protected double v = 1.0;
6
7       public UniformRV (double u, double v)
8       {
9           this.u = u;
10          this.v = v;
11      }
12
13      public double nextDouble ()
14      {
15          return u + (v - u) * RandomNumberGenerator.nextDouble ();
16      }
17  }
```

---

interval $(0, 1)$, the linear transformation

$$V_i = u + (v - u)U_i$$

suffices to produce a sequence of random numbers V_i uniformly distributed on the interval (u, v).

Exponentially Distributed Random Variables

Program 14.17 defines the **ExponentialRV** class. This class generates exponentially distributed random numbers with a mean value of μ. The mean value μ is specified in the constructor.

The **ExponentialRV** class generates a sequence of random numbers, X_i, *exponentially distributed* on the interval $(0, \infty)$ and having a mean value μ. The numbers are said to be *exponentially distributed* because the probability that X_i falls between 0 and z is given by

$$P[0 < X_i < z] = \int_0^z p(x)dx,$$

where $p(x) = \frac{1}{\mu}e^{-x/\mu}$. The function $p(x)$ is called the *probability density function*. Thus,

$$P[0 < X_i < z] = \int_0^z \frac{1}{\mu}e^{-x/\mu}dx$$
$$= 1 - e^{-z/\mu}.$$

PROGRAM 14.17
ExponentialRV class

```
1   public class ExponentialRV
2       implements RandomVariable
3   {
4       protected double mu = 1.;
5
6       public ExponentialRV (double mu)
7       {
8           this.mu = mu;
9       }
10
11      public double nextDouble ()
12      {
13          return -mu * Math.log (
14              RandomNumberGenerator.nextDouble ());
15      }
16  }
```

Notice that $P[0 < X_i < z]$ is a value between zero and one. Therefore, given a random variable, U_i, uniformly distributed between zero and one, we can obtain an exponentially distributed variable X_i as follows:

$$U_i = 1 - e^{X_i/\mu} \Rightarrow X_i = -\mu \ln(U_i - 1)$$
$$= X_i = -\mu \ln(U_i'), \quad U_i' = U_i - 1. \tag{14.26}$$

Note, if U_i is uniformly distributed on $(0, 1)$, then so too is U_i'. The implementation of the **nextDouble** method follows directly from Equation (14.26).

14.5.3   Monte Carlo Methods

In this section we consider a method for solving problems using random numbers. The method exploits the statistical properties of random numbers in order to ensure that the correct result is computed in the same way that a gambling casino sets the betting odds in order to ensure that the "house" will always make a profit. For this reason, the problem-solving technique is called a *Monte Carlo method*.

To solve a given problem using a Monte Carlo method we devise an experiment in such a way that the solution to the original problem can be obtained from the experimental results. The experiment typically consists of a series of random trials. A random number generator such as the one given in the preceding section is used to create the series of trials.

The accuracy of the final result usually depends on the number of trials conducted. That is, the accuracy usually increases with the number of trials. This trade-off between the accuracy of the result and the time taken to compute it is an extremely useful characteristic of Monte Carlo methods. If only an approximate solution is required, then a Monte Carlo method can be very fast.

Example—Computing π

This section presents a simple, Monte Carlo algorithm to compute the value of π from a sequence of random numbers. Consider a square positioned in the *x-y* plane with its bottom left corner at the origin as shown in Figure 14.4. The area of the square is r^2,

FIGURE 14.4
Illustration of a Monte Carlo method for computing π.

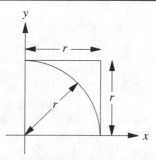

where r is the length of its sides. A quarter circle is inscribed within the square. Its radius is r and its center is at the origin of x-y plane. The area of the quarter circle is $\pi r^2/4$.

Suppose we select a large number of points at random inside the square. Some fraction of these points will also lie inside the quarter circle. If the selected points are uniformly distributed, we expect the fraction of points in the quarter circle to be

$$f = \frac{\pi r^2/4}{r^2} = \frac{\pi}{4}.$$

Therefore by measuring f, we can compute π. Program 14.18 shows how this can be done.

The **pi** method uses the **RandomNumberGenerator** defined to generate (x, y) pairs uniformly distributed on the unit square ($r = 1$). Each point is tested to see if it falls inside the quarter circle. A given point is inside the circle when its distance from the origin, $\sqrt{x^2 + y^2}$, is less than r. In this case since $r = 1$, we simply test whether $x^2 + y^2 < 1$.

How well does Program 14.18 work? When 1,000 trials are conducted, 792 points are found to lie inside the circle. This gives the value of 3.168 for π, which is only 0.8% too large. When 10^8 trials are conducted, 78535956 points are found to lie inside the circle. In this case, we get $\pi \approx 3.141\ 438\ 24$, which is within 0.005% of the correct value!

14.5.4 Simulated Annealing

Despite its name, *simulated annealing* has nothing to do either with simulation or annealing. Simulated annealing is a problem-solving technique based loosely on the way

---

PROGRAM 14.18
Monte Carlo program to compute π

```
1   public class Example
2   {
3       public static double pi (int trials)
4       {
5           int hits = 0;
6           for (int i = 0; i < trials; ++i)
7           {
8               double x = RandomNumberGenerator.nextDouble ();
9               double y = RandomNumberGenerator.nextDouble ();
10              if (x * x + y * y < 1.0)
11                  ++hits;
12          }
13          return 4.0 * hits / trials;
14      }
15  }
```

in which a metal is annealed in order to increase its strength. When a heated metal is cooled very slowly, it freezes into a regular (minimum-energy) crystalline structure.

A simulated annealing algorithm searches for the optimum solution to a given problem in an analogous way. Specifically, it moves about randomly in the solution space looking for a solution that minimizes the value of some objective function. Because it is generated randomly, a given move may cause the objective function to increase, to decrease, or to remain unchanged.

A simulated annealing algorithm always accepts moves that *decrease* the value of the objective function. Moves that *increase* the value of the objective function are accepted with probability

$$p = e^{\Delta/T},$$

where Δ is the change in the value of the objective function and T is a control parameter called the *temperature*. That is, a random number generator that generates numbers distributed uniformly on the interval $(0, 1)$ is sampled, and if the sample is less than p, the move is accepted.

By analogy with the physical process, the temperature T is initially high. Therefore, the probability of accepting a move that increases the objective function is initially high. The temperature is gradually decreased as the search progresses. That is, the system is *cooled* slowly. In the end, the probability of accepting a move that increases the objective function becomes vanishingly small. In general, the temperature is lowered in accordance with an *annealing schedule*.

The most commonly used annealing schedule is called *exponential cooling*. Exponential cooling begins at some initial temperature, T_0, and decreases the temperature in steps according to $T_{k+1} = \alpha T_k$, where $0 < \alpha < 1$. Typically, a fixed number of moves must be accepted at each temperature before proceeding to the next. The algorithm terminates either when the temperature reaches some final value, T_f, or when some other stopping criterion has been met.

The choice of suitable values for α, T_0, and T_f is highly problem-dependent. However, empirical evidence suggests that a good value for α is 0.95 and that T_0 should be chosen so that the initial acceptance probability is 0.8. The search is terminated typically after some fixed, total number of solutions have been considered.

Finally, there is the question of selecting the initial solution from which to begin the search. A key requirement is that it be generated quickly. Therefore, the initial solution is generated typically at random. However, sometimes the initial solution can be generated by some other means such as with a greedy algorithm.

Example—Balancing Scales

Consider again the *scales balancing problem* described in Section 14.2.1. That is, we are given a set of n weights, $\{w_1, w_2, \ldots, w_n\}$, which are to be placed on a pair of scales in the way that minimizes the difference between the total weight in each pan. Feasible solutions to the problem all have the form $X = \{x_1, x_2, \ldots, x_n\}$, where

$$x_i = \begin{cases} 0 & w_i \text{ is placed in the left pan,} \\ 1 & w_i \text{ is placed in the right pan.} \end{cases}$$

To solve this problem using simulated annealing, we need a strategy for generating random moves. The move generator should make small, random changes to the current solution and it must ensure that all possible solutions can be reached. A simple approach is to use the formula

$$X_{i+1} = X_i \oplus U,$$

where X_i is the initial solution, X_{i+1} is a new solution, $U = \{u_1, u_2, \ldots, u_n\}$ is a sequence of zeroes and ones generated randomly, and $\oplus$ denotes elementwise addition modulo two.

Exercises

14.1   Consider the greedy strategy for counting out change given in Section 14.1.1. Let $\{d_1, d_2, \ldots, d_n\}$ be the set of available denominations. For example, the set $\{1, 5, 10, 25, 100, 200\}$ represents the denominations of the commonly circulated Canadian coins. What condition(s) must the set of denominations satisfy to ensure that the greedy algorithm always finds an optimal solution?

14.2   Devise a greedy algorithm to solve optimally the scales balancing problem described in Section 14.2.1.

a.   Does your algorithm always find the optimal solution?

b.   What is the running time of your algorithm?

14.3   Consider the following 0/1-knapsack problem:

i	w_i	p_i
1	10	10
2	6	6
3	3	4
4	8	9
5	1	3

$C = 18$

a.   Solve the problem using the greedy by profit, greedy by weight, and greedy by profit density strategies.

b.   What is the optimal solution?

14.4   Consider the breadth-first solver shown in Program 14.5. Suppose we replace the queue (line 3) with a *priority queue*.

a.   How should the solutions in the priority queue be prioritized?

b.   What possible benefit might there be from using a priority queue rather than a FIFO queue?

14.5   Repeat Exercise 14.4, but this time consider what happens if we replace the queue with a *LIFO stack*.

14.6   Repeat Exercise 14.4 and 14.5, but this time consider a *branch-and-bound* breadth-first solver.

14.7   (This question should be attempted *after* reading Chapter 16.) For some problems the solution space is more naturally a graph rather than a tree.

   a.   What problem arises if we use the `DepthFirstSolver` given in Program 14.4 to explore a search space that is not a tree?

   b.   Modify the `DepthFirstSolver` so that it explores a solution space that is not a tree. **Hint**: See Program 16.8.

   c.   What problem arises if we use the `BreadthFirstSolver` given in Program 14.5 to explore a search space that is not a tree?

   d.   Modify the `BreadthFirstSolver` so that it explores a solution space that is not a tree. **Hint**: See Program 16.9.

14.8   Devise a backtracking algorithm to solve the *N-queens problem*: Given an $N \times N$ chess board, find a way to place N queens on the board in such a way that no queen can take another.

14.9   Consider a binary search tree that contains n keys, $k_1, k_2, \ldots, k_n$, at depths $d_1, d_2, \ldots, d_n$, respectively. Suppose the tree will be subjected to a large number of `find` operations. Let p_i be the probability that we access key k_i. Suppose we know a priori all the access probabilities. Then we can say that the *optimal binary search tree* is the tree that minimizes the quantity

$$\sum_{i=1}^{n} p_i(d_i + 1).$$

   a.   Devise a dynamic programming algorithm that, given the access probabilities, determines the optimal binary search tree.

   b.   What is the running time of your algorithm?

   Hint: Let $C_{i,j}$ be the *cost* of the optimal binary search tree that contains the set of keys $\{k_i, k_{i+1}, k_{i+2}, \ldots, k_j\}$, where $i \leq j$. Show that

$$C_{i,j} = \begin{cases} p_i & i = j, \\ \min_{i \leq k \leq j}\{C_{i,k-1} + C_{k+1,j} + \sum_{l=i}^{j} p_l\} & i < j. \end{cases}$$

14.10   Consider the typesetting problem discussed in Section 14.4.3. The objective is to determine how to break a given sequence of words into lines of text of the appropriate size. This was done either by stretching or compressing the space between the words. Explain why the greedy strategy always finds the optimal solution if we stretch but do not compress the space between words.

14.11   Consider two complex numbers, $a + bi$ and $c + di$. Show that we can compute the product $(ac - bd) + (ad + bc)i$ with only three multiplications.

14.12   Devise a divide-and-conquer strategy to find the root of a polynomial. For example, given a polynomial such as $p(x) = 2x^2 + 3x - 4$, and an interval $[u, v]$ such that $p(u)$ and $p(v)$ have opposite signs, find the value r, $u \leq r \leq v$, such that $p(r) = 0$.

14.13 Devise an algorithm to compute a *normally distributed random variable*. A normal distribution is completely defined by its mean and standard deviation. The probability density function for a normal distribution is

$$p(x) = \frac{1}{\sigma \sqrt{2\pi}} \exp\left(-\frac{1}{2\sigma^2}(x - \mu)^2\right),$$

where μ is the mean and σ is the standard deviation of the distribution. **Hint**: Consider the *central limit theorem*.

14.14 Devise an algorithm to compute a *geometrically distributed random variable*. A geometrically distributed random variable is an integer in the interval $[1, \infty)$ given by the probability density function

$$P[X = i] = \theta(1 - \theta)^{i-1},$$

where θ^{-1} is the mean of the distribution. **Hint**: Use the fact $P[X = i] = P[i - 1 < Z \le i]$, where Z is an exponentially distributed random variable with mean $\mu = -1/\ln(1 - \theta)$.

14.15 Do Exercise 8.13.

Programming Projects

14.1 Design a class that implements the **Solution** interface defined in Program 14.1 to represent the nodes of the solution space of a *0/1-knapsack problem* described in Section 14.1.2.

Devise a suitable representation for the state of a node and then implement the following methods **isFeasible**, **isComplete**, **getObjective**, **getBound**, **clone**, and **getSuccessors**. Note, the **getSuccessors** method returns an **Enumeration**, which enumerates all successors of a given node.

a. Use your class with the **DepthFirstSolver** defined in Program 14.4 to solve the problem given in Table 14.1.

b. Use your class with the **BreadthFirstSolver** defined in Program 14.5 to solve the problem given in Table 14.1.

c. Use your class with the **DepthFirstBranchAndBoundSolver** defined in Program 14.6 to solve the problem given in Table 14.1.

14.2 Do Project 14.1 for the *change counting problem* described in Section 14.1.1.

14.3 Do Project 14.1 for the *scales balancing problem* described in Section 14.2.1.

14.4 Do Project 14.1 for the *N-queens problem* described in Exercise 14.8.

14.5 Design and implement a **GreedySolver** class, along the lines of the **DepthFirstSolver** and **BreadthFirstSolver** classes, that conducts a greedy search of the solution space. To do this you will have to add a method to the `Solution` interface:

```
public interface getGreedySolution
    extends Solution
{
    Solution getGreedySuccessor ();
}
```

14.6 Design and implement a `SimulatedAnnealingSolver` class, along the lines of the `DepthFirstSolver` and `BreadthFirstSolver` classes, that implements the simulated annealing strategy described in Section 14.5.4 this you will have to add a method to the `Solution` interface:

```
public interface SimulatedAnnealingSolution
    extends Solution
{
    Solution getRandomSuccessor ();
}
```

14.7 Design and implement a dynamic programming algorithm to solve the change counting problem. Your algorithm should always find the optimal solution— even when the greedy algorithm fails.

14.8 Consider the divide-and-conquer strategy for matrix multiplication described in Section 14.3.5.

a. Rewrite the implementation of the `times` method of the `Matrix` class introduced in Program 4.10.

b. Compare the running time of your implementation with the $O(n^3)$ algorithm given in Program 4.12.

14.9 Consider a random number generator that generates random numbers uniformly distributed between zero and one. Such a generator produces a sequence of random numbers $x_1, x_2, x_2, \ldots$. A common test of randomness evaluates the correlation between consecutive pairs of numbers in the sequence. One way to do this is to plot on a graph the points

$$(x_1, x_2), (x_2, x_3), (x_3, x_4), \ldots.$$

a. Write a program to compute the first 1000 pairs of numbers generated using the `UniformRV` defined in Program 14.16.

b. What conclusions can you draw from your results?

15 | Sorting Algorithms and Sorters

15.1 Basics

Consider an arbitrary sequence $S = \{s_1, s_2, s_3, \ldots, s_n\}$ composed of $n \geq 0$ elements drawn from a universal set U. The goal of *sorting* is to rearrange the elements of S to produce a new sequence, say S', in which the elements of S appear *in order*.

But what does it mean for the elements of S' to be *in order*? We will assume that there is a relation, $<$, defined over the universe U. The relation $<$ must be a *total order*, which is defined as follows:

Definition 15.1
A total order is a relation, say $<$, defined on the elements of some universal set U with the following properties:

1. *For all pairs of elements $(i, j) \in U \times U$, exactly one of the following is true: $i < j$, $i = j$, or $j < i$.*
   (All elements are commensurate).
2. *For all triples $(i, j, k) \in U \times U \times U$, $i < j \wedge j < k \iff i < k$.*
   (The relation $<$ is transitive).

In order to *sort* the elements of the sequence S, we determine the *permutation* $P = \{p_1, p_2, p_3, \ldots, p_n\}$ of the elements of S such that

$$s_{p_1} \leq s_{p_2} \leq s_{p_3} \leq \cdots \leq s_{p_n}.$$

In practice, we are not interested in the permutation P, per se. Instead, our objective is to compute the sorted sequence $S' = \{s'_1, s'_2, s'_3, \ldots, s'_n\}$ in which $s'_i = s_{p_i}$ for $1 \leq i \leq n$.

Sometimes the sequence to be sorted, S, contains duplicates—that is, there exist values i and j, $1 \leq i < j \leq n$, such that $s_i = s_j$. In general when a sequence that contains duplicates is sorted, there is no guarantee that the duplicated elements retain their relative positions, that is, s_i could appear either before or after s_j in the sorted sequence S'. If duplicates retain their relative positions in the sorted sequence, the sort is said to be *stable*. For s_i and s_j to retain their relative order in the sorted sequence, we require that s'_{p_i} precedes s'_{p_j} in S'. Therefore, the sort is stable if $p_i < p_j$.

15.2   Sorting and Sorters

The traditional way to implement a sorting algorithm is to write a method that sorts an array of data. This chapter presents an alternate, object-oriented approach that is based on the notion of an *abstract sorter*.

Think of a sorter as an abstract machine, the sole purpose of which is to sort arrays of data. A machine is an object. Therefore, it makes sense that we represent it as an instance of some class. The machine sorts data. Therefore, the class will have a method, say **sort**, which sorts an array of data.

Program 15.1 defines the **Sorter** interface. The interface consists of the single method **sort**. This method takes as its argument an array of **Comparable** objects and it sorts the objects therein.

Abstract Sorters

Program 15.2 defines the **AbstractSorter** class. The **AbstractSorter** class implements the **Sorter** interface defined in Program 15.1. The **AbstractSorter** comprises the two fields, **array** and **n**, the concrete methods **swap** and **sort(Comparable[])**, and the no-arg abstract method **sort()**. Since the no-arg **sort** method is an abstract method, an implementation must be given in a derived class.

The **sort(Comparable[])** method does not sort the data itself. It is the no-arg **sort** method, which is provided by a derived class, that does the actual sorting. The **sort(Comparable[])** method merely sets-up things by initializing the fields of **AbstractSorter** as follows: the **array** field refers to the array of objects to be sorted and the length of that array is assigned to the **n** field.

The **swap** method is used to implement most of the sorting algorithms presented in this chapter. The swap method takes two integer arguments. It exchanges the contents of the array at the positions specified by the arguments. The exchange is done as a sequence of three assignments. Therefore, the **swap** method runs in constant time.

PROGRAM 15.1
Sorter interface

```
1  public interface Sorter
2  {
3      void sort (Comparable[] array);
4  }
```

PROGRAM 15.2
AbstractSorter class

```
1    public abstract class AbstractSorter
2        implements Sorter
3    {
4        protected Comparable[] array;
5        protected int n;
6
7        protected abstract void sort ();
8
9        public final void sort (Comparable[] array)
10        {
11            n = array.length;
12            this.array = array;
13            if (n > 0)
14                sort ();
15            this.array = null;
16        }
17
18        protected final void swap (int i, int j)
19        {
20            Comparable tmp = array [i];
21            array [i] = array [j];
22            array [j] = tmp;
23        }
24    }
```

Sorter Class Hierarchy

This chapter describes nine different sorting algorithms. These are organized into the following five categories:

- insertion sorts,
- exchange sorts,
- selection sorts,
- merge sorts, and
- distribution sorts.

As shown in Figure 15.1, the sorter classes have been arranged in a class hierarchy that reflects this classification scheme.

FIGURE 15.1
Sorter class hierarchy.

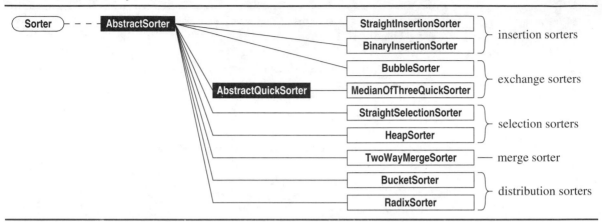

15.3 Insertion Sorting

The first class of sorting algorithm that we consider comprises algorithms that *sort by insertion*. An algorithm that sorts by insertion takes the initial, unsorted sequence, $S = \{s_1, s_2, s_3, \ldots, s_n\}$, and computes a series of *sorted* sequences $S'_0, S'_1, S'_2, \ldots, S'_n$, as follows:

1. The first sequence in the series, S'_0, is the empty sequence; that is, $S'_0 = \{\}$.
2. Given a sequence S'_i in the series, for $0 \leq i < n$, the next sequence in the series, S'_{i+1}, is obtained by inserting the $(i + 1)$th element of the unsorted sequence s_{i+1} into the correct position in S'_i.

Each sequence S'_i, $0 \leq i < n$, contains the first i elements of the unsorted sequence S. Therefore, the final sequence in the series, S'_n, is the sorted sequence we seek; that is, $S' = S'_n$.

Figure 15.2 illustrates the insertion sorting algorithm. The figure shows the progression of the insertion sorting algorithm as it sorts an array of ten integers. The array is sorted *in place*; that is, the initial unsorted sequence, S, and the series of sorted sequences, $S'_0, S'_1, \ldots$, occupy the same array.

In the ith step, the element at position i in the array is inserted into the sorted sequence S'_i, which occupies array positions 0 to $(i - 1)$. After this is done, array positions 0 to i contain the $i + 1$ elements of S'_{i+1}. Array positions $(i + 1)$ to $(n - 1)$ contain the remaining $n - i - 1$ elements of the unsorted sequence S.

As shown in Figure 15. 2, the first step ($i = 0$) is trivial—inserting an element into the empty list involves no work. Altogether, $n - 1$ non-trivial insertions are required to sort a list of n elements.

FIGURE 15.2
Insertion sorting.

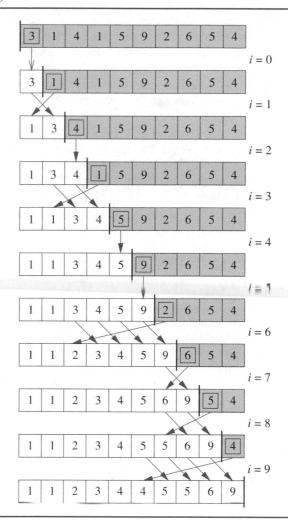

15.3.1 Straight Insertion Sort

The key step of any insertion sorting algorithm involves the insertion of an item into a sorted sequence. There are two aspects to an insertion—finding the correct position in the sequence at which to insert the new element and moving all the elements over to make room for the new one.

This section presents the *straight insertion sorting* algorithm. Straight insertion sorting uses a *linear search* to locate the position at which the next element is to be inserted.

Implementation

Program 15.3 defines the `StraightInsertionSorter` class. The `Straight-InsertionSorter` extends the `AbstractSorter` class defined in Program 15.2. It simply provides an implementation for the no-arg `sort` method.

In order to determine the running time of the `sort` method, we need to determine the number of iterations of the inner loop (lines 7–11). The number of iterations of the inner loop in the ith iteration of the outer loop depends on the positions of the values in the array. In the best case, the value in position i of the array is larger than the value in position $i - 1$ and zero iterations of the inner loop are done. In this case, the running time for insertion sort is $O(n)$. Notice that the best-case performance occurs when we sort an array that is already sorted!

In the worst case, i iterations of the inner loop are required in the ith iteration of the outer loop. This occurs when the value in position i of the array is smaller than the values at positions 0 through $i - 1$. Therefore, the worst case arises when we sort an array in which the elements are initially sorted in reverse. In this case the running time for insertion sort is $O(n^2)$.

15.3.2 Average Running Time

The best-case running time of insertion sorting is $O(n)$ but the worst-case running time is $O(n^2)$. Therefore, we might suspect that the average running time falls somewhere in between. In order to determine it, we must define more precisely what we mean by the *average* running time. A simple definition of average running time is to say that it is the running time needed to sort the average sequence. But what is the average sequence?

The usual way to determine the average running time of a sorting algorithm is to consider only sequences that contain no duplicates. Since every sorted sequence of length n is simply a permutation of an unsorted one, we can represent every such sequence by

---

PROGRAM 15.3
`StraightInsertionSorter` class `sort` method

```
1   public class StraightInsertionSorter
2       extends AbstractSorter
3   {
4       protected void sort ()
5       {
6           for (int i = 1; i < n; ++i)
7               for (int j = i;
8                   j > 0 && array [j - 1].isGT (array [j]); --j)
9               {
10                  swap (j, j - 1);
11              }
12      }
13  }
```

---

a permutation of the sequence $S = \{1, 2, 3, \ldots, n\}$. When computing the average running time, we assume that every permutation is equally likely. Therefore, the average running time of a sorting algorithm is the running time averaged over all permutations of the sequence S.

Consider a permutation $P = \{p_1, p_2, p_3, \ldots, p_n\}$ of the sequence S. An *inversion* in P consists of two elements, say p_i and p_j, such that $p_i > p_j$ but $i < j$; that is, an inversion in P is a pair of elements that are in the wrong order. For example, the permutation $\{1, 4, 3, 2\}$ contains three inversions—$(4, 3)$, $(4, 2)$, and $(3, 2)$. The following theorem tells us how many inversions we can expect in the average sequence:

Theorem 15.1
The average number of inversions in a permutation of n distinct elements is n(n − 1)/4.

Proof   Let S be an arbitrary sequence of n distinct elements and let S^R be the same sequence, but in reverse.

For example, if $S = \{s_1, s_2, s_3, \ldots, s_n\}$, then $S^R = \{s_n, s_{n-1}, s_{n-2}, \ldots, s_1\}$.

Consider any pair of distinct elements in S, say s_i and s_j, where $1 \leq i < j \leq n$. There are two distinct possibilities: either $s_i < s_j$, in which case (s_j, s_i) is an inversion is S^R; or $s_j < s_i$, in which case (s_i, s_j) is an inversion is S. Therefore, every pair contributes exactly one inversion either to S or to S^R.

The total number of pairs in S is $\binom{n}{2} = n(n - 1)/2$. Since every such pair contributes an inversion either to S or to S^R, we expect *on average* that half of the inversions will appear in S. Therefore, the average number of inversions in a sequence of n distinct elements is $n(n - 1)/4$.

What do inversions have to do with sorting? As a list is sorted, inversions are removed. In fact, since the inner loop of the insertion sort method swaps *adjacent* array elements, inversions are removed *one at a time*! Since a swap takes constant time, and since the average number of inversions is $n(n - 1)/4$, the *average* running time for the insertion sort method is $O(n^2)$.

15.3.3   Binary Insertion Sort

The straight insertion algorithm presented in the preceding section does a linear search to find the position in which to do the insertion. However, since the element is inserted into a sequence that is already sorted, we can use a binary search instead of a linear search. Whereas a linear search requires $O(n)$ comparisons in the worst case, a binary search only requires $O(\log n)$ comparisons. Therefore, if the cost of a comparison is significant, the binary search may be preferred.

Program 15.4 defines the **BinaryInsertionSorter** class. The **Binary-InsertionSorter** class extends the **AbstractSorter** class defined in Program 15.2. The framework of the **sort** method is essentially the same as that of the **StraightInsertionSorter** class.

Exactly $n - 1$ iterations of the outer loop are done (lines 6–21). In each iteration, a binary search search is done to determine the position at which to do the insertion

PROGRAM 15.4
BinaryInsertionSorter class sort method

```
1   public class BinaryInsertionSorter
2       extends AbstractSorter
3   {
4       protected void sort ()
5       {
6           for (int i = 1; i < n; ++i)
7           {
8               Comparable tmp = array [i];
9               int left = 0;
10              int right = i;
11              while (left < right)
12              {
13                  int middle = (left + right) / 2;
14                  if (tmp.isGE (array [middle]))
15                      left = middle + 1;
16                  else
17                      right = middle;
18              }
19              for (int j = i; j > left; --j)
20                  swap (j - 1, j);
21          }
22      }
23  }
```

(lines 8–18). In the ith iteration of the outer loop, the binary search considers array positions 0 to i (for $1 \leq i < n$). The running time for the binary search in the ith iteration is $O(\lfloor \log_2(i + 1) \rfloor) = O(\log i)$. Once the correct position is found, at most i swaps are needed to insert the element in its place.

The worst-case running time of the binary insertion sort is dominated by the i swaps needed to do the insertion. Therefore, the worst-case running time is $O(n^2)$. Furthermore, since the algorithm only swaps adjacent array elements, the average running time is also $O(n^2)$. (See Section 15.3.2.) Asymptotically, the binary insertion sort is no better than straight insertion.

However, the binary insertion sort does fewer array element comparisons than the insertion sort. In the ith iteration of the outer loop, the binary search requires $\lfloor \log_2(i + 1) \rfloor$ comparisons, for $1 \leq i < n$. Therefore, the total number of comparisons is

$$\sum_{i=0}^{n-1} \lfloor \log_2(i + 1) \rfloor = \sum_{i=1}^{n} \lfloor \log_2 i \rfloor$$
$$= (n + 1) \lfloor \log_2(n + 1) \rfloor + 2^{\lfloor \log_2(n+1) \rfloor + 1} + 2$$
$$= O(n \log n).$$

(This result follows directly from Theorem 11.3.)

TABLE 15.1
Running Times for Insertion Sorting

Algorithm	Running Time		
	Best Case	Average Case	Worst Case
Straight insertion sort	$O(n)$	$O(n^2)$	$O(n^2)$
Binary insertion sort	$O(n \log n)$	$O(n^2)$	$O(n^2)$

The number of comparisons required by the straight insertion sort is $O(n^2)$ in the worst case as well as on average. Therefore on average, the binary insertion sort uses fewer comparisons than the straight insertion sort. On the other hand, the previous section shows that in the best case the running time for straight insertion is $O(n)$. Since the binary insertion sort method *always* does the binary search, its best-case running time is $O(n \log n)$. Table 15.1 summarizes the asymptotic running times for the two insertion sorts.

15.4 Exchange Sorting

The second class of sorting algorithm that we consider comprises algorithms that *sort by exchanging* pairs of items until the sequence is sorted. In general, an algorithm may exchange adjacent elements as well as widely separated ones.

In fact, since the insertion sorts considered in the preceding section accomplish the insertion by swapping adjacent elements, insertion sorting can be considered as a kind of exchange sort. The reason for creating a separate category for insertion sorts is that the essence of those algorithms is insertion into a sorted list. On the other hand, an exchange sort does not necessarily make use of such a sorted list.

15.4.1 Bubble Sort

The simplest and, perhaps, the best known of the exchange sorts is the *bubble sort*.[1] Figure 15.3 shows the operation of the bubble sort.

To sort the sequence $S = \{s_0, s_1, s_2, \ldots, s_{n-1}\}$, bubble sort makes $n - 1$ passes through the data. In each pass, adjacent elements are compared and swapped if necessary. First, s_0 and s_1 are compared; next, s_1 and s_2; and so on.

Notice that after the first pass through the data, the largest element in the sequence has *bubbled up* into the last array position. In general, after k passes through the data, the last k elements of the array are correct and need not be considered any longer. In this regard the bubble sort differs from the insertion sort algorithms—the sorted subsequence of k elements is never modified (by an insertion).

Figure 15.3 also shows that although $n - 1$ passes through the data are required to guarantee that the list is sorted in the end, it is possible for the list to become sorted much earlier! When no exchanges at all are made in a given pass, then the array is

---

[1] Unfortunately, the fame of bubble sort exceeds by far its practical value.

FIGURE 15.3
Bubble sorting.

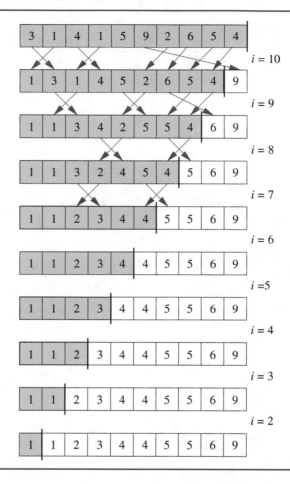

sorted and no additional passes are required. A minor algorithmic modification would be to count the exchanges made in a pass and to terminate the sort when none are made.

Program 15.5 defines the **BubbleSorter** class. The **BubbleSorter** class extends the **AbstractSorter** class defined in Program 15.2. It simply provides an implementation for the no-arg **sort** method.

The outer loop (lines 6–9) is done for $i = n, n - 1, n - 2, n - 3, \ldots, 2$. That makes $n - 1$ iterations in total. During the ith iteration of the outer loop, exactly $i - 1$ iterations of the inner loop are done (lines 7–9). Therefore, the number of iterations of the inner loop, summed over all the passes of the outer loop, is

$$\sum_{i=2}^{n}(i - 1) = \sum_{i=1}^{n-1} i = \frac{n(n - 1)}{2}.$$

Consequently, the running time of bubble sort is $\Theta(n^2)$.

PROGRAM 15.5
BubbleSorter class sort method

```
 1   public class BubbleSorter
 2       extends AbstractSorter
 3   {
 4       protected void sort ()
 5       {
 6           for (int i = n; i > 1; --i)
 7               for (int j = 0; j < i - 1; ++j)
 8                   if (array [j].isGT (array [j + 1]))
 9                       swap (j, j + 1);
10       }
11   }
```

The body of the inner loop compares adjacent array elements and swaps them if necessary (lines 8–9). This takes at most a constant amount of time. Of course, the algorithm will run slightly faster when no swapping is needed. For example, this occurs if the array is already sorted to begin with. In the worst case, it is necessary to swap in every iteration of the inner loop. This occurs when the array is sorted initially in reverse order. Since only adjacent elements are swapped, bubble sort removes inversions one at a time. Therefore, the average number of swaps required is $O(n^2)$. Nevertheless, the running time of bubble sort is always $\Theta(n^2)$.

15.4.2 Quicksort

The second exchange sort we consider is the *quicksort* algorithm. Quicksort is a *divide-and-conquer* style algorithm. A divide-and-conquer algorithm solves a given problem by splitting it into two or more smaller subproblems, recursively solving each of the subproblems, and then combining the solutions to the smaller problems to obtain a solution to the original one.

To sort the sequence $S = \{s_1, s_2, s_3, \ldots, s_n\}$, quicksort performs the following steps:

1. Select one of the elements of S. The selected element, p, is called the *pivot*.
2. Remove p from S and then partition the remaining elements of S into two distinct sequences, L and G, such that every element in L is less than or equal to the pivot and every element in G is greater than or equal to the pivot. In general, both L and G are *unsorted*.
3. Rearrange the elements of the sequence as follows:

$$S' = \{\underbrace{l_1, l_2, \ldots, l_{|L|}}_{L}, \underbrace{p}_{\text{pivot}}, \underbrace{g_1, g_2, \ldots, g_{|G|}}_{G}\}.$$

Notice that the pivot is now in the position in which it belongs in the sorted sequence, since all of the elements to the left of the pivot are less than or equal to the pivot and all of the elements to the right are greater than or equal to it.

4. Recursively quicksort the unsorted sequences L and G.

The first step of the algorithm is a crucial one. We have not specified how to select the pivot. Fortunately, the sorting algorithm works no matter which element is chosen to be the pivot. However, the pivot selection affects directly the running time of the algorithm. If we choose poorly the running time will be poor.

Figure 15.4 illustrates the detailed operation of quicksort as it sorts the sequence $\{3, 1, 4, 1, 5, 9, 2, 6, 5, 4\}$. To begin the sort, we select a pivot. In this example, the value 4 in the last array position is chosen. Next, the remaining elements are partitioned into two sequences, one that contains values less than or equal to 4 ($L = \{3, 1, 2, 1\}$) and one that contains values greater than or equal to 4 ($G = \{5, 9, 4, 6, 5\}$). Notice that the partitioning is accomplished by exchanging elements. This is why quicksort is considered to be an exchange sort.

After the partitioning, the pivot is inserted between the two sequences. This is called *restoring* the pivot. To restore the pivot, we simply exchange it with the first element of G. Notice that the 4 is in its correct position in the sorted sequence and it is not considered any further.

Now the quicksort algorithm calls itself recursively, first to sort the sequence $L = \{3, 1, 2, 1\}$; second to sort the sequence $G = \{9, 4, 6, 5, 5\}$. The quicksort of L selects 1 as the pivot, and creates the two subsequences $L' = \{1\}$ and $G' = \{2, 3\}$. Similarly, the quicksort of G uses 5 as the pivot and creates the two subsequences $L'' = \{5, 4\}$ and $G'' = \{9, 6\}$.

At this point in the example the recursion has been stopped. It turns out that to keep the code simple, quicksort algorithms usually stop the recursion when the length of a subsequence falls below a critical value called the *cut-off*. In this example, the cut-off is two (i.e., a subsequence of two or fewer elements is not sorted). This means that when the algorithm terminates, the sequence is not yet sorted. However as Figure 15.4 shows, the sequence is *almost* sorted. In fact, every element is guaranteed to be less than two positions away from its final resting place.

We can complete the sorting of the sequence by using a straight insertion sort. In Section 15.3.1 it is shown that straight insertion is quite good at sorting sequences that are almost sorted. In fact, if we know that every element of the sequence is at most d positions from its final resting place, the running time of straight insertion is $O(dn)$ and since $d = 2$ is a constant, the running time is $O(n)$.

Implementation

Program 15.6 introduces the **AbstractQuickSorter** class. The **AbstractQuickSorter** class extends the **AbstractSorter** class defined in Program 15.2. It declares the abstract method **selectPivot**, the implementation of which is provided by a derived class.

Program 15.7 defines a **sort** method of the **AbstractQuickSorter** class that takes two integer arguments, **left** and **right**, which denote left and right ends,

FIGURE 15.4
"Quick" sorting.

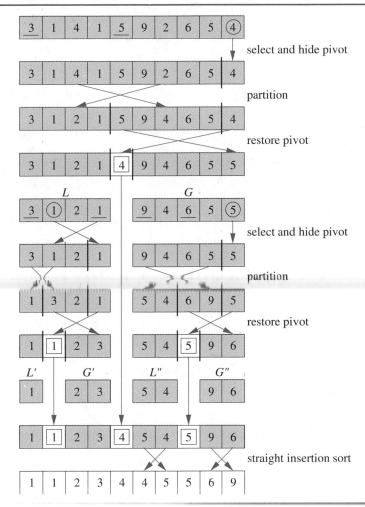

select and hide pivot

partition

restore pivot

select and hide pivot

partition

restore pivot

straight insertion sort

PROGRAM 15.6
`AbstractQuickSorter` fields

```
1  public abstract class AbstractQuickSorter
2      extends AbstractSorter
3  {
4      protected static final int cutOff = 2; // minimum cut-off
5
6      protected abstract int selectPivot (int left, int right);
7      // ...
8  }
```

PROGRAM 15.7
AbstractQuickSorter class recursive **sort** method

```
1   public abstract class AbstractQuickSorter
2       extends AbstractSorter
3   {
4       protected void sort (int left, int right)
5       {
6           if (right - left + 1 > cutOff)
7           {
8               int p = selectPivot (left, right);
9               swap (p, right);
10              Comparable pivot = array [right];
11              int i = left;
12              int j = right - 1;
13              for (;;)
14              {
15                  while (i < j && array [i].isLT (pivot)) ++i;
16                  while (i < j && array [j].isGT (pivot)) --j;
17                  if (i >= j) break;
18                  swap (i++, j--);
19              }
20              if (array [i].isGT (pivot))
21                  swap (i, right);
22              if (left < i)
23                  sort (left, i - 1);
24              if (right > i)
25                  sort (i + 1, right);
26          }
27      }
28      // ...
29  }
```

---

respectively, of the section of the array to be sorted. That is, this **sort** method sorts

$$\text{array[left], array[left+1], ... , array[right]}$$

As discussed previously, the **AbstractQuickSorter** only sorts sequences whose length exceeds the *cut-off* value. Since the implementation shown only works correctly when the number of elements in the sequence to be sorted is three or more, the *cut-off* value of two is used (line 6).

The algorithm begins by calling the method **selectPivot**, which chooses one of the elements to be the pivot (line 8). The implementation of **selectPivot** is discussed next. All that we require here is that the value p returned by **selectPivot** satisfies **left** $\leq p \leq$ **right**. Having selected an element to be the pivot, we *hide* the pivot by swapping it with the rightmost element of the sequence (line 9). The pivot is *hidden* in order to get it out of the way of the next step.

The next step partitions the remaining elements into two sequences—one comprising values less than or equal to the pivot, the other comprising values greater than or equal to the pivot. The partitioning is done using two array indices, i and j. The first, i, starts at the left end and moves to the right; the second, j, starts at the right end and moves to the left.

The variable i is increased as long as **array[i]** is less than the pivot (line 15). Then the variable j is decreased as long as **array[j]** is greater than the pivot (line 16). When i and j meet, the partitioning is done (line 17). Otherwise, i < j but **array[i]** ≥ **pivot** ≥ **array[j]**. This situation is remedied by swapping **array[i]** and **array[j]** (line 18).

When the partitioning loop terminates, the pivot is still in **array[right]**; the value in **array[i]** is greater than or equal to the pivot; everything to the left is less than or equal to the pivot; and everything to the right is greater than or equal to the pivot. We can now put the pivot in its proper place by swapping it with **array[i]** (lines 20–21). This is called *restoring* the pivot. With the pivot in its final resting place, all we need to do is sort the subsequences on either side of the pivot (lines 22–25).

Program 15.8 defines the no-arg **sort** method of the **AbstractQuickSorter** class. The no-arg **sort** acts as the front end to the recursive **sort** given in Program 15.7. It calls the recursive sort method with left set to zero and **right** set to $n-1$, where n is the length of the array to be sorted. Finally, it uses a **StraightInsertionSorter** to finish sorting the list.

15.4.3 Running Time Analysis

The running time of the recursive **sort** method (Program 15.7) is given by

$$T(n) = \begin{cases} O(1) & n \le 2, \\ \mathcal{T}\langle \texttt{selectPivot} \rangle + T(i) + T(n-i-1) + O(n) & n > 2, \end{cases} \quad (15.1)$$

PROGRAM 15.8
AbstractQuickSorter class **sort** method

```
1   public abstract class AbstractQuickSorter
2       extends AbstractSorter
3   {
4       protected void sort ()
5       {
6           sort (0, n - 1);
7           Sorter sorter = new StraightInsertionSorter ();
8           sorter.sort (array);
9       }
10      // ...
11  }
```

where n is the number of elements in sequence to be sorted, $\mathcal{T}\langle\texttt{selectPivot}\rangle$ is the running time of the **selectPivot** method, and i is the number of elements that end up to the left of the pivot, $0 \leq i \leq n - 1$.

The running time of **sort** is affected by the **selectPivot** method in two ways: First, the value of the pivot chosen affects the sizes of the subsequences; that is, the pivot determines the value i in Equation (15.1). Second, the running time of the **selectPivot** method itself, $\mathcal{T}\langle\texttt{selectPivot}\rangle$, must be taken into account. Fortunately, if $\mathcal{T}\langle\texttt{selectPivot}\rangle = O(n)$, we can ignore its running time because there is already an $O(n)$ term in the expression.

In order to solve Equation (15.1), we assume that $\mathcal{T}\langle\texttt{selectPivot}\rangle = O(n)$ and then drop the $O(\cdot)$s from the recurrence to get

$$T(n) = \begin{cases} 1 & n \leq 2, \\ T(i) + T(n - i - 1) + n & n > 2, \quad 0 \leq i \leq n - 1. \end{cases} \tag{15.2}$$

Clearly the solution depends on the value of i.

Worst-Case Running Time

In the worst case the i in Equation (15.2) is always zero.[2] In this case, we solve the recurrence using repeated substitution like this:

$$\begin{aligned} T(n) &= T(n - 1) + n \\ &= T(n - 2) + (n - 1) + n \\ &= T(n - 3) + (n - 2) + (n - 1) + n \\ &\;\;\vdots \\ &= T(n - k) + \sum_{j=n-k}^{n} j \\ &\;\;\vdots \\ &= T(2) + \sum_{j=2}^{n} j \\ &= n(n + 1)/2 \\ &= O(n^2). \end{aligned}$$

The worst case occurs when the two subsequences are as unbalanced as they can be—one sequence has all of the remaining elements and the other has none.

Best-Case Running Time

In the best case, the partitioning step divides the remaining elements into two sequences with exactly the same number of elements. For example, suppose that $n = 2^m - 1$ for some integer $m > 0$. After removing the pivot, $2^m - 2$ elements remain. If these are divided evenly, each sequence will have $2^{m-1} - 1$ elements. In this case Equation (15.2)

---

[2]There is also the symmetrical case in which i is always $n - 1$.

gives

$$
\begin{aligned}
T(2^m - 1) &= 2T(2^{m-1} - 1) + 2^m - 1 \\
&= 2^2 T(2^{m-2} - 1) + 2 \cdot 2^m - 2 - 1 \\
&= 2^3 T(2^{m-3} - 1) + 3 \cdot 2^m - 3 - 2 - 1 \\
&\ \ \vdots \\
&= 2^k T(2^{m-k} - 1) + k 2^m - \sum_{j=1}^{k} j \\
&= 2^{m-1} T(1) + (m-1) 2^m - \sum_{j=1}^{m-1} j, \quad m - k = 1 \\
&= \left(2^m(2m - 1) - m(m-1)\right)/2 \\
&= \left[(n+1)(2\log_2(n+1) - 1) - (\log_2(n+1) - 1)\log_2(n+1)\right]/2 \\
&= O(n \log n).
\end{aligned}
$$

15.4.4   Average Running Time

To determine the average running time for the quicksort algorithm, we shall assume that each element of the sequence has an equal chance of being selected for the pivot. Therefore, if i is the number of elements in a sequence of length n less than the pivot, then i is uniformly distributed in the interval $[0, n - 1]$. Consequently, the average value of $T(i) = \frac{1}{n}\sum_{j=0}^{n-1} T(j)$. Similarly, the average the value of $T(n - i - 1) = \frac{1}{n}\sum_{j=0}^{n-1} T(n - j - 1)$. To determine the average running time, we rewrite Equation (15.2) thus:

$$
T(n) = \begin{cases} 1 & n \le 2, \\ \dfrac{1}{n}\displaystyle\sum_{j=0}^{n-1} T(j) + \dfrac{1}{n}\sum_{j=0}^{n-1} T(n - j - 1) + n & n > 2 \end{cases}
$$

$$
= \begin{cases} 1 & n \le 2, \\ \dfrac{2}{n}\displaystyle\sum_{j=0}^{n-1} T(j) + n & n > 2. \end{cases} \tag{15.3}
$$

To solve this recurrence we consider the case $n > 2$ and then multiply Equation (15.3) by n to get

$$
nT(n) = 2\sum_{j=0}^{n-1} T(j) + n^2. \tag{15.4}
$$

Since this equation is valid for any $n > 2$, by substituting $n - 1$ for n we can also write

$$
(n - 1)T(n - 1) = 2\sum_{j=0}^{n-2} T(j) + n^2 - 2n + 1, \tag{15.5}
$$

which is valid for $n > 3$. Subtracting Equation (15.5) from Equation (15.3) gives

$$nT(n) - (n-1)T(n-1) = 2T(n-1) + 2n - 1,$$

which can be rewritten as

$$\frac{T(n)}{n+1} = \frac{T(n-1)}{n} + \frac{2}{n+1} - \frac{1}{n(n+1)}. \tag{15.6}$$

Equation (15.6) can be solved by telescoping like this:

$$\frac{T(n)}{n+1} = \frac{T(n-1)}{n} + \frac{2}{n+1} - \frac{1}{(n)(n+1)} \tag{15.7}$$

$$\frac{T(n-1)}{n} = \frac{T(n-2)}{n-1} + \frac{2}{n} - \frac{1}{(n-1)(n)}$$

$$\frac{T(n-1)}{n-1} = \frac{T(n-3)}{n-2} + \frac{2}{n-1} - \frac{1}{(n-2)(n-1)}$$

$$\vdots$$

$$\frac{T(n-k)}{n-k+1} = \frac{T(n-k-1)}{n-k} + \frac{2}{n-k+1} - \frac{1}{(n-k)(n-k+1)}$$

$$\vdots$$

$$\frac{T(3)}{4} = \frac{T(2)}{2} + \frac{2}{4} - \frac{1}{(3)(4)}. \tag{15.8}$$

Adding together Equation (15.7) through Equation (15.8) gives

$$\frac{T(n)}{n+1} = \frac{T(2)}{3} + 2\sum_{i=4}^{n+1} \frac{1}{i} - \sum_{i=3}^{n} \frac{1}{i(i+1)}$$

$$= 2\sum_{i=1}^{n+1} \frac{1}{i} - \sum_{i=1}^{n} \frac{1}{i(i+1)} - 2$$

$$= 2H_{n+1} + \frac{1}{n+1} - 3,$$

where H_{n+1} is the $(n+1)$th *harmonic number*. Finally, multiplying through by $n+1$ gives

$$T(n) = 2(n+1)H_{n+1} - 3n - 2.$$

In Section 2.1.8 it is shown that $H_n \approx \ln n + \gamma$, where $\gamma \approx 0.577, 215$ is called *Euler's constant*. Thus, we get that the average running time of quicksort is

$$T(n) \approx 2(n+1)(\ln(n+1) + \gamma) - 3n - 3$$
$$= O(n \log n).$$

TABLE 15.2
Running Times for Exchange Sorting

Algorithm	Best Case	Average Case	Worst Case
	Running Time		
Bubble sort	$O(n^2)$	$O(n^2)$	$O(n^2)$
Quicksort (random pivot selection)	$O(n \log n)$	$O(n \log n)$	$O(n^2)$

Table 15.2 summarizes the asymptotic running times for the quicksort method and compares them to those of bubble sort. Notice that the best-case and average-case running times for the quicksort algorithm have the same asymptotic bound!

15.4.5 Selecting the Pivot

The analysis in the preceding section shows that selecting a good pivot is important. If we do a bad job of choosing the pivot, the running time of quicksort is $O(n^2)$. On the other hand, the average-case analysis shows that if every element of a sequence is equally likely to be chosen for the pivot, the running time is $O(n \log n)$. This suggests that we can expect to get good performance simply by selecting *a random pivot*!

If we expect to be sorting random input sequences, then we can achieve random pivot selection simply by always choosing, say, the first element of the sequence to be the pivot. Clearly this can be done in constant time. (Remember, the analysis requires that $\mathcal{T}\langle \texttt{selectPivot} \rangle = O(n)$.) As long as each element in the sequence is equally likely to appear in the first position, the average running time will be $O(n \log n)$.

In practice it is often the case that the sequence to be sorted is almost sorted. In particular, consider what happens if the sequence to be sorted using quicksort is already sorted. If we always choose the first element as the pivot, then we are guaranteed to have the worst-case running time! This is also true if we always pick the last element of the sequence. And it is also true if the sequence is initially sorted in reverse.

Therefore, we need to be more careful when choosing the pivot. Ideally, the pivot divides the input sequence exactly in two; that is, the ideal pivot is the *median* element of the sequence. This suggests that the **selectPivot** method should find the median. To ensure that the running time analysis is valid, we need to find the median in $O(n)$ time.

How do you find the median? One way is to sort the sequence and then select the $\lceil n/2 \rceil$th element. But this is not possible, because we need to find the median to sort the sequence in the first place!

While it is possible to find the median of a sequence of n elements in $O(n)$ time, it is usually not necessary to do so. All that we really need to do is select a random element of the sequence while avoiding the problems previously described.

A common way to do this is the *median-of-three pivot selection* technique. In this approach, we choose as the pivot the median of the element at the left end of the sequence, the element at the right end of the sequence, and the element in the middle of

---

PROGRAM 15.9
MedianOfThreeQuickSorter class selectPivot method

```
1   public class MedianOfThreeQuickSorter
2       extends AbstractQuickSorter
3   {
4       protected int selectPivot (int left, int right)
5       {
6           int middle = (left + right) / 2;
7           if (array [left].isGT (array [middle]))
8               swap (left, middle);
9           if (array [left].isGT (array [right]))
10              swap (left, right);
11          if (array [middle].isGT (array [right]))
12              swap (middle, right);
13          return middle;
14      }
15  }
```

---

the sequence. Clearly, this does the *right thing* if the input sequence is initially sorted (either in forward or reverse order).

Program 15.9 defines the **MedianOfThreeQuickSorter** class. The **MedianOf-ThreeQuickSorter** class extends the abstract **AbstractQuickSorter** class introduced in Program 15.6. It provides an implementation for the **selectPivot** method based on median-of-three pivot selection. Notice that this algorithm does exactly three comparisons to select the pivot. As a result, its running time is $O(1)$. In practice this scheme performs sufficiently well that more complicated pivot selection approaches are unnecessary.

15.5 Selection Sorting

The third class of sorting algorithm that we consider comprises algorithms that sort *by selection*. Such algorithms construct the sorted sequence one element at a time by adding elements to the sorted sequence *in order*. At each step, the next element to be added to the sorted sequence is selected from the remaining elements.

Because the elements are added to the sorted sequence in order, they are always added at one end. This is what makes selection sorting different from insertion sorting. In insertion sorting elements are added to the sorted sequence in an arbitrary order. Therefore, the position in the sorted sequence at which each subsequent element is inserted is arbitrary.

Both selection sorts described in this section sort the arrays *in place*. Consequently, the sorts are implemented by exchanging array elements. Nevertheless, selection sorting differs from exchange sorting because at each step we *select* the next element of the sorted sequence from the remaining elements and then we move it into its final position in the array by exchanging it with whatever happens to be occupying that position.

15.5.1 Straight Selection Sorting

The simplest of the selection sorts is called *straight selection*. Figure 15.5 illustrates how straight selection works. In the version shown, the sorted list is constructed from the right (i.e., from the largest to the smallest element values).

At each step of the algorithm, a linear search of the unsorted elements is made in order to determine the position of the largest remaining element. That element is then moved into the correct position of the array by swapping it with the element that currently occupies that position.

FIGURE 15.5
Straight selection sorting.

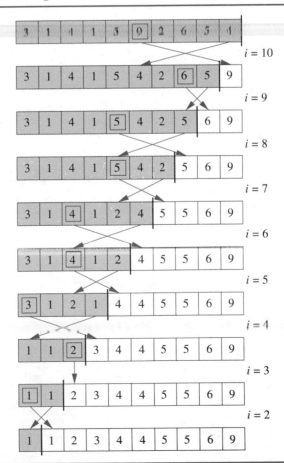

For example, in the first step shown in Figure 15.5, a linear search of the entire array reveals that 9 is the largest element. Since 9 is the largest element, it belongs in the last array position. To move it there, we swap it with the 4 that initially occupies that position. The second step of the algorithm identifies 6 as the largest remaining element and moves it next to the 9. Each subsequent step of the algorithm moves one element into its final position. Therefore, the algorithm is done after $n - 1$ such steps.

Implementation

Program 15.10 defines the **StraightSelectionSorter** class. This class is derived from the **AbstractSorter** base defined in Program 15.2 and it provides an implementation for the no-arg **sort** method. The **sort** method follows directly from the algorithm previously discussed. In each iteration of the main loop (lines 6–13), exactly one element is selected from the unsorted elements and moved into the correct position. A linear search of the unsorted elements is done in order to determine the position of the largest remaining element (lines 9–11). That element is then moved into the correct position (line 12).

In all, $n - 1$ iterations of the outer loop are needed to sort the array. Notice that exactly one swap is done in each iteration of the outer loop. Therefore, $n - 1$ data exchanges are needed to sort the list.

Furthermore, in the ith iteration of the outer loop, $i - 1$ iterations of the inner loop are required and each iteration of the inner loop does one data comparison. Therefore, $O(n^2)$ data comparisons are needed to sort the list.

The total running time of the straight selection **sort** method is $O(n^2)$. Because the same number of comparisons and swaps are always done, this running time bound applies in all cases; that is, the best-case, average-case, and worst-case running times are all $O(n^2)$.

PROGRAM 15.10
StraightSelectionSorter class sort method

```
1   public class StraightSelectionSorter
2       extends AbstractSorter
3   {
4       protected void sort ()
5       {
6           for (int i = n; i > 1; --i)
7           {
8               int max = 0;
9               for (int j = 1; j < i; ++j)
10                  if (array [j].isGT (array [max]))
11                      max = j;
12              swap (i - 1, max);
13          }
14      }
15  }
```

15.5.2 Sorting with a Heap

Selection sorting involves the repeated selection of the next element in the sorted sequence from the set of remaining elements. For example, the straight insertion sorting algorithm given in the preceding section builds the sorted sequence by repeatedly selecting the largest remaining element and prepending it to the sorted sequence developing at the right end of the array.

At each step the largest remaining element is withdrawn from the set of remaining elements. A linear search is done because the order of the remaining elements is arbitrary. However, if we consider the value of each element as its priority, we can view the set of remaining elements as a priority queue. In effect, a selection sort repeatedly dequeues the highest priority element from a priority queue.

Chapter 11 presents a number of priority queue implementations, including binary heaps, leftist heaps, and binomial queues. In this section we present a version of selection sorting that uses a *binary heap* to hold the elements that remain to be sorted. Therefore, it is called a *heapsort*. The principal advantage of using a binary heap is that it is easily implemented using an array and the entire sort can be be done in place.

As explained in Section 11.2, a binary heap is a *complete binary tree* that is easily represented in an array. The n nodes of the heap occupy positions 1 through n of the array. The root is at position 1. In general, the children of the node at position i of the array are found at positions $2i$ and $2i + 1$, and the parent is found at position $\lfloor i/2 \rfloor$.

The heapsort algorithm consists of two phases. In the first phase, the unsorted array is transformed into a heap. (This is called *heapifying* the array.) In this case, a *max-heap* rather than a min-heap is used. The data in a max heap satisfy the following condition: For every node in the heap that has a parent, the item contained in the parent is greater than or equal to the item contained in the given node.

The second phase of heapsort builds the sorted list. The sorted list is built by repeatedly selecting the largest element, withdrawing it from the heap, and adding it to the sorted sequence. As each element is withdrawn from the heap, the remaining elements are heapified.

Implementation

In the first phase of heapsort, the unsorted array is transformed into a max heap. Throughout the process we view the array as a complete binary tree. Since the data in the array are initially unsorted, the tree is not initially heap ordered. We make the tree into a max heap from the bottom up; that is, we start with the leaves and work toward the root. Figure 15.6 illustrates this process.

Figure 15.6 (a) shows a complete tree that is not yet heap ordered—the root is smaller than both its children. However, the two subtrees of the root *are* heap ordered. Given that both of the subtrees of the root are already heap ordered, we can heapify the tree by *percolating* the value in the root down the tree.

To percolate a value down the tree, we swap it with its largest child. For example, in Figure 15.6 (b) we swap 3 and 7. Swapping with the largest child ensures that after the swap, the new root is greater than or equal to *both* its children.

Notice that after the swap the heap order is satisfied at the root, but not in the left subtree of the root. We continue percolating the 3 down by swapping it with 6 as shown in Figure 15.6 (c). In general, we percolate a value down either until it arrives in a

FIGURE 15.6
Combining heaps by percolating values.

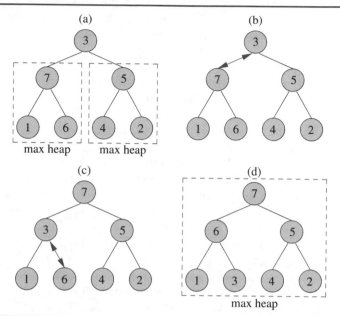

position in which the heap order is satisfied or until it arrives in a leaf. As shown in Figure 15.6 (d), the tree obtained when the percolation is finished is a max heap.

Program 15.11 introduces the **HeapSorter** class. The **HeapSorter** class extends the **AbstractSorter** class defined in Program 15.2. The **percolateDown** method shown in Program 15.11 implements the algorithm previously described. The **percolateDown** method takes two arguments: the number of elements in the array to be considered, **length**; and the position, i, of the node to be percolated.

The purpose of the **percolateDown** method is to transform the subtree rooted at position i into a max heap. It is assumed that the left and right subtrees of the node at position i are already max heaps. Recall that the children of node i are found at positions $2i$ and $2i + 1$. **percolateDown** percolates the value in position i down the tree by swapping elements until the value arrives in a leaf node or until both children of i contain a smaller value.

A constant amount of work is done in each iteration. Therefore, the running time of the **percolateDown** method is determined by the number of iterations of its main loop (lines 8–18). In fact, the number of iterations required in the worst case is equal to the height in the tree of node i.

Since the root of the tree has the greatest height, the worst case occurs for $i = 1$. In Chapter 11 it is shown that the height of a complete binary tree is $\lfloor \log_2 n \rfloor$. Therefore, the worst-case running time of the **percolateDown** method is $O(\log n)$.

Recall that **buildHeap** calls **percolateDown** for $i = \lfloor n/2 \rfloor, \lfloor n/2 \rfloor - 1, \lfloor n/2 \rfloor - 1, \ldots, 1$. If we assume that the worst case occurs every time, the running time of **buildHeap** is $O(n \log n)$.

PROGRAM 15.11
HeapSorter class percolateDown method

```
1   public class HeapSorter
2       extends AbstractSorter
3   {
4       protected static final int base = 1;
5
6       protected void percolateDown (int i, int length)
7       {
8           while (2 * i <= length)
9           {
10              int j = 2 * i;
11              if (j < length &&
12                      array [j + 1 - base].isGT (array [j - base]))
13                  j = j + 1;
14              if (array [i - base].isGE (array [j - base]))
15                  break;
16              swap (i - base, j - base);
17              i = j;
18          }
19      }
20      // ...
21  }
```

15.5.3 Building the Heap

The buildHeap method shown in Program 15.12 transforms an unsorted array into a max heap. It does so by calling the percolateDown method for $i = \lfloor n/2 \rfloor, \lfloor n/2 \rfloor - 1, \lfloor n/2 \rfloor - 2, \ldots, 1$.

PROGRAM 15.12
HeapSorter class buildHeap method

```
1   public class HeapSorter
2       extends AbstractSorter
3   {
4       protected static final int base = 1;
5
6       protected void buildHeap ()
7       {
8           for (int i = n / 2; i > 0; --i)
9               percolateDown (i, n);
10      }
11      // ...
12  }
```

Why does **buildHeap** start percolating at $\lfloor n/2 \rfloor$? A complete binary tree with n nodes has exactly $\lceil n/2 \rceil$ leaves. Therefore, the last node in the array that has a child is in position $\lfloor n/2 \rfloor$. Consequently, the **buildHeap** method starts doing percolate down operations from that point.

The **buildHeap** visits the array elements in reverse order. In effect, the algorithm starts at the deepest node that has a child and works toward the root of the tree. Each array position visited is the root of a subtree. As each such subtree is visited, it is transformed into a max heap. Figure 15.7 illustrates how the **buildHeap** method heapifies an array that is initially unsorted.

FIGURE 15.7
Building a heap.

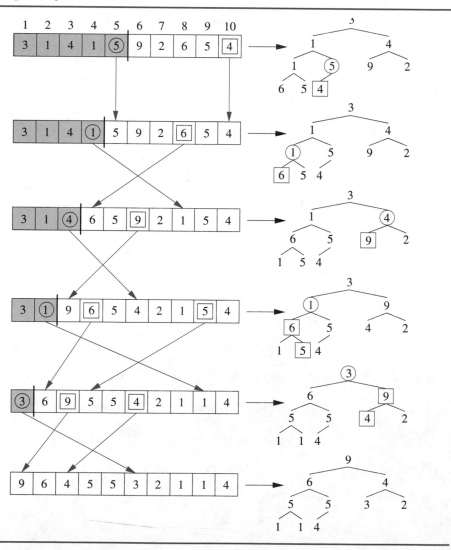

Running Time Analysis

The `buildHeap` method does exactly $\lfloor n/2 \rfloor$ `percolateDown` operations. As discussed previously, the running time for `percolateDown` is $O(h_i)$, where h_i is the height in the tree of the node at array position i. The highest node in the tree is the root and its height is $O(\log n)$. If we make the simplifying assumption that the running time for `percolateDown` is $O(\log n)$ for every value of i, we get that the total running time for `buildHeap` is $O(n \log n)$.

However, $n \log n$ is not a tight bound. The maximum number of iterations of the `percolateDown` loop done during the entire process of building the heap is equal to the sum of the heights of all of the nodes in the tree! The following theorem shows that this is $O(n)$.

Theorem 15.2

Consider a perfect binary tree T of height h having $n = 2^{h+1} - 1$ nodes. The sum of the heights of the nodes in T is $2^{h+1} - 1 - (h + 1) = n - \log_2(n + 1)$.

Proof A perfect binary tree has 1 node at height h, 2 nodes at height $h - 1$, 4 nodes at height $h - 2$, and so on. In general, there are 2^i nodes at height $h - i$. Therefore, the sum of the heights of the nodes is $\sum_{i=0}^{h}(h - i)2^i$.

The summation can be solved as follows: First, we make the simple variable substitution $i = j - 1$:

$$\sum_{i=0}^{h}(h - i)2^i = \sum_{j-1=0}^{h}(h - (j - 1))2^{j-1}$$

$$= \frac{1}{2}\sum_{j=1}^{h+1}(h - j + 1)2^j$$

$$= \frac{1}{2}\sum_{j=0}^{h}(h - j + 1)2^j - (h + 1)/2$$

$$= \frac{1}{2}\sum_{j=0}^{h}(h - j)2^j + \sum_{j=0}^{h}2^j - (h + 1)/2$$

$$= \frac{1}{2}\sum_{j=0}^{h}(h - j)2^j + (2^{h+1} - 1 - h + 1)/2. \qquad (15.9)$$

Note that the summation that appears on the right-hand side is identical to that on the left. Rearranging Equation (15.9) and simplifying gives

$$\sum_{i=0}^{h}(h - i)2^i = 2^{h+1} - 1 - h + 1$$

$$= n - \log_2(n + 1).$$

It follows directly from Theorem 15.2 that the sum of the heights of a perfect binary tree is $O(n)$. But a heap is not a *perfect* tree—it is a *complete* tree. Nevertheless, it is easy to show that the same bound applies to a complete tree. The proof is left as an exercise for the reader (Exercise 15.15). Therefore, the running time for the `buildHeap` method is $O(n)$, where n is the length of the array to be heapified.

The Sorting Phase

Once the max heap has been built, heapsort proceeds to the selection sorting phase. In this phase the sorted sequence is obtained by repeatedly withdrawing the largest element from the max heap. Figure 15.8 illustrates how this is done.

The largest element of the heap is always found at the root and the root of a complete tree is always in array position one. Suppose the heap occupies array positions 1 through k. When an element is withdrawn from the heap, its length decreases by one; that is, after the withdrawal the heap occupies array positions 1 through $k - 1$. Thus, array position k is no longer required by the max heap. However, the next element of the sorted sequence belongs in position k!

FIGURE 15.8
Heap sorting.

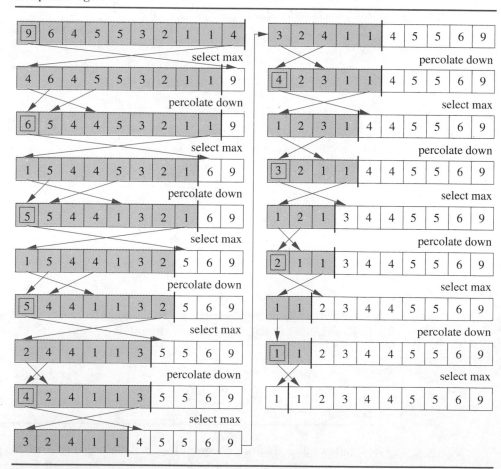

PROGRAM 15.13
HeapSorter class sort method

```
1   public class HeapSorter
2       extends AbstractSorter
3   {
4       protected static final int base = 1;
5
6       protected void sort ()
7       {
8           buildHeap ();
9           for (int i = n; i >= 2; --i)
10          {
11              swap (i - base, 1 - base);
12              percolateDown (1, i - 1);
13          }
14      }
15      // ...
16  }
```

Thus, the sorting phase of heapsort works like this: We repeatedly swap the largest element in the heap (always in position 1) into the next position of the sorted sequence. After each such swap, there is a new value at the root of the heap and this new value is pushed down into the correct position in the heap using the **percolateDown** method.

Program 15.13 gives the **sort** method of the **HeapSorter** class. The **sort** method embodies both phases of the heapsort algorithm. In the first phase of heapsort the **buildHeap** method is called to transform the array into a max heap. As discussed, this is done in $O(n)$ time.

The second phase of the heapsort algorithm builds the sorted list. In all, $n - 1$ iterations of the loop on lines 9–13 are required. Each iteration involves one swap followed by a **percolateDown** operation. Since the worst-case running time for **percolateDown** is $O(\log n)$, the total running time of the loop is $O(n \log n)$. The running time of the second phase asymptotically dominates that of the first phase. As a result, the worst-case running time of heapsort is $O(n \log n)$.

15.6 Merge Sorting

The fourth class of sorting algorithm we consider comprises algorithms that sort *by merging*. Merging is the combination of two or more sorted sequences into a single sorted sequence.

Figure 15.9 illustrates the basic, two-way merge operation. In a two-way merge, two sorted sequences are merged into one. Clearly, two sorted sequences each of length n can be merged into a sorted sequence of length $2n$ in $O(2n) = O(n)$ steps. However, in

FIGURE 15.9
Two-way merging.

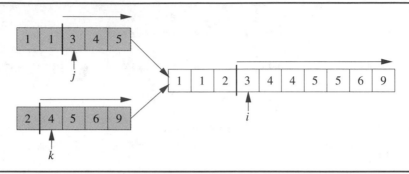

order to do this, we need space in which to store the result; that is, it is not possible to merge the two sequences *in place* in $O(n)$ steps.

Sorting by merging is a recursive, divide-and-conquer strategy. In the base case, we have a sequence with exactly one element in it. Since such a sequence is already sorted, there is nothing to be done. To sort a sequence of $n > 1$ elements:

1. Divide the sequence into two sequences of length $\lfloor n/2 \rfloor$ and $\lceil n/2 \rceil$.
2. Recursively sort each of the two subsequences.
3. Merge the sorted subsequences to obtain the final result.

Figure 15.10 illustrates the operation of the two-way merge sort algorithm.

Implementation
Program 15.14 declares the **TwoWayMergeSorter** class. The **TwoWayMergeSorter** class extends the **AbstractSorter** class defined in Program 15.2. A single field, **tempArray**, is declared. This field is an array of **Comparable** objects. Since merge operations cannot be done in place, a second, temporary array is needed. The **tempArray** field keeps track of that array.

Merging
The **merge** method of the **TwoWayMergeSorter** class is defined in Program 15.15. Altogether, this method takes three integer parameters, **left**, **middle**, and **right**. It is assumed that

$$\texttt{left} \leq \texttt{middle} < \texttt{right}.$$

Furthermore, it is assumed that the two subsequences of the array,

$$\texttt{array[left], array[left + 1], \ldots, array[middle]},$$

and

$$\texttt{array[middle + 1], array[middle + 2], \ldots, array[right]},$$

FIGURE 15.10
Two-way merge sorting.

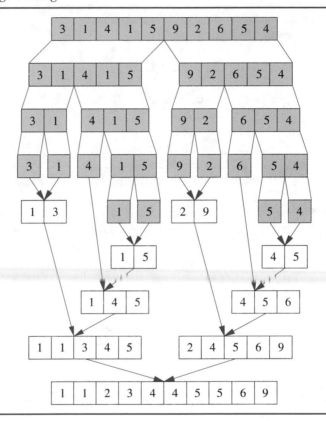

PROGRAM 15.14
TwoWayMergeSorter fields

```
1   public class TwoWayMergeSorter
2       extends AbstractSorter
3   {
4       Comparable[] tempArray;
5
6       // ...
7   }
```

PROGRAM 15.15
TwoWayMergeSorter class merge method

```
1   public class TwoWayMergeSorter
2       extends AbstractSorter
3   {
4       Comparable[] tempArray;
5
6       protected void merge (int left, int middle, int right)
7       {
8           int i = left;
9           int j = left;
10          int k = middle + 1;
11          while (j <= middle && k <= right)
12          {
13              if (array [j].isLT (array [k]))
14                  tempArray [i++] = array [j++];
15              else
16                  tempArray [i++] = array [k++];
17          }
18          while (j <= middle)
19              tempArray [i++] = array [j++];
20          for (i = left; i < k; ++i)
21              array [i] = tempArray [i];
22      }
23      // ...
24  }
```

are both sorted. The **merge** method merges the two sorted subsequences using the temporary array, **tempArray**. It then copies the merged (and sorted) sequence into the array at

$$\text{array}[\text{left}], \text{array}[\text{left} + 1], \dots, \text{array}[\text{right}].$$

To determine the running time of the **merge** method it is necessary to recognize that the total number of iterations of the two loops (lines 11–17, lines 18–19) is **right**−**left**+1, in the worst case. The total number of iterations of the third loop (lines 20–21) is the same. Since all of the loop bodies do a constant amount of work, the total running time for the **merge** method is $O(n)$, where $n =$ **right**−**left**+1 is the total number of elements in the two subsequences that are merged.

Two-Way Merge Sorting

Program 15.16 gives the code for two **sort** methods of the **TwoWayMergeSorter** class. The no-arg **sort** method sets things up for the second, recursive **sort** method. First, it allocates a temporary array, the length of which is equal to the length of the array to be sorted (line 8). Then it calls the recursive **sort** method, which sorts

---

PROGRAM 15.16
TwoWayMergeSorter class sort methods

```
1   public class TwoWayMergeSorter
2       extends AbstractSorter
3   {
4       Comparable[] tempArray;
5
6       protected void sort ()
7       {
8           tempArray = new Comparable [n];
9           sort (0, n - 1);
10          tempArray = null;
11      }
12
13      protected void sort (int left, int right)
14      {
15          if (left < right)
16          {
17              int middle = (left + right) / 2;
18              sort (left, middle);
19              sort (middle + 1, right);
20              merge (left, middle, right);
21          }
22      }
23      // ...
24  }
```

---

the array (line 9). After the array has been sorted, the no-arg **sort** discards the temporary array (line 10).

The second **sort** method implements the recursive, divide-and-conquer merge sort algorithm previously described. The method takes three parameters—**array**, **left**, and **right**. The first is the array to be sorted and the latter two specify the subsequence of the array to be sorted. If the sequence to be sorted contains more than one element, the sequence is split in two (line 17), each half is recursively sorted (lines 18–19), and then the two sorted halves are merged (line 20).

Running Time Analysis

The running time of merge sort is determined by the running time of the recursive **sort** method. (The no-arg **sort** method adds only a constant amount of overhead.) The running time of the recursive **sort** method is given by the following recurrence:

$$T(n) = \begin{cases} O(1) & n = 1, \\ T(\lfloor n/2 \rfloor) + T(\lceil n/2 \rceil) + O(n) & n > 1, \end{cases} \tag{15.10}$$

where $n = \text{right} - \text{left} + 1$.

In order to simplify the solution of Equation (15.10) we will assume that $n = 2^k$ for some integer $k \geq 0$. Dropping the $O(\cdot)$s from the equation, we get

$$T(n) = \begin{cases} 1 & n = 1, \\ 2T(n/2) + n & n > 1, \end{cases}$$

which is easily solved by repeated substitution:

$$\begin{aligned} T(n) &= 2T(n/2) + n \\ &= 4T(n/4) + 2n \\ &= 8T(n/8) + 3n \\ &\;\;\vdots \\ &= 2^k T(n/2^k) + kn \\ &\;\;\vdots \\ &= nT(1) + n\log_2 n \\ &= n + n\log_2 n. \end{aligned}$$

Therefore, the running time of merge sort is $O(n \log n)$.

15.7 A Lower Bound on Sorting

The preceding sections present three $O(n \log n)$ sorting algorithms—quicksort, heapsort, and the two-way merge sort. But is $O(n \log n)$ the best we can do? In this section we answer the question by showing that any sorting algorithm that sorts using only binary comparisons must make $\Omega(n \log n)$ such comparisons. If each binary comparison takes a constant amount of time, then running time for any such sorting algorithm is also $\Omega(n \log n)$.

Consider the problem of sorting the sequence $S = \{a, b, c\}$ composed of three distinct items; that is, $a \neq b \wedge a \neq c \wedge b \neq c$. Figure 15.11 illustrates a possible sorting algorithm in the form of a *decision tree*. Each node of the decision tree represents one binary comparison; that is, in each node of the tree, exactly two elements of the sequence are compared. Since there are exactly two possible outcomes for each comparison, each non-leaf node of the binary tree has degree two.

For example, suppose that $a < b < c$. Consider how the algorithm shown in Figure 15.11 discovers this. The first comparison compares a and b, which reveals that $a < b$. The second comparison compares a and c to find that $a < c$. At this point it has been determined that $a < b$ and $a < c$; the relative order of b and c is not yet known. Therefore, one more comparison is required to determine that $b < c$. Notice that the algorithm shown in Figure 15.11 works correctly in all cases because every possible permutation

FIGURE 15.11
A decision tree for comparison sorting.

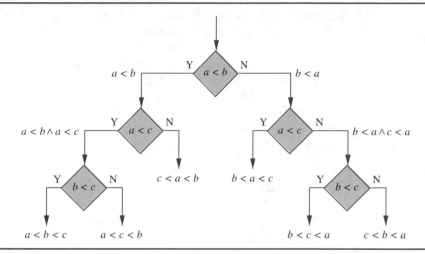

of the sequence S appears as a leaf node in the decision tree. Furthermore, the number of comparisons required in the worst case is equal to the height of the decision tree!

Any sorting algorithm that uses only binary comparisons can be represented by a binary decision tree. Furthermore, it is the height of the binary decision tree that determines the worst-case running time of the algorithm. In general, the size and shape of the decision tree depends on the sorting algorithm and the number of items to be sorted.

Given an input sequence of n items to be sorted, every binary decision tree that correctly sorts the input sequence must have *at least* $n!$ leaves—one for each permutation of the input. Therefore, it follows directly from Theorem 9.3 that the height of the binary decision tree is *at least* $\lceil \log_2 n! \rceil$:

$$\lceil \log_2 n! \rceil \geq \log_2 n!$$

$$\geq \sum_{i=1}^{n} \log_2 i$$

$$\geq \sum_{i=1}^{n/2} \log_2 n/2$$

$$\geq n/2 \log_2 n/2$$

$$= \Omega(n \log n).$$

Since the height of the decision tree is $\Omega(n \log n)$, the number of comparisons done by any sorting algorithm that sorts using only binary comparisons is $\Omega(n \log n)$. Assuming each comparison can be done in constant time, the running time of any such sorting algorithm is $\Omega(n \log n)$.

15.8   Distribution Sorting

The final class of sorting algorithm considered in this chapter consists of algorithms that sort *by distribution*. The unique characteristic of a distribution sorting algorithm is that it does *not* make use of comparisons to do the sorting.

Instead, distribution sorting algorithms rely on a priori knowledge about the universal set from which the elements to be sorted are drawn. For example, if we know a priori that the size of the universe is a small, fixed constant, say m, then we can use the bucket sorting algorithm described in Section 15.8.1.

Similarly, if we have a universe the elements of which can be represented with a small, finite number of bits (or even digits, letters, or symbols), then we can use the radix sorting algorithm given in Section 15.8.2.

15.8.1   Bucket Sort

Bucket sort is possibly the simplest distribution sorting algorithm. The essential requirement is that the size of the universe from which the elements to be sorted are drawn is a small, fixed constant, say m.

For example, suppose that we are sorting elements drawn from $\{0, 1, \ldots, m - 1\}$, that is, the set of integers in the interval $[0, m - 1]$. Bucket sort uses m counters. The ith counter keeps track of the number of occurrences of the ith element of the universe. Figure 15.12 illustrates how this is done.

In Figure 15.12, the universal set is assumed to be $\{0, 1, \ldots, 9\}$. Therefore, ten counters are required—one to keep track of the number of zeroes, one to keep track of the number of ones, and so on. A single pass through the data suffices to count all of the elements. Once the counts have been determined, the sorted sequence is easily obtained. For example, the sorted sequence contains no zeroes, two ones, one two, and so on.

Implementation

Program 15.17 introduces the **BucketSorter** class. The **BucketSorter** class extends the **AbstractSorter** class defined in Program 15.2. This bucker sorter is de-

---

FIGURE 15.12
Bucket sorting.

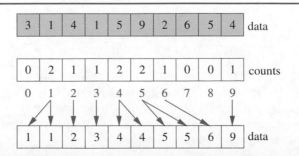

signed to sort specifically an array of **Int**s. The **BucketSorter** class contains two fields, **m** and **count**. The integer **m** simply keeps track of the size of the universe. The **count** variable is an array of integers used to count the number of occurrences of each element of the universal set.

The constructor for the **BucketSorter** class takes a single argument that specifies the size of the universal set. The variable **m** is set to the specified value, and the **count** array is initialized to have the required size.

Program 15.17 defines the no-arg **sort** method. It casts the array to an array **Int**s and calls the **sort(Int[])** method defined in Program 15.18.

The **sort(Int[])** method defined in Program 15.18 sorts an array of **Int**s. It begins by setting all of the counters to zero (lines 9–10). This can clearly be done in $O(m)$ time.

Next, a single pass is made through the data to count the number of occurrences of each element of the universe (lines 11–12). Since each element of the array is examined exactly once, the running time is $O(n)$.

In the final step, the sorted output sequence is created (lines 13–15). Since the output sequence contains exactly n items, the body of the inner loop (line 15) is executed exactly n times. During the ith iteration of the outer loop (line 13), the loop termination test of the inner loop (line 14) is evaluated $count[i] + 1$ times. As a result, the total running time of the final step is $O(m + n)$.

Thus, the running time of the bucket sort method is $O(m+n)$. Note that if $m = O(n)$, the running time for bucket sort is $O(n)$; that is, the bucket sort algorithm is a *linear-time* sorting algorithm! Bucket sort breaks the $\Omega(n \log n)$ bound associated with sorting algorithms that use binary comparisons because bucket sort does not do any binary

PROGRAM 15.17
BucketSorter class constructor and **sort** methods

```
1  public class BucketSorter
2       extends AbstractSorter
3  {
4       protected int m;
5       protected int[] count;
6
7       public BucketSorter (int m)
8       {
9           this.m = m;
10          count = new int [m];
11      }
12
13      protected void sort ()
14          { sort ((Int[]) array); }
15      // ...
16  }
```

PROGRAM 15.18
BucketSorter class sort method

```
1   public class BucketSorter
2       extends AbstractSorter
3   {
4       protected int m;
5       protected int[] count;
6
7       protected void sort (Int[] array)
8       {
9           for (int i = 0; i < m; ++i)
10              count [i] = 0;
11          for (int j = 0; j < n; ++j)
12              ++count [array [j].intValue ()];
13          for (int i = 0, j = 0; i < m; ++i)
14              for ( ; count [i] > 0; --count [i])
15                  array [j++] = new Int (i);
16      }
17      // ...
18  }
```

---

comparisons. The cost associated with breaking the $\Omega(n \log n)$ running time bound is the $O(m)$ space required for the array of counters. Consequently, bucket sort is practical only for small m. For example, to sort 16-bit integers using bucket sort requires the use of an array of $2^{16} = 65\,536$ counters.

15.8.2 Radix Sort

This section presents a sorting algorithm known as *least-significant-digit-first radix sorting*. Radix sorting is based on the bucket sorting algorithm discussed in the preceding section. However, radix sorting is practical for much larger universal sets than it is practical to handle with a bucket sort.

Radix sorting can be used when each element of the universal set can be viewed as a sequences of digits (or letters or any other symbols). For example, we can represent each integer between 0 and 99 as a sequence of two decimal digits. (For example, the number five is represented as "05".)

To sort an array of two-digit numbers, the algorithm makes two sorting passes through the array. In the first pass, the elements of the array are sorted by the *least significant* decimal digit. In the second pass, the elements of the array are sorted by the *most significant* decimal digit. The key characteristic of the radix sort is that the second pass is done in such a way that it does not destroy the effect of the first pass. Consequently, after two passes through the array, the data contained therein are sorted.

Each pass of the radix sort is implemented as a bucket sort. In the example we base the sort on *decimal* digits. Therefore, this is called a *radix-10* sort and ten buckets are required to do each sorting pass.

Figure 15.13 illustrates the operation of the radix-10 sort. The first radix sorting pass considers the least significant digits. As in the bucket sort, a single pass is made through the unsorted data, counting the number of times each decimal digit appears as the least significant digit. For example, there are no elements that have a 0 as the least significant digit, there are two elements that have a 1 as the least significant digit, and so on.

After the counts have been determined, it is necessary to permute the input sequence so that it is sorted by the least significant digits. To do this permutation efficiently, we compute the sequence of *offsets* given by

$$\texttt{offset}[i] = \begin{cases} 0 & i = 0, \\ \sum_{j=0}^{i-1} \texttt{count}[j] & 0 < i < R, \end{cases} \qquad (15.11)$$

where R is the sorting radix. Note that $\texttt{offset}[i]$ is the position in the permuted sequence of the first occurrence of an element whose least significant digit is i. By making use of the offsets, it is possible to permute the input sequence by making a single pass through the sequence.

The second radix sorting pass considers the most significant digits. As above, a single pass is made through the permuted data sequence counting the number of times

---

FIGURE 15.13
Radix sorting.

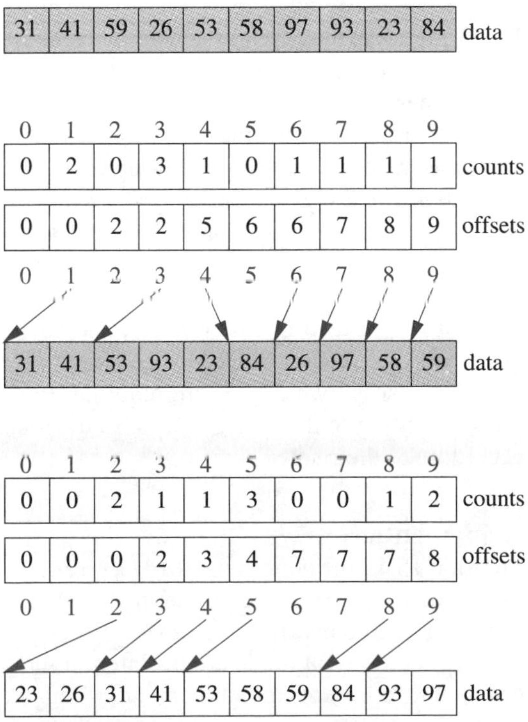

each decimal digit appears as the most significant digit. Then the sequence of *offsets* is computed as above. The sequence is permuted again using the offsets, producing the final, sorted sequence.

In general, radix sorting can be used when the elements of the universe can be viewed as *p*-digit numbers with respect to some radix, R; that is, each element of the universe has the form

$$\sum_{i=0}^{p-1} d_i R^i,$$

where $d_i \in \{0, 1, \ldots, R-1\}$ for $0 \le i < p$. In this case, the radix sort algorithm must make p sorting passes from the least significant digit, d_0, to the most significant digit, d_{p-1}, and each sorting pass uses exactly R counters.

Radix sorting can also be used when the universe can be viewed as the cross product of a finite number of finite sets—that is, when the universe has the form

$$U = U_1 \times U_2 \times U_3 \times \cdots \times U_p,$$

where $p > 0$ is a fixed integer constant and U_i is a finite set for $1 \le i \le p$. For example, each card in a 52-card deck of playing cards can be represented as an element of $U = U_1 \times U_2$, where $U_1 = \{\clubsuit, \diamondsuit, \heartsuit, \spadesuit\}$ and $U_2 = \{A, 2, 3, 4, 5, 6, 7, 8, 9, 10, J, Q, K\}$.

Before we can sort over the universe U, we need to define what it means for one element to precede another in U. The usual way to do this is called *lexicographic ordering*. For example, in the case of the playing cards we may say that one card precedes another if its suit precedes the other suit or if the suits are equal but the face value precedes that of the other.

In general, given the universe $U = U_1 \times U_2 \times U_2 \times \cdots \times U_p$, and two elements of U, say x and y, represented by the p-tuples $x = (x_1, x_2, \ldots, x_p)$ and $y = (y_1, y_2, \ldots, y_p)$, respectively, we say that x *lexicographically precedes* y if there exists $1 \le k \le p$ such that $x_k < y_k$ and $x_i = y_i$ for all $1 \le i < k$.

With this definition of precedence, we can radix sort a sequence of elements drawn from U by sorting with respect to the components of the p-tuples. Specifically, we sort first with respect to U_p, then U_{p-1}, and so on down to U_1. Notice that the algorithm does p sorting passes and in the ith pass it requires $|U_i|$ counters. For example, to sort a deck of cards, two passes are required. In the first pass the cards are sorted into 13 piles according to their face values. In the second pass the cards are sorted into 4 piles according to their suits.

Implementation

Program 15.19 introduces the **RadixSorter** class. The **RadixSorter** class extends the **AbstractSorter** class defined in Program 15.2. This radix sorter is designed to sort specifically an array of **Ints**.

Three static final fields are declared in the **RadixSorter** class—**R**, **r**, and **p**. The constant R represents the radix and $r = \log_2 R$. The constant p is the number of sorting

---

PROGRAM 15.19
RadixSorter fields

```
 1   public class RadixSorter
 2       extends AbstractSorter
 3   {
 4       protected static final int r = 8;
 5       protected static final int R = 1 << r;
 6       protected static final int p = (32 + r - 1) / r;
 7       protected int[] count = new int [R];
 8
 9       protected void sort ()
10           { sort ((Int[]) array); }
11       // ...
12   }
```

---

passes needed to sort the data. In this case $r = 8$ and $R = 2^r = 256$. Therefore, a radix-256 sort is being done. We have chosen R as a power of two because that way the computations required to implement the radix sort can be implemented efficiently using simple bit shift and mask operations. In order to sort b-bit integers, it is necessary to make $p = \lceil \log_R 2^b \rceil = \lceil b/r \rceil$ sorting passes.

One more field is defined in the **RadixSorter** class—**count**. The **count** field is an array of integers used to implement the sorting passes. An array of integers of length R is created and assigned to the **count** array.

Program 15.19 also defines the no-arg **sort** method. It casts the array to an array **Int**s and calls the **sort(Int[])** method defined in Program 15.20.

The **sort(Int[])** method shown in Program 15.20 begins by creating a temporary array of **Int**s of length n. Each iteration of the main loop corresponds to one pass of the radix sort (lines 8–29). In all, p iterations are required.

During the ith pass of the main loop the following steps are done: First, the R counters are all set to zero (lines 10–11). This takes $O(R)$ time. Then a pass is made through the input array during which the number of occurrences of each radix-R digit in the ith digit position is counted (lines 12–16). This pass takes $O(n)$ time. Notice that during this pass all of the input data are copied into the temporary array.

Next, the array of counts is transformed into an array of offsets according to Equation (15.11). This requires a single pass through the counter array (lines 17–23). Therefore, it takes $O(R)$ time. Finally, the data sequence is permuted by copying the values from the temporary array back into the input array (lines 24–28). Since this requires a single pass through the data arrays, the running time is $O(n)$.

After the p sorting passes have been done, the array of data is sorted. The running time for the **sort** method of the **RadixSorter** class is $O(p(R + n))$. If we assume that the size of an integer is 32 bits and given that $R = 256$, the number of sorting passes required is $p = 4$. Therefore, the running time for the radix sort is simply $O(n)$. Thus, radix sort is a linear-time sorting algorithm.

PROGRAM 15.20
RadixSorter class sort method

```
1  public class RadixSorter
2      extends AbstractSorter
3  {
4      protected void sort (Int[] array)
5      {
6          Int[] tempArray = new Int [n];
7
8          for (int i = 0; i < p; ++i)
9          {
10             for (int j = 0; j < R; ++j)
11                 count [j] = 0;
12             for (int k = 0; k < n; ++k)
13             {
14                 ++count [(array[k].intValue() >>> (r*i)) & (R-1)];
15                 tempArray [k] = array [k];
16             }
17             int pos = 0;
18             for (int j = 0; j < R; ++j)
19             {
20                 int tmp = pos;
21                 pos += count [j];
22                 count [j] = tmp;
23             }
24             for (int k = 0; k < n; ++k)
25             {
26                 int j = (tempArray[k].intValue()>>>(r*i))&(R-1);
27                 array [count [j]++] = tempArray [k];
28             }
29         }
30     }
31     // ...
32 }
```

15.9 Performance Data

In order to better understand the actual performance of the various sorting algorithms presented in this chapter, it is necessary to conduct some experiments. Only by conducting experiments is it possible to determine the relative performance of algorithms with the same asymptotic running time.

To measure the performance of a sorting algorithm, we need to provide it with some data to sort. To obtain the results presented here, random sequences of integers were sorted; that is, for each value of n, the `RandomNumberGenerator` class defined in Section 14.5.1 was used to create a sequence of n integers. In all cases (except for bucket sort) the random numbers are uniformly distributed in the interval $[1, 2^{31} - 1]$. For the bucket sort the numbers are uniformly distributed in $[0, 2^{10} - 1]$.

Figure 15.14, 15.15, and 15.16 show the actual running times of the sorting algorithms presented in this chapter. These running times were measured on a Sun SPARCstation 5, Model 85, which has an 85-MHz clock and 32MB of RAM under the Solaris 2.5 operating system. The programs were compiled using the Solaris Java Platform 1.1 compiler (`javac`) and run under the Java interpreter (`java`). The times shown are user CPU times, measured in seconds.

Figure 15.14 shows the running times of the $O(n^2)$ sorts for sequences of length n, $10 \le n \le 2\,000$. Notice that the bubble sort has the worst performance and that the binary insertion sort has the best performance. Figure 15.14 clearly shows that, as predicted, binary insertion is better than straight insertion. Notice too that all of the $O(n^2)$ sorts require more than 5 seconds of execution time to sort an array of $2\,000$ integers.

The performance of the $O(n \log n)$ sorts is shown in Figure 15.15. In this case, the length of the sequence varies between $n = 10$ and $n = 10\,000$. The graph clearly shows that the $O(n \log n)$ algorithms are significantly faster than the $O(n^2)$ ones. All three algorithms sort 10,000 integers in under 5 seconds. Clearly, merge sort is the best of the three, with quicksort not that far behind.

FIGURE 15.14
Actual running times of the $O(n^2)$ sorts.

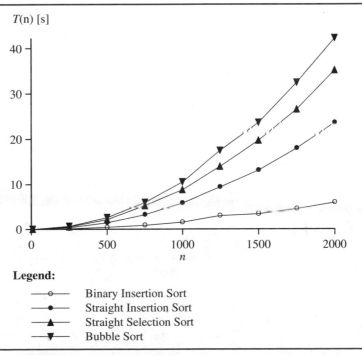

Legend:

─○─	Binary Insertion Sort
─●─	Straight Insertion Sort
─▲─	Straight Selection Sort
─▼─	Bubble Sort

FIGURE 15.15
Actual running times of the $O(n \log n)$ sorts.

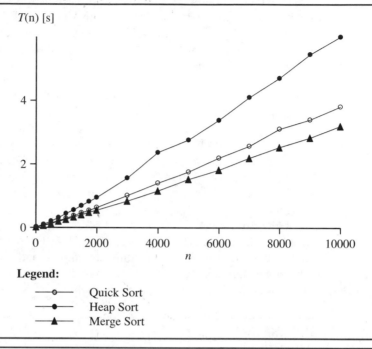

Legend:

—○—	Quick Sort
—●—	Heap Sort
—▲—	Merge Sort

FIGURE 15.16
Actual running times of the $O(n)$ sorts.

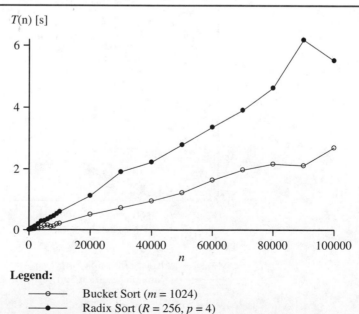

Legend:

—○—	Bucket Sort ($m = 1024$)
—●—	Radix Sort ($R = 256$, $p = 4$)

Figure 15.16 shows the actual running times for the bucket sort and radix sort algorithms. Both these algorithms were shown to be $O(n)$ sorts. The graph shows results for n between 10 and 100, 000. The universe used to test bucket sort was $\{0, 1, \ldots, 1023\}$; that is, a total of $m = 1024$ counters (buckets) were used. For the radix sort, 32-bit integers were sorted by using the radix $R = 256$ and doing $p = 4$ sorting passes.

Clearly, the bucket sort has the best running time. For example, it sorts 100,000 10-bit integers in about 3 seconds. Radix sort performs extremely well too. It sorts 100,000 32-bit integers in about 7 seconds, roughly a factor of two slower than the bucket sort.

Exercises

15.1 Consider the sequence of integers

$$S = \{8, 9, 7, 9, 3, 2, 3, 8, 4, 6\}.$$

For each of the following sorting algorithms, draw a sequence of diagrams that traces the execution of the algorithm as it sorts the sequence S: straight insertion sort, binary insertion sort, bubble sort, quick sort, straight selection sort, heapsort, merge sort, and bucket sort.

15.2 Draw a sequence of diagrams that traces the execution of a radix-10 sort of the sequence

$$S = \{89, 79, 32, 38, 46, 26, 43, 38, 32, 79\}.$$

15.3 For each of the sorting algorithms listed in Exercise 15.1 and 15.2, indicate whether the sorting algorithm is *stable*.

15.4 Consider a sequence of three distinct keys $\{a, b, c\}$. Draw the binary decision tree that represents each of the following sorting algorithms: straight insertion sort, straight selection sort, and bubble sort.

15.5 Devise an algorithm to sort a sequence of exactly three elements. Make your algorithm as efficient as possible.

15.6 Prove that the swapping of a pair of adjacent elements removes at most one inversion from a sequence.

15.7 Consider the sequence of elements $\{s_1, s_2, \ldots, s_n\}$. What is the maximum number of inversions that can be removed by the swapping of a pair of distinct elements s_i and s_j? Express the result in terms of the *distance* between s_i and s_j: $d(s_i, s_j) = j - i + 1$.

15.8 Devise a sequence of keys such that *exactly* 11 inversions are removed by the swapping of one pair of elements.

15.9 Prove that *binary insertion sort* requires $O(n \log n)$ comparisons.

15.10   Consider an arbitrary sequence $\{s_1, s_2, \ldots, s_n\}$. To sort the sequence, we determine the permutation $\{p_1, p_2, \ldots, p_n\}$, such that

$$s_{p_1} \leq s_{p_2} \leq \cdots \leq s_{p_n}.$$

Prove that *bubble sort* requires at least p passes, where

$$p = \max_{1 \leq i \leq n} (i - p_i).$$

15.11   Modify the bubble sort algorithm (Program 15.5) so that it terminates the outer loop when it detects that the array is sorted. What is the running time of the modified algorithm? **Hint**: See Exercise 15.10.

15.12   A variant of the bubble sorting algorithm is the so-called *odd–even transposition sort*. Like bubble sort, this algorithm makes a total of $n - 1$ passes through the array. Each pass consists of two phases: The first phase compares **array**$[i]$ with **array**$[i + 1]$ and swaps them if necessary for all odd values of i. The second phase does the same for the even values of i.

   a.   Show that the array is guaranteed to be sorted after $n - 1$ passes.

   b.   What is the running time of this algorithm?

15.13   Another variant of the bubble sorting algorithm is the so-called *cocktail shaker sort*. Like bubble sort, this algorithm makes a total of $n - 1$ passes through the array. However, alternating passes go in opposite directions. For example, during the first pass the largest item bubbles to the end of the array and during the second pass the smallest item bubbles to the beginning of the array.

   a.   Show that the array is guaranteed to be sorted after $n - 1$ passes.

   b.   What is the running time of this algorithm?

15.14   Consider the following algorithm for selecting the kth largest element from an unsorted sequence of n elements, $S = \{s_1, s_2, \ldots, s_n\}$.

   1.   If $n \leq 5$, sort S and select directly the kth largest element.

   2.   Otherwise, $n > 5$: Partition the sequence S into subsequences of length five. In general, there will be $\lfloor n/5 \rfloor$ subsequences of length five and one of length $n \bmod 5$.

   3.   Sort by any means each of the subsequences of length five. (See Exercise 15.5.)

   4.   Form the sequence $M = \{m_1, m_2, \ldots, m_{\lfloor n/5 \rfloor}\}$ containing the $\lfloor n/5 \rfloor$ median values of each of the subsequences of length five.

   5.   Apply the selection method recursively to find the median element of M. Let m be the median of the medians.

   6.   Partition S into three subsequences, $S = \{L, E, G\}$, such that all elements in L are less than m, all elements in E are equal to m, and all elements of G are greater than m.

7. If $k \leq |L|$ then apply the method recursively to select the kth largest element of L; if $|L| < k \leq |L| + |E|$, the result is m; otherwise, apply the method recursively to select the $(k - (|L| + |E|))$th largest element of G.

   a. What is the running time of this algorithm?

   b. Show that if we use this algorithm to select the pivot, the worst-case running time of *quick sort* is $O(n \log n)$.

15.15 Show that the sum of the heights of the nodes in a complete binary tree with n nodes altogether is $n - b(n)$, where $b(n)$ is the number of ones in the binary representation of n.

Programming Projects

15.1 Design and implement an algorithm that finds all duplicates in a random sequence of keys.

15.2 Suppose we wish to sort a sequence of data represented using the linked-list class **LinkedList** introduced in Program 4.13. Which of the sorting algorithms described in this chapter is the most appropriate for sorting a linked list? Design and implement a linked list sorter class that implements this algorithm.

15.3 Replace the **sort** method of the **MergeSorter** class with a non-recursive version. What is the running time of the non-recursive merge sort?

15.4 Replace the **sort** method of the **AbstractQuickSorter** class with a non-recursive version. What is the running time of the non-recursive quick sort? **Hint**: Use a stack.

15.5 Design and implement a radix-sorter class that sorts an array of **String**s.

15.6 Design and implement a **RandomPivotQuickSorter** class that uses a random number generator (See Section 14.5.1) to select a pseudo-random pivot. Run a sequence of experiments to compare the running times of random pivot selection with median-of-three pivot selection.

15.7 Design and implement a **MeanPivotQuickSorter** class that partitions the sequence to be sorted into elements that are less than the mean and elements that are greater than the mean. Run a sequence of experiments to compare the running times of the mean pivot quick sorter with median-of-three pivot selection.

15.8 Design and implement a **MedianPivotQuickSorter** class that uses the algorithm given in Exercise 15.14 to select the median element for the pivot. Run a sequence of experiments to compare the running times of median pivot selection with median-of-three pivot selection.

15.9 Design and implement a sorter class that sorts using a **PriorityQueue** instance. (See Chapter 11.)

16 | Graphs and Graph Algorithms

A graph is simply a set of points together with a set of lines connecting various points. Many real-world application problems can be reduced to problems on graphs.

Suppose you are planning a trip by airplane. From a map you have determined the distances between the airports in the various cities that you wish to visit. The information you have gathered can be represented using a graph, as shown in Figure 16.1 (a). The points in the graph represent the cities and the lines represent the distances between them. Given such a graph, you can answer questions such as "What is the shortest distance between LAX and JFK?" or "What is the shortest route that visits all of the cities?"

An electric circuit can also be viewed as a graph, as shown in Figure 16.1 (b). In this case the points in the graph indicate where the components are connected (i.e., the wires) and the lines represent the components themselves (e.g, resistors and capacitors). Given such a graph, we can answer questions such as "What are the mesh equations that describe the circuit's behavior?"

Similarly, a logic circuit can be reduced to a graph, as shown in Figure 16.1 (c). In this case the logic gates are represented by the points, and arrows represent the signal flows from gate outputs to gate inputs. Given such a graph, we can answer questions such as "How long does it take for the signals to propagate from the inputs to the outputs?" or "Which gates are on the critical path?"

Finally, Figure 16.1 (d) illustrates that a graph can be used to represent a *finite state machine*. The points of the graph represent the states, and labeled arrows indicate the allowable state transitions. Given such a graph, we can answer questions such as "Are all the states reachable?" or "Can the finite state machine deadlock?"

This chapter is a brief introduction to the body of knowledge known as *graph theory*. It covers the most common data structures for the representation of graphs and introduces some fundamental graph algorithms.

FIGURE 16.1
Real-world examples of graphs.

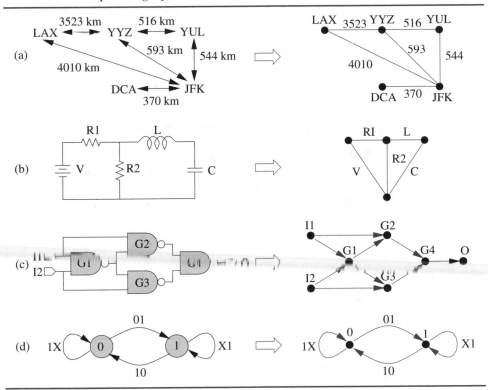

16.1 Basics

Directed Graphs
We begin with the definition of a directed graph:

Definition 16.1 (Directed Graph)
A directed graph, or digraph, *is an ordered pair* $G = (\mathcal{V}, \mathcal{E})$ *with the following properties:*

1. *The first component,* $\mathcal{V}$, *is a finite, non-empty set. The elements of* $\mathcal{V}$ *are called the vertices of G.*

2. *The second component,* $\mathcal{E}$, *is a finite set of ordered pairs of vertices; that is,* $\mathcal{E} \subseteq \mathcal{V} \times \mathcal{V}$. *The elements of* $\mathcal{E}$ *are called the edges of G.*

For example, consider the directed graph $G_1 = (\mathcal{V}_1, \mathcal{E}_1)$ composed of four vertices and six edges:

$$\mathcal{V}_1 = \{a, b, c, d\}$$
$$\mathcal{E}_1 = \{(a, b), (a, c), (b, c), (c, a), (c, d), (d, d)\}.$$

FIGURE 16.2
A directed graph.

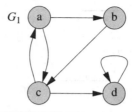

G_1

The graph G can be represented *graphically*, as shown in Figure 16.2. The vertices are represented by appropriately labeled circles, and the edges are represented by arrows that connect associated vertices.

Notice that because the pairs that represent edges are *ordered*, the two edges (a, c) and (c, a) are distinct. Furthermore, since $\mathscr{E}_1$ is a mathematical set, it cannot contain more than one instance of a given edge. Finally, an edge such as (d, d) may connect a node to itself.

Terminology

Consider a directed graph $G = (\mathscr{V}, \mathscr{E})$, as given by Definition 16.1.

- Each element of $\mathscr{V}$ is called a *vertex* or a *node* of G. Hence, $\mathscr{V}$ is the set of *vertices* (or *nodes*) of G.

- Each element of $\mathscr{E}$ is called an *edge* or an *arc* of G. Hence, $\mathscr{E}$ is the set of *edges* (or *arcs*) of G.

- An edge $(v, w) \in \mathscr{E}$ can be represented as $v \to w$. An arrow that points from v to w is known as a *directed arc*. Vertex w is called the *head* of the arc because it is found at the arrow head. Conversely, v is called the *tail* of the arc. Finally, vertex w is said to be *adjacent* to vertex v.

- An edge $e = (v, w)$ is said to *emanate* from vertex v. We use notation $\mathscr{A}(v)$ to denote the set of edges emanating from vertex v; that is, $\mathscr{A}(v) = \{(v_0, v_1) \in \mathscr{E} : v_0 = v\}$.

- The *out-degree* of a node is the number of edges emanating from that node. Therefore, the out-degree of v is $|\mathscr{A}(v)|$.

- An edge $e = (v, w)$ is said to be *incident* on vertex w. We use notation $\mathscr{I}(w)$ to denote the set of edges incident on vertex w; that is, $\mathscr{I}(w) = \{(v_0, v_1) \in \mathscr{E} : v_1 = w\}$.

- The *in-degree* of a node is the number of edges incident on that node. Therefore, the in-degree of w is $|\mathscr{I}(w)|$.

For example, Table 16.1 enumerates the sets of emanating and incident edges and the in- and out-degrees for each of the vertices in graph G_1 shown in Figure 16.2.

There is still more terminology to be introduced, but in order to do that, we need the following definition:

TABLE 16.1
Emanating and Incident Edge Sets for Graph G_1 in Figure 16.2

Vertex v	$\mathcal{A}(v)$	Out-Degree	$\mathcal{I}(v)$	In-Degree
a	$\{(a, b), (a, c)\}$	2	$\{(c, a)\}$	1
b	$\{(b, c)\}$	1	$\{(a, b)\}$	1
c	$\{(c, a), (c, d)\}$	2	$\{(a, c), (b, c)\}$	2
d	$\{(d, d)\}$	1	$\{(c, d), (d, d)\}$	2

Definition 16.2 (Path and Path Length)
A path *in a directed graph* $G = (\mathcal{V}, \mathcal{E})$ *is a non-empty sequence of vertices*

$$P = \{v_1, v_2, \ldots, v_k\},$$

where $v_i \in \mathcal{V}$ *for* $1 \leq i \leq k$ *such that* $(v_i, v_{i+1}) \in \mathcal{E}$ *for* $1 \leq i < k$. *The length of path* P *is* $k - 1$.

For example, consider again the graph G_1 shown in Figure 16.2. Among the paths contained in G_1 there is the path of length zero, $\{u\}$; the path of length one, $\{b, c\}$; the path of length two, $\{a, b, c\}$; and so on. In fact, this graph generates an infinite number of paths! (To see how this is possible, consider that $\{a, c, a, c, a, c, a, c, a, c, a, c, a\}$ is a path in G_1.) Notice too the subtle distinction between a path of length zero, say $\{d\}$, and the path of length one $\{d, d\}$.

More Terminology
Consider the path $P = \{v_1, v_2, \ldots, v_k\}$ in a directed graph $G = (\mathcal{V}, \mathcal{E})$.

- Vertex v_{i+1} is the *successor* of vertex v_i for $1 \leq i < k$. Each element v_i of path P (except the last) has a *successor*.
- Vertex v_{i-1} is the *predecessor* of vertex v_i for $1 < i \leq k$. Each element v_i of path P (except the first) has a *predecessor*.
- A path P is called a *simple* path if and only if $v_i \neq v_j$ for all i and j such that $1 \leq i < j \leq k$. However, it *is* permissible for v_1 to be the same as v_k in a simple path.
- A *cycle* is a path P of non-zero length in which $v_1 = v_k$. The *length of a cycle* is just the length of the path P.
- A *loop* is a cycle of length one; that is, it is a path of the form $\{v, v\}$.
- A *simple cycle* is a path that is both a *cycle* and *simple*.

Referring again to graph G_1 in Figure 16.2, we find that the path $\{a, b, c, d\}$ is a simple path of length three. Conversely, the path $\{c, a, c, d\}$ also has length three but is not simple because vertex c occurs twice in the sequence (but not at the ends). The graph contains the path $\{a, b, c, a\}$, which is a cycle of length three, as well as $\{a, c, a, c, a\}$, a cycle of length four. The former is a simple cycle but the latter is not.

Directed Acyclic Graphs

For certain applications it is convenient to deal with graphs that contain no cycles. For example, a tree (see Chapter 9) is a special kind of graph that contains no cycles.

Definition 16.3 (Directed Acyclic Graph (DAG))

A directed, acyclic graph is a directed graph that contains no cycles.

Obviously, all trees are DAGs. However, not all DAGs are trees. For example, consider the two directed, acyclic graphs, G_2 and G_3, shown in Figure 16.3. Clearly G_2 is a tree but G_3 is not.

Undirected Graphs

An undirected graph is a graph in which the nodes are connected by *undirected arcs*. An undirected arc is an edge that has no arrow. Both ends of an undirected arc are equivalent—there is no head or tail. Therefore, we represent an edge in an undirected graph as a set rather than an ordered pair:

Definition 16.4 (Undirected Graph)

An undirected graph *is an ordered pair* $G = (\mathcal{V}, \mathcal{E})$ *with the following properties:*

1. *The first component,* $\mathcal{V}$*, is a finite, non-empty set. The elements of* $\mathcal{V}$ *are called the* vertices *of G.*

2. *The second component,* $\mathcal{E}$*, is a finite set of sets. Each element of* $\mathcal{E}$ *is a set that is composed of exactly two (distinct) vertices. The elements of* $\mathcal{E}$ *are called the* edges *of G.*

For example, consider the undirected graph $G_4 = (\mathcal{V}_4, \mathcal{E}_4)$ composed of four vertices and four edges:

$$\mathcal{V}_4 = \{a, b, c, d\}$$
$$\mathcal{E}_4 = \{\{a, b\}, \{a, c\}, \{b, c\}, \{c, d\}\}.$$

FIGURE 16.3
Two directed, acyclic graphs.

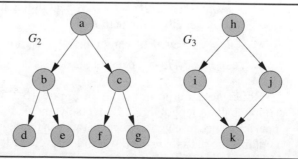

FIGURE 16.4
An undirected graph.

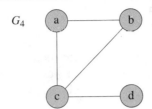

The graph G_4 can be represented *graphically*, as shown in Figure 16.4. The vertices are represented by appropriately labeled circles, and the edges are represented by lines that connect associated vertices.

Notice that because an edge in an undirected graph is a set, $\{a, b\} \equiv \{b, a\}$, and since $\mathcal{E}_4$ is also a set, it cannot contain more than one instance of a given edge. Another consequence of Definition 16.4 is that there cannot be an edge from a node to itself in an undirected graph because an edge is a set of size two and a set cannot contain duplicates.

Terminology
Consider an undirected graph $G = (\mathcal{V}, \mathcal{E})$ as given by Definition 16.4.

- An edge $\{v, w\} \in \mathcal{E}$ *emanates from* and is *incident on* both vertices v and w.
- The set of edges emanating from a vertex v is the set $\mathcal{A}(v) = \{(v_0, v_1) \in \mathcal{E} : v_0 = v \vee v_1 = v\}$. The set of edges incident on a vertex w is $\mathcal{I}(w) \equiv \mathcal{A}(w)$.

Labeled Graphs
Practical applications of graphs usually require that they be annotated with additional information. Such information may be attached to the edges of the graph and to the nodes of the graph. A graph that has been annotated in some way is called a *labeled graph*. Figure 16.5 shows two examples of this.

FIGURE 16.5
Labeled graphs.

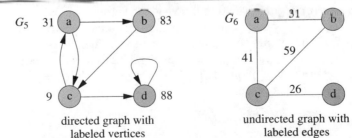

directed graph with labeled vertices

undirected graph with labeled edges

For example, we can use a directed graph with labeled vertices such as G_5 in Figure 16.5 to represent a finite state machine. Each vertex corresponds to a state of the machine and each edge corresponds to an allowable state transition. In such a graph we can attach a label to each vertex that records some property of the corresponding state such as the latency time for that state.

We can use an undirected graph with labeled edges such as G_6 in Figure 16.5 to represent geographic information. In such a graph, the vertices represent geographic locations and the edges represent possible routes between locations. In such a graph we might use a label on each edge to represent the distance between the end points.

16.1.1 Representing Graphs

Consider a directed graph $G = (\mathcal{V}, \mathcal{E})$. Since $\mathcal{E} \subseteq \mathcal{V} \times \mathcal{V}$, graph G contains at most $|\mathcal{V}|^2$ edges. There are $2^{|\mathcal{V}|^2}$ possible sets of edges for a given set of vertices $\mathcal{V}$. Therefore, the main concern when designing a graph representation scheme is to find a suitable way to represent the set of edges.

Adjacency Matrices

Consider a directed graph $G = (\mathcal{V}, \mathcal{E})$ with n vertices, $\mathcal{V} = \{v_1, v_2, \ldots, v_n\}$. The simplest graph representation scheme uses an $n \times n$ matrix A of 0's and 1's given by

$$A_{i,j} = \begin{cases} 1 & (v_i, v_j) \in \mathcal{E}, \\ 0 & \text{otherwise}; \end{cases}$$

that is, the (i, j)th element of the matrix is a 1 only if $v_i \to v_j$ is an edge in G. The matrix A is called an *adjacency matrix*.

For example, the adjacency matrix for graph G_1 in Figure 16.2 is

$$A_1 = \begin{bmatrix} 0 & 1 & 1 & 0 \\ 0 & 0 & 1 & 0 \\ 1 & 0 & 0 & 1 \\ 0 & 0 & 0 & 1 \end{bmatrix}.$$

Clearly, the number of 1's in the adjacency matrix is equal to the number of edges in the graph.

One advantage of using an adjacency matrix is that it is easy to determine the sets of edges emanating from a given vertex. For example, consider vertex v_i. Each 1 in the ith row corresponds to an edge that emanates from vertex v_i. Conversely, each 1 in the ith column corresponds to an edge incident on vertex v_i.

We can also use adjacency matrices to represent undirected graphs; that is, we represent an undirected graph $G = (\mathcal{V}, \mathcal{E})$ with n vertices, using an $n \times n$ matrix A of 0's and 1's given by

$$A_{i,j} = \begin{cases} 1 & \{v_i, v_j\} \in \mathcal{E}, \\ 0 & \text{otherwise}. \end{cases}$$

Since the two sets $\{v_i, v_j\}$ and $\{v_j, v_i\}$ are equivalent, matrix A is symmetric about the diagonal; that is, $A_{i,j} = A_{j,i}$. Furthermore, all of the entries on the diagonal are 0; that is, $A_{i,i} = 0$ for $1 \leq i \leq n$.

For example, the adjacency matrix for graph G_4 in Figure 16.4 is

$$A_4 = \begin{bmatrix} 0 & 1 & 1 & 0 \\ 1 & 0 & 1 & 0 \\ 1 & 1 & 0 & 1 \\ 0 & 0 & 1 & 0 \end{bmatrix}.$$

In this case, there are twice as many 1's in the adjacency matrix as there are edges in the undirected graph.

A simple variation allows us to use an adjacency matrix to represent an edge-labeled graph. For example, given numeric edge labels, we can represent a graph (directed or undirected) using an $n \times n$ matrix A in which the $A_{i,j}$ is the numeric label associated with edge (v_i, v_j) in the case of a directed graph, and edge $\{v_i, v_j\}$, in an undirected graph.

For example, the adjacency matrix for the graph G_6 in Figure 16.5 is

$$A_6 = \begin{bmatrix} \infty & 31 & 41 & \infty \\ 31 & \infty & 59 & \infty \\ 41 & 59 & \infty & 26 \\ \infty & \infty & 26 & \infty \end{bmatrix}.$$

In this case, the array entries corresponding to non-existent edges have all been set to ∞. Here ∞ serves as a kind of *sentinel*. The value to use for the sentinel depends on the application. For example, if the edges represent routes between geographic locations, then a route of length ∞ is much like one that does not exist.

Since the adjacency matrix has $|\mathcal{V}|^2$ entries, the amount of space needed to represent the edges of a graph is $O(|\mathcal{V}|^2)$, *regardless of the actual number of edges* in the graph. If the graph contains relatively few edges—for example, if $|\mathcal{E}| \ll |\mathcal{V}|^2$, then most of the elements of the adjacency matrix will be 0 (or ∞). A matrix in which most of the elements are 0 (or ∞) is a *sparse matrix*.

Sparse vs. Dense Graphs

Informally, a graph with relatively few edges is *sparse*, and a graph with many edges is *dense*. The following definition defines precisely what we mean when we say that a graph "has relatively few edges":

Definition 16.5 (Sparse Graph)

A sparse graph is a graph $G = (\mathcal{V}, \mathcal{E})$ in which $|\mathcal{E}| = O(|\mathcal{V}|)$.

For example, consider a graph $G = (\mathcal{V}, \mathcal{E})$ with n nodes. Suppose that the out-degree of each vertex in G is some fixed constant k. Graph G is a *sparse graph* because $|\mathcal{E}| = k|\mathcal{V}| = O(|\mathcal{V}|)$.

A graph that is not sparse is said to be *dense*:

FIGURE 16.6
Adjacency lists.

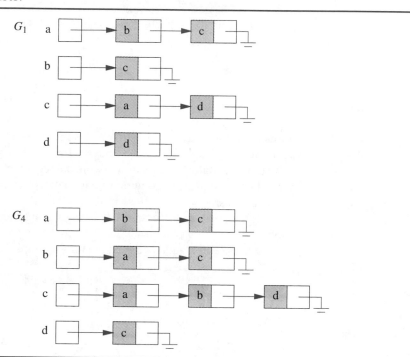

Definition 16.6 (Dense Graph)
A dense graph is a graph $G = (\mathcal{V}, \mathcal{E})$ in which $|\mathcal{E}| = \Theta(|\mathcal{V}|^2)$.

For example, consider a graph $G = (\mathcal{V}, \mathcal{E})$ with n nodes. Suppose that the out-degree of each vertex in G is some fraction f of n, $0 < f \leq 1$. For example, if $n = 16$ and $f = 0.25$, the out-degree of each node is 4. Graph G is a *dense graph* because $|\mathcal{E}| = f|\mathcal{V}|^2 = \Theta(|\mathcal{V}|^2)$.

Adjacency Lists
One technique that is often used for a sparse graph, say $G = (\mathcal{V}, \mathcal{E})$, uses $|\mathcal{V}|$ linked lists—one for each vertex. The linked list for vertex $v_i \in \mathcal{V}$ contains the elements of $\{w : (v_i, w) \in \mathcal{A}(v_i)\}$, the set of nodes adjacent to v_i. As a result, the lists are called *adjacency lists*.

Figure 16.6 shows the adjacency lists for the directed graph G_1 of Figure 16.2 and the directed graph G_4 of Figure 16.4. Notice that the total number of list elements used to represent a directed graph is $|\mathcal{E}|$ but the number of lists elements used to represent an undirected graph is $2 \times |\mathcal{E}|$. Therefore, the space required for the adjacency lists is $O(|\mathcal{E}|)$.

By definition, a sparse graph has $|\mathcal{E}| = O(|\mathcal{V}|)$. Hence, the space required to represent a sparse graph using adjacency lists is $O(|\mathcal{V}|)$. Clearly this is asymptotically better than using adjacency matrices, which require $O(|\mathcal{V}|^2)$ space.

16.2 Implementing Graphs

In keeping with the design framework used throughout this text, we view graphs as specialized containers. Formally, the graph $G = (\mathcal{V}, \mathcal{E})$ is an ordered pair composed of two sets—a set of vertices and a set of edges. Informally, we can view a graph as a container with two compartments, one that holds vertices and one that holds edges. There are four kinds of objects—vertices, edges, undirected graphs, and directed graphs. Accordingly, we define four interfaces: **Vertex**, **Edge**, **Graph**, and **Digraph**. (See Figure 16.7.)

16.2.1 Vertices

What exactly is a vertex? The answer to this question depends on the application. At the very minimum, every vertex in a graph must be distinguishable from every other vertex in that graph. We can do this by numbering consecutively the vertices of a graph. In addition, some applications require vertex-weighted graphs. A weighted vertex can be viewed as one that carries a "payload." The payload is an object that represents the weight on the vertex.

Program 16.1 defines the **Vertex** interface. Since we intend to insert vertices into containers, the **Vertex** interface extends the **Comparable** interface defined in Program 5.1.

Every vertex in a graph is assigned a unique number. The **getNumber** method returns the number of a vertex. The **getWeight** method returns an object that represents the weight associated with a weighted vertex. If the vertex is unweighted, the **getWeight** method returns **null**.

Enumerations

Program 16.1 also declares four methods, each of which returns an **Enumeration**. The **getIncidentEdges** method returns an **Enumeration** that enumerates the elements of the $\mathcal{I}(v)$. Similarly, the **getEmanatingEdges** method returns an **Enumeration** that enumerates the elements of $\mathcal{A}(v)$.

FIGURE 16.7
Object class hierarchy

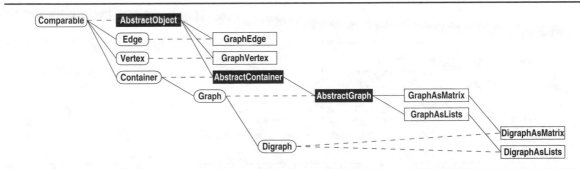

PROGRAM 16.1
`Vertex` interface

```
1  public interface Vertex
2      extends Comparable
3  {
4      int getNumber ();
5      Object getWeight ();
6      Enumeration getIncidentEdges ();
7      Enumeration getEmanatingEdges ();
8      Enumeration getPredecessors ();
9      Enumeration getSuccessors ();
10  }
```

The `getPredecessors` method returns an `Enumeration` that enumerates the elements of $\mathcal{P}(v) = \{u : (u, v) \in \mathcal{I}(v)\}$ and the `getPredecessors` method returns an `Enumeration` that enumerates $\mathcal{S}(v) = \{w : (v, w) \in \mathcal{A}(v)\}$. The elements of $\mathcal{P}(v)$ and $\mathcal{S}(v)$ are vertices, whereas the elements of $\mathcal{I}(v)$ and $\mathcal{A}(v)$ are edges.

16.2.2 Edges

An edge in a directed graph is an ordered pair of vertices; an edge in an undirected graph is a set of two vertices. Because of the similarity of these concepts, we use the same class for both—the context in which an edge is used determines whether it is directed or undirected.

Program 16.2 defines the `Edge` interface. Since we intend to insert edges into containers, the `Edge` interface extends the `Comparable` interface defined in Program 5.1.

An edge connects two vertices, v_0 and v_1. The methods `getV0` and `getV1` return these vertices. The `isDirected` method is a `boolean`-valued method that returns `true` if the edge is directed. When an `Edge` is directed, it represents $v_0 \rightarrow v_1$; that is,

---

PROGRAM 16.2
`Edge` interface

```
1  public interface Edge
2      extends Comparable
3  {
4      Vertex getV0 ();
5      Vertex getV1 ();
6      Object getWeight ();
7      boolean isDirected ();
8      Vertex getMate (Vertex vertex);
9  }
```

---

v_1 is the head and v_0 is the tail. Alternatively, when an **Edge** is undirected, it represents $\{v_0, v_1\}$.

For every instance **e** of a class that implements the **Edge** interface, the **getMate** method satisfies the following identities:

$$e.getMate(e.getV0()) \equiv e.getV1()$$

$$e.getMate(e.getV1()) \equiv e.getV0()$$

Therefore, if we know that a vertex **v** is one of the vertices of **e**, then we can find the other vertex by calling **e.getMate(v)**.

16.2.3 Graphs and Digraphs

Directed graphs and undirected graphs have many common characteristics. In addition, we can view a directed graph as an undirected graph with arrowheads added. As shown in Figure 16.7, we have chosen to define the **Graph** interface to represent undirected graphs and to derive the **Digraph** interface from it. We have chosen this approach because many algorithms for undirected graphs can also be used with directed graphs. On the other hand, it is often the case that algorithms for directed graphs cannot be used with undirected graphs.

Program 16.3 defines the **Graph** interface. The **Graph** interface extends the **Container** interface defined in Program 5.8.

There are essentially three groups of methods declared in Program 16.3: accessors and mutators, enumerations, and traversals. The operations performed by the methods are explained in the following sections.

Accessors and Mutators
The **Graph** interface declares the following accessor and mutator methods:

getNumberOfEdges This method returns the number of edges contained by the graph.

getNumberOfVertices This method returns the number of vertices contained by the graph.

isDirected This **boolean**-valued method returns **true** if the graph is a directed graph.

addVertex This method inserts a vertex into a graph. All of the vertices contained in a given graph must have a unique vertex number. Furthermore, if a graph contains n vertices, those vertices shall be numbered $0, 1, \ldots, n - 1$. Therefore, the next vertex inserted into the graph shall have the number n.

getVertex This method takes an integer, say i where $0 \le i < n$, and returns the ith vertex contained in the graph.

addEdge This method inserts an edge into a graph. If the graph contains n vertices, both arguments must fall in the interval $[0, n - 1]$.

isEdge This **boolean**-valued method takes two integer arguments. It returns **true** if the graph contains an edge that connects the corresponding vertices.

PROGRAM 16.3

Graph interface

```
1   public interface Graph
2       extends Container
3   {
4       int getNumberOfEdges ();
5       int getNumberOfVertices ();
6       boolean isDirected ();
7       void addVertex (int v);
8       void addVertex (int v, Object weight);
9       Vertex getVertex (int v);
10      void addEdge (int v, int w);
11      void addEdge (int v, int w, Object weight);
12      Edge getEdge (int v, int w);
13      boolean isEdge (int v, int w);
14      boolean isConnected ();
15      boolean isCyclic ();
16      Enumeration getVertices ();
17      Enumeration getEdges ();
18      void depthFirstTraversal (PrePostVisitor visitor, int start);
19      void breadthFirstTraversal (Visitor visitor, int start);
20  }
```

---

getEdge This method takes two integer arguments. It returns the edge instance (if it exists) that connects the corresponding vertices. The behavior of this method is undefined when the edge does not exist. (An implementation will typically throw an exception.)

isCyclic This **boolean**-valued method returns **true** if the graph is *cyclic*.

isConnected This **boolean**-valued method returns **true** if the graph is *connected*. Connectedness of graphs is discussed in Section 16.3.4.

Enumerations

All other container classes considered in this text have only one associated enumeration. When dealing with graphs, it is convenient to have two enumerations. Each of the following methods returns an **Enumeration** defined as follows:

getVertices This method returns an enumeration that can be used to traverse the elements of $\mathcal{V}$.

getEdges This method returns an enumeration that can be used to traverse the elements of $\mathcal{E}$.

Graph Traversals

The following traversal methods are analogous to the **accept** method of the container class. (See Section 5.2.4.) Each of these methods takes a *visitor* and performs a traversal;

that is, all of the *vertices* of the graph are visited systematically. When a vertex is visited, the **visit** method of the visitor is applied to that vertex.

depthFirstTraversal This method accepts two arguments—a **PrePost-Visitor** and an integer. The integer specifies the starting vertex for a depth-first traversal of the graph.

breadthFirstTraversal This method accepts two arguments—a **Visitor** and an integer. The integer specifies the starting vertex for a breadth-first traversal of the graph.

Graph traversal algorithms are discussed in Section 16.3.

16.2.4 Directed Graphs

Program 16.4 defines the **Digraph** interface. The **Digraph** interface extends the **Graph** interface defined in Program 16.3.

The **Digraph** interface adds the following methods, which apply only to directed graphs, to the inherited interface:

isStronglyConnected This **boolean**-valued method returns **true** if the directed graph is *strongly connected*. Strong connectedness is discussed in Section 16.3.4.

topologicalOrderTraversal A topological sort is an ordering of the nodes of a directed graph. This traversal visits the nodes of a directed graph in the order specified by a topological sort.

16.2.5 Abstract Graphs

Program 16.5 introduces the **AbstractGraph** class. The **AbstractGraph** class extends the **AbstractContainer** class introduced in Program 5.9 and it implements the **Graph** interface defined in Program 16.3.

The **AbstractGraph** class serves as the base class from which the various concrete graph implementations discussed in Section 16.2.6 are derived. The **AbstractGraph**

PROGRAM 16.4
Digraph interface

```
1   public interface Digraph
2       extends Graph
3   {
4       boolean isStronglyConnected ();
5       void topologicalOrderTraversal (Visitor visitor);
6   }
```

PROGRAM 16.5
`AbstractGraph` interface

```
1   public abstract class AbstractGraph
2       extends AbstractContainer
3       implements Graph
4   {
5       protected int numberOfVertices;
6       protected int numberOfEdges;
7       protected Vertex[] vertex;
8
9       public AbstractGraph (int size)
10          { vertex = new Vertex [size]; }
11
12      protected final class GraphVertex
13          extends AbstractObject
14          implements Vertex
15      {
16          protected int number;
17          protected Object weight;
18          // ...
19      }
20
21      protected final class GraphEdge
22          extends AbstractObject
23          implements Edge
24      {
25          protected int v0;
26          protected int v1;
27          protected Object weight;
28          // ...
29      }
30
31      protected abstract Enumeration getIncidentEdges (int v);
32      protected abstract Enumeration getEmanatingEdges (int v);
33      // ...
34  }
```

---

class also provides implementations for the graph traversals described in Section 16.3 and for the algorithms that test for cycles and connectedness described in Section 16.3.4.

As shown in Program 16.5, the **AbstractGraph** class defines two inner classes, **GraphVertex** and **GraphEdge**. Both classes extend the **AbstractObject** class introduced in Program 5.2.

The **GraphVertex** class implements the **Vertex** interface. It comprises two fields—**number** and **weight**. Each vertex in a graph with *n* vertices is assigned a unique number in the interval $[0, n - 1]$. The **number** field records this number. The **weight** field is used to record the weight on a weighted vertex.

The **GraphEdge** class implements the **Edge** interface. It comprises three fields—**v0**, **v1**, and **weight**. The first two record the vertices that are the end points of the edge. The third field, **weight**, is used to record the weight on a weighted edge.

16.2.6 Implementing Undirected Graphs

This section describes two concrete classes—**GraphAsMatrix** and **GraphAsLists**. These classes both represent *undirected graphs*. The **GraphAsMatrix** class represents the edges of a graph using an adjacency matrix. The **GraphAsLists** class represents the edges of a graph using adjacency lists.

Using Adjacency Matrices

The **GraphAsMatrix** is introduced in Program 16.6. The **GraphAsMatrix** class extends the **AbstractGraph** class introduced in Program 16.5.

Each instance of the **GraphAsMatrix** class represents an undirected graph, say $G = (V, \mathcal{E})$. The set of vertices, V, is represented using the **vertex** array inherited from the **AbstractGraph** base class. Each vertex is represented by a separate **GraphVertex** instance.

Similarly, the set of edges, $\mathcal{E}$, is represented using the **matrix** field, which is a two-dimensional array of **Edge**s. Each edge is represented by a separate **GraphEdge** instance.

The **GraphAsMatrix** constructor takes a single argument of type **int** that specifies the maximum number of vertices that the graph may contain. This quantity specifies the length of the array of vertices and the dimensions of the adjacency matrix. The implementation of the **GraphAsMatrix** class is left as a programming project for the reader (Project 16.3).

PROGRAM 16.6
GraphAsMatrix fields and constructor

```
1   public class GraphAsMatrix
2       extends AbstractGraph
3   {
4       protected Edge[][] matrix;
5
6       public GraphAsMatrix (int size)
7       {
8           super (size);
9           matrix = new Edge [size][size];
10      }
11      // ...
12  }
```

PROGRAM 16.7
GraphAsLists fields and constructor

```
1  public class GraphAsLists
2      extends AbstractGraph
3  {
4      protected LinkedList[] adjacencyList;
5
6      public GraphAsLists (int size)
7      {
8          super (size);
9          adjacencyList = new LinkedList [size];
10         for (int i = 0; i < size; ++i)
11             adjacencyList [i] = new LinkedList ();
12     }
13     // ...
14 }
```

Using Adjacency Lists

Program 16.7 introduces the **GraphAsLists** class. The **GraphAsLists** extends the **AbstractGraph** class introduced in Program 16.5. The **GraphAsLists** class represents the edges of a graph using adjacency lists.

Each instance of the **GraphAsLists** class represents an undirected graph, say $G = (\mathcal{V}, \mathcal{E})$. The set of vertices, $\mathcal{V}$, is represented using the **vertex** array inherited from the **AbstractGraph** base class. The set of edges, $\mathcal{E}$, is represented using the **adjacencyList** field, which is an array of linked lists. The ith linked list, **adjacencyList[i]**, represents the set $\mathcal{A}(v_i)$ which is the set of edges emanating from vertex v_i. The implementation uses the **LinkedList** class given in Section 4.3.

The **GraphAsLists** constructor takes a single argument of type **int** that specifies the maximum number of vertices that the graph may contain. This quantity specifies the lengths of the array of vertices and the array of adjacency lists. The implementation of the **GraphAsLists** class is left as programming project for the reader (Project 16.4).

16.2.7 Comparison of Graph Representations

In order to make the appropriate choice when selecting a graph representation scheme, it is necessary to understand the time/space trade-offs. Although the details of the implementations have been omitted, we can still make meaningful conclusions about the performance that we can expect from those implementations. In this section we consider the space required as well as the running times for basic graph operations.

Space Comparison

Consider the representation of a directed graph $G = (\mathcal{V}, \mathcal{E})$. In addition to the $|\mathcal{V}|$ **GraphVertex** class instances and the $|\mathcal{E}|$ **GraphEdge** class instances contained by the graph, there is the storage required by the adjacency matrix. In this case, the matrix is a $|\mathcal{V}| \times |\mathcal{V}|$ matrix of **Edge**s. Therefore, the amount of storage required by an adjacency matrix implementation is

$$|\mathcal{V}| \times \texttt{sizeof(GraphVertex)} + |\mathcal{E}| \times \texttt{sizeof(GraphEdge)} \qquad (16.1)$$
$$+ |\mathcal{V}| \times \texttt{sizeof(Vertex ref)} + |\mathcal{V}|^2 \times \texttt{sizeof(Edge ref)} + O(1).$$

On the other hand, consider the amount of storage required when we represent the same graph using adjacency lists. In addition to the vertices and the edges themselves, there are $|\mathcal{V}|$ linked lists. If we use the **LinkedList** class defined in Section 4.3, each such list has a **head** and **tail** field. Altogether there are $|\mathcal{E}|$ linked lists elements, each of which refers to the next element of the list and contains an **Edge**. Therefore, the total space required is

$$|\mathcal{V}| \times \texttt{sizeof(GraphVertex)} + |\mathcal{E}| \times \texttt{sizeof(GraphEdge)} \qquad (16.2)$$
$$+ |\mathcal{V}| \times \texttt{sizeof(Vertex ref)} + 2|\mathcal{V}| \times \texttt{sizeof(LinkedList ref)}$$
$$+ |\mathcal{E}| \times (\texttt{sizeof(LinkedList.Element ref)} + \texttt{sizeof(Edge ref)}) + O(1).$$

Notice that the space for the vertices and edges themselves cancels out when we compare Equation (16.1) with Equation (16.2). If we assume that all object references require the same amount of space, we can conclude that adjacency lists use less space than adjacency matrices when

$$|\mathcal{E}| < \frac{|\mathcal{V}|^2 - 2|\mathcal{V}|}{2}.$$

For example, given a 10-node graph, the adjacency lists version uses less space when there are fewer than 40 edges. As a rough rule of thumb, we can say that adjacency lists use less space when the average degree of a node, $\bar{d} = |\mathcal{E}|/|\mathcal{V}|$, satisfies $\bar{d} \lesssim |\mathcal{V}|/2$.

Time Comparison

The following four operations are used extensively in the implementations of many different graph algorithms:

find edge (v, w) Given vertices v and w, this operation locates the corresponding **Edge** instance. When using an adjacency matrix, we can find an edge in constant time. When adjacency lists are used, the worst-case running time is $O(|\mathcal{A}(v)|)$, since $|\mathcal{A}(v)|$ is the length of the adjacency list associated with vertex v.

This is the operation performed by the **getEdge** method of the **Graph** interface.

enumerate all edges In order to locate all of the edges when using adjacency matrices, it is necessary to examine all $|\mathcal{V}|^2$ matrix entries. Therefore, the worst-case running time needed to enumerate all of the edges is $O(|\mathcal{V}|^2)$.

On the other hand, to enumerate all the edges when using adjacency lists requires the traversal of $|\mathcal{V}|$ lists. In all, there are $|\mathcal{E}|$ edges. Therefore, the worst-case running time is $O(|\mathcal{V}| + |\mathcal{E}|)$.

This operation is performed using the enumeration returned by the **getEdges** method of the **Graph** interface.

TABLE 16.2
Comparison of Graph Representations

	Representation Scheme	
Operation	Adjacency Matrix	Adjacency List
Find edge (v, w)	$O(1)$	$O(\lvert\mathcal{A}(v)\rvert)$
Enumerate all edges	$O(\lvert\mathcal{V}\rvert^2)$	$O(\lvert\mathcal{V}\rvert + \lvert\mathcal{E}\rvert)$
Enumerate edges emanating from v	$O(\lvert\mathcal{V}\rvert)$	$O(\lvert\mathcal{A}(v)\rvert)$
Enumerate edges incident on w	$O(\lvert\mathcal{V}\rvert)$	$O(\lvert\mathcal{V}\rvert + \lvert\mathcal{E}\rvert)$

enumerate edges emanating from v To enumerate all edges that emanate from vertex v requires a complete scan of the vth row of an adjacency matrix. Therefore, the worst-case running time when using adjacency matrices is $O(\lvert\mathcal{V}\rvert)$.

Enumerating the edges emanating from vertex v is a trivial operation when using adjacency lists. All we need do is traverse the vth list. This takes $O(\lvert\mathcal{A}(v)\rvert)$ time in the worst case.

This operation is performed using the enumeration returned by the `getEmanatingEdges` method of the `Vertex` interface.

enumerate edges incident on w To enumerate all edges that are incident on vertex w requires a complete scan of the wth column of an adjacency matrix. Therefore, the worst-case running time when using adjacency matrices is $O(\lvert\mathcal{V}\rvert)$.

Enumerating the edges incident on vertex w is a non-trivial operation when using adjacency lists. It is necessary to search every adjacency list in order to find all edges incident on a given vertex. Therefore, the worst-case running time is $O(\lvert\mathcal{V}\rvert + \lvert\mathcal{E}\rvert)$.

This operation is performed using the enumeration returned by the `getIncidentEdges` method of the `Vertex` interface.

Table 16.2 summarizes these running times.

16.3 Graph Traversals

There are many different applications of graphs. As a result, there are many different algorithms for manipulating them. However, many of the different graph algorithms have in common the characteristic that they systematically visit all of the vertices in the graph; that is, the algorithm walks through the graph data structure and performs some computation at each vertex in the graph. This process of walking through the graph is called a *graph traversal*.

Although there are many different possible ways in which to systematically visit all of the vertices of a graph, certain traversal methods occur frequently enough that they are given names of their own. This section presents three of them—depth-first traversal, breadth-first traversal, and topological sort.

FIGURE 16.8
Depth-first traversal.

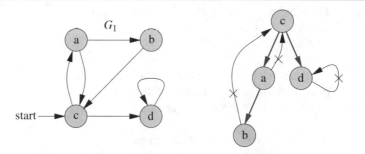

16.3.1 Depth-First Traversal

The *depth-first traversal* of a graph is like the depth-first traversal of a tree discussed in Section 9.4. A depth-first traversal of a tree always starts at the root of the tree. Since a graph has no root, when we do a depth-first traversal, we must specify the vertex at which to begin.

A depth-first traversal of a tree visits a node and then recursively visits the subtrees of that node. Similarly, depth-first traversal of a graph visits a vertex and then recursively visits all of the vertices adjacent to that node. The catch is that the graph may contain cycles, but the traversal must visit every vertex at most once. The solution to the problem is to keep track of the nodes that have been visited, so that the traversal does not suffer the fate of infinite recursion.

For example, Figure 16.8 illustrates the depth-first traversal of the directed graph G_1 starting from vertex c. The depth-first traversal visits the nodes in the order

$$c, a, b, d.$$

A depth first traversal only follows edges that lead to unvisited vertices. As shown in Figure 16.8, if we omit the edges that are not followed, the remaining edges form a tree. Clearly, the depth-first traversal of this tree is equivalent to the depth-first traversal of the graph.

Implementation

Program 16.8 gives the code for the **depthFirstTraversal** method of the **AbstractGraph** class. In fact, two **depthFirstTraversal** methods are defined. One of them accepts two arguments, the other accepts three. As indicated in Program 16.3, the two-argument method is declared **public**, whereas the three-argument one is **private**.

The user of the **Graph** interface only sees the two-argument **depthFirstTraversal** method. This method takes any **PrePostVisitor** and an integer. The idea is that the **visit** method of the visitor is called once for each vertex in the graph and the vertices are visited in depth-first traversal order starting from the vertex specified by the integer.

PROGRAM 16.8
AbstractGraph class depthFirstTraversal method

```
1   public abstract class AbstractGraph
2       extends AbstractContainer
3       implements Graph
4   {
5       protected int numberOfVertices;
6       protected int numberOfEdges;
7       protected Vertex[] vertex;
8
9       public void depthFirstTraversal (
10          PrePostVisitor visitor, int start)
11      {
12          boolean[]  visited = new boolean [numberOfVertices];
13          for (int v = 0; v < numberOfVertices; ++v)
14              visited [v] = false;
15          depthFirstTraversal (visitor, vertex [start], visited);
16      }
17
18      private void depthFirstTraversal (
19          PrePostVisitor visitor, Vertex v, boolean[] visited)
20      {
21          if (visitor.isDone ())
22              return;
23          visitor.preVisit (v);
24          visited [v.getNumber ()] = true;
25          Enumeration p = v.getSuccessors ();
26          while (p.hasMoreElements ())
27          {
28              Vertex to = (Vertex) p.nextElement ();
29              if (!visited [to.getNumber ()])
30                  depthFirstTraversal (visitor, to, visited);
31          }
32          visitor.postVisit (v);
33      }
34      // ...
35  }
```

In order to ensure that each vertex is visited at most once, an array of length $|\mathcal{V}|$ of **boolean** values called **visited** is used (line 12); that is, **visited**[i] = **true** only if vertex i has been visited. All of the array elements are initially **false** (lines 13–14). After initializing the array, the two-argument method calls the three-argument one, passing it a reference to the array as the third argument.

The three-argument method returns immediately if the visitor is done. Otherwise, it visits the specified node, and then it follows all of the edges emanating from that node and recursively visits the adjacent vertices *if those vertices have not already been visited*.

Running Time Analysis

The running time of the depth-first traversal method depends on the graph representation scheme used. The traversal visits each node in the graph at most once. When a node is visited, all edges emanating from that node are considered. During a complete traversal the algorithm enumerates every edge in the graph.

Therefore, the worst-case running time for the depth-first traversal of a graph represented using an adjacency matrix is

$$|\mathcal{V}| \times (\mathcal{T}\langle \texttt{previsit} \rangle + \mathcal{T}\langle \texttt{postvisit} \rangle) + O(|\mathcal{V}|^2).$$

When adjacency lists are used, the worst-case running time for the depth-first traversal method is

$$|\mathcal{V}| \times (\mathcal{T}\langle \texttt{previsit} \rangle + \mathcal{T}\langle \texttt{postvisit} \rangle) + O(|\mathcal{V}| + |\mathcal{E}|).$$

Recall that for a sparse graph graph $|\mathcal{E}| = O(|\mathcal{V}|)$. If the sparse graph is represented using adjacency lists and if $\mathcal{T}\langle \texttt{previsit} \rangle = O(1)$ and $\mathcal{T}\langle \texttt{postvisit} \rangle = O(1)$, the worst-case running time of the depth-first traversal is simply $O(|\mathcal{V}|)$.

16.3.2   Breadth-First Traversal

The *breadth-first traversal* of a graph is like the breadth-first traversal of a tree discussed in Section 9.4. The breadth-first traversal of a tree visits the nodes in the order of their depth in the tree. Breadth-first tree traversal first visits all nodes at depth zero (i.e., the root), then all nodes at depth one, and so on.

Since a graph has no root, when we do a breadth-first traversal, we must specify the vertex at which to start the traversal. Furthermore, we can define the depth of a given vertex to be the length of the shortest path from the starting vertex to the given vertex. Thus, breadth-first traversal first visits the starting vertex, then all vertices adjacent to the starting vertex, and then all vertices adjacent to those, and so on.

Section 6.2.3 presents a non-recursive breadth-first traversal algorithm for N-ary trees that uses a queue to keep track vertices that need to be visited. The breadth-first graph traversal algorithm is very similar.

First, the starting vertex is enqueued. Then, the following steps are repeated until the queue is empty:

1. Remove the vertex at the head of the queue and call it **vertex**.
2. Visit **vertex**.
3. Follow each edge emanating from **vertex** to find the adjacent vertex and call it **to**. If **to** has not already been put into the queue, enqueue it.

Notice that a vertex can be put into the queue at most once. Therefore, the algorithm must somehow keep track of the vertices that have been enqueued.

FIGURE 16.9
Breadth-first traversal.

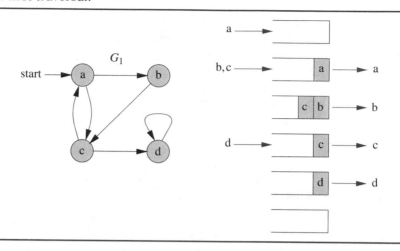

Figure 16.9 illustrates the breadth-first traversal of the directed graph G_1 starting from vertex a. The algorithm begins by inserting the starting vertex, a, into the empty queue. Next, the head of the queue (vertex a) is dequeued and visited, and the vertices adjacent to it (vertices b and c) are enqueued. When b is dequeued and visited we find that there is only adjacent vertex, c, and that vertex is already in the queue. Next vertex c is dequeued and visited. Vertex c is adjacent to a and d. Since a has already been enqueued (and subsequently dequeued) only vertex d is put into the queue. Finally, vertex d is dequeued and visited. Therefore, the breadth-first traversal of G_1 starting from a visits the vertices in the sequence

$$a, b, c, d.$$

Implementation
Program 16.9 gives the code for the **breadthFirstTraversal** method of the **AbstractGraph** class. This method takes any **Visitor** and an integer. The **visit** method of the visitor is called once for each vertex in the graph and the vertices are visited in breadth-first traversal order starting from the vertex specified by the integer.

A **boolean**-valued array, **enqueued**, is used to keep track of the vertices that have been put into the queue. The elements of the array are all initialized to **false** (lines 12–14). Next, a new queue is created and the starting vertex is enqueued (lines 16–19).

The main loop of the **breadthFirstTraversal** method comprises lines 20–34. This loop continues as long as there is a vertex in the queue and the visitor is willing to do more work (line 20). In each iteration exactly one vertex is dequeued and visited (lines 22–23). After a vertex is visited, all successors of that node are examined (lines 24–33). Every successor of the node that has not yet been enqueued is put into the queue and the fact that it has been enqueued is recorded in the array **enqueued** (lines 28–32).

PROGRAM 16.9
AbstractGraph class breadthFirstTraversal method

```
1   public abstract class AbstractGraph
2       extends AbstractContainer
3       implements Graph
4   {
5       protected int numberOfVertices;
6       protected int numberOfEdges;
7       protected Vertex[] vertex;
8
9       public void breadthFirstTraversal (
10          Visitor visitor, int start)
11      {
12          boolean[] enqueued = new boolean [numberOfVertices];
13          for (int v = 0; v < numberOfVertices; ++v)
14              enqueued [v] = false;
15
16          Queue queue = new QueueAsLinkedList ();
17
18          enqueued [start] = true;
19          queue.enqueue (vertex [start]);
20          while (!queue.isEmpty () && !visitor.isDone ())
21          {
22              Vertex v = (Vertex) queue.dequeue ();
23              visitor.visit (v);
24              Enumeration p = v.getSuccessors ();
25              while (p.hasMoreElements ())
26              {
27                  Vertex to = (Vertex) p.nextElement ();
28                  if (!enqueued [to.getNumber ()])
29                  {
30                      enqueued [to.getNumber ()] = true;
31                      queue.enqueue (to);
32                  }
33              }
34          }
35      }
36      // ...
37  }
```

Running Time Analysis

The breadth-first traversal enqueues each node in the graph at most once. When a node is dequeued, all edges emanating from that node are considered. Therefore, a complete traversal enumerates every edge in the graph.

The actual running time of the breadth-first traversal method depends on the graph representation scheme used. The worst-case running time for the traversal of a graph represented using an adjacency matrix is

$$|\mathcal{V}| \times \mathcal{T}\langle \texttt{visit} \rangle + O(|\mathcal{V}|^2).$$

When adjacency lists are used, the worst-case running time for the breadth-first traversal method is

$$|\mathcal{V}| \times \mathcal{T}\langle \texttt{visit} \rangle + O(|\mathcal{V}| + |\mathcal{E}|).$$

If the graph is sparse, then $|\mathcal{E}| = O(|\mathcal{V}|)$. Therefore, if a sparse graph is represented using adjacency lists and if $\mathcal{T}\langle \texttt{visit} \rangle = O(1)$, the worst-case running time of the breadth-first traversal is just $O(|\mathcal{V}|)$.

16.3.3   Topological Sort

A topological sort is an ordering of the vertices of a *directed acyclic graph* given by the following definition:

Definition 16.7 (Topological Sort)
Consider a directed acyclic graph $G = (\mathcal{V}, \mathcal{E})$. A topological sort of the vertices of G is a sequence $S = \{v_1, v_2, \ldots, v_{|\mathcal{V}|}\}$ in which each element of $\mathcal{V}$ appears exactly once. For every pair of distinct vertices v_i and v_j in the sequence S, if $v_i \rightarrow v_j$ is an edge in G; that is, if $(v_i, v_j) \in \mathcal{E}$, then $i < j$.

Informally, a topological sort is a list of the vertices of a DAG in which all successors of any given vertex appear in the sequence after that vertex. Consider the directed acyclic graph G_7 shown in Figure 16.10. The sequence $S = \{a, b, c, d, e, f, g, h, i\}$ is a topological sort of the vertices of G_7. To see that this is so, consider the set of vertices:

$$\mathcal{E} = \{(a, b), (a, c), (a, e), (b, d), (b, e), (c, f), (c, h),$$
$$(d, g), (e, g), (e, h), (e, i), (f, h), (g, i), (h, i)\}.$$

The vertices in each edge are in alphabetical order, and so is the sequence S.

It should also be evident from Figure 16.10 that a topological sort is not unique. For example, the following are also valid topological sorts of the graph G_7:

$$S' = \{a, c, b, f, e, d, h, g, i\}$$
$$S'' = \{a, b, d, e, g, c, f, h, i\}$$
$$S''' = \{a, c, f, h, b, e, d, g, i\}$$

$$\vdots$$

FIGURE 16.10
A directed acyclic graph.

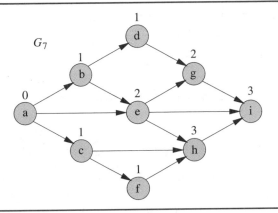

One way to find a topological sort is to consider the *in-degrees* of the vertices. (The number above a vertex in Figure 16.10 is the in-degree of that vertex.) Clearly the first vertex in a topological sort must have in-degree zero and every DAG must contain at least one vertex with in-degree zero. A simple algorithm to create the sort goes like this:

Repeat the following steps until the graph is empty:

1. Select a vertex that has in-degree zero.
2. Add the vertex to the sort.
3. Delete the vertex and all edges emanating from it from the graph.

Implementation

Instead of implementing an algorithm that computes a topological sort, we have chosen to implement a traversal that visits the vertices of a DAG in the order given by the topological sort. The topological order traversal can be used to implement many other graph algorithms. Furthermore, given such a traversal, it is easy to define a visitor that computes a topological sort.

In order to implement the algorithm described in the preceding section, an array of integers of length $|V|$ is used to record the in-degrees of the vertices. As a result, it is not really necessary to remove vertices or edges from the graph during the traversal. Instead, the effect of removing a vertex and all the edges emanating from that vertex is simulated by decreasing the apparent in-degrees of all successors of the removed vertex.

In addition, we use a queue to keep track of the vertices that have not yet been visited, but whose in-degree is zero. Doing so eliminates the need to search the array for zero entries.

Program 16.10 defines the **topologicalOrderTraversal** method of the **AbstractGraph** class. This method takes as its argument a **Visitor**. The **visit** method of the visitor is called once for each vertex in the graph. The order in which the vertices are visited is given by a topological sort of those vertices.

The algorithm begins by computing the in-degrees of all of the vertices. An array of integers of length V called **inDegree** is used for this purpose. First, all array

PROGRAM 16.10
AbstractGraph class topologicalOrderTraversal method

```
1   public abstract class AbstractGraph
2       extends AbstractContainer
3       implements Graph
4   {
5       protected int numberOfVertices;
6       protected int numberOfEdges;
7       protected Vertex[] vertex;
8
9       public void topologicalOrderTraversal (Visitor visitor)
10      {
11          int[] inDegree = new int [numberOfVertices];
12          for (int v = 0; v < numberOfVertices; ++v)
13              inDegree [v] = 0;
14          Enumeration p = getEdges ();
15          while (p.hasMoreElements ())
16          {
17              Edge edge = (Edge) p.nextElement ();
18              Vertex to = edge.getV1 ();
19              ++inDegree [to.getNumber ()];
20          }
21
22          Queue queue = new QueueAsLinkedList ();
23          for (int v = 0; v < numberOfVertices; ++v)
24              if (inDegree [v] == 0)
25                  queue.enqueue (vertex [v]);
26          while (!queue.isEmpty () && !visitor.isDone ())
27          {
28              Vertex v = (Vertex) queue.dequeue ();
29              visitor.visit (v);
30              Enumeration q = v.getSuccessors ();
31              while (q.hasMoreElements ())
32              {
33                  Vertex to = (Vertex) q.nextElement ();
34                  if (--inDegree [to.getNumber ()] == 0)
35                      queue.enqueue (to);
36              }
37          }
38      }
39      // ...
40  }
```

elements are set to zero. Then, for each edge $(v_0, v_1) \in \mathcal{V}$, array element `inDegree`$(v_1)$ is increased by one (lines 11–20). Next, a queue to hold vertices is created. All vertices with in-degree zero are put into this queue (lines 22–25).

The main loop of the `topologicalOrderTraversal` method comprises lines 26–37. This loop continues as long as the queue is not empty and the visitor is not finished. In each iteration of the main loop exactly one vertex is dequeued and visited (lines 28–29).

Once a vertex has been visited, the effect of removing that vertex from the graph is simulated by decreasing by one the in-degrees of all successors of that vertex. When the in-degree of a vertex becomes zero, that vertex is enqueued (lines 30–36).

Running Time Analysis

The topological-order traversal enqueues each node in the graph at most once. When a node is dequeued, all edges emanating from that node are considered. Therefore, a complete traversal enumerates every edge in the graph.

The worst-case running time for the traversal of a graph represented using an adjacency matrix is

$$|\mathcal{V}| \times \mathcal{T}\langle\texttt{visit}\rangle + O(|\mathcal{V}|^2).$$

When adjacency lists are used, the worst-case running time for the topological-order traversal method is

$$|\mathcal{V}| \times \mathcal{T}\langle\texttt{visit}\rangle + O(|\mathcal{V}| + |\mathcal{E}|).$$

16.3.4 Graph Traversal Applications: Testing for Cycles and Connectedness

This section presents several graph algorithms that are based on graph traversals. The first two algorithms test undirected and directed graphs for connectedness. Both algorithms are implemented using the depth first traversal. The third algorithm tests a directed graph for cycles. It is implemented using a topological-order traversal.

Connectedness of an Undirected Graph

Definition 16.8 (Connectedness of an Undirected Graph)
An undirected graph $G = (\mathcal{V}, \mathcal{E})$ is connected *if there is a path in G between every pair of vertices in $\mathcal{V}$.*

Consider the undirected graph shown in Figure 16.11. It is tempting to interpret this figure as a picture of two graphs. However, the figure actually represents the undirected graph $G_8 = (\mathcal{V}, \mathcal{E})$, given by

$$\mathcal{V} = \{a, b, c, d, e, f\}$$
$$\mathcal{E} = \{\{a, b\}, \{a, c\}, \{b, c\}, \{d, e\}, \{e, f\}\}.$$

FIGURE 16.11
An unconnected, undirected graph with two (connected) components.

G_8

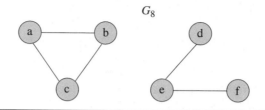

Clearly, the graph G_8 is not connected. For example, there is no path between vertices a and d. In fact, the graph G_8 consists of two unconnected parts, each of which is a connected subgraph. The connected subgraphs of a graph are called *connected components*.

A traversal of an undirected graph (either depth-first or breadth-first) starting from any vertex will only visit all other vertices of the graph if that graph is connected. Therefore, there is a very simple way to test whether an undirected graph is connected: Count the number of vertices visited during a traversal of the graph. Only if all of the vertices are visited is the graph connected.

Program 16.11 shows how this can be implemented. The **isConnected** method of the **AbstractGraph** class is a **boolean**-valued method that returns **true** if the graph is connected.

The method is implemented using the **depthFirstTraversal** method and a visitor that simply counts the number of vertices it visits. The **visit** method adds one to the **value** field of the counter each time it is called.

The worst-case running time of the **isConnected** method is determined by the time taken by the **depthFirstTraversal**. Clearly, in this case $\mathcal{T}\langle \text{visit} \rangle = O(1)$. Therefore, the running time of **isConnected** is $O(|\mathcal{V}|^2)$ when adjacency matrices are used to represent the graph and $O(|\mathcal{V}| + |\mathcal{E}|)$ when adjacency lists are used.

Connectedness of a Directed Graph
When dealing with directed graphs, we define two kinds of connectedness, *strong* and *weak*. Strong connectedness of a directed graph is defined as follows:

Definition 16.9 (Strong Connectedness of a Directed Graph)
A directed graph $G = (\mathcal{V}, \mathcal{E})$ is strongly connected *if there is a path in G between every pair of vertices in $\mathcal{V}$.*

For example, Figure 16.12 shows the directed graph $G_9 = \{\mathcal{V}, \mathcal{E}\}$ given by

$$\mathcal{V} = \{a, b, c, d, e, f\}$$
$$\mathcal{E} = \{(a, b), (b, c), (b, e), (c, a), (d, e), (e, f), (f, d)\}.$$

Notice that the graph G_9 is *not* connected! For example, there is no path from any of the vertices in $\{d, e, f\}$ to any of the vertices in $\{a, b, c\}$. Nevertheless, the graph "looks" connected in the sense that it is not made of up of separate parts in the way that the graph G_8 in Figure 16.11 is.

AbstractGraph class isConnected method

```
1   public abstract class AbstractGraph
2       extends AbstractContainer
3       implements Graph
4   {
5       protected int numberOfVertices;
6       protected int numberOfEdges;
7       protected Vertex[] vertex;
8
9       protected final static class Counter
10      {
11          int value = 0;
12      }
13
14      public boolean isConnected ()
15      {
16          final Counter counter = new Counter ();
17          PrePostVisitor visitor = new AbstractPrePostVisitor ()
18          {
19              public void visit (Object object)
20                  { ++counter.value; }
21          };
22          depthFirstTraversal (visitor, 0);
23          return counter.value == numberOfVertices;
24      }
25      // ...
26  }
```

FIGURE 16.12
A weakly connected directed graph and the underlying undirected graph.

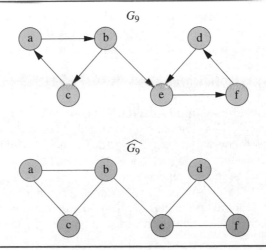

This idea of "looking" connected is what *weak connectedness* represents. To define weak connectedness we need to introduce first the notion of the undirected graph that underlies a directed graph. Consider a directed graph $G = (\mathcal{V}, \mathcal{E})$. The underlying undirected graph is the graph $\widehat{G} = (\mathcal{V}, \widehat{\mathcal{E}})$, where $\widehat{\mathcal{E}}$ represents the set of undirected edges that is obtained by removing the arrowheads from the directed edges in G:

$$\widehat{\mathcal{E}} = \left\{ \{v, w\} : (v, w) \in \mathcal{E} \vee (w, v) \in \mathcal{E} \right\}.$$

Weak connectedness of a directed graph is defined with respect to its underlying, undirected graph:

Definition 16.10 (Weak Connectedness of a Directed Graph)
A directed graph $G = (\mathcal{V}, \mathcal{E})$ is weakly connected *if the underlying undirected graph $\widehat{G}$ is connected.*

For example, since the undirected graph $\widehat{G_9}$ in Figure 16.12 is connected, the directed graph G_9 is *weakly connected*. Consider what happens when we remove the edge (b, e) from the directed graph G_9. The underlying undirected graph that we get is G_8 in Figure 16.11. Therefore, when we remove edge (b, e) from G_9, the graph that remains is neither strongly connected nor weakly connected.

Testing Strong Connectedness
A traversal of a directed graph (either depth-first or breadth-first) starting from a given vertex will only visit all of the vertices of an undirected graph if there is a path from the start vertex to every other vertex. Therefore, a simple way to test whether a directed graph is strongly connected uses $|\mathcal{V}|$ traversals—one starting from each vertex in $\mathcal{V}$— each time the number of vertices visited is counted. The graph is strongly connected if all of the vertices are visited in each traversal.

Program 16.12 shows how this can be implemented. It shows the **isStrongly-Connected** method of the **AbstractGraph** class, which returns the **boolean** value **true** if the graph is *strongly* connected.

The method consists of a loop over all of the vertices of the graph. Each iteration does a **depthFirstTraversal** using a visitor that counts the number of vertices it visits. The running time for one iteration is essentially that of the **depthFirstTraversal** since $\mathcal{T}\langle\text{visit}\rangle = O(1)$ for the counting visitor. Therefore, the worst-case running time for the **isConnected** method is $O(|\mathcal{V}|^3)$ when adjacency matrices are used and $O(|\mathcal{V}|^2 + |\mathcal{V}| \cdot |\mathcal{E}|)$ when adjacency lists are used to represent the graph.

Testing for Cycles in a Directed Graph
The final application of graph traversal that we consider in this section is to test a directed graph for cycles. An easy way to do this is to attempt a topological-order traversal using the algorithm given in Section 16.3.3. This algorithm only visits all vertices of a directed graph if that graph contains no cycles.

To see why this is so, consider the directed cyclic graph G_{10} shown in Figure 16.13. The topological traversal algorithm begins by computing the *in-degrees* of the vertices. (The number shown below each vertex in Figure 16.13 is the in-degree of that vertex.)

PROGRAM 16.12
AbstractGraph class isConnected method

```
1   public abstract class AbstractGraph
2       extends AbstractContainer
3       implements Graph
4   {
5       protected int numberOfVertices;
6       protected int numberOfEdges;
7       protected Vertex[] vertex;
8
9       public boolean isStronglyConnected ()
10      {
11          final Counter counter = new Counter ();
12          for (int v = 0; v < numberOfVertices; ++v)
13          {
14              counter.value = 0;
15              PrePostVisitor visitor = new AbstractPrePostVisitor()
16              {
17                  public void visit (Object object)
18                      { ++counter.value; }
19              };
20              depthFirstTraversal (visitor, v);
21              if (counter.value != numberOfVertices)
22                  return false;
23          }
24          return true;
25      }
26      // ...
27  }
```

FIGURE 16.13
A directed cyclic graph.

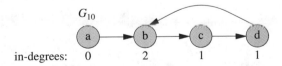

At each step of the traversal, a vertex with in-degree of zero is visited. After a vertex is visited, the vertex and all edges emanating from that vertex are removed from the graph. Notice that if we remove vertex a and edge (a, b) from G_{10}, all remaining vertices have in-degrees of one. The presence of the cycle prevents the topological-order traversal from completing.

PROGRAM 16.13
AbstractGraph class isCyclic method

```
1   public abstract class AbstractGraph
2       extends AbstractContainer
3       implements Graph
4   {
5       protected int numberOfVertices;
6       protected int numberOfEdges;
7       protected Vertex[] vertex;
8
9       public boolean isCyclic ()
10      {
11          final Counter counter = new Counter ();
12          Visitor visitor = new AbstractVisitor ()
13          {
14              public void visit (Object object)
15                  { ++counter.value; }
16          };
17          topologicalOrderTraversal (visitor);
18          return counter.value != numberOfVertices;
19      }
20      // ...
21  }
```

Therefore, a simple way to test whether a directed graph is cyclic is to attempt a topological traversal of its vertices. If all vertices are not visited, the graph must be cyclic.

Program 16.13 gives the implementation of the isCyclic method of the **AbstractGraph** class. This **boolean**-valued accessor returns **true** if the graph is cyclic. The implementation simply makes use of a visitor that counts the number of vertices visited during a topologicalOrderTraversal of the graph.

The worst-case running time of the isCyclic method is determined by the time taken by the topologicalOrderTraversal. Since $\mathcal{T}\langle\text{visit}\rangle = O(1)$, the running time of isCyclic is $O(|\mathcal{V}|^2)$ when adjacency matrices are used to represent the graph and $O(|\mathcal{V}| + |\mathcal{E}|)$ when adjacency lists are used.

16.4 Shortest-Path Algorithms

In this section we consider edge-weighted graphs, both directed and undirected, in which the weight measures the *cost* of traversing that edge. The units of cost depend on the application.

For example, we can use a directed graph to represent a network of airports. In such a graph the vertices represent the airports and the edges correspond to the available flights between airports. In this scenario there are several possible cost metrics: If we are interested in computing travel time, then we use an edge-weighted graph in which the weights represent the flying time between airports. If we are concerned with the financial cost of a trip, then the weights on the edges represent the monetary cost of a ticket. Finally, if we are interested in the actual distance traveled, then the weights represent the physical distances between airports.

If we are interested in traveling from point A to B, we can use a suitably labeled graph to answer the following questions: What is the fastest way to get from A to B? Which route from A to B has the least expensive airfare? What is the shortest possible distance traveled to get from A to B?

Each of these questions is an instance of the same problem: Given an edge-weighted graph, $G = (\mathcal{V}, \mathcal{E})$, and two vertices, $v_s \in \mathcal{V}$ and $v_d \in \mathcal{V}$, find the path that starts at v_s and ends at v_d that has the smallest weighted path length. The weighted length of a path is defined as follows:

Definition 16.11 (Weighted Path Length)
Consider an edge-weighted graph $G = (\mathcal{V}, \mathcal{E})$. Let $C(v_i, v_j)$ be the weight on the edge connecting v_i to v_j. A path in G is a non-empty sequence of vertices $P = \{v_1, v_2, \ldots, v_k\}$. The weighted path length of path P is given by

$$\sum_{i=1}^{k-1} C(v_i, v_{i+1}).$$

The *weighted* length of a path is the sum of the weights on the edges in that path. Conversely, the *unweighted* length of a path is simply the number of edges in that path. Therefore, the *unweighted* length of a path is equivalent to the weighted path length obtained when all edge weights are one.

16.4.1 Single-Source Shortest Path

In this section we consider the *single-source shortest path* problem: Given an edge-weighted graph $G = (\mathcal{V}, \mathcal{E})$ and a vertex $v_s \in \mathcal{V}$, find the shortest weighted path from v_s to every other vertex in $\mathcal{V}$.

Why do we find the shortest path to every other vertex if we are interested only in the shortest path from, say, v_s to v_d? It turns out that to find the shortest path from v_s to v_d, it is necessary to find the shortest path from v_s to every other vertex in G! If a vertex is ignored, say v_i, then we will not consider any of the paths from v_s to v_d that pass through v_i. But if we fail to consider all of the paths from v_s to v_d, we cannot be assured of finding the shortest one.

Furthermore, suppose the shortest path from v_s to v_d passes through some intermediate node v_i; that is, the shortest path is of the form $P = \{v_s, \ldots, v_i, \ldots, v_d\}$. It must be the case that the portion of P between v_s to v_i is also the shortest path from v_s to v_i. Suppose it is not. Then there exists another shorter path from v_s to v_i. However, then P would not be the shortest path from v_s to v_d, because we could obtain a shorter one by replacing the portion of P between v_s and v_i by the shorter path.

FIGURE 16.14
Two edge-weighted directed graphs.

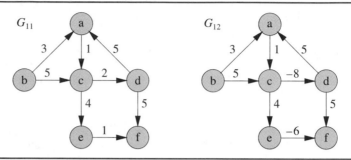

Consider the directed graph G_{11} shown in Figure 16.14. The shortest *weighted* path between vertices b and f is the path $\{b, a, c, e, f\}$, which has the weighted path of length nine. On the other hand, the shortest *unweighted* path from b to f is the path of length three, $\{b, c, e, f\}$.

As long as all of the edge weights are non-negative (as is the case for G_{11}), the shortest-path problem is well defined. Unfortunately, things get a little tricky in the presence of negative edge weights.

For example, consider the graph G_{12} shown in Figure 16.14. Suppose we are looking for the shortest path from d to f. Exactly two edges emanate from vertex d, both with the same edge weight of five. If the graph contained only positive edge weights, there could be no shorter path than the direct path $\{d, f\}$.

However, in a graph that contains negative weights, a long path gets "shorter" when we add edges with negative weights to it. For example, the path $\{d, a, c, e, f\}$ has a total weighted path length of four, even though the first edge, (d, a), has the weight five.

But negative weights are even more insidious than this: For example, the path $\{d, a, c, d, a, e, f\}$, which also joins vertex d to f, has a weighted path length of two but the path $\{d, a, c, d, a, c, d, a, e, f\}$ has length zero; that is, as the number of edges in the path increases, the weighted path length decreases! The problem in this case is the existence of the cycle $\{d, a, c, d\}$ the weighted path length of which is less than zero. Such a cycle is called a *negative cost cycle*.

Clearly, the shortest-path problem is not defined for graphs that contain negative cost cycles. However, negative edges are not intrinsically bad. Solutions to the problem do exist for graphs that contain both positive and negative edge weights, as long as there are no negative cost cycles. Nevertheless, the problem is greatly simplified when all edges carry non-negative weights.

Dijkstra's Algorithm
Dijkstra's algorithm is a greedy algorithm for solving the single-source, shortest-path problem on an edge-weighted graph in which all of the weights are non-negative. It finds the shortest paths from some initial vertex, say v_s, to all the other vertices one-by-one. The essential feature of Dijkstra's algorithm is the order in which the paths are determined: The paths are discovered in the order of their weighted lengths, starting with the shortest and proceeding to the longest.

For each vertex v, Dijkstra's algorithm keeps track of three pieces of information, k_v, d_v, and p_v:

k_v The `boolean`-valued flag k_v indicates that the shortest path to vertex v is *known*. Initially, $k_v = $ `false` for all $v \in \mathcal{V}$.

d_v The quantity d_v is the length of the shortest known path from v_s to v. When the algorithm begins, no shortest paths are known. The distance d_v is a *tentative* distance. During the course of the algorithm, candidate paths are examined and the *tentative* distances are modified.

Initially, $d_v = \infty$ for all $v \in \mathcal{V}$ such that $v \neq v_s$, while $d_{v_s} = 0$.

p_v The predecessor of vertex v on the shortest path from v_s to v; that is, the shortest path from v_s to v has the form $\{v_s, \ldots, p_v, v\}$.

Initially, p_v is unknown for all $v \in \mathcal{V}$.

Dijkstra's algorithm proceeds in phases. The following steps are performed in each pass:

1. From the set of vertices for which $k_v = $ `false`, select the vertex v having the smallest tentative distance d_v.

2. Set $k_v \leftarrow$ `true`.

3. For each vertex w adjacent to v for which $k_w \neq $ `true`, test whether the tentative distance d_w is greater than $d_v + C(v, w)$. If it is, set $d_w \leftarrow d_v + C(v, w)$ and set $p_w \leftarrow v$.

In each pass exactly one vertex has its k_v set to `true`. The algorithm terminates after $|\mathcal{V}|$ passes are completed, at which time all of the shortest paths are known.

Table 16.3 illustrates the operation of Dijkstra's algorithm as it finds the shortest paths starting from vertex b in graph G_{11} shown in Figure 16.14.

Initially all of the tentative distances are ∞, except for vertex b, which has tentative distance zero. Therefore, vertex b is selected in the first pass. The mark $\sqrt{}$ beside an entry in Table 16.3 indicates that the shortest path is *known* ($k_v = $ `true`).

TABLE 16.3
Operation of Dijkstra's Algorithm

Vertex	Initially	Passes					
		1	2	3	4	5	6
a	∞	$3\,b$	$\sqrt{}\;3\,b$	$\sqrt{}\;3\,b$	$\sqrt{}\;3\,b$	$\sqrt{}\;3\,b$	$\sqrt{}\;3\,b$
b	$0\,-$	$\sqrt{}\;0\,-$	$\sqrt{}\;0\,-$	$\sqrt{}\;0\,-$	$\sqrt{}\;0\,-$	$\sqrt{}\;0\,-$	$\sqrt{}\;0\,-$
c	∞	$5\,b$	$4\,a$	$\sqrt{}\;4\,a$	$\sqrt{}\;4\,a$	$\sqrt{}\;4\,a$	$\sqrt{}\;4\,a$
d	∞	∞	∞	$6\,c$	$\sqrt{}\;6\,c$	$\sqrt{}\;6\,c$	$\sqrt{}\;6\,c$
e	∞	∞	∞	$8\,c$	$8\,c$	$\sqrt{}\;8\,c$	$\sqrt{}\;8\,c$
f	∞	∞	∞	∞	$11\,d$	$9\,e$	$\sqrt{}\;9\,e$

FIGURE 16.15
The shortest-path graph for G_{11}.

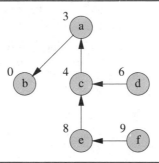

Next we follow the edges emanating from vertex b, $b \rightarrow a$ and $b \rightarrow c$ and update the distance accordingly. The new tentative distance for a becomes 3 and the new tentative distance for c is 5. In both cases, the next-to-last vertex on the shortest path is vertex b.

In the second pass, vertex a is selected and its entry is marked with $\sqrt{}$, indicating the shortest path is known. There is one edge emanating from a, $a \rightarrow c$. The distance to c via a is 4. Since this is less than the tentative distance to c, vertex c is given the new tentative distance 4 and its predecessor on the shortest path is set to a. The algorithm continues in this fashion for a total of $\mathcal{V}$ passes until all shortest paths have been found.

The shortest-path information contained in the rightmost column of Table 16.3 can be represented in the form of a vertex-weighted graph, as shown in Figure 16.15.

This graph contains the same set of vertices as the problem graph G_{11}. Each vertex v is labeled with the length d_v of the shortest path from b to v. Each vertex (except b) has a single emanating edge that connects the vertex to the next-to-last vertex on the shortest path. By following the edges in this graph from any vertex v to vertex b, we can construct the shortest path from b to v in reverse.

Data Structures for Dijkstra's Algorithm

The implementation of Dijkstra's algorithm described next uses the **Entry** structure declared in Program 16.14. Each **Entry** instance has three fields, **known**, **distance**, and **predecessor**, which correspond to the variables k_v, d_v, and p_v, respectively.

In each pass of its operation, Dijkstra's algorithm selects from the set of vertices for which the shortest path is not yet known the one with the smallest tentative distance. Therefore, we use a *priority queue* to represent this set of vertices.

The priority assigned to a vertex is its tentative distance. The class **Association** class introduced in Program 5.16 is used to associate a priority with a given vertex instance.

Implementation

An implementation of Dijkstra's algorithm is shown in Program 16.15. The **DijkstrasAlgorithm** method takes two arguments. The first is a directed graph. It is assumed that the directed graph is an edge-weighted graph in which the weights are instances of the **Int** class defined in Program 5.5. The second argument is

PROGRAM 16.14
GraphAlgorithms Entry class

```
1   public class Algorithms
2   {
3       static final class Entry
4       {
5           boolean known = false;
6           int distance = Integer.MAX_VALUE;
7           int predecessor = Integer.MAX_VALUE;
8       }
9   }
```

the number of the start vertex, v_s.

The `DijkstrasAlgorithm` method returns its result in the form of a shortest-path graph. Therefore, the return value is a `Digraph` instance.

The main data structures used are called `table` and `queue` (lines 6 and 10). The former is an array of $n = |V|$ Entry elements. The latter is a priority queue. In this case, a `BinaryHeap` of length $|\mathcal{E}|$ is used. (See Section 11.2.)

The algorithm begins by setting the tentative distance for the start vertex to zero and inserting the start vertex into the priority queue with priority zero (lines 9–13).

The main loop of the method comprises lines 14–38. In each iteration of this loop the vertex with the smallest distance is dequeued (line 17). The vertex is processed only if its table entry indicates that the shortest path is not already known (line 19).

When a vertex `v0` is processed, its shortest path is deemed to be *known* (line 21). Then each vertex `v1` adjacent to vertex `v0` is considered (lines 22–37). The distance to `v1` along the path that passes through `v0` is computed (line 29). If this distance is less than the tentative distance associated with `v1`, entries in the table for `v1` are updated, and the `v1` is given a new priority and inserted into the priority queue (lines 30–36).

The main loop terminates when all shortest paths have been found. The shortest-path graph is then constructed using the information in the table (lines 39–44).

Running Time Analysis

The running time of the `DijkstrasAlgorithm` method is dominated by the running time of the main loop (lines 14–38). (It is easy to see that lines 5–13 and 39–44 run in $O(|\mathcal{V}|)$ time.)

To determine the running time of the main loop, we proceed as follows: First, we ignore temporarily the time required for the `enqueue` and `dequeue` operations in the priority queue. Clearly, each vertex in the graph is processed exactly once. When a vertex is processed all the edges emanating from it are considered. Therefore, the time (ignoring the priority queue operations) taken is $O(|V| + |E|)$ when adjacency lists are used and $O(|V|^2)$ when adjacency matrices are used.

Now, we add back the worst-case time required for the priority queue operations. In the worst case, a vertex is enqueued and subsequently dequeued once for every edge

```
1   public class Algorithms
2   {
3       public static Digraph DijkstrasAlgorithm (Digraph g, int s)
4       {
5           int n = g.getNumberOfVertices ();
6           Entry[] table = new Entry [n];
7           for (int v = 0; v < n; ++v)
8               table [v] = new Entry ();
9           table [s].distance = 0;
10          PriorityQueue queue =
11              new BinaryHeap (g.getNumberOfEdges());
12          queue.enqueue (
13              new Association (new Int (0), g.getVertex (s)));
14          while (!queue.isEmpty ())
15          {
16              Association assoc = (Association) queue.dequeueMin();
17              Vertex v0 = (Vertex) assoc.getValue ();
18              int n0 = v0.getNumber ();
19              if (!table [n0].known)
20              {
21                  table [n0].known = true;
22                  Enumeration p = v0.getEmanatingEdges ();
23                  while (p.hasMoreElements ())
24                  {
25                      Edge edge = (Edge) p.nextElement ();
26                      Vertex v1 = edge.getMate (v0);
27                      int n1 = v1.getNumber ();
28                      Int wt = (Int) edge.getWeight ();
29                      int d = table [n0].distance + wt.intValue ();
30                      if (table [n1].distance > d)
31                      {   table [n1].distance = d;
32                          table [n1].predecessor = n0;
33                          queue.enqueue (
34                              new Association (new Int (d), v1));
35                      }
36                  }
37              }
38          }
39          Digraph result = new DigraphAsLists (n);
40          for (int v = 0; v < n; ++v)
41              result.addVertex (v, new Int (table [v].distance));
42          for (int v = 0; v < n; ++v)
43              if (v != s)
44                  result.addEdge (v, table [v].predecessor);
45          return result;
46      }
47  }
```

in the graph. Therefore, the length of the priority queue is at most $|\mathcal{E}|$. As a result, the worst-case time for each operation is $O(\log|\mathcal{E}|)$. Thus, the worst-case running time for Dijkstra's algorithm is

$$O(|\mathcal{V}| + |\mathcal{E}|\log|\mathcal{E}|),$$

when adjacency lists are used, and

$$O(|\mathcal{V}|^2 + |\mathcal{E}|\log|\mathcal{E}|),$$

when adjacency matrices are used to represent the input graph.

16.4.2 All-Pairs Source Shortest Path

In this section we consider the *all-pairs, shortest-path* problem: Given an edge-weighted graph $G = (\mathcal{V}, \mathcal{E})$, for each pair of vertices in $\mathcal{V}$ find the *length* of the shortest weighted path between the two vertices.

One way to solve this problem is to run Dijkstra's algorithm $|\mathcal{V}|$ times in turn using each vertex in $\mathcal{V}$ as the initial vertex. Therefore, we can solve the all pairs problem in $O(|\mathcal{V}|^2 + |\mathcal{V}||\mathcal{E}|\log|\mathcal{E}|)$ time when adjacency lists are used, and $O(|\mathcal{V}|^3 + |\mathcal{V}||\mathcal{E}|\log|\mathcal{E}|)$, when adjacency matrices are used. However, for a dense graph ($|\mathcal{E}| = \Theta(|\mathcal{V}|^2)$) the running time of Dijkstra's algorithm is $O(|\mathcal{V}|^3\log|\mathcal{V}|)$, regardless of the representation scheme used.

Floyd's Algorithm

Floyd's algorithm uses the dynamic programming method to solve the all-pairs shortest-path problem on a dense graph. The method makes efficient use of an adjacency matrix to solve the problem. Consider an edge-weighted graph $G = (\mathcal{V}, \mathcal{E})$, where $C(v, w)$ represents the weight on edge (v, w). Suppose the vertices are numbered from 1 to $|\mathcal{V}|$. That is, let $\mathcal{V} = \{v_1, v_2, \ldots, v_{|\mathcal{V}|}\}$. Furthermore, let $\mathcal{V}_k$ be the set composed of the first k vertices in $\mathcal{V}$; that is, $\mathcal{V}_k = \{v_1, v_2, \ldots, v_k\}$, for $0 \leq k \leq |\mathcal{V}|$.

Let $P_k(v, w)$ be the shortest path from vertex v to w that passes only through vertices in $\mathcal{V}_k$, if such a path exists. Thus, the path $P_k(v, w)$ has the form

$$P_k(v, w) = \{v, \underbrace{\ldots}_{\in \mathcal{V}_k}, w\}.$$

Let $D_k(v, w)$ be the *length* of path $P_k(v, w)$:

$$D_k(v, w) = \begin{cases} |P_k(v, w)| & P_k(v, w) \text{ exists,} \\ \infty & \text{otherwise.} \end{cases}$$

Since $\mathcal{V}_0 = \varnothing$, the P_0 paths correspond to the edges of G:

$$P_0(v, w) = \begin{cases} \{v, w\} & (v, w) \in \mathcal{E}, \\ \text{undefined} & \text{otherwise.} \end{cases}$$

FIGURE 16.16
Calculating D_{i+1} in Floyd's algorithm.

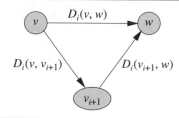

Therefore, the D_0 path lengths correspond to the weights on the edges of G:

$$D_0(v, w) = \begin{cases} C(v, w) & (v, w) \in \mathcal{E}, \\ \infty & \text{otherwise.} \end{cases}$$

Floyd's algorithm computes the sequence of matrices $D_0, D_1, \ldots, D_{|\mathcal{V}|}$. The distances in D_i represent paths with intermediate vertices in $\mathcal{V}_i$. Since $\mathcal{V}_{i+1} = \mathcal{V}_i \cup \{v_{i+1}\}$, we can obtain the distances in D_{i+1} from those in D_i by considering only the paths that pass through vertex v_{i+1}. Figure 16.16 illustrates how this is done.

For every pair of vertices (v, w), we compare the distance $D_i(v, w)$, (which represents the shortest path from v to w that does not pass through v_{i+1}) with the sum $D_i(v, v_{i+1}) + D_i(v_{i+1}, w)$ (which represents the shortest path from v to w that does pass through v_{i+1}). Thus, D_{i+1} is computed as follows:

$$D_{i+1}(v, w) = \min\{D_i(v, v_{i+1}) + D_i(v_{i+1}, w), D_i(v, w)\}.$$

Implementation

An implementation of Floyd's algorithm is shown in Program 16.16. The **Floyds-Algorithm** method takes as its argument a directed graph. The directed graph is assumed to be an edge-weighted graph in which the weights are instances of the **Int** class defined in Program 5.5.

The **FloydsAlgorithm** method returns its result in the form of an edge-weighted directed graph. Therefore, the return value is a **Digraph**.

The principal data structure use by the algorithm is a $|\mathcal{V}| \times |\mathcal{V}|$ matrix of integers called **distance**. All elements of the matrix are initially set to ∞ (lines 6–9). Next, an edge enumeration is used to visit all of the edges in the input graph in order to transfer the weights from the graph to the **distance** matrix (lines 11–18).

The main work of the algorithm is done in three, nested loops (lines 20–29). The outer loop computes the sequence of distance matrices $D_1, D_2, \ldots, D_{|\mathcal{V}|}$. The inner two loops consider all possible pairs of vertices. Notice that as D_{i+1} is computed, its entries overwrite those of D_i.

Finally, the values in the **distance** matrix are transferred to the result graph (lines 31–38). The result graph contains the same set of vertices as the input graph. For each finite entry in the **distance** matrix, a weighted edge is added to the result graph.

PROGRAM 16.16
Floyd's algorithm

```
1   public class Algorithms
2   {
3       public static Digraph FloydsAlgorithm (Digraph g)
4       {
5           int n = g.getNumberOfVertices ();
6           int[][] distance = new int[n][n];
7           for (int v = 0; v < n; ++v)
8               for (int w = 0; w < n; ++w)
9                   distance [v][w] = Integer.MAX_VALUE;
10
11          Enumeration p = g.getEdges ();
12          while (p.hasMoreElements ())
13          {
14              Edge edge = (Edge) p.nextElement ();
15              Int wt = (Int) edge.getWeight ();
16              distance [edge.getV0().getNumber()]
17                  [edge.getV1().getNumber()] = wt.intValue ();
18          }
19
20          for (int i = 0; i < n; ++i)
21              for (int v = 0; v < n; ++v)
22                  for (int w = 0; w < n; ++w)
23                      if (distance [v][i] != Integer.MAX_VALUE &&
24                          distance [i][w] != Integer.MAX_VALUE)
25                      {
26                          int d = distance[v][i] + distance[i][w];
27                          if (distance [v][w] > d)
28                              distance [v][w] = d;
29                      }
30
31          Digraph result = new DigraphAsMatrix (n);
32          for (int v = 0; v < n; ++v)
33              result.addVertex (v);
34          for (int v = 0; v < n; ++v)
35              for (int w = 0; w < n; ++w)
36                  if (distance [v][w] != Integer.MAX_VALUE)
37                      result.addEdge (v, w,
38                          new Int (distance [v][w]));
39          return result;
40      }
41  }
```

Running Time Analysis

The worst-case running time for Floyd's algorithm is easily determined. Creating and initializing the **distance** matrix is $O(|\mathcal{V}|^2)$ (lines 6–9). Transferring the weights from the input graph to the **distance** matrix requires $O(|\mathcal{V}|+|\mathcal{E}|)$ time if adjacency lists are used, and $O(|\mathcal{V}|^2)$ time when an adjacency matrix is used to represent the input graph (lines 11–18).

The running time for the three nested loops is $O(|\mathcal{V}|^3)$ in the worst case. Finally, constructing the result graph and transferring the entries from the **distance** matrix to the result requires $O(|\mathcal{V}|^2)$ time. As a result, the worst-case running time of Floyd's algorithm is $O(|\mathcal{V}|^3)$.

16.5 Minimum-Cost Spanning Trees

In this section we consider undirected graphs and their subgraphs. A *subgraph* of a graph $G = (\mathcal{V}, \mathcal{E})$ is any graph $G' = (\mathcal{V}', \mathcal{E}')$ such that $\mathcal{V}' \subseteq \mathcal{V}$ and $\mathcal{E}' \subseteq \mathcal{E}$. In particular, we consider *connected* undirected graphs and their *minimal subgraphs*. The minimal subgraph of a connected graph is called a *spanning tree*:

Definition 16.12 (Spanning Tree)
Consider a connected, undirected *graph* $G = (\mathcal{V}, \mathcal{E})$. *A spanning tree of G is a subgraph of G, say* $T = (\mathcal{V}', \mathcal{E}')$, *with the following properties:*

1. $\mathcal{V}' = \mathcal{V}$.
2. T is connected.
3. T is acyclic.

Figure 16.17 shows an undirected graph, G_{13}, together with three of its spanning trees. A spanning tree is called a *tree* because every *acyclic* undirected graph can be viewed as a general, unordered tree. Because the edges are undirected, any vertex may be chosen to serve as the root of the tree. For example, the spanning tree of G_{13} given in Figure 16.17 (c) can be viewed as the general, unordered tree

$$\{b, \{a\}, \{c\}, \{e, \{d\}, \{f\}\}\}.$$

According to Definition 16.12, a spanning tree is connected. Therefore, as long as the tree contains more than one vertex, there can be no vertex with degree zero. Furthermore, the following theorem guarantees that there is always at least one vertex with degree one:

Theorem 16.1
Consider a connected, undirected graph $G = (\mathcal{V}, \mathcal{E})$, *where* $|\mathcal{V}| > 1$. *Let* $T = (\mathcal{V}, \mathcal{E}')$ *be a spanning tree of G. The spanning tree T contains at least one vertex of degree one.*

Proof (By contradiction). Assume that there is no vertex in T of degree one; that is, all vertices in T have degree two or greater. Then by following edges into and out

FIGURE 16.17
An undirected graph and three spanning trees.

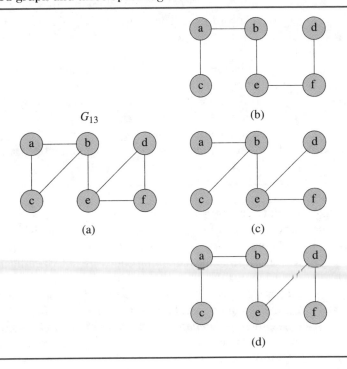

G_{13}

(a)

(b)

(c)

(d)

of vertices we can construct a path that is cyclic. But a spanning tree is acyclic—a contradiction. Therefore, a spanning tree always contains at least one vertex of degree one.

According to Definition 16.12, the edge set of a spanning tree is a subset of the edges in the spanned graph. How many edges must a spanning tree have? The following theorem answers the question:

Theorem 16.2
Consider a connected, undirected graph $G = (\mathcal{V}, \mathcal{E})$. Let $T = (\mathcal{V}, \mathcal{E}')$ be a spanning tree of G. The number of edges in the spanning tree is given by

$$|\mathcal{E}'| = |\mathcal{V}| - 1.$$

Proof (By induction). We can prove Theorem 16.12 by induction on $|\mathcal{V}|$, the number of vertices in the graph.

Base Case Consider a graph that contains only one node; that is, $|\mathcal{V}| = 1$. Clearly, the spanning tree for such a graph contains no edges. Since $|\mathcal{V}| - 1 = 0$, the theorem is valid.

Inductive Hypothesis   Assume that the number of edges in a spanning tree for a graph with $|\mathcal{V}|$ has been shown to be $|\mathcal{V}| - 1$ for $|\mathcal{V}| = 1, 2, \ldots, k$.

Consider a graph $G_{k+1} = (\mathcal{V}, \mathcal{E})$ with $k + 1$ vertices and its spanning tree $T_{k+1} = (\mathcal{V}, \mathcal{E}')$. According to Theorem 16.1, G_{k+1} contains at least one vertex of degree one. Let $v \in \mathcal{V}$ be one such vertex and $\{v, w\} \in \mathcal{E}'$ be the one edge emanating from v in T_{k+1}.

Let T_k be the graph of k nodes obtained by removing v and its emanating edge from the graph T_{k+1}; that is, $T_k = (\mathcal{V} - \{v\}, \mathcal{E}' - \{v, w\})$.

Since T_{k+1} is connected, so too is T_k. Similarly, since T_{k+1} is acyclic, so too is T_k. Therefore, T_k is a spanning tree with k vertices. By the inductive hypothesis, T_k has $k - 1$ edges. Thus, T_{k+1} has k edges.

Therefore, by induction on k, the spanning tree for a graph with $|\mathcal{V}|$ vertices contains $|\mathcal{V}| - 1$ edges.

Constructing Spanning Trees

Any traversal of a connected, undirected tree visits all vertices in that tree, regardless of the node from which the traversal is started. During the traversal certain edges are traversed while the remaining edges are not. Specifically, an edge is traversed if it leads from a vertex that has been visited to a vertex that has not been visited. The set of edges that are traversed during a traversal forms a spanning tree.

The spanning tree obtained from a breadth-first traversal starting at vertex v of graph G is called the *breadth-first spanning tree* of G rooted at v. For example, the spanning tree shown in Figure 16.17 (c) is the breadth-first spanning tree of G_{13} rooted at vertex b.

Similarly, the spanning tree obtained from a depth-first traversal is the *depth-first spanning tree* of G rooted at v. The spanning tree shown in Figure 16.17 (d) is the depth-first spanning tree of G_{13} rooted at vertex c.

Minimum-Cost Spanning Trees

The total *cost* of an edge-weighted undirected graph is simply the sum of the weights on all edges in that graph. A minimum-cost spanning tree of a graph is a spanning tree of that graph that has the least total cost:

Definition 16.13 (Minimal Spanning Tree)

Consider an edge-weighted, undirected, connected graph $G = (\mathcal{V}, \mathcal{E})$, where $C(v, w)$ represents the weight on edge $\{v, w\} \in \mathcal{E}$. The minimum spanning tree *of G is the spanning tree $T = (\mathcal{V}, \mathcal{E}')$ that has the smallest total cost,*

$$\sum_{\{v, w\} \in \mathcal{E}'} C(v, w).$$

Figure 16.18 shows edge-weighted graph G_{14} together with its minimum-cost spanning tree T_{14}. In general, it is possible for a graph to have several different minimum-cost spanning trees. However, in this case there is only one.

The two sections that follow present two different algorithms for finding the minimum-cost spanning tree. Both algorithms are similar in that they build the tree one edge at a time.

FIGURE 16.18
An edge-weighted, undirected graph and a minimum-cost spanning tree.

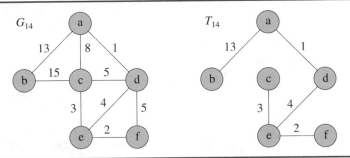

16.5.1 Prim's Algorithm

Prim's algorithm finds a minimum-cost spanning tree of an edge-weighted, connected, undirected graph $G = (\mathcal{V}, \mathcal{E})$. The algorithm constructs the minimum-cost spanning tree of a graph by selecting edges from the graph one-by-one and adding those edges to the spanning tree.

Prim's algorithm is essentially a minor variation of *Dijkstra's algorithm*. (See Section 16.4.1.) To construct the spanning tree, the algorithm constructs a sequence of spanning trees $T_0, T_1, \ldots, T_{|\mathcal{V}|-1}$, each of which is a subgraph of G. The algorithm begins with a tree that contains one selected vertex, say $v_s \in \mathcal{V}$; that is, $T_0 = \{\{v_s\}, \varnothing\}$.

Given $T_i = \{\mathcal{V}_i, \mathcal{E}_i\}$, we obtain the next tree in the sequence as follows: Consider the set of edges given by

$$\mathcal{H}_i = \bigcup_{u \in \mathcal{V}_i} \mathcal{A}(u) - \bigcup_{u \in \mathcal{V}_i} \mathcal{I}(u).$$

The set $\mathcal{H}_i$ contains all edges $\{v, w\}$ such that exactly one of v or w is in $\mathcal{V}_i$ (but not both). Select the edge $\{v, w\} \in \mathcal{H}_i$ with the smallest edge weight,

$$C(v, w) = \min_{\{v', w'\} \in \mathcal{H}_i} C(v', w').$$

Then $T_{i+1} = \{\mathcal{V}_{i+1}, \mathcal{E}_{i+1}\}$, where $\mathcal{V}_{i+1} = \mathcal{V}_i \cup \{v\}$ and $\mathcal{E}_{i+1} = \mathcal{E} \cup \{\{v, w\}\}$. After $|\mathcal{V}| - 1$ such steps we get $T_{|\mathcal{V}|-1}$, which is the minimum-cost spanning tree of G.

Figure 16.19 illustrates how Prim's algorithm determines the minimum-cost spanning tree of the graph G_{14} shown in Figure 16.18. The circled vertices are the elements of $\mathcal{V}_i$, the solid edges represent the elements of $\mathcal{E}_i$, and the dashed edges represent the elements of $\mathcal{H}_i$.

Implementation
An implementation of Prim's algorithm is shown in Program 16.17. This implementation is almost identical to the version of *Dijkstra's* algorithm given in Program 16.15. In fact, there are only five differences between the two algorithms. These are found on lines 3, 29, 30, 39, and 41.

FIGURE 16.19
Operation of Prim's algorithm.

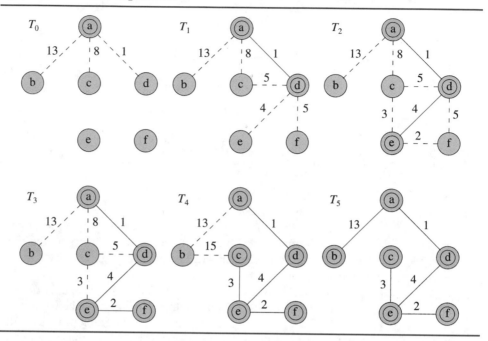

The **PrimsAlgorithm** method takes two arguments. The first is an undirected graph instance. We assume that the graph is edge-weighted and that the weights are instances of the **Int** class defined in Program 5.5. The second argument is the number of the start vertex, v_s.

The **PrimsAlgorithm** method returns a minimum-cost spanning tree represented as an undirected graph. Therefore, the return value is a **Graph**.

The running time of Prim's algorithm is asymptotically the same as Dijkstra's algorithm; that is, the worst-case running time is

$$O(|\mathcal{V}| + |\mathcal{E}| \log |\mathcal{E}|),$$

when adjacency lists are used, and

$$O(|\mathcal{V}|^2 + |\mathcal{E}| \log |\mathcal{E}|),$$

when adjacency matrices are used to represent the input graph.

16.5.2 Kruskal's Algorithm

Like Prim's algorithm, *Kruskal's algorithm* also constructs the minimum spanning tree of a graph by adding edges to the spanning tree one-by-one. At all points during its execution, the set of edges selected by Prim's algorithm forms exactly one tree. On the other hand, the set of edges selected by Kruskal's algorithm forms a forest of trees.

```
1   public class Algorithms
2   {
3       public static Graph PrimsAlgorithm (Graph g, int s)
4       {
5           int n = g.getNumberOfVertices ();
6           Entry[] table = new Entry [n];
7           for (int v = 0; v < n; ++v)
8               table [v] = new Entry ();
9           table [s].distance = 0;
10          PriorityQueue queue =
11              new BinaryHeap (g.getNumberOfEdges());
12          queue.enqueue (
13              new Association (new Int (0), g.getVertex (s)));
14          while (!queue.isEmpty ())
15          {
16              Association assoc = (Association) queue.dequeueMin();
17              Vertex v0 = (Vertex) assoc.getValue ();
18              int n0 = v0.getNumber ();
19              if (!table [n0].known)
20              {
21                  table [n0].known = true;
22                  Enumeration p = v0.getEmanatingEdges ();
23                  while (p.hasMoreElements ())
24                  {
25                      Edge edge = (Edge) p.nextElement ();
26                      Vertex v1 = edge.getMate (v0);
27                      int n1 = v1.getNumber ();
28                      Int wt = (Int) edge.getWeight ();
29                      int d = wt.intValue ();
30                      if (!table[n1].known && table[n1].distance>d)
31                      {   table [n1].distance = d;
32                          table [n1].predecessor - n0;
33                          queue.enqueue (
34                              new Association (new Int (d), v1));
35                      }
36                  }
37              }
38          }
39          Graph result = new GraphAsLists (n);
40          for (int v = 0; v < n; ++v)
41              result.addVertex (v);
42          for (int v = 0; v < n; ++v)
43              if (v != s)
44                  result.addEdge (v, table [v].predecessor);
45          return result;
46      }
47  }
```

Kruskal's algorithm is conceptually quite simple. The edges are selected and added to the spanning tree in increasing order of their weights. An edge is added to the tree only if it does not create a cycle.

The beauty of Kruskal's algorithm is the way that potential cycles are detected. Consider an undirected graph $G = (\mathcal{V}, \mathcal{E})$. We can view the set of vertices, $\mathcal{V}$, as a *universal set* and the set of edges, $\mathcal{E}$, as the definition of an *equivalence relation* over the universe $\mathcal{V}$. (See Definition 12.1.) In general, an equivalence relation partitions a universal set into a set of equivalence classes. If the graph is connected, there is only one equivalence class—all of the elements of the universal set are *equivalent*. Therefore, a *spanning tree* is a minimal set of equivalences that result in a single equivalence class.

Kruskal's algorithm computes $P_0, P_1, \ldots, P_{|\mathcal{V}-1|}$, a sequence of *partitions* of the set of vertices $\mathcal{V}$. (Partitions are discussed in Section 12.4.) The initial partition consists of $|\mathcal{V}|$ sets of size one:

$$P_0 = \{\{v_1\}, \{v_2\}, \ldots, \{v_{|\mathcal{V}|}\}\}.$$

Each subsequent element of the sequence is obtained from its predecessor by *joining* two of the elements of the partition. Therefore, P_i has the form

$$P_i = \{S_0^i, S_1^i, \ldots, S_{|\mathcal{V}|-1-i}^i\},$$

for $0 \le i \le |\mathcal{V}| - 1$.

To construct the sequence the edges in $\mathcal{E}$ are considered one-by-one in increasing order of their weights. Suppose we have computed the sequence up to P_i and the next edge to be considered is $\{v, w\}$. If v and w are both members of the same element of partition P_i, then the edge forms a cycle and is not part of the minimum-cost spanning tree.

On the other hand, suppose v and w are members of two different elements of partition P_i, say S_k^i and S_l^i (respectively). Then $\{v, w\}$ must be an edge in the minimum-cost spanning tree. In this case, we compute P_{i+1} by *joining* S_k^i and S_l^i; that is, we replace S_k^i and S_l^i in P_i by the *union* $S_k^i \cup S_l^i$.

Figure 16.20 illustrates how Kruskal's algorithm determines the minimum-cost spanning tree of the graph G_{14} shown in Figure 16.18. The algorithm computes the following sequence of partitions:

$$P_0 = \{\{a\}, \{b\}, \{c\}, \{d\}, \{e\}, \{f\}\}$$
$$P_1 = \{\{a, d\}, \{b\}, \{c\}, \{e\}, \{f\}\}$$
$$P_2 = \{\{a, d\}, \{b\}, \{c\}, \{e, f\}\}$$
$$P_3 = \{\{a, d\}, \{b\}, \{c, e, f\}\}$$
$$P_4 = \{\{a, c, d, e, f\}, \{b\}\}$$
$$P_5 = \{\{a, b, c, d, e, f\}\}.$$

Implementation

An implementation of Kruskal's algorithm is shown in Program 16.18. The **KruskalsAlgorithm** method takes as its argument an edge-weighted, undirected graph. This implementation assumes that the edge weights are instances of the **Int** class defined in Program 5.5. The method computes the minimum-cost spanning tree and returns it in the form of an edge-weighted, undirected graph.

FIGURE 16.20
Operation of Kruskal's algorithm.

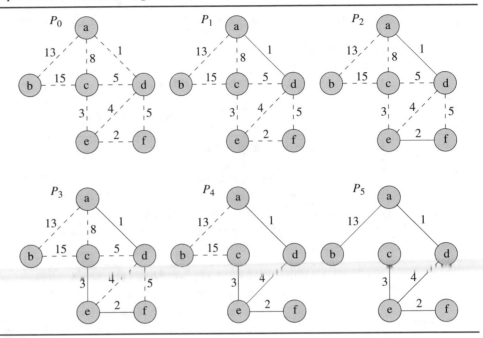

The main data structures used by the method are a priority queue to hold the edges, a partition to detect cycles, and a graph for the result. This implementation uses a **BinaryHeap** (Section 11.2) for the priority queue (lines 11–12), a **PartitionAsForest** (Section 12.4) for the partition (line 21), and a **GraphAsLists** for the spanning tree (line 7).

Running Time Analysis

The **KruskalsAlgorithm** method begins by creating a graph to hold the result spanning tree (lines 7–9). Since a spanning tree is a sparse graph, the **GraphAsLists** class is used to represent it. Initially the graph contains $|\mathcal{V}|$ vertices but no edges. The running time for lines 7–9 is $O(|\mathcal{V}|)$.

Next all of the edges in the input graph are inserted one-by-one into the priority queue (lines 11–19). Since there are $|\mathcal{E}|$ edges, the worst-case running time for a single insertion is $O(\log |\mathcal{E}|)$. Therefore, the worst-case running time to initialize the priority queue is

$$O(|\mathcal{V}| + |\mathcal{E}| \log |\mathcal{E}|),$$

when adjacency lists are used, and

$$O(|\mathcal{V}|^2 + |\mathcal{E}| \log |\mathcal{E}|),$$

when adjacency matrices are used to represent the input graph.

PROGRAM 16.18
Kruskal's algorithm

```
1   public class Algorithms
2   {
3       public static Graph KruskalsAlgorithm (Graph g)
4       {
5           int n = g.getNumberOfVertices ();
6
7           Graph result = new GraphAsLists (n);
8           for (int v = 0; v < n; ++v)
9               result.addVertex (v);
10
11          PriorityQueue queue =
12              new BinaryHeap (g.getNumberOfEdges());
13          Enumeration p = g.getEdges ();
14          while (p.hasMoreElements ())
15          {
16              Edge edge = (Edge) p.nextElement ();
17              Int weight = (Int) edge.getWeight ();
18              queue.enqueue (new Association (weight, edge));
19          }
20
21          Partition partition = new PartitionAsForest (n);
22          while (!queue.isEmpty () && partition.getCount () > 1)
23          {
24              Association assoc = (Association) queue.dequeueMin();
25              Edge edge = (Edge) assoc.getValue ();
26              int n0 = edge.getV0 ().getNumber ();
27              int n1 = edge.getV1 ().getNumber ();
28              Set s = partition.find (n0);
29              Set t = partition.find (n1);
30              if (s != t)
31              {
32                  partition.join (s, t);
33                  result.addEdge (n0, n1);
34              }
35          }
36          return result;
37      }
38  }
```

The main loop of the method comprises lines 22–35. This loop is done at most $|\mathcal{E}|$ times. In each iteration of the loop, one edge is removed from the priority queue (lines 24–25). In the worst case this takes $O(\log |\mathcal{E}|)$ time.

Then, two partition *find* operations are done to determine the elements of the partition that contain the two end points of the given edge (lines 26–29). Since the partition contains at most $|\mathcal{V}|$ elements, the running time for the find operations is $O(\log |\mathcal{V}|)$. If the two elements of the partition are distinct, then an edge is added to the spanning tree and a *join* operation is done to unite the two elements of the partition (lines 30–35). The join operation also requires $O(\log |\mathcal{V}|)$ time in the worst case. Therefore, the total running time for the main loop is $O(|\mathcal{E}| \log |\mathcal{E}| + |\mathcal{E}| \log |\mathcal{V}|)$.

Thus, the worst-case running time for Kruskal's algorithm is

$$O(|\mathcal{V}| + |\mathcal{E}| \log |\mathcal{E}| + |\mathcal{E}| \log |\mathcal{V}|)$$

when adjacency lists are used, and

$$O(|\mathcal{V}|^2 + |\mathcal{E}| \log |\mathcal{E}| + |\mathcal{E}| \log |\mathcal{V}|)$$

when adjacency matrices are used to represent the input graph.

16.6 Application: Critical Path Analysis

In the introduction to this chapter it is stated that there are many applications of graphs. In this section we consider one such application—*critical path analysis*. Critical path analysis crops up in a number of different contexts, from the planning of construction projects to the analysis of combinational logic circuits.

For example, consider the scheduling of activities required to construct a building. Before the foundation can be poured, it is necessary to dig a hole in the ground. After the building has been framed, the electricians and the plumbers can rough in the electrical and water services and this rough-in must be completed before the insulation is put up and the walls are closed in.

We can represent the set of activities and the scheduling constraints using a vertex-weighted, directed acyclic graph (DAG). Each vertex represents an activity and the weight on the vertex represents the time required to complete the activity. The directed edges represent the sequencing constraints; that is, an edge from vertex v to vertex w indicates that activity v must complete before w may begin. Clearly, such a graph must be *acyclic*.

A graph in which the vertices represent activities is called an *activity-node graph*. Figure 16.21 shows an example of an activity-node graph. In such a graph it is understood that independent activities may proceed in parallel. For example, after activity A is completed, activities B and C may proceed in parallel. However, activity D cannot begin until *both* B and C are done.

FIGURE 16.21
An activity-node graph.

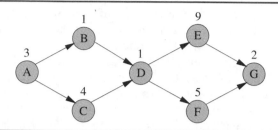

FIGURE 16.22
The event-node graph corresponding to Figure 16.21.

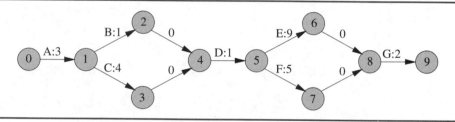

Critical path analysis answers the following questions:

1. What is the minimum amount of time needed to complete all activities?
2. For a given activity v, is it possible to delay the completion of that activity without affecting the overall completion time? If yes, by how much can the completion of activity v be delayed?

The activity-node graph is a vertex-weighted graph. However, the algorithms presented in the preceding sections all require edge-weighted graphs. Therefore, we must convert the vertex-weighted graph into its edge-weighted *dual*. In the dual graph the edges represent the activities, and the vertices represent the commencement and termination of activities. For this reason, the dual graph is called an *event-node graph*.

Figure 16.22 shows the event-node graph corresponding to the activity node graph given in Figure 16.21. Where an activity depends on more than one predecessor it is necessary to insert *dummy* edges.

For example, activity D cannot commence until both B and C are finished. In the event-node graph, vertex 2 represents the termination of activity B and vertex 3 represents the termination of activity C. It is necessary to introduce vertex 4 to represent the event that *both* B and C have completed. Edges $2 \rightarrow 4$ and $3 \rightarrow 4$ represent this synchronization constraint. Since these edges do not represent activities, the edge weights are zero.

For each vertex v in the event node graph we define two times. The first E_v is the *earliest event time* for event v. It is the earliest time at which event v can occur assuming the first event begins at time zero. The earliest event time is given by

$$E_w = \begin{cases} 0 & w = v_i, \\ \min_{(v,w) \in \mathcal{I}(w)} E_v + C(v, w) & \text{otherwise,} \end{cases} \quad (16.3)$$

where v_i is the *initial* event, $\mathcal{I}(w)$ is the set of incident edges on vertex w, and $C(v, w)$ is the weight on vertex (v, w).

Similarly, L_v is the *latest event time* for event v. It is the latest time at which event v can occur. The latest event time is given by

$$L_v = \begin{cases} E_{v_f} & w = v_f, \\ \max_{(v,w) \in \mathcal{A}(w)} E_w - C(v, w) & \text{otherwise,} \end{cases} \quad (16.4)$$

where v_f is the *final* event.

Given the earliest and latest event times for all events, we can compute the time available for each activity. For example, consider an activity represented by edge (v, w). The amount of time available for the activity is $L_w - E_v$ and the time required for that activity is $C(v, w)$. We define the *slack time* for an activity as the amount of time by which an activity can be delayed without affecting the overall completion time of the project. The slack time for the activity represented by edge (v, w) is given by

$$S(v, w) = L_w - E_v - C(v, w). \quad (16.5)$$

Activities with zero slack are *critical*; that is, critical activities must be completed on time—any delay affects the overall completion time. A *critical path* is a path in the event-node graph from the initial vertex to the final vertex comprised solely of critical activities.

Table 16.4 gives the results obtained from the critical path analysis of the activity-node graph shown in Figure 16.21. The tabulated results indicate the critical path is

$$\{A, C, D, E, G\}.$$

TABLE 16.4
Critical Path Analysis Results for the Activity-Node Graph in Figure 16.21

Activity	$C(v, w)$	E_v	L_w	$S(v, w)$
A	3	0	3	0
B	1	3	7	3
C	4	3	7	0
D	1	7	8	0
E	9	8	17	0
F	5	8	17	4
G	2	17	18	0

Implementation

Given an activity-node graph, the objective of critical path analysis is to determine the slack time for each activity and thereby to identify the critical activities and the critical path. We will assume that the activity node graph has already been transformed to an edge-node graph. The implementation of this transformation is left as a project for the reader (Project 16.10). Therefore, the first step is to compute the earliest and latest event times.

According to Equation (16.3), the earliest event time of vertex w is obtained from the earliest event times of all its predecessors. Therefore, we must compute the earliest event times *in topological order*. To do this, we define the **EarliestTimeVisitor** shown in Program 16.19.

The **EarliestTimeVisitor** has one field, **earliestTime**, which is an array used to record the E_v values. The **visit** method of the **EarliestTimeVisitor** class implements directly Equation (16.3). It uses a **getIncidentEdges** enumer-

---

PROGRAM 16.19
Critical path analysis—computing earliest event times

```
 1  public class Algorithms
 2  {
 3      private static final class EarliestTimeVisitor
 4          extends AbstractVisitor
 5      {
 6          int[] earliestTime;
 7
 8          EarliestTimeVisitor (int[] earliestTime)
 9              { this.earliestTime = earliestTime; }
10
11          public void visit (Object object)
12          {
13              Vertex w = (Vertex) object;
14              int max = earliestTime [0];
15              Enumeration p = w.getIncidentEdges ();
16              while (p.hasMoreElements ())
17              {
18                  Edge edge = (Edge) p.nextElement ();
19                  Vertex v = edge.getV0();
20                  Int wt = (Int) edge.getWeight ();
21                  max = Math.max (max,
22                      earliestTime[v.getNumber()] + wt.intValue());
23              }
24              earliestTime [w.getNumber ()] = max;
25          }
26      }
27  }
```

---

ation to determine all predecessors of a given node and computes $\min_{(v,w)\in\mathcal{I}(w)} E_v + C(v, w)$.

In order to compute the latest event times, it is necessary to define also a **Latest-TimeVisitor**. This visitor must visit the vertices of the event-node graph in *reverse topological order*. Its implementation follows directly from Equation (16.4) and Program 16.19.

Program 16.20 defines the method called **criticalPathAnalysis**, which does what its name implies. This method takes as its argument a **Digraph** that represents

---

PROGRAM 16.20
Critical path analysis—finding the critical paths

```
1   public class Algorithms
2   {
3       public static Digraph criticalPathAnalysis (Digraph g)
4       {
5           int n = g.getNumberOfVertices ();
6
7           int[] earliestTime = new int [n];
8           earliestTime [0] = 0;
9           g.topologicalOrderTraversal (
10              new EarliestTimeVisitor (earliestTime));
11
12          int[] latestTime = new int [n];
13          latestTime [n - 1] = earliestTime [n - 1];
14          g.depthFirstTraversal (new PostOrder (
15              new LatestTimeVisitor (latestTime)), 0);
16
17          Digraph slackGraph = new DigraphAsLists (n);
18          for (int v = 0; v < n; ++v)
19              slackGraph.addVertex (v);
20          Enumeration p = g.getEdges ();
21          while (p.hasMoreElements ())
22          {
23              Edge edge = (Edge) p.nextElement ();
24              int n0 = edge.getV0().getNumber();
25              int n1 = edge.getV1().getNumber();
26              Int wt = (Int) edge.getWeight ();
27              int slack = latestTime [n1] - earliestTime [n0] -
28                  wt.intValue ();
29              slackGraph.addEdge (n0, n1, new Int (slack));
30          }
31          return DijkstrasAlgorithm (slackGraph, 0);
32      }
33  }
```

FIGURE 16.23
The critical path graph corresponding to Figure 16.22.

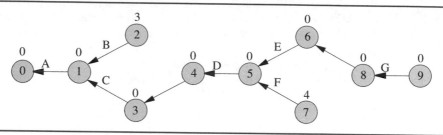

an event-node graph. This implementation assumes that the edge weights are instances of the **Int** class defined in Program 5.5.

The method first uses the **EarliestTimeVisitor** in a topological order traversal to compute the earliest event times, which are recored in the **earliestTime** array (lines 7–10). Next, the latest event times are computed and recorded in the **latestTime** array. Notice that this is done using a **LatestTimeVisitor** in a *postorder* depth-first traversal (lines 12–15). This is because a postorder depth-first traversal is equivalent to a topological order traversal in reverse!

Once the earliest and latest event times have been found, we can compute the slack time for each edge. In the implementation shown, an edge-weighted graph is constructed that is isomorphic with the original event-node graph, but in which the edge weights are the slack times as given by Equation (16.5) (lines 17–30). By constructing such a graph we can make use of Dijkstra's algorithm to find the shortest path from start to finish, since the shortest path must be the critical path (line 31).

The **DijkstrasAlgorithm** method given in Section 16.4 returns its result in the form of a shortest-path graph. The shortest-path graph for the activity-node graph of Figure 16.22 is shown in Figure 16.23. By following the path in this graph from vertex 9 back to vertex 0, we find that the critical path is {*A, C, D, E, G*}.

Exercises

16.1   Consider the *undirected graph* G_A shown in Figure 16.24. List the elements of $\mathcal{V}$ and $\mathcal{E}$. Then, for each vertex $v \in \mathcal{V}$ do the following:

a.   Compute the in-degree of v.

b.   Compute the out-degree of v.

c.   List the elements of $\mathcal{A}(v)$.

d.   List the elements of $\mathcal{I}(v)$.

16.2   Consider the directed graph G_A shown in Figure 16.24.

a.   Show how the graph is represented using an adjacency matrix.

b.   Show how the graph is represented using adjacency lists.

FIGURE 16.24
Sample graphs.

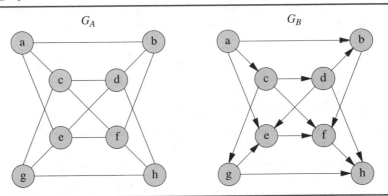

16.3 Repeat Exercises 16.1 and 16.2 for the *directed graph* G_B shown in Figure 16.24.

16.4 Consider a *depth-first traversal* of the undirected graph G_A shown in Figure 16.24 starting from vertex *a*.

   a. List the order in which the nodes are visited in a preorder traversal.

   b. List the order in which the nodes are visited in a postorder traversal.

   Repeat this exercise for a depth-first traversal starting from vertex *d*.

16.5 List the order in which the nodes of the undirected graph G_A shown in Figure 16.24 are visited by a *breadth-first traversal* that starts from vertex *a*. Repeat this exercise for a breadth-first traversal starting from vertex *d*.

16.6 Repeat Exercises 16.4 and 16.5 for the *directed graph* G_B shown in Figure 16.24.

16.7 List the order in which the nodes of the directed graph G_B shown in Figure 16.24 are visited by a *topological-order traversal* that starts from vertex *a*.

16.8 Consider an undirected graph $G = (\mathcal{V}, \mathcal{E})$. If we use a $|\mathcal{V}| \times |\mathcal{V}|$ adjacency matrix A to represent the graph, we end up using twice as much space as we need because A contains redundant information; that is, A is symmetric about the diagonal and all the diagonal entries are zero. Show how a one-dimensional array of length $|\mathcal{V}|(|\mathcal{V}| - 1)/2$ can be used to represent G. **Hint**: Consider just the part of A above the diagonal.

16.9 What is the relationship between the sum of the degrees of the vertices of a graph and the number of edges in the graph.

16.10 A graph with the maximum number of edges is called a *fully connected graph*. Draw fully connected, undirected graphs that contain two, three, four, and five vertices.

16.11 Prove that an undirected graph with *n* vertices contains at most $n(n-1)/2$ edges.

16.12 Every tree is a directed, acyclic graph (DAG), but there exist DAGs that are not trees.

    a. How can we tell whether a given DAG is a tree?

    b. Devise an algorithm to test whether a given DAG is a tree.

16.13 Consider an acyclic, connected, undirected graph G that has n vertices. How many edges does G have?

16.14 In general, an undirected graph contains one or more *connected components*. A connected component of a graph G is a subgraph of G that is *connected* and contains the largest possible number of vertices. Each vertex of G is a member of exactly one connected component of G.

    a. Devise an algorithm to count the number of connected components in a graph.

    b. Devise an algorithm that labels the vertices of a graph in such a way that all the vertices in a given connected component get the same label and vertices in different connected components get different labels.

16.15 A *source* in a directed graph is a vertex with zero in-degree. Prove that every DAG has at least one source.

16.16 What kind of DAG has a unique topological sort?

16.17 Under what conditions does a *postorder* depth-first traversal of a DAG visit the vertices in *reverse* topological order?

16.18 Consider a pair of vertices, v and w, in a directed graph. Vertex w is said to be *reachable* from vertex v if there exists a path in G from v to w. Devise an algorithm that takes as input a graph, $G = (\mathcal{V}, \mathcal{E})$, and a pair of vertices, $v, w \in \mathcal{V}$, and determines whether w is reachable from v.

16.19 An *Eulerian walk* is a path in an undirected graph that starts and ends at the same vertex *and traverses every edge* in the graph. Prove that in order for such a path to exist, all nodes must have even degree.

16.20 Consider the binary relation $<$ defined for the elements of the set $\{a, b, c, d\}$ as follows:

$$\{a < b, a < c, b < c, b < d, c < d, d < a\}.$$

How can we determine whether $<$ is a *total order*?

16.21 Show how the *single-source shortest-path* problem can be solved on a DAG using a topological-order traversal. What is the running time of your algorithm?

16.22 Consider the directed graph G_C shown in Figure 16.25. Trace the execution of *Dijkstra's algorithm* as it solves the single-source shortest-path problem starting from vertex a. Give your answer in a form similar to Table 16.3.

16.23 Dijkstra's algorithm works as long as there are no negative edge weights. Given a graph that contains negative edge weights, we might be tempted to eliminate the negative weights by adding a constant weight to all of the edge weights to make them all positive. Explain why this does not work.

16.24 Dijkstra's algorithm can be modified to deal with negative edge weights (but not negative cost cycles) by eliminating the *known* flag k_v and by inserting a vertex back into the queue every time its *tentative distance* d_v decreases. Explain why the modified algorithm works correctly. What is the running time of the modified algorithm?

FIGURE 16.25
Sample weighted graphs.

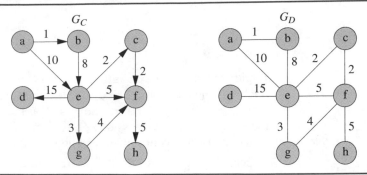

16.25 Consider the directed graph G_C shown in Figure 16.25. Trace the execution of *Floyd's algorithm* as it solves the *all-pairs shortest-path problem*.

16.26 Prove that if the edge weights on an undirected graph are *distinct*, there is only one minimum-cost spanning tree.

16.27 Consider the undirected graph G_D shown in Figure 16.25. Trace the execution of *Prim's algorithm* as it finds the *minimum-cost spanning tree* starting from vertex *a*.

16.28 Repeat Exercise 16.27 using *Kruskal's algorithm.*

16.29 Do Exercise 14.7.

Programming Projects

16.1 Devise a graph description language. Implement a method that reads the description of a graph and constructs a graph object instance. Your method should be completely generic—it should not depend on the graph implementation used.

16.2 Extend Project 16.1 by writing a method that prints the description of a given graph object instance.

16.3 Complete the implementation of the `GraphAsMatrix` class introduced in Program 16.16 by providing suitable definitions for the following methods: `GraphAsMatrix` (constructor), `purge`, `addVertex`, `getVertex`, `addEdge`, `getEdge`, `isEdge`, `getVertices`, `getEdges`, `getIncidentEdges`, and `getEmanatingEdges`. Write a test program and test your implementation.

16.4 Repeat Project 16.3 for the `GraphAsLists` class.

16.5 The `DigraphAsMatrix` class can be implemented by extending the `GraphAsMatrix` class introduced in Program 16.6 to implement the `Digraph` interface defined in Program 16.4:

```
public class DigraphAsMatrix
    extends GraphAsMatrix
    implements Digraph
{
    // ...
}
```

Implement the `DigraphAsMatrix` class by providing suitable definitions for the following methods: `DigraphAsMatrix` (constructor), `purge`, `addEdge`, `getEdge`, `isEdge`, and `getEdges`. You must also have a complete implementation of the base class `GraphAsMatrix`. (See Project 16.3.) Write a test program and test your implementation.

16.6 Repeat Project 16.5 for the `DigraphAsLists` class.

16.7 Add a method to the `Digraph` interface that returns the undirected graph underlying the given digraph. Write an implementation of this method for the `AbstractGraph` class introduced in Program 16.5.

16.8 Devise an approach using an enumeration and a stack to perform a topological-order traversal by doing a postorder depth-first traversal in reverse.

16.9 The single-source shortest-path problem on a DAG can be solved by visiting the vertices in topological order. Write a visitor for use with the `topological-OrderTraversal` method that solves the single-source shortest-path problem on a DAG.

16.10 Devise and implement a method that transforms a vertex-weighted *activity-node graph* into an edge-weighted *event-node graph*.

16.11 Complete the implementation of the critical path analysis methods. In particular, you must implement the `LatestTimeVisitor` along the lines of the `EarliestTimeVisitor` defined in Program 16.19.

A | Java and Object-Oriented Programming

This appendix is a brief overview of programming in Java. It identifies and describes the features of Java that are used throughout this text. This appendix is *not* a Java tutorial—if you are not familiar with Java, you should read one of the many Java programming books.

A.1 Variables

A *variable* is a programming language abstraction that represents a storage location. A Java variable has the following *attributes*:

name The *name* of a variable is the label used to identify a variable in the text of a program.

type The *type* of a variable determines the set of values that the variable can have *and* the set of operations that can be performed on that variable.

value The *value* of a variable is the content of the memory location(s) occupied by that variable. How the contents of the memory locations are interpreted is determined by the *type* of the variable.

lifetime The *lifetime* of a variable is the interval of time in the execution of a Java program during which a variable is said to exist. Local variables exist as long as the method in which they are declared is active. Non-static fields of a class exist as long as the object of which they are members exist. Static fields of a class exist as long as the class in which they are defined remains loaded in the Java virtual machine

scope The *scope* of a variable is the range of statements in the text of a program in which that variable can be referenced.

Consider the Java variable declaration statement:

```
int i = 57;
```

This statement defines a variable and *binds* various attributes with that variable. The name of the variable is `i`, the type of the variable is `int`, and its initial value is 57.

Some attributes of a variable, such its name and type, are bound at compile time. This is called *static binding*. Other attributes of a variable, such as its value, may be bound at run time. This is called *dynamic binding*.

There are two kinds of Java variables—local variables and fields. A *local variable* is a variable declared inside a method. A *field* is a variable declared in some *class*. (Classes are discussed in Section A.3.) The *type* of a Java variable is either one of the primitive types or it is a reference type.

A.1.1 Primitive Types

The Java primitive types are `boolean`, `char`, `short`, `int`, `long`, `float`, and `double`. The Java language specification [16] defines the range of values provided by each primitive type and the set of operations supported by each type.

Every variable of a primitive type is a distinct instance of that type. Thus, an assignment statement such as

```
y = x;
```

takes the *value* of the variable `x` and copies that value *into* the variable `y`. After the assignment, `x` and `y` remain distinct instances that happen to have equal values.

A comparison of the form

```
if (x == y)
    { /* ... */ }
```

tests whether the *values* contained in the variables `x` and `y` are equal.

A.1.2 References Types

Java allows the creating of *user-defined types*. A user-defined type is created by defining a *class*. For example, by defining a class called `Foo`, we introduce a new "type" that can be used to declare a variable like this:

```
Foo f;
```

(Classes are discussed in Section A.3.)

In Java, every variable that is not one of the primitive types is a *reference type*. Such a variable can be thought of as a *reference to* (or a *pointer to*) an object of the appropriate type. For example, the variable **f** defined above is a *reference* to an object instance of the class **Foo**.

In Java, class instances must be explicitly created. An instance of a class is created using the **new** operator like this:

```
f = new Foo ();
```

If we follow this with an assignment statement such as

```
Foo g = f;
```

then both **f** and **g** refer to the same object! Note that this is very different from what happens when you assign one primitive type to another.

A comparison of the form

```
if (f == g)
    { /* ... */ }
```

tests whether the **f** and **g** refer to the same object instances. If **f** and **g** refer to distinct object instances that happen to be equal, the test still fails. To test whether two distinct object instances are equal, it is necessary to invoke the **equals** method like this:

```
if (f.equals(g))
    { /* ... */ }
```

Null References

In Java, it is possible for a reference type variable to refer to nothing at all. A reference that refers to nothing at all is called a *null reference*. By default, an uninitialized reference is null.

We can explicitly assign the null reference to a variable like this:

```
f = null;
```

Also, we can test explicitly for the null reference like this:

```
if (f == null)
    { /* ... */ }
```

A.2 Parameter Passing

Parameter-passing methods are the ways in which parameters are transferred between methods when one method calls another. Java provides only one parameter-passing method—*pass-by-value*.

A.2.1 Passing Primitive Types

Consider the pair of Java methods defined in Program A.1. On line 7, the method **one** calls the method **two**. In general, every method call includes a (possibly empty) list of arguments. The arguments specified in a method call are called *actual parameters*. In this case, there is only one actual parameter—**y**.

On line 11 the method **two** is defined as accepting a single argument of type **int** called **x**. The arguments that appear in a method definition are called *formal parameters*. In this case, the formal parameter is a *primitive type*.

The semantics of pass-by-value work like this: The effect of the formal parameter definition is to create a local variable of the specified type in the given method. For example, the method **two** has a local variable of type **int** called **x**. When the method is called, the *values* of the *actual parameters* are assigned to the *formal parameters* before the body of the method is executed.

Since the formal parameters give rise to local variables, if a new value is assigned to a formal parameter, that value has no effect on the actual parameter. Therefore, the output obtained produced by the method **one** defined in Program A.1 is

```
1
2
1
```

PROGRAM A.1
Parameter-passing example: passing primitive types

```java
1   public class Example
2   {
3       public static void one ()
4       {
5           int y = 1;
6           System.out.println (y);
7           two (y);
8           System.out.println (y);
9       }
10
11      public static void two (int x)
12      {
13          x = 2;
14          System.out.println (x);
15      }
16  }
```

A.2.2 Passing Reference Types

Consider the methods **one** and **two** defined in Program A.2. In this case, the variables **x** and **y** are *reference types*. The type of **x** and **y** is **Obj**. Thus, **x** and **y** both refer to instances of the **Obj** class defined on lines 3–13.

The semantics of pass-by-value for reference types work like this: The effect of the formal parameter definition is to create a local variable of the specified type in the given method. For example, the method **two** has a local variable of type **Obj** called **x**. When the method is called, the *actual parameters* are assigned to the *formal parameters* before the body of the method is executed.

PROGRAM A.2
Parameter-passing example: passing reference types

```
1   public class Example
2   {
3       static class Obj
4       {
5           int field;
6
7           public Obj (int arg)
8               { field = arg; }
9           public void assign (int arg)
10              { field = arg; }
11          public String toString ()
12              { return Integer.toString (field); }
13      }
14
15      public static void one ()
16      {
17          Obj y = new Obj (1);
18          System.out.println (y);
19          two (y);
20          System.out.println (y);
21      }
22
23      public static void two (Obj x)
24      {
25          x.assign (2);
26          System.out.println (x);
27      }
28  }
```

Since **x** and **y** are reference types, when we assign **y** to **x**, we make them both refer to the same instance of the **Obj** class. Therefore, the output obtained produced by the method **one** defined in Program A.2 is

```
1
2
2
```

A.3   Objects and Classes

"An *object* is a *class instance* or an array" [16]. The *class* of an object determines what it is and how it can be manipulated. A class encapsulates methods, data, and semantics. This encapsulation is like a *contract* between the implementer of the class and the user of that class.

The **class** construct is what makes Java an *object-oriented* language. A Java class definition groups a set of values with a set of operations. Classes facilitate modularity and information hiding. The user of a class manipulates object instances of that class only through the methods provided by that class.

It is often the case that different classes possess common features. Different classes may share common values; they may perform the same operations; they may support common interfaces. In Java such relationships are expressed using *derivation* and *inheritance*.

A.3.1   Class Members: Fields and Methods

A class groups a set of values and a set of operations. The values and the operations of a class are called its *members*. *Fields* implement the values and *methods* implement the operations.

Suppose we wish to define a class to represent *complex numbers*. The **Complex** class definition shown in Program A.3 illustrates how this can be done. Two fields, **real** and **imag**, are declared, which represent the real and imaginary parts of a complex number, respectively. Program A.3 also defines two methods, **setReal** and **setImag**, which can be used to assign values to the real and imaginary parts of a complex number, respectively.

Every object instance of the **Complex** class contains its own fields. Consider the following variable declarations:

```
Complex c = new Complex ();
Complex d = new Complex ();
```

Both **c** and **d** refer to distinct instances of the **Complex** class. Therefore, each of them has its own **real** and **imag** field. The fields of an object are accessed using the *dot* operator. For example, **c.real** refers to the **real** field of **c** and **d.imag** refers to the **imag** field of **d**.

PROGRAM A.3
Complex class fields and methods

```
1   public class Complex
2   {
3       private double real;
4       private double imag;
5
6       public void setReal (double x)
7           { real = x; }
8
9       public void setImag (double y)
10          { imag = y; }
11      // ...
12  }
```

Program A.3 also defines the methods setReal and getImag. In general, a method performs some operation on an instance of the class. Again, the *dot* operator is used to specify the object on which the operation is performed. For example, c.setReal(1.0) invokes the setReal method on c and d.toString() invokes the toString method on d.

A.3.2 Constructors

A *constructor* is a method that has the same name as its class (and that has no return value). Three constructors are defined in Program A.4. The purpose of a constructor is to *initialize* an object. A constructor is invoked whenever a new instance of a class is created using the **new** operator.

Consider the following sequence of variable declarations:

```
Complex c = new Complex ();      // calls Complex ()
Complex d = new Complex (2.0);   // calls Complex (double)
Complex i = new Complex (0, 1);  // calls Complex (double, double)
```

Consider the constructor that takes two **double** arguments, **x** and **y** (lines 6–10). This constructor initializes the complex number by assigning **x** and **y** to the **real** and **imag** fields, respectively.

The No-Arg Constructor

The constructor that takes no arguments is called the *no-arg constructor*. For example, the no-arg constructor is invoked when a variable is declared like this:

```
Complex c = new Complex ();
```

If there are no constructors defined in a Java class, the Java compiler provides a *default no-arg constructor*. The default no-arg constructor does nothing. The fields simply retain their initial, default values.

Program A.4 gives an implementation for the no-arg constructor of the **Complex** class (lines 12–13). This constructor simply invokes the method called **this**. In Java, one constructor can invoke another constructor by calling the **this** method as its first executable statement. In this case, the no-arg constructor invokes the two-arg constructor to set both **real** and **imag** fields to zero.

A.3.3 Accessors and Mutators

An *accessor* is a method that accesses the contents of an object but does not modify that object. In the simplest case, an accessor just returns the value of one of the fields. In general, an accessor performs some computation using the fields as long as that computation does not modify any of the fields.

Program A.5 defines the five accessor methods of the **Complex** class—**getReal**, **getImag**, **getR**, **getTheta**, and **toString**. The **getReal** and **getImag** methods just return the values of the real and imaginary parts of a complex number. The **getR** and **getTheta** methods return the polar coordinates of a complex number. Finally, the **toString** method returns a **String** representation of a complex number.

PROGRAM A.4
Complex constructors

```
1   public class Complex
2   {
3       private double real;
4       private double imag;
5
6       public Complex (double x, double y)
7       {
8           real = x;
9           imag = y;
10      }
11
12      public Complex ()
13          { this (0, 0); }
14
15      public Complex (double x)
16          { this (x, 0); }
17      // ...
18  }
```

PROGRAM A.5
Complex class accessor methods

```
1    public class Complex
2    {
3        private double real;
4        private double imag;
5
6        public double getReal ()
7            { return real; }
8
9        public double getImag ()
10           { return imag; }
11
12       public double getR ()
13           { return Math.sqrt (real * real + imag * imag); }
14
15       public double getTheta ()
16           { return Math.atan2 (imag, real); }
17
18       public String toString ()
19           { return real + "+" + imag + "i"; }
20       // ...
21   }
```

By defining suitable accessors, it is possible to hide the implementation of the class from the user of that class. Consider the following statements:

```
System.out.println (c.real);
System.out.println (c.getReal ());
```

The first statement depends on the implementation of the Complex class. If we change the implementation of the class from the one given (which uses rectangular coordinates) to one that uses polar coordinates, then the first statement above must also be changed. On the other hand, the second statement does not need to be modified, provided we reimplement the getReal method when we switch to polar coordinates.

Mutators

A *mutator* is a method that can modify an object. In the simplest case, a mutator just assigns a new value to one of the fields. In general, a mutator performs some computation and modifies any number of fields.

The setReal and setImag methods defined in Program A.3 are mutators. Program A.6 defines three more mutators for the Complex class, setR, setTheta, and assign. All three of these assign new values to the real and imag fields, as appropriate.

PROGRAM A.6
Complex class mutator methods

```
1   public class Complex
2   {
3       private double real;
4       private double imag;
5
6       public void setR (double r)
7       {
8           double theta = getTheta ();
9           real = r * Math.cos (theta);
10          imag = r * Math.sin (theta);
11      }
12
13      public void setTheta (double theta)
14      {
15          double r = getR ();
16          real = r * Math.cos (theta);
17          imag = r * Math.sin (theta);
18      }
19
20      public void assign (Complex c)
21      {
22          real = c.real;
23          imag = c.imag;
24      }
25      // ...
26  }
```

Member Access Control

Every member of a class, be it a field or a method, has an *access control attribute* that affects the manner in which that member can be accessed. The members of a class can be **private**, **public** or **protected**. For example, the fields **real** and **imag** declared in Program A.3 are both **private**. **private** members can be used only by methods of the class in which the member is declared.

On the other hand, **public** members of a class can be used by any method in any class. All of the methods defined in Programs A.3, A.4, A.5, and A.6 are declared to be **public**.

In effect, the public part of a class defines the interface to that class and the private part of the class encapsulates the implementation of that class. By making the implementation of a class private, we ensure that the code using the class depends only on the interface and not on the implementation of the class. Furthermore, we can modify the implementation of the class without affecting the code of the user of that class.

`protected` members are similar to `private` members; that is, they can be used by methods of the class in which the member is declared. In addition, `protected` members can also be used by methods of all the classes derived from the class in which the member is declared. The `protected` category is discussed again in Section A.5.1.

Java introduces the notion of a *package*. A Java package is a collection of related classes. Unless declared otherwise, the members of a class are accessible only by the methods of classes in the same package. In this text, we do not use packages explicitly. For convenience, you should consider all of the classes discussed in this book to be elements of the same package.

A.4 Inner Classes

In Java it is possible to define one class *inside* another. A class defined inside another one is called an *inner class*. Java provides two kinds of inner classes—static and non-static.

A.4.1 Static Inner Classes

Consider the following Java code fragment:

```
public class A
{
    int y;

    public static class B
    {
        int x;

        void f () {}
    }
}
```

This fragment defines the class **A**, which contains an static inner class **B**.

A static inner class behaves like any "outer" class. It may contain methods and fields, and it may be instantiated like this:

```
A.B object = new A.B ();
```

This statement creates a new instance of the inner class **B**. Given such an instance, we can invoke the **f** method in the usual way:

```
object.f();
```

Note that it is not necessarily the case that an instance of the outer class **A** exists even when we have created an instance of the inner class. Similarly, instantiating the outer class **A** does not create any instances of the inner class **B**.

The methods of a static inner class may access all members (fields or methods) of the inner class but they can access only static members (fields or methods) of the outer class. Thus, **f** can access the field **x**, but it cannot access the field **y**.

A.4.2 Non-Static Inner Classes

By default, an inner class is *non-static*:

```
public class A
{
    int y;

    public class B
    {
        int x;

        void f () {}
    }
}
```

This fragment defines the class **A**, which contains a non-static inner class **B**.

A non-static inner class can be instantiated only inside a non-static method of the outer class. This is because every instance of a non-static inner class must be associated with an instance of the outer class. In a sense, every instance of a non-static inner class exists "inside" an instance of the outer class. A single instance of the outer class may have associated with it more than one instance of the inner class.

Because an instance of a non-static inner class has an associated instance of the outer class, the methods of the inner class can access directly any of the members (fields or methods) of the outer class instance. For example, the **f** method defined previously can access both **x** and **y** directly.

The Java keyword **this** can be used in a non-static method to refer to the current object instance. Thus, in the method **f**, **this** refers to an instance of the inner **B** class. Every non-static inner class is associated with an instance of the outer class. To access the outer class instance inside the method **f** we write **A.this**.

A.5 Inheritance and Polymorphism

A.5.1 Derivation and Inheritance

This section reviews the concept of a derived class. Derived classes are an extremely useful feature of Java because they allow the programmer to define new classes by extending existing classes. By using derived classes, the programmer can exploit the commonalities that exist among the classes in a program. Different classes can share values, operations, and interfaces.

Derivation is the definition of a new class by extending an existing class. The new class is called the *derived class* and the existing class from which it is derived is called the *base class*. In Java there can be only one base class (*single inheritance*).

Consider the **Person** class defined in Program A.7 and the **Parent** class defined in Program A.8. Because parents are people too, the **Parent** class is derived from the **Person** class. Derivation in Java is indicated using the keyword **extends**.

A derived class *inherits* all of the members of its base class; that is, the derived class contains all of the fields contained in the base class and the derived class supports all of the same operations provided by the base class. For example, consider the following variable declarations:

```
Person p = new Person ();
Parent q = new Parent ();
```

Since **p** is a **Person**, it has the fields **name** and **sex** and method **toString**. Furthermore, since **Parent** is derived from **Person**, then the object **q** also has the fields **name** and **sex** and method **toString**.

A derived class can *extend* the base class in several ways: New fields can be defined, new methods can be defined, and existing methods can be *overridden*. For example, the **Parent** class adds the field **children** and the method **getChild**.

If a method is defined in a derived class that has exactly the same *signature* (name and types of arguments) as a method in a base class, the method in the derived class *overrides* the one in the base class. For example, the **toString** method in the **Parent** class overrides the **toString** method in the **Person** class. Therefore, **p.toString()** invokes **Person.toString**, whereas **q.toString(...)** invokes **Parent.toString**.

PROGRAM A.7
Person class

```
1   public class Person
2   {
3       public final int male = 0;
4       public final int female = 1;
5
6       protected String name;
7       protected int sex;
8
9       public Person (String name, int sex)
10      {
11          this.name = name;
12          this.sex = sex;
13      }
14
15      public String toString ()
16          { return name; }
17  }
```

PROGRAM A.8
Parent class

```
1   public class Parent
2        extends Person
3   {
4        protected Person[] children;
5
6        public Parent (String name, int sex, Person[] children)
7        {
8             super (name, sex);
9             this.children = children;
10       }
11
12       public Person getChild (int i)
13            { return children [i]; }
14
15       public String toString ()
16            { /* ... */ }
17   }
```

An instance of a derived class can be used anywhere in a program where an instance of the base class may be used. For example, this means that a **Parent** may be passed as an actual parameter to a method in which the formal parameter is a **Person**.

It is also possible to assign a derived class object to a base class variable like this:

```
Person p = new Parent ();
```

However, having done so, it is not possible to call **p.Child(...)**, because **p** is a **Person** and a **Person** is not necessarily a **Parent**.

Derivation and Access Control

Members of a class can be **private**, **public**, or **protected**. As explained in Section A.3.3, private members are accessible only by methods of the class in which the member is declared. In particular, this means that the methods of a derived class cannot access the private members of the base classes even though the derived class has inherited those members! On the other hand, if we make the members of the base class public, then all classes can access those members directly, not just derived classes.

Java provides a third category of access control—**protected**. **protected** members can be used by methods of the class in which the member is declared as well as by methods of all classes derived from the class in which the member is declared.

A.5.2 Polymorphism

Polymorphism literally means "having many forms." Polymorphism arises when a set of distinct classes share a common interface. Because the derived classes are distinct, their implementations may differ. However, because the derived classes share a common interface, instances of those classes are used in exactly the same way.

Interfaces

Consider a program for creating simple drawings. Suppose the program provides a set of primitive graphical objects such as circles, rectangles, and squares. The user of the program selects the desired objects, and then invokes commands to draw, to erase, or to move them about. Ideally, all graphical objects support the same set of operations. Nevertheless, the way that the operations are implemented varies from one object to the next.

We implement this as follows: First, we define a Java *interface* that represents the common operations provided by all graphical objects. A Java interface declares a set of methods. An object that supports an interface must provide an implementation for every method declared in the interface.

Program A.9 defines the **GraphicsPrimitives** interface comprised of three methods, **draw**, **erase**, and **moveTo**, the methods declared in the interface.

The **draw** method is invoked in order to draw a graphical object. The **erase** method is invoked in order to erase a graphical object. The **moveTo** method is used to move an object to a specified position in the drawing. The argument of the **moveTo** method is a **Point**. Program A.10 defines the **Point** class, which represents a position in a drawing.

PROGRAM A.9
GraphicsPrimitives interface

```
1  public interface GraphicsPrimitives
2  {
3      void draw ();
4      void erase ();
5      void moveTo (Point p);
6  }
```

PROGRAM A.10
Point class

```
1  public class Point
2  {
3      int x;
4      int y;
5
6      public Point (int x, int y)
7      {
8          this.x = x;
9          this.y = y;
10     }
11     // ...
12 }
```

Abstract Methods and Abstract Classes

Consider the `GraphicalObject` class defined in Program A.11. The `Graphical-Object` class *implements* the `GraphicsPrimitives` interface.

The `GraphicalObject` class has a single field, `center`, which is a `Point` that represents the position in a drawing of the center point of the graphical object. The constructor for the `GraphicalObject` class takes as its argument a `Point` and initializes the `center` field accordingly.

Program A.11 shows a possible implementation for the `erase` method. In this case we assume that the image is drawn using an imaginary pen. Assuming that we know how to draw a graphical object, we can erase the object by changing the color of the pen so that it matches the background color and then redrawing the object.

Once we can erase an object as well as draw it, then moving it is easy. Just erase the object, change its `center` point, and then draw it again. This is how the `moveTo` method shown in Program A.11 is implemented.

We have seen that the `GraphicalObject` class provides implementations for the `erase` and `moveTo` methods. However, the `GraphicalObject` class does not provide an implementation for the `draw` method. Instead, the method is declared to be

---

PROGRAM A.11
`GraphicalObject` class

```
1   public abstract class GraphicalObject
2       implements GraphicsPrimitives
3   {
4       protected Point center;
5
6       public GraphicalObject (Point p)
7           { this.center = p; }
8
9       public abstract void draw ();
10
11      public void erase ()
12      {
13          setPenColor (backgroundColor);
14          draw ();
15          setPenColor (foregroundColor);
16      }
17
18      public void moveTo (Point p)
19      {
20          erase ();
21          center = p;
22          draw ();
23      }
24  }
```

---

abstract. We do this because until we know what kind of object it is, we cannot possibly know how to draw it!

Consider the `Circle` class defined in Program A.12. The `Circle` class *extends* the `GraphicalObject` class. Therefore, it inherits the field `center` and the methods `erase` and `moveTo`. The `Circle` class adds an additional field, `radius`, and it overrides the `draw` method. The body of the `draw` method is not shown in Program A.12. However, we will assume that it draws a circle with the given radius and center point.

Using the `Circle` class defined in Program A.12, we can write code like this:

```
Circle c = new Circle (new Point (0, 0), 5);
c.draw ();
c.moveTo (new Point (10, 10));
c.erase ();
```

This code sequence declares a circle object with its center initially at position (0, 0) and radius 5. The circle is then drawn, moved to (10, 10), and then erased.

Program A.13 defines the `Rectangle` class and Program A.14 defines the `Square` class. The `Rectangle` class also extends the `GraphicalObject` class. Therefore, it inherits the field `center` and the methods `erase` and `moveTo`. The `Rectangle` class adds two additional fields, `height` and `width`, and it overrides the `draw` method. The body of the `draw` method is not shown in Program A.13. However, we will assume that it draws a rectangle with the given dimensions and center point.

The `Square` class extends the `Rectangle` class. No new fields or methods are declared—those inherited from `GraphicalObject` or from `Rectangle` are sufficient. The constructor simply arranges to make sure that the `height` and `width` of a square are equal!

PROGRAM A.12
`Circle` class

```
1   public class Circle
2       extends GraphicalObject
3   {
4       int radius;
5
6       public Circle (Point p, int r)
7       {
8           super (p);
9           radius = r;
10      }
11
12      public void draw ()
13          { /* ... */ }
14  }
```

PROGRAM A.13
Rectangle class

```
1   public class Rectangle
2       extends GraphicalObject
3   {
4       protected int height;
5       protected int width;
6
7       public Rectangle (Point p, int ht, int wid)
8       {
9           super (p);
10          height = ht;
11          width = wid;
12      }
13
14      public void draw ()
15          { /* ... */ }
16  }
```

PROGRAM A.14
Square class

```
1   public class Square
2       extends Rectangle
3   {
4       public Square (Point p, int wid)
5           { super (p, wid, wid); }
6   }
```

Method Resolution

Consider the following sequence of instructions:

```
GraphicalObject g1 = new Circle (new Point (0,0), 5);
GraphicalObject g2 = new Square (new Point (0,0), 5);
g1.draw ();
g2.draw ();
```

The statement `g1.draw()` calls `Circle.draw`, whereas the statement `g2.draw()` calls `Rectangle.draw`.

It is as if every object of a class "knows" the actual method to be invoked when a method is called on that object. For example, a `Circle` "knows" to call `Circle.draw`, `GraphicalObject.erase`, and `GraphicalObject.moveTo`, whereas a `Square` "knows" to call `Rectangle.draw`, `GraphicalObject.erase`, and `Graphical-Object.moveTo`.

In this way, Java ensures that the "correct" method is actually called, regardless of how the object is accessed. Consider the following sequence:

```
Square s = new Square (new Point (0,0), 5);
Rectangle r = s;
GraphicalObject g = r;
```

Here `s`, `r`, and `g` all refer to the same object, even though they are all of different types. However, because the object is a `Square`, `s.draw()`, `r.draw()`, and `g.draw()` all invoke `Rectangle.draw`.

Abstract Classes and Concrete Classes

In Java an *abstract class* is one that does not provide implementations for all its methods. A class must be declared `abstract` if any of the methods in that class are `abstract`. For example, the `GraphicalObject` class defined in Program A.11 is declared `abstract` because its `draw` method is `abstract`.

An abstract class is meant to be used as the base class from which other classes are derived. The derived class is expected to provide implementations for the methods that are not implemented in the base class. A derived class that implements all of the missing functionality is called a *concrete class*.

In Java it is not possible to instantiate an abstract class. For example, the following declaration is illegal:

```
GraphicalObject g = new GraphicalObject (new Point (0,0));
// Wrong.
```

If we were allowed to declare `g` in this way, then we could attempt to invoke the non-existent method `g.draw()`.

Algorithmic Abstraction

Abstract classes can be used in many interesting ways. One of the most useful paradigms is the use of an abstract class for *algorithmic abstraction*. The `erase` and `moveTo` methods defined in Program A.11 are examples of this.

The `erase` and `moveTo` methods are implemented in the abstract class `GraphicalObject`. The algorithms implemented are designed to work in any concrete class derived from `GraphicalObject`, be it `Circle`, `Rectangle`, or `Square`. In effect, we have written algorithms that work regardless of the actual class of the object. Therefore, such algorithms are called *abstract algorithms*.

Abstract algorithms typically invoke abstract methods. For example, both `moveTo` and `erase` ultimately invoke `draw` to do most of the actual work. In this case, the derived classes are expected to inherit the abstract algorithms `moveTo` and `erase` and to override the abstract method `draw`. Thus, the derived class customizes the behavior of the abstract algorithm by overriding the appropriate methods. The Java method resolution mechanism ensures that the "correct" method is always called.

A.5.3   Multiple Inheritance

In Java a class can be derived from only one base class. Thus, the following declaration is not allowed:

```
class C
    extends A, B // Wrong;
{
}
```

Nevertheless, it is possible for a class to extend a base class and to implement one or more interfaces:

```
class C
    extends A
    implements D, E
{
}
```

The derived class C inherits the members of A and it implements all of the methods defined in the interfaces D and E.

It is possible to use derivation in the definition of interfaces. And in Java, it is possible for an interface to extend more than one base interface:

```
interface D
    extends E, F
{
}
```

In this case, the derived interface D comprises all of the methods inherited from E and F as well as any new methods declared in the body of D.

A.5.4   Run-Time Type Information and Casts

Consider the following declarations, which make use of the Rectangle and Square classes defined in Programs A.13 and A.14:

```
Rectangle r = new Rectangle (new Point (0,0), 5, 10);
Square s = new Square (new Point (0,0), 15);
```

Clearly, the assignment

```
r = s;
```

is valid because Square is derived from Rectangle. Thus, since a Square is a Rectangle, we may assign s to r.

On the other hand, the assignment

```
s = r;  // Wrong.
```

is not valid because a `Rectangle` instance is not necessarily a `Square`.

Consider now the following declarations:

```
Rectangle r = new Square (new Point (0,0), 20);
Square s;
```

The assignment `s=r` is still invalid because `r` is a `Rectangle`, and a `Rectangle` is not necessarily a `Square`, despite the fact that in this case it actually is!

In order to do the assignment, it is necessary to convert the type of `r` from a `Rectangle` to a `Square`. This is done in Java using a *cast operator*:

```
s = (Square) r;
```

The Java virtual machine checks at run-time that `r` actually does refer to a `Square` and if it does not, the operation throws a `ClassCastException`. (Exceptions are discussed in Section A.6.)

To determine the type of the object to which `r` refers, we must make use of *run-time type information*. In Java, every class supports the method `getClass`, which returns an instance of `java.lang.Class` that represents the class of the object. Thus, we can determine the class of an object like this:

```
if (r.getClass() == Square.class)
    s = (Square) r;
```

This code does not throw an exception because the cast operation is only attempted when `r` actually is a `Square`.

A.6   Exceptions

Sometimes unexpected situations arise during the execution of a program. Careful programmers write code that detects errors and deals with them appropriately. However, a simple algorithm can become unintelligible when error checking is added because the error-checking code can obscure the normal operation of the algorithm.

Exceptions provide a clean way to detect and handle unexpected situations. When a program detects an error, it *throws* an exception. When an exception is thrown, control is transferred to the appropriate *exception handler*. By defining a method that *catches* the exception, the programmer can write the code to handle the error.

In Java, an exception is an object. All exceptions in Java are ultimately derived from the base class called `java.lang.Throwable`. For example, consider the class `A` defined in Program A.15. Since the `A` class extends the `Throwable` class, `A` is an exception that can be *thrown*.

A method throws an exception by using the `throw` statement. The `throw` statement is similar to a `return` statement. A `return` statement represents the normal

PROGRAM A.15
Using exceptions in Java

```
1   public class Example
2   {
3        static class A extends Throwable
4            {}
5
6        static void f () throws A
7            { throw new A (); }
8
9        static void g ()
10       {
11           try
12           {
13               f ();
14           }
15           catch (A exception)
16           {
17               // ...
18           }
19       }
20   }
```

termination of a method and the object returned matches the return value of the method. A **throw** statement represents the abnormal termination of a method and the object thrown represents the type of error encountered.

The **f** method in Program A.15 throws an **A** exception. Java requires that a method that throws exceptions that are not caught within that method (see below) must declare all of the exceptions it throws unless those exceptions are derived from the special classes **java.lang.Error** or **java.lang.RuntimeException**.[1] Thus, the **f** method declares that it throws **A**.

Exception handlers are defined using a **try** block. The body of the **try** block is executed either until an exception is thrown or until it terminates normally. One or more exception handlers follow a **try** block. Each exception handler consists of a **catch** clause, which specifies the exceptions to be caught, and a block of code, which is executed when the exception occurs. When the body of the **try** block throws an exception for which an exception is defined, control is transferred to the body of the exception handler.

In this example, the exception thrown by the **f** method is caught by the **g** method. In general when an exception is thrown, the chain of methods called is searched in reverse (from caller to callee) to find the closest matching **catch** statement. When a program throws an exception that is not caught, the program terminates.

---

[1] Both **java.lang.Error** and **java.lang.RuntimeException** are derived from **java.lang.-Throwable**.

C | Character Codes

TABLE C.1
7-bit ASCII Character Set

Bits 6–3	Bits 2–0							
	0	1	2	3	4	5	6	7
0	NUL	SOH	STX	ETX	EOT	ENQ	ACK	BEL
1	BS	HT	NL	VT	NP	CR	SO	SI
2	DLE	DC1	DC2	DC3	DC4	NAK	SYN	ETB
3	CAN	EM	SUB	ESC	FS	GS	RS	US
4	SP	!	"	#	$	%	&	'
5	(	)	*	+	,	–	.	/
6	0	1	2	3	4	5	6	7
7	8	9	:	;	<	=	>	?
010	@	A	B	C	D	E	F	G
011	H	I	J	K	L	M	N	O
012	P	Q	R	S	T	U	V	W
013	X	Y	Z	[	\	]	^	_
014	`	a	b	c	d	e	f	g
015	h	i	j	k	l	m	n	o
016	p	q	r	s	t	u	v	w
017	x	y	z	{	|	}	~	DEL

Bibliography

[1] Alfred V. Aho, John E. Hopcroft, and Jeffrey D. Ulman. *Data Structures and Algorithms*. Addison-Wesley, Reading, MA, 1983.

[2] Alfred V. Aho and Jeffrey D. Ullman. *Foundations of Computer Science*. Computer Science Press, New York, NY, 1992.

[3] ANSI Accredited Standards Committee X3, Information Processing Systems. *Working Paper for Draft Proposed International Standard for Information Systems—Programming Language C++,* December 1996. Document Number X3J16/96-0225 WG21/N1043.

[4] Ken Arnold and James Gosling. *The Java™ Programming Language*. The Java™ Series. Addison-Wesley, Reading, MA, 1996.

[5] Borland International, 1800 Green Hills Road, P.O. Box 660001, Scotts Valley, CA 95067-0001. *Borland C++ Version 3.0 Programmer's Guide,* 1991.

[6] Timothy A. Budd, *Classic Data Structures in C++*. Addison-Wesley, Reading, MA, 1994.

[7] Computational Sciences Education Project. Mathematical optimization. Virtual book, 1995. `http://csep1.phy.ornl.gov/CSEP/MO/MO.html`.

[8] Computational Sciences Education Project. Random number generation. Virtual book, 1995. `http://csep1.phy.ornl.gov/CSEP/RN/RN.html`.

[9] Gaelan Dodds de Wolf, Robert J. Gregg, Barbara P. Harris, and Matthew H. Scargill, Editors. *Gage Canadian Dictionary*. Gage Educational Publishing Company, Toronto, Ontario, Canada, 1997.

[10] Rick Decker and Stuart Hirshfield. *Working Classes: Data Structures and Algorithms Using C++*. PWS Publishing Company, Boston, MA, 1996.

[11] Adam Drozdek. *Data Structures and Algorithms in C++*. PWS Publishing Company, Boston, MA, 1996.

[12] Margaret A. Ellis and Bjarne Stroustrup. *The Annotated C++ Reference Manual*. Addison-Wesley, Reading, MA, 1990.

[13] James A. Field. *Makegraph User's Guide.* Technical Report 94-04, Department of Electrical and Computer Engineering, University of Waterloo, Waterloo, Ontario, 1994.

[14] Erich Gamma, Richard Helm, Ralph Johnson, and John Vlissides. *Design Patterns: Elements of Reusable Object-Oriented Software.* Addison-Wesley, Reading, MA, 1995.

[15] Michael Goosens, Frank Mittelbach, and Alexander Samarin. *The L^AT_EX Companion.* Addison-Wesley, Reading, MA, 1994.

[16] James Gosling, Bill Joy, and Guy Steele. *The Java™ Language Specification.* The Java™ Series. Addison-Wesley, Reading, MA, 1996.

[17] James Gosling, Frank Yellin, and The Java Team. *The Java™ Application Programming Interface, Volume 1: Core Packages.* The Java™ Series. Addison-Wesley, Reading, MA, 1996.

[18] James Gosling, Frank Yellin, and The Java Team. *The Java™ Application Programming Interface, Volume 2: Windows Toolkit and Applets.* The Java™ Series. Addison-Wesley, Reading, MA, 1996.

[19] Irwin Guttman, S. S. Wilks, and J. Stuart Hunter. *Introductory Engineering Statistics,* Second ed. John Wiley & Sons, New York, NY, 1971.

[20] Gregory L. Heileman. *Data Structures, Algorithms, and Object-Oriented Programming.* McGraw-Hill, New York, NY, 1996.

[21] Ellis Horowitz and Sartaj Sahni. *Data Structures in Pascal,* Third ed. W. H. Freeman and Company, New York, NY, 1990.

[22] Ellis Horowitz, Sartaj Sahni, and Dinesh Mehta. *Fundamentals of Data Structures in C++.* W. H. Freeman and Company, New York, NY, 1995.

[23] Richard Jones and Rafael Lins. *Garbage Collection: Algorithms for Automatic Dynamic Memory Management.* John Wiley & Sons, New York, NY, 1996.

[24] Brian W. Kernighan and Dennis M. Ritchie. *The C Programming Language.* Prentice-Hall, Englewood Cliffs, NJ, 1978.

[25] Leonard Kleinrock. *Queueing Systems, Volume 1: Theory.* John Wiley & Sons, New York, NY, 1975.

[26] Donald E. Knuth. *Fundamental Algorithms,* Second ed., Vol. 1 of *The Art of Computer Programming.* Addison-Wesley, Reading, MA, 1973.

[27] Donald E. Knuth. *Sorting and Searching,* Vol. 3 of *The Art of Computer Programming.* Addison-Wesley, Reading, MA, 1973.

[28] Donald E. Knuth. *Seminumerical Algorithms,* Second ed., Vol. 2 of *The Art of Computer Programming.* Addison-Wesley, Reading, MA, 1981.

[29] Donald E. Knuth. *The METAFONTbook.* Addison-Wesley, Reading, MA, 1986.

[30] Donald E. Knuth. *The T_EXbook.* Addison-Wesley, Reading, MA, 1986.

[31] Elliot B. Koffman, David Stemple, and Caroline E. Wardle. Recommended curriculum for CS2, 1984. *Communications of the ACM,* 28(8): 815–818, August, 1985.

[32] Leslie Lamport. *L^AT_EX: A Document Preparation System,* Second ed. Addison-Wesley, Reading, MA, 1994.

[33] Yedidyah Langsam, Moshe J. Augenstein, and Aaron M. Tenenbaum. *Data Structures Using C and C++,* Second ed. Prentice-Hall, Upper Saddle River, NJ, 1996.

[34] Tim Lindholm and Frank Yellin. *The Java™ Virtual Machine Specification.* The Java™ Series. Addison-Wesley, Reading, MA, 1996.

[35] Kenneth McAloon and Anthony Tromba. *Calculus,* Vol. 1BCD. Harcourt Brace Jovanovich, New York, NY, 1972.

[36] Thomas L. Naps. *Introduction to Program Design and Data Structures.* West, St. Paul, MN, 1993.

[37] Stephen K. Park and Keith W. Miller. Random number generators: Good ones are hard to find. *Communications of the ACM,* 31(10): 1192–1201, October, 1988.

[38] P. J. Plauger. *The Draft Standard C++ Library.* Prentice-Hall, Englewood Cliffs, NJ, 1995.

[39] Stephen R. Schach. *Classical and Object-Oriented Software Engineering,* Third ed. Irwin, Chicago, IL, 1996.

[40] G. Michael Schneider and Steven C. Bruell. *Concepts in Data Structures and Software Development.* West, St. Paul, MN, 1991.

[41] Bjarne Stroustrup. *The C++ Programming Language,* Second ed. Addison-Wesley, Reading, MA, 1991.

[42] Bjarne Stroustrup. *The Design and Evolution of C++.* Addison-Wesley, Reading, MA, 1994.

[43] Allen B. Tucker, Bruce H. Barnes, Robert M. Aiken, Keith Barker, Kim B. Bruce, J. Thomas Cain, Susan E. Conry, Gerald L. Engel, Richard G. Epstein, Doris K. Lidtke, Michael C. Mulder, Jean B. Rogers, Eugene H. Spafford, and A. Joe Turner. *Computing Curricula 1991: Report of the ACM/IEEE-CS Joint Curriculum Task Force.* ACM/IEEE, 1991.

[44] Bill Venners. *Inside the Java Virtual Machine.* McGraw-Hill, New York, NY, 1997.

[45] Larry Wall and Randal L. Schwartz. *Programming Perl.* O'Reilly & Associates, Sebastopol, CA, 1991.

[46] Mark Allen Weiss. *Data Structures and Algorithm Analysis,* Second ed. Benjamin/Cummings, Redwood City, CA, 1995.

[47] Mark Allen Weiss. *Algorithms, Data Structures and Problem Solving with C++.* Addison-Wesley, Menlo Park, CA, 1996.

[48] Geoff Whale. *Data Structures and Abstraction using C.* Thomas Nelson Australia, Melbourne, Australia, 1996.

Index

627